Adaptations for
SAXON MATH™
Course 3

Adaptation by
Susan Blanchard, EdD

Student Workbook

For Use with *Saxon Math Course 3*

SAXON™

A Harcourt Education Imprint

www.SaxonPublishers.com
1-800-284-7019

ISBN-13 978-1-5914-1921-1

ISBN-10   1-514-1921-2

Printed in the United States of America

1 2 3 4 5 6 7 8 202 14 13 12 11 10 09 08 07

TABLE OF CONTENTS

This workbook is designed to supplement and support the instruction and exercises in Saxon Math Course 3 and cannot be used independently of the textbook. Included are Lesson and Investigation Worksheets.

Each Lesson Worksheet contains brief instruction on the lesson's topics, workspace for every Practice Set and Written Practice problem, and assistance for many of the solutions. Many worksheets also include teacher notes indicating resources (such as Teaching Guide hints, manipulatives, or masters) that will help students understand the lesson.

Support for individual problems takes many forms, including:

- identifying a starting point

- restating the problem

- crafting partial solutions

- citing a *Student Reference Guide* page

- referring students to a page in the textbook (with the textbook icon, 📖)

- reminding students to include units in the answer (by showing words like *units*, *money*, and *time* in relevant answer boxes)

Investigation Worksheets are much like Lesson Worksheets. They summarize the contents of Investigations, aid in solving problems, and supply teacher-support information.

Name _____

Individual Recording Form

Assignment	Date	Assignment	Date	Assignment	Date	Assignment	Date
1		14		33		TP 51	
TP 1A		15		TP 33		52	
TP 1B		TP 15		34		TP 52	
TP 1C		Test 1		35		53	
2		16		TP 35		54	
TP 2		17		Test 5		55	
3		TP 17		36		Test 9	
4		18		TP 36		56	
TP 4		19		37		TP 56	
5		20		TP 37		57	
TP 5		Test 2		38		58	
FA A		Inv. 2		39		59	
6		TP Inv. 2		TP 39		60	
7		21		40		Test 10	
TP 7		TP 21		TP 40		Inv. 6	
8		22		Test 6		61	
TP 8		23		Inv. 4		A61	
9		TP 23		41		62	
TP 9A		24		42		63	
TP 9B		TP 24		43		TP 63	
10		25		44		A63	
TP 10		TP 25		TP 44		64	
FA B		Test 3		45		65	
FA C		26		Test 7		TP 65	
Inv. 1		27		46		Test 11	
11		28		TP 46		66	
FA D		29		47		TP 66	
12		30		48		A66	
TP 12A		TP 30		49		67	
TP 12B		Test 4		50		68	
FA E		Inv. 3		TP 50		TP 68	
13		31		Test 8		A68	
TP 13		TP 31		Inv. 5		69	
FA F		32		51		70	

Name _____

Assignment	Date	Assignment	Date	Assignment	Date	Assignment	Date
Test 12		84		Test 17		Test 20	
Inv. 7		TP 84		96		Inv. 11	
71		A84		97		111	
A71		85		A97		112	
72		Test 15		98		113	
73		86		A98		114	
A73		87		99		Test 21	
74		A87		TP 99		115	
75		88		A99		TP 115	
TP 75		89		100		116	
Test 13		90		Test 18		TP 116	
76		TP 90		Inv. 10		117	
77		Test 16		101		TP 117	
78		Inv. 9		102		Test 22	
79		91		103		118	
80		92		104		TP 118	
TP 80		TP 92		105		119	
A80		A92		Test 19		TP 119	
Test 14		93		106		120	
Inv. 8		TP 93		107		TP 120	
81		94		108		Test 23	
82		TP 94		109		Inv. 12	
83		95		110			
A83		A 95		TP 110			

• Number Line: Comparing and Ordering Integers (page 6)

Name _____

A number line shows numbers in order from least to greatest.

- The number line has zero at the center.
  Numbers to the right of zero are **positive**.
  Numbers to the left of zero are **negative**.

- A **set** is a collection of numbers.
  Sets are shown inside **braces** { }.
  Ellipsis points(…) show that a set is infinite.

- **Counting numbers** are the numbers we use to count:
  {1, 2, 3, 4, 5,…}

- **Whole numbers** are the counting numbers and zero:
  {0, 1, 2, 3, 4, 5,…}

- **Integers** are the whole numbers and their opposites:
  {…, –2, –1, 0, 1, 2,…}

Teacher Notes:
- Students who have difficulty with subtraction, multiplication, or division will benefit from working Targeted Practices 1A, 1B, and 1C *before* Lesson 1.

- Introduce Hint #8, "Positive and Negative Numbers," and Hint #9, "Comparing Numbers."

- Refer students to "Number Line" on page 9 and "Number Families" and "Definitions" on page 10 in the *Student Reference Guide*.

- Post reference chart, "Number Families."

- A number-line manipulative is available in the Adaptations Manipulative Kit.

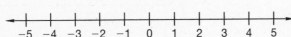

Opposites are two numbers that are the same distance from zero but in opposite directions.

3 and –3 are opposites.

The **absolute value** of a number is the distance of that number from zero.

$$|5| = 5$$
The absolute value
of 5 is 5.

$$|-5| = 5$$
The absolute value
of –5 is 5.

The absolute value of a number is always positive.

- We use symbols to compare the values of numbers.

–5 < 4	3 + 2 = 5	0 > –2
–5 is less than 4.	3 plus 2 equals 5.	Zero is greater than –2.

- To **graph** a number, draw a point to correspond to that number on the number line.

Practice Set (page 9)

a. Arrange these integers in order from least to greatest: –4, 3, 2, –1, 0

_____, **–1**, _____, _____, _____

b. Which number –4, –1, 0, 2, 3 is an **even number but not a whole number**? _____
Cross out the odd numbers.

c. Compare: –2 ◯ –4
The larger the negative digit, the smaller the number is.

d. Graph the numbers in this sequence on a number line: ... –4, –2, 0, 2, 4, ...

Simplify.

e. | –3 | = _____   **f.** | 3 | = _____

g. Write two numbers that are **ten** units from zero. _____ , _____

h. Write an example of a whole number that is not a counting number. _____

Written Practice   (page 9)

1.

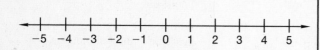

Use work area.

2. least to greatest

Use a number line.

–5, 3, –2, 1

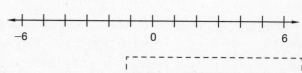

_____ , _____ , _____ , _____

3. whole numbers

{__, 1, 2, __, 4, . . .}

4. even numbers

{. . . __, –2, 0, __, 4, __, . . .}

5. Which number is an **even** number?

–5, 3, –2, 1

_____

6. Which whole number is **not** a counting number?

See page 10 in the Student Reference Guide.

_____

7. Write the graphed numbers.

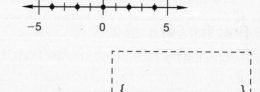

{. . . __, __, __, __, __, . . .}

8. Name the type of numbers in problem 7.

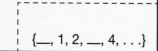

e _____ integers

9. *See page 10 in the* Student Reference Guide.

_____ . z _____ is a whole number but

not a c _____ number.

Use work area.

10. *See page 10 in the* Student Reference Guide.

_____. All c_____ numbers are

w_____ numbers.

¦ Use work area. ¦

11. _____. Integers include c_____

numbers, their o_____, and zero.

¦ Use work area. ¦

12. What is the **absolute value** of 21?

$|21| =$

_____

13. $|-13| =$

_____

14. $|0| =$

_____

15. 5 ◯ −7

_____

16. −3 ◯ −2

_____

17. $|-3|$ $|-2|$

↓   ↓

— ◯ —

_____

18.

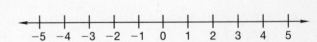

¦ Use work area. ¦

19. If $|n| = 5$, then n can be which two numbers?

$n =$ _____, _____

20. Write two numbers that are five units from zero.

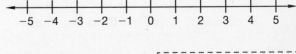

_____, _____

21.

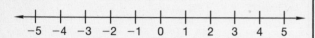

Use work area.

22. Write 2 numbers that are 3 units from 0.

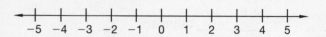

————, ————

23.

Use work area.

24. What number is the **opposite** of 10?

_____

25. 10 + _____ = _____

_____

26. What number is the opposite of −2?

_____

27. −2 + _____ = _____

_____

28. Choose all correct answers.

−7

A counting numbers **B** whole numbers

C integers **D** none of these

_____

29. Choose all correct answers

30

A counting numbers **B** whole numbers

C integers **D** none of these

————, ————, ————

30. Choose all correct answers

$\frac{1}{3}$

A counting numbers **B** whole numbers

C integers **D** none of these

_____

• **Operations of Arithmetic** (page 12)

Name _____

The fundamental operations of arithmetic are addition, subtraction, multiplication, and division.

• More than one symbol can show multiplication and division:

Symbols for Multiplication and Division

"three times five"	$3 \times 5, 3 \cdot 5, 3(5), (3)(5)$
"six divided by two"	$6 \div 2, 2\overline{)6}, \frac{6}{2}$

• A **property** of addition or multiplication is something that is always true no matter what numbers are used.

• Properties are written with letters instead of numbers.
  These letters are called **variables**.
  The letters could represent any number.

Teacher Notes:
• Introduce Hint #10, "Fact Families," and Hint #11, "Properties of Operations."

• Refer students to "Properties of Operations" on page 20 in the *Student Reference Guide*.

• Review "Division" on page 5 in the *Student Reference Guide*.

• Triangle fact cards are available in the Adaptations Manipulative Kit.

Some Properties of Addition and Multiplication

Name of Property	Representation	Example
Commutative Property of Addition	$a + b = b + a$	$3 + 4 = 4 + 3$
Commutative Property of Multiplication	$a \cdot b = b \cdot a$	$3 \cdot 4 = 4 \cdot 3$
Associative Property of Addition	$(a + b) + c = a + (b + c)$	$(3 + 4) + 5 = 3 + (4 + 5)$
Associative Property of Multiplication	$(a \cdot b) \cdot c = a \cdot (b \cdot c)$	$(3 \cdot 4) \cdot 5 = 3 \cdot (4 \cdot 5)$
Identity Property of Addition	$a + 0 = a$	$3 + 0 = 3$
Identity Property of Multiplication	$a \cdot 1 = a$	$3 \cdot 1 = 3$
Zero Property of Multiplication	$a \cdot 0 = 0$	$3 \cdot 0 = 0$

• The Commutative and Associative Properties **do not** work with subtraction or division.

Practice Set (page 16)

Name each property illustrated in a–d.

a. $4 \cdot 1 = 4$ I_____ Property of _____

b. $4 + 5 = 5 + 4$ C_____ Property of _____

c. $(8 + 6) + 4 = 8 + (6 + 4)$ A_____ Property of _____

d. $0 \cdot 5 = 0$ _____ Property of M_____

e. What's is the difference when the sum of 5 and 7 is subtracted from the product of 5 and 7?

$(5 \times 7) - (5 + 7)$

_____ $-$ _____ $=$ _____

f. *See Example 4 on pg. 15*

$$\begin{array}{r} 36 \\ -87 \\ \hline \end{array} \qquad \begin{array}{r} 87 \\ -36 \\ \hline \end{array}$$

Answer: _____

g. What properties did Lee use to simplify his calculations?

What are the properties that cover multiplication?

$5 \cdot (7 \cdot 8)$ Given

$5 \cdot (8 \cdot 7)$ _____ Property of _____

$(5 \cdot 8) \cdot 7$ _____ Property of _____

$40 \cdot 7 \qquad 5 \cdot 8 = 40$

$280 \qquad 40 \cdot 7 = 280$

h. Explain how to check this subtraction problem.

What is the opposite of subtraction?

i. Explain how to check this division problem.

What is the opposite of division?

For **j** and **k**, find the unknown.

j. $12 + m = 48$

$$\begin{array}{r} 48 \\ 12 \\ \hline \end{array}$$

$m =$ _____

k. $12n = 48$

1. (_____) – (_____) =
    product   sum

_____

2. (_____) ÷ (_____) =
    product   sum

_____

3. *fact family*

$30 - \underline{\quad} = 10$

$\underline{\quad} - 10 = \underline{\quad}$

Use work area.

4. *fact family*

$\overline{)200}$ $\overline{)200}$

Use work area.

5. a. *What makes 100?*   (___ · ___) · ___

b. The product is ___.

c. C_____ Property of ____

   A_____ Property of ____

Use work area.

6. set of counting numbers

{1, ___, ___, . . .}

7. set of whole numbers

{ ___, 1, 2, . . .}

8. set of integers

{. . ., ___, ___, ___, . . .}

9. *See page 10 in the* Student Reference Guide.

___. Zero is a w_____ number but not a

c_____ number.

Use work area.

10. _____. All _____ numbers are _____.

Use work area.

11. least to greatest

Use a number line.

0, 1, −2, −3, 4

———, ———, ———, ———, ———

12. a. | −12 | = ———

b. | 11 | = ———

———————

13. *See page 20 in the* Student Reference Guide.

$100 \times 1 = 100$

——— Property of Multiplication

14. $a + 0 = a$

——— Property of Addition

15. $(5)(0) = 0$

Zero ——— of ———

16. $5 + (10 + 15) = (5 + 10) + 15$

——— Property of Addition

17. $10 \times 5 = 5 \times 10$

——— Property of Multiplication

18. a. The four operations of arithmetic are

(+) —————, (−) —————,

(×) —————, and (÷) —————.

b. The Commutative and Associative Properties

apply to ——— and ———.

Use work area.

19. $|n| = 10$
$|-n| = 10$

———, ———

20. a. 0 ◯ –1

b. –2 ◯ –3

c. $|-2|$ ◯ $|-3|$

a._____

b._____

c._____

21.

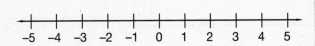

Use work area.

22. opposite of 20

_____

23. Which integer is neither positive nor negative?

_____

24. Choose all correct answers.

100

A counting numbers   **B** whole numbers

C integers   **D** none of these

_____

25. –5

A counting numbers   **B** whole numbers

C integers   **D** none of these

_____

26. $\frac{1}{2}$

A counting numbers   **B** whole numbers

C integers   **D** none of these

_____

27. 5010
    − 846

28. rearrange.

846   5010
−5010 → − 846

29. 780
    × 49

30. long division

25)5075

• Addition and Subtraction Word Problems (page 19)

Name _____

The plot in a word problem tells us what equation to write to solve the problem.

• A formula is an equation written with letters, also called variables.

• Each kind of word problem has a formula.

• Stories about **combining** have an addition pattern:

some + more = total

$s + m = t$

• Stories about **separating** have a subtraction pattern:

starting amount − some went away = what is left

$s - a = l$

• Stories about **comparing** also have subtraction patterns:

greater − lesser = difference

$g - l = d$

later − earlier = difference

$l - e = d$

• To solve a word problem:

1. Look for keywords that will help you find the plot of the story: combining, separating, or comparing.
    Use the key words chart on page 35 in the Student Reference Guide.

2. Write an equation for the problem using the formula and numbers from the story. Use a variable for the missing number

3. Find the missing number.
    Use the missing numbers chart on page 4 in the Student Reference Guide.

4. Check to see that your answer makes sense.

> **Teacher Notes:**
> • Introduce Hint #12, "Word Problem Cues," Hint #13, "Finding Missing Numbers," and Hint #14, "Abbreviations and Symbols."
>
> • Refer students to "Equivalence Table for Units" on page 1, "Time" on page 2, "Missing Numbers" on page 4, and "Word Problem Keywords" on page 35 in the *Student Reference Guide.*
>
> • Post reference chart, "Word Problem Keywords."

Practice Set (page 22)

a. What are the three kinds of word problems described in this lesson?

c _____   s _____   c _____

b. In example 2 on 📖† pg. 21, we solved a word problem to find how much money Alberto spent on milk and bread. Using the same information, write a word problem that asks how much money Alberto gave to the clerk.

At the store, Alberto bought milk and bread that cost $_____. The clerk gave Alberto $_____

in change. How much money did _____ give to _____?

† *When you see* 📖, *refer to your* **Saxon Math** *Course 3 textbook.*

c. Write a story problem for this equation.

$20.00 − a = $8.45

Abby went to the store with $_____. She bought a _____. The clerk gave her $_____ in

change. _____ _____ money did Abby spend?

For problems **d–f,** identify the plot, write an equation, and solve the problem.

d. From 1990 to 2000 the population of Garland increased from 180,635 to 215,768. How many **more** people lived in Garland in 2000 than in 1990?

plot: _____   equation: _____ − _____ = d

answer: _____ people

e. Binh went to the theater with $20.00 and left the theater with $10.50. How much money did Binh spend at the theater? Explain why your answer is reasonable.

plot: _____   equation: _____ − a = _____

answer: _____; The answer is reasonable because half of $20 is $_____. The money left,

$10.50, is a little m_____ than half, so the money spent should be a little l_____ than half.

f. In the three 8th-grade classrooms at Washington school, there are 29 students, 28 students, and 31 students. What is the **total** number of students in the three classrooms?

plot: _____   equation: _____ + _____ + _____ = t

answer: _____ students

g. Circle the equation that shows how to find how much change a customer should receive from $10.00 for a $6.29 purchase.

A $10.00 + $6.29 = c   **B** $10.00 − $6.29 = c

Written Practice   (page 23)

1. plot: _____

_____ min _____ sec −

_____ min _____ sec = d

d = _____

2. plot: _____

$_____ + $_____ + $_____ = t

t = _____

3. plot: _____

1 ft = _____ in.   _____ in. − _____ in. = d

d = _____

4. plot: _____

$_____ + m = $_____

m = _____

5. plot: _____

_____ − _____ = d

d = _____

6. plot: _____

1 dozen = _____

_____ − _____ = d

d = _____

7. Sam earned $_____ mowing yards.

He spent $4.05 on _____.

How much _____?

Use work area.

8. $|n| = 3$

$|-n| = 3$

_____ , _____

9. least to greatest
Use a number line.
−6, 5, −4, 3, −2

_____ , _____ , _____ , _____ , _____

10. a. −5 ◯ 1

b. −1 ◯ −2

a. _____

b. _____

11. a. −10 ◯ 10

  b. |−10| ◯ |10|

a. _____

b. _____

12. |−5| ◯ (the distance from 0 to −5 on a number line.)

Use a number line.

_____

13. See 📖 *page 13.*

a. _____

b. _____

14. See 📖 *page 13.*

a. _____

b. _____

15. a. *What makes 100?*

  (_____ · _____) · _____

  b. C___ Property of _____

  A___ Property of _____

  c. (_____ · _____) · _____ = _____

Use work area.

16. 36 − 17   17 − 36

  ↓   ↓

  _____ ◯ _____

_____

Use work area.

17. Commutative Property of Addition

  5 + _____ = _____ + _____

Use work area.

18. Associative Property of Addition

  (_____ + _____) + _____ =

  _____ + (_____ + _____)

Use work area.

19.

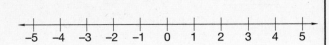

Use work area.

20. *rearrange*

10
-15

_____

21. *fact family*

___ + ___ = ___

___ − ___ = ___

___ − ___ = ___

Use work area.

22. *fact family*

___ × ___ = ___

___ ÷ ___ = ___

___ ÷ ___ = ___

Use work area.

23. Which whole number is not a counting number?

_____

24. opposite of −5

_____

25. $5t = 5$

___ Property of _____

$t =$ _____

26. $5 + u = 5$

___ Property of _____

$u =$ _____

27. $4x = 0$

_____ Property of _____

x = _____

28.
$$\begin{array}{r} \$100.00 \\ - \$90.90 \\ \hline \end{array}$$

29.
$$\begin{array}{r} 89 \\ \times \ \$.67 \\ \hline \end{array}$$

30. _long division_

$$18\overline{)\$72.18}$$

• Multiplication and Division Word Problems (page 27)

Some word problems have an equal groups plot.

• Stories about **equal groups** have a multiplication pattern:

number of groups × number in group = total

$$n \times g = t$$

• The keywords for equal-groups problems are *in each*.

• If the missing number is a product, multiply.

Example: There were 24 rows of chairs with 15 chairs in each row. How many chairs were there in all?

$$n \times g = t$$
24 groups × 15 in a group = t
24 × 15 = 360

There were 360 chairs in all. To solve this problem, we multiplied.

• If the missing number is a factor, divide.

Example: There were 360 chairs arranged in rows with 15 chairs in each row. How many rows were there in all?

$$n \times g = t$$

n × 15 in a group = 360 total

```
       24
   15)360
       30
       60
      −60
        0
```

There were 24 rows. To solve this problem, we divided.

• Some equal-groups problems have a remainder.

Example: Cory sorted 375 quarters into groups of 40 so that he could put them in rolls. How many rolls can Cory fill with the quarters?

$$n \times g = t$$

n × 40 in a group = 375 total

```
      9 r 15
   40)375
      360
       15
```

Cory can make 9 full rolls of quarters and have 15 quarters left over. The problem asks how many rolls Cory can **fill**. The answer is 9 rolls.

Practice Set (page 28)

a. Carver gazed at the ceiling tiles. He saw 30 rows of tiles with 32 tiles in each row. How many ceiling

tiles did Carver see? _____ tiles

_____ × _____ = t   *offset* $\begin{array}{r} 32 \\ \times\ 30 \\ \hline \end{array}$

b. Four student tickets to the amusement park cost $95.00. The cost of each ticket can be found by
solving which of these equations? (Circle one.)

A $\dfrac{4}{\$95.00}$ 5 t

B $\dfrac{t}{4} = \$95.00$

C $4 \times \$95 = t$

D $4t = \$95.00$

c. Amanda has 632 dimes. How many rolls of 50 dimes can she fill? Explain why your answer is
reasonable.

$n \times$ _____ = _____   *long division* $\overline{)632}$

_____ rolls; 632 _____ by 50 is _____ with _____ dimes left over.

Written Practice   (page 28)

1. _____ × g = _____

$\overline{)98}$

g = _____

2. 1 dozen = _____

_____ × _____ = t

t = _____

3. $n \times$ _____ = 5000
Cancel matching zeros.

$\dfrac{5000}{800}\ \overline{)}$

5000 divided by 800 is

_____ with _____ left over.

Only _____ markers

be used.

n = _____

4. In which equation is the total cost missing?

A $c = \dfrac{\$1.98}{3}$

B $c = 3 \times \$1.98$

C $\$1.98 = c \cdot 3$

D $\dfrac{3}{c} = \$1.98$

_____

5. $n \times$ _____ = _____

Cancel matching zeros.

$$\frac{200}{60} \overline{)}$$

200 divided by 60 is

_____ with _____ left

over. _____ buses will
be used.

_____

6. 306
    297
    ‾‾‾‾

_____

7. $8
       9
       7
      ‾‾

_____

8.   14
       ‾‾‾

_____

9. Jake had $5. He spent all but $_____.

_____ did Jake spend?

10. Tajuana paid $_____ for concert tickets.

Each ticket cost $_____. How many

_____ did Tajuana buy?

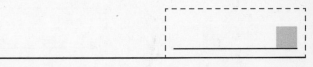

Use work area.   Use work area.

11. least to greatest

Use a number line.

-1, 2, -3, -4, 5

——, ——, ——, ——, ——

12. a. -7 ◯ -8

b. 5 ◯ -6

a. _____

b. _____

13. a. |-7| ◯ |-8|

b. |11| ◯ |-11|

a. _____

b. _____

14.

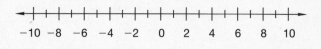
-10 -8 -6 -4 -2 0 2 4 6 8 10

_____

15. |n| = 1

|-n| = 1

——, ——

16. odd numbers

{ ... , ——, *-1*, ——, ——, ——, ——, ... }

17. Graph the set of odd numbers.

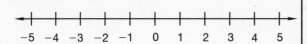

Use work area.

18. *See page 4 in the* Student Reference Guide.

a. _____

b. _____

19. *See page 4 in the* Student Reference Guide.

a. _____

b. _____

20. a. (_____ + _____) + _____

b. _____ Property of _____

_____ Property of _____

Use work area.

21. 12 − 5   5 − 12

_____ ◯ _____

_____

22. *fact family*

_____ × _____ = _____

_____ ÷ _____ = _____

_____ ÷ _____ = _____

Use work area.

23. *fact family*

_____ + _____ = _____

_____ − _____ = _____

_____ − _____ = _____

Use work area.

24. opposite of 10

Use work area.

25.

× _____   × _____

┌─────────────────────────────┐
⌐ _____ groups of _____   ⌐
└─────────────────────────────┘

26.

− 54   − 48

┌─────────────────────────────┐
⌐ _____ in. to _____ in. ____ ⌐
└─────────────────────────────┘

27.

× _____   × _____

┌─────────────────────────────┐
⌐ _____ tickets for _____   ⌐
└─────────────────────────────┘

28. whole numbers

┌──────────────────────────────────────┐
⌐ { _____ , _____ , _____ , _____ , . . . } ⌐
└──────────────────────────────────────┘

29. *See page 10 in the* Student Reference Guide.

┌─────────────────────────────┐
⌐ _____   ⌐
└─────────────────────────────┘

30. $|n| = \dfrac{1}{2}$

$|\text{-}n| = \dfrac{1}{2}$

┌─────────────────────────────┐
⌐ _____ , _____   ⌐
└─────────────────────────────┘

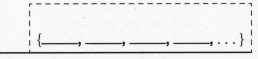

• Fractional Parts (page 31)

Name _____

We can use fractions to describe part of a group.

- Fractions have two parts: a **numerator** (top number) and a **denominator** (bottom number).

$$\begin{array}{ll} \text{numerator} & \quad 1 \quad \text{number of parts described} \\ \text{denominator} & \quad 3 \quad \text{number of equal parts} \end{array}$$

- To find a fraction of a group:
    1. **Divide** by the denominator.
    2. **Multiply** by the numerator.

    Example: Two fifths of the 30 questions on the test were multiple-choice. How many questions were multiple-choice?

    1. Divide by the denominator: $30 \div 5 = 6$
    2. Multiply by the numerator: $6 \times 2 = 12$
        12 of the questions were multiple choice.

- One way to compare fractions is to compare each fraction to $\frac{1}{2}$.

- Take half of the denominator and compare it to the numerator.
    If the numerator is greater than half the denominator, the fraction is greater than $\frac{1}{2}$.
    If the numerator is less than half the denominator, the fraction is less than $\frac{1}{2}$.
    If the numerator is equal to half the denominator, the fraction is equal to $\frac{1}{2}$.

    Example: Arrange these fractions from least to greatest.

    $$\frac{3}{6}, \frac{3}{5}, \frac{3}{8}$$

    Compare each fraction to $\frac{1}{2}$.

    $\frac{3}{6}$: half of 6 is 3. The numerator is equal to 3, so $\frac{3}{6}$ is equal to $\frac{1}{2}$.

    $\frac{3}{5}$: half of 5 is $2\frac{1}{2}$. The numerator is more than $2\frac{1}{2}$, so $\frac{3}{5}$ is more than $\frac{1}{2}$.

    $\frac{3}{8}$: half of 8 is 4. The numerator is less than 4, so $\frac{3}{8}$ is less than $\frac{1}{2}$.

    $$\frac{3}{8} < \frac{3}{6} < \frac{3}{5}$$

Practice Set (page 33)

a. How many minutes is $\frac{1}{6}$ of an hour? _____ ▪

1 hr = _____ min

Divide by the denominator.

Multiply by the numerator.

Practice Set (continued) (page 33)

b. Three fifths of the 30 questions on the test were multiple-choice. How many multiple-choice questions were there? Explain why your answer is reasonable.

Divide by the denominator.   *Multiply by the numerator.*

_____ questions; $\frac{3}{5}$ is _____ than $\frac{1}{2}$, and _____ is greater than $\frac{1}{2}$ of 30.

c. Greta drove 288 miles and used 8 gallons of fuel. Greta's car traveled an average of how many miles

per gallon of fuel? _____   ▨ $)\overline{288}$

d. Arrange these fractions from least to greatest. _____, _____, _____

Compare each to $\frac{1}{2}$.

$\frac{5}{10}, \frac{5}{6}, \frac{5}{12}$

_____, _____, _____

least   greatest

Written Practice   (page 33)

1. *Divide by the denominator.*
Multiply by the numerator.

$\frac{1}{4}$ of a mile

1 mi = ____ yd

_____ ▨

2. least to greatest

Compare to $\frac{1}{2}$.

_____, _____, _____

---

3. $\frac{2}{3}$ of 600

Divide by the denominator.
Multiply by the numerator.

_____

4. *short division*

$)\overline{1\ 9\ 2}$

_____

5. ____ × ____ = *t*

t = _____

6. 1 hr = ____ min

   $2\frac{1}{2}$ hr = ____ min

   500

   ____

_____

7. *long division*

   $\overline{)200}$

_____

8. $300
    54

_____

9. $\frac{3}{4}$ of 8000

Divide by the denominator.
Multiply by the numerator.

_____

10. total

  A $c = 19 \cdot \$2.98$ **B** $\dfrac{19}{\$2.98} = c$

  C $\$2.98 \cdot c = 19$ **D** $\dfrac{\$2.98}{19} = c$

_____

11. *offset*

  x _____

_____

12. $10

   ____

_____

13. Cyndie is microwaving frozen _____.

Each _____ takes 20 seconds. How

long should she microwave _____?

Use work area.

14. Erika had _____ pounds of compost.

She used all but _____ pounds in her

garden. How many _____ of compost

did she use?

Use work area.

15.   23

_____

16. least to greatest
Use a number line.

−5, 7, 4, −3, 0

17. Compare to $\frac{1}{2}$.

$\frac{1}{2}$ ◯ $\frac{7}{15}$

_____

18. $|n| = 6$
$|-n| = 6$

_____ , _____

19. _____ + _____ = 6

_____ , _____

20. _____ × _____ = 6

_____ , _____

21. *Use parentheses.*

_____ · _____ · _____ = _____ · _____ · _____

22.

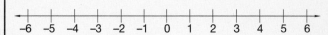

23. What two numbers are 50 units from zero?

_____ , _____

24. *fact family*

_____ + _____ = _____

_____ + _____ = _____

_____ − _____ = _____

25. *fact family*

_____ × _____ = _____

_____ ÷ _____ = _____

_____ ÷ _____ = _____

26. opposite of 5 = _____

5 + _____ = _____

_____

27. –8 ◯ –6

_____

28. *List some integers and counting numbers.*

_____ ;

The _____ 1, 2, 3, . . .

are also _____ numbers.

29. *List some integers and fractions.*

_____ ; An example of a f_____

that is not an _____ is

_____ .

30. 6 · (17 · 50)   Given

6 · (____ · ____)   Commutative Property of
                      Multiplication

(____ · ____) · 17   _____ Property of
                              Multiplication

300 · ____   Multiplied ____ and ____

_____   Multiplied ____ and ____

• Converting Measures (page 36)

Name _____

We measure weight, length, amount of liquids (capacity), and temperature.

- There are two systems of measurement:

    The **metric system** is used throughout the world.

    The United States uses both the **U.S. Customary System** and the metric system.

- The U.S. Customary System uses fractions.

- The metric system uses decimal numbers.

- To convert from one unit to another, use five steps.

    Example: The 5000-meter run is an Olympic event. How many kilometers is 5000 meters?

1. Name the two units in the problem and write them in a column:

    km
    m

2. Fill in what you know from the Equivalence Table. Write the amounts next to the units:

    km   1
    m   1000

3. Write what you are looking for. Put a question mark in the unknown spot:

    km   1   ?
           1000   5000

4. Draw a loop around the two diagonal numbers. **The loop should never include the question mark.**

    km   1   ?
    m   1000   5000

5. Multiply the numbers in the loop. Divide by the number outside the loop.

    $5000 \times 1 = 5000$
    $5000 \div 1000 = 5$
    There are **5 km** in 5000 m.

Teacher Notes:
- Introduce Hint #19, "Converting Measures and Rate" and Hint # 20, "Measuring Liquids and Capacities of Containers."
- Refer students to "Liquids" on page 1 and "Proportion (Rate) Problems" on page 19 in the *Student Reference Guide.*
- Review "Equivalence Table for Units" on page 1 in the *Student Reference Guide.*
- Post reference chart, "Liquids."

Equivalent Measures

Measure	U.S. Customary	Metric
Length	12 in. = 1 ft 3 ft = 1 yd 5280 ft = 1 mi	1000 mm = 1 m 100 cm = 1 m 1000 m = 1 km
	1 in. = 1 mi ≈	2.54 cm 1.6 km
Capacity	16 oz = 1 pt 2 pt = 1 qt 4 qt = 1 gal	1000 mL = 1 L
	1 qt ≈	0.95 Liters
Weight/ Mass	16 oz = 1 lb 2000 lb = 1 ton	1000 mg = 1 g 1000 g = 1 kg 1000 kg = 1 tonne
	2.2 lb ≈ 1.1 ton ≈	1 kg 1 metric tonne

Practice Set (p. 38)

a. A room is 15 **feet** long and 12 **feet** wide. What are the length and width of the room in **yards**?

_____ ft = 1 yd

Multiply the loop. Divide by the outside number.

length   **width**

length: _____ ☐   width: _____ ☐

ft   3   15
yd   1   ?

b. Nathan is 6 ft 2 in. tall. How many inches tall is Nathan? _____ ☐

First, convert 6 feet to inches. Then add the 2 inches.

1 ft = _____ in.

ft   1   ___
in 12   ?

c. Seven kilometers is how many meters? _____ ☐

1 km = _____ m

Multiply the loop. Divide by the outside number.

km   1   ___
m   ?

Written Practice   (page 38)

1. 1 hr = _____ min

Multiply the loop.

Divide by the outside number.

hr   1   ?
min   80

_____ ☐

2. 1 pt = _____ oz

Find half of that.

_____ ☐

3. 1 kg = _____ g

Double that.

_____ ☐

4. $\frac{3}{4}$ of 300

Divide by the denominator.
Multiply by the numerator.

_____

5. _____ × _____ = _____

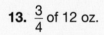

6. 23
18

7. Shade two of the parts.
What fraction is that?

8. $\overline{)20}$

9. Drawing a picture may help.

272
79

10. $\overline{)150}$

11. 1 week = _____ days

1 day = _____ hr

Multiply the loop.

day $\dfrac{1}{}$

hr $\dfrac{}{?}$

12. 20
15
12

13. $\dfrac{3}{4}$ of 12 oz.

Divide by the denominator.
Multiply by the numerator.

14. least to greatest

Use a number line.
Compare $\dfrac{5}{7}$ to $\dfrac{1}{2}$.

$-2, \dfrac{5}{7}, 1, 0, \dfrac{1}{2}$

_____, _____, _____, _____, _____

15. $-5 \bigcirc 4$

16. $|-2| \bigcirc |-3|$

17. $5 \bigcirc |-5|$

Use work area.

18. Commutative Property of Addition

_____ + _____ =

_____ + _____

Use work area.

19. even counting numbers
Draw the braces.

_____, _____, _____, . . .

20. | 0 | = _____

_____

21.

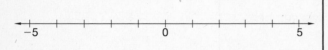

Use work area.

22. *fact family*

_____ + _____ = _____

_____ − _____ = _____

_____ − _____ = _____

15

3   12

Use work area.

23. *fact family*

_____ ÷ _____ = _____

_____ × _____ = _____

_____ × _____ = _____

40

5   8

Use work area.

24. opposite of 100

_____

25. *See p. 10 in the Student Reference Guide.*

_____

26. *See p. 10 in the Student Reference Guide.*

_____

27. _____; 3 is a

_____

number and it is an

_____.

Use work area.

28. _____; Every _____ number is greater than zero, and every negative number is _____ than zero.

Use work area.

29. _____; $\frac{2}{2}$ is equal to 1.

30. | x | = 7
| −x | = 7

x = _____, _____

Use work area.

• Rates and Average
• Measures of Central Tendency (page 41)

Name _____

A rate is a relationship between two measures.

Teacher Notes:
• Introduce Hint #21, "Average."
• Refer students to "Average" on page 7 and "Statistics" on page 23 in the *Student Reference Guide*.
• Review Hint #19, "Converting Measures and Rate."

• Rates use the word *per* to mean "in one."

    65 miles per hour (65 mph) means "65 miles in one hour."

    32 feet per second (32 ft/sec) means "32 feet in one second."

• To solve rate problems, use the loop method from Lesson 6.

• The **average** (or **mean**) describes what number is in the "center" of a group of numbers.
    1. Add the numbers.
    2. Divide by the number of items.

• The average must be between the smallest and largest numbers.
    Example: Find the average of 5, 1, 3, 5, 4, 8, and 2.
        1. Add the numbers. $5 + 1 + 3 + 5 + 4 + 8 + 2 = 28$
        2. Divide by the number of items. $28 \div 7 = 4$
        The **average** is 4. Four is between the smallest number (1) and the largest number (8).

• The **median** is the middle number when the numbers are put in order.
    Example: Find the median of 5, 1, 3, 5, 4, 8, and 2.
        1. Write the numbers in order. 1, 2, 3, 4, 5, 5, 8
        2. Count the numbers. There are 7 numbers.
        Counting from the first number or the last number, 4 is the middle number.

The **median** is 4. In this group of numbers, the average and the median are the same. This is not always true.

• The **mode** is the number that occurs most often.
    Example: Find the mode of 5, 1, 3, 5, 4, 8, and 2.
    The **mode** is 5. Five is the only number that occurs more than once in these numbers.

• The **range** is the difference between the largest and smallest numbers in a group.
    Example: Find the range of 5, 1, 3, 5, 4, 8, and 2.
    The **range** is 7.
    The largest number is 8 and the smallest number is 1.
    $8 - 1 = 7$.

• A **line plot** is a way to show a group of numbers. Each number is shown by an "X" above a number line.
    Example: Display this group of numbers on a line plot. {5, 1, 3, 5, 4, 8, 2}

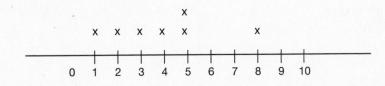

Practice Set (page 44)

a. Alba ran 21 miles in three hours. What was her average speed in miles per hour?

_____ per ▪

Multiply the loop.
Divide by the outside number.

mi　21　?
hr　3　1

b. How far can Freddy drive in 8 hours at an average speed of 50 miles per hour? _____ ▪

mi　___　?
hr　1　8

c. If a commuter train averages 62 miles per hour between stops that are 18 miles apart, about how

many **minutes** does it take the train to travel the distance between the two stops? _____ ▪

62 miles per hour is about 60 miles per hour and 60 miles per hour is 1 mile per minute.

mi　1　?
min　1　8

d. If the average number of students in three classrooms is 26, and one of the classrooms has 23 students, then which of the following must be true? (Circle one.) *The average must be between the smallest and largest numbers.*

A At least one classroom has fewer than 23 students.

B At least one classroom has more than 23 students and less than 26 students.

C At least one classroom has exactly 26 students.

D At least one classroom has more than 26 students.

e. What is the **mean** of 84, 92, 92, and 96? _____

f. The heights of five basketball players are 184 cm, 190 cm, 196 cm, 198 cm, and 202 cm. What is the

average height of the five players? _____

The price per pound of apples sold at different sold at different grocery stores is reorted below. Use this information to answer problems **g–i.**

$0.99	$1.99	$1.49	$1.99
$1.49	$0.99	$2.49	$1.49

g. Display the data in a line plot.

$1.00　　$1.50　　$2.00　　$2.50

Practice Set (continued) (page 45)

h. Compute the mean, median, mode, and range of the data.

i. Rudy computed the average price and predicted that he would usually have to pay $1.62 per pound of apples. Why is Rudy's prediction incorrect?

The mode is the most common price for apples. The mode is $ _____.

Written Practice (page 45)

1. *long division*

$\overline{)132}$

2. $\frac{4}{5}$ of 35

Divide by the denominator.
Multiply by the numerator.

3. *Convert pounds to ounces.*
Then add 7 ounces.

1 lb. = _____ oz.

$\begin{array}{c} \text{lb.} \\ \text{oz.} \end{array} \quad \begin{array}{c} 1 \\ \hline ? \end{array} \quad \begin{array}{c} 7 \\ ? \end{array}$

4. *Multiply the loop.*
Divide by the outside number.

$\begin{array}{c} \text{km} \\ \text{hr} \end{array} \quad \underline{\quad} \quad \begin{array}{c} ? \\ 1 \end{array}$

5. $\begin{array}{c} \text{mi} \\ \text{hr} \end{array} \quad \underline{\quad} \quad \begin{array}{c} ? \\ 1 \end{array} \begin{array}{c} \\ 5 \end{array}$

6. *See p. 1 in the* Student Reference Guide.

7. *average*

$\begin{array}{r} 8 \\ 12 \\ 16 \\ 19 \\ + 20 \end{array} \quad \overline{)}$

8. plot: _____

equation: _____ × _____ = t

t =

9. plot: _____

equation: _____ + m = _____

m = _____

10. plot: _____

equation: _____ − l = _____

l = _____

11. 2 terms = _____ yr

plot: _____

equation: _____ − e = _____

e = _____

12. Each bag of _____ weighed _____ pounds. If there were _____ bags, how much did all the bags weigh?

Use work area.

13. Ginger gets an allowance of $ _____ each week. At the end of one week, she had $ _____ left. How much money did Ginger spend?

Use work area.

14. least to greatest

Use a number line.
Compare each fraction to $\frac{1}{2}$.

$0, -1, \frac{2}{3}, 1, \frac{2}{5}$

_____ , _____ , _____ , _____ , _____

15. −11 ◯ −10

_____

16. $a + b = c$

addend + _____ = _____

$d \cdot e = f$

factor · _____ = _____

Use work area.

17. _____ × _____ = _____ × _____

Use work area.

18. *Use parentheses.*

_____ + _____ + _____ = _____ + _____ + _____

Use work area.

19.

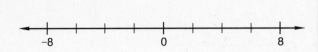

‑8　　0　　8

Use work area.

20. *Rearrange*

0
−20

_____

21. *fact family*

_____ − _____ = _____

_____ + _____ = _____

_____ + _____ = _____

7
2　　5

Use work area.

22. *fact family*

_____ ÷ _____ = _____

_____ × _____ = _____

_____ × _____ = _____

12
3　　4

Use work area.

23. _____ ; _____ is a _____ number that

is not a _____ number.

Use work area.

24. | −90 | =

_____

25. opposite of 6

_____

26 a. $x =$ _____

_____ Property of
Multiplication

b. $y =$ _____

_____ Property of Addition

Use work area.

27. *Rearrange*

2020
−10,101

_____

28.

$0.79
×　48

_____

29. *long division*

$12\overline{)\$60.60}$

---

30. $4 \cdot (12 \cdot 75)$ Given

$4 \cdot (\underline{\hphantom{xx}} \cdot \underline{\hphantom{xx}})$　　　　　$\underline{\hspace{3cm}}$ Property

$(\underline{\hphantom{xx}} \cdot \underline{\hphantom{xx}})$　　　　　$\underline{\hspace{2cm}}$ $\underline{\hspace{2cm}}$ Property

$\underline{\hphantom{xx}} \cdot \underline{\hphantom{xx}}$　　　Multiplied $\underline{\hspace{2cm}}$ and $\underline{\hspace{2cm}}$

$\underline{\hphantom{xx}}$　　　Multiplied $\underline{\hspace{2cm}}$ and $\underline{\hspace{2cm}}$

Use work area.

• Perimeter and Area (page 47)

Name _____

A rectangle is a four-sided shape with two dimensions, length (*l*) and width (*w*).

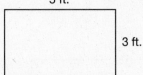

5 ft.

3 ft.

• The **perimeter** of a **rectangle** is the distance around the rectangle.

> Perimeter is measured in units of length such as ft, in., cm, and m.

• To find a perimeter, **add all sides**.

> The perimeter of the rectangle above is 16 ft.
>
> $l + w + l + w$ = perimeter
>
> $5 + 3 + 5 + 3 = 16$ ft.

• The **area** of a rectangle is the amount of surface.

> Area is measured in square units such as ft^2, $in.^2$, cm^2, and m^2.

• **Area = length × width**

> The area of the rectangle above is $15 ft^2$.
>
> $l × w$ = Area
>
> 5 ft $× 3$ ft $= 15 ft^2$

• To find the perimeter and area of some shapes, we divide the shape into more than one area and find each unknown side length.

1. Subtract to find each unknown side length.

   $h = 12$ cm $- 5$ cm $= 7$ cm

   $v = 10$ cm $- 6$ cm $= 4$ cm

2. Perimeter: Add all sides.

   Perimeter $= 5 + 10 + 12 + 6 + 7 + 4 = 44$ cm

3. Area: Find the area of each small rectangle.

   Then add the two areas.

   Area of $A = 4$ cm $× 5$ cm $= 20 cm^2$

   Area of $B = 6$ cm $× 12$ cm $= 72 cm^2$

   Total area $= 20 cm^2 + 72 cm^2 = 92 cm^2$

5 cm

v | *A*

h

6 cm | *B* | 10 cm

12 cm

Practice Set (page 51)

a.
12 ft

8 ft

How many feet of baseboard does Jared need?

Perimeter = _____

How many tiles will he need?

Area = _____ floor tiles

Find the perimeter and area of each rectangle.

b.
3 cm

4 cm

P = _____

A = _____

c.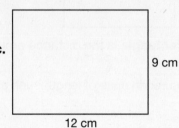
9 cm

12 cm

P = _____

A = _____

d. The length and width of the rectangle in **c** are three times the length and width of the rectangle in **b.**

The perimeter of **c** is how many times the perimeter of **b**? _____

The area of **c** is how many times the area of **b**? _____

e. Pete made a rectangle using 12 tiles side by side. This is a 12 × 1 rectangle.

Name two other rectangles Pete can make with 12 tiles. ____ × ____ and ____ × ____
Use square tiles for help.

f. Find the perimeter and area of a room with these dimensions.

$x =$ ____ $y =$ ____   P = ____   A = ____

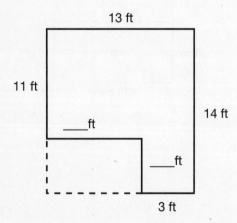
13 ft

11 ft

14 ft

____ ft

____ ft

3 ft

1. *Perimeter: Add all sides.*

Area = length × width

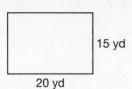

15 yd

20 yd

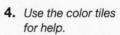
_____

_____

2. Label the sides in the figure. Find its perimeter and area

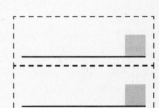
_____

_____

3. The perimeter of 2 is how many times the perimeter of 1?

The area of 2 is how many times the area of 1?

_____

_____

4. *Use the color tiles for help.*

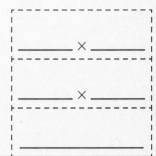

_____ × _____

_____ × _____

_____

5. _____ × _____ = t

_____

6. *Multiply the loop.*

lb $\dfrac{1}{?}$

oz

_____

7. $\frac{2}{3}$ of $45

Divide by the denominator.
Multiply by the numerator.

8. a. Put in order. _____, _____, _____, _____,

_____, _____, _____, _____, _____, _____

mean: _____ median: _____

mode: _____ range: _____

b. Which describes the difference from

greatest to least? _____

```
   12
   12
   12
   10
   10   10)‾‾‾
    9
    9
    8
    8
 +  7
```

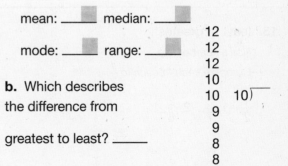

Use work area.

9. _____ × _____ = t

10. (_____) ÷ (_____) =

sum   difference

11. *See p. 1 in the* Student Reference Guide.

12. Multiply the loop.

Divide by the outside number.

mi
—   ?
hr   1

13. Murat drives _____ miles every day to

_____.

How many _____ will Murat

drive in 4 days?

Use work area.

14. A carpenter has a board that measures

_____ inches. After cutting, the board

measures _____ inches. How many

_____ did the carpenter

cut off?

Use work area.

15. least to greatest.

Use a number line.

Compare each fraction to $\frac{1}{2}$.

$\frac{1}{2}$, −1, $\frac{5}{7}$, −2, $\frac{2}{6}$, 1

16. −100 ◯ 10

17. −3 ◯ −4

18. | −3 | ◯ | −4 |

19. Commutative Property

____ + ____ = ____ + ____

20.

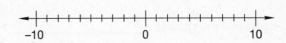

Use work area.

21. | 15 | =

22. *fact family*

____ + ____ = ____

____ − ____ = ____

____ − ____ = ____

Use work area.

23. opposite of 3

24. | n | = 5

| −n | = 5

____ , ____

25. _____ ;

_____ is a

_____ number but is not an

_____ .

Use work area.

26. _____ ; The

_____ contain the

_____ numbers.

Use work area.

27. _____ ; The sum of two

positive integers is a p_____

i_____ .

Use work area.

28. $|x| = 15$

$|-x| = 15$

_____ , _____

29.   68
       $\times\ 37$

30. Three out of four did not order the special. What fraction did?

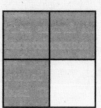

• Prime Numbers (page 54)

Name _____

A factor is a counting number that divides evenly into another number.

- Think of factors in *pairs* that multiply to make the number:

  6 has two factor pairs:

  $1 \times 6 = 6$ and $2 \times 3 = 6$

  The factor pairs can be shown with rectangles:

  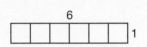

  The factors of 6 are 1, 2, 3, and 6.

- A **prime number** is a counting number greater than 1 that has exactly two factors (one factor pair).

  7 has one factor pair: $1 \times 7 = 7$

  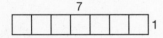

  The factors of 7 are 1 and 7. Therefore, 7 is a prime number.

- The factors of a prime number are always 1 and the number itself.

  Some prime numbers:

  2, 3, 5, 7, 11, 13, …

- A counting number that has more than two factors is a **composite number.**

  Any composite number can be written as the product of factors that are prime numbers. This is called **prime factorization.**

- We can use a **factor tree** to write the prime factorization of a number:

  1. List two factors of the given number under "branches" of the tree.
  (If you have trouble, start with 2, 3, or 5.)

  2. Check if either factor is prime.
  If the factor is prime, circle it.
  If it is not, continue to draw branches and factor until each number is prime.

  3. Write the prime factors in order.
  You may have to write some numbers more than once.

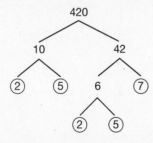

$$420 = 2 \times 2 \times 3 \times 5 \times 7$$

• Another way to do prime factorization is **division by primes**:

1. Write the number in a division box.
2. Divide by the smallest prime number that is a factor. (Try 2, 3, or 5.)
3. Divide that answer by the smallest prime number that is a factor.
4. Repeat until the quotient is 1.
5. The divisors are the prime factors of the number.

Division by Primes

$$
\begin{array}{r}
1 \\
7\overline{)7} \\
5\overline{)35} \\
3\overline{)105} \\
2\overline{)210} \\
2\overline{)420} \\
\end{array}
$$

$420 = 2 \times 2 \times 3 \times 5 \times 7$

• Tests for divisibility will help you find factors of numbers or tell if a number is prime:

Tests for Divisibility

A number is able to be divided by . . .

2	if the last digit is even.
4	if the last two digits can be divided by 4.
8	if the last three digits can be divided by 8.
5	if the last digit is 0 or 5.
10	if the last digit is 0.
3	if the **sum of the digits** can be divided by 3.
6	if the number can be divided by 2 **and** by 3.
9	if the **sum of the digits** can be divided by 9.

Practice Set (page 57)

a. Is 9 a prime or composite number?

Use 9 color tiles to make a square.

b. Write the first 10 prime numbers. 2, _____, _____, _____, 11, 13, _____, _____, 23, _____

See p. 9 in the Student Reference Guide.

c. Complete this factor tree for 36.

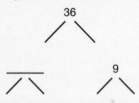

d. Find the prime factors of 60 using division by primes.

$60 =$ _____ · _____ · _____ · _____

$$
\begin{array}{r}
\overline{)} \\
\overline{)} \\
\overline{)} \\
\overline{)60} \\
\end{array}
$$

Write the prime factorization of each number in **e–g.**

e. 25 = _____ · _____

$$\overline{)25}$$

f. $100 =$ ____ · ____ · ____ · ____

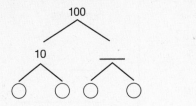

g. $16 =$ ____ · ____ · ____ · ____

h. A multi-digit number might be **prime** if its last digit is ____.

A 4   **B** 5   **C** 6   **D** 7

See the tests for divisibility.

i. Show that 12 is composite by drawing three different rectangles using 12 squares.

Use color tiles for help.

Written Practice   (page 57)

1. $\frac{2}{3}$ of

   Divide by the denominator.
   Multiply by the numerator.

2. *Multiply the loop.*

   m   1   2
   cm   ?

3. *Multiply the loop.*

$$\frac{80}{1} \quad ?$$

2 hours ⟶ ____

3 hours ⟶ ____

4 hours ⟶ ____

4. a. plot: ____

   equation: ____ $+ m =$ ____
   320
   <u>150</u>

   b. average
      150
    +

   $2\overline{)}$

a. ____

b. ____

Use work area.

5. a. median: _____
Put the numbers in order.

_____, _____, _____, _____, _____, _____, _____

b. mean: _____

86
182
205
214
208
190
+126   7)‾‾‾‾

c. The _____ is closer to

most of the numbers.

¦ Use work area. ¦

---

6. *Multiply the loop.*

ft   1   5280
yd   ?

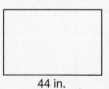

---

7. first eight prime
numbers

_____, _____,

_____, _____,

_____, _____,

_____, _____

¦ Use work area. ¦

---

8.   100 cm
      − 68 cm

---

9. $2970.98
      − 1429.59

---

10. *Cancel matching zeros.*

$\dfrac{5280}{30}$)‾‾‾‾

---

11. *short division*

3)$1 2 3 . 4 5

---

12. *Perimeter: Add all sides.*

Area = length × width

32 in.

44 in.

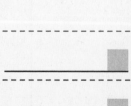

---

13. *Perimeter: Add all sides.*

12 m   15 m

19 m

---

14. *Perimeter: Add all sides.*

area = length × width

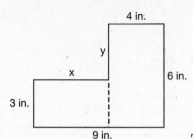

4 in.

y

x

6 in.

3 in.

9 in.

15.

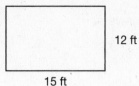

12 ft

15 ft

a. *Perimeter: Add all sides.*

b. *Area = length x width*

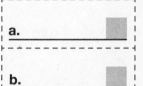

a. _____

b. _____

_____

_____

16. $5 + 4 = 4 + a$

_____ Property of Addition

a _____

17. $17 \cdot 18 = b \cdot 17$

_____ Property of Multiplication

b _____

18. $20 \cdot c = 20$

_____ Property of Multiplication

c _____

19. $21d = 0$

_____ Property of Multiplication

$d =$ _____

20. **a.** $|9| =$

b. $|-12| \bigcirc |-11|$

a. _____

b. _____

21.   13
      $\times 5$

_____

22. *long division*

$15\overline{)225}$

_____

23. Choose all correct answers.

27

A whole number

B counting number

C integer

_____

24. Choose all correct answers.

0

A whole number

B counting number

C integer

_____

25. Choose all correct answers.

−2

   A whole number

   B counting number

   C integer

   _____

26. Choose all correct answers.

Use tests for divisibility.

5280

   A 2 **B** 3 **C** 4 **D** 5

   _____

27. *See p. 9 in the* Student Reference Guide.

   ____, ____, ____, ____, ____

28.

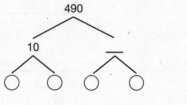

   490 = __ · __ · __ · __

29.

```
  )‾‾‾‾
  )‾‾‾‾
  )‾‾‾‾
  )‾‾‾‾
  )48
```

   48 = __ · __ · __ · __ · __

30. 40 · (23 · 50)   Given

   40 · (____ · ____)   _____ Property

   (____ · ____) · ____   _____ Property

   ____ · ____   Multiplied _____ and _____

   ____   Multiplied _____ and _____

   Use work area.

- **Rational Numbers**
- **Equivalent Fractions** (page 60)

Name _____

Rational numbers are numbers that can be expressed as a ratio (division) of two integers.

All integers, whole numbers, and counting numbers are **rational numbers.**

All fractions are rational numbers.

- **Equivalent fractions** are different names for the same number.

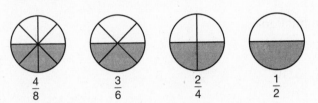

$$\frac{4}{8} \qquad \frac{3}{6} \qquad \frac{2}{4} \qquad \frac{1}{2}$$

$\frac{4}{8}, \frac{3}{6}, \frac{2}{4}$, and $\frac{1}{2}$ are equivalent fractions.

$\frac{4}{8}, \frac{3}{6}$ and $\frac{2}{4}$ all **reduce** to $\frac{1}{2}$.

- To reduce a fraction:

  1. Write the prime factorization of the numerator and denominator.

  2. Cancel all the pairs of factors.

$$\frac{4}{8} = \frac{\overset{1}{\cancel{2}} \cdot \overset{1}{\cancel{2}}}{\underset{1}{\cancel{2}} \cdot \underset{1}{\cancel{2}} \cdot 2} = \frac{1}{2} \qquad \frac{3}{6} = \frac{\overset{1}{\cancel{3}}}{2 \cdot \underset{1}{\cancel{3}}} = \frac{1}{2} \qquad \frac{2}{4} = \frac{\overset{1}{\cancel{2}}}{\underset{1}{\cancel{2}} \cdot 2} = \frac{1}{2}$$

- To form equivalent fractions, multiply by a fraction equal to 1 (same numerator and denominator).

$$\frac{1}{2} \cdot \mathbf{1}\,\frac{2}{2} = \frac{2}{4} \qquad \frac{1}{2} \cdot \mathbf{1}\,\frac{3}{3} = \frac{3}{6} \qquad \frac{1}{2} \cdot \mathbf{1}\,\frac{4}{4} = \frac{4}{8}$$

- As a shortcut, use the "loop" method.

  Example: Write a fraction equivalent to $\frac{1}{2}$ that has a denominator of 100.

  Multiply the loop.
  Divide by the outside number.

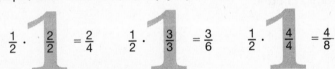

$100 \times 1 = 100$
$100 \div 2 = 50$

$\frac{50}{100}$ is the equivalent to $\frac{1}{2}$

- Fractions that have the same denominator have **common denominators.**

$$\frac{5}{8} \text{ and } \frac{7}{8} \qquad\qquad \frac{5}{8} \text{ and } \frac{7}{10}$$

Common Denominators   Not Common Denominators

Teacher Notes:
- Introduce Hint #28, "Finding the Greatest Common Factor," and Hint #29, "Improper Fractions."
- Refer students to "Mixed Numbers and Improper Fractions" and "Fraction Families Equivalent Fractions" on page 12 in the *Student Reference Guide.*
- Review Hint #17, "Fraction Manipulatives," and Hint #19, "Comparing Fractions."
- Review "Number Families" on page 10, "Factors" on page 5, and "Fraction Terms" on page 12 in the *Student Reference Guide.*

- To compare fractions that do not have common denominators, cross-multiply:

Example: Compare: $\dfrac{2}{3} \bigcirc \dfrac{3}{5}$

$10 \searrow \dfrac{2}{3} \bigcirc \dfrac{3}{5} \nearrow 9$

$2 \times 5 = 10$
$3 \times 3 = 9$
$10 > 9$, so $\dfrac{2}{3} > \dfrac{3}{5}$

- An **improper** (top heavy) **fraction** is a fraction that is greater than 1 or equal to 1.

- A **mixed number** is a whole number and a fraction.

- To write an improper fraction as a mixed number or integer:
    1. Divide the denominator into the numerator.
    2. Write the quotient as the whole number.
    3. Write the remainder as the numerator of the fraction.
    4. Keep the same denominator.

Example: Express $\dfrac{3}{10}$ as a mixed number.

$$\begin{array}{r} 3R1 \\ 3\overline{)10} \\ 9 \\ \hline 1 \end{array}$$

$$\dfrac{10}{3} = 3\dfrac{1}{3}$$

The quotient is 3, so that is the whole number.
The remainder is 1, so that is the numerator.
The denominator stays the same: 3.

___

Practice Set (page 65)

Each number in **a–c** is a member of one or more of the following sets of numbers. Write all the letters that apply.

A Whole numbers   **B** Integers   **C** Rational numbers

a. 5 _____   **b.** 2 _____   **c.** $-\dfrac{2}{5}$ _____

Use prime factorization to reduce each fraction in **d–f.**

d. $\dfrac{20}{36} = \dfrac{\cancel{2}\cdot 2\cdot 5}{\cancel{2}\cdot\cancel{2}\cdot 3\cdot 3} =$ _____

$$\begin{array}{r} 1 \\ 5\overline{)5} \\ 2\overline{)10} \\ 2\overline{)20} \end{array} \qquad \begin{array}{r} 1 \\ 3\overline{)3} \\ 3\overline{)9} \\ 2\overline{)18} \\ 2\overline{)36} \end{array}$$

e. $\dfrac{36}{108} = \dfrac{\;\cdot\;\cdot\;\cdot\;}{\;\cdot\;\cdot\;\cdot\;} =$ _____

$$\begin{array}{r} \overline{)} \\ \overline{)} \\ \overline{)} \\ \overline{)36} \end{array} \qquad \begin{array}{r} \overline{)} \\ \overline{)} \\ \overline{)} \\ \overline{)} \\ \overline{)108} \end{array}$$

f. $\dfrac{75}{100} = \dfrac{\;\cdot\;\cdot\;}{\;\cdot\;\cdot\;\cdot\;} =$ _____

$$\begin{array}{r} \overline{)} \\ \overline{)} \\ \overline{)75} \end{array} \qquad \begin{array}{r} \overline{)} \\ \overline{)} \\ \overline{)} \\ \overline{)100} \end{array}$$

Practice Set (continued) (page 65)

Complete each equivalent fraction in **g–i.**

Multiply the loop.
Divide by the outside number.

g. $\frac{3}{5} = \frac{}{20}$

h. $\frac{3}{4} = \frac{}{20}$

i. $\frac{1}{4} = \frac{}{100}$

j. Compare:
Cross-multiply.

 $\frac{3}{5} \bigcirc \frac{3}{4}$

k. Draw and label points on the number line for these numbers: $-1, \frac{3}{4}, 0, \frac{3}{2}, \frac{-1}{2}$

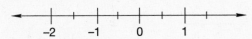

l. Convert the improper (top-heavy) fraction to a mixed number. Shade the circles to show that the numbers are equal.

$\frac{9}{4} = $ _____ $\quad 4\overline{)9}^{\,R}$

   $=$

m. Equivalent fractions can be formed by multiplying by a fraction form of 1 (same numerator and denominator). What property of multiplication states that any number multiplied by 1 is equal to the original number?

_____ Property of Multiplication

n. Write a subtraction equation using whole numbers and a **difference** that is an integer.

_____ − _____ = _____

1.

| | | | | | | | | | | | | | | |1

15

2.

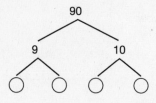

90 = ___ · ___ · ___ · ___

3. Use Tests for Divisibility.

_____

4.

$3\overline{)165}$

165 = ___ · ___ · ___

5. $\dfrac{22}{165} = \dfrac{\ \cdot\ }{\ \cdot\ \cdot\ } = $ _____

$\overline{)22}$ $\overline{)165}$

_____

6. $\dfrac{35}{210} = \dfrac{\ \cdot\ }{\ \cdot\ \cdot\ }$

_____

7. Multiply the loop.

Divide by the outside number.

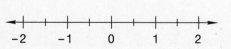

_____

8.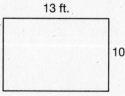

_____

9.

-2   -1   0   1   2

Use work area.

10. Perimeter: Add all sides.

Area= length × width

13 ft.

10 ft.

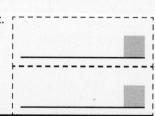

11. Put the numbers in order:

_____, _____, _____, _____, _____, _____, _____

median: _____ mode: _____ range: _____

mean: _____

84
85
88
89   7)‾‾‾‾
82
78
+82

Use work area.

12. Which measure is the halfway point in order?

_____

13. 1 hr = _____ min

2 hr = _____ min

$\frac{1}{2}$ hr = _____ min

_____

14. $\frac{3}{4}$ of 80

Divide by the denominator.
Multiply by the numerator.

_____

15. _____ × c = _____

_____

16. 178
      69

_____

17. Dwayne had _____ pounds of apples. After

he made a pie, he had _____ pounds left.

How many _____ of apples

did Dwayne use?

Use work area.

18. Each _____ cost $2. If

the total price was $ _____, how many

_____ were bought?

Use work area.

19. least to greatest

$0, \dfrac{3}{4}, -\dfrac{4}{3}, 1, -1$

Convert $-\dfrac{4}{3}$ *to a mixed number.*

_____, _____, _____, _____, _____

20. $-7 \bigcirc -6$

_____

21. $|7| \bigcirc |-6|$

_____

22. $-\dfrac{3}{4} \bigcirc -\dfrac{1}{4}$

_____

23. $\left|-\dfrac{3}{4}\right| =$

_____

24. $|n| = 7$
$|-n| = 7$

_____, _____

25. sometimes, always, or never?

_____; Every _____ number is an integer.

Use work area.

26. _____; A mixed number has a <u>f</u>_____ part, so it cannot be a _____ number.

Use work area.

27. _____; The set of _____ numbers contains the _____.

Use work area.

28. *long division*

$\overline{)\$30.00}$

29. $\$8.57$
$\times\ 63$

30. $(\ \ \ \ ) - (\ \ \ \ ) =$
  product   *sum*

  $\$17$ $\$17$
  $\times\ 6$ $+\ 6$

• **Percents** (page 72)

Name _____

Percents are special fractions that have a denominator of 100 and are written with a percent symbol (%).

- **Percent** means *per hundred.*

$$1\% = \frac{1}{100} \qquad 50\% = \frac{50}{100} = \frac{1}{2} \qquad 100\% = \frac{100}{100} = 1$$

- To write a percent as a fraction:

  1. Write the number with a denominator of 100.

  2. Reduce the fraction, if possible.

$$40\% = \frac{40}{100} = \frac{2}{5} \qquad 25\% = \frac{25}{100} = \frac{1}{4} \qquad 67\% = \frac{67}{100}$$

- To write a mixed-number percent as a fraction:

  1. Convert the mixed number to an improper fraction.

  2. Multiply the denominator by 100.

  3. Reduce the fraction, if possible.

$$33\frac{1}{3}\% = \frac{100}{3}\% \cdot \frac{1}{100} = \frac{100}{300} = \frac{1}{3}$$

- To write a fraction as a percent:

  1. Multiply by 100%.

  2. Divide. Write any remainder as a reduced fraction.

$$\frac{1}{10} \cdot \frac{100\%}{1} = \frac{100\%}{10} = 10\% \qquad\qquad \frac{5}{6} \cdot \frac{100\%}{1} = \frac{500\%}{6} = 83\frac{2}{6}\% = 83\frac{1}{3}\%$$

$$\begin{array}{r} 10 \\ 10\overline{)100} \end{array} \qquad\qquad \begin{array}{r} 83 \text{ R2} \\ 6\overline{)50^20} \end{array}$$

> **Teacher Notes:**
>
> - Introduce Hint #31, "Percent."
>
> - Refer students to "Fraction-Decimal-Percent Equivalents" and "Fraction ⟷ Decimal ⟷ Percent" on page 13 in the *Student Reference Guide.*
>
> - Introduce Reference Chart, "Often Used Fractions."
>
> - Students may use the fraction, decimal, and percent towers available in the Adaptations Manipulative Kit. If the kit is not available, Hint #17 describes how to make your own.

Practice Set (page 75)

Write each fraction as a percent.

a. $\dfrac{4}{5} \times \dfrac{100\%}{1} = \dfrac{400\%}{5} =$ _____%

$$5\overline{)4\,0\,0}$$

b. $\dfrac{7}{10} \times \dfrac{100\%}{1} = \dfrac{700\%}{10} =$ _____%

$$10\overline{)7\,0\,0}$$

c. $\dfrac{1}{6} \times \dfrac{100\%}{1} = \dfrac{100\%}{6} =$ _____%

$$\begin{array}{r} \text{R} \\ 6\overline{)1\,0\,0} \end{array}$$

Write each percent as a reduced fraction.

d. $5\% = \dfrac{5}{100} = $ _____

e. $50\% = \dfrac{}{100} = $ _____

f. $12\dfrac{1}{2}\% = \dfrac{25}{2}\% \cdot \dfrac{1}{100} = \dfrac{}{200} = $ _____

Arrange these numbers in order from least to greatest.

g. 75%, 35%, 3%, 100% _____, _____, _____, _____

h. $\dfrac{1}{2}$, $33\dfrac{1}{3}\%$, $\dfrac{1}{10}$, 65% _____, _____, _____, _____

Convert each fraction to a percent.

$\dfrac{1}{2} \times \dfrac{100\%}{1} = \dfrac{100\%}{} = $ _____%

$\dfrac{1}{10} \times \dfrac{100\%}{1} = $ _____ $ = $ _____%

i. Three of the five basketball players scored more than 10 points. What **percent** of the players scored more than 10 points? _____

Convert the fraction to a percent.

$\dfrac{3}{5} \times \dfrac{100\%}{1} = $

j. Janice scored 30% of the team's 50 points.

How many points did Janice score? _____

Convert the percent to a fraction.

30% of 50

$30\% = \dfrac{}{100} = $ _____

Written Practice (page 76)

1. _____ × _____ = 1000

2. 5 tons and 800 pounds.

1 ton = _____ lb

Multiply the loop.

ton	1	5
lb		?

3. average

98
97   5)‾‾‾
100
109
+ 101

4. plot: ˢ_____

_____ − a = _____

5. $\dfrac{60}{72}$ = $\dfrac{\cdot \quad \cdot \quad \cdot}{\cdot \quad \cdot \quad \cdot \quad \cdot}$ =

$\overline{)}$ $\overline{)}$

$\overline{)}$ $\overline{)}$

$\overline{)}$ $\overline{)}$

$\overline{)60}$ $\overline{)72}$

_____

6. *Multiply the loop.*

Divide by the outside number.

$\dfrac{2}{3} = \dfrac{}{18}$

_____

7. _____ Property of Multiplication

Use work area.

8. *Perimeter: Add all sides*

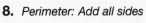

$x =$ _____ 7 cm

$y =$ _____

4 cm, x, y, 10 cm, 12 cm

_____

9. *Area = length × width*

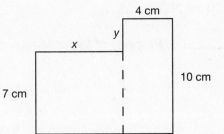

4 cm, y, x, 7 cm, 10 cm, 12 cm

_____

10. perimeter and area

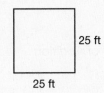

25 ft

25 ft

_____

_____

11. *Multiply the loop.*

$\dfrac{mi}{hr} \quad \dfrac{16}{1} \quad \dfrac{?}{}$

2 hours ⟶ _____

3 hours ⟶ _____

4 hours ⟶ _____

Use work area.

12. *Multiply the loop.*

Divide by the outside number.

_____

13. $\frac{7}{10}$ of 150

Divide by the denominator.

Multiply by the numerator.

_____

14. *Perimeter: Add all sides.*

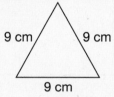

9 cm   9 cm

9 cm

_____

15. **a.** $|-4|$ ◯ -3

b. *Cross-multiply.*

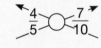

a. _____

b. _____

16. $7 + 2 = 2 +$ _____

_____ Property of Addition

Use work area.

17. $13 \cdot 200 = 200 \cdot$ _____

_____ Property of Multiplication

Use work area.

18. $5 + (4 + 7) = (5 + 4) +$ _____

_____ Property of Addition

Use work area.

19. equivalent fractions

_____ , _____

20. (   ) − (   ) =
  product   *difference*

         _____

21. 3 · _____ = 21

         _____

22. 8 · (7 · 5)   Given

     8 · (5 · 7)   _____ Property

     (8 · 5) · 7   _____ Property of
                            Multiplication

     _____ · 7   Multiplied 8 and 5

     _____   Multiplied _____ and 7

         _____

23. Choose **all** correct answers.

     $\dfrac{22}{23}$

     A whole numbers   **B** counting numbers

     C integers   **D** rational numbers

         _____

24. Choose **all** correct answers.
     −5

     A whole numbers   **B** counting numbers

     C integers   **D** rational numbers

         _____

25. Choose **all** correct answers.
     0

     A whole numbers   **B** counting numbers

     C integers   **D** rational numbers

         _____

26. *See page 9 in the* Student Reference Guide.

_____ , _____ , _____ , _____

27. a.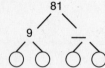

b.

$\overline{)80}$

a. 81 = _____ · _____ · _____ · _____

b. 80 = _____ · _____ · _____ · _____

28. *Cancel matching zeros.*

$$\frac{9450}{30} = \underline{\quad}$$

_____

29. 100.00
−69.83

_____

30. $\frac{3}{4}$ of 48

Divide by the denominator.
Multiply by the numerator.

_____

• Decimal Numbers (page 78)

Name _____

The value of a digit in a number depends on its place in the number. Each place is ten times the value of the place to its right.

• **Decimal numbers** have a whole-number part and a fraction part. The fraction part is separated from the whole-number part by a **decimal point**.

Teacher Notes:

• Introduce Hint #32, "Place Value," Hint #33, "Writing Numbers," and Hint #34, "Tenths and Hundredths."

• Refer students to "Spelling Numbers" on page 9 and "Place Value" on page 11 in the *Student Reference Guide*.

• Review "Fraction-Decimal-Percent Equivalents" and "Fraction ⟷ Decimal ⟷ Percent" on page 13 in the *Student Reference Guide*.

• Introduce Reference Chart, "Examples of Spelling Numbers."

Decimal Place Values

millions		hundred thousands	ten thousands	thousands		hundreds	tens	ones	decimal point	tenths	hundredths	thousandths	ten-thousandths	hundred-thousandths	millionths
1,000,000	,	100,000	10,000	1,000	,	100	10	1	.	$\frac{1}{10}$	$\frac{1}{100}$	$\frac{1}{1000}$	$\frac{1}{10,000}$	$\frac{1}{100,000}$	$\frac{1}{1,000,000}$

• To read a decimal number:
   1. Read the whole number part.
   2. Say "and" for the decimal point.
   3. Read the fraction part and name the place value of the final digit.

   Example: 12.05

   Twelve and Five Hundredths

• When comparing decimal numbers, line up the decimal points and compare one digit at a time.

   Example: Order these numbers from least to greatest.

   0.5   0.41   0.05   0.405
   0.5
   0.41
   0.05
   0.405

   0.05, 0.405, 0.41, 0.5

• To convert **decimals to fractions:**
   The whole number does not change.
   Write the **digits after the decimal point** as the *numerator*.
   Write the **place value of the last digit** as the *denominator*.
   Reduce the fraction.

   Example: $2.75 = 2\frac{75}{100} = 2\frac{3}{4}$

- To convert **fractions to decimals:**

    The whole number does not change. **Divide** the numerator by the denominator. Write the decimal point and zeros in the dividend. Divide until there is no remainder.

    Examples: $\dfrac{3}{25} = 0.12$ $3 + \dfrac{4}{5} = 3 + 0.8 = 3.8$

$$
\begin{array}{r}
.12 \\
25\overline{)3.00} \\
\underline{25} \\
50 \\
\underline{50} \\
0
\end{array}
\qquad
\begin{array}{r}
0.8 \\
5\,\overline{)4.0}
\end{array}
$$

- To convert **decimals to percents,** *shift* the decimal point two places to the *right.*

    Examples: $0.2 \longrightarrow 0.2\underset{\frown}{} = 20\%$

    $1.5 \longrightarrow 1.5\underset{\frown}{} = 150\%$

- To compare fractions, decimals, or percents, **convert** all the numbers to decimals.

- To convert **percents to decimals,** *shift* the decimal point two places to the *left.*

    Examples: $5\% \longrightarrow \underset{\frown}{5\%} \longrightarrow 0.05$

    $225\% \longrightarrow \underset{\frown}{225\%} \longrightarrow 2.25$

Practice Set (page 82)

Use words to write each decimal number.

a. 11.12 _____ and _____

b. 0.375 _____

Write each fraction as a decimal number.

c. $\dfrac{3}{5}$ = _____ · _____ $5\overline{)3.\overset{.}{0}}$

d. $2\dfrac{1}{4}$ = _____ · _____ _____ $4\overline{)1.\overset{.}{0}\,0}$

e. $\dfrac{1}{200}$ = _____ · _____ _____ _____ $200\overline{)1.\overset{.}{0}\,0\,0}$

Write each decimal as a fraction or mixed number.

f. 0.05 = _____

g. 0.025 = _____

h. 1.2 = _____

i. 0.001 = _____

Write each decimal as a percent.

  Shift $\longrightarrow$.

j. 0.8 = _____

k. 1.3 = _____

l. 0.875 = _____

m. 0.002 = _____

Write each percent as a decimal.

Shift ←——— .

n. 2% = _____

o. 20% = _____

p. 24% = _____

q. 0.3% = _____

r. Order from least to greatest:

−0.4, 2.3, 0.6, $\frac{1}{2}$

$\frac{1}{2}$ = _____

2.3
0.6
_____ , _____ , _____ , _____

s. What length is 75% of 12 inches? _____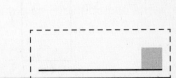

Convert the percent to a fraction.

75% = $\frac{75}{100}$ = _____

t. If the sales-tax rate is 7.5%, what is the sales tax on a $48.00 purchase? _____

Convert the percent to a decimal.

$48
× _____

7.5% = _____ · _____ _____ _____

u. Estimate 8.25% sales tax on a $39.79 purchase. _____

Round 8.25% to 8%. Then convert to a decimal.
Round $39.79 to $40.

$40
× _____

8% = _____ · _____ _____

Written Practice (page 83)

1. 28)‾140‾

2. average

71
69
69
67
+ 64

)‾‾‾‾‾

_____

_____

3. plot: _____

_____ − _____ = d

4. $\frac{50}{75}$ = _____ ÷ _____ ÷ _____ = _____

50 — 10

75 — 25

5. 4.02

_____ and _____

_____

Use work area.

6. _short division_

8)5. 0 0 0

___ • ___ ___ ___

7. 0.17 =

_____

8. 15% of $60
Convert to a fraction.

15% = ____ =
_____100

9. Multiply the loop.
Divide by the outside number.

$\frac{1}{7} = \frac{}{35}$

10. $\frac{5}{5}$ $\frac{7}{7}$

↓   ↓

____ ◯ ____

11. _Perimeter: Add all sides._

7 m
2 m
3 m
5 m
y
4 m

_____

12. _Area = length × width_

7 m
2 m
3 m
5 m
4 m

_____

13. _Multiply the loop._

acres
hr   ____ ____

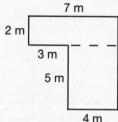

14. _Multiply the loop._
Divide by the outside number.

$\frac{\$}{hr} \frac{}{} \frac{}{1}$

15. *Perimeter: Add all sides.*

9 m

9 m

Use work area.

16. $6 \cdot 4 = 4 \cdot$ _____

_____ Property of Multiplication

Use work area.

17. $4 + (5 + 1) = (4 + 5) +$

_____ Property of addition

Use work area.

18. $6\frac{1}{2} + 1\frac{1}{8} = 1\frac{1}{8} +$

_____ Property of addition

Use work area.

19. **a.** $|{-2}| \bigcirc 2$

b. *Cross-multiply*

a. _____

b. _____

20. What equivalent fractions are shown?

_____ , _____

21. Find two numbers that work in both equations.

_____ × _____ = 10

_____ + _____ = 7

_____ , _____

22. _____ × _____ = 6

_____ − _____ = 1

_____ , _____

23. least to greatest

−0.12 $-\frac{1}{2} = -$_____

−1.2

_____ , _____ , _____

24. Name two sets of numbers for -4.

See page 10 in the Student Reference Guide.

_____

_____

¦ Use work area. ¦

25. *See page 9 in the Student Reference Guide.*

_____, _____, _____, _____,

_____, _____, _____, _____ .

¦ Use work area. ¦

---

26. $\overline{\smash{)}}$
$\overline{\smash{)}}$
$\overline{\smash{)}}$
$\overline{\smash{)}60}$

¦ $60 =$ ___ $\cdot$ ___ $\cdot$ ___ $\cdot$ ___ ¦

27. $\frac{2}{3}$ of 18

Divide by the denominator.
Multiply by the numerator.

---

28. $11.40
$\underline{12}$

29. *Multiply the loop.*

Divide by the outside number.

mi $\quad \dfrac{3}{} \quad \dfrac{1}{?}$
min

mi $\quad \dfrac{1}{} \quad \dfrac{5}{?}$
min

---

30. $18.7
$\underline{+9.04} \qquad -1.809$

• Adding and Subtracting Fractions and Mixed Numbers (page 85)

Name _____

Teacher Notes:
• Introduce Hint #35, "Finding the Least Common Multiple."
• Refer students to "Multiples" on page 7 in the *Student Reference Guide*.

Fractions and mixed numbers must have common denominators before adding or subtracting.

• To add or subtract fractions with common denominators:

Add or subtract the *numerators*.

The denominator does not change.

Reduce the fraction in the answer.

Convert to mixed numbers in the answer.

Example: $\dfrac{3}{4} + \dfrac{3}{4}$ common denominators

$\dfrac{3}{4} + \dfrac{3}{4} = \dfrac{6}{4}$ Add the numerators.

$\dfrac{6}{4} = \dfrac{3}{2}$ Reduce the answer.

$\dfrac{3}{2} = 1\dfrac{1}{2}$ Convert to mixed number.

Example: $\dfrac{3}{4} - \dfrac{1}{6}$ not common denominators

$\dfrac{3}{4} = \dfrac{9}{12}$ Rename the fractions

$-\dfrac{1}{6} = \dfrac{2}{12}$

$\dfrac{7}{12}$ Subtract the numerators.

• Sometimes we must **regroup** a mixed number to subtract.

Example: $3\dfrac{1}{2} - 1\dfrac{3}{4}$ not common denominators

$3\dfrac{1}{2} = 3\dfrac{2}{4}$ Rename the fraction.

$3\dfrac{2}{4} = 2\dfrac{6}{4}$ Regroup the mixed number.

$3\dfrac{2}{4} = 2 + \dfrac{4}{4} + \dfrac{2}{4} = 2\dfrac{6}{4}$

$-1\dfrac{3}{4} = 1\dfrac{3}{4}$

$1\dfrac{3}{4}$ Subtract.

Simplify:

a.

$$\frac{4}{9} + \frac{5}{9} =$$

b.

$$\frac{2}{3} - \frac{2}{3} =$$

c. *Convert.*

$$\frac{1}{8} = \frac{}{8}$$

$$+ \frac{1}{4} = \frac{}{8}$$

d. *Reduce.*

$$\frac{5}{6} = \frac{}{6}$$

$$- \frac{1}{2} = \frac{}{6}$$

e. *Convert.*

$$\frac{4}{5} = \frac{}{10}$$

$$+ \frac{1}{2} = \frac{}{10}$$

f.

$$\frac{1}{3} = \frac{1}{12}$$

$$- \frac{1}{4} = \frac{}{12}$$

g.

$$3\frac{1}{3} = 3\frac{}{6}$$

$$- 2\frac{1}{2} = 2\frac{}{6}$$

h. *Reduce.*

$$6\frac{5}{6} = 6\frac{}{6}$$

$$- 2\frac{1}{3} = 2\frac{}{6}$$

i. *Convert.*

$$3\frac{1}{2} = 3\frac{}{6}$$

$$+ 1\frac{2}{3} = 1\frac{}{6}$$

j. *Regroup.*

$$7\frac{1}{3} = \frac{}{6}$$

$$- 1\frac{1}{2} = \frac{}{6}$$

k. In problem **h**, did you need to regroup the whole number to subtract? Why or why not?

_____; $\frac{5}{6}$ is _____ than $\frac{1}{3}$, so I _____ regroup.

l. A door frame is $32\frac{1}{4}$ inches wide and is trimmed with molding on each side that is $1\frac{5}{8}$ inches wide.

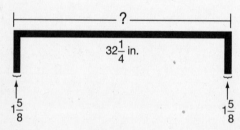

How long is the molding across the top? _____

Add the molding first. Then add the door width.

$$1\frac{5}{8}$$
$$+ 1\frac{5}{8}$$
$$=$$

$$32\frac{1}{4}$$
$$+ $$
$$=$$

© 2007 Harcourt Achieve Inc.

Practice Set (page 89)

m. If the top of a bulletin board is $74\frac{3}{4}$ inches above the floor and the bottom is $38\frac{1}{2}$ inches

floor, then what is the vertical measurement of the bulletin board? _____

Reduce.

$$74\frac{3}{4} = 74\frac{}{4}$$

$$- \ 38\frac{1}{2} = 38\frac{}{4}$$

$$= \ $$

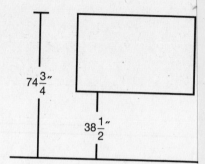

$74\frac{3}{4}''$

$38\frac{1}{2}''$

Written Practice (page 90)

1. 80% of 65,000

Convert to a fraction.

2. 1 cm 5 _____ mm

Multiply the loop.

dimes $\quad \underline{1} \quad \underline{?}$
mm $\qquad \quad 10$

3. 1 hr = 525 mi

2 hr = _____ mi

3 hr = _____ mi

4 hr = _____ mi

4. plot: s _____

$1 - (\quad + \quad) = r$

$\dfrac{3}{8} = \dfrac{}{8} \qquad 1 = \dfrac{}{8}$

$+\dfrac{1}{4} = \dfrac{}{8} \qquad \dfrac{}{8} = \dfrac{}{8}$

Use work area.

5. plot: _____

_____ – _____ = d

7400

6900

6. $\dfrac{5}{8} + \dfrac{2}{8} =$

7. $\dfrac{5}{8} - \dfrac{2}{8} =$

8. $\dfrac{2}{3} = \dfrac{}{6}$

$+ \dfrac{1}{6} = \dfrac{}{6}$

Reduce.

$$\frac{2}{3} = \frac{}{6}$$
$$-\frac{1}{6} = \frac{}{6}$$

_____

10. Reduce.

$$1\frac{1}{4} + 2\frac{1}{4} =$$

_____

$$2\frac{1}{4} - 1\frac{1}{4} =$$

_____

12.
$$3\frac{4}{5} = 3\frac{}{10}$$
$$-2\frac{1}{10} = 2\frac{}{10}$$

_____

$$3\frac{4}{5} = 3\frac{}{10}$$
$$+2\frac{1}{10} = 2\frac{}{10}$$

_____

14. $3\frac{1}{2} + (4\frac{9}{10} + 2\frac{1}{2})$ Given

$3\frac{1}{2} + (\underline{} + \underline{})$

_____ Property

$(\underline{} + \underline{}) + \underline{}$

_____ Property

$\underline{} + \underline{}$ Added

$\underline{}$ Added

. a. $\frac{3}{25} =$

$25\overline{)3.00}$

b. $3\frac{2}{5} =$

$5\overline{)2.0}$

a. _____ . _____

b. _____ . _____

. a. $0.15 =$

b. $0.015 =$

a. _____

b. _____

Use work area.

17. Choose all the correct answers.
The set of whole numbers is closed under

A. addition.   **B.** subtraction.

C. multiplicaton.   **D.** division.

_____ , _____

18. $\dfrac{75}{125} = \dfrac{\ \cdot\ \cdot\ }{\ \cdot\ \cdot\ } =$

$\overline{}$ $\overline{}$

$\overline{}$ $\overline{}$

$\overline{)75}$ $\overline{)125}$

_____

19. Multiply the loop.

Divide by the outside number.

$\dfrac{3}{5} = \dfrac{\ \ }{100}$

_____

20. Perimeter: Add all sides

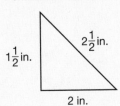

$1\frac{1}{2}$ in. $2\frac{1}{2}$ in.

2 in.

_____

21. Area $=$ length $\times$ width

16 ft

14 ft

_____

22. See page 9 in the Student Reference Guide.

_____, _____, _____, _____, _____

Use work area.

23.

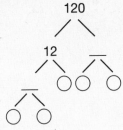

$120 = \dfrac{\ \ \cdot\ \ }{\ \ \cdot\ \ \cdot\ \ }$

24. average

1
3
5
+ 7

$\overline{)}$

_____

25. average

22
24
26
28
+20

$\overline{)}$

_____

26. short division

$4\overline{)2\,8\,0}$

_____

27. $\dfrac{1}{2} = \dfrac{\ }{6}$ $\dfrac{1}{3} = \dfrac{\ }{6}$ $\dfrac{5}{6}$

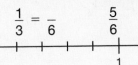

0   1

Use work area.

28. $16\overline{)\$64.32}$

29.   2007
    $-\ 1918$

How many years were there

from _____ to _____?

30. $17\overline{)\$52.70}$

L13-74

• Evaluation
• Solving Equations
by Inspection (page 92)

Teacher Note:
• Review "Missing Numbers" on page 4 in the *Student Reference Guide*.

An equation may have numbers and letters.

• A variable is a letter that stands in for a number in an equation.

• A constant is another name for a number in an equation.

$$\text{constant} \longrightarrow 4s \longleftarrow \text{variable}$$

• We can **evaluate** the equation by *substituting* numbers for the variables and calculating the answer.

Example: A formula for the perimeter of a rectangle is $P = 2l + 2w$.

Find P when l is 15 cm and w is 12 cm.

$P = 2l + 2w$	Given formula
$P = 2(15) + 2(12)$	Substitute.
$P = 30 + 24 = 54 \text{ cm}$	Calculate the answer.

If an equation has only one variable, we can **solve** the equation.

• To solve an equation, use the "Missing Numbers" chart in the *Student Reference Guide*.

• Some equations will take more than one step to solve.

Example: Solve the equation $3m + 2 = 20$.

$3m + 2 = 20$	Given equation
Think: *What number plus 2 equals 20?*	
$3m = 18$	$18 + 2 = 20$, so $3m = 18$.
$m = 6$	solved

Practice Set (page 94)

a. A formula for the area (A) of a parallelogram is $A = bh$.
Find the area of a parallelogram with a base (b) of 12 in. and a height (h) of 4 in. _____

$A = bh$

$A =$ _____ $\times$ _____

$A =$ _____

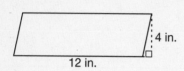

b. Name the constant in this expression: $4ac$ _____

c. Evaluate $4ac$ for $a = 1$ and $c = 12$.

$4ac = 4 \times$ _____ $\times$ _____ $=$ _____

Solve each equation.

d. $w + 5 = 16$

$w =$ _____

e. $m - 6 = 18$

$m =$ _____

f. $25 - n = 11$

$n =$ _____

g. $5x = 30$

$x =$ _____

h. $\dfrac{d}{4} = 8$

$d =$ _____

i. $\dfrac{12}{z} = 6$

$z =$ _____

j. $2a - 1 = 9$
What number plus 1 is 9?

$2a =$ _____

$a =$ _____

k. $20 = 3f - 1$
What number minus 1 is 20?

$3f =$ _____

$f =$ _____

l. Admission to the county fair is $3. Each ride costs $2. Nate has $15. Solve the following equation to find how many rides he can take.

$2r + 3 = 15$
What number plus 3 is 15?

$2r =$ _____

$r =$ _____

1. $\frac{5}{8}$ of 256

   Divide by the denominator.

   Multiply by the numerator.

   _____

2. 1 hr = 35 pages

   2 hr = _____ pages

   3 hr = _____ pages

   4 hr = _____ pages

   Use work area.

3. _____ × g = _____

   _____

4. plot: _____

   _____ − _____ = d

   $$\begin{array}{r} 50 \\ -\ 13 \\ \hline \end{array}$$

   _____

5. $15 = m - 4$

   $$\begin{array}{r} 15 \\ 4 \\ \hline \end{array}$$

   $m =$ _____

6. $15 - m = 4$

   $$\begin{array}{r} 15 \\ 4 \\ \hline \end{array}$$

   $m =$ _____

7. $3w = 36$

   $w =$ _____

8. $5x + 5 = 20$

   What number plus 5 is 20?

   $5x =$

   $x =$ _____

9. $\frac{x}{3} = 4$

   $x =$ _____

10. $\frac{x}{2} + 3 = 12$

   What number plus 3 is 12?

   $\frac{x}{2} =$

   $x =$ _____

11. $\frac{3}{8} = \frac{}{24}$

$+\frac{1}{3} = \frac{}{24}$

12. $1\frac{1}{4} = 1\frac{}{16}$

$-\frac{3}{16} = \frac{}{16}$

13. $\frac{3}{8} + \left(1\frac{1}{2} + 2\frac{5}{8}\right)$ given

$\frac{3}{8} + (\underline{\hspace{1cm}} + \underline{\hspace{1cm}})$ _____ Property

$\underline{\hspace{1cm}} + \underline{\hspace{1cm}} + \underline{\hspace{1cm}}$ _____ Property

$\underline{\hspace{1cm}} + \underline{\hspace{1cm}}$ added

$\underline{\hspace{1cm}}$ added   Use work area.

14. least to greatest

$\frac{1}{2}, \ -1, \ 0, \ \frac{3}{8}, \ 0.8, \ 1, \ -.05$

Convert to fractions.

$\underline{\hspace{1cm}}, \ \underline{\hspace{1cm}}, \ 0, \ \underline{\hspace{1cm}}, \ \underline{\hspace{1cm}}, \ \underline{\hspace{1cm}}, \ 1$

Use work area.

15. Find ac
when $a = 2$
$c = 9$

16. $P = 4s$
Find P if $s = 12$.

$P = \underline{\hspace{2cm}}$

17. $y = x - 9$
Find y if $x = 22$.

$y = \underline{\hspace{2cm}}$

18. $d = rt$
Find d if $r = 60$
$t = 4$.

$d = \underline{\hspace{2cm}}$

© 2007 Harcourt Achieve Inc.

19. least to greatest

$$\frac{2}{3}, \quad \frac{3}{4}, \quad \frac{5}{12}$$

$$\frac{}{12} \quad \frac{}{12}$$

_____, _____, _____

20.

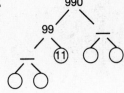

990 = _____ · _____ · _____ · _____ · _____

21. (_____) − (_____) =

_____

22. *See page 5 in the* Student Reference Guide.

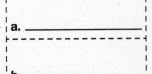

_____

23. *Perimeter: Add all sides.*

$2\frac{1}{2}$ in.

$2\frac{1}{2}$ in.

_____

24. a. $|-5| \bigcirc |-6|$

b. $-5 \bigcirc -6$

a. _____

b. _____

25. Median

27, 30, 29, 31, 30, 32, 39

Put the numbers in order.

_____, _____, _____, _____, _____, _____, _____

_____

26. 8.25% rounds to 8%.

Convert to a decimal.

$40

× _____

_____

27. *Shift* ←.

a. 125% =

b. 8.25% =

a. _____

b. _____

28. *Perimeter: Add all sides.*

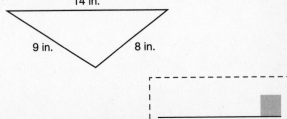

14 in.

9 in.   8 in.

_____

29.

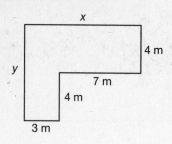

30. *Area = length × width*

width: _____ yd

ft	3	12
yd		?

length: _____ yd

ft		15
yd		?

• Powers and Roots (page 97)

Name _____

An exponent shows repeated multiplication. It shows how many times the base is used as a factor.

base ➤ 5^2 ◄ exponent

• An exponent of 2 is read "squared."

• An exponent of 3 is read "cubed."

• Other exponents are called **powers.**

Examples:

$3^4 = 3 \times 3 \times 3 \times 3 = 81$

three to the fourth power

$5^2 = 5 \times 5 = 25$

five squared

$2^3 = 2 \times 2 \times 2 = 8$

two cubed

$8^1 = 8$

eight to the first power

Teacher Notes:
• Introduce Hint #36, "Square Roots."
• Refer students to "Multiplication Table" on page 3 and "Exponents" on page 8 in the *Student Reference Guide.*
• The color tiles available in the Adaptations Manipulative Kit can be used to show the relationship between area and side length of a square.

• Powers of 10 have a pattern. The number has as many zeros as the power.

$10^2 = 100$

two zeros

$10^4 = 10,000$

four zeros

• Variables can be grouped with exponents.

$2xxxyyz = 2x^3y^2z$

x is a factor three times

y is a factor two times

• **Roots** are the opposite of powers. They use a radical sign. $\sqrt{}$

• To find a root, tell what factor is multiplied by itself to make the number.

Examples:

$\sqrt{144} = 12$

square root of 144

$(12 \times 12 = 144)$

$\sqrt[3]{64} = 4$

cube root of 64

$(4 \times 4 \times 4 = 64)$

$\sqrt[5]{32} = 2$

fifth root of 32

$(2 \times 2 \times 2 \times 2 \times 2 = 32)$

$\sqrt{4^2} = 4$

square root of four squared

• A **perfect square** is a square of a counting number. In the Multiplication Table in the *Student Reference Guide* the circled numbers are perfect squares.

Practice Set (page 101)

Simplify:

a. $10^5 =$ _____

b. $3^4 = 3 \times 3 \times 3 \times 3 =$ _____

c. $(15 \text{ cm})^2 =$ _____ cm^2

d. $\sqrt{121} =$ _____

e. $\sqrt[3]{8} =$ _____

f. $\sqrt{5^2} =$ _____

Practice Set (continued) (page 101)

Rewrite with exponents.

g. $5xyyyzz =$ _____

h. $aaab =$ _____

i. $3xyxyx =$ _____

j. Mr. Chin wants to cover the floor of his garage with a non-slip coating. His garage measures 20 feet on each side. Use the formula $A = s^2$ to find the number of square feet of floor that needs to be coated.

20 ft

$A = s^2$

$A = ($ _____ $)^2 =$ _____ $\times$ _____

$A =$ _____

Written Practice (page 101)

1. 40% of 25,000

Convert to a fraction.

$40\% = \dfrac{1}{100} =$

---

2. short division

$8\overline{)1\ 2\ 8}$

---

3. *Multiply the loop.*

min | 1 | 4
beats

$\dfrac{1}{2}$ min = _____ beats

---

4. $(4\ \text{in.})^3 =$

---

5. $\sqrt[3]{1} =$

---

6. $\sqrt{8^2} =$

---

7. $2xxxmrr =$

---

8. $\dfrac{x}{4} = 12$

$x =$ _____

9. $2x + 5 = 5$

What number plus 5 is 5?

$2x =$

$x = \underline{\hspace{3cm}}$

10. $9 - m = 7$

$$\begin{array}{r} 9 \\ 7 \\ \hline \end{array}$$

$m = \underline{\hspace{3cm}}$

11. *Reduce*

$\dfrac{4}{5} = \dfrac{}{10}$

$-\dfrac{1}{2} = \dfrac{}{10}$

$\underline{\hspace{4cm}}$

12. $1\dfrac{1}{4} = 1\dfrac{}{12}$

$+1\dfrac{1}{3} = 1\dfrac{}{12}$

$\underline{\hspace{4cm}}$

13. $\left(\dfrac{1}{3} + \dfrac{1}{2} + \dfrac{2}{3}\right) \bigcirc \left(\dfrac{1}{3} + \dfrac{2}{3} + \dfrac{1}{2}\right)$

Use the Commutative Property and you won't have to add.

$\underline{\hspace{4cm}}$

14. least to greatest

$0, -2, \dfrac{1}{3}, 0.3, 3, -1.5$

Convert 0.3 to a fraction.

$-2, \underline{\hspace{1cm}}, \underline{\hspace{1cm}}, \underline{\hspace{1cm}}, \underline{\hspace{1cm}}, 3$

Use work area.

15. Find $4ac$

when $a = 1$

$c = 9$

$\underline{\hspace{4cm}}$

16. $(\quad) - (\quad) =$

$\underline{\hspace{4cm}}$

17. $y = \dfrac{1}{3}x + 2$

Find y if $x = 6$.

$y = \underline{\hspace{3cm}}$

18. 20% of $65

20% =

19. least to greatest

$\dfrac{3}{8}, \dfrac{2}{5}, \dfrac{1}{4}$

$\downarrow \quad \downarrow \quad \downarrow$

$\dfrac{}{40} \dfrac{}{40} \dfrac{}{40}$

$\underline{\hspace{1cm}}, \underline{\hspace{1cm}}, \underline{\hspace{1cm}}$

20. Use exponents.

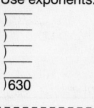

$$630 = \underline{\quad} \cdot \underline{\quad} \cdot \underline{\quad} \cdot \underline{\quad} \cdot \underline{\quad}$$

21. $A = s^2$

Find A if $s = 15$ cm.

$A = $ _____

22.

$$\begin{array}{r} m \\ -\ 12 \\ \hline 12 \end{array}$$

$m = $ _____

23. Perimeter: *Add all sides.*

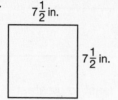

7½ in.

7½ in.

_____

24. 0.625 ◯ $\frac{3}{5}$

Convert to a decimal.

$5\overline{)3.0}$

_____

25. median

11, 3, 18, 2, 5

Put the numbers in order.

___ , ___ , ___ , ___ , ___

_____

26. fraction: 0.07 =

words: _____

_____

Use work area.

27. ____ is a whole number that is not positive.

Use work area.

28. *Perimeter: Add all sides.*

10 cm

4 cm

5 cm

_____

29.

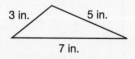

3 in.   5 in.

7 in.

_____

30. $A = s^2$

$s = 15$ ft

_____

• Irrational Numbers (page 103)

Name _____

Irrational numbers are numbers that cannot be expressed *exactly* as decimals or fractions.

- The square root of any counting number that is not a perfect square is an irrational number.

$$\sqrt{1} = 1 \qquad \sqrt{2} \approx 1.41 \qquad \sqrt{3} \approx 1.73 \qquad \sqrt{4} = 2$$

$\sqrt{2}$ and $\sqrt{3}$ are irrational numbers.

- The irrational numbers and the rational numbers make up the set of **real numbers**.

- All real numbers can be placed on a number line.

- To place an irrational number on a number line, find which two counting numbers the irrational number is between.

Teacher Notes:
- Review "Number Families" on page 10 in the *Student Reference Guide*.
- Students will need a calculator to complete the lesson.

Example:

Name the two counting numbers that $\sqrt{12}$ is between on a number line.

$$\sqrt{1} = 1 \qquad \sqrt{4} = 2 \qquad \sqrt{9} = 3 \qquad \sqrt{16} = 4$$

$\sqrt{12}$ is greater than $\sqrt{9}$ and less than $\sqrt{16}$.

So $\sqrt{12}$ must be between 3 and 4 on a number line.

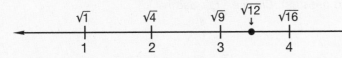

The area of this square is 100cm².

100 cm²

The side length is the square root of its area.

$$\sqrt{100 cm^2} = \sqrt{10 cm}$$

So the length of the side is $\sqrt{10}$ cm.

The area of this square is 2 cm².

$$\boxed{2\ cm^2}$$

The side length is the square root of its area.

$$\sqrt{2cm^2} = \sqrt{2}cm$$

So the length of the side is $\sqrt{2}$ cm.

Practice Set (page 105)

Simplify:

a. If a real number is **not rational**, then it is _____.

b. Circle the irrational number below.

  A −3   **B** $\sqrt{9}$ **C** $\frac{9}{2}$ **D** $\sqrt{7}$

c. Circle the number that is between 2 and 3 on the number line. How do you know?

  A $\sqrt{2}$ **B** $\sqrt{3}$ **C** $\sqrt{4}$ **D** $\sqrt{5}$

  $\sqrt{4} = 2$ and $\sqrt{9} =$ _____, so _____ must be between 2 and 3.

d. Arrange these real numbers in order from least to greatest. *Change $\frac{3}{4}$ to a decimal.*

  0, 1, $\sqrt{2}$, $\frac{3}{4}$, 0.5, -0.6

  _____, 0, _____, _____, 1, _____

Find the length of each side of these squares. The area is given.

e. *square root*

$$\boxed{400\ mm^2}$$

f. *square root*

$$\boxed{3\ cm^2}$$

Use a calculator to find the square roots of these numbers. Round to the nearest hundredth. (Enter the number, and then the press the $\sqrt{}$ key.)

g. $\sqrt{10} \approx$ ___ . ___ ___ ___

h. $\sqrt{20} \approx$ ___ . ___ ___ ___

i. $\sqrt{40} \approx$ ___ . ___ ___ ___

j. Look at your answers to problems **g**, **h**, and **i**. Which number is twice as much as the square root of 10? _____

© 2007 Harcourt Achieve Inc.

1. $2\overline{)108}$

2. $\frac{2}{7}$ of 294

3. plot: _____

$$\underline{} - \underline{} = 1$$

$$\begin{array}{r} 41 \\ -28 \\ \hline \end{array}$$

4. plot: _____

$$\underline{} - (\underline{} \times 2) = d$$

$$\begin{array}{r} 30 \\ \underline{} \\ \end{array}$$

5. $\sqrt[3]{64} =$

6. $10^3 =$

7. $\dfrac{6}{7} = \dfrac{}{14}$

$+ \dfrac{1}{14} = \dfrac{}{14}$

8. $2\dfrac{5}{8} = 2\dfrac{}{8}$

$- 1\dfrac{1}{4} = 1\dfrac{}{8}$

9. Perimeter: *Add all sides.* Area = *length* × *width.*

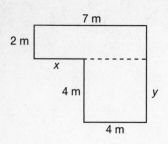

10. a. $4xy7xy =$

b. $3aabbbc =$

a. _____

b. _____

11. a. $\sqrt{16}$ 7
↓
___ ◯ 7

b. $\sqrt{81}$ 3^2
↓   ↓
___ ◯ ___

a. _____

b. _____

12. $4z - 2 = 30$
What number minus 2 is 30?

$4z =$

z = _____

13. $200 - a = 140$

200
140

a = _____

14. $50 = 5m + 10$
What number plus 10 is 50?

$5m =$

m = _____

15. $7 = \dfrac{x}{3}$

x = _____

16. 75% of $800
Convert to a fraction.

$75\% =$

17. Find 4*ac*
   when *a* = 3
       c = 39

‾‾‾‾‾‾‾‾‾‾‾‾

18. 8 · (49 · 25)   Given

8 · (____ · ____)   _____ Property

(____ · ____) · ____   _____ Property

____ · ____   Multiplied

____   Multiplied

Use work area.

19. *p* = *mv*

Find *p* when *m* = 40
           v = 11

p = ‾‾‾‾‾‾‾‾‾‾

20. mean

     2
     4
     6
  + 8   ‾‾‾‾‾‾‾
‾‾‾‾‾

median
Put the numbers in order.

‾‾ , ‾‾ , ‾‾ , ‾‾

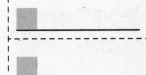

21. Use the exponents.

400 = ‾‾‾‾ · ‾‾‾‾

22. (   ) × (   ) =

‾‾‾‾‾‾‾‾‾‾‾‾

23. 8)‾1.‾0‾0‾0

Percent: shift → .

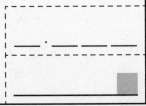

‾‾‾ · ‾‾‾ ‾‾‾ ‾‾‾

24. *d* = *rt*
   Find *d* when *r* = 55 $\frac{mi}{hr}$
               t = 2 hr

d = ‾‾‾‾‾‾‾‾‾‾

25. *See p. 9 in the* Student Reference Guide.

_____

26. *Be careful!*

$$\begin{array}{r} 123 \\ -321 \\ \hline \end{array} \quad \longrightarrow \quad \begin{array}{r} 321 \\ -123 \\ \hline \end{array}$$

_____

27. 3)‾2̅0̅0̅1̅

_____

28. List all correct answers.

See p. 10 in the Student Reference Guide.

-2

_____, _____, _____

29. List all correct answers.

$\sqrt{2}$

_____, _____

30. List all correct answers.

$\dfrac{1}{2}$

_____, _____

• Rounding and Estimating

(page 108)

Name _____

Estimate means to round off.

Teacher Notes:
• Introduce Hint #37, "Estimating or Rounding."
• Refer students to "Estimate" on page 7 in the *Student Reference Guide.*
• Review "Place Value" on page 11 in the *Student Reference Guide.*

• We can **estimate** the answer to a problem by *rounding* the numbers *before* we work the problem.

• To round a **whole number**:

1. Underline the place value you are rounding to.

2. Circle the digit to the right.

3. If the circled digit is *5 or more*, **add 1** to the underlined number.
   If the circled digit is *less than 5*, **do not change** the underlined number.

4. Everything *after* the underline becomes zero.

Examples: 67   6̲   ⑦   ⟶   70

              328   3̲   ②   8   ⟶   300

              2180   2 1̲   ⑧   0   ⟶   2200

• To round a **decimal number**:

1. Use a place-vlaue chart.

2. Round in the same way as a whole number.

3. Do not write zeros at the end of a decimal number.

Examples: Round 3.14159 to two decimal places.

              3.14159   3.14̲①59   ⟶   3.14

              Round 3.14159 to the nearest ten-thousandth.

              3.14159   3.1415̲⑨   ⟶   3.1416

• To round a **mixed number**:

1. Compare the fraction to $\frac{1}{2}$.

2. If the fraction is *greater than or equal to* $\frac{1}{2}$, **add 1** to the whole number (numerator greater than or equal to half the denominator).

3. If the fraction is *less than* $\frac{1}{2}$, **do not change** the whole number (numerator *less than* half the denominator).

Examples: $6\frac{2}{3}$ ⟶   7   (because $\frac{2}{3} > \frac{1}{2}$)

              $6\frac{1}{8}$ ⟶   6   (because $\frac{1}{2} < \frac{1}{8}$)

Richard is paid $11.85 per hour. About how much money does he earn in 52 weeks if he works 40 hours per week?

We round the numbers before we work the problem.

Round the money to the nearest whole number.	$11.85 $\longrightarrow$	$12
Round the number of weeks to the nearest ten.	52 $\longrightarrow$	50
Round the hours per week to the nearest ten.	40 $\longrightarrow$	40

Now we work the problem with the rounded numbers.

$12 · 40 · 50 = $24,000

Richard earns about $24,000 per year.

Practice Set (page 111)

a. In 2000 the population of Dallas was 1,188,580. Round that number to the nearest **hundred thousand.**

1, 1⑧8, 5 8 0 $\longrightarrow$ _____

b. Round 3.14159 to **four decimal places.**

3. 1 4 1 5⑨ $\longrightarrow$ ____ · ____ ____ ____ ____

c. The price of regular unleaded gasoline was 2.19\frac{9}{10}$. Round that price to the **nearest cent.**
   Compare to $\frac{1}{2}$.

$2.19 $\quad \frac{9}{10}$ $\longrightarrow$ ▨_____

d. Estimate the height of the ceiling in your classroom in meters and in feet.
   How tall are you? How many of you would it take to touch the ceiling?

meters: ▨_____ feet: _____

e. Estimate the sum of 3879 and 5276.

3⑧7 9 $\longrightarrow$

$+$

5②7 6 $\longrightarrow$ _____

g. Gus works 39 hours for $9.85 per hour. He calculates that his weekly paycheck should be $38,415. What is a reasonable estimate of what Gus earns?

$$\begin{array}{r} 39 \\ \underline{\$9.85} \end{array} \longrightarrow \times \underline{\hspace{3cm}}$$

What was Gus's error?
Gus multiplied by $985 instead of $ _____.

h. A rectangular room is $11\frac{3}{4}$ feet long and $10\frac{1}{2}$ feet wide. Grace calculated the area to be about 124 square feet. Explain why her calculation is or is not reasonable.

$$\begin{array}{r} 11\frac{3}{4} \longrightarrow \\ 10\frac{1}{2} \longrightarrow \times \underline{\hspace{2cm}} \end{array}$$

Round $11\frac{3}{4}$ to _____ and $10\frac{1}{2}$ to _____.

The area should be close to _____ ft².

124 ft² is close to _____, so Grace's

answer is reasonable.

i. It is 6:05 p.m. and Eduardo is driving to Dallas. If he is 157 miles away and driving at an average speed of 62 miles per hour, is it reasonable that he can reach Dallas by 9:00 p.m.? Explain.

$$62 \longrightarrow$$

$$\underline{\times \quad 3\ hours}$$

Round 62 to _____ miles per hour. He

has about _____ hours until 9:00, so

Eduardo can drive about _____ miles.

It is reasonable to reach Dallas by 9:00.

Written Practice (page 111)

1.
$$\begin{array}{r} 12 \\ \underline{\times 10} \end{array}$$

2.
$$\begin{array}{r} 72°F \\ \underline{- \ 57°F} \end{array}$$

3. 1, 3, _____, _____, _____, ...

4. One yard is equal to _____ feet. So four feet

is just more than _____ yard.

$$\begin{array}{cc} \text{ft} & \overline{} \quad \dfrac{?}{48} \\ \text{yd} & 1 \end{array}$$

Use work area.

5. $11^2 =$

6. $\sqrt{121} =$

---

7. *Convert.*

$$\frac{1}{2} = \frac{}{4}$$

$$+\frac{3}{4} = \frac{}{4}$$

8. *Convert.*

$$1\frac{2}{3} = 1\frac{}{6}$$

$$+\frac{5}{6} = \frac{}{6}$$

---

9. *Perimeter: Add all sides.*

Area = length × width

18 yd

15 yd

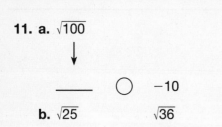

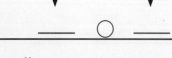

10. a. $5xxy =$

b. $6xyyxy =$

a. _____

b. _____

---

11. a. $\sqrt{100}$

$\downarrow$

_____ $\bigcirc$ -10

b. $\sqrt{25}$ $\sqrt{36}$

$\downarrow$ $\downarrow$

_____ $\bigcirc$ _____

a. _____

b. _____

12. $5x = 45$

$x =$ _____

---

13. $\dfrac{x}{12} = 3$

$x =$ _____

14. $x + 7 = 15$ 15

$\underline{7}$

$x =$ _____

15. $18 - x = 10$ 　　18
　　　　　　　　　　　　 10

$x =$ _____

16. Complete this story for problem 12.

Julie ate 5 _____ at lunch everyday. In how

many days did Julie eat _____ _____?

Use work area.

17. $P = 2 (l + w)$

Find P when $l = 7$ in.
　　　　　　　 $w = 5$ in.

$P =$ _____

18. Use exponents.

$\overline{}$
$\overline{}$
$\overline{}$
$\overline{)90}$

$990 =$ ____ · ____ · ____ · ____

19. *factors of 18*

____ and ____

____ and ____

____ and ____

Use work area.

20. Mean: ____　　Median: ____

　3
　4
　3
　2
　5
　3
　4
　6
　3
+ 2

____, ____, ____, ____, ____,

____, ____, ____, ____, ____

Mode: ____

Range: ____

$\overline{)}$

Use work area.

21. Which measure tells the most common number?

_____

22. $17 + 28 + 3$　　　given

$17 +$ ____ $+$ ____　　_____ Property

____ $+$ ____ $=$

_____

23. $(4,0), (-2, 3), \left(0, -\dfrac{n}{2}\right)$

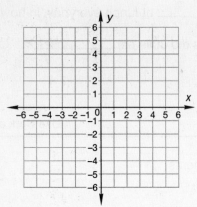

Which point seems farthest from (,)?

_____

24. area and perimeter
$(-1,2), (3,2)\ (3,-5), (-1,-5)$

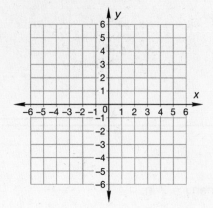

_____ units

_____ units²

25. least to greatest

$1.3, 0, 1, \dfrac{3}{4}, \dfrac{4}{3}, 1\dfrac{1}{12}$

Convert 1.3 to a fraction.

$0, \underline{\hphantom{xx}}, \underline{\hphantom{xx}}, 1\dfrac{1}{12}, \underline{\hphantom{xx}}, \underline{\hphantom{xx}}$

Use work area.

26. Which is greatest?

A 30% of $20   **B** $\dfrac{1}{4}$ of $20

C $4

_____

27. $7⑧9 →

$\underline{\times\ \ 6}$

$\underline{\hphantom{xx}}$ is close to $5000, so the budget is reasonable.

Use work area.

28. a. $4\dfrac{5}{8}$ →

b. $3.①99$ →

a. _____

b. _____

29. 8.25% → 8% = _____ · _____ _____

Shift ← .

$7⑧9 →

$\underline{\times\ \hphantom{xx}}$

_____

30. fraction

$0.24 = \dfrac{\hphantom{xx}}{100} =$

percent

Shift → .

0.24 =

_____

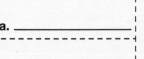

• **Lines and Angles** (page 114)

Lines, line segments and rays are contained in planes.

• A **plane** is a flat (two-dimensional) surface like a table top.

• A **line** has no end. It extends in opposite directions forever.

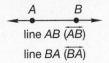

line AB ($\overleftrightarrow{AB}$)

line BA ($\overleftrightarrow{BA}$)

• A **ray** has one endpoint. It extends in one direction forever.

ray AB ($\overrightarrow{AB}$)

• A **segment** has two endpoints. Its length can be measured.

segment AB ($\overline{AB}$)

segment BA ($\overline{BA}$)

The **length** of AB is mAB or $\overline{AB}$.

• When lines cross, they **intersect**.

• **Parallel** lines do not intersect, like railroad tracks.

• **Perpendicular** lines intersect to form square corners, like the corner or a piece of paper.

• Lines that intersect but are not perpendicular are **oblique** lines. Oblique can also mean a line or segment is not horizontal or vertical.

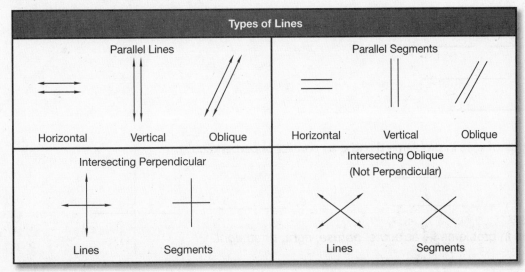

Types of Lines
Parallel Lines / Parallel Segments

Horizontal — Vertical — Oblique — Horizontal — Vertical — Oblique

Intersecting Perpendicular — Intersecting Oblique (Not Perpendicular)

Lines — Segments — Lines — Segments

• An **angle** is formed by two rays with a common endpoint, called a **vertex**.

• Angles can be named using:

The letter of the vertex

Three letters with the vertex in the middle

A number.

• The **measure** of ∠ABC is m∠ABC.

• Angles and turns are measured in **degrees**.

A full turn (a circle) contains 360°.

Teacher Notes:
• Introduce Hint #37, "Geometry Vocabulary."
• Refer students to "Types of Lines" on page 17 and "Angles" on page 27 in the *Student Reference Guide*.
• Introduce reference chart, "Angles and Triangles."

Lesson Summary (page 115)

• Angles are classified by their degree measures.

An **acute** angle has between 0° and 90° ("a cute" little angle).

A **right** angle has exactly 90° (like a square corner).

An **obtuse** angle has between 90° and 180°.

A **straight** angle has exactly 180° (like a line).

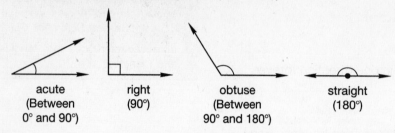

acute
(Between
0° and 90°)

right
(90°)

obtuse
(Between
90° and 180°)

straight
(180°)

• A **linear pair** is two angles that share a side and make a straight angle. Because a straight angle has 180°, the sum of the measures of a linear pair is 180°.

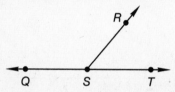

∠QRS is ∠RST are a linear pair.
m∠QRS + m∠RST = 180°

Practice Set (page 117)

Name each figure in problems **a–c**.

a. P ———— Q   _____

b. P ———— Q   _____

c. P ———— Q   _____

Describe each pair of lines in problems **d** and **e** as *parallel* or *perpendicular*.

d. _____

e. _____

Describe each angle in problems **f–i** as *acute, obtuse, right,* or *straight*.

f. ∠CMD _____

g. ∠CMA _____

h. ∠AMB _____

i. ∠AMD _____

j. If the measure of ∠DMC is 45°, then what is the measure of ∠CMA? Explain your answer.

Because ∠DMC and ∠_____ are a linear pair, they add to 180°.

So m∠CMA = 180° − m∠DMC = 180° − 45° = _____°.

1. 9
$\times$ 6

_____

2. 66°F
17°F

_____

3. fraction: $\frac{35}{50} =$
Reduce.

percent: $\frac{35}{50} = \frac{}{100}$

_____

4. 1 gal =

_____ cups

cups		
gal	1	3

_____

5.

mi	$\frac{3}{45}$	$\frac{1}{}$
min		

mi	$\frac{1}{}$	$\frac{}{60}$
min		

$\frac{\text{min.}}{\text{mi}}$

_____

$\frac{\text{mi}}{\text{hr.}}$

_____

6. $12^2 =$

_____

7. $\sqrt{144}$

_____

8. $\frac{5}{8} = \frac{}{24}$

$- \frac{2}{6} = \frac{}{24}$

_____

9. _Convert and reduce._

$3\frac{1}{4} = 3\frac{}{12}$

$+ 1\frac{11}{12} = 1\frac{}{12}$

_____

10. a. |-10| $\sqrt{100}$
↓   ↓
_____ ◯ _____

b. $\sqrt{5}$ ◯ 2 $\sqrt{4} = 2$

a. _____ b. _____

11. $x - 13 = 20$ 20
                              13

$x =$ _____

12. $5 + x = 13$ 13
                            5

$x =$ _____

13. $\frac{2x}{5} = 10$

What number divided by 5 is 10?

$2x =$

$x =$ _____

14. $8x = 64$

$x =$ _____

15. 5, (+5) _____, (+5) _____, (+5) _____

Use work area.

16. area and perimeter

15 ft

10 ft

$A =$ _____

$P =$ _____

17. Use exponents.

)_____   )_____

)_____   )_____

)_____   )_____

)128 $128 =$ _____

18. *See page 9 in the* Student Reference Guide.

_____

19. least to greatest
Use a number line.

0, 1, -1, $\frac{-4}{5}$, $\frac{5}{4}$

_____, _____, _____, _____, _____

Use work area.

20. a. *Convert.*

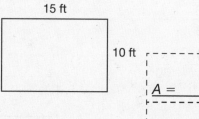

$\left|\frac{-4}{5}\right|$ $\left|\frac{5}{4}\right|$

_____ ◯ _____

b.

$\frac{7}{10}$

↓

0.8 ◯ _____

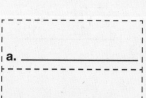

a. _____

b. _____

21. fraction: 0.125 =

Reduce.

percent: 0.125 =

Shift ——→.

22. 15% of $40

Shift ←——.

$40

x _____

23. Round.

8.25% ——→ 8% =

Shift ←——.

$104 ——→

x _____

26.

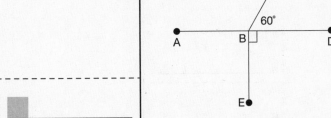

a. ∠ABC   b. ∠ABD

c. ∠CBD   d. ∠DBE

24. √4, √5, √9, √10, √15, √16

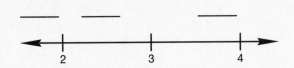

Use work area.

25. *square root*

40 cm²

√40 is between which two whole numbers?

_____ and _____

a. _____   c. _____

b. _____   d. _____

27.

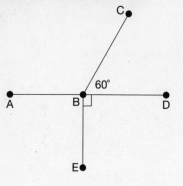

a. m∠ABC = 180° − _____ =

b. m∠ABE = 180° − _____

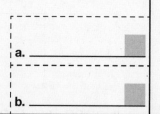

a. _____

b. _____

28. *round*

58 mph ⟶

1 hr 52 min ⟶ _____ hr

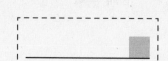

29. List all correct answers.

See page 10 in the Student Reference Guide.

_____, _____, _____, _____

30. List all correct answers.

√7

_____, _____

● **Polygons** (page 120)

Teacher Notes:
● Refer students to "Similar and Congruent Triangles" on page 28 in the *Student Reference Guide*.

Polygons are *closed, flat* shapes with *straight* sides.

● Two sides of a polygon meet at a **vertex (vertices is plural form)**.

● The name of a polygon states its **number** of sides and angles.
   A **quadrilateral** is a polygon with 4 sides and 4 angles.

Names of Polygons

Name of Polygon	Number of Sides	Name of Polygon	Number of Sides
Triangle	3	Octagon	8
Quadrilateral	4	Nonagon	9
Pentagon	5	Decagon	10
Hexagon	6	Hendecagon	11
Heptagon	7	Dodecagon	12

A polygon with more than 12 sides may be referred to as an *n*-gon, with *n* being the number of sides. Thus, a polygon with 15 sides is a 15-gon.

● A **regular polygon** has equal sides and equal angles.
   A **square** is a *regular* quadrilateral.

Regular and Irregular Polygons

Type	Regular	Irregular
Triangle	△	◿
Quadrilateral	□	▱
Pentagon	⬠	⬠
Hexagon	⬡	⬡

● Polygons are named by their vertices.
   Start with any vertex and name the other vertices around the polygon **in order**. You can go clockwise or counterclockwise.

● **Congruent** polygons have the *same shape and size.*
   The angles and sides of congruent polygons are equal. Congruent polygons are not always in the same position on the page.

● **Similar** polygons have the *same shape* but not always the same size.
   All congruent polygons are also similar polygons.
   Figure A is congruent to figure D. (Figure A ≅ Figure D)
   Figures A, C, and D are similar. (Figure A ~ Figure C ~ Figure D)

● A **dilation** is an enlargement of a similar polygon.
   Figure C is a dilation of Figures A and D.

Practice Set (page 123)

a. Name this polygon. _____
How many sides?

Is the polygon regular or irregular? _____

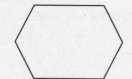

b. Circle the one that is not a way to name this rectangle.
Use your finger to trace around the shape.

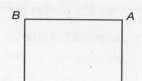

   A □ABCD   **B** □ADCB
   C □BACD   **D** □BADC

c. What is the name for the shape of a stop sign? o_____

d. The block H shown is a polygon.

Count the sides and name the polygon. d_____

e. Use four letters to name the figure that looks like a **square**.

Start the name with the letter *A*. □ _____
Use your finger to trace around the shape.

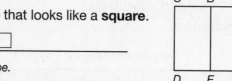

f. Circle the triangle that appears to be a **dilation** of triangle A.
  A   **B**   **C**   **D**

g. Which of the figures below appear to be **congruent?** _____, _____

Which figures appear to be **similar?** _____, _____, _____

  A   **B**   **C**   **D**

1. $1.12
  × 7

2. 890 cm
   − 835 cm

3. 33
   − 17

4. 1 km = _____ m

| lengths m | $\frac{1}{25}$ | $\frac{}{1000}$ |
| lengths min | $\frac{}{40}$ | $\frac{1}{}$ |

5. *See page 9 in the* Student Reference Guide.

_____, _____, _____, _____

+ _____

6. $-2, |-3|, \frac{1}{2}, \sqrt{2}$

_____

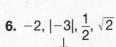

-2 -1 0 1 2 3

Use work area.

7. $\frac{375}{1000}$ = $\frac{\cdot \; \cdot \; \cdot}{\cdot \; \cdot \; \cdot \; \cdot}$ =

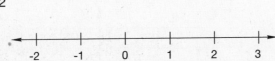

)375

)1000

8. a. *Convert.* $\frac{7}{2}$

4 ◯ ─

a. _____

b. $\sqrt{49}$

7 ◯

b. _____

9. $\frac{1}{5} = \frac{}{45}$

  + $\frac{4}{9} = \frac{}{45}$

10. *Reduce.*

$$\frac{1}{2} = \frac{}{10}$$

$$-\frac{1}{10} = \frac{}{10}$$

11. fraction: 40% =

decimal: 40% =

Shift ←.

12. 150% of $70

Shift ←.

$70

×

13. a. $y \cdot y \cdot y \cdot y =$

b. $3xxyxy =$

a. _____

b. _____

14. (0, 4), (2, 4), (2, −3)

Find the fourth vertex: (,)

area: _____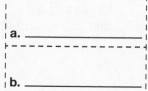

perimeter: _____

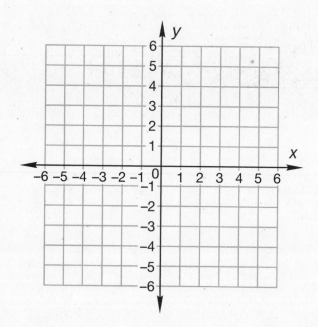

15. $2^5 =$

Use work area.

16. $10^6 =$

17. $\sqrt{144} =$

18. $(12 \text{ in.})^2 =$

19. $8^3 =$

20. $\sqrt[3]{8} =$

21. $(30^2) \div ($ ____ $) =$
product

22. area

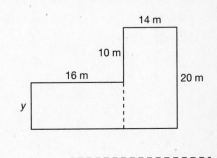

23. perimeter

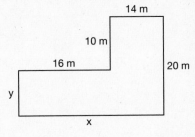

24. $72 = 36 + m$

72
36

$m =$

25. $w - 11 = 39$

39
11

$w =$

26. $7c = 56$

$c =$

27. $8 = \dfrac{72}{x}$

$x =$

28. Estimate.

62 mph $\longrightarrow$

3 hr 50 min $\longrightarrow$

29. $A = bh$

Find A when $b = 7mm$
$h = 9mm$

$A =$ ▨

30. List all correct answers.

0

——, ——, ——, ——

• Triangles (page 126)

Name _____

A triangle is a polygon with 3 sides.

• The measure of the three angles in a triangle add up to 180°.

• Triangles can be classified by their sides and by their angles:

Teacher Notes:

• Refer students to "Classifying Triangles" on page 28 and "Geometric Formulas" on page 29 in the *Student Reference Guide*.

• Review "Angles" on page 27 in the *Student Reference Guide*.

Classifying Triangles by Sides		
Type	Characteristic	Example
Equilateral triangle	Three sides of equal length	
Isosceles triangle	At least two sides of equal length	
Scalene triangle	Three sides of unequal length	
Classifying Triangles by Angles		
Type	Characteristic	Example
Acute triangle	All acute angles	
Right triangle	One right angle	
Obtuse triangle	One obtuse angle	

• A *regular triangle* is called an **equilateral triangle.**

Each angle in an equilateral triangle measures 60°. (60° + 60° + 60° = 180°)

• An **isosceles triangle** has at least two equal sides *and* two equal angles.

• Area of a triangle = $\frac{1}{2}$ (base × height)

$A = \frac{1}{2} bh$

The base (*b*) is any side of the triangle.

The height (*h*) is the perpendicular distance from the base to the opposite vertex.

Practice Set (page 129)

Classify each triangle in problems **a–c** by angles and by sides.

a. by angles: *r* _____ triangle

by sides: *i* _____ triangle

b. by angles: *a* _____ triangle

by sides: *e* _____ triangle

c. by angles: *o* _____ triangle

by sides: *s* _____ triangle

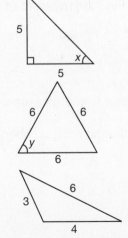

d. In problems **a** and **b**, the letters x and y represent how many degrees?
The sum of the angles in a triangle is 180°.

isosceles right triangle

$$x + x + 90° = 180°$$

$$2x + 90° = 180°$$

$$2x = \underline{\qquad}°$$

$$x = \underline{\qquad}°$$

equilateral triangle

$$y + y + y = 180°$$

$$3y = 180°$$

$$y = \underline{\qquad}°$$

Find the area of each triangle in problems **e–g**.

$$A = \frac{1}{2}bh$$

e. $A = \frac{1}{2}(4 \text{ in.} \times 3 \text{ in.}) = \underline{\qquad}$

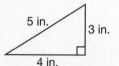

5 in. 3 in. 4 in.

f. $A = \frac{1}{2}(\underline{\qquad} \times \underline{\qquad}) = \underline{\qquad}$

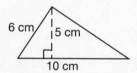

6 cm 5 cm 10 cm

g. $A = \underline{\qquad}$

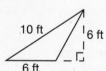

10 ft 6 ft 6 ft

h. Mr. Torres arranges square floor tiles diagonally in a room. Near each wall he needs to cut the tiles to fit in the shape shown. Classify the triangle by angle and by sides. Find the measure of each angle.

by angles: _____ triangle

by sides: _____ triangle

The *r*_____ angle is 90°, and the other two angles are equal because the triangle is

*i*_____. The other two angles each measure _____° because 45° + 45° + 90° = 180°.

1. *long division*

$$45 \overline{)\$50.40}$$

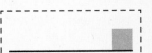

2.
19 L
12 L
___

3. 1 min = _____ sec

baskets $\dfrac{3}{10}$ _____
sec

4. 1 gal = _____ qt

3 gal = _____ qt

5. Use exponents.

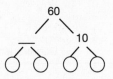

60 = _____ · _____ · _____

6. $(-1, 1), (-1, -6), (5, 1), (5, -6)$

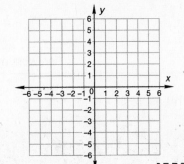

perimeter

7. a. mean: _____ median: _____

$52
 49
 48
 50
 49
 50
+ 51

_____, _____, _____, _____,

_____, _____, _____,

mode: _____

range: _____

b. _____

8. Does the mean or median change more?

$52
 49
 48
 50
 49
 50
 51
+ 30

_____, _____, _____, _____,

_____, _____, _____,

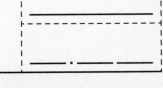

9. a. $\dfrac{2}{3}$ ◯ $\dfrac{3}{2}$

b. $|-7|$ ◯ $|7|$

a. _____

b. _____

10. $\dfrac{3}{25} = \dfrac{}{100}$

What decimal is that?

$$25 \overline{)3.00}$$

_____ . _____ _____

11. Which number is $\sqrt{5}$ between?

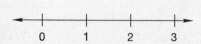

12. a.

by angles: _____

by sides: _____

b.

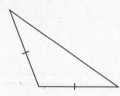

by angles: _____

by sides: _____

Use work area.

Use work area.

13. Which angle measures:

a. 60°?

b. 120°?

c. 180°?

∠ _____

∠ _____

∠ _____

14. $A = \frac{1}{2}bh$

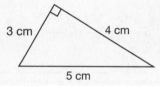

3 cm

4 cm

5 cm

15. $9^3 =$

16. $13^2 =$

17. $\sqrt{64}$ =

_____

18. $\sqrt[3]{216}$ =

_____

19. *long division*

$15\overline{)1125}$

_____

20. *Reduce.*

$$-\frac{3}{4} = \frac{}{12}$$

$$-\frac{5}{12} = \frac{}{12}$$

_____

21. a. $a \cdot a \cdot a \cdot a \cdot b \cdot b$ =

    b. $2xyxyxyx$ =

a. _____

b. _____

22. $(-1, -1)$, $(3, -1)$, $(3, 3)$ Find the fourth vertex.

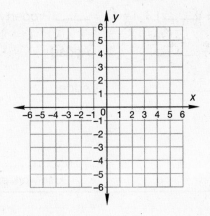

(_____, _____)

23. $m + 90 = 10$ $\begin{array}{r} 90 \\ \underline{10} \end{array}$

$m =$ _____

24. $90 - 3x = 60$

What number plus 60 is 90?

$3x =$

$x =$ _____

25. $38 = 2x - 2$

What number minus 2 is 38?

$2x =$

$x =$ _____

26. $\dfrac{x}{100} = 1$

$x =$ _____

27. Find $4ac$

when $a = 3$

$c = 12$

$x =$ _____

28. $A = s^2$

Find A when $s = 25$ ft

$A =$ _____

29. $3\dfrac{1}{6} + (4\dfrac{1}{6} + 1\dfrac{2}{3})$ Given

$(\underline{\quad} + \underline{\quad}) + 1\dfrac{2}{3}$ _____ Property

$\underline{\quad} + \underline{\quad}$ Added

$\underline{\quad}$ Added

Use work area.

30. List all correct answers.

-9

_____ , _____ , _____

- ## Distributive Property
- ## Order of Operations (page 139)

Name _____

The Distributive Property shows how to spread multiplication over addition or subtraction.

$$a(b + c) = ab + ac$$
Distributive Property

Teacher Notes:
- Refer students to "Order of Operations" on page 22 in the *Student Reference Guide*.
- Review "Properties of Operations" on page 20 in the *Student Reference Guide*.

Example: There are two ways to simplify 2(12 + 8):

2(12 + 8)	2(12 + 8)
2(20)	$2 \cdot 12 + 2 \cdot 8$
40	24 + 16
Add first.	40
	Use Distributive Property.

- The Distributive Property works with variables.

    Example: $3(x - 2)$

    $3 \cdot x - 3 \cdot 2$

    $3x - 6$

- We can also use the Distributive Property in reverse to **factor** an expression.

    1. Write the greatest factor common to both numbers.

    2. Divide each number by the factor and write the quotients inside the parentheses.

    Example: Factor $6x + 9$.

    $3(\ \ + \ \ )$ 3 is the greatest common factor of 6 and 9.

    $3(2x + 3)$ $6x \div 3 = 2x$ and $9 \div 3 = 3$.

- The common factor can be a variable.

    Example: Factor $ax + ay$.

    $a(\ \ + \ \ )$ a is the common factor of ax and ay

    $a(x + y)$ $ax \div a = x$ and $ay \div a = y$

If there is more than one operation in an expression, we follow this order of operations:

1. Simplify within **parentheses** (and symbols of inclusion).

2. Simplify **exponents.**

3. **Multiply** and **divide** in order *from left to right.*

4. **Add** and **subtract** in order *from left to right.*

- A good way to remember the order of operations is with this sentence:

"**P**lease **e**xcuse **m**y **d**ear **A**unt **S**ally."

Each initial letter stands for an order-of-operations word.

    Parentheses

    Exponents

    Multiplication

    Division

    Addition

    Subtraction

Example: $20 - 2 \cdot 3^2 + (7 + 8) \div 5$

$20 - 2 \cdot 3^2 + 15 \div 5$	Simplified parentheses
$20 - 2 \cdot 9 + 15 \div 5$	Simplified exponent
$20 - 18 + 3$	Multiplied and divided
5	Added and subtracted

Practice Set (page 143)

Multiply.

a. $2(3 + w) = \underline{\hspace{1cm}} + \underline{\hspace{1cm}}$ **b.** $5(x - 3) = \underline{\hspace{1cm}} - \underline{\hspace{1cm}}$

Factor.

c. $9x + 6 = 3(\underline{\hspace{1cm}} + \underline{\hspace{1cm}})$ **d.** $8w - 10 = \underline{\hspace{1cm}}(4w - \underline{\hspace{1cm}})$

e. Which property is illustrated by the following equation? _D_____ _P_____

$$x(y + z) = xy + xz$$

f. Why might you use the Distributive Property to simplify $3(30 - 2)$?

If I subtract first, I will multiply 3 times _____. If I multiply first, I will multiply 3 times _____ and 3

times _____, which are easier.

Simplify.

g. $2 + 5 \cdot 2 - 1$

$2 + \underline{\hspace{1cm}} - 1$

_____

h. $(2 + 5) \cdot (2 - 1)$

$\underline{\hspace{1cm}} \cdot \underline{\hspace{1cm}}$

_____

i. $4 + (11 - 3^2) \cdot 2^2$

$4 + (11 - \underline{\hspace{1cm}}) \cdot 2^2$

$4 + \underline{\hspace{1cm}} \cdot \underline{\hspace{1cm}}$

$4 + \underline{\hspace{1cm}}$

_____

j. $10 - [8 - (6 - 3)]$

$10 - [8 - \underline{\hspace{1cm}}]$

$10 - \underline{\hspace{1cm}}$

_____

k. $\sqrt{36 + 64}$

$\sqrt{\underline{\hspace{1cm}}}$

_____

l. $|8 - 12|$

$|\underline{\hspace{1cm}}|$

_____

m. The expression $2^2 + 2 \times 2 - 2 \div 2$ equals 7. Circle the expression that equals 11.

A $2^2 + 2 \times (2 - 2) \div 2$ **B** $(2^2 + 2) \times 2 - 2 \div 2$ **C** $2^2 + (2 \times 2) - 2 \div 2$

1. drive time: 7 hr

flight time: $\frac{1}{2} + 1\frac{1}{2} + 1 + 1 =$ _____ hr

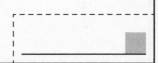

2. total chops: $8 + 5 + 2 =$ _____

total time: $30 + 20 + 10 =$ _____ s

chops per second: $\frac{8}{30} = \frac{}{60}$

$\frac{5}{20} = \frac{}{60}$

$\frac{2}{10} = \frac{}{60}$

Which is greatest? _____

3. 4 months is what fraction of a year?

_____ of 66

¦ Use work area. ¦

4. a. $7 + (18 + 13)$

$7 + ($ _____ $+$ _____ $)$

$($ _____ $+$ _____ $) +$ _____

b. _____ Property and _____ Property

c. sum: _____

¦ Use work area. ¦

5. Rearrange these numbers to make the multiplication easier.

$12 \cdot 13 \cdot 5 \cdot 10$

6. $2(\$$ _____ $) + 2(\$$ _____ $) = 2(\$$ _____ $+ \$$ _____ $)$

$\$$ _____ $+ \$$ _____ $= 2(\$$ _____ $)$

$\$$ _____ $= \$$ _____

7. Estimate the area.

$6.\textcircled{3} \longrightarrow$ _____ cm

$4\frac{1}{4} \longrightarrow$ _____ cm

6.3 cm

$4\frac{1}{4}$ cm

8. a. Distribute: $2(\overset{\times}{x + 7}) =$

b. Factor: $9x + 12 =$ _____ $($ _____ $+$ _____ $)$

a. _____

b. _____

9. *See pages 27 and 28 in the Student Reference Guide.*

by sides : _____

by angles: _____

$m\angle A =$ _____

$m\angle B =$ _____

$m\angle C =$ _____

Use work area.

10. mean

20
22
19
25
+ 24

$\overline{}$

11. *order of operations*

$1 + 2 + 3 \times 4 + 5 =$

$1 + 2 +$ _____ $+ 5 =$

12. *Reduce.*

$$\frac{2 + 5}{1 + 20} = \underline{}$$

13. *Reduce.*

$$\frac{20}{21} = \frac{20}{21}$$

$$-\frac{2}{3} = \frac{}{21}$$

14. $1\dfrac{3}{5} = 1\dfrac{}{10}$

$+1\dfrac{1}{10} = 1\dfrac{}{10}$

15. $12\overline{)3\,6\,6\,0}$

16. $\sqrt{169} =$

17. $\sqrt[3]{27} =$

18. $3^4 =$

19. $(-5, 7), (3,7), (3, -2), (-5, -2)$
area and perimeter

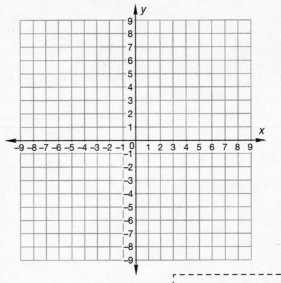

$A = $ _____

$P = $ _____

20. 20 − 33 |20 − 33|

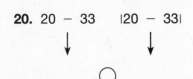

21. $|r| = 2$
so $+ r = 2$
$- r = 2$

$r = $ _____, _____

22. $\dfrac{bbrr}{yyyy} =$

23. *Perimeter: Use the Pythagorean Theorem to find the unknown side.*

$a^2 + b^2 = c^2$

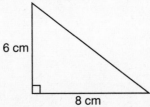

6 cm

8 cm

Area of triangle $= \dfrac{1}{2}bh$

24. $27 + w = 35$

$w = $ _____

25. $\frac{32}{y} = 2$

$y =$ _____

26. $8n + 2 = 90$

What number plus 2 is 90?

$8n =$

$n =$ _____

27. $2b - 3 = 5$

What number minus 3 is 5?

$2b =$

$b =$ _____

28. Find $b^2 - 4ac$

when $a = 2$
$\quad\quad b = 3$
$\quad\quad c = 1$

_____

29. *Convert to yards.*

30 ft

30 ft

_____

30. *See page 10 in the* Student Reference Guide.

i _____

w _____ numbers

r _____ numbers

r _____ numbers

Use work area.

• Multiplying and Dividing Fractions (page 146)

Name _____

Teacher Notes:
- Introduce Hint #39, "Canceling Fractions," and Hint #40, "Reciprocal."
- Review "Fraction Terms" on page 12 in the *Student Reference Guide*.

To multiply fractions, multiply across both numerators and denominators.

$$\frac{1}{3} \cdot \frac{2}{3} = \frac{1 \cdot 2}{3 \cdot 3} = \frac{2}{9}$$

- We can **cancel** or reduce fractions before multiplying to make the problem easier.

- When we cancel, any numerator can be paired with any denominator.

   Example: What number is $\frac{3}{4}$ of $\frac{8}{9}$?

    $= \frac{2}{3}$

- **Reciprocal** means to "flip" or invert a fraction.

   $3 \dashrightarrow \frac{1}{3}$ 　　　　 $\frac{5}{6} \dashrightarrow \frac{6}{5}$

   $\frac{1}{3}$ is the reciprocal of 3. 　　 $\frac{6}{5}$ is the reciprocal of $\frac{5}{6}$.

- Another name for reciprocal is "multiplicative inverse."

- **Inverse Property of Multiplication:** The product of any number and its reciprocal is 1

   $$\frac{3}{1} \times \frac{1}{3} = 1 \qquad \frac{5}{6} \times \frac{6}{5} = 1$$

- To divide fractions:

   1. Copy the first fraction.
   2. Change ÷ to ×.
   3. "Flip" the second fraction.
   4. Cancel, if possible.
   5. Multiply across.

   $$\frac{2}{3} \div \frac{1}{3} =$$

   $$\frac{2}{3} \times \frac{3}{1} = \frac{2}{1} = 2$$

Practice Set (page 150)

a. Multiply $\frac{1}{4}$ and $\frac{1}{2}$. Shade the square to model the multiplication as a fraction of the larger square.

$\frac{1}{4} \cdot \frac{1}{2} =$ _____

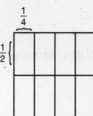

b. One half of the students in the class are boys. One third of the boys walk to school. Boys who walk to school are what fraction of the students in the class?

$\frac{1}{2} \cdot \frac{1}{3} =$

Multiply.

c. $\frac{1}{2} \cdot \frac{3}{4} =$

d. $\frac{5}{6} \cdot \frac{2}{3} =$

e. What number is $\frac{1}{2}$ of $\frac{3}{4}$?

$\frac{1}{2} \cdot \frac{3}{4} =$

f. What number is $\frac{2}{3}$ of $\frac{3}{4}$?

$\frac{2}{3} \cdot \frac{3}{4} =$

Cancel the 3s.

Cancel the 2s.

For **g** and **h** write the **reciprocal** of the number.

g. $\frac{3}{8}$ ⇒

h. 4 ⇒

i. How many $\frac{2}{3}$ are in 1? _____

reciprocal

j. $1 \div \frac{3}{5}$

↓   ↓

$\frac{1}{1} \times - =$

k. $1 \div \frac{1}{6}$

↓   ↓

$\frac{1}{1} \times - =$

l. How many $\frac{1}{2}$s are in $\frac{3}{4}$?

$\frac{3}{4} \div \frac{1}{2}$

↓   ↓

$\frac{3}{4} \times - =$

Cancel the 2s.

Divide.

m. $\dfrac{2}{3} \div \dfrac{3}{4}$

$- \times - =$

n. $\dfrac{3}{4} \div \dfrac{2}{3}$

$- \times - =$

Written Practice   (page 150)

1. 1 week = _____ days

mi $\qquad$ $\dfrac{14}{}$ $\qquad$ $\dfrac{?}{5}$
days

Multiply the loop.
Divide by the outside number

2. Total minutes: _____

1 hr = _____ min

5 hr = _____ min

Which is greatest?

$\dfrac{2}{56}$, $\dfrac{100}{}$, $\dfrac{20}{160}$

Use work area.

3. Distribute: $3(x + 7) =$

4. Factor: $5x + 35 =$

5. *order of operations*

$\dfrac{6 + 4}{7 - 2} =$

6. $6 + 5 \times 4 - 3 + 2 \div 1 =$

7. $|6 - 19|$ $\qquad$ $(6 - 19)$

_____ $\bigcirc$ _____

8. $\dfrac{3}{4} \cdot \dfrac{1}{3} =$

Cancel the 3s.

9. $\frac{1}{3}$ of $\frac{3}{5}$

Cancel the 3s.

_____

10. reciprocal of $\frac{1}{7}$

_____

11. multiplicative inverse of $\frac{2}{3}$
reciprocal

_____

12. Find $x^2 + 2yz$

when $x = 4$
$\quad\quad y = 5$
$\quad\quad z = 7$

_____

13. $\frac{3}{4} \div \frac{1}{3}$

$\frac{3}{4} \times \text{—} =$

_____

14. Perimeter and area

$A = \frac{1}{2} bh$

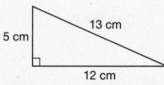

5 cm   13 cm

12 cm

_____   _____

15. *See pages 27 and 28 in the* Student Reference Guide.

$x + x + x = 180$
$\quad\quad\quad 3x = 180$

$\quad\quad\quad x = \underline{\quad\quad}°$

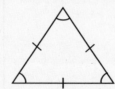

by sides: _____

by angles: _____

Each angle measures : _____

Use work area.

16. Area

17 in.

17 in.

_____

17. The figure is not a ^{p}_____

because it has a ^{c}_____

side.

Use work area.

18. *See page 27 and 28 in the* Student Reference Guide.

_____. In a regular triangle all angles

are ^e_____ and ^a_____.

Use work area.

19. Are the triangles similar or congruent? Circle the correct symbol.

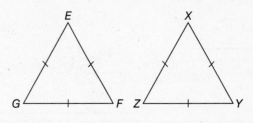

A ≅   **B** ~

C =   **D** <

Use work area.

20. *The angles in a linear pair add up to 180.*

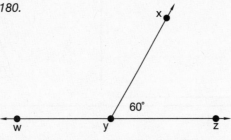

21. Name this figure.

E   F

A $\vec{EF}$

B $\vec{FE}$

C either **A** or **B**

22. The roads are:

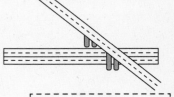

A intersecting

B parallel

C skew

23. Round to the nearest million.

$403,⑤00,000 ⟶

24. Estimate the product.

1<u>7</u>.⑧9 ⟶

$9\frac{7}{8}$ ⟶ ×_____

25. *See page 10 in the* Student Reference Guide.

26. $\sqrt[3]{64}$ =

27. *Reduce.*

$$1\frac{1}{3} = \frac{}{6}$$

$$+\ 1\frac{1}{6} = \frac{}{6}$$

_____

28. $8\overline{)7.000}$

_____

29. $\frac{3}{5}$ of 35

Cancel the 5.

_____

30. Find the measure of the third angle.
The sum of the angles in a triangle is 180°.

_____

• Multiplying and Dividing Mixed Numbers (page 153)

Name _____

Before we multiply or divide mixed numbers, we first write each number as a fraction.

To multiply or divide **improper fractions:**

Teacher Note:
- Review Hint #29, "Improper Fractions."

1. Change mixed numbers to improper (top-heavy) fractions.
2. Multiply or divide. Cancel numbers when multiplying.
3. Reduce and convert the answer as necessary.

Multiply

$$2\frac{1}{2} \times 1\frac{2}{3}$$ Change mixed numbers to improper fractions first.

$$\frac{5}{2} \times \frac{5}{3} = \frac{25}{6}$$ Multiply.

$$\frac{25}{6} = 4\frac{1}{6}$$ Simplify.

Divide

$$3\frac{1}{3} \div 2\frac{1}{2}$$ Change mixed numbers to improper fractions first.

$$\frac{10}{3} \div \frac{5}{2}$$ Find the reciprocal of the divisor.

$$\frac{\overset{2}{10}}{3} \times \frac{2}{\underset{1}{5}} = \frac{4}{3}$$ Cancel and multiply.

$$\frac{4}{3} = 1\frac{1}{3}$$ Simplify.

Practice Set (page 156)

a. What is the **area** of a rectangle $2\frac{1}{2}$ inches long and $1\frac{1}{2}$ inches wide? _____

$$2\frac{1}{2} \quad \times \quad 1\frac{1}{2}$$

___ × ___

b. A recipe calls for $1\frac{3}{4}$ cups of milk. How many cups of milk are needed if the recipe is doubled? _____

$$1\frac{3}{4} \quad \times \quad 2$$

___ × ___

Cancel the 2.

c. A tile setter is covering a 5 ft by 5 ft square shower wall. Each tile covers a $4\frac{5}{8}$ in. by $4\frac{5}{8}$ in. square.

About how many rows of tiles are needed to reach 5 feet? _____ rows

5 ft = 60 in.

$$\frac{60}{1} \div 4\frac{5}{8}$$

$$\downarrow \qquad \downarrow$$

$$\frac{60}{1} \div \frac{}{8}$$

$$\downarrow \qquad \downarrow$$

$$\frac{60}{1} \times \frac{}{} =$$

How many tiles are needed to cover the 5 ft by 5 ft square? _____ tiles

Find the square of the number of rows.

Write the **reciprocal** of each number.

d. $2\frac{2}{3} \longrightarrow \frac{}{3} \rightsquigarrow$

e. $\frac{5}{6} \rightsquigarrow$

f. $5 \rightsquigarrow$

Simplify.

g. $1\frac{1}{2} \times 1\frac{2}{3}$

$$\downarrow \qquad \downarrow$$

$$\frac{}{} \times \frac{}{} =$$

Cancel the 3s.

h. $2\frac{1}{2} \cdot 2\frac{1}{2}$

$$\downarrow \qquad \downarrow$$

$$\frac{}{} \cdot \frac{}{} =$$

i. $1\frac{1}{2} \div 2\frac{2}{3}$

$$\downarrow \qquad \downarrow$$

$$\frac{}{} \div \frac{}{} =$$

$$\downarrow \qquad \downarrow$$

$$\frac{}{} \times \frac{}{} =$$

j. $2\frac{2}{3} \div 1\frac{1}{2}$

$$\downarrow \qquad \downarrow$$

$$\frac{}{} \div \frac{}{} =$$

$$\downarrow \qquad \downarrow$$

$$\frac{}{} \times \frac{}{} =$$

1. 217
   109

---

2. $\dfrac{3}{10}$ of 250

Cancel the 10.

---

3. 1483
    27

---

4. $\dfrac{5}{6} = \dfrac{}{6}$

$+\ \dfrac{1}{2} = \dfrac{}{6}$

---

5. $\dfrac{5}{6} = \dfrac{}{6}$

$-\ \dfrac{1}{2} = \dfrac{}{6}$

---

6. $\dfrac{5}{6} \cdot \dfrac{1}{2} =$

——— ◯ ———

---

7. $\dfrac{5}{6} \div \dfrac{1}{2} =$

↓   ↓

——— × ——— =

Cancel the 2.

---

8. $\dfrac{5}{7} \cdot \dfrac{7}{10} =$

Cancel the 5 and the 7s.

---

9. $\dfrac{5}{7} \div \dfrac{7}{10} =$

↓   ↓

——— × ——— =

---

10. $\dfrac{3}{7} \cdot 2 =$

11. $\dfrac{3}{7} \div 2$

$\downarrow$ $\downarrow$

——— × ——— =

12. $2\dfrac{1}{2} \cdot 1\dfrac{2}{3}$

$\downarrow$ $\downarrow$

——— · ——— =

13. $2\dfrac{1}{2} \div 1\dfrac{2}{3}$

$\downarrow$ $\downarrow$

——— × ——— =

Cancel the 5s.

14. *order of operations*

$16 - [8 - 4(2 - 1)] =$

15. $6 + 7 \times (3 - 3) =$

16. $(6, 2), (6, -6), (-1, 2)$
Find the fourth vertex.
vertex: (,)
Area = length × width

area ———

Perimeter: Add all sides.

perimeter: ———

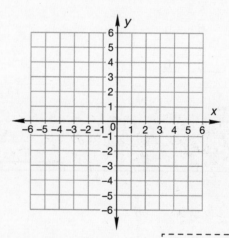

Use work area.

17. a. $(5 - 7)$ $|5 - 7|$

$\downarrow$ $\downarrow$

——— ◯ ———

b. $\sqrt{64}$ $\sqrt[3]{64}$

$\downarrow$ $\downarrow$

——— ◯ ———

a. ———

b. ———

18. $|x| = 12$
So $+x = 12$
$-x = 12$

$x =$ ———, ———

19. a. *yyyy* =

  b. 2*ababa* =

a. _____

b. _____

20. Area = length × width

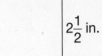

$2\frac{1}{2}$ in.

$2\frac{1}{2}$ in.

_____

21. a. $a + 5 = 5 + a$

  _____ Property of addition

  b. $a \cdot 0 = 0$

  _____ Property of Multiplication

Use work area.

22. Perimeter: Add all sides.

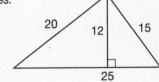

20   12   15

25

Area of a triangle = $\frac{1}{2}bh$

a. _____

b. _____

23. $5 + x = 22$

x = _____

24. $4x + 13 = 25$

What number plus 13 is 25?

$4x =$

x =

25. $\frac{1}{2}p = \frac{1}{6}$

p = _____

26. $\frac{x}{30} = \frac{2}{3}$

Think of equivalent fractions.

x =

27. Find $b^2 - 4ac$

When $a = 1$
$b = 6$
$c = 8$

_____

28. $A = \frac{1}{2}bh$

Find A when $b = 6$ cm
$h = 4$ cm

$A =$ _____

29. **a.** Distribute: 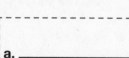 $5(x + 3) =$

b. Factor: $6x - 10y =$

a. _____

b. _____

30. _Pythagorean Theorem_

$a^2 + b^2 = c^2$

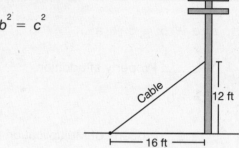

Cable

12 ft

16 ft

_____

• Adding and Subtracting
Decimal Numbers (page 159)

Name _____

When adding and subtracting decimal numbers, we must make sure we are adding or subtracting digits with the same place value.

To add or subtract decimal numbers:

1. Put a decimal point at the end of any whole number.

2. Line up the decimal points.

3. Fill in empty places with zeros.

<table>
<tr><td>**Teacher Notes:**</td></tr>
<tr><td>• Introduce Hint #41, "Decimal Arithmetic Reminders Chart."</td></tr>
<tr><td>• Refer students to "Decimal Arithmetic Reminders Chart" on page 7 in the *Student Reference Guide*.</td></tr>
</table>

Examples:

1.6 + 0.45   3 − 1.62

$$\begin{array}{r} \overset{1}{1.60} \\ + 0.45 \\ \hline 2.05 \end{array} \qquad \begin{array}{r} \overset{2\,9\,1}{3.00} \\ - 1.62 \\ \hline 1.38 \end{array}$$

Practice Set (page 160)

a. Arrange these numbers from **least to greatest.**

Change $\frac{1}{2}$ to a decimal.

$\frac{1}{2}$, 0, −1, 2, 0.3, 1.75

$\underline{\quad-1\quad}$, _____, _____, _____, _____, _____

| 0.00 |
| −1.00 |
| 2.00 |
| 0.30 |
| 1.75 |

b. Compare 0.036 ◯ 0.0354   0.036
                                        0.0354

Simplify:

c. 7.5 + 12.75
$$\begin{array}{r} 7.50 \\ + 12.75 \\ \hline \end{array}$$

d. 4.2 + 12
$$\begin{array}{r} 4.2 \\ + 12. \\ \hline \end{array}$$

e. 0.3 + 0.8
$$\begin{array}{r} 0.3 \\ + 0.8 \\ \hline \end{array}$$

f. 11 .46 − 3.6
$$\begin{array}{r} 11.46 \\ - 3.60 \\ \hline \end{array}$$

g. 5.2 − 4.87
$$\begin{array}{r} 5.2 \\ - 4.87 \\ \hline \end{array}$$

h. 3 − 2.94
$$\begin{array}{r} 3. \\ - 2.94 \\ \hline \end{array}$$

i. How can you check your answers in problems **f–h**?

Add the ᵈ_____ to the minuend; their sum should equal the subtrahend.

j. The weather report stated that the recent storm dropped 1.50 inches of rain raising the seasonal total

to 26.42 inches. What was the seasonal total prior to the recent storm? I _____ 1.50

inches _____ the total. Explain your answer.

$$
\begin{array}{r}
26.42 \text{ in.} \\
1.50 \text{ in.} \\
\hline
\end{array}
$$

Written Practice (page 161)

1. mi

$$\dfrac{\dfrac{1}{2}}{3\dfrac{1}{2}} \quad \dfrac{2}{}$$

min

_____

2. $\dfrac{7}{10}$ of 180

Cancel the 10.

_____

3. Pacific Team
   total runs   —

_____

4.
$$
\begin{array}{r}
1.23 \\
12.3 \\
+\ 123. \\
\hline
\end{array}
$$

_____

5.
$$
\begin{array}{r}
41.5°\text{ F} \\
38.6°\text{ F} \\
\hline
\end{array}
$$

_____

6. $\dfrac{4}{5} \cdot 2 =$

_____

7. $\dfrac{4}{5} \div 2$

$\quad\downarrow \qquad \downarrow$

_____ $\times$ _____ $=$

_____

8. $1\dfrac{1}{3} \div \dfrac{3}{4}$

$\quad\downarrow \qquad \downarrow$

_____ $\cdot$ _____ $=$

Cancel the 3s and the 4s.

_____

9. $1\frac{1}{3}$ ÷ $\frac{3}{4}$

——— × ——— =

10. area

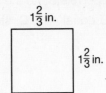

$1\frac{2}{3}$ in.

$1\frac{2}{3}$ in.

11. $\frac{4}{9} \cdot \frac{2}{3}$ =

12. $\frac{4}{9}$ ÷ $\frac{2}{3}$

——— × ——— =

Cancel the 2 and the 3.

13. *order of operations*

$4 + 3 \times (5 - 1)$ =

14. |16 − 20| (16 − 20)

——— ◯ ———

15. perimeter and area

Area of triangle = $\frac{1}{2}bh$

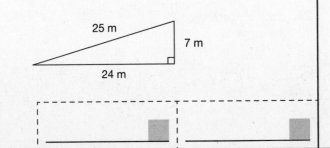

25 m

7 m

24 m

16. *See page 28 in the* Student Reference Guide.

by sides: _____

by angles: _____

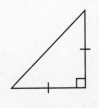

Use work area.

© 2007 Harcourt Achieve Inc.

17. How is a scale model related to the real object?

    A congruent   **B** equal   **C** similar

18. Which is regular?

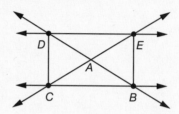

D all of the shapes

---

19. *A straight line is 180°.*

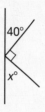

x =

20.

Does $\overrightarrow{BA}$ intersect $\overrightarrow{CD}$? _____

Name the point of intersection. _____

21. Round to the nearest tenth.

    6.0②9 →

Use work area.

22. Estimate:

    24.④2 →

    $8\frac{1}{8}$ →

23. *See page 10 in the* Student Reference Guide.

24. $\sqrt[3]{125}$ =

25. *order of operations*

    $4^2 + 3^2 =$

26. $1\frac{1}{2}$ = ———

   $+ 1\frac{1}{5}$ = ———

   _____
   _____

27. $\frac{1}{3}$ = ———

   $- \frac{1}{4}$ = ———

   _____
   _____

28. Use exponents.

)———
)———
)———
)84

   84 = ——— · ——— · ———

29. How many glasses can be **filled?**

   2 L = ——— ml

   ——— ml · $\frac{glass}{120 \ ml}$

   Cancel matching zeros.

   _____

30. **25% of $56**

   Change 25% to a fraction.

   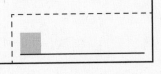
   _____

• Multiplying and Dividing Decimal Numbers (page 163)

Name _____

Teacher Notes:
• Refer students to "Multiplication and Division of Decimal Numbers by 10, 100, 1000" on page 6 and "Multiplying by Powers of Ten" on page 8 in the *Student Reference Guide*.

• Review "Decimal Arithmetic Reminders Chart" on page 7 in the *Student Reference Guide*.

Decimal places are places to the right of the decimal point.

• To multiply decimal numbers:

    1. Multiply the numbers.

    2. Count the total number of decimal places in both factors.

    3. Put the same number of decimal places in the product.

    4. Fill any empty places in the product with zeros.

Examples:

$$\begin{array}{r} 0.12 \\ \times\ 0.3 \\ \hline .036 \end{array}\Big\}3 \text{ decimal places}$$

.036 3 decimal places

$$\begin{array}{r} 1.5 \\ \times\ 1.5 \\ \hline 75 \\ 15 \\ \hline 2.25 \end{array}\Big\}2 \text{ decimal places}$$

2.25 2 decimal places

• To divide a decimal number by a whole number:

    1. Move the decimal point **up** into the *quotient*.

    2. Divide.

    3. Write zeros in the dividend to continue dividing until there is no remainder.

    4. Fill any empty places in the quotient with zeros.

up

$$\begin{array}{r} 0.96 \\ 5\overline{)4.8\overset{3}{0}} \end{array}$$

Example: $4.8 \div 5$

• To divide **by** a decimal number:

    1. Move the decimal point in the *divisor* **over** to the right to make a whole number.

    2. Move the decimal point in the *dividend* **over** the same number of places.

    3. Move the decimal point **up** into the quotient.

    4. Divide.

over, over up

$$0.6\overset{6.}{\overline{)3.6.}}$$

Example: $3.6 \div 0.6$

There are shortcuts to multiply or divide by multiples and powers of 10.

• If you are **multiplying** by a multiple of 10, **shift** the decimal point **right** one place for each zero.

• If you are **dividing** by a multiple of 10, **shift** the decimal point **left** one place for each zero.

Examples: $1.234 \cdot 100 = 123.4$ $1.234 \div 100 = 0.01234$

              Shift ⟶   *Shift* ⟵

Practice Set (page 167)

Simplify:

a. 0.4 × 0.12 _____ . _____ _____ _____
   0.12
   × 0.4

b. $(0.3)^2$ _____ . _____ _____ _____
   0.3
   × 0.3

c. $6.75 \times 10^3 = $ _____
   Shift →

d. 0.144 ÷ 6
   up

   6)0. 1 4 4

e. 1.2 ÷ 0.06
   over, over, up

   0.06)1. 2 0

f. 2.4 ÷ 0.5
   over, over, up

   0.5)2. 4 0

g. Use the answer to **b** to find $\sqrt{0.09}$. _____

h. What is the cost of 10.2 gallons of gas at $2.249 per gallon? _____

   $2.249
   ×   10.2

   over, over up

i. If 1.6 pounds of peaches cost $2.00, then what is the cost per pound? _____

   1.6)$2.00

Written Practice   (page 167)

1. min
   names   1 $1\frac{1}{2}$

2. average
   27, 29, 30, 30

3.   64.78 m
   56.36 m
   _____

4. $\dfrac{1}{2} = \dfrac{}{}$

   $+ \dfrac{2}{3} = \dfrac{}{}$
   _____

5. $\frac{1}{2} \cdot \frac{2}{3} =$

Cancel the 2s.

6. $\frac{1}{2} \div \frac{2}{3}$

$\downarrow \quad \downarrow$

$— \times — =$

7. $\frac{2}{3} = —$

$- \frac{1}{2} = —$

8. $\begin{array}{r} 0.11 \\ \times\ 0.9 \\ \hline \end{array}$

9. $\begin{array}{r} 3.1 \\ \times\ 3.1 \\ \hline \end{array}$

10. $\begin{array}{r} 4.36 \\ +\ .4 \\ \hline \end{array}$

11. $\begin{array}{r} 4.2 \\ -\ 0.42 \\ \hline \end{array}$

12. *up*

$4\overline{)0.1\,4\,4}$

13. *over, over, up*

$0.4\overline{)4.3\,6}$

14. least to greatest

0.25

0.249

0.251

———, ———, ———

Use work area.

15.

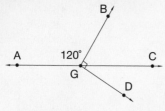

b. A straight line is 180°.

m∠BGC = _____

m∠CGD = _____

16. (−7, −1), (−7, −10), (2, −10), (2, −1)

area and perimeter

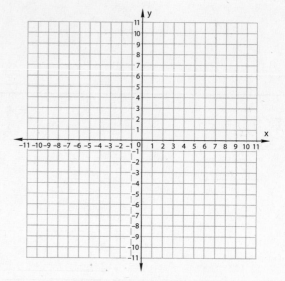

a. _____ and _____

17. a. Distribute: $3(t + 4) =$

b. Factor: $10x − 15$

a. _____

b. _____

18. a. |11 − 7| |7 − 11|

↓   ↓

___ ◯ ___

b. $\sqrt{121}$ $\sqrt[3]{1000}$

↓   ↓

___ ◯ ___

a. _____

b. _____

19. $|z| = 7$

so $z = 7$

$-z = 7$

$z =$ _____ , _____

20. $\dfrac{k \cdot k \cdot u \cdot u \cdot u}{r \cdot r \cdot r \cdot r \cdot t} =$

_____

21. area

$3\frac{1}{2}$ ft

$3\frac{1}{2}$ ft

_____

22. a. $4 + (3 + 1) = (4 + 3) + 1$

_____ Property of Addition

b. $0.5 \times 1 = 0.5$

_____ Property of Multiplication

Use work area.

23. perimeter

$a^2 + b^2 = c^2$

Area of triangle $= \frac{1}{2} bh$

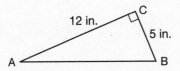

_____

_____

24. *See pages 27 and 28 in the* Student Reference Guide.

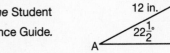

by angles: _____

by sides: _____

$m\angle B =$ _____

_____

25. $70 = 2r + 10$

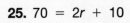

$r =$ _____

26. $1 - x = \dfrac{2}{3}$

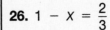

$x =$ _____

27. $\frac{1}{4}p = \frac{1}{8}$

28. $\frac{100}{m} = \frac{1}{2}$

$p = $ _____

$m = $ _____

29. Find $\frac{1}{2}bh$

when $b = 3$
$h = 6$

_____

30. Find $b^2 - (4ac)$

when $a = 1$
$b = 4$
$c = 4$

_____

• Transformations (page 169)

Name _____

Teacher Notes:
- Refer students to "Scale Factor" on page 31 in the *Student Reference Guide.*
- The activity on 📖 page 172 is optional.

Transformations are ways to move a geometric figure or change its size.

- **Reflection** means to *flip* a figure over an imaginary line. Reflection makes a mirror image.

- **Rotation** means to *turn* a figure around a point. Rotation can be clockwise or counterclockwise.

- **Translation** means to *slide* a figure to a new position.

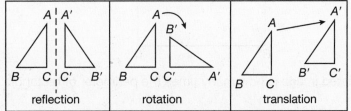

- After a figure is transformed, it gets a new name. In the diagram above, △ *ABC* becomes △ *A'B'C'* after the transformation. (We read △ *A'B'C'* as "triangle A-prime, B-prime, C-prime.")

- △ *A'B'C'* is the same size and shape as △ *ABC*. The triangles are **congruent**.

- Reflection, rotation, and translation are **congruence transformations** or **isometries.**

- **Dilation** enlarges a figure.

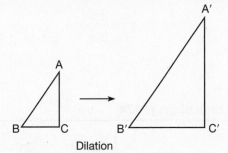

Dilation

- △ *A'B'C'* is the same shape but not the same size as △ *ABC*. The triangles are **similar.**

- Dilation is a **similarity transformation.**

- Each side of △ *A'B'C'* is twice as long as the corresponding side of △ *ABC*. The **scale factor** of the dilation is 2.

Practice Set (page 173)

For **a–d** write the meaning of each transformation by selecting one of these words: turn, flip, enlargement, slide

a. Translation _____

b. Rotation _____

c. Reflection _____

d. Dilation _____

Rectangle *PQRS* is dilated with a scale factor of 3 to form the rectangle *P'Q'R'S'*.
Use this information for **e–g**.

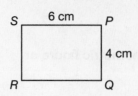

e. Label the length and width of *P'Q'R'S'*. *The scale factor is 3.*

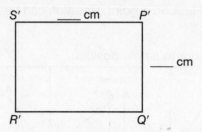

f. The **perimeter** of the dilated image is how many times the perimeter of rectangle *PQRS*? _____

perimeter of *PQRS* _____

perimeter of *P'Q'R'S'* _____

g. The **area** of the dilated image is how many times the area of rectangle *PQRS*? _____

area of *PQRS* _____

area of *P'Q'R'S'* _____

| Written Practice | (continued) (page 174) |

1. 1295
    × 24

2. $\frac{4}{25}$ of 50

3. $\frac{mi}{hr}$ $\frac{}{1}$ $\frac{}{}$

4. $1\frac{7}{8} = -$

$+1\frac{1}{6} = -$

5. $\dfrac{7}{8} = -$

$-\dfrac{1}{6} = -$

6. $\dfrac{7}{8} \cdot \dfrac{1}{6} = -$

7. $\dfrac{7}{8} \div \dfrac{1}{6}$

$- \times -$

Cancel a 2.

8. 0.9
       +0.85

9. 0.9
       −0.85

10. 0.85
        × 0.9

11. *over, over, up*

$0.9\overline{)0.\,8\,2\,8}$

12. a. *mmnmn =*

b. *2xyyxy =*

a. _____

b. _____

13. *order of operations*

$5 \times 4 - [3 \times (2 - 1)] =$

14. $|\,25 - 16\,| - \sqrt{25 - 16} =$

15. (−3, −3), (−3, 6), (0, −3), (0, 6)
area and perimeter

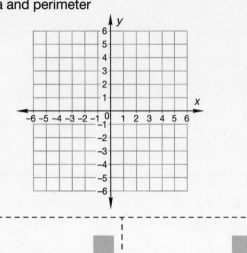

_____ _____

16. a. Distribute: $5(4 - p) =$

b. Factor: $8y - 12 =$

a. _____

b. _____

17. a. $|1 - 9|$ $(9 - 1)$

⬇   ⬇

_____ ◯ _____

b. $\sqrt{9} + \sqrt{16}$ $\sqrt{9 + 16}$

⬇   ⬇

_____ ◯ _____

a. _____

b. _____

18. $|x| = \dfrac{1}{2}$

so $x = \dfrac{1}{2}$

$-x = \dfrac{1}{2}$

$x = $ _____, _____

19. Estimate.

$\underline{14.③} \longrightarrow$

_____

$\underline{1.⑨} \longrightarrow$

_____

20. Estimate.

$\underline{2⑨83} \longrightarrow$

$\underline{7.⓪2} \longrightarrow \times$ _____

_____

21. least to greatest

1.2, 0, 0.12, 1, 2

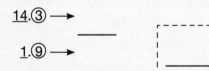

_____, _____, _____, _____, _____

22. a. $3(x - 9) = 3x - 27$

_____ Property

b. $3(4 \cdot 2) = (3 \cdot 4)2$

_____ Property of
Multiplication

⌐ Use work area. ¬

⌐ Use work area. ¬

23. perimeter and area

Dimensions are in mm.

24   26

10

$Area = \frac{1}{2}bh$

24. $\dfrac{5 + m}{2} = 10$

$m =$ _____

25. $6m + 2 = 50$

$m =$ _____

26. $2m = 104$

Write a story for this equation.

In both _____ there were

104 _____.

How many _____ were in

one _____?

$m =$ _____

27. $m + \dfrac{1}{4} = \dfrac{3}{4}$

$m =$ _____

28. Find $b^2 - 4ac$

When $a = 2$
        $b = 3$
        $c = 1$

_____

29. Use exponents.

) ‾‾‾‾‾

) ‾‾‾‾‾

) ‾‾‾‾‾

) ‾‾‾‾‾

) 200 ‾‾‾

30. $a^2 + b^2 = c^2$

Dimensions are in inches.

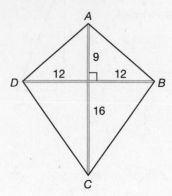

a. $AB =$

b. $BC =$

c. perimeter

200 = _____ · _____

a. _____

b. _____

c. _____

• **Laws of Exponents** (page 177)

Name _____

We show repeated multiplication with a base and an exponent.

$$\text{base} \rightarrow 5^2 \leftarrow \text{exponent}$$

• A number like the one shown above is sometimes called a **power**.

• **The laws of exponents work only when the base is the same for all the powers.**

• Any base to the first power equals the base.

$$3^1 = 3 \qquad 10^1 = 10$$

• Any base to the zero power equals 1.

$$3^0 = 1 \qquad 10^0 = 1$$

• To **multiply** powers with the same base, *add* the exponents.

$$3^2 \cdot 3^3 = 3^{2+3} = 3^5 = 243$$

• To **divide** powers with the same base, *subtract* the exponents.

$$\frac{3^4}{3^2} = 3^{4-2} = 3^2 = 9$$

• To **use an exponent** on a power, *multiply* the exponents.

$$(3^2)^2 = 3^{2 \cdot 2} = 3^4 = 81$$

Teacher Notes:
• Refer students to "Laws of Exponents" on page 19 in the *Student Reference Guide*.

• Review "Exponents" on page 8 in the *Student Reference Guide*.

• Students may use a calculator for help with repeated multiplications.

Practice Set (page 178)

Find the missing exponents.

a. $x^5 \cdot x^2 = x^{\overline{}}$

b. $\dfrac{x^5}{x^2} = x^{\overline{}}$

c. $(x^2)^3 = x^{\overline{}}$

Simplify.

d. $2^3 \cdot 2^2 = 2^{\overline{}} = $ _____

e. $\dfrac{2^5}{2^2} = 2^{\overline{}} = $ _____

f. $(2^5)^2 = 2^{\overline{}} = $ _____

Write each answer as a power of 10.

g. $10^6 \cdot 10^3 = 10^{\overline{}}$

h. $\dfrac{10^6}{10^2} = 10^{\overline{}}$

1. plants <u>12</u> __

weeks

2. total wins: 5 + 3 = _____

total games: 5 + 7 + 3 = _____

wins __
games

_____

3. $\frac{3}{70}$ of 2800

_____

4. Draw a point at (1, 4).

Reflect the point across the y-axis.

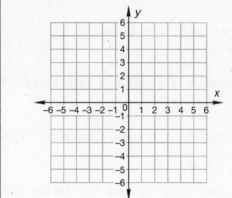

Where is the second point?

(____ , ____)

5. Is this a reflection, rotation, translation, or dilation? _____

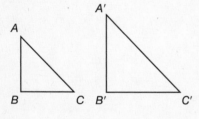

_____

6. Rotate (turn) your textbook 90° clockwise and draw what the figure looks like.

Use work area.

7. $3^2 + 3^1 + 3^0$

↓   ↓   ↓

____ + 3 + 1 =

_____

8. *over, over, up*

$0.7\overline{)2.1}$

_____

9. *shift* ⟶

$6.02 \times 10^6 =$

_____

10.   4.21
   + 42.1   − 0.421

_____

11. $1\frac{1}{2} \cdot \frac{4}{5}$

↓   ↓

___ $\cdot \frac{4}{5} =$

Cancel.

_____

12. $1\frac{1}{2} \div \frac{4}{5}$

↓   ↓

___ × ___ =

_____

13. $\frac{2}{5} \div \frac{4}{5}$

↓   ↓

___ × ___ =

Cancel.

_____

14. $\frac{4}{5} \div \frac{2}{5}$

↓   ↓

___ × ___ =

Cancel.

_____

15. *order of operations*

$4^2 - 4(2)(2) =$

_____

16. $\sqrt[3]{8} + \sqrt{9} =$

_____

17. $1\frac{1}{10} = $ ___

   $+ \frac{1}{2} = $ ___

   _____

_____

18. $|16 - 20|$ $(16 - 20)$

   ↓   ↓

___ ◯ ___

_____

19. *See page 28 in the* Student Reference Guide.

by sides: _____

by angles: _____

Use work area.

20. Perimeter and area

$Area = \frac{1}{2}bh$

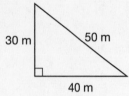

30 m   50 m

40 m

21. perimeter = 51 meters

22. Draw two squares that are not congruent.

Congruent means same shape and size.

Use work area.

23. Two lines that are in different planes and do not intersect are

A parallel.   **B** skew.

C perpendicular.   **D** diagonal.

24. See page 27 in the *Student Reference Guide.*

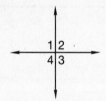

$m\angle 1 + m\angle 3 =$

25. Round to the nearest hundred thousand.

7,654,321 $\longrightarrow$

26. Estimate.

15.81 $\longrightarrow$

$6\frac{1}{4} \longrightarrow -$ _____

27. See page 10 in the *Student Reference Guide.*

28.

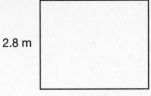

2.8 m

3.54 m

_____

29. *Use exponents.*

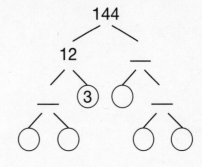

144 = _____ · _____

30. a. $35 - d = 17$

b. $8n = 72$

a. $d =$ _____

b. $n =$ _____

• Scientific Notation for Large Numbers (page 181)

Name _____

Numbers used in science are often very large or very small.

- **Scientific notation** is a way to express a number as a product of a decimal and a power of 10.

  Example: $9{,}261{,}000{,}000{,}000 = 9.261 \times 10^{12}$

- The exponent on the 10 shows where the decimal point is located when the number is written in standard form.

- Remember that multiplying a number by a power of 10 **shifts** the decimal point to the *right*.

- To write a number in scientific notation in standard form:

  1. Shift the decimal point to the right the number of places shown by the exponent.

  2. Use zero as a placeholder.

  Example: Write 4.26×106 in standard form.

  $4.26 \times 10^6 \longrightarrow 4260000 \longrightarrow 4{,}260{,}000$

- To write a large number in scientific notation:

  1. Place a decimal point to the *right of the first digit*.

  2. To find the power of 10, count the number of places the decimal point shifted.

  3. Do not write ending zeros.

  Example: Write $405{,}700{,}000$ in scientific notation.

  $405{,}700{,}000 \longrightarrow 4.05700000 \longrightarrow 4.057 \times 10^8$

Practice Set (page 183)

a. Write "two point five times ten to the sixth" with digits.

  _____ . _____ $\times$ 10^{-}

b. Use words to write 1.8×10^8.

  one point _____

Write each number in **standard form.**

c. 2.0×10^5 _____

d. 7.5×10^8 _____

e. 1.609×10^3 _____

f. 3.05×10^4 _____

Write each number in **scientific notation.**

g. $365{,}000$ _____ $\times$ _____

h. $295{,}000{,}000$ _____ $\times$ _____

i. $70{,}500$ _____ $\times$ _____

j. 25 million _____ $\times$ _____

1. Dead Sea: −1292 ft

Mount of Olives: 2680 ft

What is the difference?

2. $\frac{7}{10}$ is mountainous.

$\frac{7}{10} =$ _____ %

What percent is **not** mountainous?

3. mi   1   1500
towers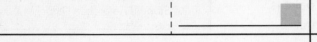

4. See page 28 in the Student
Reference Guide.

by angles: _____

by sides: _____

area:

Area = $\frac{1}{2}$ bh

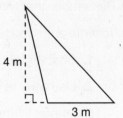

4 m

3 m

| Use work area. |

5. The sum of the angle measures in a triangle is 180°.

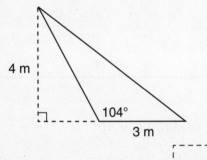

4 m

104°

3 m

6. kg   1
lb   2.2

Round to the nearest kg. ———

7. a. $m^3 \cdot m^4 =$

b. $\frac{m^6}{m^2} =$

a. _____

b. _____

8. order of operations

$1\frac{1}{3} \cdot 2\frac{1}{4}$

↓   ↓

___ · ___ =

Cancel.

$\frac{1}{3}$

$+$ _____

9. $\dfrac{1}{5} \div \dfrac{4}{5}$

↓   ↓

— × —

Cancel.

_____

10.   2.   2.
       +1.2   −1.2

over, over, up

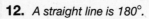

_____

11.   1.5
       ×1.5   −1.5

_____

12. *A straight line is 180°.*

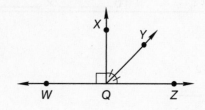

m∠WQY _____

13. Find $x^2 - 2x$

when $x = 5$

_____

14. Round to the nearest whole numbers.

a. $3\dfrac{3}{4}$ ⟶

b. $3\dfrac{3}{10}$ ⟶

c. 3.10 ⟶

a. _____

b. _____

c. _____

15. $(-1, 5), (-1, -2), (-6, -5)$

Find the fourth vertex: (_____ , _____)

perimeter: _____ area: _____

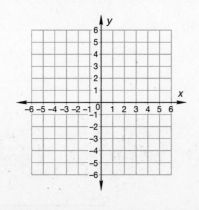

Use work area.

16. **a.** Distribute: 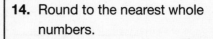 $3\,(x + r + 5)$

b. Factor: $4x + 6y$

a. _____

b. _____

17. a. *Shift* →

  2.97 × 10⁵ =

b. *Shift* ←

  4,030,000 =

a. _____

b. _____ × _____

18. 1³ + 2³ + 3¹ + 4⁰

  ↓   ↓   ↓   ↓

  __ + __ + 3 + 1 =

  _____

19. Estimate.

  6870 → _____

  6.9 →

  _____

20. √25   ³√27

  ↓   ↓

  _____ ◯ _____

  _____

21. *reciprocal*

  $2\frac{1}{2}$

  _____

22. *See page 20 in the* Student Reference Guide.

a. $xy = yx$

  _____ Property of Multiplication

b. $1 \cdot x = x$

  _____ Property of Multiplication

  Use work area.

23. *The sum of the angle measures in a triangle is 180°.*

  3x = 180°

24. $10 \cdot 5 = 10 + h$

  h = _____

25. $1 - f = \dfrac{9}{10}$

f = _____

26. $\dfrac{10^6}{10^2} = 10^x$

x = _____

27. $\dfrac{18}{x} = \dfrac{9}{10}$

x = _____

28. *order of operations*

    a. $2 + 3 \cdot 10 \div 2 =$

    b. $2 \times (3 + 12) + 10 =$

a. _____   b. _____

29. least to greatest

    2, 0.2, −2, 0, 0.02

_____, 0 , _____, _____, _____

Use work area.

30. $a^2 + b^2 + c^2 =$

1 cm
1 cm

$\sqrt{}$ ▨

• Ratio (page 186)

Name _____

Teacher Note:
• Refer students to "Ratio" on page 22 in the *Student Reference Guide*.

A fraction compares a part of a whole (the numerator) to a whole (the denominator).

• A **ratio** uses division to compare two numbers. Ratios are often written as fractions.

• Ratios are *reduced* but **are not** *converted* to mixed numbers.

> **Example:** In a class of 28 students there are 12 girls and 16 boys. Write the ratio of girls to boys.
>
> $$\frac{girls}{boys} \quad \frac{12}{16} = \frac{3}{4}$$

• The girl-boy ratio above can be written in several ways:

with the word **to**	3 to 4
as a fraction	$\frac{3}{4}$
as a decimal	0.75
with a colon	3:4

• If a ratio compares two things with the same units, such as feet and feet, the units cancel.

• If a ratio compares two things with different units, such as miles and hours, the units do not cancel.

• To find an **approximate ratio,** *round* each number.

Practice Set (page 188)

In a bag are 14 marbles. Six marbles are red and eight marbles are blue.

a. What is the ratio of **red** marbles **to blue** marbles?

Reduce. $\dfrac{red}{blue}$ _____ =

b. What is the ratio of **blue** marbles **to red** marbles?

Reduce. $\dfrac{blue}{red}$ _____ =

A 20 ft flagpole casts a shadow 24 feet long.

c. What is the ratio of the **height** of the flagpole **to the length** of the shadow?

Reduce. $\dfrac{height}{length}$ _____ =

d. What is the ratio of the **length** of the shadow **to the height** of the flagpole?

Reduce. $\dfrac{length}{height}$ _____ =

e. If 479 stocks advanced in price and 326 declined in price, then what was the approximate ratio of **advancers to decliners?**

Estimate. 479 → advancers _____ =
326 → decliners

f. Refer to the table in Example 4 on 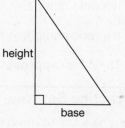 page 188. Find Rosa's approximate reading rate in **minutes per page** for the 5-day total.

Estimate. $\dfrac{\text{min}}{\text{page}}$ ⎯⎯ =

Written Practice (page 189)

1. $\overline{)1\,0\,0\,0}$

2. *Reduce.*

$$\frac{30°}{360°} =$$

3. 18% of \$3000

Change to a decimal.

$\times\ 3000$

4. What sort of triangle is this?

   A acute

   B right

   C obtuse

   D cannot be determined

height

base

5. *Reduce. Then change to a percent.*

$\dfrac{\text{germinated}}{\text{planted}}$ ⎯⎯⎯

6. $5^2 \cdot 5^1 \cdot 5^0 = 5^- =$

7. $10^2 - 10^1 - 10^0$

↓   ↓   ↓

__ $- 10 - 1 =$

8. $xxwxw =$

9. $(xy)(xy)$

_____

10. $5\frac{1}{5} - 2\frac{1}{2}$

$\downarrow$ $\downarrow$

___ · ___ =

Cancel.

_____

11. order of operations

$\frac{2}{3}$ + $\frac{3}{4}$

$\downarrow$ $\downarrow$

___ × ___ =

$\frac{1}{2}$

$+$
___

_____

12.   1.35
    $+\,0.07$

over, over, up

$)$ ___

_____

13.   101
    $+\,10.1$ $\times\,0.01$

_____

14. once a week: $2.89
             $\times\;10.2$

four weeks: $\times\quad4$

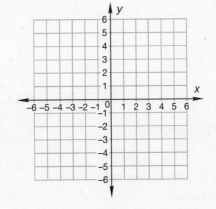

15. Divide to find the scale factor.

over, over, up

$)\overline{6.25000}$

Now round to the nearest thousandth.

___ . ___ ___ ___

16. $(-2,1),\ (3,1)\ (1,4)$

Area $= \frac{1}{2}\,bh$

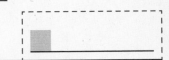

17. Which is equal to $53(100 + 20)$?

Distributive Property

A $53 + 100 \times 53 + 20$

B $53 \times 100 + 20$

C $53 \times 100 + 53 \times 20$

_____

18. $53 \times 100 =$ _____

$53 \times 20 =$ _____

_____ those products to find 53(120).

Use work area.

19. least to greatest

$\frac{2}{3}, -1, 0.5, 0, \frac{3}{7}$

_____, _____, _____, _____, _____

Use work area.

20. teaspoons
bowl   _____   _____
               1

_____ teaspoons

21. a. $22 - n = 10$

b. $\frac{d}{4} = -8$

a. $n =$ _____

b. $d =$ _____

22. median
Put in order.

13, 9, 11, 5, 3, 16

_____, _____, _____, _____, _____, _____

_____

23. $\frac{mi}{hr}$ _____

24. Distribute: $3(2x - y) =$

_____

25. Factor: $18x - 27 =$

_____

26. a. Scientific notation
252,000 =

b. Round to the nearest ten thousand.
252,000 ⟶

$\frac{}{1,000,000} =$

a. _____ $\times$ _____

b. _____

27.

by angles: _____

by sides: _____

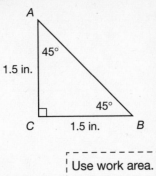

Use work area.

28. $c \times 1.75 = p$

Find p when $c = \$16$

$p =$ _____

29. *A straight line is 180°. The sum of the angle measures in a triangle is 180°.*

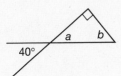

$m\angle a =$ _____

$m\angle b =$ _____

30. Find the perimeter.

$a^2 + b^2 = c^2$

Does Miles have enough chicken wire?

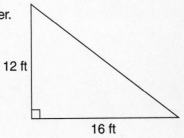

_____

Teacher Notes:
• The calculator exercises on
  page 194 are optional.

When a division problem does not work out evenly, we usually attach a decimal point and zeros to the dividend and continue dividing.

• For some divisions, the problem will never work out evenly.

• When there is a pattern of repeating digits, write a bar over the first pattern of repeating digits.

$$\text{Examples: } \frac{1}{6} \longrightarrow 6\overline{)1.0^40^40^40^40} \cdots \quad = 0.1\overline{6}$$
$$\phantom{\text{Examples: } \frac{1}{6} \longrightarrow } 0.1\ 6\ 6\ 6\ 6 \cdots$$

$$\frac{35}{11} \longrightarrow 11\overline{)35.0000} \cdots = 3.1\overline{8}$$

```
        3.1818 ...
11)35.0000 ... = 3.18
   33
   20
   11
    90
    88
    20
    11
     90
     88
      2
```

• The repeating digits are called the **repetend.**

• To round a repeating decimal:

Example: Round $25.\overline{405}$ to five decimal places.

  1. Remove the bar and write the repeating digits.

  $25.\overline{405} = 25.405405\ldots$

  2. Round to five places.

  $25.405\underline{4}05 \longrightarrow 25.40541$

Practice Set (page 194)

Write each fraction in **a–d** as a repeating decimal with a bar over the repetend.

a. $\frac{3}{11}$ ⟶ $11\overline{)3.000}$ = _____

b. $\frac{2}{9}$ ⟶ $9\overline{)2.00}$ = _____

c. $2\frac{2}{3}$ $3\overline{)2.00}$

$2\frac{2}{3}$ = 2._____

d. $\frac{1}{30}$ ⟶ $30\overline{)1.000}$ = _____

Round each decimal number to the nearest thousandth.

e. $0.\overline{3}$ = 0.333③ ... ⟶ _____

f. $0.\overline{6}$ = 0.6666... ⟶ _____

g. $0.\overline{36}$ = 0.3636... ⟶ _____

h. $1.\overline{86}$ = 1.8686... ⟶ _____

Arrange in order from least to greatest.

i. 0.6, $0.\overline{6}$, 0.66

j. $\frac{1}{2}$, $0.\overline{5}$, $\frac{1}{3}$, 0.3, $0.0\overline{6}$

Written Practice (page 195)

1. $\frac{1}{2}$ of 20 were boys: _____

Divide by the denominator.

$\frac{1}{2}$ of boys wore T-shirts: _____

$\frac{1}{2}$ of $\frac{1}{2}$ = _____

‹ Use work area.

2. Estimate the area.

19 ft 10 in. ⟶ _____ ft

22 ft 1 in. ⟶ _____ ft

3. average

$7\frac{1}{2}$ = _

$5\frac{3}{4}$ = _

5 =

+ $2\frac{3}{4}$ = _

_____

=

Convert. $4\overline{)}$

4. area

Dimensions are in mm.

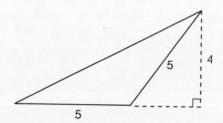

5. by angles: _____
by sides: _____

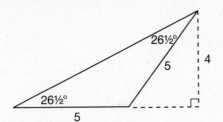

What is the measure of the third angle? _____

6. 25% of $80

_____ Use work area.

_____

---

7. side length _____
perimeter

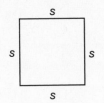

_____

8. *order of operations*

$$\frac{2}{3} \cdot \frac{1}{2} = \qquad \frac{1}{4}$$

$$+ \underline{\quad}$$

Cancel.

_____

---

9. $\frac{1}{8} \div \frac{1}{4}$ $\qquad \frac{7}{8}$

$\underline{\quad} \times \underline{\quad}$

Cancel.

_____

10. 1.23
0.4
+5

over, over, up
short division

$\overline{)\ \ }$

_____

---

11. $4^0 + 4 \cdot 5 \cdot 2 - 1^3 =$

12. $0.8 - \{0.6 - [0.4 - (0.2)^2]\} =$

0.2
× 0.2
‾‾‾‾‾

_____

---

13. *short division*

   a. $9\overline{)2.00}$ = _____ = _____%

   b. The _____ form is best

   because _____ divides

   into 27 evenly.

                         Use work area.

14. decimal and fraction

   shift ←

   70% =

   $70\% = \dfrac{}{100} =$

15. area and perimeter

   (5,11), (5,1), (−2,1), (−2,11)

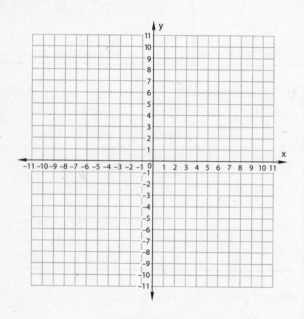

16. a. Distribute:

   $5(x + y + z) =$

   b. Factor: $wx + wy =$

   a. _____

   b. _____

17. $\dfrac{x^5 \cdot x^2}{x} =$

18. scientific notation

   28,000,000 =

   _____ × _____

19. 1,000,000 = 10^6

   $2^{} \cdot 5^{}$

20. $\sqrt{169}$ $(3.7)^2$

   ↓   ↓

   — ◯ —

21. a. $\frac{1}{2} \cdot \frac{1}{4} = \frac{1}{4} \cdot \frac{1}{2}$

_____ Property of Multiplication

b. $\frac{1}{3} + \left(\frac{2}{3} + \frac{1}{2}\right) = \left(\frac{1}{3} + \frac{2}{3}\right) + \frac{1}{2}$

_____ Property of Addition

Use work area.

22. least to greatest

$0.3, \frac{2}{5}, 35\%, 0, 1$

____, ____, ____, ____, ____

Use work area.

23.

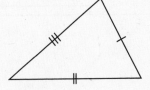

by sides: _____

by angles: _____

Use work area.

24. $2.2 = 2m + 0.2$

What number plus 0.2 is 2.2?

$2m =$

$m =$ _____

25. $\frac{4}{5} = 1 - r$

$r =$ _____

26. $\frac{7}{20} = \frac{7}{10}h$

$h =$ _____

27. $\frac{t + 3}{4} = 5$

What number is 4 divided by 5?

$t + 3 =$

$t =$ _____

28. Find $b^2 - 4ac$
when $a = 4$
$b = 9$
$c = 5$

_____

29. $E = mgh$

Find E when $m = 2$
$g = 9.8$
$h = 5$

$E =$ _____

30. Use the Pythagorean Theorem.

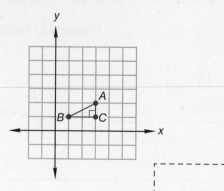

_____ ▪

• Adding Integers
• Collecting Like Terms (page 202)

Name _____

Teacher Notes:
• Introduce Hint #44, "Adding Signed Numbers on a Number Line."

• Refer students to "Adding Two Signed Numbers" on page 26 in the *Student Reference Guide*.

Integers are the whole numbers and their opposites.

..., −3, −2, −1, 0, 1, 2, 3...

• We can show addition of integers on a number line.

   1. Start at zero.

   2. Move right for positive numbers.

   3. Move left for negative numbers.

   4. Where you end up is the answer.

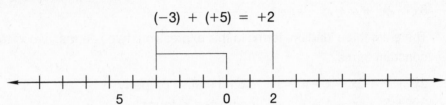

$$(-3) + (+5) = +2$$

• We can also add integers without a number line.

• Remember that the **absolute value** of a number is its distance from zero on a number line.

$$|\text{-}3| = 3$$
$$|5| = 5$$

• If the signs are the *same*, **add** the absolute values and keep the same sign.

   Example: $(-5) + (-4) = -9$

• If the signs are *different*, **subtract** the absolute values and keep the sign of the number with the greater absolute value.

   Example: $(-5) + (+4) = -1$

• Numbers with the same absolute value but different signs are **opposites**.

• The sum of two opposites is always zero.

   Example: $(-4) + (+4) = 0$

An algebraic term is part of an algebra expression or equation.

• Each term has a positive or negative number (the **coefficient**) and may have one or more variables (letters).

   When a term is written without a number, the coefficient is 1.

   When a term is written without a sign, the sign is positive.

• A term without a variable is called a **constant term**. Its value cannot change.

$$3y, x, -w^2z, 2$$

The coefficient of $3y$ is $+3$.
The coefficient of x is $+1$.
The coefficient of $-w^2z$ is -1.
2 is a *constant*.

• **Like terms** can be combined, or collected, by addition.

Like terms are identical variable parts including exponents.

$-3xy$ and xy are like terms.
a^2b and ab are **not** like terms.

Example: Collect like terms.

$$3x + 2x^2 + 4 + x^2 - x - 1$$

There are three kinds of terms in this expression: two x terms, two x^2 terms, and two constant terms.

$2x^2 + x^2 + 3x - x + 4 - 1$	Commutative property
$3x^2 + 3x - x + 4 - 1$	combined x^2 terms
$3x^2 + 2x + 4 - 1$	combined x terms
$3x^2 + 2x + 3$	combined constant terms

• Always arrange terms in descending order of exponents. The term with the greatest exponent is on the left and the constant term is on the right.

Practice Set (page 207)

Simplify.

a. $(-12) + (-3) = $ _____

b. $(-12) + (+3) = $ _____

c. $(+12) + (-3) = $ _____

d. $(-3) + (+12) = $ _____

e. Show $(-3) + (+12)$ on the number line below.

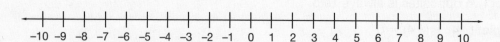

f. At 6:00 a.m. the temperature was $-12°C$. By noon the temperature increased 8 degrees. Write an equation for this situation and find the temperature at noon.

$(-12) + ($ _____ $) = $ _____

g. The hikers started on the desert floor, 182 feet **below** sea level. After an hour of hiking they had climbed 1,108 ft. Write an equation for the situation and find the hikers' elevation after an hour of hiking.

$($ _____ $) + ($ _____ $) = $ _____

Collect like terms:

h. $3x + 2xy + xy - x =$ _____

i. $6x^2 - x + 2x - 1 =$ _____

j. $2a^3 + 3b - a^3 - 4b =$ _____

k. $x + y - 1 - x + y + 1 =$ _____

l. $P = L + W + L + W$

$P =$ _____

m. $P = s + s + s + s$

$P =$ _____

n. What is the perimeter of this rectangle?

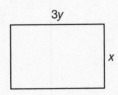

$3y + x + 3y + x =$ _____

Written Practice (page 208)

1. $\dfrac{\$}{lb}$ $\dfrac{\$0.45}{1}$ _____

2. $4\dfrac{1}{4} \cdot 2\dfrac{1}{2}$

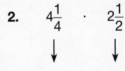

_____ $\cdot$ _____ $=$

 Convert.

3. 78.08% nitrogen
   20.95% oxygen

4. reflection, rotation, translation, or dilation? scale factor?

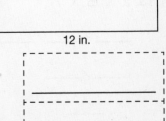

5. twelve-and-a-half trillion

scientific notation

See page 21 in the Student Reference Guide.

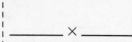

6. Snails ____
Goldfish

7. $4 + 10 \div 5 \times 2 =$

8. $\dfrac{5 + 3 \cdot 10}{5^2 - 10}$

9. $\dfrac{1}{6} \div \dfrac{1}{3}$ $\dfrac{3}{4} =$

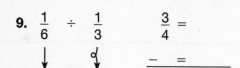

____ × ____ =

Cancel.

10. $\dfrac{1}{12} \cdot \dfrac{1}{2} =$ $\dfrac{2}{3} =$

____ = ____

11. $\sqrt{9} + \sqrt{16}$ $\sqrt{9 + 16}$

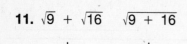

____ ◯ ____

12. a. Distribute: $4(x + 2y + 3) =$

b. Factor: $6x + 3y =$

a. _____

b. _____

13. $2 \times (5 \times 7)$ Given

____ × ____ × ____ _____ Property

____ × ____

____

Use work area.

14. $|-3| + |-5| =$

A a negative number

B a positive integer

C zero

D any positive number

15. Find $a + b + c$

when $a = 5$
$b = -2$
$c = -4$

_____

16. $W = mg$

Find W when $m = 5$
$g = 9.8$

$W = $ _____

17. by angles: _____

by sides: _____

area: _____

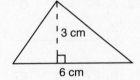

3 cm

6 cm

Use work area.

18. Collect like terms:
$3x^2 + 2x + 3x - 1 = $

_____

19. $47 - 79 = $

_____

20. $\dfrac{x^6 \cdot x^2}{x \cdot x^3} = $

_____

21. $6\dfrac{1}{4} = $ —

$- 3\dfrac{3}{8} = $ —

_____

22. 6
$- 3.67$

_____

23. a. $(-3) + (-12) = $

b. $(-12) + (-3) = $

a. _____

b.

24. $8h + 10 = 50$

$h = $ _____

25. long division

up

$11\overline{)3.000}$

_____

26. $\dfrac{27}{45} = \dfrac{\quad \div \quad}{\quad \div \quad} =$

$\overline{)27}$ $\overline{)45}$

_____

27. How many words did Julie remove?

$(-25) + (+17) =$

Now find the total.
500

_____

_____

28. a. $62 \times 0 = 0$

_____ Property of Multiplication

b. $27 \times 1 = 27$

_____ Property of Multiplication

Use work area.

29. a. Find the missing exponent:
$x^8 \cdot x^2 \cdot x^{\square} = x^{15}$

b. $2^3 \ + \ 2^2 \ + \ 2^1 \ + \ 2^0$
↓   ↓   ↓   ↓

____ + ____ + ____ + ____ =

a. _____   b. _____

30. Round to the nearest cent.

$\begin{array}{r} \$4.29 \\ \times \ \ 1.3 \\ \hline \end{array}$

_____

● **Probability** (page 210)

Name _____

The probability of an event is the ratio of favorable outcomes (what we want to happen) to the number of possible outcomes.

- The range of probability is from zero (impossible) to 1 (certain).

- Probability is usually written as a *reduced fraction.*

- When probability is written as a *percent,* it is called **chance.**

- **Odds** is the ratio of *favorable to unfavorable outcomes.* Odds are written with a colon.

Teacher Notes:
- Introduce Hint #45, "Probability."
- Refer students to "Probability, Chance, Odds" on page 25 in the *Student Reference Guide.*
- Review "Ratio" on Page 22 in the *Student Reference Guide.*

Example: The spinner is spun once. What is the probability the spinner will stop in sector *A*? The probability of spinning *A* is *P(A)*.

$$P(A) = \frac{\text{number of favorable outcomes}}{\text{number of possible outcomes}} = \frac{1}{4}$$

The chance of spinning *A* is 25%

$$\frac{1}{4} = 25\%$$

The odds of spinning *A* are 1:3

1 favorable: 3 unfavorable

- The sample space is a list of all possible outcomes.

    Example: The sample space for the spinner above is *{A, B, C, D}.*

- The **complement** of an event is the opposite of the event. The sum of the probabilities of an event and its complement is 1.

    Example: The probability of spinning *A*, *P(A)*, is $\frac{1}{4}$. The complement of *P(A)* is the probability of not spinning *A* or *P(not A)*. The probability of *P(not A)* is $\frac{3}{4}$.

$$P(A) + P(not\ A) = \frac{1}{4} + \frac{3}{4} = 1$$

- **Theoretical probability** is found by calculating mathematically what will happen in an experiment.

- **Experimental probability** is found by performing an experiment or looking at data and finding the result.

Practice Set (page 214)

a. A number cube is rolled once. What is the probability of rolling an even number?

even numbers: {_____, _____, _____}

possible numbers {_____, _____, _____, _____, _____, _____}

$P(\text{even}) = \dfrac{\text{number of even numbers}}{\text{number of possible numbers}} = \underline{\hspace{1cm}} =$

Write the probability as a decimal. _____

b. A number cube is rolled once. What are the odds of rolling a 6? _____ : _____
favorable: unfavorable

c. If the chance of rain tomorrow is 20%, then is it more likely to rain or not rain?
What is the chance it will **not rain** tomorrow?

The chance of not rain is _____% because the chance of rain and not rain equals 100%.

_____% is greater than 20%, so _____ is more likely.

d. A coin is flipped three times. The tree diagram below shows all the possible outcomes for the three flips.

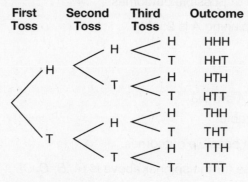

What is the sample space of the experiment?

{_____, _____, _____, _____, _____, _____, _____, _____}

e. Referring to the experiment in **d**, what is the probability of getting heads **exactly twice**?

$P(\text{heads exactly twice}) = \underline{\hspace{0.8cm}}$

What is the probability of **not** getting heads **exactly twice**? _____

f. Quinn runs a sandwich shop. Since she added turkey melt to the menu 36 out of 120 customers have ordered the new sandwich. What is the probability the next customer will order a turkey melt?

$$\frac{36}{120} =$$

reduce

If Quinn has 50 customers for lunch, about how many are likely to order a turkey melt? _____
Multiply 50 by the probability.

g. Is the probability found in problem **e** theoretical probability or experimental probability? _____

Is the probability found in problem **f** theoretical probability or experimental probability? _____

Written Practice (page 214)

1. First oz: $0.39
additional oz:

oz $\dfrac{1}{0.24}$ ___
$

0.24
× ___ +0.39

2. pages   ____ ____
days

3. sec ____ ____
yd

4. a. experimental:

$$\frac{\text{eighth-graders}}{\text{names chosen}} = \_\_\_ =$$

b. theoretical:

$$\frac{\text{eighth-graders}}{\text{total names}} =$$

a. _____ b. _____

5. 18 marbles, 2 yellow

$$P\text{ (yellow)} = \frac{\text{yellow}}{\text{total}} =$$

$$P\text{ (not yellow)} = \frac{\text{not yellow}}{\text{total}} =$$

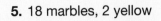

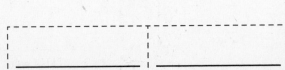

6.

10 m

6 m

a. area

b. perimeter

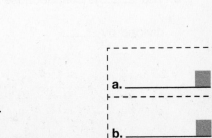

a. _____

b. _____

7. Estimate

6①0 ⟶

1⑨5 ⟶   +   3⑨8 ⟶ _____

_____

8. $\frac{1}{3} \cdot \frac{4}{5} =$ $\frac{1}{5} =$

_____

_____

---

9. $\frac{1}{3} \div \frac{3}{4}$ $\frac{7}{9} -$ _____ = _____ = _____

_____ × _____ =

_____

10.   3.1   2.05
        × 0.1   −

_____

_____

---

11. 7^2 − 6^1 + 5^0

_____ − _____ + _____ =

_____

12. a. $\sqrt{3^2 + 4^2}$ $\sqrt{3^2} + \sqrt{4^2}$

_____ ◯ _____

b. $|-1 + 5|$ $|-1| + |5|$

_____ ◯ _____

---

13. decimal and percent

up

9)‾5.‾0‾0

_____

_____

a. _____

b. _____

---

14. a. 60%

decimal: _____

shift ⟵

fraction: _____

b. The _____ is best because $15 can be

divided by _____.

_____

15. (3, −5), (7, −5), (7,2)

fourth vortex: (,   ) area: _____

perimeter: _____

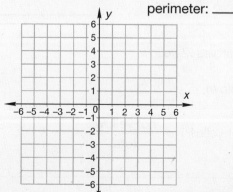

Use work area.

16. a. Distribute: $3(x + 12) =$

b. Factor: $x^2 + 6x =$

a. _____

b. _____

17. standard notation

shift →

6.02×10^{10}

_____

18. a. $(m^4)^3 =$

b. $\dfrac{r^2 r^5}{r^3} =$

a. _____

b. _____

19. a. Graph 2 and 6. Find and graph the average.

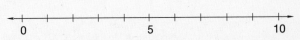

b. Graph -5 and 1. Guess the average.

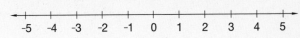

Use work area.

20. *See page 10 in the Student Reference Guide.*

{ _____ , _____ , _____ , _____ ...}

Use work area.

21. $23 + (7 + 18)$ given

(_____ + _____) + _____   _____ Property

_____ + _____

_____

Use work area.

22. Use exponents.

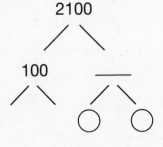

2100 = _____ · _____ · _____ · _____

23. { _____ , _____ , _____ , _____ , _____ ,

_____ , _____ , _____ , _____ }

$P(A) = \text{—}$

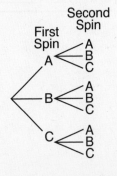

Use work area.

24. Which is greater?

$P(A) = \underline{\quad}$

$P(AA, BB, CC) = \underline{\quad}$

Use work area.

25. least to greatest

0, 2.3, −3.2, 4.5, −5.4

$\underline{\quad}, \underline{\quad}, \underline{\quad}, \underline{\quad}, \underline{\quad},$

Use work area.

26. A mirror image is which transformation?

_____

27. $3x + 20 = 80$

$x = \underline{\qquad\qquad}$

28. Find $\sqrt{b^2 - 4ac}$

when $a = 2$
$b = 5$
$c = 2$

_____

29. $E = \dfrac{1}{2}mv^2$

Find E when $m = 2$
$v = 3$

$E = \underline{\qquad\qquad}$

30.

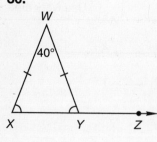

a. $m\angle X = \underline{\qquad}$

b. $m\angle WX = \underline{\qquad}$

c. $m\angle WYZ = \underline{\qquad}$

• **Subtracting Integers** (page 218)   Name _____

To subtract integers, use algebraic addition.

• Instead of subtracting a number, **add** its *opposite*.

• Instead of subtracting a *positive number,* add a *negative number.*

> **Example:** Simplify: $(+7) - (+3)$
> $(+7) + (-3) = 4$

• Instead of subtracting a *negative number,* add a *positive number.*

> **Example:** Simplify: $(-3) - (-2)$
> $(-3) + (+2) = -1$

Teacher Notes:
• Refer students to "Subtracting Signed Numbers" on page 26 in the *Student Reference Guide.*
• Review Hint #44, "Adding Signed Numbers on a Number Line."
• Review "Adding Two Signed Numbers" on page 26 in the *Student Reference Guide.*

Practice Set (page 219)

Use algebraic addition to simplify:

a. $(-12) - (-3)$
$(-12) + (+3) =$ _____

b. $(-12) - (+3)$
$(-12) + ($ ___ $) =$ _____

c. $(-3) - (-12)$
$(-3) + ($ ___ $) =$ _____

d. $(-3) - (+12)$
$(-3) - ($ ___ $) =$ _____

e. Show $(-3) - (-12)$ on the number line below:

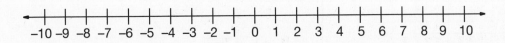

f. Victor owed $386. His creditor forgave (subtracted) $100 of the debt. Write an equation for the situation and find out how much Victor still owes.

$(-386) - (-100)$
$($ ___ $) + ($ ___ $) =$ _____

Victor still owes _____ .

1. $(-5°F) + (17°F) =$

   A 22°F   **B** 12°F   **C** 10°F   **D** 8°F

_____

2. *Scientific notation*

   25,000,000

_____ × _____

3. *Multiply the loop.*

Bags   1   6
$

   $13.89
  × _____

_____

4. Total sales tax: _____

   $189
  × _____

¦ Use work area. ¦

5. Plot the points and then connect them in order.
$(-2, 2), (1, 5), (5, 5), (8, 2), (-2, 2)$

What kind of quadrilateral is it?

Are any sides parallel?

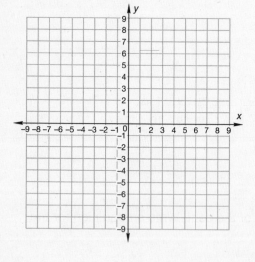

_____

6. $(-10) - ($ $) =$
   $(-10) + ($ $) =$

_____

7. a. $8 - (-1)$
    $8 + ($ $) =$

  b. $-1 - (-2)$
    $-1 + ($ $) =$

  a. _____

  b. _____

8. a. $-6 - 5$
    $-6 + ($ $) =$

  b. $-8 + (-12) =$

  a. _____

  b. _____

9. Collect like terms:

$3a + 2a^2 + a - a^2 =$

10. Decimal and percent

up

$9\overline{)7.00}$

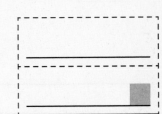

11. $9 \div \dfrac{1}{4}$

——— × ——— =

12. Find BC.

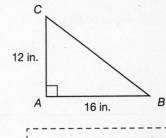

C

12 in.

A   16 in.   B

13. $\sqrt{\left(\dfrac{1}{3}\right)^2 \cdot \left(\dfrac{1}{4}\right)^2} =$

14. $5x - 3 = 27$

$m =$

15. Estimate.

$29 \rightarrow$

$\times \quad 0.3$

16. a. $-17 + (-5) =$ _____

b. $16 + -4 =$ _____

c. $-12 + 27 =$ _____

d. $-\dfrac{1}{4} + 0.75 =$ _____

Use work area.

17. a. 20%

Decimal: _____

shift

Fraction: _____

b. The _____ is best because $45

can be divided by _____.

Use work area.

18. $9^2 - 7^2 + 6^0 =$

19.   1.09
         0.055
       + 3.2
       _____

20.   1.5   3.14
        × 0.2   ____

21. *over, over, up*

0.025$\overline{)0.500}$

22. cartons × boxes × containers × ounces

Use a calculator.

23. least to greatest

$\frac{1}{8}$, 0.12, −1.8, 0.22, −$\frac{1}{10}$

_____, $-\frac{1}{10}$, _____, _____, _____

Use work area.

24. Plot the points and draw the triangle.

(−2, 1), (2, 4), (6, 1)

a. by sides: _____

b. area: _____

c. perimeter: _____

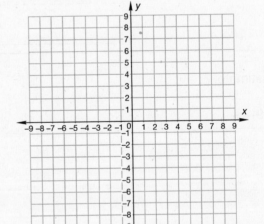

25. Plot the points and draw the triangle.
(−2, 1), (1, −3), (−2, −7)

Compare this triangle with the triangle in problem 24. What transformation is this?

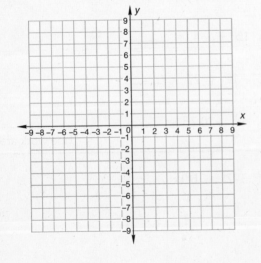

Use work area.

26. scale drawing _____
actual height

27. over, over, up

28. 6.7 cm
  5.8 cm
  _____

29. Distributive Property

$$\frac{1}{2}\left(6 + \frac{3}{4}\right) =$$

30. length: $\frac{1}{2}$ of 11 = _____

width: $\frac{1}{2}$ of $8\frac{1}{2}$ = _____

area: _____

Use work area.

- **Proportions**
- **Ratio Word Problems** (page 223)

A proportion is a statement that two ratios are equal.

- **Cross-multiply** to check that ratios are equal.

- If the **cross-products** are equal, then the ratios are equal (proportional).

Example: Are these ratios proportional?

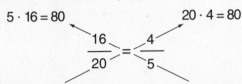

$$5 \cdot 16 = 80 \qquad 20 \cdot 4 = 80$$

$$\frac{16}{20} = \frac{4}{5}$$

The cross-products are equal, so the ratios are proportional.

- To find a missing number in a proportion:

  1. Cross-multiply.

  2. Divide by the known factor.

$$\frac{3}{5} = \frac{6}{w}$$

$$3 \cdot w = 5 \cdot 6 \qquad \text{cross-multiply}$$

$$3 \cdot w = 30$$

$$w = \frac{30}{3} \qquad \text{divide}$$

$$w = 10$$

  You have done this before: *Multiply the loop. Divide by the outside number.*

- Ratio word problems have several numbers, so we will use ratio boxes.

  1. Make a ratio box.
  Write the given numbers in the box. Be careful!
  Write a letter in the box that answers the question asked.

  2. Write a proportion using the numbers in the ratio box.

  3. Find the missing number in the proportion.

Example: The ratio of boys to girls in the class is 3 to 4. If there are 12 girls, how many boys are there?

	Ratio	Actual Count
Boys	3	b
Girls	4	12

$$\rightarrow \frac{3}{4} = \frac{b}{12}$$

$$3 \cdot 12 = 4 \cdot b$$

$$36 = 4b$$

$$\frac{36}{4} = b$$

$$9 = b$$

There are 9 boys in the class.

Practice Set (page 226)

a. Circle the pair of ratios that forms a proportion.

cross-multiply

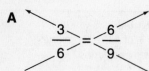

A $\frac{3}{6} = \frac{6}{9}$ **B** $\frac{3}{6} = \frac{6}{12}$ **C** $\frac{3}{6} = \frac{6}{3}$

b. How do you know your choice is correct?

The cross-products are _____.

Solve each proportion.

Multiply the loop. Divide by the outside number.

c. $\frac{4}{6} = \frac{c}{48}$ $c =$ _____

d. $\frac{9}{3} = \frac{18}{d}$ $d =$ _____

e. $\frac{e}{9} = \frac{5}{15}$ $e =$ _____

f. $\frac{4}{f} = \frac{3}{12}$ $f =$ _____

g. A wholesaler offers discounts for large purchases. The table shows the price of an item for various quantities. Is the price proportional to the quantity?

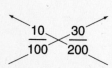

$\frac{10}{100} \diagdown \frac{30}{200}$

Quantity	Price
10	$30
100	$200
1000	$1000

The price is _____ because the cross-products are _____ .

h. A retailer sells an item for $5. Brenda needs several of the items. Complete the table.

$\frac{1}{2}$ $\frac{5}{}$

Quantity	Price
1	$5
2	
3	

Is the total price proportional to the quantity purchased?

The price is _____ because the cross-products are _____ .

Practice Set (continued) (page 226)

Solve problems **i** and **j** by completing the ratio boxes and writing a proportion.

i. The ratio of the length to width of a rectangular room is 5 to 4. If the room is 20 feet long, how wide is the room? _____

	Ratio	Actual Count
Length	5	20
Width	4	w

$$\frac{5}{4} = \frac{}{w}$$

$$w =$$

j. The teacher-student ratio in the primary grades is 1 to 20. If there are 100 students in the primary grades, how many teachers are there? _____

	Ratio	Actual Count
Teachers		t
Students	20	

Written Practice (page 227)

1. cents $\dfrac{33\frac{1}{3}}{} \quad \dfrac{}{27}$
   min

2. 12.43
   11.91
   _____

3.

	Ratio	Actual Count
Base		24
Height		h

4. reflection, rotation, translation, or dilation?

5. $(-3) + (-4) - (-5) - (+6)$
   $(-3) + (-4) + (\quad) + (\quad) =$

6. *See page 16 in the* Student Reference Guide.

   _____; A s_____ is both a

   rectangle and a r_____ .

   Use work area.

7. $\dfrac{7^7 \cdot 7^0}{7^5 \cdot 7^2} =$

8.   3   3   *over, over, up*

    −2.7   −2.7

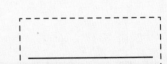

9. $3^3 + 4[21 - (7 + 2 \cdot 3)] =$

10. $\dfrac{9}{5} \cdot \dfrac{1}{3} - \dfrac{1}{10} =$

    $\dfrac{9}{5} \cdot \dfrac{1}{3} =$ $-\dfrac{1}{10} =$

11. $\sqrt{1^3 + 2^3 + 3^3} =$

12. $-2 - (-13 + 20) =$

13. a. $P(A) = \dfrac{A \text{ parts}}{\text{total parts}} =$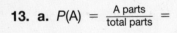

    b. $P(B) = \dfrac{B \text{ parts}}{\text{total parts}} =$

    c. $P(A \text{ or } C) = \dfrac{A \text{ or } C \text{ parts}}{\text{total parts}} =$

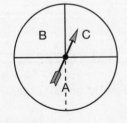

14. Collect like terms:

    a. $7xy - 3y + 4y - 18yx =$
       xy and yx are like terms.

    b. $13b^2 + 8ac - ac + 4 =$

    a. _____   **b.** _____

15. pallets × boxes × cases × bottles × ounces

a. _____

b. _____

c. _____

16. a. $\angle B + \angle C = 180°$
Similar figures have the same angles.

b. *Use a proportion.*

$$\frac{12}{4} = \frac{WX}{}$$

a. m $\angle Y =$ _____

b. $WX =$ _____

17. $3|b| = 21$

$b =$ _____ , _____

18. *Collect like terms.*
$b + 2b = 15$

$b =$ _____

19. $\dfrac{81}{b} = 9$

$b =$ _____

20. $|b| + |b| = 12$

$b =$ _____ , _____

21. decimal and percent

$3\overline{)1.0\,0}$

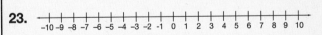

_____

22. Order from greatest to least.

Remember to look at the exponents.

_____ , _____ ,

_____ , _____

Planet	Mass (kg)
Pluto	4.960×10^{27}
Neptune	1.028×10^{27}
Jupiter	1.894×10^{30}
Earth	5.976×10^{27}

23.

$$-10\ -9\ -8\ -7\ -6\ -5\ -4\ -3\ -2\ -1\ 0\ 1\ 2\ 3\ 4\ 5\ 6\ 7\ 8\ 9\ 10$$

Use work area.

Use work area.

24. $70.92
+38.15   + 52.83

Which is the total?
A $109.07   **B** $150.10

C $161.90   **D** $207.70

25. reflection, rotation, translation, or dilation?

_____

26. $\dfrac{10}{y} = \dfrac{2}{7}$

$y =$ _____

27. $\dfrac{4}{5} = \dfrac{16}{y}$

$y =$ _____

28. $(134°F) - ($ $)$

$($ $) + ($ $) =$

_____

29. Find $a^2 + b^2 - 2ab$
when $a = 4$
   $b = 2$

_____

30. *See page 18 in the* Student Reference Guide.

_____

16. a. $\angle B + \angle C = 180°$
Similar figures have the same angles.

b. *Use a proportion.*

$$\frac{12}{4} = \frac{WX}{}$$

a. m $\angle Y =$ _____

b. $WX =$ _____

17. $3|b| = 21$

$b =$ _____ , _____

18. *Collect like terms.*
$b + 2b = 15$

$b =$ _____

19. $\frac{81}{b} = 9$

$b =$ _____

20. $|b| + |b| = 12$

$b =$ _____ , _____

21. decimal and percent

$3\overline{)1.0\,0}$

_____

_____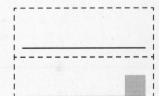

22. Order from greatest to least.

Remember to look at the exponents.

_____ , _____ ,

_____ , _____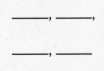

Planet	Mass (kg)
Pluto	4.960×10^{27}
Neptune	1.028×10^{27}
Jupiter	1.894×10^{30}
Earth	5.976×10^{27}

23.

```
 ┬──┬──┬──┬──┬──┬──┬──┬──┬──┬──┬──┬──┬──┬──┬──┬──┬──┬──┬──┬──┬
-10 -9 -8 -7 -6 -5 -4 -3 -2 -1  0  1  2  3  4  5  6  7  8  9  10
```

Use work area.

Use work area.

24. $70.92
   +38.15   + 52.83

Which is the total?
   A $109.07   **B** $150.10

   C $161.90   **D** $207.70

25. reflection, rotation, translation, or dilation?

26. $\dfrac{10}{y} = \dfrac{2}{7}$

$y = $ _____

27. $\dfrac{4}{5} = \dfrac{16}{y}$

$y = $ _____

28. $(134°F) - ($ ____ $)$

$($ ____ $) + ($ ____ $) =$

29. Find $a^2 + b^2 - 2ab$
   when $a = 4$
         $b = 2$

30. *See page 18 in the* Student Reference Guide.

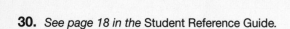

• Similar and Congruent Polygons (page 229)

Name _____

We can identify similar and congruent polygons by comparing their sides and angles.

- **Similar** polygons are the same shape but not always the same size.

- **Congruent** polygons are the same shape and the same size.

Teacher Notes:

- Introduce Hint #46, "Proportion Setups," and Hint #47, "Scale Factor."

- Refer students to "Scale Factor" on page 31 in the *Student Reference Guide.*

- Review "Similar and Congruent Triangles" on page 28 in the *Student Reference Guide.*

- Students will need a centimeter ruler for this lesson.

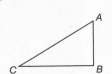
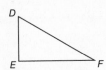
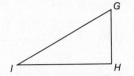

- Similar and congruent triangles have **corresponding parts,** the parts of the triangles that match.

Corresponding Angles	**Corresponding Sides**
$\angle A$, $\angle D$, $\angle G$,	$\overline{AB}$, $\overline{DE}$, $\overline{GH}$,
$\angle B$, $\angle E$, $\angle H$,	$\overline{BC}$, $\overline{EF}$, $\overline{HI}$
$\angle C$, $\angle F$, $\angle I$	$\overline{CA}$, $\overline{FD}$, $\overline{IG}$

- **Similar** polygons have corresponding angles that are equal and corresponding sides that are *proportional.*

- **Congruent** polygons have corresponding angles that are equal and corresponding sides that are *equal.*

- To find the length of an unknown side in similar figures, set up a proportion of corresponding sides.

Example: The triangles are similar.

Find *x*.

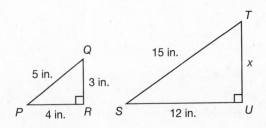

Because the triangles are similar, the corresponding sides are proportional.

$\overline{TU}$ corresponds to $\overline{QR}$ ⟶ $\dfrac{x}{12} = \dfrac{3}{4}$
$\overline{PR}$ corresponds to $\overline{SU}$ ⟶

$$4 \cdot x = 12 \cdot 3$$
$$4x = 12 \cdot 3$$
$$4x = 36$$
$$x = \frac{36}{4}$$
$$x = 9 \text{ in.}$$

- **Scale factor** is the number of times larger (or smaller) the terms of one ratio are when compared to another ratio.

- To find the scale factor, divide corresponding sides.

Example: Find the scale factor from $\triangle PQR$ to $\triangle STU$ in the figure above.

Place side of figure going to in numerator.
Place side of figure going from in denominator. $\dfrac{12}{4} = 3$

The scale factor is 3. We used corresponding sides $\overline{SU}$ and $\overline{PR}$, but any pair of corresponding sides will work.

Practice Set (page 233)

Refer to the following figures for problems **a–e**.

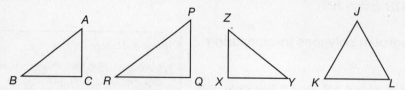

a. Which triangle is **congruent** to △ABC? △ _____

b. Which triangle is **similar** but *not congruent* to △XYZ? △ _____

c. Which triangle is **not similar** to △PQR? △ _____

d. Which angle in △XYZ corresponds to ∠A in △ABC? ∠ _____

e. Which side of △PQR corresponds to side XY in △XYZ? side _____

f. Are these two triangles similar?

Are corresponding sides proportional?

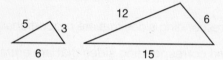   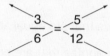

The triangles are _____, because corresponding sides are _____.

g. These quadrilaterals are similar. Use a proportion to find the missing side length. Then find the scale factor **from** the smaller figure **to** the larger. (Units are inches.)

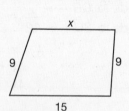

$$\frac{4}{x} = \underline{\quad}$$

$$x = \underline{\quad}$$

scale factor: $\dfrac{\text{to}}{\text{from}} = \underline{\quad}$

For **h–j**, refer to the similar rectangles below. First, use a centimeter ruler to measure the length and width of each rectangle. Label the sides.

_____ cm

_____ cm

_____ cm

_____ cm

h. What is the scale factor **from** the smaller figure **to** the larger? _____

i. The perimeter of the larger rectangle is how many times the perimeter of the smaller rectangle?

_____

j. The area of the larger rectangle is how many times the area of the smaller rectangle? _____

k. On a scale drawing of a house, one inch represents 8 feet. How wide is the garage if it

is $2\frac{1}{2}$ inches wide on the drawing? _____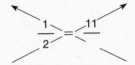

$$\frac{\text{in.}}{\text{ft}} \quad \frac{1}{8} =$$

Written Practice (page 234)

1. Complete the table.

Days	Total Miles
1	11
2	
3	

$$\frac{1}{2} = \frac{11}{}$$

The total distance is _____ to the days

worked because the _____ are equal.

⌐ Use work area. ⌐

4. $P(A) = \dfrac{\text{Design A}}{\text{total}} =$

$P(B) = \dfrac{\text{Design B}}{\text{total}} =$

Which design has the greater probability?

b. _____

⌐ Use work area. ⌐

6. (0, 0), (4, 0), (0, 3)
Draw the triangle.

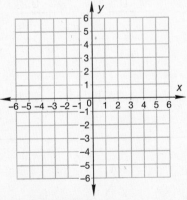

Label the lengths of the sides.
Find the length of the hypotenuse
$a^2 + b^2 = c^2$

Perimeter: Add all sides. _____

$Area = \frac{1}{2}bh$ _____

⌐ Use work area. ⌐

2. $P(\text{prime}) = \dfrac{\text{number of primes}}{\text{total number}} =$

3. after increase: _____ hrs

← after increase

$\underline{-\quad 8}$ ← before increase

5. Distribute then collect like terms:

$3(x + 2) + x + 2 =$

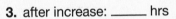

7. a. *Area of triangle* $= \frac{1}{2}bh$

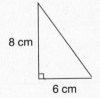

8 cm

6 cm

b. *Perimeter: Add all sides.*
$a^2 + b^2 = c^2$

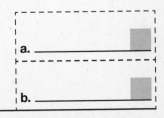

a. _____

b. _____

8. a. $(-3) + (-15) =$

   b. $(-3) - (-15)$

     $(\quad) + (\quad) =$

a. _____

b. _____

9. a. $(-15) + (-3) =$

   b. $(-15) - (-3)$

     $(\quad) + (\quad) =$

a. _____

b. _____

10. $1\dfrac{2}{3} = \dfrac{\quad}{\quad}$

  $+ \ 2\dfrac{3}{4} = \dfrac{\quad}{\quad}$

_____

11. $\dfrac{7}{8} \ \div \ \dfrac{7}{8}$ $\dfrac{1}{8}$

$\underline{\quad\quad} \times \underline{\quad\quad} =$

      $+ \underline{\quad\quad}$

_____

12. $\dfrac{2}{3} \cdot \dfrac{3}{5} =$ $\dfrac{9}{10} =$

        $- \quad =$ _____

_____

13. 2.54 $0.03\overline{)}$

    $+ \ 1.21$

_____

14. $7^2 - 4(7 + 3) + 1^{20} - \sqrt{64} =$

_____

15. 0.3 0.2 0.3

    $\times \ 0.3$ $\times \ 0.2$ $- \ 0.2$

_____

16. a. $10^5 \cdot 10^6 = 10^{\square}$

   b. $\dfrac{10^5}{10^2} = 10^{\square}$

a. _____

b. _____

17.

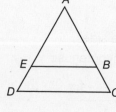

a. side _____

b. _____

18. a. even _____
odd

b. $P(\text{even}) = \dfrac{\text{even}}{\text{total}} =$

c. $P(\text{not even}) = \dfrac{\text{not even}}{\text{total}} =$

Use work area.

19. a.

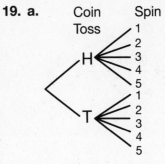

Coin Toss   Spin

{_____, _____, _____, _____, _____,

_____, _____, _____, _____, _____}

b. $P(\text{heads, even}) = \dfrac{\text{H2, H4}}{\text{total outcomes}} =$

Use work area.

20. a. $8\overline{)1.000}$

percent: _____

b. The _____ is best because $\dfrac{4}{8}$ is easy.

Use work area.

21. $|x| = 4$

x = _____, _____

22. $2x + 5 = 29$

x = _____

23. $\dfrac{3}{x} = \dfrac{12}{20}$

x = _____

24. $\dfrac{7}{28} = \dfrac{9}{x}$

x = _____

25. $\dfrac{144}{360} =$  $=$

$\overline{)144}$ $\overline{)360}$

26. Graph the negative integers.

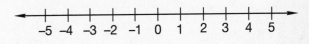

27. Estimate:

$$\frac{(39)\ (1.9)\ +\ 1.1}{8.89} \longrightarrow \frac{(40)\ (\quad)\ +\ (\quad)}{}$$

_____

28. _The rectangles are similar._

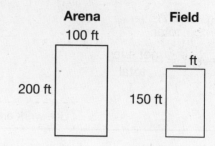

Arena   **Field**

100 ft

200 ft   150 ft   ___ ft

a. Solve for the missing side.

$$\frac{200}{150} = \underline{\quad\quad}$$

b. _Perimeter: add all sides._

_____

Use work area.

29. length $\dfrac{11}{8\frac{1}{2}}$ $5\frac{1}{2}$
width

_____

30.

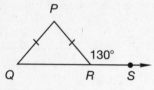

P

130°

Q   R   S

a.   m∠PRQ

A straight line is 180°.

b.   m∠Q

c.   m∠P

The sum of the angle meaures in a triangle is 180°.

a. _____

b. _____

c. _____

- **Multiplying and Dividing Integers**
- **Multiplying and Dividing Terms** (page 237)

Name _____

Teacher Notes:
- Refer students to "Multiplying or Dividing Two Signed Numbers" and "Multiplying Three or More Signed Numbers • Powers of Negative Numbers" on page 26 in the *Student Reference Guide.*
- The calculator activity on 📖 page 240 is optional.

When multiplying and dividing integers, follow these rules to place a sign on the answer.

- To multiply and divide two signed numbers:

    1. Multiply or divide as with whole numbers.

    2. Place a sign on the answer.

    > If the signs are the *same*, the answer is **positive**.

    > If the signs are *different*, the answer is **negative**.

Examples:

multiplication	division
$(+6)(+2) = +12$	$\dfrac{+6}{+2} = +3$
$(-6)(-2) = +12$	$\dfrac{-6}{-2} = +3$
$(-6)(+2) = -12$	$\dfrac{-6}{+2} = -3$
$(+6)(-2) = -12$	$\dfrac{+6}{-2} = -3$

- A power of a positive number is always positive.

- A power of a negative number can be positive or negative.

    An **even** exponent gives a **positive** product.

    An **odd** exponent gives a **negative** product.

Example: $(-3)^2 = (-3)(-3) = 9$ even exponent

$(-3)^3 = (-3)(-3)(-3) = (9)(-3) = -27$ odd exponent

Example: Solve for x in $x^2 = 9$.

$(3)^2 = 9$ and $(-3)^2 = 9$

$x = 3$ and -3

- When using the $\sqrt{}$ sign, give only a **positive** answer.

Terms do not have to be like terms to multiply or divide.

- To **multiply** terms with variables:

    1. Multiply the numbers.

    2. Group variable factors with exponents.

    Example: $(6x^2y)(-2xyz)$

    $(6x^2y)(-2xyz) = (6)(-2) \cdot x^2 \cdot x \cdot y \cdot y \cdot z$

    $= -12x^3y^2z$

    Each factor in the terms is in the final product.

- The Distributive Property applies to multiplying terms.

   Example: $3x(2x - 4)$

   $3x(2x - 4) = (3x)(2x) - (3x)(4) = 6x^2 - 12x$

- To **divide** terms with variables:

   1. Factor terms in the numerator and denominator.

   2. Cancel matching factors.

   3. Regroup remaining factors with exponents.

   Example:

   $$\frac{10a^3bc^2}{8ab^2c} = \frac{2^1 \cdot 5 \cdot \cancel{a}^1 \cdot a \cdot a \cdot \cancel{b}^1 \cdot \cancel{c}^1 \cdot c}{2_1 \cdot 2 \cdot 2 \cdot \cancel{a}_1 \cdot \cancel{b}_1 \cdot b \cdot \cancel{c}_1} = \frac{5a^2c}{4b}$$

Practice Set (page 241)

a. $(-12)(-3) = $ _____

b. $(-12)(+3) = $ _____

c. $\dfrac{-12}{-3} = $ _____

d. $\dfrac{-12}{+3} = $ _____

e. $(-6)^2 = (-6)(-6) = $ _____

f. $(-1)^2 = $ _____

g. $(-3)^3 = (-3)(-3)(-3) = $ _____

h. $(-2)^4 = $ _____

i. Solve: $x^2 = 100 \quad x = $ _____, _____
   (Write two possible solutions.)

j. What are the square roots of 100? _____, _____

   What is $\sqrt{100}$? _____

k. Drilling for core samples in the sea floor, the driller used 12 drill rods 8 meters long to reach from the surface of the ocean to the lowest core sample. Write an equation using integers that shows the depth of the core sample with respect to sea level.

   (_____)$(-8) = $ _____

Simplify:

l. $(-12xy^2z)(3xy) = (-12)(3) \cdot x \cdot x \cdot y \cdot y \cdot y \cdot z = $ _____

m. $\dfrac{-12xy^2z}{3xy} = \dfrac{-2 \cdot 2 \cdot 3 \cdot x \cdot y \cdot y \cdot z}{3 \cdot x \cdot y} = $ _____

Distribute:

n. $2x(2x - 5) = (2x)(2x) - (2x)(5) = $ _____

o. $-2x(2x - 5) = (-2x)(\quad) - (-2x)(\quad) = $ _____

1. *Offset*

$1.081
$\times \quad 70$

2. boxes $\times$ packs $\times$ cards

3. 156 $\quad$ 12
$\times \underline{\quad}$ $\quad \times \underline{\quad}$

4.

	Ratio	Actual Count
Customers		9
Tellers		t

5. $\dfrac{x}{12} = \dfrac{2}{3}$

6. $\dfrac{1}{5} = \dfrac{4}{x}$

7. $(2, 3), (5, 3), (5, -1)$

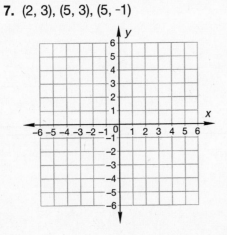

a. _____

b. _____

8. The figures are **similar**.

a. *corresponding angles*

b. $\dfrac{12}{6} = \dfrac{AD}{}$

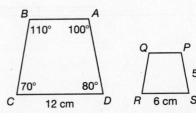

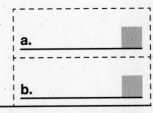

a. _____

b. _____

9. **a.** Distribute: $-2(3x - 4) =$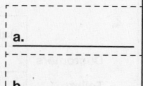

  b. Factor: $7x - 21 =$

a. _____

b. _____

10. $P(odd) = \dfrac{odd}{total} =$

  $P(even) = \dfrac{even}{total} =$

  $P(odd) \bigcirc P(even)$

Use work area.

11. *order of operations*

  $(-4)\left(\dfrac{1}{2}\right)(-3)$

  $(\quad)(-3) =$

  _____

12. $\dfrac{-72xy}{6} =$

  _____

13. *order of operations*

  $\dfrac{3}{4} \div \dfrac{1}{2}$

  $\dfrac{2}{3} =$

  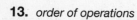

  $+ \quad = $ _____

  $\underline{\quad} \times \underline{\quad} =$

  _____

14. $\dfrac{2}{3} \cdot \dfrac{3}{4} =$

  $\dfrac{1}{2}$

  $\underline{\quad\quad}$

  _____

15. $(-2)^2 \cdot (-2)^3$

  $\underline{\quad} \cdot \underline{\quad} =$

  _____

16. $\dfrac{10^3 \cdot 10^2}{10^4} =$

  _____

17. $3\frac{3}{4} \div 1\frac{1}{2}$ $1\frac{2}{3} =$

$+ \underline{\hspace{1cm}} = \underline{\hspace{2cm}}$

$\underline{\hspace{1cm}} \times \underline{\hspace{1cm}} = $

_____

18. $0.16\overline{)6\,4.0\,0}$

_____

19. a. $25\overline{)1.0\,0}$

percent: _____

b. Use the decimal.

$\underline{\times \quad\quad 80}$

Use work area.

20. least to greatest

$12.5\%, \frac{1}{6}, 0.15$

$\underline{\hspace{1cm}}, \underline{\hspace{1cm}}, \underline{\hspace{1cm}}$

Use work area.

21. Draw segment YZ so that it is longer than $\overline{XW}$ and **parallel** to $\overline{XW}$. Draw $\overline{ZW}$.

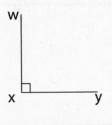

Use work area.

22. $-3|x| = -6$

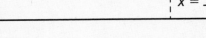

$x = \underline{\hspace{1cm}}, \underline{\hspace{1cm}}$

23. *Collect like terms.*

$x + x = 26$

$x = \underline{\hspace{3cm}}$

24. $2x - 1 = 19$

$x = \underline{\hspace{3cm}}$

25. $x^2 - 1 = 24$

26. See page 9 in the Student Reference Guide.

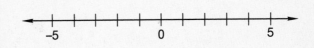

Use work area.

27. mean

81
78
79
74
70
77
+ 80

28. Find $\sqrt{b^2 - 4ac}$

when $a = 2$

$b = -5$

$c = -3$

29. a.{_____, _____, _____, _____, _____, _____}

   b. P(vowel, add) = _____

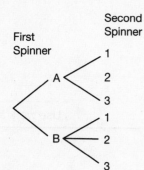

First
Spinner

Second
Spinner

A — 1
   2
   3

B — 1
   2
   3

Use work area.

30. Classify **by sides.**

   a. $\triangle ABC$: _____

   b. $\triangle BCD$: _____

   c. $\triangle ADC$: _____

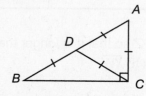

Use work area.

•Areas of Combined Polygons
(page 245)

Name _____

We use formulas to find the area of rectangles and triangles.

Teacher Notes:
• Review "Geometric Formulas" on page 29 in the *Student Reference Guide*.

• Area of a rectangle: **Area = length × width**

• Area of a triangle: **Area = $\frac{1}{2}$ (base × height)**

• The area of some polygons can be found by dividing the polygon into smaller parts and finding the area of each part.

Example: Find the area of this figure.

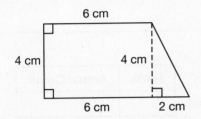

Area of rectangle = 6 cm · 4 cm = 24 cm²
+ Area of triangle = $\frac{1}{2}$ · 4 cm · 2 cm = 4 cm²
_____
= 28 cm²

• We can use the Pythagorean Theorem to find the lengths of unknown sides in right triangles.

$a^2 + b^2 = c^2$

Practice Set (page 247)

Find the area of each polygon by dividing the polygons into rectangles and triangles. (Angles that look like right angles are right angles.)

a.

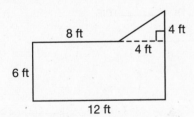

Area of rectangle = (6 ft) (12 ft) = ____ ft²
+ Area of triangle = $\frac{1}{2}$ (4 ft) (4 ft) = ____ ft²
_____
= ____

b.

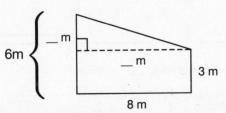

Area of rectangle = ( )( ) = ____ m²
+ Area of triangle = $\frac{1}{2}$ ( )( ) = ____ m²
_____
= ____

c. Find the area of the shaded region by **subtracting** the area of the smaller triangle from the area of the larger triangle. Dimensions are in cm.

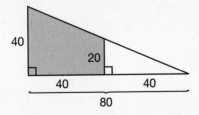

Area of large triangle = $\frac{1}{2}$ (80) (40) = ____ cm²
− Area of small triangle = $\frac{1}{2}$ ( )( ) = ____ cm²
_____
= ____

Practice Set (continued) (page 247)

d. Use a calculator to estimate the unknown base of the triangle. Round to the nearest foot and label the base. Then find the area of the figure.

Dimensions are in feet. _____

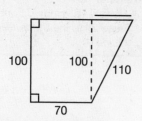

$a^2 + b^2 = c^2 \longrightarrow c^2 - a^2 = b^2$

$(110)^2 - (100)^2 = ($ ____ $)^2 = $ _____

Area of rectangle
+ Area of triangle

Written Practice (page 248)

1. $\frac{3}{5}$ of 1800

2.

	Ratio	Actual Count
Spotted		
Striped		s

3.

	Ratio	Actual Count
Lizards		l
Snakes		

4. 1 week = _____ days

_____ days = _____ hr

_____ hr = _____ min

90)‾‾‾‾‾‾

5. $P = 4s$ Complete the table.

Side Length	Perimeter
3	12
4	
5	

Use work area.

6. An octagon has _____ sides.

a. sides in. $\frac{1}{12}$ ___

b. sides ft $\frac{1}{}$ ___

a. _____

b. _____

7. The triangles are **similar**.

a. m∠CED = _____

b. m∠D = _____

c. side _____

[triangle diagram with points A, E, B, C, D, angle 60°]

Use work area.

8. $\frac{6}{10} = \frac{x}{15}$

x = _____

9. $\frac{x}{5} = \frac{4}{20}$

x = _____

10.

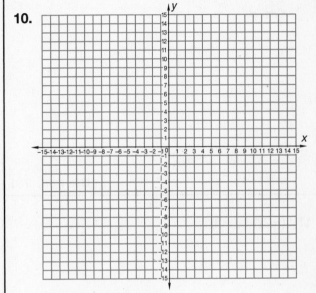

(0, 0), (-5, 0), (0, -12)

a. _____

b. _____

11.

[house-shaped figure with sides 10, 10, 12, 12, 14]

a. Area of rectangle
+ Area of triangle

b. perimeter

a. _____

b. _____

12. a. Distribute: $-3(x - y + 5) =$

b. Factor: $4x - 2 =$

a. _____

b. _____

13. reduced fraction and decimal

    a. 99%

    b. $\dfrac{180}{360}$

Use work area.

14. $\dfrac{35x}{-7} =$
Cancel.

_____

15. $\dfrac{x^3}{x^4 x} =$
Cancel.

Use work area.

16. $10 + 10\,(10^2 - 10 \cdot 3^2) =$

_____

17. $(-2)^3 + (-3)^2 =$

_____

18. $\dfrac{3}{4} \cdot \dfrac{2}{5} =$
Cancel.

    $\dfrac{9}{10}$

    $\dfrac{\quad}{\quad}$

_____

19. $\dfrac{6}{7} \div \dfrac{2}{7}$

$+\dfrac{1}{2}$

$\downarrow \qquad \downarrow$

$\underline{\quad} \times \underline{\quad} =$

20. Collect like terms.

    $x^2 + x + 1 + 3x + x^2 + 2 =$

_____

21. $5x - x + 2y - y =$

_____

22. $x^2 = 1$

$x =$ _____, _____

23. $|x| + 1 = 3$

$x =$ _____, _____

24. $(-2) + (-3) - (-4) + (-5)(-2) =$

_____

25. mean
89
97
112
104
113

_____

26. See page 10 in the _Student Reference Guide._

_____ , _____

27. _Hint:_ $1000 = 2^3 \cdot 5^3$

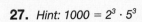
$77,000 =$ _____ · _____ · _____ · _____

28. Find $n(n - 1)$

when $n = 10$

_____

29. a. two of A, B, C, D with no repeats

{AB, ____, ____, ____, ____, ____}

b. $P(B) = \dfrac{B}{total} =$

Use work area.

30.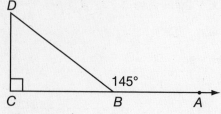

a. m∠CBD

b. m∠CDB

a. ____

b. ____

• Using Properties of Equality to Solve Equations (page 251)

We can use inverse operations to solve equations.

• Inverse operations "undo" each other.

Addition and subtraction are inverse operations.

$n + 5 - 5 = n + 0 = n$

Multiplication and division are inverse operations.

$n \times 5 \div 5 = n \times 1 = n$

• We use inverse operations to get the variable alone on one side of the equation. This is called "isolating" the variable.

• To keep the equation balanced, **whatever you do to one side of an equation you must do to the other side of the equation**.

Example: Solve: $x + 5 = 12$

Step:	Justification:
$x + 5 = 12$	Given equation
$x + 5 - 5 = 12 - 5$	Subtracted 5 from both sides
$x = 7$	Simplified
$7 + 5 = 12$	Check

• The variable is usually written on the left side of an equation. When it is on the right side, we can use the **Symmetric Property** to switch sides.

Example: Solve: $1.5 = x - 2.3$

Step:	Justification:
$1.5 = x - 2.3$	Given equation
$1.5 + 2.3 = x - 2.3 + 2.3$	Added 2.3 to both sides
$3.8 = x$	Simplified
$x = 3.8$	Symmetric Property

• Remember that dividing by a fraction is the same as *multiplying by the reciprocal*. It is usually easier to multiply than divide.

Example: $\frac{2}{3}w = \frac{3}{4}$

Step:	Justification:
$\frac{2}{3}w = \frac{3}{4}$	Given equation
$\frac{3}{2} \cdot \frac{2}{3}w = \frac{3}{2} \cdot \frac{3}{4}$	Multiplied both sides by $\frac{3}{2}$
$1w = \frac{9}{8}$	Simplified
$w = \frac{9}{8}$	Simplified

Practice Set (page 254)

a. What does "isolate the variable" mean?

To get the variable a_____ on one side of the e_____.

b. Which operation is the **inverse of subtraction?** _____

c. Which operation is the **inverse of multiplication?** _____

Solve each equation. Justify the steps.

d. $x + \dfrac{1}{2} = \dfrac{3}{4}$ Given

$x + \dfrac{1}{2} - \dfrac{1}{2} = \dfrac{3}{4} - \dfrac{1}{2}$ Subtracted _____ from both sides

$x =$ _____   Simplified

e. $x - 1.3 = 4.2$ Given

$x - 1.3 +$ ___ $= 4.2 +$ _____ Added _____ to both sides

$x =$ ___   Simplified

f. $1.2 = \dfrac{x}{4}$ Given

$1.2 \cdot 4 = \dfrac{x}{4} \cdot 4$ M_____ both sides by 4

_____ $= x$ Simplified

$x =$ _____   Symmetric Property

g. $\dfrac{3}{5}x = \dfrac{1}{4}$ Given

$\left(\ \ \right)\left(\dfrac{3}{5}x\right) = \left(\dfrac{1}{4}\right)\left(\ \ \right)$ Multiplied both sides by _____

$x =$ _____   Simplified

h. Peggy bought 5 pounds of oranges for $4.50. Solve the equation $5x = \$4.50$ to find the price per pound. _____ per pound

$5x = 4.50$

i. From 8 a.m. to noon, the temperature rose 5 degrees to 2°C. Solve the equation $t + 5 = 2$ to find the temperature at 8 a.m. _____

$t + 5 = 2$

1. How many minutes?

_____ min

_____

2.

	Ratio	Actual Count
Whole		w
Skim	7	

_____

3. a. L   1   3.78
mL

b. 1 gal = _____ qt

1 gal = 3.78 L

qt ◯ L

a. _____

4. $2\frac{1}{2}$ hr = _____ half-hours

_____

5. $x - 2.9 = 4.21$

$x - 2.9 + \quad = 4.21 + 2.9$

$x = $ _____

6. $\frac{2}{3} + x = \frac{5}{6}$

$\frac{2}{3} + x - \quad = \frac{5}{6} -$

$x = $ _____

7. $\frac{3}{5}x = \frac{6}{7}$

$(\quad)\left(\frac{3}{5}x\right) = \left(\frac{6}{7}\right)(\quad)$

$x = $ _____

8. $\frac{x}{2.2} = 11$

$(\quad)\left(\frac{x}{2.2}\right) = (11)(\quad)$

$x = $ _____

9. $\frac{7}{x} = \frac{21}{30}$

$x = $ _____

10. Draw the triangle.

$(-4, 1), (2,1), (2, -7)$

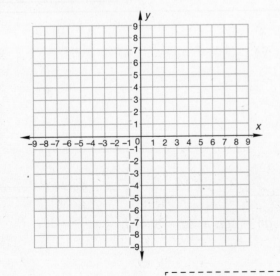

a. _____

b. _____

11. a. *Area of rectangle*

+ Area of triangle

_____

b. perimeter

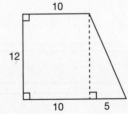

a. _____

b. _____

12. Simplify.

    a. $-4x(2x - 9) =$

    b. $3x + 3 =$

    a. _____

    b. _____

13. decimal and reduced fraction

    32%

    _____

    _____

14. $26 + 3(8^2 - 4 \cdot 4^2) =$

    _____

15. $21 - 20(0.5)^2 =$

    0.5

    $\underline{\times 0.5}$

    _____

16. $\dfrac{-48mx}{-8x} =$

    _____

17. $\dfrac{4}{7} \div 1\dfrac{5}{7}$ $\dfrac{2}{5} =$

    ↓   ↓ $\underline{} = \underline{}$

    $\underline{} \times \underline{} =$

    _____

18. $\dfrac{4}{6} \cdot \dfrac{4}{12} =$ $\dfrac{1}{9}$

    $\underline{+}$

    _____

19. $\dfrac{x^5}{x^2 x} \cdot \dfrac{y^4}{y} =$

    _____

20. Collect like terms.

    $xyz + yxz - zyx - x^2yz =$

    _____

21. $gh - 4gh + 7g - 8h + h =$

    _____

22. Similar triangles

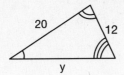

$$\frac{x}{12} = \text{—}$$

$$\frac{44}{y} = \text{—}$$

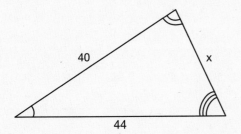

20 12

y

40 x

44

$x = $ _____

$y = $ _____

23. $x^2 = 100$

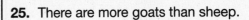

$x = $ _____ , _____

24. $3 + |x| = 9$

$x = $ _____ , _____

25. There are more goats than sheep.

$$\frac{\text{sheep}}{\text{goats}}$$

A $\frac{12}{5}$ **B** $\frac{12}{12}$ **C** $\frac{17}{12}$ **D** $\frac{12}{17}$

26. $1 \cdot 2 \cdot 2 \cdot 2 \cdot 2 \cdot 2 \cdot 2 \cdot 2 \cdot 2 \cdot 2 \cdot 2 \cdot 2 \cdot 2 \cdot 2 = 2^{\square}$

Use a calculator to find that number.

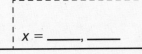

27.

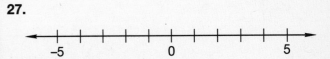

–5   0   5

Use work area.

28. 6 total
3 black
2 blue
1 red

a. $P(\text{blue}) = \dfrac{\text{blue}}{\text{total}} =$

b. $P(\text{not blue}) = \dfrac{\text{not blue}}{\text{total}} =$

a. _____

b. _____

29. Find $2\pi r$
when $\pi = 3.14$
$r = 5$

_____

30. See page 18 in the *Student Reference Guide.*

a. ∠ _____   **b.** ∠ _____

c. ∠ _____   **d.** ∠ _____ , ∠ _____

L38-222

• **Circumference of a Circle**
(page 257)

Name _____

A circle is a geometric shape in which every point on the shape is the same distance from the center.

Teacher Notes:
• Refer students to "Circle" on page 17 in the *Student Reference Guide*.
• Introduce reference chart, "Circle."

• The **radius** (r) is the distance from the center to the circle.

• The **diameter** (d) is the distance across a circle through the center. The diameter is exactly twice the radius ($d = 2r$).

• The *distance around* a circle is the **circumference** (C).

   • Circumference is the perimeter of a circle

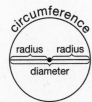

• A circumference is exactly π **(pi)** times the diameter.
   $C = \pi d$
   and
   $C = 2\pi r$ (because $d = 2r$)

• π is not a variable, like x in an equation. π is an irrational number. It has a constant value of 3.14159265...

• Because π is irrational, we cannot write it exactly. In problems we do one of the following:
   leave π as π in the answer
   use 3.14 as an approximation
   use $\frac{22}{7}$ as an approximation

• To mentally estimate with π, round π to 3.

Practice Set (page 260)

a. The diameter (d) of a circle on the playground is 12 ft. What is the radius (r) of the circle? _____
   $d = 2r$
   $12 = 2r$
   $r =$

b. A spoke on the bike wheel is about 12 inches long. The diameter of the wheel is about how many

   inches? _____
   $d = 2r$

c. What is the name for the perimeter of a circle? c_____

d. How many diameters equal a circumference? _____
   $C = \pi d$

e. Write two formulas for the circumference of a circle. Use the diameter (*d*) in one and the radius (*r*) in

another. *C* = _____   *C* = _____

f. Circle the term that does not apply to π.

A rational number   **B** irrational number   **C** real number

g. Explain your answer to **f.**

_____ is an irrational number, and all irrational numbers are also _____ numbers.

h. Write the decimal and fraction approximations for π.

decimal: _____   fraction: _____

i. What is incorrect about the following equation?

π = 3.14

π does not _____ 3.14.

j. To roughly estimate calculations involving π or to check if a calculation is reasonable, we can use what

number for π? _____

Round π to the nearest whole number.

k. A bicycle tire with a diameter of 30 inches rolls about how many inches in one turn? _____

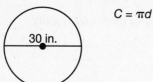

C = π*d*

30 in.

l. The diameter of a circle painted on the playground is 7 yards. The distance around the circle is about

how many yards? Did you use 3.14 or $\frac{22}{7}$ for π? Why? *C* = π*d*

The circumference is about _____ yd. I used _____ for π because the 7s cancel.

m. The diameter of the earth at the equator is about 7927 miles. About how many miles is the
circumference of the earth at the equator? Use a calculator. Round to the nearest hundred miles.

_____ *C* = π*d*

Written Practice   (page 261)

1.   North

7 mi

20 mi

South

2. $\frac{\text{pieces}}{\text{hr}}$ _____ _____

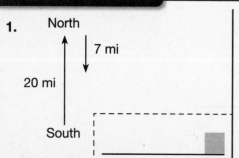

3. 1 + 2 + 3 + ____ +

____ + ____ + ____ +

____ + ____ =

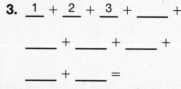

4. Write as a reduced fraction and a rounded percent.

$$P(greater\ than\ 2) = \frac{\text{number greater than 2}}{\text{total numbers}} =$$

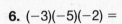

5.

	Ratio	Actual Count
Buffalo		b
Non-Buffalo		

6. $(-3)(-5)(-2) =$

7. $\frac{(-5)(-12)}{-10} =$

8. $\frac{-6}{-3} + \frac{-10}{5} =$

9. $\frac{-12x}{-2} =$

10. $2\frac{1}{2} \div 1\frac{1}{3}$

$$——×—— =$$

$$1\frac{1}{4} =$$

$$—— + —— =$$

11. $\frac{1}{5} \cdot \frac{1}{2} =$

$$\frac{1}{5} =$$

$$—— = ——$$

12.

$$\begin{array}{r} 4.28 \\ -\ 1 \\ \hline \end{array} \qquad \begin{array}{r} 0.2 \\ \times\ 2 \\ \hline \end{array} \qquad \overline{}$$

13. $\sqrt{5^2 + 12^2} =$

14. $\frac{x^0 \cdot x^5}{x^2} =$

15. $2^6 \cdot 3 \cdot 5^6 =$

First find $2^6 \cdot 5^6$.

---

16. Plot (-2, -5) and (-9, -5).

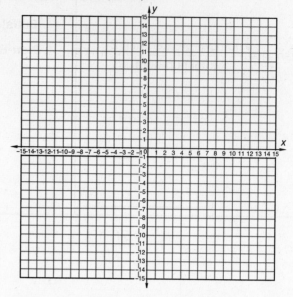

What is the length of this segment? _____ units

If the segment is one side of a rectangle, what is the length of

the adjacent side that makes an area of 21 units²? _____ units

Find two pairs of possible vertices:

(,), (,), (,), (,)

17.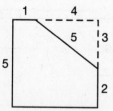

a. area of square: _____

b. area of triangle: _____

c. Area of square
  −Area of triangle
  _____

---

18. a. 25%

  fraction: _____

  decimal: _____

b. The _____ is best because $24 can be

divided by 4.

19. # XYZ

a. *mirror image*

b. *Turn your paper to check.*

a. _____

b. _____

20. Estimate:

$$\frac{2.8^2 + 1.1^2}{1.9} \longrightarrow \frac{(\ \ )^2 + (\ \ )^2}{}$$

_____

21. { _____, H2, _____, _____,

_____, _____, _____, _____,

_____, _____, _____, T6 }

$$P(H1) = \frac{H1}{\text{total outcomes}} =$$

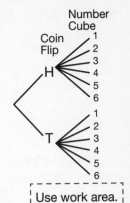

Coin Flip H T Number Cube 1 2 3 4 5 6 / 1 2 3 4 5 6

Use work area.

22. $3\left(2 \cdot \frac{1}{3}\right)$ Given

$3(\_\_ \cdot \_\_)$ _____ Property

$(\_\_ \cdot \_\_) \_\_$ _____ Property

$(\_\_) \_\_$

_____

Use work area.

23. $x^2 = 16$

$x = \_\_\_, \_\_\_$

24. $0.9 + x \quad = 2.7$

$0.9 + x - \quad = 2.7 -$

$x = _____$

25. $0.9x = 2.7$

$$\frac{0.9x}{} = \frac{2.7}{}$$

$x = _____$

26. one quarter of a million miles
a. standard notation
b. scientific notation

a. _____

b. _____ × _____

27.

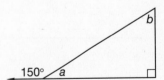

$150°$ a b

a. $m\angle a = $ _____

b. $m\angle b = $ _____

28. Draw a diameter and label it 2 in.

$C = \pi d$

Use 3.14 for π.

29. Find the length of the third side of the right triangle.

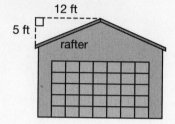

12 ft

5 ft

rafter

30. *Area of large square*
   — Area of small square

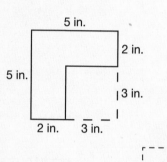

5 in.

2 in.

5 in.

3 in.

2 in.   3 in.

• **Area of a Circle** (page 264)

Name _____

The area of a circle is related to the square of the radius (r^2) and π.

$$A = \pi r^2$$

Example: Find the area of this circle. Express the answer in terms of π.

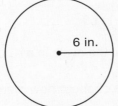

$A = \pi r^2$

$A = \pi(6)^2$

$A = 36\pi$ inches^2

6 in.

• A **sector** of a circle is part of a circle closed in by two radii and an **arc,** which is part of the circle.

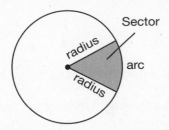

Sector

radius

arc

radius

• An angle formed by two radii is a **central angle**.

• The measure of a central angle determines the part of the area of the circle the sector contains. Remember that a full circle is 360°.

Example: Find the area of sector *RMS*. Express in terms of π.

R

45°

M   S

4 cm

The full circle has an area of $A = \pi r^2 = \pi(4)^2 = 16\pi$ cm^2.

m∠*RMS* = 45°, so the area the sector contains is

Area of sector $= \dfrac{45°}{360°}$ (area of circle)

$= \dfrac{1}{8}(16\pi)$

$= 2\pi$ cm^2

• A **semicircle** is exactly half a circle, closed off by a diameter and an arc.

• Because a diameter is a straight line, the central angle is 180°.

Area of semicircle $= \dfrac{180°}{360°}$ (area of circle) $= \dfrac{1}{2}$ (area of circle)

Practice Set (page 267)

For **a** and **b**, find the area of each circle.

a.

$A = \pi r^2$

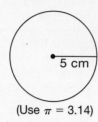
5 cm

(Use $\pi = 3.14$)

b.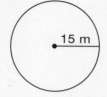

$A = \pi r^2$

15 m

(Express in terms of π)

c. What is the scale factor from the circle in **a** to the circle in **b**? _____

The area of the circle in **b** is how many times the area of the circle in **a**? _____

d. A 140 ft diameter helicopter landing pad covers an area of about how many square feet? What did you use for π and why?

First, find the radius.

140 ft

The area is about _____. I used _____ for π because I could divide by 7.

e. A semicircular window with a radius of 36 inches allows light through an area of how many square

feet? Use a calculator. Round to the nearest square foot. _____

A semicircle is half a circle.

$r = 36$ in.

In the figure below, segment *AC* is a diameter of circle O and measures 12 cm. Central angle *BOC* measures 60°. Find the area of the sectors named in **f–h** below. Express each area in terms of π.

f. Sector *BOC* _____

m∠*BOC* = 60°

$A = \dfrac{60°}{360°} (\pi r^2)$

$= \dfrac{1}{6} (\quad)$

$=$

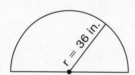

B

A ⟋ O ⟋ 60° ⟍ C

12 cm

g. Sector *BOA* _____

m∠*BOA* =

$A = \dfrac{}{360°} (\pi r^2)$

h. Sector *AOC* _____

m∠*AOC* = 180°

$A = \dfrac{180°}{360°} (\pi r^2)$

1. 3:45 p.m. to 4:00 p.m. ⟶ _____ min

4:00 p.m. to 6:00 a.m. ⟶ _____ hr

6:00 a.m. to 6:30 a.m. ⟶ _____ min

2.

	Ratio	Actual Count
Heroes		
Evil		e

3. mean

186

210

246

<u>206</u>

4. $A = \pi r^2$

$C = \pi d$

6m

Leave π as π.

$A =$ _____

$C =$ _____

5. **a.** $A = \pi r^2$

b. $C = 2\pi r$

10m

Use 3.14 for π.

a. _____

b. _____

6.

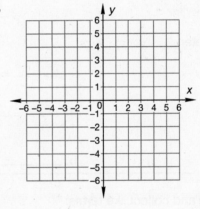

Use work area.

7. similar

a. $\dfrac{x}{3.5} =$ —

b. $\dfrac{25}{y} =$ —

c. $\dfrac{24}{12} =$

Reduce.

25   24

x

y   12

3.5

a. $x =$ _____

b. $y =$ _____

c. _____

8. least to greatest

A $\dfrac{2}{5}$ **B** 0.88

C 0.8   **D** 0.44

_____, _____, _____, _____

9. $\frac{1}{4}x = 5$

$(\quad)(\frac{1}{4}x) = 5(\quad)$

$x = \underline{\hspace{3cm}}$

10. $2.9 + x = 3.83$

$2.9 + x - \quad = 3.83 -$

$x = \underline{\hspace{3cm}}$

11.

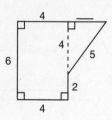

a. Area of rectangle
+ Area of triangle $\underline{\hspace{2cm}}$

b. perimeter

a. $\underline{\hspace{3cm}}$

b. $\underline{\hspace{3cm}}$

12. $(2, 1)$, $(2, -5)$ $(-6, -5)$

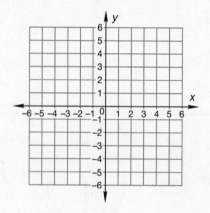

a. $\underline{\hspace{3cm}}$

b. $\underline{\hspace{3cm}}$

13. Distribute and collect like terms:
$x(2x - 3) - x^2 - x =$

$\underline{\hspace{4cm}}$

14. $\frac{27x^2y^2}{3xy} =$

$\underline{\hspace{4cm}}$

15. $(7^2 - 2^2) - (4^2 - 1^2) =$

$\underline{\hspace{4cm}}$

16. $\left(\frac{1}{2}\right)^2 - \left(\frac{1}{2}\right)^3 =$

$\underline{\hspace{4cm}}$

17. $5 + 5(10)^2 =$

18. $\dfrac{3}{4} \cdot 1\dfrac{1}{2}$

$\downarrow \qquad \downarrow$

— · — =

$\dfrac{1}{2} =$

— =

19. $\dfrac{5}{14} \div \dfrac{1}{2}$

$\downarrow \qquad \downarrow$

— × — =

$\dfrac{2}{7}$

+ ———

20. $(-2) - (-6) + (-4) =$

21. $\dfrac{(-2)(-6)}{-4} =$

22. $x^2 + 1 = 26$

$x =$ ——— , ———

23. $|x| - 16 = 2$

$x =$ ——— , ———

24. *See page 16 in the* Student Reference Guide.

$x =$

25. Which does **not** have rotational symmetry?

Turn your paper to check.

  A

  B

  C

D

26. Standard form

4.93×10^8

27.

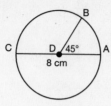

a. m∠*BDC* =

b. $A = \dfrac{45°}{360°}(\pi r^2)$

Leave π as π.

a. _____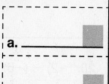

b. _____

28. Estimate the circumference.
$C = \pi d$

A 48 ft   **B** 50 ft   **C** 52 ft   **D** 54 ft

_____

29. Find *Fd*

when *F* = 2.2
d = 10

_____

30. a. {H1, _____, _____, _____, Coin Flip

_____, _____, _____, T4}

b. *P*(*T*, *odd*) = ____ =
Reduce.

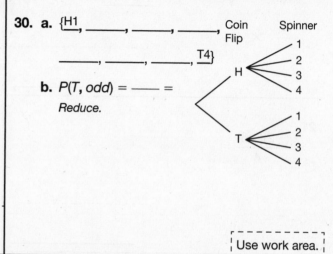

Use work area.

A function is a mathematical rule that tells the relationship between two numbers.

• The function changes an input number to an output number.

• **For each input number there is one and only one output number.**

• Any variables can be used for the input and output numbers,
but we often use **x for the input** and **y for the output** because it makes it easier to display on a
coordinate plane.

• A function table for $y = 2x$ and a graph of its coordinates are shown below. The rule for this function is:
To find y, multiply x by 2

$$y = 2x$$

Input Number (x)	Output Number (y)	Coordinates (x, y)
0	0	(0, 0)
1	2	(1, 2)
2	4	(2, 4)
-1	-2	(-1, -2)
-2	-4	(-2, -4)

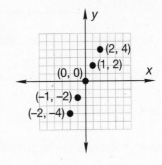

• Because x can be any number, there are many
more coordinate pairs for the function $y = 2x$.
To show all the possible pairs, we draw a line through the points.

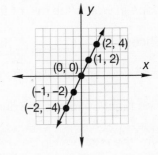

• If all the input-output pairs of a function fall on a line,
then the function is **linear.**

• If a *linear* function includes the point (0, 0), the function is
proportional. To check whether a function is proportional,
input 0 for x and see if the output number is 0.

• Many functions are not linear. The formula for the area of a
square is $A = s^2$ where A is the area and s is the side length.
A function table and a graph of $A = s^2$ are shown here.

• Even though $A = s^2$ includes the point (0, 0), the function is
not proportional because the function is not linear.

$$A = s^2$$

s	A
0	0
1	1
2	4
3	9

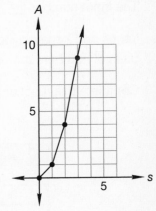

Practice Set (page 283)

a. The relationship between feet and inches is a function. Write an equation that shows how to find the number of inches (*n*, output) if you know the number of feet (*i*, input).

What do you multiply feet by to find number of inches? $n = $ _____ *i*

Complete the function table for the number of inches in 1, 2, 3, and 4 feet.

Is the relationship linear? _____
Will the coordinates fall on a line?

Is the relationship proportional? _____
Is the function linear? Does it include (0, 0)?

feet (*i*)	inches (*n*)
1	
2	
3	
4	

b. Yolanda played a game with Xavier. She used this equation to find her response to each number Xavier played: $y = x - 2$

Describe in words the rule Yolanda uses.

To find *y*, s_____ 2 from *x*.

Complete the function table.

Is the function linear? _____

Is it proportional? _____

x	*y*
0	
1	
2	
3	

c. This table shows the capacity in ounces of a given number of pint containers.

Describe in words the rule of the function. To find the number of ounces, m_____ the number of pints by _____.

Write an equation for the function using *p* for pints and *z* for ounces. $z = $ _____ *p*

Use the function to find the number of ounces in 5 pints. _____

Pints	Ounces
1	16
2	32
3	48
4	64

d. Tell why the relationship between the numbers in this table is **not** a function. *A function has only one output number for each input number.*

The input number _____ has two different o_____ numbers.

x	*y*
0	0
1	1
1	−1
2	2

e. Yanos and Xena played a numbers game. This graph shows all the possible pairs of numbers they could say following the rule of the game.

Complete this function table using numbers from the graph.

x	*y*
−2	
−1	
0	
1	

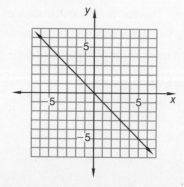

Describe the function rule Yanos followed: To find *y*, multiply *x* by _____.

Write an equation for the rule: $y =$ _____ *x*

f. Make up a numbers game for Yanos and Xena to play. Describe the rule and write an equation for the rule.

To find *y*, _____.

$y =$

Complete the function table for the rule. Then graph all possible pairs of numbers for the rule.

x	y
−1	
0	
1	
2	

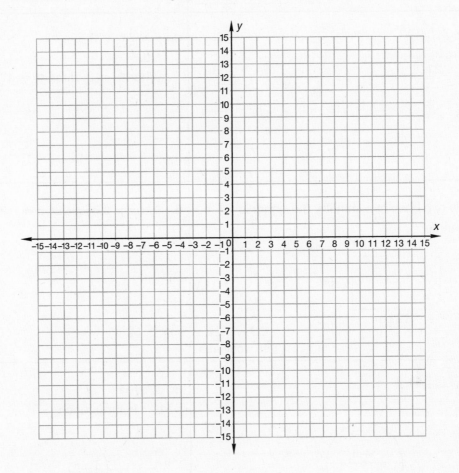

g. For the function $y = \frac{1}{2}x + 1$, complete the function table and use it to graph the equation.

x	y
-2	
0	
2	
4	

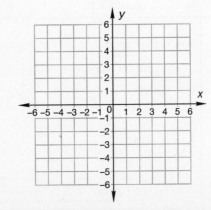

1. $

  piano $\dfrac{18}{\frac{1}{2}}$ —

  $

  chef $\dfrac{32}{1}$ —

2. fruit —

  vegetables

3.

  $-\ 21$

4. $y = \dfrac{1}{2}x + 3$

  When $x = 2$, does $y = 4$?

5. Draw two lines of symmetry through this rectangle.

7 cm

12 cm

Use work area.

6. *See page 28 in the* Student Reference Guide.

7. a. $A = \pi r^2$

  b. $C = 2\pi r$

14 m

Use $\dfrac{22}{7}$ for π.

a. _____

b. _____

8. a. area

  b. circumference

1 cm

Leave π as π.

a. _____

b. _____

9. $4 - (\quad) = t$

  $4 + (\quad) = t$

  $t =$ _____

10. $-3m = 4.2$

  $\dfrac{-3m}{} = \dfrac{4.2}{}$

  $m =$ _____

11. $30.7 - x = 20$

  $30.7 - x +\quad = 20 +$

  $x =$ _____

12. Area of large rectangle

Area of small rectangle

\+ Area of triangle

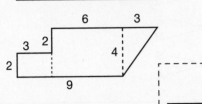

13. perimeter

14. a. Distribute: $-4(2m - 7x + 9) =$

b. Factor: $3x^2 + 3x + 3$

a. _____

b. _____

15. $\dfrac{32xmz}{-4mz} =$

16. $4\dfrac{2}{7} \div 1\dfrac{11}{49}$

$\downarrow \qquad \downarrow$

$\dfrac{}{} \div \dfrac{}{}$

$\downarrow \qquad \downarrow$

$\dfrac{}{} \times \dfrac{}{} =$

$\dfrac{2}{5} =$

$+ \quad =$

_____

17. $\dfrac{2}{3} \cdot 2\dfrac{1}{4}$

$\downarrow \qquad \downarrow$

$\dfrac{}{} \cdot \dfrac{}{} = \dfrac{}{} \cdot 1\dfrac{4}{5}$

18. $36 \div [2(1 + 2)^2] =$

19. $\dfrac{(-3) + (-5)}{-4} =$

20. $\left(\dfrac{1}{3}\right)^2 - \left(\dfrac{1}{3}\right)^3 =$

21. $(-3)^2 + (-3)^1 + (-3)^0 =$

22. $(2x^2 y)^3 =$

23. a. decimal

$20\overline{)11}$

b. percent

$\dfrac{11}{20} =$

a. _____

b. _____

24.

| | First Pick | Second Pick |

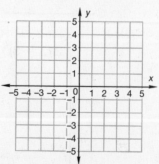

First Pick   Second Pick

S ⟨ A, M

A ⟨ S, M

M ⟨ S, A

a. { ____ , ____ , ____ , ____ , ____ , ____ }

b. $P(A) = \dfrac{\text{number with } A}{\text{total number}} =$ _____

Use work area.

25. Collect like terms.

$2xy - xy - y + 7y - xy =$

_____

26. $9x^2 - 4x + 7x - 6x^2 + 3 =$

_____

27. $E = \dfrac{1}{2}mv^2$

Find E when $m = 5$

$v = 4$

$E =$ _____

28. $A = \dfrac{120°}{360°}\pi r^2$

_____

29. $50 - 16 - 34 =$

30. a. rule: To find y, _____ 3 from x.

b. equation: $y = x$ _____

c. Graph the coordinate pairs. Draw a line through the points.

Use work area.

Volume is the amount of space occupied by a geometric solid.

- The units used to measure volume are cubes of certain sizes. Volume is expressed in **cubic units,** for instance ft^3 or cm^3.

- To find the volume of a rectangular prism:

  1. Find the number of cubes in one layer of a rectangular prism.

  2. Multiply that by the number of layers in the prism.

  Example: Find the number of 1-cm cubes that can fit in this box.

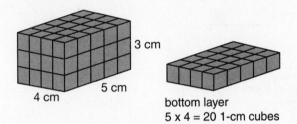

layers	1	3
cubes	20	?

20 x 3 = 60 1-cm cubes

3 cm

5 cm

4 cm

bottom layer
5 x 4 = 20 1-cm cubes

The volume of the box is 60 cm³.

- The formula for volume of a rectangular prism is:

  volume = *length* × *width* × *height*

  V = lwh

Practice Set (page 290)

a. What is the volume of a tissue box with the dimensions shown? _____

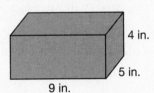

4 in.

5 in.

9 in.

number of cubes in bottom layer = 9 × 5 = _____

layers	1	4
cubes		

Teacher Notes:
- Introduce Hint #50, "Volume."
- Review "Perimeter, Area, Volume" on page 16 in the *Student Reference Guide.*
- Students will require a rectangular box, such as a shoe box or a cereal box, for Practice Set **f.**
- The activity on  pg. 289 is optional.

b. What is the volume of a **cube** with edges 2 inches long? _____

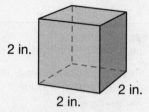

2 in.

2 in.

2 in.

layers   <u>1</u>   <u>2</u>
cubes

c. Find the volume of a cube with edges 6 inches long. _____

d. How many times greater are the dimensions of the cube in problem **c** than the cube

in problem **b**? _____

How many times greater is the volume? _____

e. What is the volume of this block T? _____
Add the volumes of the two parts.

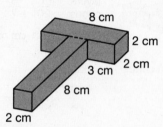

8 cm

2 cm

2 cm

3 cm

8 cm

2 cm

f. Get a box from your teacher. Measure the length, width, and height of the box in inches. Estimate
the volume of the box by rounding each measurement to the nearest inch before using the volume

formula. _____
$V = lwh$

length: _____

width: _____

height: _____

1. $\dfrac{\$}{hr}$ $\dfrac{15}{1}$ —

$\dfrac{\$}{lawn}$ $\dfrac{25}{1}$ $\dfrac{}{4}$

2. $\dfrac{cups}{bottles}$ —

3. $V = lwh$
$l = 50 \, m$
$w = 25 \, m$
$h = 2 \, m$

$\dfrac{m^3}{gal}$ $\dfrac{1}{264}$ —

_____ m³

_____ gal

4. $y = \dfrac{1}{4}x + 1$

When $x = 8$, does $y = 3$?

5. a. • Draw a line from every vertex of the triangle to the vanishing point.

• Use the lines as a guide to draw a smaller triangle.

vanishing point
•

b. t _____ prism

Use work area.

6. *Congruent means same shape and size.*
Similar means same shape.

7. a. $A = \pi r^2$

b. $C = \pi d$

28 ft

Use $\dfrac{22}{7}$ for π.

a. _____

b. _____

8. total treats: $8 \times$ _____ $=$ _____

$\dfrac{treats}{week}$ $\dfrac{1}{}$ —

9. a. rule: To find y, multiply x by _____,

then s_____ 2.

b. equation: $y =$ _____ $x - 2$

c.

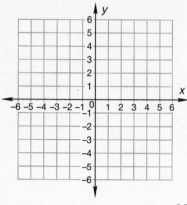

Use work area.

10. $3 \times 2(6 - 4)^3 =$

_____

11. $\dfrac{5}{8} + 3\dfrac{2}{3} \div 1\dfrac{1}{21} =$

Convert.

_____

12. $\dfrac{4}{9} \cdot \dfrac{10}{9} \cdot \dfrac{3}{8} =$

_____

13. $48 \div [3(4 - 2)^2] =$

_____

14. $\left(\dfrac{1}{2}\right)^3 - \left(\dfrac{1}{2}\right)^4 =$

_____

15. $\dfrac{105xyz}{-5yz} =$

_____

16. $-5s = 21.5$

$\dfrac{-5s}{} = \dfrac{21.5}{}$

$s =$ _____

17. $\qquad 45.6 - m = 25$

$45.6 - m + \quad = 25 +$

$m =$ _____

18. $V = lwh$

$l = 11$

$w = 8.5$

$h = 0.004$

_____

19. a. Distribute: $-3(4n - 6w + 5) =$

   b. Factor: $8y^2 + 8y + 8 =$

   a. _____

   b. _____

20. a. $P(A) = \dfrac{A}{total} =$

   b. $P(A, B, C) = \dfrac{A, B, C}{total} =$

   a. _____

   b. _____

21. a. $C = \pi d$

   b. $A = \pi r^2$

8 m

Leave π as π.

   a. _____

   b. _____

22.

	Ratio	Actual Count
Cars		c
Trucks		

_____

23. $x^2 + 3 = 7$

$x =$ _____ , _____

24. $-5|x| = 25$

$\dfrac{-5|x|}{-5} = \dfrac{25}{-5}$

$|x| =$

Is this possible? _____

Use work area.

25. $3x^2 = 27$

$x =$ _____ , _____

26. $|x| - 4 = 12$

$x =$ _____ , _____

27. Write in the plus and minus signs.

   $-255 \_\_ 65 \_\_ 25 = d$

$d =$ _____

28. Collect like terms:

   $3xy - xy - 2y + 5y =$

_____

29. $5x^2 - 3x + 5x - 4x^2 + 6 =$

_____

30. Which graph shows a proportional

function? _____

A. Is it a straight line? _____

Does it go through (0, 0)? _____

B. Is it a straight line? _____

Does it go through (0, 0)? _____

C. Is it a straight line? _____

Does it go through (0, 0)? _____

D. Is it a straight line? _____

Does it go through (0, 0)? _____

Use work area.

● **Surface Area** (page 294)

Name _____

Surface area is the combined area of all the faces of a geometric solid.

- To find the surface area of a solid:

    1. Find the area of each face.

    2. Add all the areas.

- **Lateral surface area** is the combined area of all the side faces but not the bases (top or bottom).

- To find the lateral surface area:

    1. Find the perimeter of a base.

    2. Multiply by the height.

This is a shortcut for adding the area of all the lateral faces.

Example: Find the lateral surface area and total surface area of this figure.

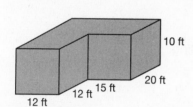
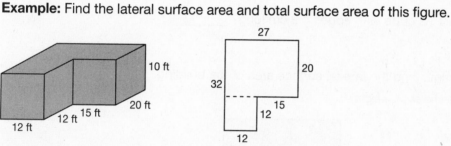

We find the lateral surface area first.

perimeter of base $= 32 + 27 + 20 + 15 + 12 + 12 = 118$ ft

lateral surface area $=$ perimeter $\times$ height $= 118 \times 10 = 1180$ ft^2

Now we add the area of the two bases to find the total surface area.

area of base $=$ area of small square $+$ area of large rectangle
$= (12 \times 12) + (20 \times 27) = 684$ ft^2

total surface area $=$ lateral surface area $+$ area of bases
$= 1180 + 2(684) = 1180 + 1386 = 2548$ ft^2

- A **net** is a two-dimensional image of the surfaces of a solid. Imagine unfolding a cereal box and laying it flat.

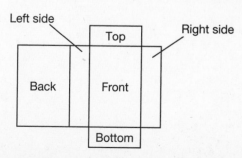

- A net can help us visualize the surfaces of a solid.

Practice Set (page 297)

a. What is the **lateral** surface area of a tissue box with the

dimensions shown? _____

lateral surface area = perimeter of base   height

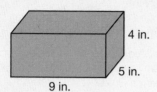

4 in.

5 in.

9 in.

b. What is the **total** surface area of a cube with edges 2 inches long? _____

Each face on a cube has the same area. There are 6 faces.

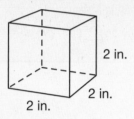

2 in.

2 in.

2 in.

c. Estimate the surface area a **cube** with edges 4.9 cm long? _____

Round 4.9.

d. Kwan is painting a garage. Find the **lateral** surface area of the building. _____

lateral surface area = perimeter × height

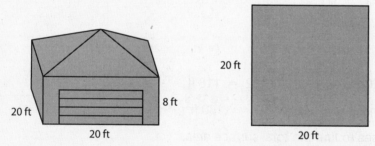

20 ft

8 ft

20 ft

20 ft

20 ft

20 ft

e. Get a box from your teacher. Measure the length, width, and height of the box in inches. Estimate the number of square inches of material used to make the box by rounding each

measurement to the nearest inch before calculating. _____

Add the areas of each face.

length: _____

width: _____

height: _____

1. north

30 min = _____ hr

$\dfrac{mi}{hr} \quad \dfrac{}{1} \quad —$

south

20 min = _____ hr

$\dfrac{mi}{hr} \quad \dfrac{}{1} \quad —$

distance: _____

direction: _____

2. $\quad$ 2 $\quad$ deciduous

$\underline{+7}$ $\quad$ evergreen

$\quad$ total

	Ratio	Actual Count
Deciduous	2	
Total tress		t

_____

3. total miles: 3hr $\times$ 9mi/hr = _____ mi

$\dfrac{hr}{mi} \quad \dfrac{1}{} \quad \dfrac{3}{}$

N
W —|— E
S

speed: _____

direction: _____

4. V = *lwh*

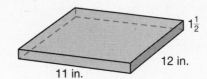

$1\frac{1}{2}$

12 in.

11 in.

_____

5. *lateral surface area* = *perimeter* $\times$ *height*

total surface area = *lateral surface area* + 2 *(area of base)*

12 in.

11 in.

_____

_____ edges

_____ faces

_____ vertices

Use work area.

7. y = −2x + 3

when x = 4,

does y = −11? _____

x	y
−1	
0	
1	
2	

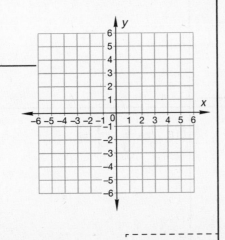

Use work area.

8. a. A = πr^2

b. C = 2πr

6 in.

Leave π as π.

a. _____

b. _____

9.  See the top of page 298.

y = _____

10. $\frac{x}{1.1} = 11$

$$\left(\frac{\ }{\ }\right)\left(\frac{x}{1.1}\right) = \left(\frac{11}{\ }\right)\left(\frac{\ }{\ }\right)$$

x = _____

11. $x + 3.2 = 5.14$

$x + 3.2 - \underline{} = 5.14 - \underline{}$

x = _____

12.

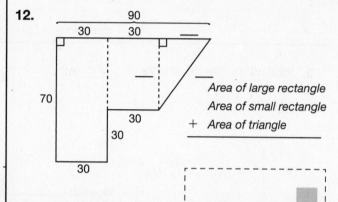

Area of large rectangle
Area of small rectangle
+ Area of triangle
_____

_____

13. perimeter

_____

14. a. Distribute: $-5(x^2 - x + 4) =$

b. Factor: $7x + 7 =$

a. _____

b. _____

15. $\frac{20\,wx^2}{5\,x^2} =$

_____

16. $\left(\frac{1}{4}\right)^2 - \left(\frac{1}{2}\right)^4 =$

_____

17. $\frac{7}{8} - \frac{12}{13} \div \frac{16}{13} =$

_____

18. $\frac{1}{2} \cdot \frac{2}{3} \cdot \frac{3}{4} =$

_____

19. $\dfrac{1 + 3^2}{(1 + 3)^2} =$

20. $\dfrac{(-3)(-4)}{(-3) - (-4)} =$

---

21. $\dfrac{x^2}{2} = 18$

$x = \underline{\hspace{1cm}}, \underline{\hspace{1cm}}$

22. $\dfrac{|x|}{5} = 10$

$x = \underline{\hspace{1cm}}, \underline{\hspace{1cm}}$

---

23. a. percent

  shift ⟶

  $0.005 =$

b. reduced fraction

  $0.005 =$

a. _____

b. _____

24. a. decimal number

  $\dfrac{5}{6} \longrightarrow 6\overline{)5.00}$

b. percent

  shift ⟶

a. _____

b. _____

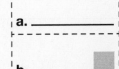

---

25. Use exponents.

  $9000 = 9 \times 1000$

  $9000 = \underline{\hspace{1cm}} \cdot \underline{\hspace{1cm}} \cdot \underline{\hspace{1cm}}$

26. a. $\dfrac{\text{number of numbers}}{\text{number of students}} =$

b. $\dfrac{\text{number of 7s}}{\text{number of students}} =$

c. Does **b** match **a**? _____

Use work area.

---

27. Collect like terms.

  $x^2 + 4x + 4 + 2x^2 - 3x - 4 =$

28. Find mgh

  When $m = 3$
  $g = 9.8$
  $h = 10$

29.

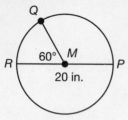

a. m∠QMP =

b. area of the semicircle *RMP* = $\dfrac{\quad}{360°}$ (πr^2)

a. _____

b. _____

30. a. Circle the top view.

A   B   C

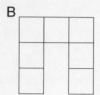

b. *Add the areas.*

Front

Back

Left side

Right side

Top

Bottom

+ Inside _____

c. *Each cube is 1 cm³.*

How many cubes are there?

b. _____

c. _____

- **Solving Proportions Using Cross Products**
- **Slope of a Line** (page 300)

Name _____

A cross product is the result of multiplying the denominator of one fraction and the numerator of another fraction.

- You already know how to solve a proportion using cross products.

Example: Solve: $\dfrac{4}{6} = \dfrac{6}{n}$

$$4 \cdot n = 6 \cdot 6$$
$$4n = 36$$
$$\dfrac{4n}{4} = \dfrac{36}{4}$$
$$n = 9$$

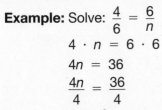

slope: $\dfrac{\text{rise}}{\text{run}} = \dfrac{+2}{+3} = \dfrac{2}{3}$

The **slope** is the slant of a line on a graph.

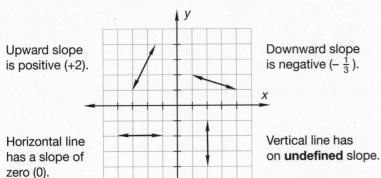

Upward slope is positive (+2).

Downward slope is negative ($-\frac{1}{3}$).

Horizontal line has a slope of zero (0).

Vertical line has on **undefined** slope.

- Think of reading each line in the coordinate plane from left to right:

- To calculate a slope, find the reduced ratio of the *rise* to the *run*.

$$\text{slope} = \dfrac{\text{rise}}{\text{run}}$$

1. Locate two points on the line. (0, −1) and (3, 1)
2. Start from the point on the left, (0, −1), and draw the horizontal leg of a triangle to the right.
3. Draw the vertical leg of a triangle up to the second point, (3, 1).
4. Find the rise and the run. The rise is +2 and the run is +3.
5. The slope is $\frac{2}{3}$. The slope is positive because the line rises upward.

Practice Set (page 304)

Use cross products to solve the proportions in **a–d.**

a. $\dfrac{8}{12} = \dfrac{12}{w}$ $w =$ _____

b. $\dfrac{3}{12} = \dfrac{x}{1.6}$ $x =$ _____

c. $\dfrac{y}{18} = \dfrac{16}{24}$ $y =$ _____

d. $\dfrac{0.8}{z} = \dfrac{5}{1.5}$ $z =$ _____

Find the slope of lines **e–g.**

Choose two points on each line to find the slope.

e. _____

f. _____

g. _____

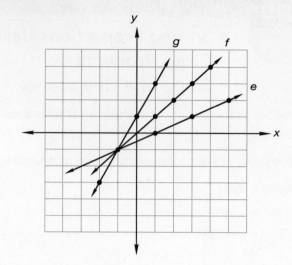

h. Which statement best describes the relationship between the slope and steepness of the line? _____

    A The greater the uphill steepness, the *less* the slope.

    B The greater the uphill steepness, the *greater* the slope.

    C The less the uphill steepness, the *greater* the slope.

i. Plot points on the origin (0, 0) and (2, −4). Draw a line through

the points. Find the slope of the line. _____

$$slope = \frac{rise}{run}$$

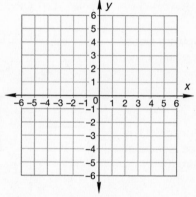

j. What is the slope of a line passing through (1, 1) and (5, −1)? _____

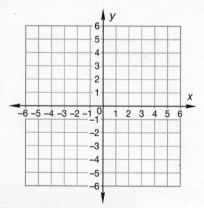

Written Practice (page 305)

1.

	Ratio	Actual Count
Undersized		*u*
Total		

2. $\frac{5}{9}$ of 36

    A 20   **B** 25   **C** 30   **D** 45

3. $C = 2\pi r$

17.5 ft

Use $\frac{22}{7}$ for π.

_____ ▪

4.   2(area of front)
2(area of side)
+ 2(area of bottom)

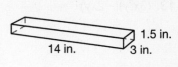

14 in.   1.5 in.   3 in.

_____ ▪

5. $V = lwh$

$2\frac{1}{2} \times 1\frac{3}{4} \times 4 =$

_____ ▪

6.

Purses (p)	Dollars (d)
0	
1	4
2	
3	

equation:

$d =$ _____

Is it linear?

_____

Is it proportional?

_____

Use work area.

7. $A = \pi r^2$
Round the answer to the nearest sq. ft.

12 ft

Use 3.14 for π.

_____

8. $y = \frac{2}{3}x - 1$

a. When $x = 9$,
does $y = 5$?

b. If $x = 15$, what is y?

a. _____   b. (15,   )

9. $6\frac{3}{4} - \frac{3}{5} \div \frac{1}{5} =$

_____

10. $(2.5)^2 - \left(\frac{3}{2}\right)^2 =$

$\begin{array}{r} 2.5 \\ \times 2.5 \end{array}$ $\frac{3}{2} \times \frac{3}{2} =$

_____

11. $(-10) - (-4) =$

_____

12. $\dfrac{(-4)(-8) \div (-2)}{-2} =$

_____

13. $(3x^2y)(-2xy)^3 =$

14. $5(40) \div [-5(1 - 3)^3] =$

15. $\left[\dfrac{3}{5} - \left(-\dfrac{1}{2}\right)^2 + \dfrac{9}{10}\right]^0 =$

Any number to the zero power equals what?

16. $\dfrac{10^8}{10^3} =$

17. Use a calculator.

$P(\text{F}) = \dfrac{31}{75} =$

$P(\text{R}) = \dfrac{40}{83} =$

_____ is more likely to

get a hit because _____

is greater than _____.

Use work area.

18. $C = \pi d$

$d = 1$ in.

19. $-3 - 5 + 2 =$

20.

	Ratio	Actual Count
Farmers		f
People		

21. ____ $\times c = 12$

$c =$ _____

22. *scale factor* $= \dfrac{larger}{smaller}$

23.   Area of square
 — Area of triangle

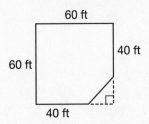

60 ft

60 ft   40 ft

40 ft

Use work area.

24. a. 4%

fraction:

decimal:

b. The _____ is best because I can divide 25.

Use work area.

25. $5x + 3 = 28$

$5x + 3 - \_\_ = 28 - \_\_$

$5x = \_\_$

$\dfrac{5x}{5} = \dfrac{\_\_}{\_\_}$

26. mean
    98
    90
    102
    97
    113

27. $(-4, -1), (-4, 7), (4, 7), (4, -1)$

area: _____

perimeter: _____

kind of quadrilateral:

_____

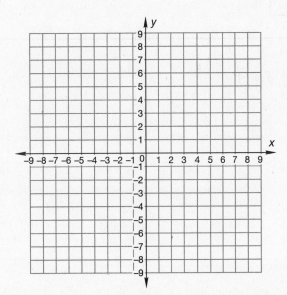

Use work area.

28. $d = 0.50w + 1$

$d = $ _____

29. Plot (4, 2) and (0, −6).
Draw the line.

slope $= \dfrac{rise}{run}$

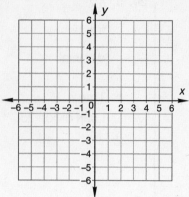

30. Use the graph to complete the table.

Hats	$
1	10
2	
3	
4	
5	

Hilbert charges $_____ for the first and $_____ for each additional hat. The relation is not proportional because it does not go through (_____ , _____)

Use work area.

• **Ratio Problems**
Involving Totals (page 308)

Name _____

Some ratio problems require using the total to solve the problem.

1. Read the problem carefully and fill in the ratio box. You may have to add or subtract to find a number you need.

2. Write a letter in the box for the number you want to find.

3. Write a proportion using the row with the letter and the row with two numbers.

4. Solve the proportion.

Example: A bus company has small and large buses in the ratio of 2 to 7. If the company has 84 large buses, how many buses does it have?

$$
\begin{array}{rl}
2 & \text{small} \\
+\ 7 & \text{large} \\
\hline
9 & \text{total}
\end{array}
$$

	Ratio	Actual Count
Small	2	
Large	7	84
Total	9	t

$$\rightarrow \frac{7}{9} = \frac{84}{t}$$

$$7t = 9 \cdot 84$$

$$t = 108$$

Practice Set (page 310)

a. The ratio of boys to girls at the assembly was 5 to 4. If there were 180 students at the assembly, how many **girls** were there? _____

$$
\begin{array}{rl}
5 & \text{boys} \\
+\ 4 & \text{girls} \\
\hline
& \text{total}
\end{array}
$$

	Ratio	Actual Count
Boys	5	
Girls	4	g
Total	9	180

The answer is reasonable because _____ girls is a little less than half the total.

b. The coin jar was filled with pennies and nickels in the ratio of 7 to 2. If there were 28 nickels in the jar, how many **coins** were there? _____

	Ratio	Actual Count
Pennies		
Nickles		28
Coins		c

c. The ratio of football players to soccer players at the park was 5 to 7. If the total number of players was 48, how many were **football** players? _____

	Ratio	Actual Count
Football		f
Soccer		
Total		

Written Practice (page 310)

1.

	Ratio	Actual Count
House finches		
Gold finches		g
Total		

2. 113.5
     95.7
  _____

3.

	Ratio	Actual Count
On		h
Off		
Total		

4. $\dfrac{}{25}$ of 5175

5. a. faces: _____

   edges: _____

   vertices: _____

b. Complete the net of the solid.

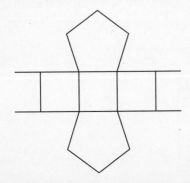

Use work area.

6. $V = lwh$

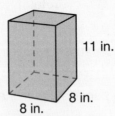

11 in.

8 in.

8 in.

7. $y = -x$

x	y
-2	
0	
2	

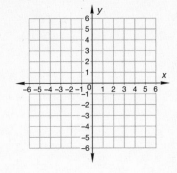

Is (5,5) on the line? _____

slope $= \dfrac{\text{rise}}{\text{run}} =$ _____

⌐ ‐ ‐ ‐ ‐ ‐ ‐ ‐ ‐ ‐ ‐ ‐ ‐ ¬
¦ Use work area. ¦
└ ‐ ‐ ‐ ‐ ‐ ‐ ‐ ‐ ‐ ‐ ‐ ‐ ┘

8.

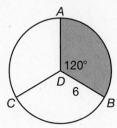

Leave π as π.

a. $A = \pi r^2$

b. Fraction ADB $= \dfrac{\quad}{360°} =$

c. $A = \left(\dfrac{\quad}{\quad}\right)(\pi r^2)$

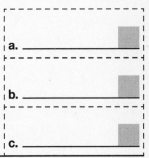

a. _____

b. _____

c. _____

9. *What is done to x to make y?*

⌐ ‐ ‐ ‐ ‐ ‐ ‐ ‐ ‐ ‐ ‐ ‐ ‐ ¬
¦ $y =$ _____ ¦
└ ‐ ‐ ‐ ‐ ‐ ‐ ‐ ‐ ‐ ‐ ‐ ‐ ┘

10.

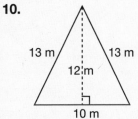

a. by sides: _____

b. area: _____

c. perimeter: _____

⌐ ‐ ‐ ‐ ‐ ‐ ‐ ‐ ‐ ‐ ‐ ¬
¦ Use work area. ¦
└ ‐ ‐ ‐ ‐ ‐ ‐ ‐ ‐ ‐ ‐ ┘

11. $\dfrac{2}{3}x = 10$

$\left(\quad\right)\left(\dfrac{2}{3}x\right) = 10\left(\quad\right)$

⌐ ‐ ‐ ‐ ‐ ‐ ‐ ‐ ‐ ‐ ‐ ‐ ‐ ¬
¦ $x =$ _____ ¦
└ ‐ ‐ ‐ ‐ ‐ ‐ ‐ ‐ ‐ ‐ ‐ ‐ ┘

12. $x - \dfrac{2}{3} = \dfrac{1}{9}$

$x - \dfrac{2}{3} + \quad = \dfrac{1}{9} +$

⌐ ‐ ‐ ‐ ‐ ‐ ‐ ‐ ‐ ‐ ‐ ‐ ‐ ¬
¦ $x =$ _____ ¦
└ ‐ ‐ ‐ ‐ ‐ ‐ ‐ ‐ ‐ ‐ ‐ ‐ ┘

13. $x^2 + 1 = 145$

$x^2 + 1 - = 145 - $

$x = \underline{}, \underline{}$

14. $7 - |x| = 1$

$x = \underline{}, \underline{}$

15. $\dfrac{mn}{2m^2} =$

16. $\dfrac{4}{5} - \dfrac{1}{5} \div \dfrac{1}{4} =$

17. $\dfrac{2}{7} \cdot \dfrac{3}{4} + \dfrac{11}{14} =$

18. $\left(\dfrac{3}{5}\right)^2 + \dfrac{3}{5} =$

19. $\dfrac{-5 + \sqrt{25 - 16}}{2}$ $\dfrac{-5 - \sqrt{25 - 16}}{2}$

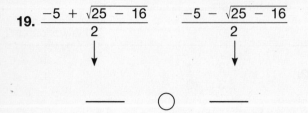

$\underline{} \quad \bigcirc \quad \underline{}$

20. *Change to decimals.*

0.5% of 1000 $\bigcirc$ 101% of 5

21. a. decimal

45% =

reduced fraction

45% =

b. The _____ is best because I can divide $40.

Use work area.

22.

14 m

Leave π as π.

a. $A = \pi r^2$
b. $C = \pi d$

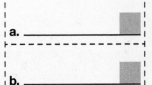

a. _____

b. _____

23. *Use 3 for π to estimate.*

a. area

b. circumference

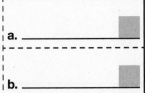

a. _____

b. _____

24. $E = \frac{1}{2}mv^2$

Find E when $m = 6$
                    $v = 2$

$E = $ _____

25. Factor.

7 · 3 + 7 · 5 =

A 7 + 3 × 7 + 5   **B** 7 × 7 + 3 × 5

C 7(3 + 5)   **D** 8(7 + 7)

_____

26. $80.00

__ . __

_____

27.   *2(area of front)*
           2(area of side)
        + *2(area of top)*
          total surface area

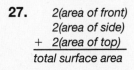

_____

28. Circumference of Venus: _____
$C = \pi d$

Which planet is larger?

Earth   Venus

40,070 km   ◯   _____

_____

29. $T = I \times$ _____

30. Complete the table.

Number (n) of Servings	Number of Cups of Sauce (s)	Ratio $\frac{s}{n}$
4	3	$\frac{3}{4}$
8	6	
12		
16		
20		

What is the constant ratio $\frac{s}{n}$? _____

$$\frac{3}{4} = \frac{s}{18}$$

$s =$ _____

$l =$ _____

Use work area.

• Solving Problems Using Scientific Notation (page 313)

Name _____

Teacher Note:
• Review "Place Value" on page 11 and "Scientific Notation for Numbers Powers of 10" on page 21 in the *Student Reference Guide*.

A number written in scientific notation has a coefficient and a power of 10.

• To multiply numbers in scientific notation:

    1. Multiply the coefficients.

    2. Multiply the powers of 10. (**Add** the exponents).

    3. If the coefficient has more than one whole-number place, write the coefficient in scientific notation and then combine the powers of 10.

        Example: $(7.5 \times 10^4)(2 \times 10^3)$

$(7.5 \times 10^4)(2 \times 10^3)$	Given
$(7.5 \times 2)(10^4 \times 10^3)$	Associative and Commutative Properties
15×10^7	Simplified (but *incorrect form*)
$1.5 \times 10^1 \times 10^7$	$15 = 1.5 \times 10^1$
1.5×10^8	Proper form ($10^1 \times 10^7 = 10^8$)

• To divide numbers in scientific notation:

    1. Divide the coefficients.

    2. Divide the powers of 10. (**Subtract** the exponents).

    3. If the coefficient has fewer than one whole-number place, write the coefficient in scientific notation and then combine the powers of 10.

        Example: $\dfrac{1.0 \times 10^8}{4.0 \times 10^3}$

$\dfrac{1.0 \times 10^8}{4.0 \times 10^3}$	Given
0.25×10^5	Simplified (but *incorrect form*)
$2.5 \times 10^{-1} \times 10^5$	$0.25 = 2.5 \times 10^{-1}$
2.5×10^4	Proper form ($10^{-1} \times 10^5 = 10^4$)

• If the decimal point is moved **left,** the exponent is **positive.**

    $25 = 2.5 \times 10^1$

• If the decimal point is moved **right,** the exponent is **negative.**

    $0.16 = 1.6 \times 10^{-1}$

Practice Set (page 316)

Find each product in **a–d.**

a. $(2.4 \times 10^6)(2.0 \times 10^5)$

  $4.8 \times 10^{\underline{}}$

b. $(1.25 \times 10^4)(2 \times 10^6)$

  $\underline{} \times 10^{\underline{}}$

c. $(4.0 \times 10^5)(4.0 \times 10^5)$

  $16 \times 10^{\underline{}}$

  $1.6 \times 10^1 \times 10^{\underline{}}$

  $1.6 \times 10^{\underline{}}$

d. $(2.5 \times 10^6)(5 \times 10^7)$

  $\underline{} \times 10^{\underline{}}$

  $\underline{} \times 10^{\underline{}} \times 10^{\underline{}}$

  $\underline{} \times 10^{\underline{}}$

e. The speed of light is about 3.0×10^5 kilometers per second. One day is 86,400 seconds. Express this number in scientific notation and estimate how far the sun's light travels in one day.

  $86{,}400 = 8.64 \times 10^{\underline{}}$

  $(3.0 \times 10^5)(8.64 \times 10^{\underline{}}) = \underline{} \times \underline{}$ km

f. What operation did you use for the exponents in problems **a–e?** $\underline{}$

Find each quotient in **g–j.**

g. $\dfrac{3.6 \times 10^{10}}{3.0 \times 10^6}$

  $1.2 \times 10^{\underline{}}$

h. $\dfrac{6.0 \times 10^8}{4.0 \times 10^8}$

  $\underline{}$

i. $\dfrac{1.2 \times 10^7}{3.0 \times 10^3}$

  $0.4 \times 10^{\underline{}}$

  $4.0 \times 10^{-1} \times 10^{\underline{}}$

  $4.0 \times 10^{\underline{}}$

j. $\dfrac{3 \times 10^9}{8 \times 10^4}$

  $\underline{} \times 10^{\underline{}}$

  $\underline{} \times 10^{\underline{}} \times 10^{\underline{}}$

  $\underline{} \times 10^{\underline{}}$

k. If Mars is 225 million kilometers from the sun, how long does it take light from the sun to reach Mars?

  $225 \text{ million} = 2.25 \times 10^{\underline{}}$

  $\dfrac{2.25 \times 10^{\underline{}}}{3.0 \times 10^5} = \underline{} \times 10^{\underline{}}$ sec.

l. What operation did you use for the exponents in problems **g–k?** $\underline{}$

© 2007 Harcourt Achieve Inc.

1.

	Ratio	Actual Count
Cat		
Rabbit		r
Total		22

2.

	Ratio	Actual Count
Guinea Pig		
Goliath Beetle		b
Total		

3. *over, over, up*

$0.005\overline{)1.0\,0\,0}$

4. *Subtract the exponents.*

$$\frac{3.36 \times 10^7}{1.6 \times 10^3}$$

_____ × _____

5. *Add the exponents.*

$(9.0 \times 10^2)(1.1 \times 10^7) =$

_____ × _____

6. $y = \frac{3}{2}x - 2$

x	y
−2	
0	
2	

$slope = \frac{rise}{run}$

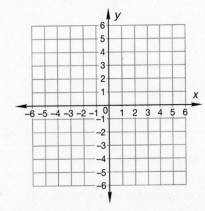

7. a. $A = \pi r^2$

   b. $C = \pi d$

100 units

Use 3.14 as π.

a. _____

b. _____

8. $V = lwh$

_____

9. 📖 See the bottom of page 316.

$y =$ _____ $+ 45$

10. a. *area of triangle* $= \dfrac{1}{2}bh$

Area of rectangle
$+$ *Area of triangle*

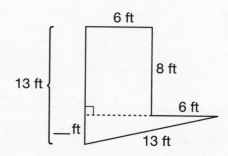

6 ft

8 ft

13 ft

6 ft

___ ft

13 ft

   b. perimeter

a. _____

b. _____

11. $\dfrac{1}{2}x = \dfrac{3}{7}$

$\left(\quad\right)\left(\dfrac{1}{2}x\right) = \left(\dfrac{3}{7}\right)\left(\quad\right)$

$x =$ _____

12. $x + \dfrac{1}{12} = \dfrac{1}{2}$

$x + \dfrac{1}{12} - \quad = \dfrac{1}{2} - \quad$

$x =$ _____

13. $x - 1.2 = 1.95$

$x - 1.2 + \quad = 1.95 +$

$x =$ _____

14. $\dfrac{x}{16} = \dfrac{30}{20}$

$x =$ _____

15. a. Distribute: $-6(x^2 - 18x + 81) =$

b. Factor: $9x - 3 =$

a. _____

b. _____

16. a. decimal

$20\overline{)11.00}$

percent

$\frac{11}{20} =$ _____

b. Discounts are usually given as a

_____.

Use work area.

17. $\frac{mr}{3mr} =$

_____

18. $\frac{(-12) - (-2)(3)}{(-2)(-3)} =$

_____

19. $\frac{1}{2} \div \frac{3}{4} - \frac{1}{3} =$

_____

20. $(0.15)^2 =$

_____

21. Collect like terms:

$x^3 + 2x^2y - 3xy^2 - x^2y =$

_____

22. Use the Distributive Property First

$5(x - 3) + 2(3 - x) =$

_____

23. $x^2 - 9 = 0$

$x^2 - 9 + = 0 + $

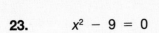

$x =$ _____ , _____

24.

	First Toss	
Second Toss	**H**	**T**
H	HH	TH
T	HT	TT

a. $P(T)$

b. $P(HH)$

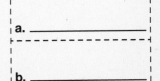

a. _____

b. _____

25. Similar

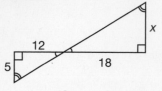

a. scale factor

b. $\dfrac{12}{18} = $ ___

a. _____

b. $x = $ _____

26. a.
$$\frac{\text{in.}}{\text{ft}} \quad \frac{6}{30} \quad \frac{1}{}$$

b.
$$\frac{\text{ft}}{\text{in.}} \quad \frac{}{1} \quad \frac{10}{}$$

$$\frac{\text{ft}}{\text{in.}} \quad \frac{}{1} \quad \frac{20}{}$$

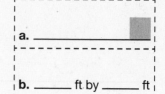

a. _____

b. _____ ft by _____ ft

27. area of a trapezoid

$$A = \frac{b_1 + b_2}{2} \cdot h$$

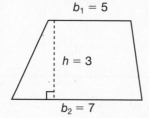

$A = $ _____

28. Pythagorean Theorem

$$a^2 + b^2 = c^2$$

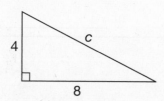

A $\sqrt{80}$　　**B** $\sqrt{81}$　　**C** $\sqrt{9.1}$　　**D** $\sqrt{9.3}$

_____

29. Surface area

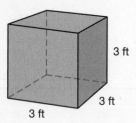

3 ft
3 ft
3 ft

_____

30.

loaves (l)	hours (h)
0	0
1	144
2	

Which graph goes with the table? _____

The graph is proportional because it is a

straight _____ and it goes through

(_____, _____)

equation: $l = $ _____

constant ratio: $\dfrac{h}{l} = $

Use work area.

• **Graphing Functions** (page 319)   Name _____

A function is a mathematical rule that pairs one output number with each input number.

• The **domain** of a function is every possible input number.

• The **range** of a function is every possible output number.

The domain and range will depend on what the function describes.

• To graph a function:

  1. Create a table with input and output numbers according to the function.

  2. Plot the input and output numbers as coordinate pairs on a grid.

  3. If the points make a line, draw a line through them to show all the possible coordinate pairs for the function.

Example: Consider the formula for the perimeter of a square, in which P is the perimeter and s is the side length.

$P = 4s$

The *domain* (input numbers) is any number that can be a side length.
Lengths must be positive numbers, so the domain is **all positive real numbers.**

The *range* (output numbers) is any number that can be a perimeter.
A perimeter is a length, so the range is also **all positive real numbers.**

This table shows a few input and output pairs for the function. Because the domain is positive real numbers, we do not include negative numbers in the table.

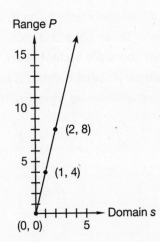

P = 4s

s	P
0	0
1	4
2	8

The graph shows the coordinate pairs from the table. Because the pairs are in a straight line, we drew a *ray* through the points. We did not draw a *line* because lengths cannot be negative.

• The perimeter formula is a **direct proportion** because the *graph starts at the origin* (0, 0) and *all points in the graph are aligned.*

a. The directions on the can of paint describe a function: One gallon covers 400 sq. ft. Complete the function table relating quantity of paint in gallons (g) to area (A) covered in square feet. Then graph the coordinate pairs from the table.

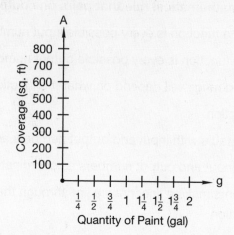

Gallons (g)	Area (A)
0	0
1	
2	

b. Referring to problem **a,** which equation below describes the relationship between the number of gallons (g) of paint and the area (A) covered in square feet? _____

A $A = 400 + g$ **B** $A = 400g$ **C** $A = \dfrac{400}{g}$ **D** $A = \dfrac{g}{400}$

c. Referring to problem **a,** painting 700 square feet of wall would require about how many **quarts** of paint? _____

1 gal = _____ qt
On the graph, each quart covers how many sq. ft.?

d. Janine works in a high-rise building. When she wants to go to upper floors she enters an elevator and pushes a button (input), and the elevator takes her a distance above street level (output). Assuming that the building has 12 floors and that floors are 10 feet apart, graph the relationship between the floor Janine is on and her distance (elevation) above street level.

Do not draw a line through the points on this graph because Janine could not input a floor number such as $2\frac{1}{2}$. The first floor is on the ground (0 ft).

Floor number	Feet above street level
1	0
2	10
3	
4	
5	
6	
7	
8	
9	
10	
11	
12	

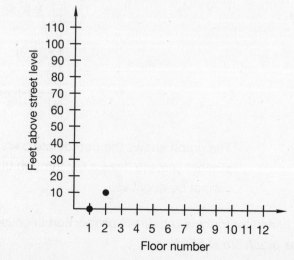

e. In problem **d**, what is the **domain** of the function?

List all possible input numbers.

{ _____ , _____ , _____ , _____ , _____ , _____ , _____ , _____ , _____ , _____ , _____ , _____ }

f. Is the relationship in problem d proportional?

_____ because even though the points are in a straight _____ , the graph does not

begin at the o_____ .

Written Practice (page 324)

1.

	Ratio	Actual Count
Buses		
Cars		c
Vehicles		650

_____

2.

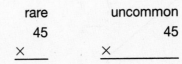

rare   uncommon
45   45
× _____   × _____

_____

3. *Double the sum.*

$1.00
1.25
1.50
+ 1.50
‾‾‾‾‾‾

_____

4. *Add the exponents.*
Use proper form.

$(4.0 \times 10^3)(3.0 \times 10^4) =$

_____ × _____

5. $y = x - 1$

x	y
0	
−1	
1	

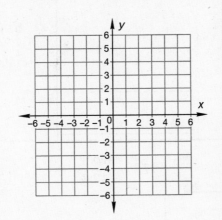

Is (3, 1) on the line? _____

Use work area.

6. a. $A = \pi r^2$

   b. $C = 2\pi r$

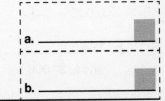

a. _____

b. _____

7. $V = lwh$

8. $C = \pi d$

_____ ◯ *1 yd*

9. area

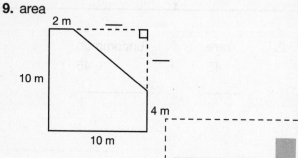

2 m

10 m

4 m

10 m

10. perimeter minus 10 m

11. $\frac{4}{3}x = 12$

$\left(\quad\right)\left(\frac{4}{3}x\right) = (12)\,(\quad)$

$x = $ _____

12. $x - \frac{2}{5} = 12$

$x - \frac{2}{5} + \quad = 12 + $

$x = $ _____

13. $4x^2 = 64$

$\frac{4x^2}{} = \frac{64}{}$

$x^2 = $

$x = $ _____ , _____

14. $\frac{24}{x} = \frac{15}{20}$

$x = $ _____

15. a. Distribute:

$-5(4r - 2d - 1) = $

b. Factor: $4x - 28 = $

a. _____

b. _____

16. a. percent

0.005 = _____

fraction

0.005 = ___

b. The _____ is best because I can divide $1000.

Use work area.

17. $\dfrac{24wx^2y}{-12xy} = $

18. *order of operations*

$$\frac{1}{2} \cdot \frac{2}{3} = \underline{\quad} \cdot \frac{3}{4} =$$

$$\frac{3}{8} =$$

$$\underline{\quad} = \underline{\qquad\qquad}$$

19. $1\frac{2}{3} \div 3\frac{1}{3}$ $\qquad =$

$$\underline{\quad} \div \underline{\quad}$$

$$\downarrow \qquad \downarrow$$

$$\underline{\quad} \times \underline{\quad} =$$

$$+ 1\frac{5}{6} =$$
$$\underline{\qquad\qquad}$$

20. $\dfrac{(-12) - (-2)(-3)}{-(-2)(-3)} =$

21. $\dfrac{1.2 - 0.12}{0.012} =$

22. $(-1)^2 + (-1)^3 =$

23. Distributive Property first

$$\overset{\times}{\overbrace{2(x + 1)}} + \overset{\times}{\overbrace{3(x + 2)}} =$$

24. $(0, 0)$ and $(2, -4)$

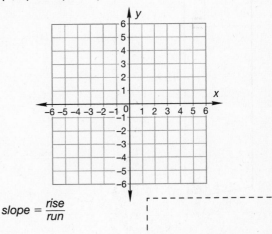

$$slope = \frac{rise}{run}$$

25. a. $A = \pi r^2$

b. $m\angle AOC = 180°$

$m\angle BOC = \underline{\quad}°$

$m\angle DOB = 180°$

$m\angle AOD = \underline{\quad}°$

$\dfrac{m\angle BOC + m\angle AOD}{360°} =$ **a.** _____

c. $A = (\quad)(\pi r^2)$

b. _____

c. _____

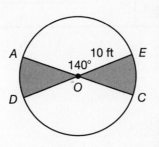

26. a. $\triangle ABE$ and $\triangle ACD$ are redrawn. Label the sides and vertices.

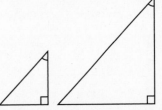

b. $\triangle ABE$ and $\triangle ACD$ are similar because they have angles with the same

m _____.

c. scale factor: $\dfrac{CD}{BE} =$

┌─────────────┐
│ Use work area. │
└─────────────┘

27. $E = mc^2$

Find E when $m = 0.001$
$\qquad c = 3.0 \times 10^8$

order of operations

Add the exponents.

$(3.0 \times 10^8)(3.0 \times 10^8) = \underline{\qquad} \times 10^\square$

$0.001 = 1.0 \times 10^\square$

$(1.0 \times 10^\square)(\underline{\qquad} \times 10^\square) =$

$E = \underline{\qquad} \times \underline{\qquad}$

28. a. decimal

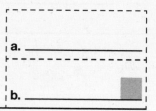

$12\overline{)1.000}$

b. percent

a. _____

b. _____

29. *lateral surface area = (perimeter of base) × (height)*

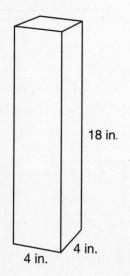

18 in.

4 in.

4 in.

_____

30. a. equation: $y = \underline{\qquad}$

b.

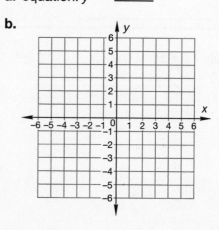

c. _____ because the graph is a

straight l_____ and it intersects the

o_____ .

Use work area.

●**Percent of a Whole** (page 326)

Name _____

Percents are often used to describe parts of a whole.

- We use a percent box and proportions to solve these problems.

- To solve a percent problem:

Teacher Note:
- Refer students to "Percent as Part of a Whole" on page 14 in the *Student Reference Guide*.

1. Read the problem carefully and fill in the percent box. The total is always 100%. You may have to subtract from 100% to find a missing percent.

2. Write a letter in the box for the number you want to find.

3. Write a proportion using the row with the letter and the row with two numbers.

4. Solve the proportion.

Example: Thirty percent of the students ride the bus. If 210 *do not* ride the bus, how many students are there **in all?**

	Percent	Actual Count
Bus	30	
Not Bus	70	210
Total	100	t

100
$\underline{-30}$
70

$$\frac{70}{100} = \frac{210}{t}$$

$70t = 210 \times 100$

$70t = 21{,}000$

$t = 300$

There are 300 students in all.

Practice Set (page 327)

a. Mariah has read 135 of the 180 pages in the book. What percent of the book has she *read?* _____

	Percent	Actual Count
Read	r	135
Not Read		45
Total	100	180

180
$\underline{-135}$
45

$$\frac{r}{100} = \frac{135}{180}$$

$r =$ _____

b. McGregor is growing alfalfa on 180 acres, which is 30% of his farmland. McGregor has how many acres of farmland? _____

	Percent	Actual Count
Alfalfa	30	180
Not Alfalfa	70	
Total	100	t

100
$\underline{-70}$
30

Practice Set (continued) (page 328)

c. The frequency of the letter *e* in written English is about 13%. On a page of a novel that has about 2000 letters per page, about how many occurrences of the letter *e* can we expect to find? _____

$$\begin{array}{r} 100 \\ -13 \\ \hline \end{array}$$

	Percent	Actual Count
e	13	*e*
Not *e*		
Total	100	

d. The Springfield Sluggers won 64% of their games and lost 9 games. How many games did the Sluggers **win?** _____

$$\begin{array}{r} 100 \\ -64 \\ \hline \end{array}$$

	Percent	Actual Count
Won		*w*
Lost		9
Total	100	

Written Practice (page 328)

1.

	Percent	Actual Count
Whales	5	
Fishing	7	*f*
Total		

_____

2.

$$\begin{array}{r} \times \quad 4 \\ \hline \end{array} \qquad \begin{array}{r} \times \quad\quad \\ \hline \end{array} \qquad \begin{array}{r} + \quad\quad \\ \hline \end{array}$$

_____

3. $\frac{1}{2}$ of 62 =

$\frac{1}{3}$ of 66 =

$$\begin{array}{r} + \\ \hline \end{array}$$

_____

4. $\begin{array}{r} 25 \\ -19 \\ \hline \end{array}$

	Percent	Actual Count
Correct	*c*	19
Incorrect		
Total	100	25

_____

5. $(-2, 2)$ and $(2, 0)$

slope $= \dfrac{rise}{run}$

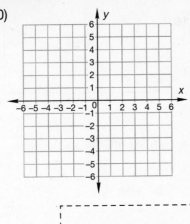

_____

6. $\dfrac{a^2b^2c}{12a^2c^2} =$

Cancel.

_____

7. *Cancel.*

$\dfrac{4}{9} \div \dfrac{2}{3} - \dfrac{1}{2} =$

_____

8. $3^2 \div 3 + 3 - 3(3) =$

_____

9. $\left(\dfrac{2}{5}\right)^2 - \left(\dfrac{1}{5}\right)^2 =$

_____

10. *Subtract the exponents.*

$\dfrac{5.2 \times 10^7}{1.3 \times 10^4} =$

_____ × _____

11. *Add the exponents.*

Use proper form.

$(5.0 \times 10^7)(3.0 \times 104) =$

_____ × _____

12. $(12.4 + 2)(1 - 0.998) =$

_____

13. $y = x - 3$

x	y
-1	
0	
1	

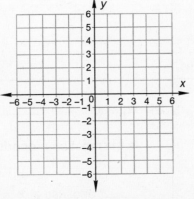

Is (3, 0) on the line? _____

Use work area.

14. Use 3.14 for π.

$d = 40\text{cm}$

a. $A = \pi r^2$

b. $C = \pi d$

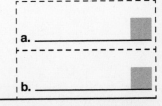

a. _____

b. _____

15. $V = lwh$

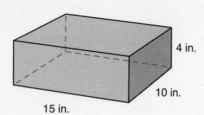

4 in.

10 in.

15 in.

_____

16.

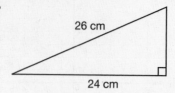

26 cm

24 cm

a. by angles

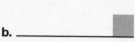

a. _____

b. area

b. _____

c. perimeter

c. _____

17. $x - 3\frac{1}{3} = 2\frac{1}{2}$

$x =$ _____

18. $x - \frac{2}{3} = \frac{5}{6}$

$x =$ _____

19. $4x^2 = 400$

$4x^2 = 400$

$x^2 =$

$x =$

$x =$ _____, _____

20. $\frac{1.2}{3} = \frac{x}{2}$

$x =$ _____

21. a. decimal

250% =

fraction

250% =

b. The percent is best because I can

d_____ (200%) then add

h_____ (50%).

Use work area.

22. Collect like terms.

$abc - cab + bac - 2b^2 =$

Commutative Property

$abc - abc + abc - 2b^2 =$

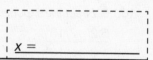
_____

23. $5x^2y - 4yx^2 + 2x - x =$

_____

24. equation: $y =$ _____ $x +$ _____

Is the function proportional?

_____ because at $x = 0$, $y =$ _____.

Use work area.

25. a. $\dfrac{30°}{360°} = $ _____

So how many 30° sectors cover a full circle?

b. $A = ($ _____ $)(\pi r^2)$

a. _____

b. _____

26. $r = \dfrac{d}{t}$

Find r when $d = 26.2$ mi
$t = 2$ hr

_____

27.
$$\begin{array}{r} 3.14 \\ \underline{2.76} \end{array}$$

_____

28. reflection, rotation, translation, or dilation of minute hand?

12:30 p.m.   12:45 p.m.

_____

29. *2(area of front)*
 2(area of side)
 $\underline{+\ 2(area\ of\ bottom)}$

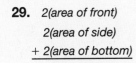
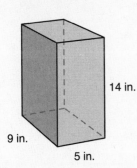

14 in.

9 in.

5 in.

_____

30. Is the graph proportional? _____
Is it a straight line?
Does it intersect the orgin?

equation: $S = \dfrac{5}{3}$ _____

Constant of proportionality: $k = \dfrac{S}{t} = $ _____

Use work area.

• Solving Rate Problems with Proportions and Equations (page 330)

Name _____

Rate problems can be solved with a proportion or by writing an equation using the unit rate.

Teacher Notes:
• Review Hint #19, "Converting Measures and Rates."

• Review "Proportion (Rate) Problems" on page 19 in the *Student Reference Guide*.

• A rate is a ratio of two measures. These are all rates:

$$\frac{100 \text{ miles}}{2 \text{ hours}} \qquad \frac{\$36}{4 \text{ hours}} \qquad \frac{15 \text{ kilograms}}{7 \text{ liters}}$$

• A **unit rate** is a rate with a denominator (the bottom number) of 1. Each of the rates above has been reduced to its unit rate:

$$\frac{50 \text{ miles}}{1 \text{ hour}} \qquad \frac{\$9}{1 \text{ hour}} \qquad \frac{2.5 \text{ kilograms}}{1 \text{ liter}}$$

• We already know how to solve rate problems with a proportion:

Multiply the loop. Divide by the outside number.

Example: If 6 books weigh 15 pounds, how much would 20 books weigh?

books $\dfrac{6}{15} \quad \dfrac{20}{?}$ $20 \times 15 = 300$

pounds $\dfrac{300}{6} = 50$ pounds

Even though there is no equal sign, this is a proportion.

• We can also solve rate problems by writing an equation.

   1. Find the unit rate. Be sure that the unit you want to end up with is in the numerator (top of the fraction).
   2. Write an equation using the unit rate and letters that stand for the two things in the problem.
   3. Substitute the number in from the problem and calculate the answer.

Example: If 6 books weigh 15 pounds, how much would 20 books weigh?

We want to end up with weight (pounds), so we put that in the numerator.

$$\text{unit rate} = \frac{15 \text{ pounds}}{6 \text{ books}} = \frac{2.5 \text{ pounds}}{1 \text{ book}} = 2.5 \text{ pounds per book}$$

Write an equation, using *w* for weight and *n* for number of books.

$w = 2.5n$

Substitute 20 books for n.

$w = 2.5 \times 20 = 50$ pounds

Practice Set (page 333)

For problems **a-c**, estimate an answer first and then solve the problem by writing a proportion.

a. If 5 pounds of seedless grapes cost $3.80, how much would 9 pounds cost? _____

Estimate: 9 pounds is a little less than twice _____ pounds, so about $ _____ is a good estimate.

$$\begin{array}{ccc} \text{lb} & 5 & 9 \\ \$ & 3.80 & ? \end{array}$$

b. If 8 cows eat 200 pounds of hay a day, how many pounds of hay would 20 cows eat in a day? _____

Estimate: 20 cows is more than _____ 8 cows, so more than _____ pounds is a good estimate.

$$\text{cows } \underline{8} \quad \underline{20}$$
$$\text{lb}$$

c. Darcie can type 135 words in 3 minutes. At that rate, how many minutes would it take her to type 450 words? _____

Estimate: _____ words is about three times as many as _____ words, so _____ minutes is a good estimate.

$$\begin{array}{c} \text{words} \\ \text{min} \end{array} \quad \underline{} \quad \underline{}$$

d. *unit rates*

Find the price per pound of grapes in **a.** _____ per pound $\qquad \dfrac{\$3.80}{5 \text{ lb}} =$

Find the pounds of hay per cow in **b.** _____ per cow $\qquad \dfrac{\text{lb}}{8 \text{ cows}} =$

Find the words per minute in **c.** _____ words per min. $\qquad \dfrac{\text{words}}{\text{min.}} =$

e. Solve problem **a** again using a rate equation and the unit rate instead of a proportion. Use *d* for dollars and *p* for pounds of grapes.

$d = $ _____ p

$d = $ _____ $\times$ _____ $= $ _____

Solve problem **b** again using a rate equation and the unit rate instead of a proportion. Use *p* for pounds of hay and *n* for number of cows.

$p = $ _____ n

$p = $ _____ $\times$ _____ $= $ _____

Written Practice (page 333)

1. 7 miles is about twice _____ miles, so _____ minutes is a good estimate.

$$\begin{array}{c} \text{mi} \\ \text{min} \end{array} \quad \underline{3} \quad \underline{7}$$

_____

2. _____ weeks is more than twice _____ weeks, _____ pounds is a good estimate.

$$\begin{array}{c} \text{lb} \\ \text{weeks} \end{array} \quad \underline{} \quad \underline{}$$

_____

3. 60 marbles

$\dfrac{18 \text{ green}}{\text{not green}}$

  a. P (green) =

  b. P (not green) =

a. _____

b. _____

4.

	Ratio	Actual Count
Stripes		s
Stars		

10,000

$-\ \underline{}$

_____

5.

       $3.50

      $+\ \underline{}$

_____ ▨

6. $1.4x = 84$

$x =$ _____

7. $x + 2.6 = 4$

$x =$ _____

8. $\dfrac{x}{3} = 1.2$

$x =$ _____

9. $x - 7 = -2$

$x =$ _____

10.

$\begin{array}{r} 25 \\ -\ 21 \\ \hline \end{array}$

	Percent	Actual Count
Answered	a	
Not Answered		
Total	100	

_____ ▨

11. 100
   70

	Percent	Actual Count
Remembered		
Forgot		
Total	100	t

12.

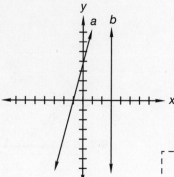

a. slope = $\frac{\text{rise}}{\text{run}}$

b. perpendicular to x-axis

c. intersects the y-axis

d. *See page 18 in the* Student Reference Guide.

a. _____

b. line _____

c. line _____

d. quadrant _____

13. $y = 3$

x	y
-1	3
0	3
1	3

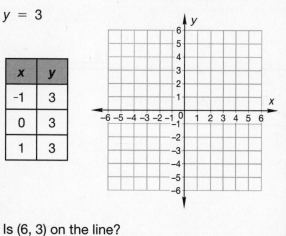

Is (6, 3) on the line?

14. circumference

ft $\frac{3}{1}$ —
people

20 feet

Use 3.14 for π.

15. $V = wh$

Use work area.

16.

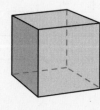

_____ edges

_____ vertices

_____ faces

17. *See page 18 in the* Student Reference Guide.

18. *The angles in a triangle add up to 180°.*

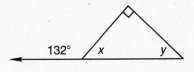

132° x y

x =

y =

19. decimal and fraction

21%

_____

_____

20. Find $\frac{1}{2}mv^2$

when m = 8

v = 2

_____

21. Complete this triangular prism.

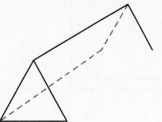

Use work area.

22.

x	6	2	1	−2
y	3	1	$\frac{1}{2}$	−1

a. to find y, _____ x by _____.

b. y =

c. Graph the coordinate pairs

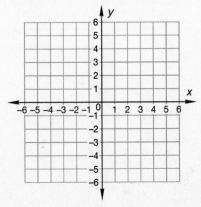

Use work area.

23. *Distributive property first*

$5(x + 3) - 2(x + 4) =$

_____

24. *Distribute first.*

$-7x + 2(x^2 + 4x - 1) =$

_____

25. $\dfrac{-(-3)}{-6} =$

_____

26. $-(-4) - 3$

(____) + (____) =

_____

27. $\left(1\dfrac{1}{2}\right)^2 - 1\dfrac{1}{2} =$

_____

28. *Subtract the exponents.*

$\dfrac{(5.2 \times 10^9)}{(4 \times 10^7)} =$

_____

29. $3|x| = 6$

$x =$ _____ , _____

30.

Wheel Revolutions Per Minute (rpm)

260
195
130
65

5   10   15   20
Speed of Bike (mph)

What rate does this graph show? ____

Is it propotional? _____

Is it straight?

Does it intersect the origin?

unit rate: $\dfrac{130 \text{ rpm}}{10 \text{ mph}} = \dfrac{}{1 \text{ mph}}$

equation: $r =$ _____

constant of proportionality: $k = \dfrac{r}{s} =$

Use work area.

• Solving Multi-Step Equations (page 336)

Name _____

We can use inverse operations to solve multi-step equations.

• We have used **inverse operations** to *isolate* a variable on one side of an equation.

Addition and subtraction are inverse operations.

Multiplication and division are inverse operations.

• Some equations will take multiple steps to isolate the variable.

1. Collect like terms, if possible.

2. Add or subtract to isolate the variable and its coefficient.

3. Multiply or divide to isolate the variable.

Example: Solve: $3x + 4 - x = 28$

$3x + 4 - x = 28$	Given
$(3x - x) + 4 = 28$	Commutative and Associative Properties
$2x + 4 = 28$	Collected like terms
$2x + 4 - 4 = 28 - 4$	Subtracted 4 from both sides
$2x = 24$	Simplified
$\dfrac{2x}{2} = \dfrac{24}{2}$	Divided both sides by 2
$x = 12$	Simplified

Practice Set (page 338)

Solve each equation.

a. $3x + 5 = 50$

  $3x + 5 - 5 = 50 - 5$

      $3x =$ _____

       $x =$ _____

b. $4x - 12 = 60$

  $4x - 12 +$ _____ $= 60 +$ _____

       $4x =$ _____

        $x =$ _____

c. $30n + 22 = 292$ $n =$ _____

d. $\dfrac{x}{5} + 4 = 13$ $x =$ _____

e. $-2x + 17 = 3$ $x =$ _____

f. $3m - 1.5 = 4.2$ $m =$ _____

g. *Collect like terms.*
  $4x + 10 + x = 100$ $x =$ _____

h. $7x - 12 - x = 24$ $x =$ _____

i. A computer repair shop charges $40 per hour plus the cost of parts. If a repair bill of $125 includes $35 for parts, then how long did the repair shop work on the computer? Solve this equation to find the answer. Express your answer in both decimal form and in hours and minutes.

$40x + 35 = 125$

decimal: $x =$ _____ ▇

hours and minutes: $x =$ _____ ▇ _____ ▇

Written Practice   (page 338)

1.

	Ratio	Actual Count
In-State		
Out-of-State		x
Total		

2. $ \quad \overline{}$
friends $\overline{50}$

$500

$+$ _____

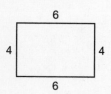

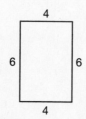

3. Quadrilaterals with corresponding sides of equal lengths are sometimes, always, or never **congruent?**

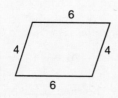

4. $5x + 25 = 100$

$x =$ _____

5. $\dfrac{x}{2} + 8 = 16$

$x =$ _____

6. $2x - 1.2 = 3$

   3.
   1.2 ^{up}
   _____ $2 \,)\overline{}$

$x =$ _____

7. $-4m + 5.5 = 9.5$

   9.5
   5.5
   _____

$m =$ _____

8. $-2w + 22 = 30$

$w =$ _____

9. $\frac{1}{2}x - \frac{1}{3} = \frac{2}{5}$

$x =$ _____

10. $-3^2 + (-3)^2 =$
   $-3^2 = -(3)^2$

_____

11. $\frac{1}{3} + \frac{5}{6} \cdot \frac{4}{5} =$

_____

12. $\dfrac{mc^2xc}{mx^2} =$

_____

13. $1\frac{1}{2} \cdot 2\frac{2}{3} - 3\frac{3}{4} =$

_____

14. *Subtract the exponents.*
   Use proper form.

$\dfrac{2.7 \times 10^8}{9 \times 10^3} =$

_____ × _____

15. $\dfrac{0.24 - 0.024}{0.02}$

   0.24   *over, over, up*
 − 0.024 $0.02 \,)\overline{}$

_____

16.

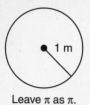

1 m

Leave π as π.

a. area

b. circumference

a. _____

b. _____

17. Estimate.

$V = lwh$

4 ft 2 in. ⟶ _____ ft

13 in. ⟶ _____ ft

2 ft 11 in. ⟶ _____ ft

_____

18. a. area

b. perimeter

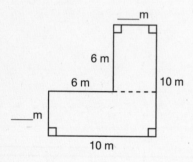

____ m

6 m

6 m

10 m

____ m

10 m

a. _____

b. _____

19. a.

x	y
0	
1	40
2	

b. y = _____

Use work area.

20. a. decimal

7.5% =

b. fraction

$\dfrac{7.5}{} = \dfrac{}{}$

a. _____

b. _____

21. a. The triangles are similar because they have

the same $\underset{\text{a}}{\underline{\hspace{3cm}}}$.

b. scale factor: $\dfrac{\text{to}}{\text{from}}$ = _____

c. $\dfrac{x}{15}$ = _____

x =

Use work area.

22. Find $\dfrac{r^2 - 24r}{t}$

when $r = 3$
when $t = -1$

_____

23.

x	y
0	
1	3
2	

$y =$ _____

Is the function linear? _____

Is it proportional? _____

Use work area.

24. _lateral surface area = perimeter × height_

40 ft

60 ft

_____

25. _Subtract the exponents._

$$\dfrac{2.25 \times 10^{12}}{1.25 \times 10^9} =$$

$12.5\overline{)2.250}$

Now convert to standard notation.

_____

26.

	Percent	Actual Count
Missed	m	
Not Missed		
Total	100	20

27. _____ $= 5.50g +$ _____

$g =$ _____

28. $1\frac{1}{9} = \frac{}{9}$

9)‾‾‾‾‾‾‾‾

29. $y = -2x$

x	y
−2	
0	
2	

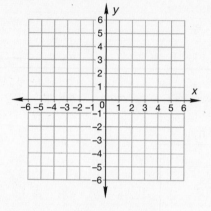

Is (−1, −2) on the line? _____

slope $= \frac{\text{rise}}{\text{run}} =$ _____

Use work area.

30.

Number of Shirts	$
0	0
1	0
2	0
3	

Which graph shows this relationship? _____

Is the relationship proportional? _____

Is it a line?

Does it intersect the origin?

Use work area.

- **Negative Exponents**
- **Scientific Notation for Small Numbers** (page 346)

Name _____

Teacher Note:
- Review "Laws of Exponents" on page 19 and "Scientific Notation" on page 21 in the *Student Reference Guide*.

We can use the Laws of Exponents to simplify expressions with negative exponents.

- Look at the pattern in these examples:

$$\frac{10^4}{10^3} = \frac{\cancel{10}^1 \cdot \cancel{10}^1 \cdot \cancel{10}^1 \cdot 10}{\cancel{10}_1 \cdot \cancel{10}_1 \cdot \cancel{10}_1} = 10 = 10^1$$

$$\frac{10^3}{10^3} = \frac{\cancel{10}^1 \cdot \cancel{10}^1 \cdot \cancel{10}^1}{\cancel{10}_1 \cdot \cancel{10}_1 \cdot \cancel{10}_1} = 1 = 10^0$$

$$\frac{10^2}{10^3} = \frac{\cancel{10}^1 \cdot \cancel{10}^1}{\cancel{10}_1 \cdot \cancel{10}_1 \cdot 10} = \frac{1}{10} = 10^{-1}$$

$$\frac{10^1}{10^3} = \frac{\cancel{10}^1}{\cancel{10}_1 \cdot 10 \cdot 10} = \frac{1}{100} = 10^{-2}$$

- To **divide** powers with the same base, we subtract the exponents.

- A number to the **zero power equals 1**.

- A number with a **negative exponent** is the *reciprocal* of the same number with a positive exponent.

$$10^{-3} = \frac{1}{10^3} = \frac{1}{1000} \qquad\qquad 10^3 = 1000$$

10^{-3} and 10^3 are reciprocals

Law of Exponents for Negative Exponents

$$x^{-n} = \frac{1}{x^n}$$

Example: Simplify: 3^{-3}

$$3^{-3} = \frac{1}{3^3} = \frac{1}{3 \cdot 3 \cdot 3} = \frac{1}{27}$$

Example: Simplify: $2x^{-1}yx^2y^{-2}z$

$$2x^{-1}yx^2y^{-2}z = \frac{2yx^2z}{xy^2} = \frac{2 \cdot \cancel{y} \cdot \cancel{x} \cdot x \cdot z}{\cancel{x} \cdot \cancel{y} \cdot y} = \frac{2xz}{y}$$

- Very small numbers between 0 and 1 are written in scientific notation, using powers of 10 with negative exponents.

- To write a small number in **standard form**:

   1. **Shift** the decimal point to the *left* the number of places shown by the negative exponent.

   2. Use zero as a placeholder.

      Example: Write 6.32×10^{-7} in standard form.

      $6.32 \times 10^{-7} = 0.000000632$

      7 places to the left

- To write a small number in **scientific notation**:

   1. Place the decimal point after the first nonzero digit.

   2. Use the power of 10 to show the real location of the decimal.

      Example: Write 0.0000033 in scientific notation.

      $0.0000033 = 3.3 \times 10^{-6}$

      6 places to the right

Practice Set (page 350)

Simplify:

a. $3^{-2} = \dfrac{1}{3^2} = \dfrac{1}{3 \cdot 3} =$

b. $2^{-3} = \dfrac{1}{2^3} =$

c. $5^0 =$ _____

d. $2^{-3} \cdot 2^3 = \dfrac{2^3}{2^3} =$

e. Arrange in order from least to greatest:

$\dfrac{1}{2}, 0, 1, 2^{-2}, -1, 0.1$

$\underline{\quad -1 \quad}, \underline{\quad 0 \quad}, \underline{\quad\quad}, \underline{\quad\quad}, \underline{\quad\quad}, \underline{\quad 1 \quad}$

Find the missing exponent in problems **f–g.**

f. Add the exponents.

$10^{-3} \times 10^{-4} = 10^{-}$

g. Subtract the exponents.

$\dfrac{10^2}{10^5} = 10^{-}$

Simplify. Write the answer using only positive exponents.

h. $x^{-3}y^2xy^{-1} = \dfrac{y^2x}{x^3y} =$ _____

i. $\dfrac{6x^{-2}y^3z^{-1}}{2xy} =$ _____

j. Write 10^{-4} as a decimal number. _____
   $10^{-4} = 1.0 \times 10^{-4}$ *shift left 5 spaces*

k. Write 5×10^{-5} in standard form. _____
   shift left 5 spaces

l. Write 2.5×10^{-2} in standard form. _____
   shift left 2 places

m. Write 0.008 in scientific notation. _____ $\times$ _____
   shift right 3 places

Practice Set (continued) (page 351)

n. Write 0.000125 in scientific notation. _____ × _____

o. If lightning strikes a mile away the sound reaches us in about 5 seconds, but its light reaches us in about 5 millionths of a second. Write 5 millionths in scientific notation. _____ × _____

5 millionths = 0.000005

p. A nanometer is 10^{-9} meters. Write that number in standard form. _____

$10^{-9} = 1.0 \times 10^{-9}$

Written Practice (page 351)

1. 9 pages is more than _____ times

2 pages, so _____ hours is a good estimate.

pages
_____ _____
hr

2. _____ gallons is about 3 times

9 gallons, so $ _____ is a good estimate.

gal
_____ _____
$

3.

	Ratio	Actual Count
Black		b
White		
Total		

4.

	Ratio	Actual Count
Apple		a
Raisins		
Total		

5. $9.26
          3.50
          _____

lb $\dfrac{1}{0.64}$ _____
$

6. $12x - 3 = 69$

$x =$ _____

7. $\dfrac{x}{4} + 1 = 12$

$x =$ _____

8. $\dfrac{x}{3} - 4 = 5$

$x =$ _____

9. $-x + 1 = 6$

$x =$ _____

10. $1 - m = -1$

$m =$ _____

11. *Collect like terms.*

$3x + 2x - 1 = 99$

_____

12.

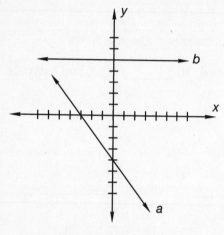

a. intersects y-axis at -4

b. perpendicular to y-axis

See page 17 in the Student Reference Guide.

c. slope $= \dfrac{\text{rise}}{\text{run}}$

d. *See page 18 in the* Student Reference Guide.

a. line _____   **c.** _____

b. line _____   **d.** quadrant _____

13. $y = 4x + 1$

x	y
-1	
0	
1	

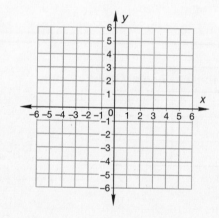

Is (3, 13) on the line? _____

Use work area.

14. Use 3.14 for π. Round the answer to the nearest sq. cm.

Area of 8-cm circle
− Area of 4-cm circle
Area of shaded part

_____

15. Complete the drawing.

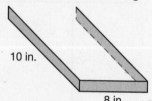

10 in.

8 in.   2 in.

$V = lwh$

_____

16. decimal notation

shift ⟵

3.4 × 10⁻⁵

_____

17. Distribute, then collect like terms.

9(x − 3) + 5(x + 5)=

_____

18. $3x^2 - 3x + x - 1 =$

_____

19. $\dfrac{(2xy)(3x^2y)}{6xy^2} =$

_____

20. $-6 - (-5) =$

_____

21. $2\dfrac{1}{2} \cdot 1\dfrac{2}{5} \cdot 2\dfrac{3}{8} =$

_____

22. *Add the exponents.*

$(2.3 \times 10^4)(1.5 \times 10^3) =$

_____ × _____

23. 0.62 ◯ $\dfrac{5}{8}$

_____

24. a. decimal

$\dfrac{7}{10} =$

b. percent

$\dfrac{7}{10} =$

a. _____

b. _____

25.

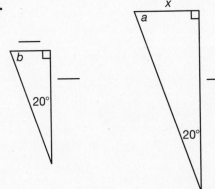

a. Label the angles of the triangles.

$a =$ _____ °

$b =$ _____ °

b. The triangles are s_____ because they have equal

_____ .

c. scale factor: _____

$\dfrac{x}{3.6} =$ — $x =$ _____

┌ Use work area. ┐

26.

Find $\sqrt{b^2 - 4ac}$

when $a = 6$

$b = 5$

$c = -1$

_____

27. Find the length of the diagonal to the nearest tenth of an inch.

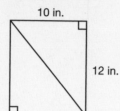

10 in.

12 in.

_____

28. $P(\text{H}) =$ _____

_____

29. $x^2 - 16 = 0$

$x =$ _____ , _____

30.

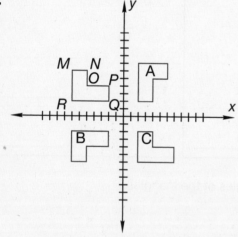

a. Is A, B, or C a slide of figure $MNOPQR$?

b. Label the vertices for figure C from the graph.

M' (,), N' (,), O' (,), P' (,),
Q' (,), R' (,)

Use work area.

52

- **Using Unit Multipliers to Convert Measures**
- **Converting Mixed-Unit to Single-Unit Measures** (page 354)

Name _____

Teacher Notes:
- Refer students to "Multiple Unit Multipliers" on page 23 in the *Student Reference Guide*.
- Review "Equivalence Table for Units" on page 1 in the *Student Reference Guide*.

A unit multiplier is a ratio of equivalent measures with different units.

- Every **unit multiplier** can be written in two ways by switching the numerator and denominator.

    Example: Write two unit multipliers for this equivalence:

    1 ft = 12 in. $\dfrac{1 \text{ ft}}{12 \text{ in.}}$ $\dfrac{12 \text{ in.}}{1 \text{ ft}}$

- We use unit multipliers to convert from one unit to another.

    Use the unit multiplier with the desired unit in the numerator.

    Cancel units as you multiply.

    Example: The apple tree is 64 inches tall. Use a unit multiplier to convert inches to **feet.**

    $64 \text{ in.} \times \dfrac{1 \text{ ft}}{12 \text{ in.}} = \dfrac{64}{12} \text{ ft} = 5\dfrac{4}{12} \text{ ft} = 5\dfrac{1}{3} \text{ ft}$

    We used the unit multiplier with feet in the numerator because we wanted the answer in feet.

- Some units, such as feet and inches or hours and minutes, are often used together to write a measurement.

- To write the measurement in a single unit, we can change the *smaller unit* to a fraction of the larger unit.

    Example: Samantha drove 100 miles in one hour and 45 minutes. How many **hours** did it take Samantha to drive 100 miles?

    $45 \text{ min} = \dfrac{45}{60} \text{ hr} = \dfrac{3}{4} \text{ hr} = 0.75 \text{ hr}$

    $1 \text{ hr } 45 \text{ min} = 1\dfrac{3}{4} \text{ hr} = 1.75 \text{ hr}$

Practice Set (page 357)

a. One day is 24 hours. Write two unit multipliers that have days and hours as units.

$\dfrac{\text{day}}{\text{hr}}$ $\dfrac{\text{hr}}{\text{day}}$

Circle the unit multiplier you would use to convert days to **hours**. Why did you choose that one?

I chose the unit multiplier that had hours in the n_____ because that is the unit I want for the answer.

b. Write two unit multipliers for this equivalence: 16 oz = 1 pt

$\dfrac{\text{oz}}{\text{pt}}$ $\dfrac{\text{pt}}{\text{oz}}$

© 2007 Harcourt Achieve Inc.

c. A gallon is 128 oz. Convert 128 oz to pints using a unit multiplier. _____

$$128 \text{ oz} \times \frac{\text{pt}}{\text{oz}} =$$

d. An inch is 2.54 cm. A bookcase that is 50 inches high is how many centimeters high? Use a unit

multiplier to perform the conversion. _____

$$50 \text{ in.} \times \frac{\text{cm}}{\text{in.}} =$$

e. Convert 24 quarts to gallons using a unit multiplier. (1 gal = 4 qt) _____

$$24 \text{ qt.} \times \frac{\text{gal}}{\text{qt}} =$$

f. Carter claims he can run 10,000 centimeters in 14 seconds. Express his claim in more appropriate

terms. _____
Change centimeters to meters.

$$10,000 \text{ cm} \times \frac{\text{m}}{\text{cm}}$$

g. The newborn child was 21 inches long and weighed 8 pounds 4 ounces. Convert the length to feet
and the weight to pounds. Write each as mixed numbers and decimal numbers. (12 in. = 1 ft and
16 oz = 1 lb)

length: mixed number _____   decimal _____

$$21 \text{ in.} \times \frac{\text{ft}}{\text{in.}} =$$

weight: mixed number _____   decimal _____

$$8 \text{ lb } 4 \text{ oz} = 8\frac{4}{16} \text{ lb} =$$

h. Marsha swam 400 meters in 6 minutes and 12 seconds. Convert that time to **minutes.** Answer with a

decimal. _____

$$4 \text{ min } 12 \text{ sec} = 4\frac{12}{60} \text{ min} =$$

i. A room is 11 ft 6 in. long and 11 ft 3 in. wide. Find the perimeter of the room in **feet.** Answer with a

decimal. _____

$$11 \text{ ft } 6 \text{ in.} = 11\frac{6}{12} \text{ ft} =$$

$$11 \text{ ft } 3 \text{ in.} = 11\frac{3}{12} \text{ ft} =$$

j. Convert 1 ft 3 in. to feet. Then use a unit multiplier to convert that measure to **yards.** Answer with a

decimal. (3 ft = 1 yd) _____

$$1 \text{ ft } 3 \text{ in.} = \_\_\_\_ \text{ ft} \times \frac{\text{yd}}{\text{ft}} =$$

1.

	Ratio	Actual Count
Hen		
Rooster		r
Total		

_____

2. popcorn + beverage = $ _____

$$\begin{array}{r} 19 \\ \times \underline{} \end{array}$$

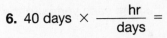

3. $\dfrac{\$}{\text{min}}$ $\underline{\quad 0.04 \quad}$

$$\begin{array}{r} \$1.00 \\ + \underline{} \end{array}$$

4. 9 hours is _____ times 3 hours, so _____

dresses is a good estimate.

$\dfrac{\text{dresses}}{\text{hr}}$ ___ ___

_____

5. mixed numbers and decimal

3 hr 30 min $= 3\dfrac{30}{60}$ hr $=$

_____

_____

6. 40 days $\times \dfrac{\text{hr}}{\text{days}} =$

Is 40 days longer than the 1400 hours? _____

_____

7. $20x + 50 = 250$

$x =$ _____

8. $\dfrac{x}{3} + 5 = 7$

$x =$ _____

9. *Collect like terms first.*

$x + 5 + x = 25$

$x =$ _____

10. $14 - m = 24$

$m =$ _____

11. See *"Number Cube Chart" on page 25 in the* Student Reference Guide.

    a. {_____, _____, _____, _____, _____,

    _____, _____, _____, _____, _____,

    _____}

    b. 2 and 12 are least likely because there is

    only _____ way to make them. _____ is

    most likely because there are the most

    ways to make it.

Use work area.

12.

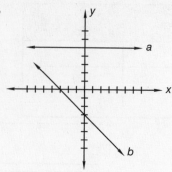

a. intersects y-axis at 5

b. $slope = \dfrac{rise}{run}$

c. See page 18 in the Student Reference Guide.

a. line _____

b. _____

c. quadrant _____

---

13. • Plot $\triangle ABC$: $A(2,1)$, $B(1, 4)$, $C(2, 2)$
    • Count the distance from each vertex to the x-axis.
    • Plot a point that distance **below** the x-axis.

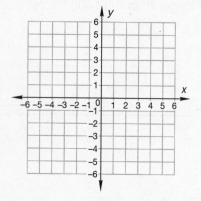

$A'(2, -1)$ $B'(1, \quad)$ $C'(2, \quad)$

Use work area.

14.

14 in.

a. area rounded to nearest square inch
    Use 3.14 for π.

b. circumference
    Use $\dfrac{22}{7}$ for π.

a. _____

b. _____

---

15. volume
    Label the dimensions.

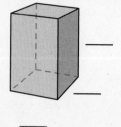

_____

16. surface area

    2(area of front)
    2(area of side)
    + 2(area of top)

17. $4(x - 4) - 2(x - 6) =$

18. $b + h + b + h =$

19. $5^{-2} = \dfrac{1}{5^2} =$

20. $(-3) - (-7) =$

21. *Subtract the exponents.*

$\dfrac{(4.2 \times 10^7)}{(1.4 \times 10^2)} =$

22. $\left(\dfrac{2}{3}\right)^2 + \dfrac{2}{3} =$

23. a. decimal: _____

$\dfrac{19}{20} =$

percent: _____

b. Test scores are usually reported as

p_____

Use work area.

24. a. *similar figures*

b. scale factor

c. $\dfrac{x}{2} =$

a. $a =$ _____

b. _____

c. $x =$ _____

25. Simplify and write with positive exponents.

$\dfrac{x^{-1}y^2}{xy} = \dfrac{y^2}{x^2 y} =$

26.

27 in.

36 in.

27. $10^{-5} = 1.0 \times 10^{-5} =$

_____

28. What type of quadrilateral is this?

_____ t

29. a. $7x^2 = 7$

b. $|x| - 15 = 5$

a. $x =$ _____, _____

b. $x =$ _____, _____

30. Label each view as front, right, or top.

Build the solid out of blocks if you need help.

Use work area.

• Solving Problems Using Measures of Central Tendency (page 360)

Name _____

Teacher Note:

• Review "Statistics" on page 23 in the *Student Reference Guide.*

We can choose the measure of central tendency (mean, median, or mode) that best summarizes a data set.

• A popular television show received these ratings over its season.

   TV Ratings

   16.0, 15.2, 15.3, 15.5, 15.7, 15.1, 14.8, 15.6, 15.0, 14.6, 14.4, 15.8, 15.3, 14.7, 14.2, 15.7, 14.9, 15.4, 14.9, 16.1

• The **mean** of a data set is the *sum of the numbers* divided by the *number of numbers.*

   The mean for the TV ratings is $\dfrac{\text{sum of numbers}}{\text{number of numbers}} = \dfrac{304.2}{20} = 15.21$

• We can display the data on a **line plot**. Each data point is shown with an X above its value on the line plot.

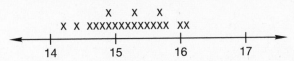

• The **median** of a data set is the *middle number* after the data are put in order from least to greatest. In order, the TV ratings are

   14.2, 14.4, 14.6, 14.7, 14.8, 14.9, 14.9, 15.0, 15.1, **15.2, 15.3,** 15.3, 15.4, 15.5, 15.6, 15.7, 15.7, 15.8, 16.0, 16.1

   There are an even number of data in this set so there are two middle numbers: 15.2 and 15.3.
   The median is the mean of the two middle numbers: 15.25

• The **mode** is the *most common number* in a data set. Look at the line plot again. Three numbers occur twice and all the other numbers occur only once.

   The TV ratings have three modes: 14.9, 15.3, and 15.7.

• The **range** is the *difference* between the highest and the lowest numbers in a data set.

   The range for the TV ratings is 16.1 − 14.2 = 1.9

• A **histogram** is a special kind of bar chart for displaying the number of data in different *intervals*.

   First, we make a **frequency chart** for the intervals selected, and tally the number of data points in each interval. Then we show the intervals with bars in the histogram.

TV Ratings

Intervals	Tally
14.0 - 14.4	II
14.5 - 14.9	ЖЖТ
15.0 - 15.4	ЖЖТI
15.5 - 15.9	ЖЖТ
16.0 - 16.4	II

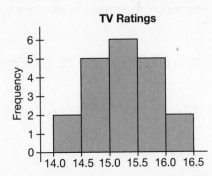

• The histogram shows that 6 data points fall within the interval 15.0–15.4 and this interval has more ratings than any other interval. In other words, the ratings tend to fall in the interval 15.0–15.4.

Practice Set (page 364)

The amount of electricity (in kWh) used by one household each month of a year is listed below:
420, 450, 480, 440, 420, 490, 580, 590, 510, 450, 430, 480

a. Make a line plot of the data by placing an X for each data point above the number line

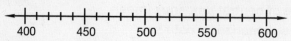

400   450   500   550   600

b. Find the mean to the nearest whole number:

_____

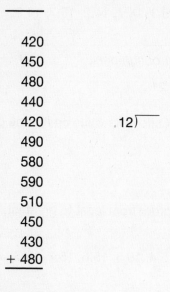

420
450
480
440
420   .12)‾‾‾‾‾
490
580
590
510
450
430
+ 480
_____

Find the median: _____

There are an even number of data, so average the two middle numbers.

420 , _____ , _____ , _____ , _____ , 450 , _____ , _____ , _____ , _____ , _____ , 590

Find the mode: _____

Find the range: _____
greatest minus least

c. Which measure would you report to describe the **difference** between the most electricity used and

the least electricity used? _____

d. Which measure would you report to someone who wanted to compute the total amount of electricity
used in the year?

The _____ because the total over the year is 12 times this number.

e. If you replaced the 590 in the data set with 500, would the mean change? _____ Would the median

change? _____

Would the mode change? _____

© 2007 Harcourt Achieve Inc.

Practice Set (continued) (page 364)

f. The data set below is the temperature for every day in February. Complete the data set so that the values fit the statement "Half of the days of February were colder than 30°F."

20 , 20 , 20 , 22 , _____ , _____ , _____ , 24 , 25 , _____ , _____ , 27 , 27 , 28 ,

30 , 30 , 30 , _____ , 31 , 31 , _____ , _____ , _____ , 33 , 33 , 33 , 34 , _____

Find the mean: _____   Find the median: _____

Find the mode: _____   Find the range: _____

Written Practice (page 364)

1.

	Ratio	Actual Count
Adults		a
Children		

_____

2.

	Ratio	Actual Count
Starters		
Alternates		a

_____

3. 20
$\frac{}{1}$

_____

4. Each angle equals how many degrees?

$x + x + x = 180°$
$ = 180°$

_____

5. cm to m

$$\frac{490 \text{ cm}}{1} \cdot \frac{\text{m}}{\text{cm}} =$$

_____

6. Use the graph to fill in the chart.

Time	°F
10:00	
11:00	
12:00	
1:00	
2:00	

mean: _____

median: _____

mode: _____

Half the time it was warmer than _____°F.

Use work area.

7. $-2x = 16$

$$\underline{-2x} = \underline{16}$$

$x =$ _____

8. $\dfrac{w}{2} = 1.5$

$(\quad)\left(\dfrac{w}{2}\right) = (1.5)(\quad)$

$w =$ _____

9. $-z + 3 = 7$

$-z + 3 - \quad = 7 - $

$-z = $

$\dfrac{-z}{-1} = $ ___

$z =$ _____

10. $23 - p = 73$

$23 - p - \quad = 73 - $

$-p = $

$\dfrac{-p}{1} = $ ___

$p =$ _____

11. Round.

4.9 m _____

$\dfrac{\quad\text{m}}{\quad} \cdot \dfrac{3.3 \text{ ft}}{1 \text{ m}} =$

A 2 ft **B** 8 ft **C** 16 ft **D** 20 ft

_____

12.

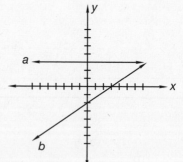

a. $slope = \dfrac{rise}{run}$

b. Line *b* intersects the *y*-axis at what point?

c. In which quadrant do the lines intersect?

a. _____

b. (0,) _____

c. quadrant ___

13. Graph $y = -x$ and $(4, -5)$

x	y
-3	
0	
3	

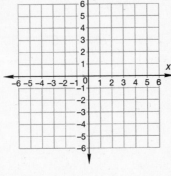

Is $(4, -5)$ on the line? _____

Use work area.

14. a. area

b. circumference

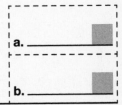

18 in.

Leave π as π.

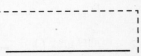

a. _____

b. _____

15. volume

4 ft by 3 ft by 2 ft

_____

16. decimal number

$1.0 \times 10^{-4} =$

_____

17. $3(x - y) - 2(x + y) =$

_____

18. $5x^2 - 3x - 2x^2 + 4x =$

_____

19. $\dfrac{2^3 \cdot 2^0}{2^1 \cdot 2^2} =$

_____

20. $\dfrac{x^3 y^3 z}{xy^3 z^3} =$

_____

21. $-5 - (-7) =$

_____

22. Add the exponents.

$(1.5 \times 10^3)(1.5 \times 10^{-2})$

_____ × _____

23. a. decimal

98% = _____

reduced fraction

98% = _____

b. The _____ is best because I can divide $50,000 by 50.

---

24. Find $\frac{x}{2m}$

when $x = 5$

$m = -5$

---

25. Write with positive exponents:

$6x^{-1}y\,y\,z^{-2} =$ _____

---

26. g to kg

$10,000g \cdot$ _____ =

kg to lb   (1kg $\approx$ 2.2lb)

_____ $\cdot \dfrac{lb}{1\ kg} =$

Sergio's claim _____ reasonable.

Use work area.

---

27. Sample space _____ is better because I can find the

p_____ using it.

$P(H \text{ and } T) =$ _____

Use work area.

---

28. Mixed number and decimal

5 ft 3 in. $= 5\dfrac{}{12}$ ft $=$

© 2007 Harcourt Achieve Inc.

29. a. $x^2 + 2 = 27$

$x^2 + 2 - = 27 - $

$x^2 = $

b. $-5\,|x| = -15$

$\dfrac{-5\,|x|}{-5} = \dfrac{-15}{-5}$

$|x| = $

a. $x = $ _____ , _____

b. $x = $ _____ , _____

30. $9\dfrac{3}{4} \longrightarrow$ _____ in.

$4\dfrac{3}{4} \longrightarrow$ _____ in.

$4\dfrac{1}{4} \longrightarrow$ _____ in.

a. volume

b. surface area

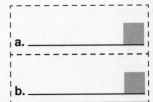

a. _____

b. _____

• Angle Relationships (page 367)

Name _____

A straight line (or straight angle) measures 180°.

- Two angles whose measures total 180° are **supplementary angles.**

Teacher Note:
- Refer students to "Angle Pairs" on page 27 and "Transversals" on page 32 in the *Student Reference Guide.*

- Intersecting lines form pairs of adjacent angles and pairs of opposite angles.

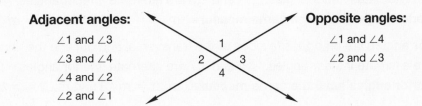

Adjacent angles:
∠1 and ∠3
∠3 and ∠4
∠4 and ∠2
∠2 and ∠1

Opposite angles:
∠1 and ∠4
∠2 and ∠3

- **Adjacent angles** share a common vertex and a common side. These angles do not overlap. Adjacent angles form a straight line, so adjacent angles are supplementary.
  The measures of adjacent angles total 180°.
  m∠1 + m∠3 = 180° because they form a straight line.

- **Opposite angles** are a pair of non-adjacent angles formed by intersecting lines. Opposite angles are also called **vertical angles.**
  Vertical angles have the same measure. m∠1 = m∠4 and m∠2 = m∠3

- The sum of the angle measures in a triangle is 180°.

- Two angles whose measures total 90° are **complementary angles.**
  m∠5 + m∠6 + 90° = 180°
  m∠5 + m∠6 = 90° so ∠5 and ∠6 are complementary.
  The measures of the two acute angles in a right triangle total 90°.

- When two parallel lines are intersected by a third line, corresponding angles and alternate angles are formed.
- The line that intersects the parallel lines is called a **transversal.** In this figure, line *t* is the transversal and lines *p* and *q* are parallel. All the acute angles have the same measure. All the obtuse angles have the same measure.

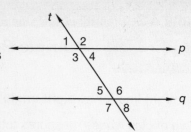

- **Corresponding angles** are on the *same side* of the transversal and in *matching positions* on the parallel lines.

  ∠1 and ∠5 are corresponding acute angles. ∠2 and ∠4 are corresponding obtuse angles.
  Corresponding angles have the same measure. m∠1 = m∠5 and m∠2 = m∠4

- **Alternate interior angles** are on *opposite sides* of the transversal and *inside* the parallel lines.

  ∠3 and ∠6 are alternate interior angles. ∠4 and ∠5 are alternate interior angles.
  Alternate interior angles have the same measure. m∠3 = m∠6 and m∠4 = m∠5

- **Alternate exterior angles** are on *opposite sides* of the transversal and *outside* the parallel lines.

  ∠1 and ∠8 are alternate interior angles. ∠2 and ∠7 are alternate interior angles.
  Alternate interior angles have the same measure. m∠1 = m∠8 and m∠2 = m∠7

Practice Set (page 371)

Refer to Figure 1 for exercises **a–c.**

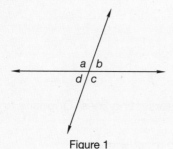

Figure 1

m∠b = _____
Vertical angles have the same measure (congruent).

m∠c = m∠a

m∠c = _____

m∠d = N_____

Refer to Figure 2 for exercises **d–f.**

a. Name two pairs of **vertical angles.**

∠a and ∠_____

∠b and ∠_____

b. Name four pairs of **supplementary angles.**

∠a and ∠_____

∠a and ∠_____

∠b and ∠_____

∠b and ∠_____

c. If m∠a is 110°, then what are the measures of angles b, c, and d?
Adjacent angles add to 180° (supplementary).

m∠a + m∠b = 180°
110° + m∠b = 180°

d. Which angle is the complement of m∠g?

∠_____
Complementary angles add to 90°.
The measures of the two acute angles in a right triangle total 90°.

e. Which angle is the **supplement** of m∠g?

∠_____
Supplementary angles form a straight line.

Practice Set (continued) (page 371)

f. If m∠h is 130°, then what are the measures of ∠g and ∠f?

m∠g + m∠h = 180°

m∠g + 130° = 180°

m∠g = _____

m∠g + m∠f = 90°

_____ + m∠f = 90°

m∠f = _____

In figure 3 parallel lines *R* and *S* are cut by transversal *T*. Refer to this figure for exercises **g–j**.

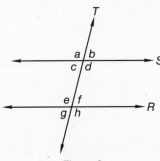

Figure 3

g. Which angle **corresponds** to ∠f? ∠_____

Corresponding angles are on the same side of the transversal in matching positions on the parallel lines.

h. Name two pairs of **alternate interior angles**.

Alternate interior angles are on opposite sides of the transversal and inside the parallel lines.

∠c and ∠_____

∠d and ∠_____

i. Name two pairs of **alternate exterior angles**.

Alternate exterior angles are on opposite sides of the transversal and outside the parallel lines.

∠a and ∠_____

∠b and ∠_____

j. If m∠a is 105°, what is the measure of m∠f?

Corresponding angles have the same measure.

m∠a = ∠e

m∠e = _____

Adjacent angles add to 180°.

m∠e + m∠f = 180°

_____ + m∠f = 180°

m∠f = _____

1.

	Ratio	Actual Count
Stars		
Stripes		s

2. yd to ft

$$\frac{40 \text{ yd.}}{1} \cdot \underline{\quad} =$$

3. flour
cranberries ——— $\dfrac{}{49}$

4. Put the data in order.

——, ——, ——, ——, ——, ——, ——, ——, ——, ——,

a.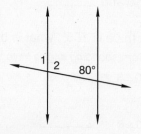

```
   2   3   4   5   6   7
```

b. range: ——   mean: ——

median: ——   mode: ——

c. ——

Use work area.

5. *corresponding angles*

Corresponding angles have the

same —————.

m∠1 = —————

6. *adjacent angles*

m∠1 + m∠2 = 180°

Adjacent angles are ˢ—————————.

m∠2 = —————

7. $3 = 2x + 3$

x = —————

8. *Collect like terms.*

$3x + 7 - x = 21$

x = —————

9. $20 - x = 1$

Libby watched —— birds. All but

—— bird flew away. How many birds

—————?

x = —————

10. $-2w = -3$

w = —————

11. $xyx^0y^{-2}x^1 =$ _____

12.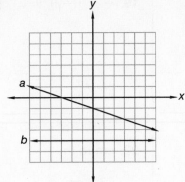

b. _____

c. line

d. quadrant _____

13. $y = x - 2$

x	y
−2	
0	
2	

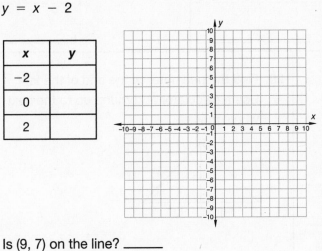

Is (9, 7) on the line? _____

14.

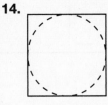

a. diameter

b. area

c. Area of square − Area of circle

a. _____

b. _____

c. _____

Use work area.

15. Units are inches.

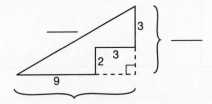

a. Area of triangle − Area of rectangle

b. perimeter of figure

a. _____

b. _____

16. $-(x - y) - (x + y) =$

17. $2x^2 - 3x - x^2 + 5 =$

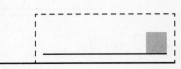

18. *Subtract the exponents.*

$$\frac{2.9 \times 10^{12}}{2.9 \times 10^3} =$$

_____ × _____

19. $-2 - (-2) =$

_____

20. $\frac{x^9 y}{x^8 y} =$

_____

21. $\left(-\frac{1}{2}\right)^3 + \frac{7}{8} =$

_____

22. cm to m

76.2 cm · —— =

Write in scientific notation.
shift ←

_____ × _____

23. 100%
   a. decimal
   b. reduced fraction

a. _____

b. _____

24. *Convert to in.*

cabin: 20ft · $\frac{\text{in.}}{\text{ft}}$ = _____

trees: 30ft · $\frac{\text{in.}}{\text{ft}}$ = _____

a. scale = $\frac{}{6}$ =

b. $\frac{}{} = \frac{360}{t}$

a. _____

b. _____

25. Find the perimeter of the end of the tent. Use a calculator and round up to the next whole meter.

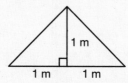
1 m
1 m   1 m

_____

26. $\frac{x}{12} = \frac{12}{9}$

$x =$ _____

27. $\frac{x^2}{2} = 18$

$x =$ _____ , _____

28. $-3|x| = -3$

$x =$ _____ , _____

29. $\frac{m}{5} = 0.2$

$m =$ _____

30. Choose the correct solid that fits the views.

A  B   C

_____

• Nets of Prisms, Cylinders, Pyramids, and Cones (page 375)

Name _____

Many geometric solids have one or more bases and lateral sides or lateral surfaces.

- Imagine cutting open a solid and spreading the bases and sides out flat. The two-dimensional figure created is a **net**.

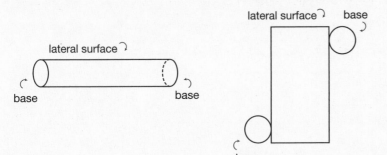

Teacher Notes:
- Review Hint #49, "Faces on a cube."
- Review "Geometric Solids" on page 30 in the *Student Reference Guide*.
- ETA Relational GeoSolids manipulatives may help students understand the concepts in this lesson.
- Students will need paper, scissors, and tape to complete this lesson.
- The Activity on 📖 page 377 is optional.

- A net can be folded up and taped together to form the geometric solid.

- To draw a net, draw all the lateral sides and the bases attached to each another.

  The bases will be congruent shapes.

  The lateral sides will not always be congruent.

Practice Set (page 378)

a. This net has one circular base and part of a circle for its lateral surface.

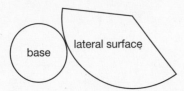

The net can form which of the following solids? _____

   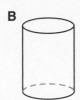

A   **B**   **C**

b. Complete the net for this cube by drawing two more square faces. *(There are many correct answers.)*

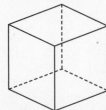   

Every face of a cube is a congruent square.

c. This figure is called a tetrahedron. All of its faces are congruent equilateral triangles.

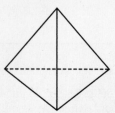

Complete the net for this tetrahedron by drawing three triangles.

d. This figure is a triangular prism.

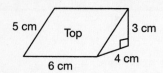

Label the side lengths of the back, top, and right side views.

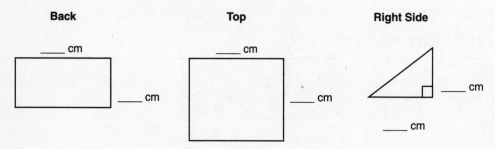

Back

_____ cm

_____ cm

Top

_____ cm

_____ cm

Right Side

_____ cm

_____ cm

Label the side lengths on this net of the triangular prism.

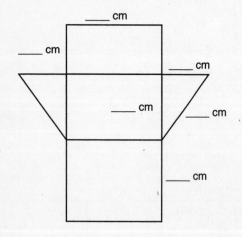

_____ cm

_____ cm

_____ cm

_____ cm

_____ cm

_____ cm

e. Trace the net you completed in exercise **c** on another piece of paper. Cut out the net, fold along the lines, and tape together to create a model of a tetrahedron.

1.

	Ratio	Actual Count
Debt		
Equity		e

_____ million

2. customers $\quad \underline{1} \quad \underline{3}$
min

$+ \quad \underline{5}$

_____

3.
$$\begin{array}{r} 105 \\ 97 \\ 96 \\ 99 \\ + 103 \end{array}$$
$$\overline{})\overline{}$$

The mean is _____. The total number of

pages is _____ times the mean.

Use work area.

4. $(-2)^2 + (-2)^3 =$

_____

5. $\dfrac{4}{3} = \dfrac{x}{1.5}$

_____

6. Find x.
First, find y.
Supplementary
$m\angle y + 105° = 180°$

$m\angle y = \underline{}°$
Now find x.
Corresponding angles

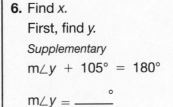

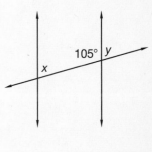

$\underline{x} =$ _____

7. $4 = -m + 11$

$\underline{m} =$ _____

8. $9x + 9 = 90$

Nine groups of students plus _____ more

group is _____ in all. How many students are in

each group?

$\underline{x} =$ _____

9. $-5 - x = -9$

$x =$ _____

10. *Collect like terms.*

$3y - y - 1 = 9$

$y =$ _____

11. top, right, or front?

a. _____

b. _____

c. _____

12. Both are correct. Roger showed the possible outcomes with their p_____. Simon just showed the possible o_____.

Use work area.

13. $A = \pi r^2$
Use 3.14 for π.

_____

14. $y = \frac{4}{5}x - 2$

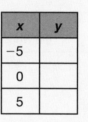

x	y
−5	
0	
5	

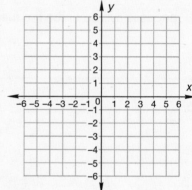

Is (5, 2) on the line?

_____

Use work area.

15. perimeter and area

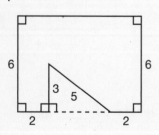

a. _____

b. _____

16. a. unit rate: $\dfrac{\text{mi}}{1 \text{ hr}}$

b. $100 \text{ mi} \cdot \dfrac{1 \text{ hr}}{\text{mi}} =$

a. _____

b. _____

17. ft to yd

$$440 \text{ ft} \cdot \frac{\text{yd}}{\text{ft}} =$$

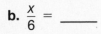

18. volume

80 in. by 33 in. by 5 in.

$244\overline{)}$

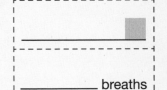

_____ breaths

19. $9^{-2}x^{-1}y^0x =$ _____

20. $\dfrac{x^5m^2}{mx} =$

21. $\left(\dfrac{1}{3}\right)^2 \div \dfrac{2}{3} =$

22. $0.05\overline{)1.2}$

23. a. decimal

$\dfrac{1}{100} =$

percent

$\dfrac{1}{100} =$

b. $\dfrac{1}{100}$ ◯ 0.009

Use work area.

24. Factor.

a. $6x - 15 =$ _____ (   )

b. $x^2 - x =$ _____ (   )

a. _____ **b.** _____

25. a. scale factor

b. $\dfrac{x}{6} =$ _____

26. mixed number and decimal

$$1 \text{ min } 18 \text{ sec} = 1\frac{}{60} \text{ min} =$$

27. (   )(−5) =

_____

28. $100 = 1.0 \times 10^2$

$(1.0 \times 10^2)(50 \times 10^{-6}) = $ _____ $\times$ _____

$\dfrac{2}{10^3} = 2.0 \times 10^{\text{—}}$

Which is thicker?

_____

29. a. $2(x + b) - (-x - b) =$

  b. $2x + 1 - 3x + 4 =$

a. _____

b. _____

30. Which graph shows decreasing heart rate

with increasing age? _____

Is the graph proportional? _____

Is it a line?
Does it intersect the origin?

Use work area.

• **The Slope-Intercept Equation of a Line** (page 382)

Name _____

An equation written in slope-intercept form tells us the slope and y-intercept of a line.

• The **slope** of a line is $\dfrac{\text{rise}}{\text{run}}$.

• The **y-intercept** is the point where the line crosses the y-axis.

• The slope-intercept form of an equation is a special form that uses these two numbers.

Slope-intercept form

$$y = mx + b$$

m is the slope. *b* is the y-intercept.

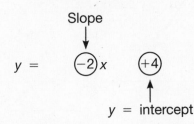

The slope is −2. The line crosses the y-axis at +4.

Example: Change this equation to slope-intercept form.

$-2x + y = -3$	Given equation
$-2x + y + 2x = -3 + 2x$	Added 2x to both sides
$y = -3 + 2x$	Simplified
$y = 2x - 3$	Commutative Property

Example: Graph $y = 2x - 3$ using slope and y-intercept.

The slope, *m*, is +2 or $\dfrac{+2}{+1}$.

The y-intercept, *b*, is −3.

1. Mark a point at the y-intercept. (0, −3)

2. From that point, move right 1 unit (run: +1) and up 2 units (rise: +2) and mark another point. (1, −1)

3. Draw a line connecting the two points.

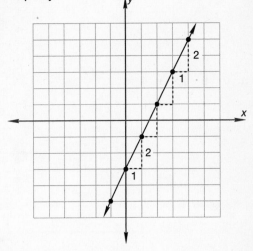

Practice Set (page 386)

a. Which of the following equations is written in slope-intercept form? _____

A $x = 2y + 3$ **B** $y + 2x = 3$ **C** $y = 2x + 3$

b. What is the slope and y-intercept of the graph of this equation?

$y = mx + b$

slope: _____   y-intercept: _____

Write equations for lines **c–f** in slope-intercept form. $y = mx + b$

c. slope: _____   y-intercept: _____

    $y =$ _____$x +$ _____

d. slope: _____   y-intercept: _____

    $y =$ _____$x +$ _____

e. slope: _____   y-intercept: _____

    $y =$ _____

f. slope: _____   y-intercept: _____

    $y =$ _____

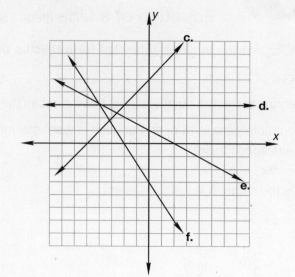

Graph the following equations using the given slope and y-intercept.

g. $y = x - 2$

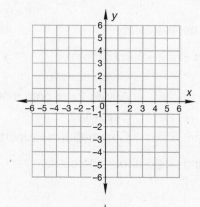

h. $y = -2x + 4$

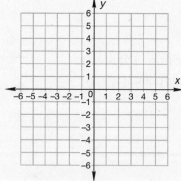

i. $y = \frac{1}{2}x - 2$

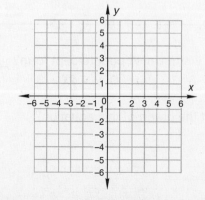

1.

	Ratio	Actual Count
Arable		a
Non-arable		
Total		

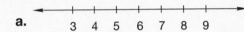

2. lamp $\dfrac{1}{\$} \quad \dfrac{8}{}$

bulbs $\dfrac{}{\$} \quad \dfrac{8}{}$

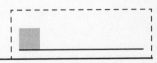

---

3. Put the data in order.

____, ____, ____, ____, ____, ____, ____, ____, ____

a.

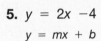
3 4 5 6 7 8 9

b. range: _____ mean: _____

median: _____ mode: _____

Use work area.

4. *Alternate interior angles are congruent.*

m∠x = _____

---

5. $y = 2x - 4$

$y = mx + b$

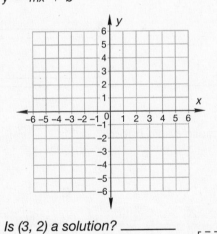

Is (3, 2) a solution? _____

Use work area.

6. Use 3.14159 for π

a. area

b. $C = 2\pi r$

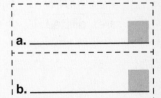

a. _____

b. _____

---

7. a. unit rate: $\dfrac{cm}{yr}$

b. one million = 1.0×10^6

$1.0 \times 10^6 \text{ yr} \cdot \dfrac{cm}{yr} \cdot \dfrac{1\ m}{100\ cm} \cdot \dfrac{1\ km}{1000\ m} = $ _____ km

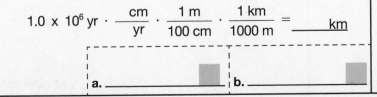

a. _____ b. _____

8. m to km

$1600 m \cdot \dfrac{}{m} = $

_____

---

9. $\dfrac{0.6}{x} = \dfrac{0.12}{5}$

$x =$ _____

10. Collect like terms first.

$2x - x = 1.5$

$x =$ _____

11. $0.6x + 1.2 = 3$

$x =$ _____

12. Collect like terms first.

$7m - 9m = -12$

$m =$ _____

13. a. decimal

$\dfrac{2}{5} =$

percent

$\dfrac{2}{5} =$

b. Which form is a ratio? _____

Use work area.

14. Factor:

a. $2x^2 + 14x =$

b. $15x - 20 =$

a. _____

b. _____

15. The ratio of the areas of similar figures is the scale factor **squared**.

$\dfrac{\text{area original}}{\text{area dilated}} = \dfrac{1}{2^2} =$

_____

16. The figure has two round bases. Which solid could it form? _____

A 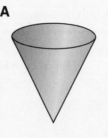 B  C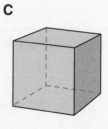

Name that solid. c _____

Use work area.

17. Distribute first.

$-5(x + 2) - 2x + 9 =$

_____

18. $(-4)^2 - (-4)^3 =$

_____

19. $\dfrac{(-15)(-12)}{(-15) - (-12)} =$

_____

20. $\dfrac{wr^2d}{r^3d} =$

_____

21. $2 \cdot 1\dfrac{1}{2} - \left(1\dfrac{1}{2}\right)^2 =$

_____

22. $\dfrac{6}{8} = \dfrac{9}{x}$

$x =$ _____

23. $\dfrac{4.8 \times 10^7}{1.6 \times 10^4} =$

_____ × _____

24. $\sqrt{10^2 - 8^2} =$

_____

25. Express with positive exponents.

$a^0b^1ab^{-1}c^{-1} =$ _____

_____

26. least to greatest

$0.3, \dfrac{1}{3}, 0.33, 3\%$

_____, _____, _____, _____

Use work area.

27. The quadrilateral on the right is a dilation with a scale factor of 1.5. Label the side lengths.

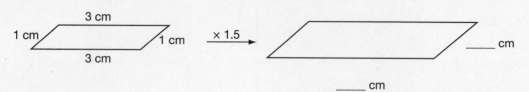

_____ cm

× 1.5 →

_____ cm

_____ cm

28.

∠x and 140° are supplementary.

m∠x + 140° = 180°

∠x and ∠y are complimentary.

m∠x + m∠y = 90°

∠y and ∠z are supplementary.

m∠y + m∠z =

x = _____

y = _____

z = _____

29. (3, 4) and (−4, −3)

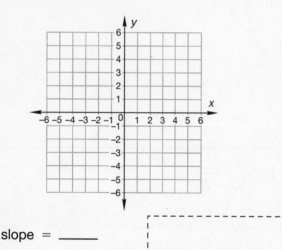

slope = _____

30. Graph _____ is a proportion because

it is a straight _____ and it intersects

the _____.

• Operations with Small Numbers in Scientific Notation (page 389)

A number written in scientific notation has a coefficient and a power of 10.

Teacher Note:
• Review "Place Value" on page 11 and "Scientific Notation" on page 21 in the *Student Reference Guide*.

• To multiply numbers in scientific notation:

    1. Multiply the coefficients.

    2. Multiply the powers of 10. (**Add** the exponents).

    3. If the coefficient has more than one whole-number place, write the coefficient in scientific notation and then combine the powers of 10.

    Example: $(4 \times 10^{-6})(5 \times 10^{-4})$

$(4 \times 10^{-6})(5 \times 10^{-4})$	Given
$(4 \times 5)(10^{-6} \times 10^{-4})$	Associative and Commutative Properties
20×10^{-10}	Simplified (but *incorrect form*)
$2.0 \times 10^{1} \times 10^{-10}$	$20 = 2.0 \times 10^{1}$
2.0×10^{-9}	Proper form ($10^{1} \times 10^{-10} = 10^{-9}$)

• To divide numbers in scientific notation:

    1. Divide the coefficients.

    2. Divide the powers of 10. (**Subtract** the exponents carefully).

    3. If the coefficient has fewer than one whole-number place, write the coefficient in scientific notation and then combine the powers of 10.

    Example: $\dfrac{4 \times 10^{-8}}{5 \times 10^{-2}}$

$\dfrac{4 \times 10^{-8}}{5 \times 10^{-2}}$	Given
0.8×10^{-6}	Simplified (but *incorrect form*)
$8.0 \times 10^{-1} \times 10^{-6}$	$0.8 = 8.0 \times 10^{-1}$
8.0×10^{-7}	Proper form ($10^{-1} \times 10^{-6} = 10^{-7}$)

Practice Set (page 390)

Find each product or quotient.

a. $(4 \times 10^{10})(2 \times 10^{-6})$

    8×10 _____

b. $(1.2 \times 10^{-6})(3 \times 10^{3})$

    _____ $\times 10$ _____

c. $(1.5 \times 10^{-5})(3 \times 10^{-2})$

    _____ $\times 10$ _____

d. $(7.5 \times 10^{-3})(2 \times 10^{-4})$

$15 \times 10\text{——}$

$1.5 \times 10^1 \times 10\text{——}$

$1.5 \times 10\text{——}$

e. $\dfrac{7.5 \times 10^5}{3 \times 10^{-2}}$

$2.5 \times 10\text{——}$

f. $\dfrac{4.8 \times 10^{-3}}{3 \times 10^2}$

$\text{——} \times 10\text{——}$

g. $\dfrac{8.1 \times 10^{-4}}{3 \times 10^{-7}}$

$\text{——} \times 10\text{——}$

h. $\dfrac{1.2 \times 10^{-6}}{3 \times 10^{-4}}$

$0.4 \times 10\text{——}$

$4.0 \times 10^{-1} \times 10\text{——}$

$4 \times 10\text{——}$

i. A dollar bill weighs about 0.001 kg. What is the weight of 1,000,000 dollar bills? Express each number in scientific notation and perform the calculation in scientific notation.

$0.001 = 1 \times 10\text{——}$ $1,000,000 = 1 \times 10\text{——}$

$(1 \times 10\text{——})(1 \times 10\text{——}) = 1 \times 10\text{——}$

Written Practice   (page 391)

1.

	Ratio	Actual Count
Spring or Summer		s
Autumn or Winter		
Total		

2. 60% of 365

4. Put the data in order.

$\text{——}, \text{——}, \text{——}, \text{——}, \text{——},$

$\text{——}, \text{——}, \text{——}$

3.

	Ratio	Actual Count
Completed		
Not Completed		n
Total	100	

a.

50 55 60 65 70 75 80 85 90 95 100

b. range: _____ mean: _____

median: _____ mode: _____ , _____

c. The most common amounts that people donated were $____ and $____.

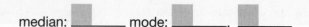

Use work area.

5. $\dfrac{6}{7} = \dfrac{x}{10.5}$

$x = $ _____

6.

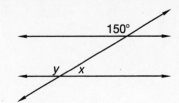
150°

First find *y*.

Corresponding angles are congruent.

$m\angle y = $ _____°

Now find *x*.

Adjacent angles are supplementary.

$m\angle y + m\angle x = 180°$

$m\angle x = $ _____

7. a. sample space

{AA, AC, AA, AB, AA, AB, AA, AC,

_____, _____, _____, _____, _____,

_____, _____, _____}

b. P(*A* at least once) =

Use work area.

8. Graph $y = x - 1$ and $(-2, -3)$.

$y = mx + b$

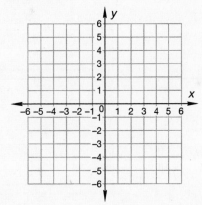

Is $(-2, -3)$ a solution? _____

Use work area.

9. *over, over, up*

$0.3m - 0.3 = 0.3$

$m = $ _____

10. *Collect like terms first.*

$4x + 7x = 99$

$x = $ _____

11. $\dfrac{2}{3}x + \dfrac{1}{2} = \dfrac{2}{3}$

_x_ = _____

12. _Collect like terms first._

$$7 = -2p - 5p$$

_p_ = _____

13.

6 m

Use 3.14 for π.

circumference to nearest meter

_____

14. area to nearest meter

_____

15. $x(x + 2) + 2(x + 2) =$

_____

16.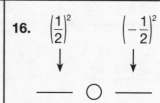

$$\left(\dfrac{1}{2}\right)^2 \qquad \left(-\dfrac{1}{2}\right)^2$$

_____ ◯ _____

_____

17. a. $\dfrac{\text{mi}}{\text{hr}} \quad \dfrac{}{3} \quad \dfrac{}{5}$

b. unit rate: $\dfrac{\text{mi}}{1\ \text{hr}}$

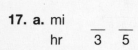

a. _____

b. _____

18. ft to yd

$$5280\ \text{ft} \cdot \dfrac{\text{yd}}{\text{ft}} =$$

_____

19. a. Label the sides of this triangular prism.

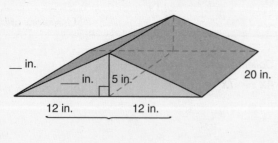

___ in.

___ in. 5 in.

20 in.

12 in.   12 in.

_____

b. Draw the second base on this net.

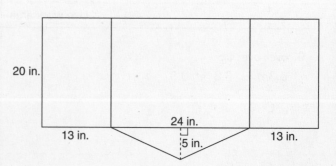

20 in.

13 in.   24 in.   13 in.

5 in.

Use work area.

20. a.

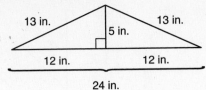

13 in.   13 in.
5 in.
12 in.   12 in.
24 in.

(volume of prism) = (area of a base) × (prism length).

Area of base $= \frac{1}{2}bh = \frac{1}{2}(24 \text{ in.})(5 \text{ in.}) =$

Area of base × length =

b. The surface area is the perimeter of a base × the length plus the area of the bases.

perimeter of base = _____ in.

(perimeter)(length) = _____ in.
Now add 2 × area
of base.

21. $\dfrac{b^3 r^4}{mb^3 r^2} =$

_____

22. $\sqrt{\dfrac{4}{9}}$ $\dfrac{\sqrt{4}}{\sqrt{9}}$

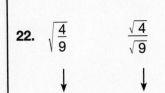

_____ ◯ _____

_____

23. $\dfrac{11}{12}$

a. percent

b. decimal

a. _____

b. _____

a. _____

b. _____

24. The relationship looks like this:

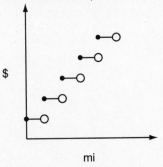

$

mi

Is it continuous?
Is it proportional?

So it must be _____.

Use work area.

25. a. {_____, _____, _____, _____, _____,

_____, _____, _____, _____}

b. *P*(A at least once) =

c. *P*(not A) =

Use work area.

26. Find $-b + \sqrt{b^2 - 4ac}$

when $a = 3$

$b = 4$

$c = 1$

_____

27. $y = mx + b$

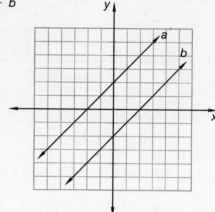

a. $m =$

$b =$

b. $y =$ ____ $x +$ ____

a. $y =$ _____

b. $y =$ _____

28. $y = mx + b$

slope $= \dfrac{1}{2}$

y-intercept $= -1$

$y =$ _____

29. $9x^2 = 36$

$x =$ ____ , ____

30. 📖 Count the faces you can see.

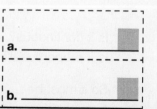

a. _____

b. _____

• Solving Percent Problems with Equations (page 394)

Name _____

Teacher Note:
• Review "Fraction-Decimal-Percent Equivalents" and "Fraction ↔ Decimal ↔ Percent" on page 13 in the *Student Reference Guide*.

Percent word problems can be "translated" into math language.

"Of" means **multiply** ($\times$).

"Is" or "was" means **equal** ($=$).

Use a variable for the missing number.

• Before solving the equation, convert the percent to a reduced fraction or a decimal.

Fractions are usually easier.

Use a decimal if any number given in the problem is a decimal.

Example: Thirty-two ounces is 25% of a gallon. How many ounces is a gallon?

$$25\% = \frac{1}{4}$$

32 oz is 25% of a gallon

$$\downarrow \quad \downarrow \quad \downarrow \quad \downarrow \quad \downarrow$$

$$32 \quad = \quad \frac{1}{4} \quad \times \quad g$$

$$32 = \frac{1}{4}g$$

$$\frac{4}{1} \cdot 32 = \frac{4}{1} \cdot \frac{1}{4}g$$

$$g = 128$$

• You may use a calculator for decimal percent problems.

• To solve a problem that asks for a percent, translate the missing percent as "*P*."

Example: Blanca correctly answered 23 of 25 questions. What percent of the questions did she answer correctly?

What percent of 25 is 23?

$$P \cdot 25 = 23$$

$$P = \frac{23}{25} = \frac{92}{100} = 92\%$$

Practice Set (page 396)

Solve by writing and solving equations.

a. Six percent of $4500 is how much money? _____

Change to a fraction.

$$6\% = \frac{6}{100} = \frac{3}{50}$$

$$\frac{3}{50} \times \$4500 = \$270$$

Explain why your answer is reasonable.

6% is between 10% and 5%. _____% of $4500 is $450, so _____% is $225.
My answer is between those numbers.

b. Twenty percent of what number is 40? _____

$$20\% = \frac{20}{100} =$$

( )$n = 40$

c. How much is a 15% tip on a $13.25 meal? Round your answer to the nearest dime. _____
Change to a decimal and use a calculator.

$$15\% = 0.15$$

$$t = \underline{\quad} \times \underline{\quad}$$

d. How much money is $16\frac{2}{3}\%$ of $1200? _____
Change to a fraction.

$$16\frac{2}{3}\% = \frac{1}{6}$$

$m = ($ $)($ $)$

e. What percent of 50 is 32? _____

$$P \times 50 = 32$$

$$P = \frac{32}{50} = \frac{\underline{\quad}}{100} = \underline{\quad}\%$$

f. Dixon made a $2,000 down payment on an $8,000 car. The down payment was what percent of

the price? _____

$$\underline{\quad} = P \times \underline{\quad}$$

$$P =$$

g. Kimo paid $24 for the shirt which was 75% of the regular price. What was the regular price? _____

$$75\% =$$

$$\underline{\quad} = ( )r$$

1.

	Ratio	Actual Count
Hydrogen		h
Oxygen		
Total		3×10^{23}

_____

2.

	Percent	Actual Count
Favored		f
Did not favor		
Total	100	

_____

3.

$
\overline{\quad} \quad \overline{\quad}
$

Checks   1   13

$10.00

+ _____

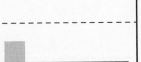

4. Put the data in order:

_____, _____, _____, _____, _____, _____, _____

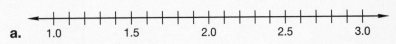

a. 1.0   1.5   2.0   2.5   3.0

b. mean: _____ median: _____ mode: _____ range: _____

c. Is mean or median greater? _____   Use work area.

5. a. 15, 27, _____   15, 18, _____

27, _____, _____   27, _____, _____

18, _____, _____   18, _____, _____

b. $P(\text{correct}) = \dfrac{\text{number correct}}{\text{total number}} =$

Use work area.

6. $\dfrac{x}{5} = \dfrac{14}{20}$

$x =$ _____

7. *Corresponding angles are congruent.*

$m\angle y =$ _____ °

Adjacent angles are supplementary.

$m\angle y + m\angle x = 180°$

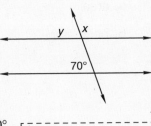

$m\angle x =$ _____

8. $y = \dfrac{1}{2}x - 2$

slope is _____

y-intercept at _____

$y = mx + b$

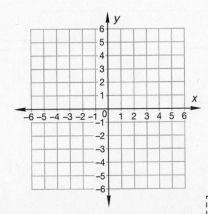

9. *Use 3 for π.*

_____ miles; I used 3 for _____, so to find the

d _____ I divided _____ by 3,

which is about _____ miles.

Use work area.

10. *Collect like terms first.*

$3m - 6 + 2m = 4$

m = _____

11. $x - 3x = 18$

x = _____

12. $\frac{2}{3}x + \frac{1}{2} = \frac{5}{6}$

x = _____

13. $\frac{y}{8} = 0.375$

y = _____

14. The beach ball _____ fit. I used 3 for π to estimate the diameter of the ball. It is about _____ in.

Use work area.

15.

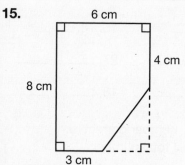

a. area

b. perimeter

a. _____

b. _____

16. $4\frac{1}{2}$ months $\cdot \dfrac{\text{in.}}{\text{month}} =$

_____

17. ft to in.

2.5 ft $\cdot$ _____ =

_____

18. $\left(\dfrac{2}{5}\right)^2 =$

_____

19. $\dfrac{ssr^5}{s^2r^4} =$

_____

20. $\dfrac{2}{15} + \dfrac{2}{5} \cdot \dfrac{1}{6} =$

_____

21. $x^2 + 2x + x + 2 =$

_____

22. a. decimal

55% =

fraction

55% =

b. 55% of $1200

b. _____

23. decimal rounded to three places

$7\overline{)1.0\,0\,0\,0}$

_____

24. Find $\dfrac{n + m}{m}$

when $n = 100$

$m = -10$

_____

25. a. The triangles are

$\underline{\text{s}\hspace{3cm}}$ because they

have $\underline{\text{c}\hspace{3cm}}$ angles.

b. $\dfrac{x}{12} = \dfrac{10}{5}$

c. Find the third side of the small triangle first.

26. scientific notation

shift $\longrightarrow$

0.00001 =

____ × ____

27.

	Percent	Actual Count
Missed		
Did not miss		
Total	100	

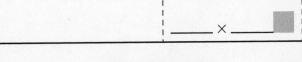

_____

b. $x =$ _____

c. $y =$ _____

28. area

6 ft

Use 3.14 for π.

29. Round to the nearest hundred.

$$\frac{25,000 \text{ mi}}{24 \text{ hr}} =$$

30. Translate each vertex 3 units right and 2 units down to draw □ *A'B'C'D'*.

A' (,   ) *B'* (,   )
C' (,   ) *D'* (,   )

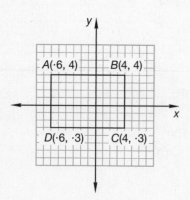

Use work area.

• **Experimental Probability** (page 400)

Name _____

Probability is a ratio of favorable outcomes to possible outcomes.

• **Theoretical probability** is found by looking at a situation mathematically.

We find the number of ways a favorable outcome can occur and divide by the total possible outcomes.

Example: Find the theoretical probability of flipping heads with a coin.

$$P(\text{heads}) = \frac{\text{favorable outcomes}}{\text{total outcomes}} = \frac{1}{2}$$

There is **one** way to flip heads.

There are **two** possible outcomes: heads or tails.

• **Experimental probability** is found by recording the number of times an event occurs in the real world and dividing by the number of **trials** (tries).

$$\text{experimental probability} = \frac{\text{number of times an event occurs}}{\text{number of trials}}$$

Example: Grey flips a coin 10 times. She gets heads 6 times. What is the experimental probability of flipping heads?

$$P(\text{heads}) = \frac{6}{10} = \frac{3}{5}$$

She got 6 heads.

She tried the experiment 10 times.

• The experimental probability for flipping heads was different from the theoretical probability.

This is because 10 coin flips is not very many trials. The more trials Grey performs, the closer the experimental probability will get to the theoretical probability.

• Experimental probability is used because some real-world events are too complicated to be modeled accurately with math.

___

Practice Set (page 403)

a. When a member of the opposing team fouls a basketball player who is shooting, the player shoots two free throws. Near the end of a close game a player has made 6 out of 20 free throws, and he has made 60% of his 2-point shots. When the player has the ball in 2-point range, should the opposing team foul him or risk the shot? Explain your answer in terms of probability.

$$P(\text{free throw}) = \frac{6}{20} = \qquad\qquad P(\text{2-point shot}) = 60\% = \frac{60}{100} =$$

The opposing team should foul the player because the probability of him making a

_____ is less than the probability of him making a _____.

b. Quinn runs a sandwich shop. Since she added a turkey melt to the menu, 36 out of 120 customers have ordered the new sandwich. What is the probability that the next customer will order a turkey

melt? _____

P(turkey melt) = _____ / _____ =

c. Quinn ordinarily has 200 customers on a busy afternoon. About how many turkey melts should she

expect to sell? _____
*Use the probability from **b**.*

_____ of 200 =

d. Based on probabilities, explain why car insurance companies charge higher rates for teenage drivers than for adult drivers.

The probability of having an accident is _____ for a teenage driver than for an adult driver.

e. Meghan is a 50% free throw shooter. What is her probability of making a free throw? 50% = _____

Meghan wants to model shooting 10 free throws with an experiment. What is an experiment that has the same probability as Meghan making a free throw?

flipping _____ on a coin

How many times should Meghan flip the coin to model shooting 10 free throws? _____ times

Written Practice   (page 403)

1.

	Ratio	Actual Count
Carbon		
Oxygen		12×10^{23}
Total		t

2. Put the data in order:

_____, _____, _____, _____, _____

a. mean: _____   median: _____

mode: _____   range: _____

b. Which measure is a difference? _____

Use work area.

3.

	Percent	Actual Count
Brought Lunch		b
Did not		
Total	100	

4. *Probability is a fraction.*

5. *scale factor:* $\frac{to}{from}$

$\frac{x}{4} = $ _____

_____

$\underline{x =}$ _____

6.

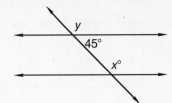

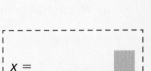

Adjacent angles are supplementary.
$m\angle y + 45° = 180°$
Corresponding angles are congruent. $m\angle y = m\angle x$

$\underline{x =}$ _____

7. $y = -2x + 4$
$y = mx + b$

Is $(0, -2)$ a

solution? _____

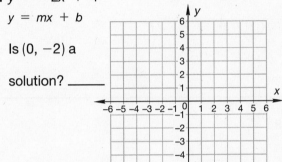

Use work area.

8. $3(x - 4) = 15$

$\underline{x =}$ _____

9. *Collect like terms first.*
$2x - x - 2 = 12$

$\underline{x =}$ _____

10. $\frac{x}{3} = 0.7$

$\underline{x =}$ _____

11. $\frac{1}{2}x = \frac{1}{3}$

$\underline{x =}$ _____

12. Leave π as π.

a. area

b. circumference

a. _____

b. _____

13.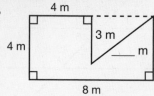

4 m

3 m

____ m

4 m

8 m

Figure A

8 m

4 m   4 m

8 m

Figure B

a. Which has greater area? **b.** Which has greater perimeter?

a. _____ b. _____

14. unit rate:

$$\frac{2400 \text{ mi}}{48 \text{ hr}} = \frac{}{1 \text{ hr}}$$

_____

15. min to sec

$$3.5 \text{ min} \cdot \frac{\text{sec}}{\text{min}} =$$

_____

16. mixed number and decimal

6 ft 9 in. = 6 ___ ft =

_____ _____

17. $3^{-2} \cdot 2^{-2} =$

_____

18. $\dfrac{h^3 p^2}{ph} =$

_____

19. $\dfrac{5}{18} - \dfrac{5}{18} \cdot \dfrac{1}{5} =$

_____

20. $0.3 - 0.2(0.1) =$

_____

21. a. percent   reduced fraction
       0.95 =   0.95 =

b. least to greatest

$0.95, \dfrac{39}{40}, \dfrac{9}{10}$

_____, _____, _____

22.

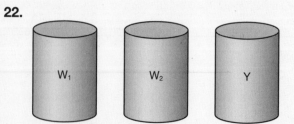

Choose 2 cans at a time.

a. { $\underline{W_1 W_2}$, $\underline{W_1 \quad}$, $\underline{W_2 \quad}$ }

b. $P(Y) =$

Use work area.   Use work area.

23. rate

$$\frac{\text{mi}}{\text{hr}} =$$

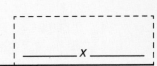

24. Round to the nearest cent.

7% of $315.90

Change to a decimal and use a calculator.

7% =

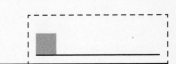

25. What percent of 25 is 23?

$P \cdot \underline{\hspace{2cm}} = \underline{\hspace{2cm}}$

26. $x(x + 1) - 1(x + 1) =$

27. volume and surface area

length: $8\frac{1}{8}$ in. $\longrightarrow$ _____ in.

width: $2\frac{7}{8}$ in. $\longrightarrow$ _____ in.

height: $11\frac{1}{8}$ in. $\longrightarrow$ _____ in.

28. scientific notation

shift $\longrightarrow$
0.0000000000625

_____ x _____

29. $30,000 = 3 \times 10^{\underline{\hspace{0.5cm}}}$

$(1.3 \times 10^{-8})(3 \times 10^{\underline{\hspace{0.5cm}}}) =$

_____ x _____

30. Vertex B moved _____ units right and _____ units up.

The translation is (,).

So $A(1, 3) \longrightarrow A'(,)$

$C(4, 3) \longrightarrow C'(,)$

● **Area of a Parallelogram** (page 406)

Name _____

A parallelogram is a quadrilateral with two pairs of parallel sides.

● The area of a **parallelogram** is its base *(b)* times its perpendicular height *(h)*.

$$A = bh$$

Teacher Notes:
● Review "Geometric Formulas" on page 29 in the *Student Reference Guide*.
● The activity on 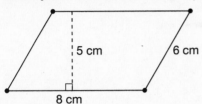 page 407 is optional.

Example: Find the area of this parallelogram.

5 cm
6 cm
8 cm

$A = bh$

$A = 8 \text{ cm} \cdot 5 \text{ cm}$

$A = 40 \text{ cm}^2$

The height is **not** the length of the adjacent side, 6 cm. The height is the perpendicular distance across the parallelogram, 5 cm.

Practice Set (page 409)

a. Circle the correct answer. The base and height of a parallelogram are always

  A perpendicular   **B** parallel   **C** sides   **D** congruent

b. What is the area of this parallelogram? _____

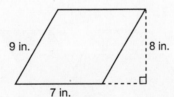
9 in.
8 in.
7 in.

$A = bh$

$A =$ _____ × _____

c. The sides of this square and this rhombus are each 3 cm long. Find the perimeter and area of each figure. (They are both parallelograms.)

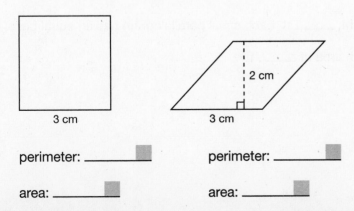
3 cm
2 cm
3 cm

perimeter: _____   perimeter: _____

area: _____   area: _____

d. Parallelogram *ABCD* has vertices *A* (4,2), *B* (2, −2), *C* (−2, −2), and *D* (0, 2).

Find the area of the parallelogram. _____

A = bh

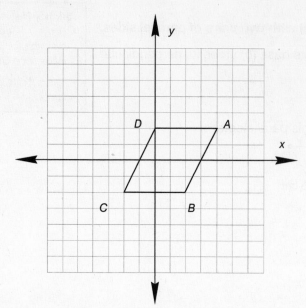

What would be the area of a dilation of this parallelogram with a scale factor of 3? _____
The area of an image is equal to the area of the figure × (scale factor)².

A = (area of figure)(scale factor)² = (_____)(3)² =

e. A brass sculpture of the letter N is formed from one long metal parallelogram folded into three

congruent parallelograms. What is the area of one of the smaller parallelograms? _____

What is the total area of the long metal parallelogram? _____
three small parallelograms together

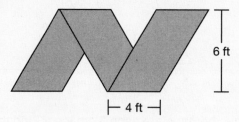

6 ft

⊢ 4 ft ⊣

f. How do you know your answer to problem **e** is correct?

Each small parallelogram has the same height, _____ ft. Each small parallelogram has an equal base,

_____ ft. So each small parallelogram has an area of _____ ft².

1. 15% off of $16.80

change to a decimal and use a calculator.

$16.80

_____

$ _____

2. scientific notation

shift ⟶

0.000025

_____ × _____

3. triangle (0,5), (−10,1), (10,1)

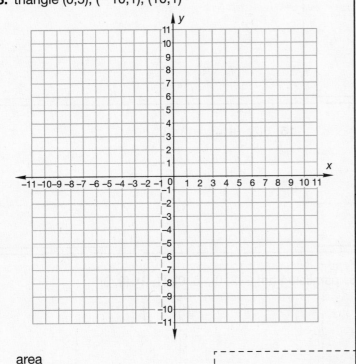

area

_____

4. tip: $ _____

Round to nearest percent.

$$\frac{}{62} =$$

Use work area.

5. Which does 10^{-2} equal?

A 8

B $\frac{1}{10} \times \frac{1}{10}$

C −20

D $10 \times (-2)$

_____

6. 25% of $60

_____

7. $-13 + (-4)(-2) =$

_____

8. $256 \div [2(6 - (-2))^2] =$

$6 - (-2)$

$6 + (+2) =$

_____

9. $(1.6 \times 10^4)(2.0 \times 10^5) =$

_____ × _____

10. $(1.5)^2(-2)^4 =$

11. $\dfrac{(5^3)^2}{5^3} =$

12. $\dfrac{1}{3}x - 1 = 4$

13. $-5k - 11 = 14$

_x_ =

_k_ =

14. $\dfrac{x}{7} = -2$

15. $5(2t + 4) = 140$

_x_ =

_t_ =

16. $-4m + 1.8 = -4.2$

18. parallelogram $(-2, 0), (6, 0), (1, 3), (9, 3)$

_m_ =

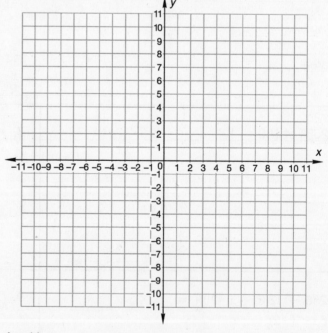

17. $27 = 8b - 5$

$A = bh$

area of dilation = (area of figure)(scale factor)²

_b_ =

19. mi to km

$$4163 \text{ mi} \cdot \frac{\text{km}}{\text{mi}} =$$

20. $25m + 75 = 125$

21. Which could **not** form a cube?

A 　B 　C

D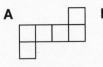

22. *Adjacent angles are supplementary.*

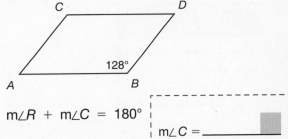

$$m\angle R + m\angle C = 180°$$

$$m\angle C = \underline{\hspace{2cm}}$$

23.

Average Annual Precipitation for Selected Texas Cities	
City	Inches
Brownsville	26
Dallas-Fort Worth	32
El Paso	9
Houston	47
Midland-Odessa	14
Port Arthur	55

Put the data in order.

____, ____, ____, ____, ____, ____

median

24. $\dfrac{\$}{\text{guppies}}$　___ ___

25.

	Ratio	Actual Count
Play		
Do not play		
Total	100	t

26. Find the diagonal.

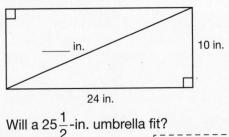

____ in.　10 in.

24 in.

Will a $25\frac{1}{2}$-in. umbrella fit?

27.

	Ratio	Actual Count
Whole Wheat		w
White		
Total		

28. pancakes _____ _____
min

29. area of walls and ceiling

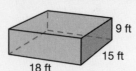

9 ft

15 ft

18 ft

Round up rolls

rolls $\dfrac{1}{80}$ _____
area

30. Complete the table:

Number of Hours (h)	Amount of Pay (P)
1	
2	
3	
4	

$P = $ _____

Is the function proportional?

_____

Use work area.

• Sequences (page 415)

A sequence is an ordered list of numbers, or terms, that follow a pattern.

Teacher Note:
• Introduce Hint #53, "Finding Patterns in Sequences.

• In an **arithmetic sequence**, the same number is *added* to each term to make the next term.

> **Example:** Describe the pattern in this sequence, and then find the next three terms.
>
> 3, 6, 9, 12, …
>
> The first term is 3 and each succeeding term is 3 more.
>
> +3 +3 +3   +3   +3   +3
> 3, 6, 9, 12, **15, 18, 21**
>
> The difference between each term and each succeeding term is 3. Arithmetic sequences have a *constant difference* between terms.

• In a **geometric sequence**, each term is *multiplied* by the same number to make the next term.

> **Example**: Describe the pattern in this sequence, and then find the next three terms.
>
> 1, 3, 9, 27, …
>
> The first term is 1 and the next term is 3 × 1. This pattern repeats.
>
> ×3 ×3 ×3   ×3   ×3   ×3
> 1, 3, 9, 27, **81, 243, 729**
>
> The ratio of each term and each previous term is 3. Geometric sequences have a *constant ratio* between terms.

• The **position** of a term is where the term is in the sequence: 1st, 2nd, 3rd, etc.

• The position is also called the number of a term *(n)*.

• The *value (a)* of a term is the actual number that appears in the sequence.

- We can make a table for *n* and *a* and plot the sequences on a graph.

Example: Make a table and graph the two sequences.

Arithmetic Sequence

n	1	2	3	4
a	3	6	9	12

Geometric Sequence

n	1	2	3	4
a	1	3	9	27

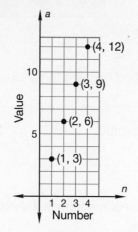
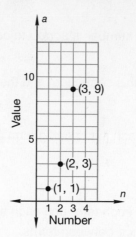

The arithmetic sequence makes a line. The geometric sequence makes a curve.

- We can also write a **formula** for sequences in the same way we have already written equations for tables with *x* and *y*.

- We use *n* for the position of the term (input number).

- We use a_n for the value of the term (output number). The little *n* is a **subscript**.

Example: Use the table above to write a formula for each sequence.

arithmetic sequence

Every *a* is a multiple of 3.

$3 = 1 \times 3$
$6 = 2 \times 3$
$9 = 3 \times 3$
$a_n = 3n$

geometric sequence

Every *a* is a power of 3.

$1 = 3^0$
$3 = 3^1$
$9 = 3^2$
$a_n = 3^{(n-1)}$

- Using formulas, we can find the value of any term in the sequence.

Example: Find the fifth term in each sequence.

The fifth term is $n = 5$.

arithmetic sequence

$a_n = 3n$

$a_5 = 3(5) = 15$

geometric sequence

$a_n = 3^{(n-1)}$

$a_5 = 3^{(5-1)} = 3^4 = 81$

- Notice that we wrote 5 as the subscript on *a* to show that we are finding the value of the fifth term.

Practice Set (page 418)

Describe each sequence as **arithmetic** (constant difference), **geometric** (constant ratio), or **neither**.

a. 1, 2, 4, 8, 16, ... _____

b. 2, 4, 6, 8, 10, ... _____

c. 1, 4, 9, 16, 25, ... _____

d. What is the **constant difference** in this sequence? _____

1, 5, 9, 13, ...

e. What is the **constant ratio** in this sequence? _____

5, 25, 125, 625, ...

Substitute 1, 2, 3, and 4 for n to write the first four terms of each sequence described by the formula.

f. $a_n = 2n$

_____, _____, _____, _____

g. $a_n = 2^n$

_____, _____, _____, _____

Written Practice (page 419)

1.

	Ratio	Actual Count
White		w
Black		
Total		

_____

2. $ \frac{15}{1}$ ___
days

$ \frac{24}{1}$ ___
days

3. $1.30 $89.00

$\begin{array}{r} \times\ 60 \\ \hline \end{array}$ _____

4. Put the data in order:

50 , _____, _____, _____, 75

mean: _____

median: _____

mode: _____

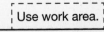
Use work area.

5. *Alternate interior angles are congruent.*

m∠x = _____

6. Substitute −4 for _____.

If _____ equals −1, then (−4, −1) is a solution.

Use work area.

7. *lateral surface area = perimeter of base × height*

_____

8.

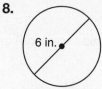

6 in.

Use 3.14 for π.

a. area

b. circumference

a. _____

b. _____

9. scale factor: $\dfrac{to}{from}$ =

$\dfrac{m}{} = \dfrac{}{}$

m = _____

10. $0.4x + 1.3 = 1.5$

$$\begin{array}{r} 1.5 \\ \underline{1.3} \\ 0.4\overline{)} \end{array}$$

x = _____

11. $0.002x + 0.03 = 0.92$

$$\begin{array}{r} 0.92 \\ \underline{0.03} \\ 0.002\overline{)} \end{array}$$

x = _____

12. $3x + 8 - x = 20$

x = _____

13. $2(x + 3) = 16$

x = _____

14. $\dfrac{2}{5}x = \dfrac{2}{3}$

x = _____

15. $\dfrac{x}{4} = 1.25$

$x =$ _____

16. unit rate

$$\dfrac{\text{in.}}{\text{yr}} = \dfrac{\text{in.}}{1 \text{ yr}}$$

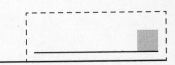
_____

17. in. to ft

$$54 \text{ in.} \cdot \dfrac{\text{ft}}{\text{in.}} =$$

_____

18. $x + 1 + x^2 + 4x + 4 =$

_____

19. a. decimal
$$\dfrac{17}{100} =$$

percent
$$\dfrac{17}{100} =$$

b. _____ of the customers registered for the discount card.

Use work area.

20. $y = mx + b$

line a:

$m =$

$b =$

line b:

$m =$

$b =$

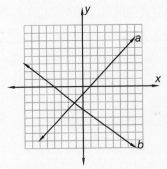

a. $y =$ _____

b. $y =$ _____

21. Find the height to the nearest inch.

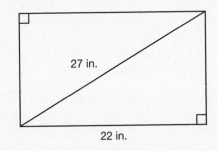

27 in.

22 in.

22. $(-3) - |-3| - 3^{-1} =$

23. $\dfrac{t^2 u^2 r}{r u t^3} =$

24. $\dfrac{3.6 - 0.36}{0.03}$

$\begin{array}{r} 3.6 \\ -0.36 \\ \hline \end{array}$ $0.03\overline{\smash{)}}$

25. 📖 See page 421.

- ## Graphing Solutions to Inequalities on a Number Line (page 422)

Teacher Note:
- Introduce reference chart, "Graphing Inequalities."

An inequality is a type of equation that has a range of possible solutions.

- Inequalities use the greater than ($>$) and less than ($<$) signs.

- To solve an **inequality**, we *isolate the variable* in the same way we solve an equation.

    Example: Solve this inequality: $2x - 5 > 1$

$2x - 5 > 1$	Given inequality
$2x - 5 + 5 > 1 + 5$	Added 5 to both sides
$2x > 6$	Simplified
$\dfrac{2x}{2} > \dfrac{6}{2}$	Divided both sides by 2
$x > 3$	Simplified.

    "x is greater than 3."

    x can be any number greater than 3, including fractions and irrational numbers.

- We graph inequalities on a **number line.**

    Example: Graph $x > 3$ on a number line.

    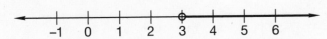

    The **circle** at 3 shows that x does not equal 3.

    The arrowhead going to the right shows that x can be any number greater than 3.

- Inequalities use two other symbols: greater than or equal ($\geq$) and less than or equal ($\leq$).

- When graphing with $\geq$ and $\leq$, use a **dot** to show that the variable can equal that number.

    Example: Solve and graph the solution: $3 \leq x - 2$

$3 \leq x - 2$	Given inequality
$5 \leq x$	Added 2 to both sides.

    "x is greater than or equal to 5."

    The dot at 5 shows that x can equal 5.

Practice Set (page 425)

a. Alisha has a number in mind. If she **adds three** to her number the result is **less than five.** Write and solve an inequality about Alisha's number. Then graph the solution set.

$x + $ _____ $ < $ _____

$x < $ _____

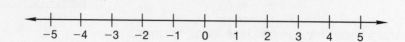

Use an open circle.

Solve these inequalities and graph their solutions on number lines.

b. $4x > -12$

$x > $ _____

Use a circle.

c. $6x + 1 \geq -5$

$6x \geq $ _____

$x \geq $ _____

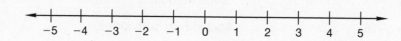

Use a dot.

d. $2x - 5 \leq 3$

$x \leq $ _____

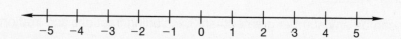

e. $7 \leq x - 8$

_____ $ \leq x$

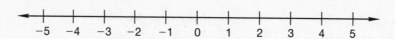

f. Jan is participating in a 6 mile run/walk for charity. If she completes the course and **runs at least half** the distance, then what inequality shows how far she might *walk?* Graph the inequality.

Find half the distance: _____ mi

Jan runs that distance or more. So she walks that distance or less.

$w \leq $ _____

It is not possible to walk a negative distance.

1.

	Ratio	Actual Count
Input		i
Output		
Total		

2.

	Percent	Actual Count
Preserved		
Not Preserved		n
Total	100	

3. Complete the drawings of the cubes.
How many small cubes fit in the large cube?

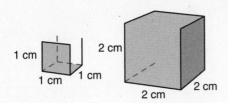

1 cm   2 cm
1 cm   1 cm
2 cm   2 cm   2 cm

Use work area.

4. Put the data in order.

279 ___, ___, ___, ___, ___, ___, 321

Mean: ___

Median: ___

Mode: ___

Use work area.

5. *Corresponding angles are congruent.*

m∠y = ___°

Adjacent angles are supplementery.
m∠y + m∠x = 180°

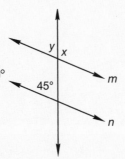

y x
45°
m
n

m∠x = ___

6. $y = 4x - 4$
$y = mx + b$
Is $(-2, -4)$ on this line? ___

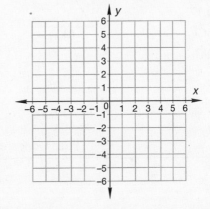

Use work area.

7. Leave π as π.
Circumference of larger wheel: ___

Circumference of smaller wheel: ___

___ times

8.

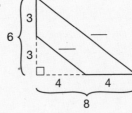

3
6
3
4   4
8

a. A = ___

P = ___

b. t ___

9. Unit rate

$$\frac{100 \text{ m}}{10 \text{ sec}} =$$

10. min to hr

$$300 \text{ min} \cdot \underline{\hspace{2cm}} =$$

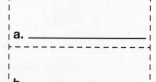

11. a. {WW, W___, W___,

R___, R___, R___,

B___, B___, B___ }

b. P (WW, RR, BB) =

b. _____

12. 125%

a. decimal

b. reduced fraction

a. _____

b. _____

13. Use a calculator.
Round to the nearest in.

Ten feet is _____ inches,

so the board _____
long enough.

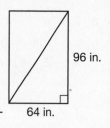

96 in.

64 in.

Use work area.

14. $(-1)^2 + (-1)^1 + (-1)^0 + (-1)^{-1} =$

_____

15. $\dfrac{race}{car} + e =$

16. $\left(\dfrac{2}{3}\right)^2 - \dfrac{1}{3} \div \dfrac{3}{4}$

$$\left(\dfrac{2}{3}\right)\left(\dfrac{2}{3}\right) =$$

$$\dfrac{1}{3} \div \dfrac{3}{4}$$

$$\downarrow \qquad \downarrow$$

$$\underline{\hspace{1cm}} \times \underline{\hspace{1cm}} =$$

_____

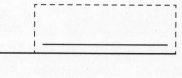

17. $x(x + 2) - 2(x + 2) =$

_____

18. $1.3x - 0.32 = 0.98$

$x =$ _____

19. $0.001x + 0.09 = 1.1$

$x =$ _____

20. $-4(2 + x) - 2(x + 3) = 4$

$x =$ _____

21. $\frac{2}{7}x = \frac{3}{14}$

$x =$ _____

22. $y = mx + b$

line a:

$m =$

$b =$

line b:

$m =$

$b =$

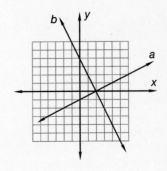

$y =$ _____

$y =$ _____

23. $x + 2 < 6$

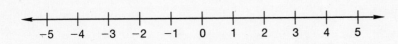

Use a circle.

$x <$ _____

24. $x + 5 \geq 3$

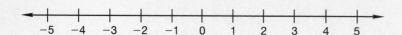

Use a dot.

$x \geq$ _____

25. Square *ABCD* has *A*(−2, 2), *B*(2, 2), *C*(2,−2), and *D*(−2,−2).

a. Draw dilated image *A′ B′ C′ D′* with a scale factor of 4.
Multiply each coordinate by 4.

b. *A′*(,) *B′*(,) *C′*(,) *D′*(,)

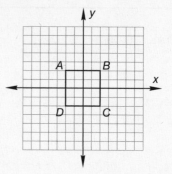

Use work area.

• **Rational Numbers,**
   Non-Terminating Decimals, and Percents
• **Fractions with Negative Exponents** (page 429)

Name _____

Teacher Note:
• Review "Fraction-Decimal-Percent Equivalents" on page 13 in the *Student Reference Guide*.

To convert a fraction to a decimal number, we divide the numerator by the denominator.

• Many fractions convert to a decimal number that ends.

$$\frac{1}{4} \longrightarrow \begin{array}{r} 0.25 \\ 4\overline{)1.00} \\ \underline{8} \\ 20 \\ \underline{20} \\ 0 \end{array} \longrightarrow 0.25$$

• Some fractions convert to a decimal number that repeats the same digits over and over without end. This is a repeating or **non-terminating** decimal.

• Repeating decimals are written with a bar over the repeating digits **(repetend)**.

$$\frac{1}{11} \longrightarrow \begin{array}{r} 0.0909 \\ 11\overline{)1.0000} \\ \underline{99} \\ 100 \\ \underline{99} \\ 1 \end{array} \longrightarrow 0.090909\ldots \qquad \frac{1}{11} = 0.\overline{09}$$

• To change the repeating decimal above to a percent,

   1. Shift the decimal point 2 places to the right to show the whole number part of the percent.

   2. Write the remainder over the divisor to show the fraction part of the percent.

$$\begin{array}{r} 0.0909 \\ 11\overline{)1.0000} \\ \underline{99} \\ 100 \\ \underline{99} \\ 1 \end{array} \longrightarrow 9\frac{1}{11}\%$$

• We cannot use repeating decimals in arithmetic. Often we will round the decimal to a certain number of places.

   Example: Round $0.\overline{09}$ to the nearest thousandth.

   $0.0\underline{\textcircled{9}}0909\ldots \longrightarrow 0.091$

• To write a percent as a fraction, divide by 100 and reduce. (Percent means *per one hundred*.)

   Example: Write $16\frac{2}{3}\%$ as a reduced fraction.

   $$16\frac{2}{3}\% = 16\frac{2}{3} \div 100$$

   $$\frac{\overset{1}{\cancel{50}}}{3} \times \frac{1}{\cancel{100}_2} = \frac{1}{6}$$

From the fraction, we can change to a decimal.

$$\frac{1}{6} = 0.1\overline{6}$$

- The **reciprocal** of a fraction is the fraction "flipped."

$$\frac{2}{5} \rightarrow \frac{5}{2}$$

- A negative exponent indicates the reciprocal of the positive exponent.

$$10^{-2} = \frac{1}{10^2} = \frac{1}{100}$$

- To find a negative power of a fraction, "flip" the fraction and write a positive exponent. Then simplify.

   Example: Simplify: $\left(\frac{1}{3}\right)^{-2}$

$$\left(\frac{1}{3}\right)^{-2} \rightarrow \left(\frac{3}{1}\right)^{2} = (3)^2 = 9$$

Practice Set (page 432)

Convert each fraction to a decimal and a percent. Then write the decimal rounded to the nearest **thousandth**.

a. $\frac{1}{3}$

decimal: _____

$3\overline{)1.00}$

rounded: _____

percent: _____ ▧

b. $\frac{5}{6}$

decimal: _____

$6\overline{)5.000}$

rounded: _____

percent: _____ ▧

c. $\frac{2}{11}$

decimal: _____

$11\overline{)2.0000}$

rounded: _____

percent: _____ ▧

Convert each percent to a fraction and a decimal. Then write the decimal rounded to the nearest **hundredth**.

d. $66\frac{2}{3}\%$

fraction: _____

$66\frac{2}{3} \div 100$

↓   ↓

$\frac{200}{3} \times \frac{1}{100}$

decimal: _____

rounded: _____

e. $8\frac{1}{3}\%$

fraction: _____

$8\frac{1}{3} \div 100$

↓   ↓

_____ × _____

decimal: _____

rounded: _____

f. $22\frac{2}{9}\%$

fraction: _____

$22\frac{2}{9} \div 100$

↓   ↓

_____ × _____

decimal: _____

rounded: _____

Practice Set (continued) (page 432)

g. Arrange in order from least to greatest. _____, _____, _____

Write each as a decimal rounded to thousandths.

$16\%, \dfrac{1}{6}, 0.165$

h. The bill for the meal was $24.00. Dario left a tip of $16\frac{2}{3}\%$. How much was the tip? _____

Change to a fraction.

$$16\frac{2}{3} \div 100$$

_____ × _____

Simplify.

i. $\left(\dfrac{1}{2}\right)^{-3} \rightarrow \left(\dfrac{2}{1}\right)^{3} = (2)^3 = $ _____   **j.** $\left(\dfrac{1}{10}\right)^{-2} = $ _____   **k.** $\left(\dfrac{3}{2}\right)^{-1} = $ _____

Written Practice (page 432)

1. Stems   _____ _____

Vases

2.

$$\begin{array}{r} 100 \\ -65 \\ \hline \end{array}$$

	Ratio	Actual Count
Wore		
Did not wear		d
Total	100	

3. $0.05 $1.95

$\times$ _____ $-$ _____

4. Put the data in order:

_____, _____, _____, _____, _____, _____, _____
1.7   3.5

a. mean: _____   median: _____

mode: _____   range: _____

b. Is the mean or median greater?

_____

5. *Corresponding angles are on the same side of the transversal in matching positions.*

∠ _____

Use work area.

6. $y = -\dfrac{2}{3}x + 1$

$y = mx + b$

Is $(-6, 4)$ a solution? _____

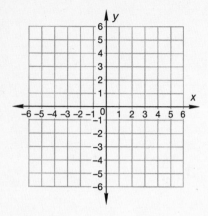

‖ Use work area. ‖

7. a. fraction

$83\dfrac{1}{3} \div 100$

↓   ↓

_____ × _____ =

b. rounded: _____ . _____ _____

decimal: _____

‖ Use work area. ‖

8. a. decimal: _____

$9\overline{)4.\,0\,0}$

percent: _____ ▨

b. rounded: _____ . _____ _____ _____

‖ Use work area. ‖

9. R_1, R_2, W, and B

a. $\left\{ \dfrac{R_1R_2}{\quad}, \text{——}, \text{——}, \dfrac{R_2W}{\quad}, \text{——}, \dfrac{WB}{\quad} \right\}$

b. $P(R) =$

c. $P(\text{not} \underline{\quad}) =$

‖ Use work area. ‖

10. Diagonal to nearest inch

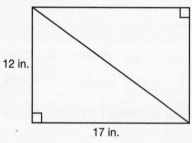

12 in.

17 in.

‖ Use work area. ‖

11. Surface area

A cube has 6 equal square faces

4 in.

12. Half a circle

Use 3.14 for π

a. area

b. perimeter

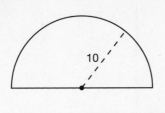

10

a. _____ b. _____

13. Unit rate

$$\frac{30 \text{ problems}}{30 \text{ minutes}} =$$

_____

14. in. to ft

2460 in. · ———— =

_____

15. Factor:

a. $7m^2 - 49 =$

b. $x^4 - 4x^3 =$

a. _____

b. _____

16. $(-3)^2 - 3^2 - \left(\frac{1}{3}\right)^{-1} =$

_____

17. $\frac{8cabs^2}{2bssa} =$

_____

18. $2\frac{1}{2} - 1\frac{1}{3} \cdot 1\frac{1}{4} =$

_____

19. $\frac{(0.6)(0.3)}{9} =$

_____

20. $0.02x + 0.1 = 1$

$x =$ _____

21. $1.2 + 0.2x = 0.8$

$x =$ _____

22. $\frac{3}{5}x = 6$

> $x = $ _____

23. $3|x| = 12$

> $x = $ _____, _____

24. $x - 11 > -4$

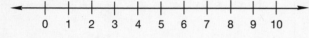

Use a circle.

> $x > $ _____

25. 📖 See page 434.

> _____

• Using a Unit Multiplier
to Convert a Rate (page 435)

Name _____

We can use a unit multiplier to convert a rate to a different unit.

- Look at the units you are given and the units you need to get for the answer.
  Which units change? Which units stay the same?

- Then use the correct unit multipliers.

- Remember to **cancel** units.

Teacher Note:
- Review "Equivalence Table for Units" on page 1 and "Multiple Unit Multipliers" on page 23 in the *Student Reference Guide.*

Example: Yasmine ran a mile in 6 minutes. Use a unit multiplier to find her average rate in miles per hour.

Minutes change to hours.

$$\frac{mi}{min} \text{ to } \frac{mi}{hr}$$

$$\frac{1 \text{ mi}}{\cancel{6} \text{ min}_1} \cdot \frac{\cancel{60}^{10} \text{ min}}{1 \text{ hr}} = \frac{10 \text{ mi}}{1 \text{ hr}} = 10 \text{ mi per hr}$$

Example: Driving at 60 miles per hour, a car travels about how many kilometers in two hours? (1 mi = 1.6 km)

Miles change to kilometers.

$$\frac{mi}{hr} \text{ to } \frac{km}{hr}$$

$$2 \text{ hr} \cdot \frac{60 \text{ mi}}{1 \text{ hr}} \cdot \frac{1.6 \text{ km}}{1 \text{ mi}} = 192 \text{ km}$$

Practice Set (page 437)

Use unit multipliers to perform the following rate conversions.

a. 3 miles per minute to miles per hour

$$\frac{mi}{min} \text{ to } \frac{mi}{hr}$$

$$\frac{3 \text{ mi}}{1 \text{ min}} \cdot \frac{60 \text{ min}}{1 \text{ hr}} = \frac{ \text{ mi}}{hr} = \underline{} \text{ mi/hr}$$

b. 880 yards in 2 minutes to feet per minute

$$\frac{yd}{min} \text{ to } \frac{ft}{min}$$

$$\frac{\overset{440}{\cancel{880} \text{ yd}}}{\cancel{2} \text{ min}} \cdot \frac{3 \text{ ft}}{1 \text{ yd}} = \frac{ \text{ ft}}{min} = \underline{} \text{ ft/min}$$

Practice Set (continued) (page 437)

c. 440 yards per minute to yards per second

$$\frac{yd}{min} \text{ to } \frac{yd}{sec}$$

$$\frac{440 \text{ yd}}{1 \text{ min}} \cdot \underline{\hspace{2cm}} = \frac{yd}{sec} = \underline{\hspace{1.5cm}} \text{ yd/sec}$$

d. 24 miles per gallon to miles per quart

$$\frac{mi}{gal} \text{ to } \frac{mi}{qt}$$

$$\frac{24 \text{ mi}}{1 \text{ gal}} \cdot \underline{\hspace{2cm}} = \frac{mi}{qt} = \underline{\hspace{1.5cm}} \text{ mi/qt}$$

e. Peter packed 32 pints of pickles in one minute. Find Peter's pickle packing rate in ounces per minute. (1 pt = 16 oz)

$$\frac{pt}{min} \text{ to } \frac{oz}{min}$$

$$\frac{32 \text{ pt}}{1 \text{ min}} \cdot \underline{\hspace{2cm}} = \frac{oz}{min} = \underline{\hspace{1.5cm}} \text{ oz/min}$$

f. Shannon rode her bike 6 miles in 24 minutes. Find her average rate in miles per hour.

$$\frac{mi}{min} \text{ to } \frac{mi}{hr}$$

$$\frac{\overset{1}{\cancel{6}} \text{ mi}}{\underset{4}{\cancel{24}} \text{ min}} \cdot \underline{\hspace{2cm}} = \frac{mi}{hr} = \underline{\hspace{1.5cm}} \text{ mi/hr}$$

g. Find the average riding rate from **f** in kilometers per hour. Then find the number of kilometers Shannon could ride in 30 minutes at that rate. (1 min = 1.6 km)

$$\frac{mi}{hr} \text{ to } \frac{km}{hr}$$

$$\frac{mi}{hr} \cdot \underline{\hspace{2cm}} = \frac{km}{hr} = \underline{\hspace{1.5cm}} \text{ km/hr}$$

$$\frac{1}{2} \text{ hr} \cdot \underline{\hspace{0.5cm}} \frac{km}{hr} = \underline{\hspace{1.5cm}} \text{ km}$$

1. game _____ ? _____
min

2.

	Percent	Actual Count
Voted		
Did not vote		d
Total	100	

3. $0.10 $2.65

   × _____   − _____

4. Put the data in order:

10 ____, ____, ____, ____, ____, ____, 18

a. mean: _____   median: _____

    mode: _____   range: _____

b. _____

Use work area.

5.

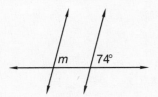

m∠m = _____

6. Circle the correct solid.

A   B   C

Name the solid: _____

7. $y = 3x - 5$
$y = mx + b$

Is $(3, -1)$ a solution?

_____

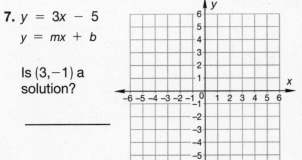

8. Coin toss and number cube roll

a. { H1 , H2 , ____, ____, ____, ____

    T1 , ____, ____, ____, ____, T6 }

b. P (H4, H5, or H6) =

Use work area.

9. $\frac{ft}{min}$ to $\frac{ft}{sec}$

$$\frac{1200\ ft}{1\ min} \cdot \frac{min}{sec} =$$

10. $\frac{ton}{day}$ to $\frac{lb}{day}$

$$\frac{0.3\ ton}{1\ day} \cdot \frac{lb}{ton} =$$

11. a. Complete the drawing of a rectangular prism.

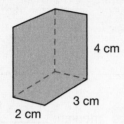

4 cm

3 cm

2 cm

b. volume

b. _____

c. surface area

c. _____

12. a. *fraction*   **b.** ___ . ___ ___ ___ ___

$$77\frac{7}{9} \div 100$$

___ × ___ =

decimal

Use work area.

13. $\left(\frac{1}{2}\right)^2 + \left(\frac{1}{2}\right)^1 + \left(\frac{1}{2}\right)^0 + \left(\frac{1}{2}\right)^{-1} =$

14.

7 cm

Use $\frac{22}{7}$ for π.

a. circumference of top

a. _____

b. area of top

b. _____

15.

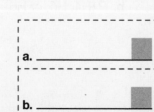

10

4   5

5

4

12

a. area

b. perimeter

a. _____

b. _____

16. Factor:

a. $-3x + 27 =$

b. $10x - 100 =$

a. _____

b. _____

17. a. The triangles

are ˢ_____ because

the angles are ᶜ_____.

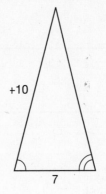
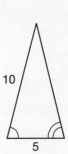

b. scale factor: ———

c. $\dfrac{x + 10}{10} = \dfrac{7}{5}$

$x =$

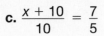

Use work area.

---

18. $-(-2)^2 - 2^2 - (\sqrt{2})^2 =$

_____

19. $\dfrac{bake^2}{acake} =$

_____

---

20. $2.1 + 0.7x = 9.8$
$2.1 + 0.7x - \quad = 9.8 -$
$0.7x =$

$x =$ _____

21. $4(x-4) - 3x = 10$

$x =$ _____

---

22. $\dfrac{4}{5}x = 16$

$x =$ _____

23. $\dfrac{12}{40} = \dfrac{30}{x}$

$x =$ _____

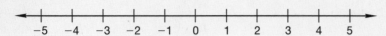

24. $x + 3 < 2$

$$\xleftarrow{\quad\;\;+\;\;\;+\;\;\;+\;\;\;+\;\;\;+\;\;\;+\;\;\;+\;\;\;+\;\;\;+\;\;\;+\;\;\;+\quad}\rightarrow$$
$$\;\;\;\;\;-5\;\;-4\;\;-3\;\;-2\;\;-1\;\;\;\;0\;\;\;\;1\;\;\;\;2\;\;\;\;3\;\;\;\;4\;\;\;\;5$$

Use a circle.

$x =$ _____

25. **a.** total rainfall

b.   inches in July
    <u>+ inches in August</u>
      total rainfall

Which month has this same amount of rainfall? _____

a. _____

b. _____

• Applications Using Similar Triangles (page 440)

Name _____

Similar triangles and proportions can be used to solve many types of real world problems.

• We can use **indirect measure** to find the measures of a large or far away triangle.

> 1. Measure a small or nearby triangle that is similar to the large triangle.

> 2. Solve proportions to find the measures of the large triangle.

• Triangles are **similar** if they have *congruent* angles.

• The *corresponding parts* of similar triangles are **proportional**.

Practice Set (page 443)

a. Trevor took big steps to find the length of the shadow of the big pine tree in front of the school. He estimated that the shadow was 16 yards long, or about 48 feet. He also walked the length of the shadow cast by the two-story building and estimated that its shadow was 18 feet long. Trevor thinks

the building is 24 feet tall. About how many feet tall is the big pine tree? _____

The triangles made by the building and its shadow and the tree and its shadow are similar. Write and solve a proportion.

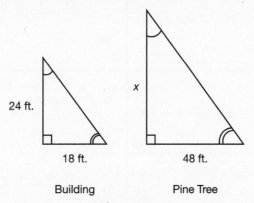

Building   Pine Tree

b. Holding a ruler upright at arm's distance **(24 in.)**, Ronnie aligned the bottom of the ruler with a mark on the utility pole that was about 5 feet above the ground. He saw that the top of the pole aligned with the 6-inch mark on the ruler. Then he took **40 long strides** to reach the pole. If each stride was about one yard

(3 feet), then the top of the pole is about how many feet high? x = _____   height = _____

Read the problem carefully and label the sides of the triangles. Then write and solve a proportion. (You do not have to change inches to feet or feet to inches.) The diagram is not drawn to the correct scale.

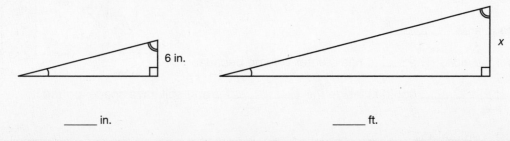

_____ in.   _____ ft.

c. Write down your height in inches: _____ in.

Imagine you are standing outside, and your shadow measures twice your height. _____ in.

You notice that the shadow of a stop sign is twice the length of your shadow: _____ in.

Label these triangles. Then write and solve a proportion to find the height of the stop sign. _____

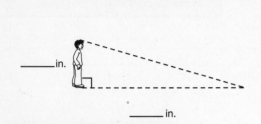

_____ in.

_____ in.

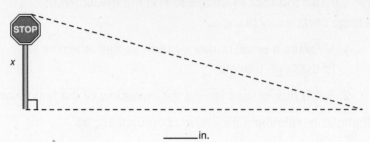

x

_____ in.

Written Practice (page 443)

1.

	Ratio	Actual Count
Stew		
Chili		c
Total		

_____

2.

	Percent	Actual Count
Dozed		
Did not Doze		d
Total	100	

_____

3.

big min	___ ___
small min	___ ___

_____

4. Put the data in order:

6.98 , _____ ,

_____ , _____ ,

7.02

mean: _____

median: _____

mode: _____

5. *First find m ∠ y.*

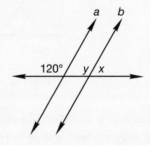

120° y / x

m∠x = _____

6. a. Label the sides.

b. surface area: _____

c. Label the sides. The _____ has greater volume because

the p_____ could fit inside the p_____ and still have space around it.

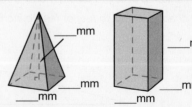

_____ Use work area. _____

7. $y = -x + 3$

$y = mx + b$

Is $(3, -6)$ a solution? _____

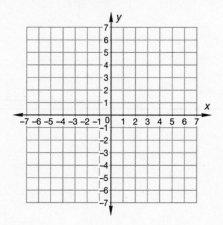

¦ Use work area. ¦

8. 1, 2, 3

a. { <u>1 and 2</u> , _____ , _____ }

b. The prize is behind door 1. What is the probability of getting the prize? _____

¦ Use work area. ¦

9. First change m to cm. Solve a proportion.

$\frac{x}{10} =$ _____

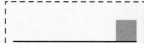

10. perimeter in centimeters

Use 3.14 for π.

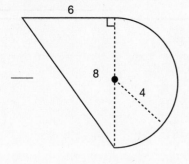

11. $\frac{m}{min}$ to $\frac{m}{sec}$

$\frac{90\ m}{1\ min} \cdot \frac{min}{sec} =$

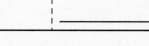

12. $\frac{ft}{sec}$ to $\frac{in.}{sec}$

$\frac{1.2\ ft}{1\ sec} \cdot \frac{in.}{ft} =$

13. Factor:

a. $4y - 32 =$

b. $2x^2 - 16x =$

a. _____

b. _____

14. a. Reduced fraction

$3\frac{1}{3}\% =$

decimal: _____

b. _____

_____

15. decimal and percent

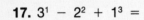

$16)\overline{7.0000}$

‾‾‾‾‾‾‾‾‾‾‾‾‾‾‾‾‾

‾‾‾‾‾‾‾‾‾‾‾‾‾‾‾‾‾

16. $p \times$ _____ = _____

$p =$

‾‾‾‾‾‾‾‾‾‾‾‾‾‾‾‾‾

17. $3^1 - 2^2 + 1^3 =$

‾‾‾‾‾‾‾‾‾‾‾‾‾‾‾‾‾

18. $\dfrac{x^4 y^3 z^2}{x^2 y^3 z^4} =$

‾‾‾‾‾‾‾‾‾‾‾‾‾‾‾‾‾

19. $\dfrac{7}{12} - \dfrac{3}{8} \cdot \left(\dfrac{9}{4}\right)^{-1} =$

‾‾‾‾‾‾‾‾‾‾‾‾‾‾‾‾‾

20. $\dfrac{4.2 + 3}{0.6} =$

‾‾‾‾‾‾‾‾‾‾‾‾‾‾‾‾‾

21. $0.8 + 0.3x = 5$

$x =$ ‾‾‾‾‾‾‾‾‾‾‾‾‾

22. $\dfrac{7}{8}x + \dfrac{1}{2} = \dfrac{7}{8}$

$x =$ ‾‾‾‾‾‾‾‾‾‾‾‾‾

23. $x + 5 > 1$

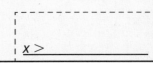

Use a circle.

$x > $ _____

24. $2x + 1 \leq -1$

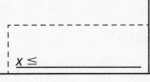

Use a dot.

$x \leq$ _____

25. Are the ratios of $\frac{mi}{gal}$

proportional? _____

$\frac{18}{1}$ $\frac{80}{3}$ $\frac{162}{9}$ $\frac{450}{15}$

Different driving conditions

give different _____

per _____ rates.

Use work area.

• Special Right Triangles (page 446)   Name _____

We will learn about two special right triangles. The triangles are named by the measures of their three angles.

- We use the Pythagorean Theorem to find the side lengths of these triangles.

- A **45-45-90 triangle** is half of a square. The square below has sides that are one unit in length.

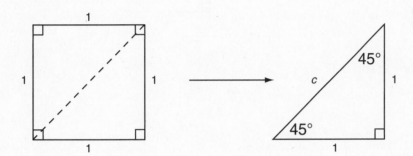

$$c^2 = a^2 + b^2$$
$$c^2 = (1)^2 + (1)^2$$
$$c^2 = 1 + 1$$
$$c^2 = 2$$
$$c = \sqrt{2} \text{ units}$$

- The proportion of side lengths will be the same in any 45-45-90 triangle:

  The legs have equal length.

  The hypotenuse is $\sqrt{2} \times$ (length of leg).

  To estimate a length, use 1.41 for $\sqrt{2}$.

- A **30-60-90 triangle** is half of an equilateral triangle. The equilateral triangle has sides of length 2 units.

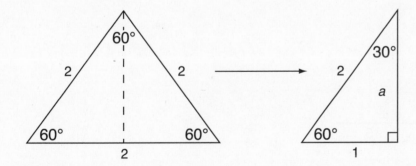

$$a^2 + b^2 = c^2$$
$$a^2 = c^2 - b^2$$
$$a^2 = (2)^2 - (1)^2$$
$$a^2 = 3$$
$$a = \sqrt{3} \text{ units}$$

- The proportion of side lengths will be the same in any 30-60-90 triangle:

  The hypotenuse is $2 \times$ (shorter leg).

  The longer leg is $\sqrt{3} \times$ (shorter leg).

  To estimate a length, use 1.73 for $\sqrt{3}$.

a. Label the angle measures and side lengths in this 45-45-90 triangle.

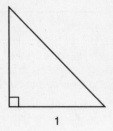

1

b. Label the angle measures and side lengths in this 30-60-90 triangle.

1

c. What are the approximations for $\sqrt{2}$ and $\sqrt{3}$?

$\sqrt{2} \approx$ _____

$\sqrt{3} \approx$ _____

d. How many units is it from the origin to (2, 2) on the coordinate plane?

Give an exact answer. _____ units

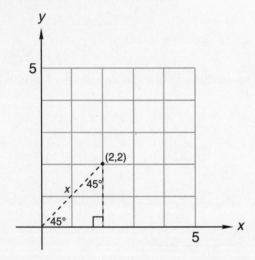

e. If each side of an equilateral triangle is 2 inches long, then what is the area of the triangle? Give an

exact answer. _____

Find the height of the equilateral triangle.

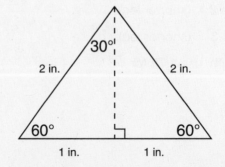

f. A regular hexagon has sides 2 feet long. What is the exact area of the hexagon? _____

*Use your answer from problem **e** to help solve problem **f**.*

What is the approximate area of the hexagon? _____

2

Written Practice (page 449)

1.

	Ratio	Actual Count
Bananas		b
Raisins		
Total		

_____

2.

	Percent	Actual Count
Raisins		
Bananas		b
Total	100	

_____

3.   0.9   1.1
    × _____   × _____

_____

4. Put the data in order

_____, _____, _____, _____, 2.6
2.4

a. mean: _____   median: _____

mode: _____   range: _____

5. First find y.

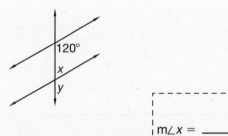

120°
x
y

m∠x = _____

b.

← + + + + + + + + + + + + →
    2.0   2.5   3.0

Use work area.

6. Use the figure to write and solve a proportion.

_____ = _____

7. slope $\frac{1}{2}$

y-intercept: 3

_____

y = _____

8. $x^{-2}y^{-1}xy^2z =$

_____

9. $\frac{4}{3}x = 28$

$x =$ _____

10. $\frac{x^2}{9} = 4$

$x =$ _____ ,

11. Area of semicircle
+ Area of triangle
_____

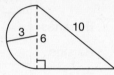

area of semicircle $= \frac{1}{2}(\pi r^2)$

_____

12. $16\frac{2}{3}\%$

Find the fraction first.

a. decimal

b. fraction

$16\frac{2}{3} \div 100$

$\underline{\quad} \times \underline{\quad}$

a. _____

b. _____

13. a. decimal

$3\overline{)2.00}$

percent

a. _____

a. _____

b. _____

14. Find $-b - \sqrt{b^2 - 4ac}$

When $a = 1$
$b = -10$
$c = 9$

_____

15. $\frac{km}{hr}$ to $\frac{mi}{hr}$

$\frac{100\ km}{1hr} \cdot \frac{mi}{km} =$

_____

16. $\dfrac{\$}{hr}$ to $\dfrac{¢}{min}$

$\dfrac{\$12}{1\ hr} \cdot \dfrac{1\ hr}{60\ min} \cdot \dfrac{100¢}{1\$} =$

17. a. Factor: $15x^2 - 10x =$

b. Distribute: $7(x - 3) =$

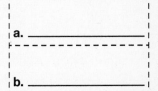

a. _____

b. _____

18. $(-3)^2 - 3^2 - 3^0 =$

19. $\dfrac{z^3 b^4 r}{x^2 b^2 z^3} =$

20. $\dfrac{9}{16} + \dfrac{1}{16} \cdot \left(\dfrac{2}{3}\right)^{-1} =$

21. $(-6) - (-2) - (-6)(-2)$

22. $0.9 + 0.3x = 2.4$

$x =$ _____

23. $3(-2x + 1) = 21$

$x =$ _____

24. Label each angle measure in the square and equilateral triangle.

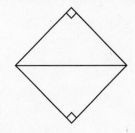

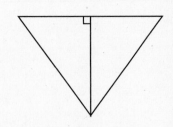

Use work area.

25. *See page 451.*

Is the relationship proportional?

_____ , because every ration of time

to volume is $\underset{\underline{\quad\quad\quad\quad\quad}}{e}$.

$\dfrac{10}{8} = \dfrac{s}{100}$

$s =$ _____

• **Percent of Change** (page 452)

Name _____

Teacher Note:
• Refer students to "Percent of Change" on page 14 in the *Student Reference Guide*.

We can use percents to describe a change. The change may be a decrease or an increase.

• To find percent of change, use a percent box:

1. The original percent is **always 100%.**

2. Put other known numbers into the "original," "change," and "new" boxes.

   If the change is an **increase, add** to the original.

   If the change is a **decrease, subtract** from the original.

3. Write a proportion using two rows:

   the row that is full and the row that answers the question.

Example: Donna bought a dress at a 30% off sale for $42. What was the **original price** of the dress?

	Percent	Actual Count
Original	100	x
Change (−)	30	
New	70	42

cancel matching zeros

$$\frac{\cancel{100}}{\cancel{70}} = \frac{x}{42}$$

$$10 \cdot 42 = 7x$$

$$\frac{420}{7} = x$$

$$x = \$60$$

Example: The median home price rose 20% in one year to $288,000. By how many dollars did the median price **increase?**

	Percent	Actual Count
Original	100	
Change (+)	20	c
New	120	288,000

cancel

$$\frac{\cancel{20}^{1}}{\cancel{120}_{6}} = \frac{c}{288,000}$$

$$288,000 = 6c$$

$$c = \$48,000$$

a. An item with a regular price of $15.00 is discounted 30%. What is the **sale price?** _____

	Percent	Actual Count
Original	100	15
Change (–)	30	
New	70	n

cancel

$$\frac{\cancel{100}}{70} = \frac{15}{n}$$

$$10n = 105$$

$$n =$$

b. A shopkeeper buys an item for $25.00 and marks up the price 80% to sell in the store. What is the

store price? _____

	Percent	Actual Count
Original	100	
Change (+)	80	
New	180	n

cancel

$$\frac{100}{180} = \frac{}{n}$$

c. Lillian saves $12 buying a rug on sale for $36.00. The sale price of the rug was **what percent** of the

regular price? _____

Find the original price first.

	Percent	Actual Count
Original	100	
Change (–)		12
New	n	36

cancel

$$\frac{100}{n} = \frac{48}{36}$$

d. The town's population increased from 80,000 to 90,000 in ten years. What was the **percent of**

increase? _____

$$\begin{array}{r} 80{,}000 \\ + \underline{} \\ 90{,}000 \end{array}$$

	Percent	Actual Count
Original	100	
Change (+)	c	
New		

$$\frac{100}{c} = \underline{}$$

e. A $15 item on sale for $12 is **marked down what percent?** _____

$$\begin{array}{r} \$\ 15 \\ - \underline{} \\ 12 \end{array}$$

	Percent	Actual Count
Original	100	
Change (–)	c	
New		

$$\frac{100}{c} = \underline{}$$

f. If Jenna buys an item for **40% off** the regular price, will she pay more or less than half the price? _____
What percent is half?

g. If Jenna buys an item for **40% of** the regular price, will she pay more or less than half the price? _____
"Of" means multiply.

h. If Jenna saves $20 buying an item for 40 percent off the regular price, then what were **the regular price** and **the sale price?**

regular price: _____

sale price: _____

	Percent	Actual Count
Original	100	r
Change (−)		
New		s

$$\frac{100}{r} = \underline{\quad}$$

$$\frac{100}{s} = \underline{\quad}$$

i. *Evan uses a 25% off coupon to buy a shirt regularly priced at $24.*
Write two questions that can be answered using that sentence and a percent box.

1. What was the _____ price of the shirt?

2. How much did Evan _____ by using the coupon?

Written Practice (page 454)

1.

	Ratio	Actual Count
Students		
Teachers		t
Total		

_____

2.

	Percent	Actual Count
Taking Roll		
Other		
Total	100	t

_____

3. $0.1 $0.05
     ×   ×   −0.10
   _____   _____   _____

_____

4. Put the data in order:

_____ , _____ , _____ , _____ , _____

mean: _____   median: _____

mode: _____   range: _____

Use work area.

5.
$$\begin{array}{r} 100 \\ -\ 20 \\ \hline \end{array}$$

	Percent	Actual Count
Original	100	x
Change($-$)	20	
New		320

6. 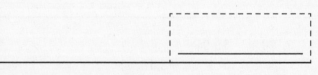 See the top of page 455.

a. $\dfrac{14}{7} = \dfrac{\quad}{x}$ $\dfrac{14}{7} = \dfrac{y}{\quad}$

b. Are they right triangles? _____

If we apply the Pythagorean Theorem, will both sides of the equation be equal?

a. $x =$ _____

a. $y =$ _____

7. slope: $\dfrac{2}{3}$

y-intercept: _____
Use slope-intercept form.

$y =$ _____

8. slope: -3

y-intercept: _____

$y =$ _____

9. $y = -2x$

Is $(-4, 2)$ on the line? _____

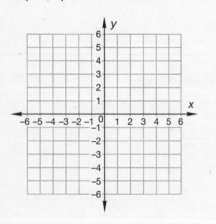

10. *See page 18 in the* Student Reference Guide.

_____

11. *perimeter to the nearest meter*

$C = 2\pi r$

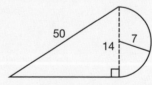

_____

_____

Use work area.

12. 0.6% of $1300

Change to a decimal.

13. a. decimal: _____

$9\overline{)5.0\,0}$

b. percent: _____

c. least to greatest

0.55,   0.56, $\dfrac{5}{9}$

_____, _____, _____

Use work area.

14. (−6,1), (6,1), (6,6)

a. perimeter

b. area

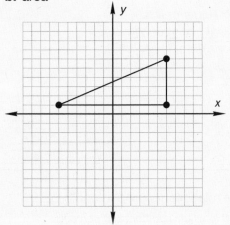

a. _____   **b.** _____

15. a. Factor: $5x^2 + 5x + 10 =$

b. Distribute: $-3(x + 3) =$

a. _____

b. _____

16. *10 vowels in the deck.*

a. $P(\text{vowel}) =$

b. 52 cards   10 vowels

$\underline{-1}$ $\underline{-1}$

c. $P(\text{2nd vowel}) =$

Use work area.

17. $\dfrac{m}{min}$ to $\dfrac{mi}{min}$

$\dfrac{400\ m}{1\ min} \cdot \dfrac{mi}{1600\ m} = \dfrac{mi}{min}$

cancel

18. a. $(-2)^2 - 4(3) + (\sqrt{11})^2 =$

b. $\dfrac{m^2 b^4 r^3}{r^4 b^4 m} =$

a. _____

b. _____

19. $\dfrac{5}{12} - \dfrac{3}{4} \cdot \left(\dfrac{9}{5}\right)^{-1} =$

_____

20. *Adjacent angles are supplementary.*

Vertical angles are congruent.

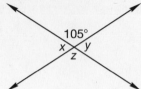

m∠x = _____

m∠y = _____

m∠z = _____

21. coin flip and spinner spun

   a. { __HA__ , _____ , _____ , __TA__ , _____ , _____ }

   b. P(TB or TC) =

Use work area.

22. $5(x - 6) = 40$

$x =$ _____

23. *Collect like terms first.*

   $8x + 3x - 2 = 75$

$x =$ _____

24. $0.007x + 0.28 = 0.7$

$x =$ _____

25. Is the relationship proportional? _____

Round to whole numbers and percents.

$\dfrac{42}{10} = \dfrac{100}{k}$ $k =$ _____

$\dfrac{42}{10} = \dfrac{p}{1}$ $p =$ _____%

$14p =$ _____%

Use work area.

• Probability
Multiplication Rule (page 457)

Name _____

Teacher Notes:
• Refer students to "Number Cube Chart" on page 25 in the *Student Reference Guide*.

• Review "Probability, Chance, Odds" on page 25 in the *Student Reference Guide*.

A tree diagram shows all the possible outcomes for a probability event that has more than one part.

• This tree diagram is for flipping two coins:

First Coin	Second Coin	Outcomes
H	H	HH
	T	HT
T	H	TH
	T	TT

There are four possible outcomes in the sample space.

• A shortcut to finding the number of outcomes is to multiply the number of outcomes for each part.

First Coin		**Second Coin**		**Possible Outcomes**
2 possible (H or T)	×	2 possible (H or T)		= 4 possible

• This is the **Fundamental Counting Principle.**

This method does not name each outcome. It only tells us how large the sample space is.

Example: How many possible outcomes are there for an experiment in which two number cubes are rolled?

Each number cube has 6 possible outcomes (1, 2, 3, 4, 5, or 6).

The total number of possible outcomes is $6 \times 6 = 36$ outcomes.

• The tree diagram shows that the probability of getting "heads and heads" is one out of four.

• Multiplying the probability of each coin toss gets the same result.

$$P(\text{H on 1}^{st}\text{ coin}) \cdot P(\text{H on 2}^{nd}\text{ coin}) = \frac{1}{2} \cdot \frac{1}{2} = \frac{1}{4}$$

• This is the **Multiplication Rule for Probability.**

To find the probability of two or more events, **multiply the probabilities** of each event.

Example: A bag contains 2 red and 3 blue marbles. Robert takes a marble from the bag, looks at it, and then replaces it in the bag. Then he takes another marble. What is the probability he selects a **red marble** and **then** a **blue marble?**

$$P(\text{red}) = \frac{2}{5}$$

$$P(\text{blue}) = \frac{3}{5}$$

$$P(\text{red and blue}) = P(\text{red}) \cdot P(\text{blue}) = \frac{2}{5} \cdot \frac{3}{5} = \frac{6}{25}$$

Practice Set (page 460)

A coin is tossed and this spinner is spun. Compute the probability of the events in **a** and **b**.

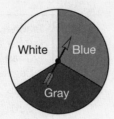

a. P(heads and blue)

P(heads) $= \dfrac{1}{2}$ P(blue) $= \dfrac{1}{3}$

P(heads and blue) $= P$(heads) $\cdot P$(blue) $= \dfrac{1}{2} \cdot \dfrac{1}{3} =$ _____

b. P(heads and not blue)

P(heads) $=$ P(not blue) $=$

P(heads and not blue) $= P$(heads) $\cdot P$(not blue) $=$ $\cdot$ $=$ _____

c. Two number cubes are rolled. What is the probability of rolling a number **greater than 4** on

each number cube? _____

P(greater than 4 on one cube) $= \dfrac{2}{6} = \dfrac{1}{3}$

P(greater than 4 on two cubes) $= ($ $) \cdot ($ $) =$

d. A coin will be flipped four times. What is the probability the coin will land **heads-up all four**

times? _____

P(heads) $=$

P(heads four times) $= ($ $) \cdot ($ $) \cdot ($ $) \cdot ($ $) =$

1.

	Ratio	Actual Count
Silver		s
Red		
Total		

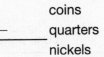

2.

	Percent	Actual Count
Wore		
Didn't wear		
Total	100	t

3.

_____ coins	$0.25	$0.10
− _____ quarters	× _____	_____
_____ nickels		

4.

	Percent	Actual Count
Left		l
Remained		
Total	100	

5. *Make a proportion.*

_____ = _____

6. What **rate** for one month? _____

Is the relationship proportional? _____

$9 \text{ mo} \cdot \dfrac{\$\ \_\_\_}{\text{mo}} =$

7. primes: 2,3,5

composites: 4,6

8. $y = \dfrac{2}{5}x - 1$

Is (10, 4) on the line? _____

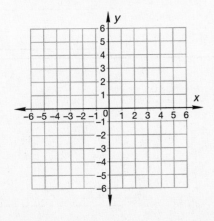

Use work area.

9. (−2, 3) and (1, 0)

Draw the line and write the equation.

$m =$

$b =$

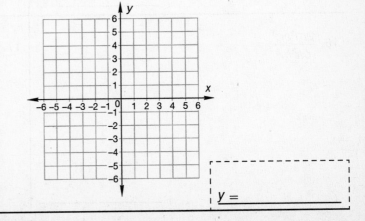

y =

10. area to nearest square inch

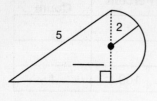

5   2

_____

_____

11. a. percent: _____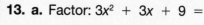

$\dfrac{7}{9}$

b. decimal: _____ $9\overline{)7.00}$

c. least to greatest

$\dfrac{6}{8}, \quad \dfrac{7}{8}, \quad \dfrac{7}{9}$

—— , —— , ——

Use work area.

12. adjacent to $\angle f$

∠ _____ and ∠ _____

13. a. Factor: $3x^2 + 3x + 9 =$

b. Distribute: $x(x-5) =$

a. _____

b. _____

14. $\dfrac{\text{in.}}{\text{min}}$ to $\dfrac{\text{in.}}{\text{hr}}$

$\dfrac{18 \text{ in.}}{1 \text{ min}} \cdot$ _____ $= \dfrac{\text{in.}}{\text{hr}}$

15. $\dfrac{\text{mi}}{\text{hr}}$ to $\dfrac{\text{rev}}{\text{hr}}$

(675 rev = 1 mi)

$\dfrac{10 \text{ mi.}}{1 \text{ hr}} \cdot$ _____ $= \dfrac{\text{rev}}{\text{hr}}$

16. $\dfrac{2m^2ac^3}{ca^2m^2} =$

17. $(-3)(-4) - (-5)(6) =$

18. $\frac{3}{5}x + \frac{7}{10} = \frac{19}{10}$

$x = $ _____

19. $\frac{1}{4} + \frac{3}{8}x = 1$

$x = $ _____

20. $0.003x - 0.02 = 0.07$

$x = $ _____

21. $0.03x - 0.02 = 0.07$

$x = $ _____

22. $5x + 2x - 3 = 18$

$x = $ _____

23. $x - 3 < 1$

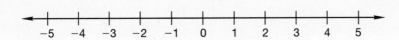

Use a circle.

$x < $ _____

24. $3x - 2 \geq 4$

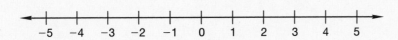

Use a dot.

$x \geq $ _____

25. Find A: (,   )

How many units is A from

the line x = 3? _____

A′ will be that number of
units **right** of x = 3.

A (1,−1)   **B** (2,−1)

C (5,−1)   **D** (8,−1)

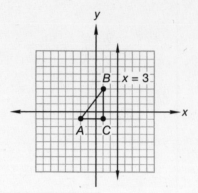

Direct variation is a proportional relationship between two variables.

• The **dependent variable** (output number, y) depends on the **independent variable** (input number, x).

• Direct variation means:

> if one variable *increases*, the other variable also *increases*.

> if one variable *decreases*, the other variable also *decreases*.

> if one variable is *zero*, the other variable is also *zero*.

• Direct variation relationships have a special equation:

> $y = kx$

> k is the **constant of proportionality** (constant multiplier).

• The direct variation equation is similar to the slope-intercept equation:

> $y = mx + b$ $y = (\text{slope})\, x + (y\text{-intercept})$

• In direct variation, the y-intercept is zero and the slope is k.

• To tell if a relationship is a direct variation, make a ratio out of each pair of numbers. If the ratios reduce to the same number, then it is direct variation.

• The reduced number will be k, the constant of proportionality.

Example: The table shows four pairs of numbers. Is the relationship an example of direct variation? What is the constant of proportionality? Write an equation and graph the line.

e	d	$\frac{d}{e}$
2	4	$\frac{4}{2} = 2$
1	2	$\frac{2}{1} = 2$
−1	−2	$\frac{-2}{-1} = 2$
−2	−4	$\frac{-4}{-2} = 2$

Every ratio of d to e reduces to the same number, 2. So this is an example of direct variation, and the constant of proportionality is 2.

Substituting 2 for k gives the equation:

$d = 2e$

This equation is graphed below.

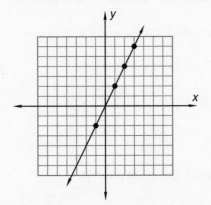

Practice Set (page 467)

a. Trinny drew some equilateral triangles and measured their side lengths and perimeters. She decided that the perimeter of an equilateral triangle varies directly with its side length. Write an equation for the relationship and identify the constant of proportionality, k.

$k =$ _____   equation: $P =$ _____

s	P	$\frac{P}{S}$
2	6	$\frac{6}{2} =$
3	9	$\frac{9}{3} =$
4	12	$\frac{12}{4} =$
7	21	$\frac{21}{7} =$

b. The relationship between Sergio's age and Fernando's age is illustrated in the graph. Are their ages proportional? Is this an example of direct variation?

_____ because the graph does not intersect the _o_____.

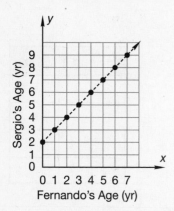

Sergio's Age (yr)

0 1 2 3 4 5 6 7
Fernando's Age (yr)

c. The weight of water in a trough is directly **proportional** to the quantity of water in the trough. If 20 gallons of water weigh 166 pounds, what is the weight of 30 gallons of water? _____

$\frac{\text{gal}}{\text{lb}}$ ___ ___

Find the constant of proportionality in pounds per gallon. _____

$\frac{\text{gal}}{\text{lb}}$ ___ 1

Write an equation for the relationship using p for pounds and g for gallons.

$p =$ _____

1. 980 total

<u>630</u> house-team

     visiting team

_____

2.

	Percent	Actual Count
Recognized		
Not recognized		n
Total	100	

_____

3.

	Percent	Actual Count
Last year	100	d
Change (+)		
This year		

_____

4.

x	2	18	30
y	5	45	80
$\dfrac{y}{x}$	$\dfrac{5}{2}$	$\dfrac{45}{18} =$	$\dfrac{80}{30} =$

Direct variation?

_____

5.

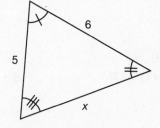

$x =$ _____

$y =$ _____

6. The smaller triangle is dilated by scale factor _____.

Use work area.

7. *special triangle*

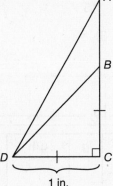

a. m∠$DAC =$ _____

b. m∠$DBC =$ _____

c. $DB =$ _____

d. $DA =$ _____

8. slope: $\dfrac{1}{4}$

   y-intercept: _____

$y =$ _____

9. $(-2, -4)$ and $(6, 0)$

Draw the line and write the equation.

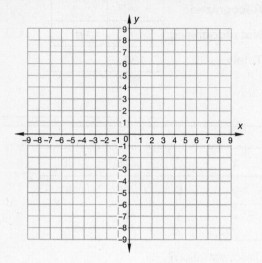

$y =$ _____

10. Round to nearest whole unit.

a. area

b. perimeter

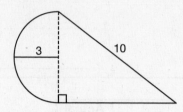

a. _____

b. _____

11. a. decimal: _____

$9\overline{)4.00}$

b. percent: _____

c. least to greatest

$0.4, 0.5, \dfrac{4}{9}$

_____, _____, _____

Use work area.

12. a. $\left\{ \dfrac{HHH}{}, —, —, —, —, —, —, — \right\}$

b. P (at least HH) =

c. same probability as b.

P (at least   )

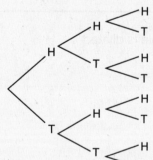

Use work area.

13. a. Factor: $5x^2 + 10x + 15$

b. Distribute: $-4(2x + 3) =$

a. _____ **b.** _____

14. $\dfrac{1}{2}$ gal/hr   **a.**

h	g	g/h
1		
2		
3		
4		

b. _____ because all the _____ reduce to the same number.

Use work area.

15. $\dfrac{\text{gal}}{\text{hr}}$ to $\dfrac{\text{gal}}{\text{day}}$

$\dfrac{1 \text{ gal}}{2 \text{ hr}} \cdot \underline{\hspace{1cm}} = \dfrac{\text{gal}}{\text{day}}$

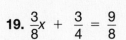

16. $\dfrac{8x^3yz^2}{4xyz^2} =$

17. $\left(-\dfrac{2}{3}\right)^2 \cdot \left(\dfrac{2}{3}\right)^{-1} =$

18. a. $m\angle x \bigcirc m\angle a$

Corresponding angles are congruent.

b. If the lines are not p $\underline{\hspace{3cm}}$,

then the angles would not

be c $\underline{\hspace{3cm}}$.

Use work area.

19. $\dfrac{3}{8}x + \dfrac{3}{4} = \dfrac{9}{8}$

$x = \underline{\hspace{2cm}}$

20. $\dfrac{1}{3}x - \dfrac{3}{4} = \dfrac{5}{12}$

$x = \underline{\hspace{2cm}}$

21. $0.007x + 0.03 = 0.1$

$x = \underline{\hspace{2cm}}$

22. $\dfrac{x}{5} = \dfrac{1}{2}$

$x = \underline{\hspace{2cm}}$

23. $\dfrac{2}{3} = \dfrac{5}{x}$

$x = \underline{\hspace{2cm}}$

24. $\dfrac{\text{mi}}{\text{hr}}$ to $\dfrac{\text{mi}}{\text{min}}$

$\dfrac{120 \text{ mi}}{1 \text{ hr}} \cdot \underline{\hspace{1cm}} = \dfrac{\text{mi}}{\text{min}}$

25. **Hot-Air Balloon Altitude**

Time (Minutes)	Altitude (Feet)	$\frac{A}{T}$
0	0	$\frac{0}{0} =$
1	200	$\frac{200}{1} =$
2	400	$\frac{400}{2} =$
2.5	500	$\frac{500}{2.5} =$
3	600	$\frac{600}{3} =$
4	800	$\frac{800}{4} =$
5.75	1150	$\frac{1150}{5.75} =$

The relationship is _____

because every ratio reduces

to the same number, _____ ft/min.

To find the altitude at _____ minutes,

multiply _____ by

_____ to get _____ feet.

Use work area.

• Solving Direct Variation Problems (page 470)

Name _____

In direct variation, every ratio of input to output numbers reduces to the same number, called the constant of proportionality.

• This is a *proportional relationship.*

• Solve direct ratios by setting up a proportion.

Example: The amount Ellen charges for banquet food varies directly to the number of people that attend. If Ellen charges $780 for 60 people, how much does she charge for 100 people?

$$\frac{\$}{\text{people}} \quad \frac{780}{60} = \frac{d}{100} \qquad 100 \cdot 13 = 1 \cdot d$$
$$d = \$1300$$

cancel

Practice Set (page 473)

a. The distance a coiled spring stretches varies directly with the amount of weight hanging on the spring. If a spring stretches 2 cm when a 30 gram weight is hung from it, how far will it stretch when a 75 gram weight is hung from the spring? _____

$$\frac{\text{cm}}{\text{g}} \quad \frac{2}{30} = \frac{x}{75} \qquad 75 = 15x$$

cancel

b. The number of words Tom types varies directly with the amount of time he spends typing. If Tom types 100 words in 2.5 minutes, how many words does he type in 15 minutes? _____

$$\frac{\text{words}}{\text{min}} \quad \frac{100}{2.5} = \frac{x}{15}$$

c. Traffic was dense for the evening commute. Mitchell traveled three miles on the highway in 15 minutes. Predict how much longer it will take Mitchell to reach his exit five miles away. _____

$$\frac{\text{mi}}{\text{min}} \quad \frac{3}{15} = \frac{}{x}$$

cancel

1. $\dfrac{\text{Insects}}{\text{Humans}} = \dfrac{x}{10}$

2.

	Percent	Actual Count
Foreign		
Not Foreign		
Total	100	t

3.

	Percent	Actual Count
Original	100	
Changed (−)	15	
New		

4. Is this direct variation?

L	W	$\dfrac{W}{L}$
6	4	$\dfrac{4}{6} =$
10	8	$\dfrac{8}{10} =$
14	12	$\dfrac{12}{14} =$

5.

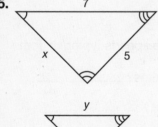

$x =$ _____

$y =$ _____

Scale Factor: _____

6. $y = \dfrac{1}{3}x - 1$

Is (6,1) a solution? _____

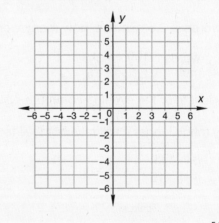

Use work area.

7. Round to the nearest unit. Use 3.14 for π.

  a. area

  b. perimeter

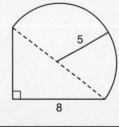

a. _____

b. _____

8. a. decimal

$6\overline{)1.000}$

  b. percent

a. _____

b. _____

9. $x - 3 \geq -1$

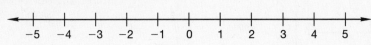

Use a dot.

$x \geq$ _____

11. $\dfrac{12w^2x^2y^3}{8x^2y^2} =$

_____

10. $2x + 3 < 1$

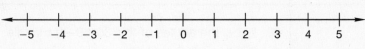

Use a circle.

$x <$ _____

12. $\dfrac{4}{5} - \dfrac{3}{5} \cdot \left(\dfrac{1}{3}\right)^{-1} =$

_____

13. $3x + 3 - x - 3 =$

_____

14. $0.2 + 0.3(0.4) =$

_____

15. $\dfrac{1}{3}x + \dfrac{4}{9} = \dfrac{7}{9}$

$x =$ _____

16. $\dfrac{4}{5} + \dfrac{2}{15}x = \dfrac{14}{15}$

$x =$ _____

17. $0.005x - 0.03 = 0.01$

$x =$ _____

18. $\dfrac{\text{in.}}{\text{sec}}$ to $\dfrac{\text{ft}}{\text{sec}}$

$\dfrac{30 \text{ in.}}{1 \text{ sec}} \cdot$ _____ $=$ _____ $\dfrac{\text{ft}}{\text{sec}}$

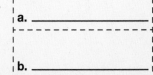

19. Factor:

a. $2x^2 + 6x + 10 =$

b. $x^3 - x^2 =$

a. _____

b. _____

20. B_1, B_2, G

   a. { $\underline{B_1B_2}$, $\underline{B_1G}$, _____ , _____ , _____ , _____ }

   b. $P(B_1B_2)$ =

   | b. _____

21. Find m∠y first.

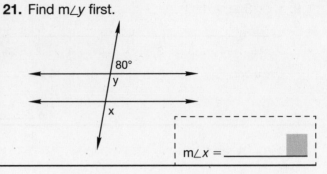

   | m∠x = _____

22. *Multiply the probabilities.*

   $P(6)$ = _____

   $P(6 \text{ three times})$ = ___ · ___ · ___ =

   | _____

23. Label the angles of this 30-60-90 triangle. Find *a*.

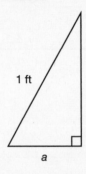

1 ft

a

   | a = _____

24. $\dfrac{3}{x} = \dfrac{5}{7}$

   | x = _____

25. Complete the table.

   The relationship is _____

   because the __r__ is not constant.

H (hours)	D ($)	$\dfrac{D}{H}$
1	20.00	$\dfrac{20}{1}$ = 20
2		
3		
4		

   | Use work area. |

• Percent Change of Dimensions (page 479)

Name _____

We calculate the dimensions of a dilation or reduction by finding the percent of increase or decrease.

Teacher Notes:
• Review Hint #47, "Scale Factor."
• Review "Scale Factor" on page 31 in the *Student Reference Guide*.

• A **dilation** (size increase) or a **reduction** (size decrease) makes similar figures.

• **Similar** figures have *proportional* measures (radius, side length, or diameter).

• The ratio of similar measures is the **scale factor.**

> The **perimeters** of similar figures are related by the *scale factor*.
> The **areas** of similar figures are related by the *scale factor squared*.
> The **volumes** of similar figures are related by the *scale factor cubed*.

• For percent change problems, change percents to *decimals*.

• **The original figure is always 100%.**

> To find a **percent increase,** find the percent of the new figure and *subtract 100%*.

> To find a **percent decrease,** find the percent of the new figure. Then *subtract it from 100%*.

Example: The towel shrunk 10% when it was washed. The area of the towel was reduced by what percent?

The original towel is 100%.

The dimensions decrease by 10%.

$100\% - 10\% = 90\%$	original $-$ decrease $=$ new
$90\% = 0.9$	change to a decimal for scale factor
$(0.9)^2 = 0.81$	Area is scale factor squared
$0.81 = 81\%$	Change to a percent
$100\% - 81\% = 19\%$	Percent decrease (subtract from 100%)

Example: If the dimensions of a cube are increased 100%, by what percent is the volume increased?

We draw a sample cube that has sides 1 inch long. A 100% percent increase means that the new figure is 200% of the old figure, so the side length doubles. The new cube has sides 2 inches long.

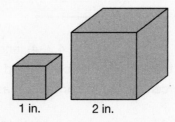

1 in.   2 in.

The cubes are similar figures and the scale factor is 2.

The volume is related by the scale factor cubed:

$2^3 = 8$

The volume of the larger cube is 8 times (800%) the volume of the smaller cube.

The smaller cube is 100%, so the volume *increased* by

$800\% - 100\% = 700\%$

Practice Set (page 482)

a. There are two concentric circles on the playground. The diameter of the larger circle is 40% greater than the diameter of the smaller circle. The area of the larger circle is what **percent greater** than the area of the smaller circle?

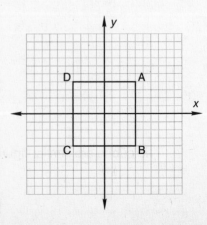

smaller circle = 100%
larger circle = 100% + 40% = 140%
Change 140% to a decimal. This is the scale factor. _____

The area is related by the scale factor squared.

$(\text{scale factor})^2 =$ _____

Change that number back to a percent: _____%

percent greater = _____% − 100% = _____

b. Becky reduced the size of the image on the computer screen by 40%. By what **percent** was the area of the image **reduced?**

original image = 100%
new image = 100% − 40% = _____%

Change this percent to a decimal: _____

The area is related by the scale factor squared.

$(\text{scale factor})^2 =$ _____

Change that number back to a percent: _____%

percent reduction = 100% − _____% = _____

c. Square *ABCD* has vertices at *A*(4, 4), *B*(4, −4), *C*(−4, −4), and *D*(−4, 4). If it is dilated by 150%, then by what percent would the **perimeter increase?** By what percent would the **area increase?**

150% increase is scale factor 1.5. Multiply each coordinate by 1.5 to draw square *A′B′C′D′*. For instance A(4, 4) × 1.5 = A′(6, 6).

The perimeter is related by the scale factor.
scale factor = 150%
percent increase in perimeter = _____% − 100% = _____

Practice Set (continued) (page 482)

The area is related by the scale factor squared.

scale factor = 150% = 1.5

(scale factor)^2 = _____

Change that number back to a percent: _____%

percent increase in area = _____% − 100% = _____

d. Suppose the dimensions of the larger cube in the example were increased by 100%.

What would be the edge length of the expanded cube? _____
100% increase is a doubling.

The volume of the expanded cube would be **what percent** of the 2 inch cube?
original + increase = 100% + 100% = 200%

Change 200% to a decimal: _____

The volume is related by the scale factor cubed.

(scale factor)^3 = _____

Change that number back to a percent: _____%

The volume of the expanded cube is _____% of the volume of the 2-inch cube.

*The problem asked for the **percent**, not the percent increase.*

Written Practice (page 483)

1.

	Ratio	Actual count
Pencils		
Pens		p
Total		

_____

2.

	Percent	Actual count
Watched		
Did not watch		d
Total	100	

_____

3.

	Percent	Actual count
Original	100	
Change(+)		
New		2470

_____

4.

s	P	$\frac{P}{s}$
1	3	
2	6	
5	15	
50	150	

s = side length P = perimeter

Is this direct variation? _____

What is the constant? _____

What type of polygon is this?

equilateral _____

¡ Use work area. ¡

5.

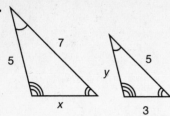

x = _____   y = _____

6. $y = 2x - 2$

$y = mx + b$

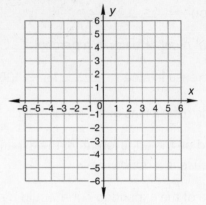

This is not direct variation because the

line _____.   Use work area.

7.

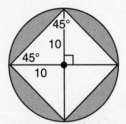

Use 3.14 for π.

Area of circle
− Area of square

_____

8. a. decimal

106% =

b. fraction

106% =

c.   1.06
      × 21

a. _____

b. _____

c. _____

9. number cube

$P(3 \text{ or more}) =$

10. dimensions increased by 10%

new = original + increase

= 100% + _____% = _____%

change to a decimal : _____

Area is scale factor squared

$(\text{Scale factor})^2 =$ _____

Change to a percent : _____

percent increase = _____% − 100% =

11. $7 - x \geq 5$

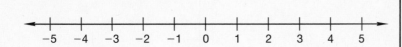

Use a dot.

$x \leq$ _____

12.

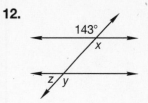

$m\angle z =$ _____

13. Put the numbers in order.

1.1, _____, _____, _____, _____, 1.9

a.

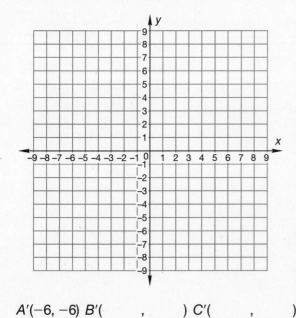

b. mean: _____   median: _____

mode: _____   range: _____

c. _____

Use work area.

14. $\dfrac{m}{sec}$ to $\dfrac{m}{min}$

$\dfrac{100 \text{ m}}{50 \text{ sec}}$ · _____ =

Cancel.

_____

15. $A(-2, -2)$, $B(2, -2)$, $C(0, 2)$

Find $\triangle A'B'C'$ with scale factor 3.

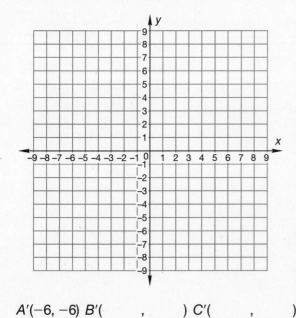

$A'(-6, -6)$ $B'($, $)$ $C'($, $)$

Use work area.

16. $\triangle A'B'C' = 100\%$

scale factor $= \dfrac{1}{3}$

What percent is $\dfrac{1}{3}$?

_____

17. $\dfrac{15x^2y^{-1}}{5xy} =$

_____

18. $\dfrac{5}{6} - \dfrac{2}{3} \div \dfrac{4}{5} =$

_____

19. $-3 + (-4)(-5) =$

_____

20. $\dfrac{1.2 + 0.24}{0.3} =$

_____

21. $\dfrac{1}{4} - \dfrac{2}{3}x = \dfrac{11}{12}$

$x =$ _____

22. $\dfrac{3}{4} = \dfrac{15}{x}$

$x =$ _____

23. $0.02x - 0.3 = 1.1$

$x =$ _____

24. $6x - 12 = 84$

$x =$ _____

25. 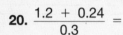 _See the top of page 485._

Total members = 60
4 members did not rent
1, 2, 3, or 4 movies

_____

• Multiple Unit Multipliers (page 486)

Name _____

Teacher Note:
• Review "Multiple Unit Multipliers" on page 23 in the *Student Reference Guide.*

Sometimes we use more than one unit multiplier to convert measures and rates.

• To convert units of **area**, use *two* unit multipliers. The units will cancel.

    Example: Convert 855 ft^2 to yd^2.

    Use the unit multiplier $\dfrac{1\ yd}{3\ ft}$ twice.

$$855\ \cancel{ft}^2 \cdot \dfrac{1\ yd}{3\ \cancel{ft}} \cdot \dfrac{1\ yd}{3\ \cancel{ft}} = \dfrac{855}{9}\ yd^2 = 95\ yd^2$$

    ft and ft cancel ft^2.

• To convert units of **volume**, use *three* unit multipliers. The units will cancel.

    Example: Convert 216 ft^3 to yd^3.

    Use the unit multiplier $\dfrac{1\ yd}{3\ ft}$ three times.

$$216\ \cancel{ft}^3 \cdot \dfrac{1\ yd}{3\ \cancel{ft}} \cdot \dfrac{1\ yd}{3\ \cancel{ft}} \cdot \dfrac{1\ yd}{3\ \cancel{ft}} = \dfrac{216}{27}\ yd^3 = 8yd^3$$

    ft and ft and ft cancel ft^3.

• To convert both units in a rate, use two unit multipliers.

• The units will cancel and leave only the correct units in the answer.

    Example: Convert 440 yards per minute to miles per hour.

    Both units are changing: yards to miles and minutes to hours.

$$\dfrac{440\ \cancel{yd}}{1\ \cancel{min}} \cdot \dfrac{6\cancel{0}\ \cancel{min}}{1\ hr} \cdot \dfrac{1\ mi}{176\cancel{0}\ \cancel{yd}} = \dfrac{2640\ mi}{176\ hr} = 15\ \dfrac{mi}{hr}$$

    Cancel matching zeros.

• **Cancel numbers and units as you go.**

Practice Set (page 488)

a. Look at problems **b–h.** Decide if you will use 2 or 3 unit multipliers for each problem.
Write the letter of each problem in the appropriate blanks.
Two unit multipliers for area or changing both units in a rate.
Three unit multipliers for volume.

2 unit multipliers: _____, _____, _____, _____, _____

3 unit multipliers: _____, _____

Use multiple unit multipliers to perform each conversion.

b. 9 sq. ft to sq. in.

$$9 \, ft^2 \cdot \frac{12 \text{ in.}}{1 \, ft} \cdot \frac{12 \text{ in.}}{1 \, ft} = \underline{\hspace{1cm}} \text{ in.}^2$$

c. 9 sq. ft to sq. yd

$$9 \, ft^2 \cdot \frac{\text{yd}}{ft} \cdot \frac{\text{yd}}{ft} = \underline{\hspace{2cm}}$$

d. 1 m^3 to cm^3

$$1 \, m^3 \cdot \frac{100 \text{ cm}}{1 \, m} \cdot \frac{100 \text{ cm}}{1 \, m} \cdot \frac{100 \text{ cm}}{1 \, m} = 10 \text{ cm}^3$$

e. 1,000,000 mm^3 to cm^3

$$1{,}000{,}000 \text{ mm}^3 \cdot \frac{\text{cm}}{\text{mm}} \cdot \frac{\text{cm}}{\text{mm}} \cdot \frac{\text{cm}}{\text{mm}} = \underline{\hspace{2cm}}$$

f. 12 dollars per hour to cents per minute

$$\frac{12 \text{ dollars}}{1 \, hr} \cdot \frac{1 \, hr}{60 \text{ min}} \cdot \frac{100 \text{ cents}}{1 \text{ dollar}} = \underline{\hspace{1cm}} \text{ cents/min}$$

g. 10 yards per second to feet per minute

$$\frac{10 \text{ yd}}{1 \text{ sec}} \cdot \frac{\text{sec}}{\text{min}} \cdot \frac{\text{ft}}{\text{yd}} = \underline{\hspace{1cm}} \text{ ft/min}$$

h. 1 gallon per day to quarts per hour

$$\frac{1 \text{ gal}}{1 \text{ day}} \cdot \underline{\hspace{1cm}} \cdot \underline{\hspace{1cm}} = \underline{\hspace{1cm}} \text{ qt/hr}$$

1.

	Ratio	Actual count
Fish		f
Ducks		
Total		

2.

	Percent	Actual count
Bands		
No Bands		
Total	100	t

_____

_____

3.

	Percent	Actual count
Original	100	b
Change (+)		
New		

4.

x	y	$\dfrac{y}{x}$
6	22	$\dfrac{22}{6} = \dfrac{11}{3}$
15	165	$\dfrac{165}{15} =$
18	176	$\dfrac{176}{18} =$

The ^{r} _____ is not constant

so this _____ direct variation.

_____

_____

5.

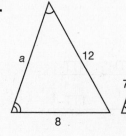

$\dfrac{\text{smaller}}{\text{larger}} =$

a. _____

b. _____

6. $\dfrac{\text{mi}}{\text{hr}}$ to $\dfrac{\text{yd}}{\text{min}}$

$\dfrac{21 \text{ mi}}{1 \text{ hr}} \cdot \dfrac{\text{hr}}{\text{min}} \cdot \dfrac{\text{yd}}{\text{mi}} =$

_____

7. $\frac{\text{ft}}{\text{min}}$ to $\frac{\text{yd}}{\text{sec}}$

$$\frac{90 \text{ ft}}{1 \text{ min}} \cdot \frac{\text{min}}{\text{sec}} \cdot \frac{\text{yd}}{\text{ft}} =$$

_____

8. $y = \frac{1}{2}x$

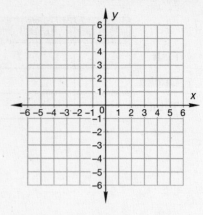

This is direct variation because the graph is

a _____ that goes through the

o_____.

Use work area.

9. area

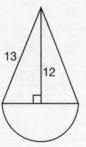

_____

10. **a.** decimal

$33\frac{1}{3}\% =$

b. fraction

$33\frac{1}{3}\% =$

a. _____

b. _____

c. _____

11.

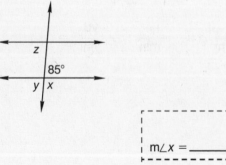

m∠x = _____

m∠y = _____

m∠z = _____

12. Coin flipped 3 times

a. $\{$ HHH , HHT , HTH , HTT ,

_____, _____, _____, TTT $\}$

b. $P(2 \text{ or more } H) =$

c. If the coin is flipped four times instead, does $P(2 \text{ or more } H)$ increase

or decrease? _____

Use work area.

13. $85.97

$$\times \underline{\hspace{2cm}}$$

14. standard form

$shift \longrightarrow$

$2.5 \times 10^5 =$

15. Factor:

a. $7x^2 + 35x - 14 =$

b. $-3x - 15 =$

a. _____

b. _____

16. $\dfrac{8a^2b^{-1}c}{6ab^2c} =$

17. $-\dfrac{1}{2} - \left(-\dfrac{3}{4}\right) =$

18. $x + y - x + 3 - 2 =$

19. $0.12 + (0.6)(0.02) + 2 =$

20. $2 + \dfrac{1}{3}t = \dfrac{2}{3}$

$t =$ _____

21. $0.9x - 1.3 = 0.5$

$x = $ _____

22. $\dfrac{x}{6} = \dfrac{6}{9}$

$x = $ _____

23. $2(x + 7) - 4 = 24$

$x = $ _____

24. $x + 5 \geq 3$

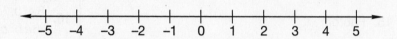

$x \geq$ _____

25. neither

Round to the nearest whole number.

_____% of 680.

_____

• **Formulas for Sequences**
(page 491)

Name _____

A sequence is an ordered set of numbers, called terms, that follows a rule.

• Every **term** in a sequence has a position and a value.

The position, *n,* is the term's place in the sequence, such as 1st, 2nd, or 3rd.

The value, *a,* of a term is the number.

• A formula for a sequence uses the variables n and a_n to describe the sequence.

• If the formula is known, we can substitute a term's position into the formula to find the value of that term.

Example: The formula $a_n = 2^n$ describes the sequence {2, 4, 8, 16, ...}.

Find the tenth term in this sequence.

Substitute 10 for *n* and solve with a calculator.
$a_{10} = 2^{10} = 1024$

• If the formula or rule is not known, find a pattern in the terms.

Example: What is the rule for this sequence?
{1, −2, 2, −1, 3, 0, 4, ...}

The pattern subtracts 3 and then adds 4.

$$\begin{array}{cccccccc} -3 & +4 & -3 & +4 & -3 & +4 & -3 & +4 \end{array}$$

1, −2, 2, −1, 3, 0, 4, **1, 5**

Practice Set (page 493)

a. What is the 7th term in this sequence? _____
1, 4, 9, 16, ...
Look at the circled numbers in the "Multiplication Table" on page 3 of the Student Reference Guide. Now find the 7th term.

b. The following sequence has the rule $a_n = 5n - 2$. Find the tenth term.
3, 8, 13, 18, ...

$a_{10} = 5(10) - 2 =$ _____

c. Circle the formula that generates the terms of the following sequence.
0, 3, 8, 15, ...

A $a_n = n - 1$ **B** $a_n = 2n - 1$ **C** $a_n = n^2 - 1$

d. Substitute 1, 2, 3, and 4 for *n* to find the first four terms in the sequence with the formula
$a_n = n^2 + 2n + 1$.

$a_1 =$ _____ $a_2 =$ _____ $a_3 =$ _____ $a_4 =$ _____

e. Write another formula that generates the same first four terms as the sequence in problem **d.**

$$a_n = (\qquad)^2$$

Compare the terms in the sequence in problem d to the terms of the sequence in problem a.

f. Triangular numbers are found with the formula $a_n = \dfrac{n(n+1)}{2}$
Find the 20th triangular number.

$$a_{20} = \frac{20(20+1)}{2} = \underline{\hspace{3cm}}$$

Written Practice (page 494)

1. new = original + increase =

100% + _____ % = _____%

Change to a decimal. _____

Area is the square of the scale factor.

$(\text{scale factor})^2 =$ _____ Change to a percent.

increase = _____% − 100% =

2.

	Percent	Actual count
Volunteered		
Did not		
Total	100	t

3.

	Percent	Actual count
Original	100	
Change (−)		
New		n

4.

W	D	$\dfrac{D}{W}$
4	20	
7	35	
9	45	

Is this direct variation?

constant = _____

5. average of bases: $\dfrac{6+10}{2} =$

6. $\dfrac{yd}{sec}$ to $\dfrac{ft}{sec}$

$$\frac{6 \text{ yd}}{3 \text{ sec}} \cdot \underline{\hspace{1.5cm}} =$$

7. $\dfrac{ft}{min}$ to $\dfrac{mi}{hr}$

$$\dfrac{440\ ft}{1\ min} \cdot \dfrac{min}{hr} \cdot \dfrac{mi}{ft} =$$

8. $y = -x + 5$

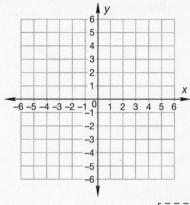

Use work area.

9. *Each triangle has the same area.*

10. a. decimal

$12\overline{)1.0000}$

b. percent

c. $\dfrac{1}{12}\ \bigcirc\ \dfrac{1}{10}$

a. _____

b. _____

c. _____

11. Factor:

a. $4x^2 + 12x - 4 =$

b. $-2x - 16 =$

a. _____

b. _____

12. perimeter and area

$A = bh$

Opposite sides have equal length.

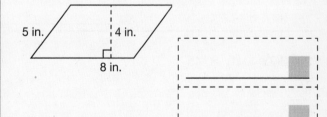
5 in.　4 in.　8 in.

13. perimeter and area

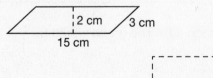
2 cm　3 cm　15 cm

14. $\sqrt{39}$ is between which whole numbers?

$3^2 =$　$4^2 =$　$5^2 =$　$6^2 =$　$7^2 =$

A 3 and 4　　**B** 4 and 5

C 5 and 6　　**D** 6 and 7

15. *$4 is always charged.*
$0.85 charges per pound.

_____

16. $\dfrac{24m^4b^{-1}}{18m^{-3}b^3} =$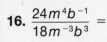

_____

17. $(-3)^1 - (-2)^2 - 4^0 =$

_____

18. $\dfrac{2}{3} - \dfrac{1}{6}x = \dfrac{1}{2}$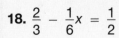

$x =$ _____

19. $\dfrac{4}{5}x + \dfrac{1}{10} = \dfrac{1}{2}$

$x =$ _____

20. $\dfrac{4}{3} = \dfrac{6}{x}$

$x =$ _____

21. $\dfrac{3}{4}x = 12$

$x =$ _____

22. $0.09x + 0.9 = 2.7$

$x =$ _____

23. $3(2x - 1) = 45$

$x =$ _____

24. $a_n = 2n - 3$

Find the 20th term.

$a_{20} =$

$a_{20} =$ _____

25. It cost $_____ for admission to the Carnival and $_____ for each ride. The graph would be

proportional if there was no cost for _____.

‎Use work area.

• Simplifying Square Roots (page 496)

Name _____

A perfect square is a number that is the product of a number times itself.

Teacher Notes:
- Introduce Hint #54, "Simplifying Square Roots Using Prime Factorization."
- Refer students to "Using Prime Factorization to Find Square Roots" on page 24 in the *Student Reference Guide.*
- Review "Multiplication Table" on page 3 and "Laws of Exponents" on page 19 in the *Student Reference Guide.*

- The first few **perfect squares** are shown circled on the "Multiplication Table" in the *Student Reference Guide* on page 3.

- Because perfect squares have two identical factors, their square roots are easy to find.

$$4 = 2 \cdot 2 \quad \sqrt{4} = \sqrt{2}\sqrt{2} = 2$$
$$81 = 9 \cdot 9 \quad \sqrt{81} = \sqrt{9}\sqrt{9} = 9$$

- The **product property of square roots** states that square roots can be factored and multiplied.

$$\sqrt{12} = \sqrt{4}\sqrt{3} = 2\sqrt{3}$$
$$\sqrt{18} = \sqrt{9}\sqrt{2} = 3\sqrt{2}$$

- Use the multiplication table to look for perfect squares that divide evenly into the factors of square roots. The perfect squares can be factored out as whole numbers and the square root is simplified.

Example: Simplify $\sqrt{600}$

100 is a perfect square and factor of 600.

$$\sqrt{600} = \sqrt{100}\sqrt{6} = 10\sqrt{6}$$

Example: Simplify $\sqrt{72}$

Look for perfect squares on the "Multiplication Table."

$\sqrt{72} = \sqrt{4}\sqrt{18}$	factor out $\sqrt{4}$
$2\sqrt{18}$	rewrite $(\sqrt{4} = 2)$
$2\sqrt{18} = 2\sqrt{9}\sqrt{2}$	factor out $\sqrt{9}$
$2 \cdot 3\sqrt{2} = 6\sqrt{2}$	rewrite $(\sqrt{9} = 3)$

- If a problem asks for an exact answer, give the simplified square root.

- If a problem asks for an approximate answer, simplify the square root and then use a calculator to multiply by one of these approximations:

Approximate Values of Square Roots

Square Root	Approximate Value
$\sqrt{2}$	1.41
$\sqrt{3}$	1.73
$\sqrt{5}$	2.24
$\sqrt{10}$	3.16

Practice Set (page 499)

Simplify. One of the square roots below cannot be simplified.

a. $\sqrt{20} = \sqrt{4}\,\sqrt{5} = $ _____ $\sqrt{5}$

b. $\sqrt{24} = \sqrt{4}\,\sqrt{6} = $ _____

c. $\sqrt{27} = \sqrt{9}\,\sqrt{3} = $ _____

d. $\sqrt{30} = $ _____

e. $\sqrt{125} = $ _____

f. $\sqrt{48} = $ _____

g. $\sqrt{50} = $ _____

h. $\sqrt{90} = $ _____

i. $\sqrt{1000} = $ _____

j. Use a calculator and the numbers in the table of square root approximations to calculate to the nearest tenth the values of the square roots in problems **g, h,** and **i.**

g. $\sqrt{50} = $ _____ · _____

h. $\sqrt{90} = $ _____ · _____

i. $\sqrt{1000} = $ _____ · _____

k. Jenny folded a 10-inch square piece of paper in half diagonally, making a triangle. What is the length of the longest side of the triangle? Give an exact answer and an approximate answer:

exact: _____ ◻   approximate: _____ ◻

It is a 45-45-90 triangle.

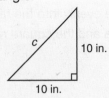

c   10 in.

10 in.

l. Which square root in problems **a–i** could not be simplified? Why?

_____ because none of the factors are <u>p</u>_____ <u>s</u>_____.

Written Practice   (page 500)

1. players _____ _____
    basketballs

2.

	Percent	Actual Count
Original	100	
Change (+)	*n*	
New		

3.

	Percent	Actual Count
Original	100	
Change (−)		
New		n

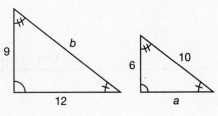

4.

x	y	$\frac{y}{x}$
0	0	
1	3.1	
2	6.2	
3	9.3	

Is this direct variation?

_____

Constant: _____

5.

9
b
12

6
10
a

_a =_ _____

_b =_ _____

6. $\frac{smaller}{larger} =$

Area is related by (scale factor)².

_____

_____

7. *Factor perfect squares.*

$\sqrt{2500} = \sqrt{25}\sqrt{100} =$

_____

8. $\sqrt{18} = \sqrt{}\ \sqrt{2} =$

_____

9. $\sqrt{75} = \sqrt{}\ \sqrt{3} =$

_____

10. $\frac{36x^3y^{-1}}{24x^2y^2} =$

_____

11. in.³ to ft³

$$86{,}400 \text{ in.}^3 \cdot \frac{\text{ft}}{\text{in.}} \cdot \frac{\text{ft}}{\text{in.}} \cdot \frac{\text{ft}}{\text{in.}} =$$

_____

12. $y = -3x + 1$

Is $(2, -5)$ a solution? _____

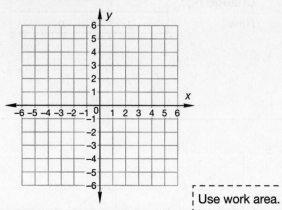

Use work area.

13. Find the 12th term.

$$a_n = n(n + 1)$$

$$a_{12} =$$

$a_{12} =$ _____

14. a. decimal

$$15\overline{)4.000}$$

b. percent

c. _____ of the athletes had played in the finals.

a. _____

b. _____

c. _____

15. Factor:

a. $6x^2 - 30x - 18 =$

b. $2x^3 + 2x =$

a. _____

b. _____

16. $\frac{2}{6}$ (area of circle)

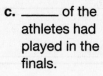

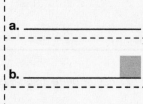

12 in.

Use 3 for π.

A 108 in.²　　**B** 36 in.²

C 12 in.²　　**D** 4 in.²

_____

17. new = original + increase = 100% + _____% =

Change to a decimal: _____

Area is related by scale factor squared.

(scale factor)² = _____

Change to a percent: _____

increase = _____% − 100% =

18. perimeter and area

$A = bh$

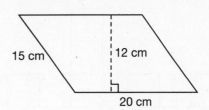

15 cm   12 cm

20 cm

_____

_____

19. a. $A = bh$

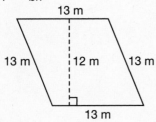

13 m

13 m   12 m   13 m

13 m

b. *See page 18 in the* Student Reference Guide.

a. _____ **b.** r _____

20. $\frac{3}{8} - \frac{2}{3}x = \frac{11}{12}$

x = _____

21. $\frac{5}{9} = \frac{x}{12}$

x = _____

22. $\frac{4}{3}m = -8$

m = _____

23. $0.07 - 0.003x = 0.1$

x = _____

24. $4x - x - 7 = 5$

x = _____

25. Label the front, top, and right-side views.

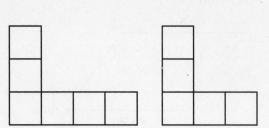

• Area of a Trapezoid (page 502)

Name _____

A trapezoid is a quadrilateral with one pair of parallel sides.

The parallel sides are called the bases, b_1 and b_2.

The perpendicular distance between the bases is the height, h.

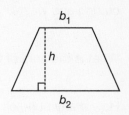

• To find the area of a trapezoid, multiply the **average** of the bases by the height.

$$A = \frac{1}{2}(b_1 + b_2)h$$

Example: Find the area of this trapezoid.

The bases are 24 ft and 8 ft. The height is 12.

$$A = \frac{1}{2}(b_1 + b_2)h = \frac{1}{2}(24 + 8)(12) = \frac{32 \cdot 12}{2} = 192 \text{ ft}^2$$

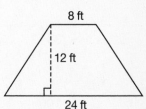

Practice Set (page 504)

Find the area of each trapezoid.

$$A = \frac{1}{2}(b_1 + b_2)h$$

a. _____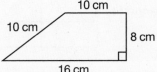

b. _____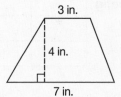

$$A = \frac{1}{2}(10 + 16)(8) =$$

c. _____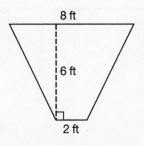

d. _____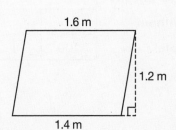

e. The shingles on the south side of Tamika's roof need to be replaced. The shingles she wants come in bundles that cover $33\frac{1}{3}$ square feet. Tamika calculates the area of the section of roof and then determines the number of bundles she needs. She wants to buy **two extra bundles** to allow for cutting and waste.

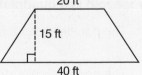

What is the area of the section of roof? _____ ▨

How many bundles of shingles should Tamika buy? _____

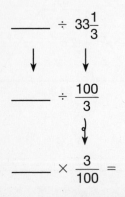

_____ ÷ $33\frac{1}{3}$

↓   ↓

_____ ÷ $\frac{100}{3}$

↓

_____ × $\frac{3}{100}$ =

Written Practice   (page 505)

1.

	Ratio	Actual Count
Recommend		
Do not		
Total		t

2.

	Percent	Actual Count
Original	100	
Change (+)	c	
New		

▨

3.

	Percent	Actual Count
Red Cheeks		
Without		
Total	100	t

4. y varies directly with x.
find a and b.

x	2	8	10	a
y	6	24	b	45

$a =$ _____

$b =$ _____

5. $A = \frac{1}{2}(b_1 + b_2)h$

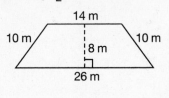

14 m

10 m   8 m   10 m

26 m

t _____

_____

6. $A = bh$

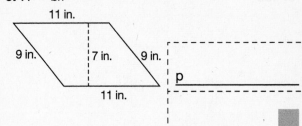

11 in.

9 in.   7 in.   9 in.

11 in.

p _____

_____

7. *See page 29 in the* Student Reference Guide.

_____

8. $0.04 - 0.02x = 0.5$

x = _____

9. $\frac{7}{3}x + 1 = \frac{17}{3}$

x = _____

10. $\frac{3}{4}r = 33$

r = _____

11. $7x + 1 - x = 19$

x = _____

12. $\frac{4}{x} = \frac{28}{56}$

x = _____

13. $\frac{4}{x} = \frac{2.8}{5.6}$

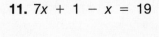

x = _____

14. *Factor perfect squares.*
$\sqrt{45} =$

_____

15. $\sqrt{50}$ =

16. a. percent

$\dfrac{8}{11}$ =

b. decimal

$11\overline{)8.0000}$

c. rounded to thousandths

a. _____

b. _____

c. ___ . ___ ___ ___

17. *Area is related by scale factor squared.*

(scale factor)² = _____

Change to a percent.

increase = _____% − 100% = _____%

18. What percent?

$\dfrac{42}{60}$ =

19. $\dfrac{mi}{hr}$ to $\dfrac{ft}{sec}$

$\dfrac{15\ mi}{1\ hr}$ · $\dfrac{hr}{min}$ · $\dfrac{min}{sec}$ · $\dfrac{ft}{mi}$ =

20. $y = \dfrac{2}{3}x - 3$

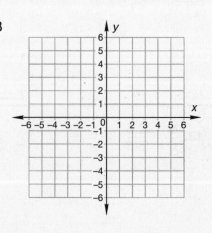

Is (9,3) a solution? _____

Use work area.

© 2007 Harcourt Achieve Inc.

21. a. $a =$ _____ $b =$ _____

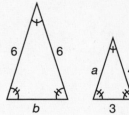

b. The triangles are ^{s} _____ because

corresponding _____ are congruent.

c. by sides: _____

d. scale factor: _____

---

22. Convert the dimensions to feet.

24 in. = _____ ft

12 in. = _____ ft

9 in. = _____ ft

volume = lwh

surface area
Add the area of each side.

$V =$ _____

$SA =$ _____

23. Find the 20th term.

$a_n = 3(n - 1)$

$a_{20} =$

$a_{20} =$ _____

---

24. Label the length of the sides of this net.

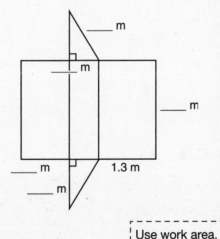

25. The relationship _____

direct variation because

the ^{l} _____

does not ^{i} _____

the origin.

• Volumes of Prisms and Cylinders (page 507)

Name _____

Teacher Note:
• Review "Geometric Solids" on page 30 in the *Student Reference Guide*.

The volume of a solid is the space occupied by the solid.

• Prisms and cylinders are geometric solids with **two bases** and **lateral sides**.

   The bases are parallel and congruent.

   The height of a prism or cylinder is the perpendicular distance between the two bases.

• The volume of a prism or cylinder is equal to the area of one base times the height:

   area of base × height = volume

   units² × units = units³

Example: Find the volume of this triangular prism.

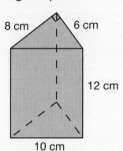

The base is a right triangle, with perpendicular sides of 6 cm and 8 cm.

area of base = $\frac{1}{2}$ (6 × 8) = 24 cm²

The height is 12 cm.

V = area of base × height = 24 cm² × 12 cm = 288 cm³

Example: A cylindrical soup can has a diameter of 2 in. and a height of 3 in. Find the volume of the soup can. Leave π as π.

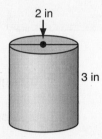

The base is a circle with a diameter of 2 in., so its radius is $\frac{2}{2}$ in. = 1 in.

area of base = πr^2 = $\pi(1)^2$ = π

The height is 3 in.

V = area of base × height = π in.² × 3 in. = 3π in.³

Practice Set (page 511)

a. A pup-tent has the dimensions shown. Label the diagram of the triangular base. Then find the volume of the tent.

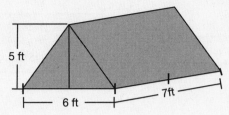 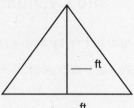

area of base = _____ ▨

V = area of base × height = _____ ▨

b. A cylindrical backyard pool 3 feet high and 20 feet in diameter holds how many cubic feet of water when full? Use 3.14 for π and round the answer to the nearest ten cubic feet.

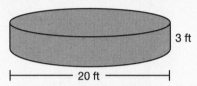

area of base = _____ ▨

V = area of base × height = _____ ▨

c. The walls of a garage are 8 feet high and the peak of the gable roof is 12 feet high. The floor of the garage is a 20 foot square. Find the volume of the garage.

Add the volume of a rectangular prism and a triangular prism.

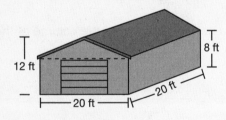 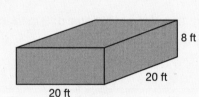 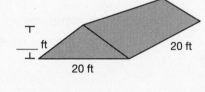

rectangular prism

area of base = _____ ▨

V = _____ ▨

total volume = _____ ▨

triangular prism

area of base = _____ ▨

V = _____ ▨

d. A cylindrical candle that is 15 cm high has a diameter of 8 cm. Label the figure and find the volume. Leave π as π. _____ ▨

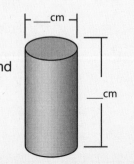

e. Brenda is putting **cubical** boxes that are 6 inches on edge into a larger **cubical** box with inside dimensions that are 12 inches on edge. How many of the smaller boxes will fit in the larger box? _____

How many times larger is the volume of the larger box?

V = (length of edge)³

Volume of smaller cube = _____

Volume of larger cube = _____

Written Practice (page 511)

1.

	Percent	Actual Count
Original	100	
Change (+)		
New		n

2.

	Ratio	Actual Count
Sheep		s
Goats		
Total		

3.

	Percent	Actual Count
Trombones		x
Not trombones		
Total	100	

4.

Hours	Pay	$\frac{p}{h}$
3	27	
4	36	
5	45	
6	54	

The relationship is

d _____

variation with a

constant of _____. The

pay rate is _____

dollars per _____.

¦ Use work area. ¦

5. V = *area of base* × *height*

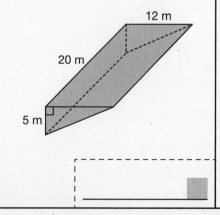

12 m

20 m

5 m

6. Find the volume in terms of π. Round to the nearest unit (use 3.14 for π).

V = *area of base* × *height*

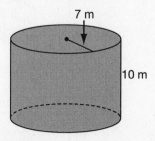

7 m

10 m

_____ π

7. yd³ to ft³

$$1 \text{ yd}^3 \cdot \frac{\text{ft}}{\text{yd}} \cdot \frac{\text{ft}}{\text{yd}} \cdot \frac{\text{ft}}{\text{yd}} =$$

_____

8. similar triangles

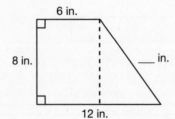

a = _____ b = _____

9. a. $A = bh$

   b. _See page 18 in the_ Student Reference Guide.

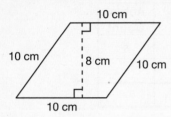

a. _____

b. r _____

10. a. _See page 18 in the_ Student Reference Guide.

   b. $A = \frac{1}{2}(b_2 + b_2)h$

   c. perimeter

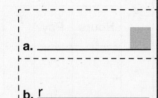

a. _____ b. _____ c. _____

11. Use a calculator.

   a. $\frac{1}{7} = \underline{\ \ }.\underline{\ }\underline{\ }\underline{\ }\underline{\ }\underline{\ }\underline{\ }$

   b. $\frac{2}{7} = \underline{\ \ }.\underline{\ }\underline{\ }\underline{\ }\underline{\ }\underline{\ }\underline{\ }$

   c. The _____ are the same but the order is different.

12. Volume smaller = _____

Volume larger = _____

$$\frac{\text{Volume smaller}}{\text{Volume larger}} = \underline{\ } = \underline{\ \ \ }\%$$

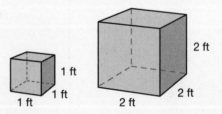

Use work area.

13. $a_n = 7(2^n)$

$a_1 = 7(2^1) =$

$a_2 =$

$a_3 =$

_____, _____, _____

14. Factor:

a. $-2x^2 - 2x - 2 =$

b. $5x^2 - 10x =$

a. _____

b. _____

15. Write the equation for the line.

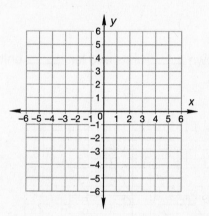

$y =$ _____

16. $(-3)(-2) - (-1)^2 =$

_____

17. *Factor perfect squares.*

$\sqrt{27} =$

_____

18. $\sqrt{32} =$

_____

19. $\dfrac{12m^3}{18xm^{-2}} =$

_____

20. $\dfrac{4.5}{6.3} = \dfrac{x}{7}$

$x =$ _____

21. $\dfrac{4}{3}x - \dfrac{2}{7} = -\dfrac{34}{21}$

$x =$ _____

22. $\dfrac{x}{4} = \dfrac{0.42}{0.14}$

$x = $ _____

23. $0.03 + 0.011x = 0.36$

$x = $ _____

24. $\dfrac{m}{5} = 2.2$

$m = $ _____

25. $A\,(\quad,\quad)$

$A'\,(\quad,\quad)$

Move down _____ units and left _____ units.

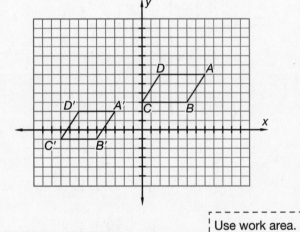

Use work area.

• Inequalities with Negative Coefficients (page 514)

Name _____

Inequalities use the comparison symbols <, >, ≤, and ≥.

6 > 5

Six is greater than 5.

• Multiply both sides by −1 and something happens.

$(-1)(6) > (-1)(5)$

$-6 > -5$

Negative six is greater than negative five.

This is wrong!

• When multiplying or dividing an inequality by a *negative number*, **reverse the comparison symbol**.

6 > 5

$(-1)(6) < (-1)(5)$

$-6 < -5$

Negative six is less than negative five.

• Solving inequalities is just like solving equations: *Isolate the variable.*

• If the variable has a negative sign $(-x)$, **reverse the symbol**.

Example: Solve and graph: $-3x - 10 > 8$

$-3x - 10 > 8$	Given inequality
$-3x > 18$	Added 10 to both sides
$x < -6$	Divided both sides by −3 and reversed the symbol

Use a circle because x cannot equal −6.

Practice Set (page 517)

Solve and graph each inequality. When you divide by a negative number, reverse the symbol.

a. $-5x - 6 < -1$

$-5x < $ _____

$x > $ _____

b. $7x + 2 \leq 8x + 4$

$-x \leq $ _____

$x \geq $ _____

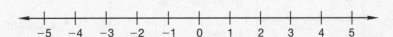

© 2007 Harcourt Achieve Inc.

Practice Set (continued) (page 517)

c. $-5x + 25 > 5(x - 5)$
$-5x + 25 > 5x - 25$

$-10x > \underline{\hspace{1cm}}$

$x < \underline{\hspace{1cm}}$

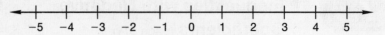

d. $-2x + 3 \geq -(x - 7)$
$-2x + 3 \geq -x + 7$

$-x \geq \underline{\hspace{1cm}}$

$x \leq \underline{\hspace{1cm}}$

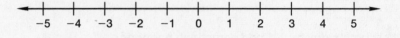

Written Practice (page 517)

1.

	Ratio	Actual Count
Broken		b
Working		
Total		

_ _ _ _ _ _ _ _ _ _ _
_____

2.

	Percent	Actual Count
Original	100	
Change		
Total		t

_____

3. $8\% + 20\% = 28\%$

$\$ 8.40$
$\underline{9.20}$ $\times 1.28$

_____

4.

x	y	$\frac{y}{x}$
2	3	
4	6	
6	9	

This _____ direct variation with a constant of _____. In 10 min, she travels _____ miles.

Use work area.

5. 50¢ + 3¢ per minute

a.

min	¢	$\frac{¢}{min}$
0	50	
5	65	
10		
20		

b. $y = \underline{\hspace{1cm}} x + \underline{\hspace{1cm}}$

c. This _____ direct variation because the _____ are not constant.

Use work area.

6. 5 out of 8 are made.

a. P(made) = _____

b. P(miss) = _____

P(made) $\times$ 360° = _____°

P(miss) $\times$ 360° = _____°

Use work area.

7. $-x + 15 > 0$

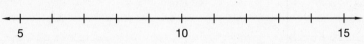

Use a circle.

$x <$ _____

9. $\dfrac{4}{x} = \dfrac{0.22}{0.55}$

8. $-2x \geq 2$

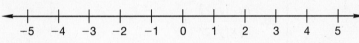

Use a dot.

$x \leq$ _____

$x =$ _____

10. $\dfrac{3}{4} - \dfrac{2}{3}x = \dfrac{11}{12}$

$x =$ _____

11. $12 = 16 - 4x$

$x =$ _____

12. $\dfrac{7}{8}x = 49$

$x =$ _____

13. new = original + increase

100% + _____% = _____%

Change to a decimal.

Area is related by scale factor squared.

(scale factor)² = _____

Change to a percent.

increase = _____% − 100% =

14. $a_n = n^2 - n$

$a_{10} =$

_____

$a_{10} =$ _____

15. Name the shape and find its area.

$A = \frac{1}{2}(b_1 + b_2)h$

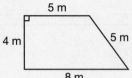

t _____

_____

16. Name the shape and find its area.

$A = bh$

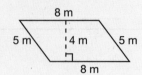

p _____

_____

17. *Factor perfect squares.*

$\sqrt{54} =$

_____

18. $\dfrac{7x^{-3}y^3z^3}{14x^4y^3z^2} =$

_____

19. *Use the "Multiplication Table" on page 3 in the Student Reference Guide.*

  a. $\sqrt{90}$

  b. $\sqrt{80}$

  c. $\sqrt{70}$

a. between _____ and _____

b. between _____ and _____

c. between _____ and _____

20. $\dfrac{\text{in.}}{\text{sec}}$ to $\dfrac{\text{ft}}{\text{min}}$

$\dfrac{10 \text{ in.}}{2 \text{ sec}} \cdot \dfrac{\text{sec}}{\text{min}} \cdot \dfrac{\text{ft}}{\text{in.}} =$

_____

21. $y = -\dfrac{1}{2}x + 2$

Is (2,1) a solution? _____

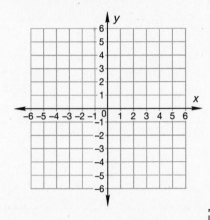

⌐ ─ ─ ─ ─ ─ ─ ─ ┐
Use work area.
└ ─ ─ ─ ─ ─ ─ ─ ┘

22. $V = area\ of\ base \times height$

Leave π as π.

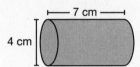

23. $V = area\ of\ base \times height$

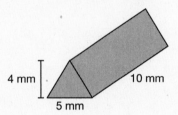

24. a. decimal

$11\overline{)4.000}$

b. percent

$\dfrac{4}{11} =$

a. _____

b. _____

25. a.   strawberries

+   bananas
_____

b. Round blueberries to a whole percent.

_____% of 30 =

c. Fraction **not** grapes

a. _____

b. _____

c. _____

• **Products of Square Roots** (page 519)

Teacher Note:
• Review "Laws of Exponents" on page 19 in the *Student Reference Guide.*

We can multiply square roots to simplify expressions.

• The **product rule of square roots** means that square roots can be factored:

$$\sqrt{ab} = \sqrt{a}\,\sqrt{b}$$

$$\sqrt{18} = \sqrt{9}\,\sqrt{2} = 3\sqrt{2}$$

• This rule also means that square roots can be multiplied.

• Try to factor perfect squares *before multiplying:*

Example: Simplify: $\sqrt{3} \cdot \sqrt{12}$

$\sqrt{3} \cdot \sqrt{12}$	Given
$\sqrt{3} \cdot 2\sqrt{3}$	$\sqrt{12} = \sqrt{4}\,\sqrt{3} = 2\sqrt{3}$
$2\sqrt{3} \cdot \sqrt{3}$	Commutative Property
$2 \cdot 3$	$\sqrt{3} \cdot \sqrt{3} = 3$
6	Simplified

• Sometimes we cannot factor out perfect squares before multiplying, but we can factor perfect squares *after multiplying.*

Example: Simplify: $3\sqrt{6} \cdot \sqrt{15}$

$3\sqrt{6} \cdot \sqrt{15}$	Given
$3\sqrt{90}$	$\sqrt{6} \cdot \sqrt{15} = \sqrt{90}$
$3 \cdot 3\sqrt{10}$	$\sqrt{90} = \sqrt{9} \cdot \sqrt{10}$
$9\sqrt{10}$	Simplified

Practice Set (page 522)

Simplify.

Factor perfect squares after multiplying.

a. $\sqrt{2}\,\sqrt{14} = \sqrt{28}$

$\sqrt{28} = \sqrt{4}\,\sqrt{7} = \underline{\quad}\,\sqrt{7}$

b. $\sqrt{15}\,\sqrt{3} = \sqrt{45}$

$\sqrt{45} = \underline{\quad}$

c. $3\sqrt{5}\,\sqrt{5} = \underline{\quad}$

d. $5\sqrt{3} \cdot 2\sqrt{3} = \underline{\quad}$

e. The square has vertices at (5, 4), (1, 5), (0, 1), and (4, 0). Find the length of a side of the square. Then find the area of the square.

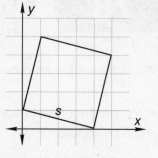

Pythagorean Theorem

$s^2 = 1^2 + 4^2 = 1 + 16 =$ _____

$s =$ _____ units

$A = s^2 =$ _____ units^2

f. The rectangle has vertices at (0, 5), (3, −1), (−1, −3), and (−4, 3). Find the length and width of the rectangle. Then find the area of the rectangle.

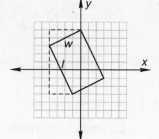

$l^2 = 6^2 + 3^2 =$ _____ + _____ = _____

$w^2 = ($ $)^2 + ($ $)^2 =$ _____ + _____ = _____

$l =$ _____ units $\qquad\qquad$ $w =$ _____ units

$A = lw =$ _____ × _____ = _____ = _____ units^2

g. Describe two ways to find the area of the shaded square.

1. The length of each side of the shaded square is _____ cm.

The area is _____ cm^2.

2. The length of each side of the large square is 1 cm + 2 cm

= _____ cm. The area of the large square is _____ cm^2.

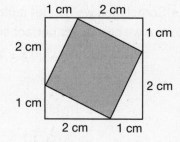

The area of one triangle is _____ cm^2. Subtract four times the area of one triangle from the area of the large square:

_____ cm^2 − _____ cm^2 = _____ cm^2

Written Practice (page 522)

1. larger = 100% + _____% = _____% change to a decimal

Area is related by scale factor squared

(scale factor)^2 = _____ change to a percent.

increase = _____% − 100% =

2.

	Percent	Actual Count
Last Year	100	
Change		
This Year		

3. 12% of 4000

_____

4. direct variation

boxes _____ = _____
apples

_____

5. *Factor perfect squares.*
$\sqrt{8}\ \sqrt{6}\ =$

_____

6. $\sqrt{21}\ \sqrt{3}\ =$

_____

7. $\sqrt{6}\ \sqrt{12}\ =$

_____

8. $\dfrac{8m^4b^3}{4m^2b^{-1}}$

_____

9. $\dfrac{0.32}{0.56} = \dfrac{8}{m}$

$\underline{m} = $ _____

10. $0.5 - 0.02x = 0.1$

$x = $ _____

11. $\dfrac{6}{7} - \dfrac{1}{2}x = -\dfrac{1}{7}$

$x = $ _____

12. $\dfrac{2}{3}m = 6$

$m = $ _____

13. Name the shape and find its area.

$A = \dfrac{1}{2}(b_1 - b_2)h$

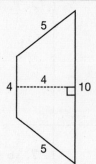

_____
_____
_____

14. Name the shape and find its area.

$A = bh$

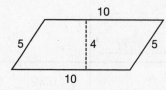

_____
_____
_____

15. **a.** $\sqrt{60}$

b. $\sqrt{50}$

c. $\sqrt{40}$

a. between _____ and _____

b. between _____ and _____

c. between _____ and _____

16. $\dfrac{\$}{hr}$ to $\dfrac{¢}{min}$

$\dfrac{\$15}{1\ hr} \cdot \dfrac{hr}{\underline{\hphantom{xx}}\ min} \cdot \dfrac{¢}{\underline{\hphantom{xx}}\ \$} =$

17. $y = -\dfrac{1}{2}x - 5$

Is $(-10, 0)$ a solution? _____

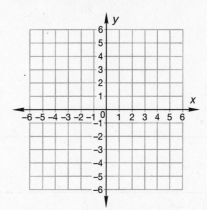

18. Label the triangles and make a proportion.

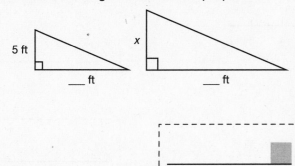

5 ft

_____ ft

x

_____ ft

Use work area.

19. $V = $ *area of base* $\times$ *height*

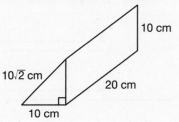

10 cm

$10\sqrt{2}$ cm

20 cm

10 cm

20. $V = $ *area of base* $\times$ *height*

leave π as π.

6 in.

20 in.

21. proportion

22. number cube and spinner

Multiply the probabilities.

$P(\text{even cube}) \cdot P(\text{even spinner}) =$

_____ $\cdot$ _____ $=$

percent: _____

decimal: _____ . _____ _____

‾‾‾‾‾‾

Use work area.

23. $4(x + 1) > 0$

$x >$ _____

24. $2(3 + x) \leq 2$

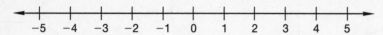

$x \geq$ _____

25. *Build the figure out of cubes for help.*

a. _____

b. _____

• **Transforming Formulas** (page 525)   Name _____

Formulas are equations that use variables instead of numbers.

• Sometimes we will want to solve a formula for one of the variables.

• Formulas can be solved in the same way as equations:

    Isolate the variable you are solving for.

    Do the same thing to both sides.

• After solving a formula, substitute numbers for the variables and solve.

    Example: The formula for the area of a rectangle is $A = lw$, where A is the area, l is the length, and w is the width. Solve the formula for l.

$A = lw$	Given formula
$\dfrac{A}{w} = \dfrac{l\cancel{w}}{\cancel{w}}$	Divided both sides by w
$l = \dfrac{A}{w}$	Symmetric Property

    Use the formula to find the length of a rectangle with area 42 and width 3.

$l = \dfrac{A}{w}$	Transformed formula
$l = \dfrac{42}{3}$	Substituted 42 for A and 3 for w
$l = 14$	Simplified

Practice Set (page 528)

a. The formula for the area of a rectangle is $A = lw$. Solve the formula for w. Then describe the meaning of the transformed formula.

    $A = lw$

    $w =$ _____

The width of a rectangle is the _____ divided by the _____.

b. Solve the formula $P = a + b + c$ for a.

    $P = a + b + c$

    $a =$ _____

c. The Pythagorean Theorem is $a^2 + b^2 = c^2$. Solve the formula for c.

$a^2 + b^2 = c^2$

$c = $ _____

d. The formula for the perimeter of a rectangle is $P = 2l + 2w$. Solve the formula for l.

$P = 2l + 2w$

$l = $ _____

Use the formula to find the length of a rectangular field with a perimeter of 620 feet and a width of 140 feet.

$l = $ _____

Written Practice (page 528)

1.

	Percent	Actual Count
Original	100	
Change	c	
New		

_____

2.

	Percent	Actual Count
Responded		
Did not respond		d
Total	100	

_____

3. Percent greater

new = 100% + _____% = _____%
Change to a decimal.
Area is related by scale factor squared.

(scale factor)^2 = _____

Change to a percent: _____

increase = _____% − 100% = _____

_____

4. Solve for r.

$C = 2\pi r$

$r = $ _____

5. R_1, R_2, and B

   a. $\left\{ \dfrac{R_1R_1}{\rule{1.5cm}{0.4pt}}, \dfrac{R_1R_2}{\rule{1.5cm}{0.4pt}}, \dfrac{R_1B}{\rule{1.5cm}{0.4pt}}, \right.$

       $\overline{\rule{1.5cm}{0pt}}, \overline{\rule{1.5cm}{0pt}}, \overline{\rule{1.5cm}{0pt}},$

       $\left. \overline{\rule{1.5cm}{0pt}}, \overline{\rule{1.5cm}{0pt}}, \dfrac{BB}{\rule{1.5cm}{0.4pt}} \right\}$

   b. $P(BB) =$

   b. _____

6. a. percent

     $\dfrac{5}{9} =$

   b. decimal

     $9\overline{)5.\,0\,0\,0}$

   c. Is $\dfrac{5}{9}$ closer to $\dfrac{1}{2}$ or $\dfrac{2}{3}$? _____

     Change all to decimals.

       :Use work area.:

---

7. Name the shape and find its area.

   $A = \dfrac{1}{2}(b_1 + b_2)$

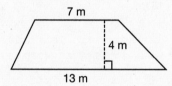

    7 m

       4 m

    13 m

8. $0.03x + 0.1 = 0.7$

   $x =$

---

9. $\dfrac{2}{3}x - \dfrac{1}{2} = \dfrac{1}{6}$

   $x =$

10. *Distribute first.*

    $3(x - 2) = x + 6$

   $x =$

---

11. $2x + 3 = x - 5$

   $x =$

12. *Factor perfect squares.*

    $\sqrt{30}\ \ \sqrt{3} =$

13. $\sqrt{8} \cdot \sqrt{5} =$

14. $(-2)(-3) + (-2) - (-3) =$

15. $\dfrac{32r^2m^3}{16r^2m^{-1}} =$

16. Name the shape and find its area.

$A = bh$

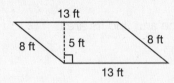

17. $\dfrac{¢}{min}$ to $\dfrac{\$}{hr}$

$$\dfrac{50¢}{1 \text{ min}} \cdot \dfrac{\text{min}}{\text{hr}} \cdot \dfrac{\$}{¢} =$$

18. $y = \dfrac{1}{3}x$

Is (15, 3)
a solution?

_____

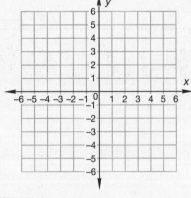

Use work area.

19.

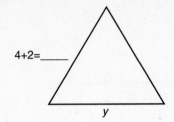

4+2=_____

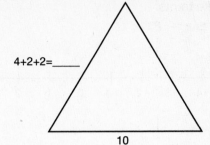

4+2+2=_____

10

$x =$ _____ $y =$ _____

20. $V = area\ of\ base \times height$

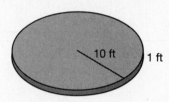

10 ft   1 ft

Use 3.14 for π.

21. Round to the nearest unit.

ft³ to yd³

$\dfrac{}{}\ \text{ft}^3\ \cdot\ \dfrac{\text{yd}}{\text{ft}}\ \cdot\ \dfrac{\text{yd}}{\text{ft}}\ \cdot\ \dfrac{\text{yd}}{\text{ft}}\ =$

22. $V = area\ of\ base \times height$

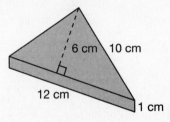

6 cm   10 cm

12 cm

1 cm

23. Earth _____ _____
Moon

24. Collect like terms.

$2x + 2 \geq x + 6$

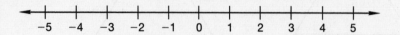

$\underline{x \geq }$

25. a. *Turn your textbook 90° clockwise.*

b. Z is the center of ^{r} _____, so its coordinates do not change.

a. _____

- **Adding and Subtracting Mixed Measures**
- **Polynomials** (page 532)

Teacher Note:
- Review "Equivalence Table for Units" on page 1 in the *Student Reference Guide*.

A mixed measure uses two different units from the same type of measurement.

- To add mixed measures:

  1. Line up the matching units.
  2. Add like units.
  3. Simplify from *right to left*.

Example:

$$
\begin{array}{ll}
27 \text{ min} & 15 \text{ sec} \\
48 \text{ min} & 18 \text{ sec} \\
+\ 42 \text{ min} & 53 \text{ sec} \\
\hline
117 \text{ min} & 96 \text{ sec} \\
\end{array}
$$

117 min   96 sec   Change 96 sec
                    to 1 min 36 sec
↓
118 min   36 sec   Change 118 minutes
                    to 1 hr 58 min
↓
1 hr 58 min   36 sec   Simplified

- To subtract mixed measures:

  1. Line up matching units.
  2. Subtract like units from *right to left*.
  3. When necessary regroup units using equivalences.

Example:

12 lb   5 oz   5 ounces −
− 7 lb 12 oz   12 ounces = ?

↓

^{11}12 lb ^{21}5 oz   Regroup 1 lb (16 oz)
−   7 lb   12 oz
─────────────────
    4 lb   9 oz   Subtracted

A term has a signed number and may have one or more variables.

- A **monomial** is a number, variable, or combination of numbers and variables.

$$2x^3 \qquad -5 \qquad x^2y \qquad 7xyz \qquad z$$

  Each of the above examples is one term.

- A **binomial** is *two* terms connected by a plus or minus sign.

$$x + 5 \qquad xy - 7y \qquad x^2 - 4$$

- A **trinomial** is *three* terms connected with plus or minus signs.

$$x^2 + 7x + 10 \qquad x + xyz + y$$

- All of these examples are **polynomials**.

  A polynomial is any monomial, binomial, or trinomial.

- The **degree** of a polynomial is the same as the greatest exponent in the polynomial.

  Examples: Name the degree of each polynomial:

$$4x^3 + x^2 + x - 3$$

  The greatest exponent is 3, so this is a **third degree** (cubic) polynomial.

$$x^2 - 2x + 3$$

  The greatest exponent is 2, so this is a **second degree** (quadratic) polynomial.

$$x + y + 3$$

  The greatest exponent is 1, so this is a **first degree** (linear) polynomial.

- These three examples are all written with the greatest exponent on the left and the least exponent on the right. This is called **descending order**.

- Polynomials should always be written in descending order.

  Example: Write this polynomial in descending order:

$$x + 2x^3 + 2 + x^2 \qquad 2x^3 + x^2 + x + 2$$

- To add polynomials:
  1. Line up like terms.
  2. Add like terms.

  Example: Add the binomials $x + 6$ and $2x - 3$.

$$\begin{array}{r} x + 6 \\ 2x - 3 \\ \hline 3x + 3 \end{array}$$

Practice Set (page 534)

Add and simplify.

a.	3 hr	32 min	45 sec
+	1 hr	43 min	27 sec
	hr	min	sec
	hr	min	sec *simplify*

b.	5 lb	8 oz
+	8 lb	9 oz
	lb	oz
	lb	oz *simplify*

c. Neil needs to buy molding to mount around the room, so he makes a sketch of the room recording its length and width. What is the **perimeter** of the room?

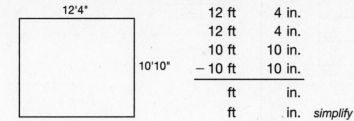

12 ft	4 in.
12 ft	4 in.
10 ft	10 in.
− 10 ft	10 in.
———	———
ft	in.
ft	in. *simplify*

Subtract.

Regroup when necessary.

d.

3 hr	15 min	12 sec
−1 hr	42 min	30 sec
hr	min	sec

e.

6 ft	2 in.
−4 ft	7 in.
ft	in.

f. Tony cut a 2 ft $7\frac{1}{2}$ in. length from an 8 ft long board. What is the remaining length of the board?

$$
\begin{array}{r}
8 \text{ ft} \\
- \quad 2 \text{ ft} \quad 7\frac{1}{2} \text{ in.} \\
\hline
\text{ft} \quad\quad \text{in.}
\end{array}
$$

Identify each polynomial below as a monomial, binomial, or trinomial and name its degree.

g. $x^2 - 25$

_____

_____ degree

h. $x^2 - 6x + 7$

_____

_____ degree

i. $2x + 3y - 4$

_____

_____ degree

j. Arrange the terms in descending order.

$5 - 4x^2 + x^3 - 6x \longrightarrow$ _____

k. Add the trinomials
$x + y - 2$ and $x - y + 4$.

$$
\begin{array}{r}
x + y - 2 \\
x - y + 4 \\
\hline
\end{array}
$$

Written Practice (page 535)

1. a.

	Percent	Actual Count
Original	100	
Change		
Sale		s

b.

	Percent	Actual Count
Sale	100	
Change		
Closeout		c

a. _____ b. _____

2.

	Percent	Actual Count
Planted		
Unplanted		
Total	100	t

3.   2 red
$\underline{+\ 7\ green}$
total

$P(\text{red}) =$

4. $5^2 + 7^2 =$ _____ $9^2 =$ _____

The triangle _____ a right triangle
because the side lengths do not fit the

P_____ theorem.

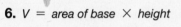

Use work area.

5. Solve for r.

$A = \pi r^2$

$r = \sqrt{}$

6. $V =$ *area of base* $\times$ *height*

Round to nearest ft^3

Use 3.14 for π.

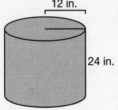
12 in.
24 in.

7. $7x - 3 = 2x - 33$

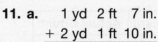
$x =$

8. $0.003x - 0.2 = 0.01$

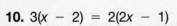
$x =$

9. $\dfrac{4}{5}x - \dfrac{2}{3} = \dfrac{1}{3}$

$x =$

10. $3(x - 2) = 2(2x - 1)$

$x =$

11. a.   1 yd 2 ft 7 in.
$\underline{+\ 2\ yd\ \ 1\ ft\ 10\ in.}$
  yd   ft   in. *simplify*

b.   2 hr 15 min
$\underline{-\ 1\ hr\ 37\ min}$
  hr   min

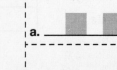
a. _____
b. _____

12. a. monomial, binomial or trinomial?

$3x + 2$

b. $3x + 2$
$\underline{x - 1}$

a. _____

b. _____

13. *Factor perfect squares.*

$\sqrt{1000} =$

_____

14. $\sqrt{40} \ \sqrt{10} =$

_____

15. $\sqrt{3} \ \sqrt{24} =$

_____

16. $\dfrac{12x^3y^4}{3x^4y^{-3}} =$

_____

17. $A = \dfrac{1}{2}(b_1 + b_2)h$

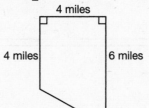

4 miles

4 miles   6 miles

_____

18. area

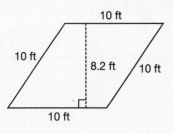

10 ft

10 ft   8.2 ft   10 ft

10 ft

_____

19. $2x + 1 \leq x + 2$

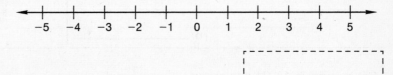

$-5 \quad -4 \quad -3 \quad -2 \quad -1 \quad 0 \quad 1 \quad 2 \quad 3 \quad 4 \quad 5$

$x \leq$ _____

20. $\dfrac{\$}{yd^2}$ to $\dfrac{\$}{ft^2}$

$\dfrac{\$27}{1 \ yd^2} \cdot \dfrac{yd}{ft} \cdot \dfrac{yd}{ft} =$

_____

21. $y = -2x + 6$

Is (3, 0) a solution? _____

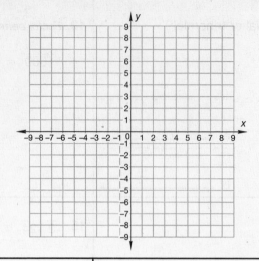

Use work area.

22. Find *a* first.

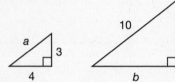

$a =$ _____ $b =$ _____ $c =$ _____

23. volume: _____

$V = area\ of\ base \times height$

Label the sides of this net of the prism.

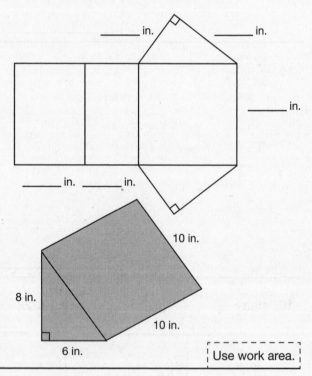

_____ in. _____ in.

_____ in.

_____ in. _____ in.

10 in.

8 in.

10 in.

6 in.

Use work area.

24. a. decimal

$9\overline{)2.0\ 0}$

b. percent

$\frac{2}{9} =$

a. _____

b. _____

25. a. total in 16-21 age group

classical

country

pop

+ R&B
_____

b. difference in classical

c. total in R&B

a. _____

b. _____

c. _____

A central angle is an angle whose vertex is the center of a circle.

• A full circle measures 360°.

• For any circle, the sum of the measures of the **central angles** is 360°.

Example: Draw a circle with central angles that divide the circle evenly into thirds.

The three angle measures are equal and must total 360°.

angle measure = 360° ÷ 3 = 120°

• A central angle divides the *area* of a circle into **sectors.**

• A central angle also divides the *circumference* of a circle into **arcs.**

An arc that is one half of the circumference (180°) is a **semicircle.**

A **minor arc** is less than a semicircle (< 180°).

A **major arc** is more than a semicircle (> 180°).

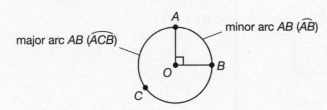

major arc AB ($\overgroup{ACB}$)   minor arc AB ($\overgroup{AB}$)

• To find the length of an arc, multiply the circumference of the circle by the fraction of degree measures.

• Unless otherwise stated, when we say 'arc' we mean a minor arc.

Example: What is the measure of $\overgroup{AD}$ in degrees? What fraction of the circumference is the arc intercepted by $\angle ABD$? If the radius of the circle is 6 cm, what is the length of the arc in terms of π?

measure of $\overgroup{AD}$ = measure of $\angle ABD$ = 60°

The arc is $\frac{60°}{360°} = \frac{1}{6}$ of the circle.

$C = 2\pi r = 12\pi$ cm

Arc = $\frac{1}{6}(12\pi$ cm$) = 2\pi$ cm

Practice Set (page 547)

For **a–d** refer to the figure.

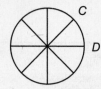

a. A circle is divided into **eighths**. What is the measure of each acute central angle?

$\frac{1}{8}$ (360°) = _____

b. What is the degree measure of arc *CD*? _____

c. What is the degree measure of major arc *CD*? _____
   It is the rest of the circumference.

d. If the diameter of the circle is 20 cm, what is the length of arc *CD*? Use 3.14 for π.

$C = \pi d = (3.14)(20 \text{ cm}) = $ _____

arc *CD* = ( )(cm) = _____

Written Practice   (page 547)

1.

	Percent	Actual Count
Original	100	
Change		
New		*n*

2.

crates   — —
tons

3. *A*(2, 2), *B*(2, −2), *C*(−2, −2), *D*(−2, 2)
dilation with scale factor 1.5

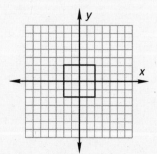

4. a. perimeter

original: _____   dilated: _____

b. The perimeters are related by the

_____   _____.

_____ × 1.5 = 24

c. area

original: _____   dilated: _____

d. The areas are related by the scale factor

_____.

Use work area.   Use work area.

5. $d = 12$ in.

Leave π as π.

a. $\frac{1}{6}(360°) =$

b. $\frac{1}{6}C = \frac{1}{6}(\pi d) =$

c. $\frac{1}{6}A = \frac{1}{6}(\pi r^2) =$

a. _____

b. _____

c. _____

6. $3d(d + 4) =$

_____

7. *Factor perfect squares.*

$\sqrt{50} =$

_____

8. $5\sqrt{20} =$

_____

9. $\dfrac{5x^4m^{-1}}{3mx} =$

_____

10. $\dfrac{(-5)(-10)}{(-5) - (-10)} =$

_____

11. $x - 2x - 1 < 3$

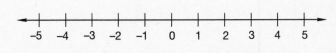

$x >$ _____

12. Solve for y.

$y + 5 = 2x$

$y =$ _____

13. $1^2 + (\sqrt{3})^2 =$ _____ $2^2 =$ _____

These _____ the sides of a right

triangle because the numbers fit the

_____ Theorem.

_____

14. $\dfrac{\$}{hr}$ to $\dfrac{¢}{min}$

$$\dfrac{\$45}{1\ hr} \cdot \dfrac{hr}{min} \cdot \dfrac{¢}{\$} =$$

_____

15.

x	y	$\dfrac{x}{y}$
2	5	
4	10	
6	15	
0	0	

This is $\underline{d}$_____

$\underline{v}$_____ with a

constant of _____.

Use work area.

16. a. decimal

$15\overline{)\,4.000}$

b. percent

$$\dfrac{4}{15} =$$

c. Is $\dfrac{4}{15}$ closer to $\dfrac{1}{3}$ or $\dfrac{1}{4}$?

Use work area.

17. $A = \dfrac{1}{2}(b_1 + b_2)h$

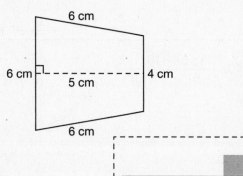

_____

18. $V = area\ of\ base \times height$

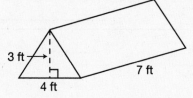

_____

19. similar triangles
Find *a* first.

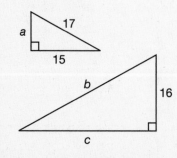

$a =$ _____

$b =$ _____

$c =$ _____

20. $\dfrac{1}{3}m - \dfrac{2}{3} = 0$

$m =$ _____

21. $3x - 5 = x$

$x =$ _____

22. a. Factor: $10x^2 - 15x =$

b. Distribute: $10(2x + 1.5) =$

a. _____

b. _____

23.   5 ft 4   in.
       − 3 ft $8\frac{1}{2}$ in.
    _____

_____

24. 2, 5, 10, 17, . . .

A. $a_n = 2n$

B. $a_n = n^2 + 1$

C. $a_n = n + (n + 2)$

$a_{10} =$

$a_{10} =$ _____

25. a. *Look at the sizes of the sectors.*

_____ most

_____

_____

_____

_____ least

b. Central angle of orange looks like a

r_____ angle.

$\dfrac{}{360°} =$ _____%

Use work area.

**• Graphing Equations
Using Intercepts** (page 550)

Linear equations can be written in different forms.

- A line can be written in slope-intercept format:
  $y = mx + b$
  where m is the slope and b is the y-intercept.

- A line can also be written in **standard form,**
  $Ax + By = C$
  where A, B, and C are constants (numbers).

- Standard form makes it easy to find the x- and y-intercepts of a line.

  The y-intercept is where $x = 0$. Substitute 0 for x and solve for y.
  The x-intercept is where $y = 0$. Substitute 0 for y and solve for x.

- Using those two points, we can draw the line.

- To graph the line of an equation in standard form:

  1. Make a table of x and y values.

  2. Substitute 0 for x to find the y-intercept.

  3. Substitute 0 for y to find the x-intercept.

  4. Use those two points to draw the line.

  Example: Graph this equation: $3x + 4y = 24$.

Substitute 0 for x.	Substitute 0 for y.
$3x + 4y = 24$	$3x + 4y = 24$
$3(0) + 4y = 24$	$3x + 4(0) = 24$
$y = 6$	$x = 8$

  The y-intercept is 6. The x-intercept is 8.

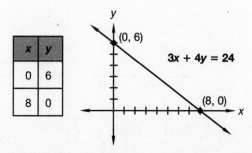

- The graph of an equation shows every possible (x, y) solution for the equation.

• If two equations are graphed on the same coordinate plane, the intersection of the lines is the (x, y) point that solves both equations.

Example: Martin is thinking of two numbers. He gives these hints. The sum of the numbers is 3. If you double the first number and add the second number, the sum is 8. Graph this system of equations to find the two numbers.

Graph both lines.

$$\begin{cases} x + y = 3 \\ 2x + y = 8 \end{cases}$$

Find the x- and y-intercepts for each equation.

x + y = 3

x	y
0	3
3	0

2x + y = 8

x	y
0	8
4	0

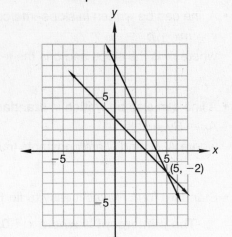

The lines intersect at $(5, -2)$.

So the numbers Martin was thinking of are 5 and -2.

Practice Set (page 553)

Find the x- and y-intercepts of the following equations. Then graph them.

a. $2x + y = 8$

x	y
0	
	0

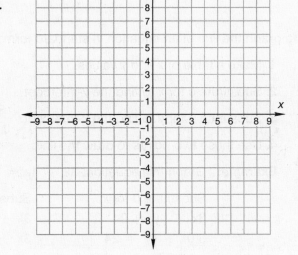

b. $3x - 2y = 12$

x	y
0	
	0

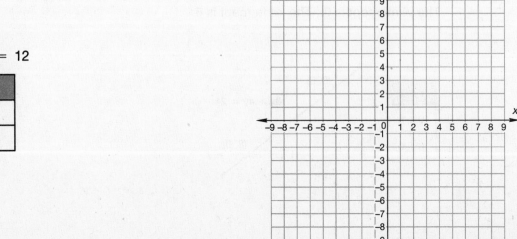

c. $-x + 3y = 6$

x	y
0	
	0

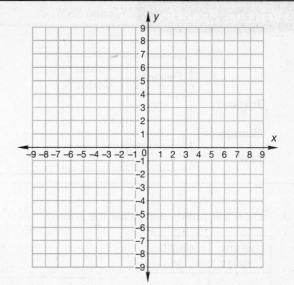

d. $x + 2y = -4$

x	y
0	
	0

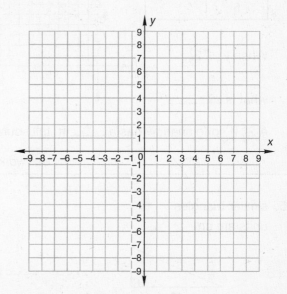

e. Tanisha is thinking of two numbers. The sum of the numbers is 5. If the lesser number is subtracted from the greater number the result is 7. Graph this system of equations to find the two numbers.

(_____ , _____)

$$\begin{cases} x + y = 5 \\ x - y = 7 \end{cases}$$

$x + y = 5$

x	y
0	
	0

$x - y = 7$

x	y
0	
	0

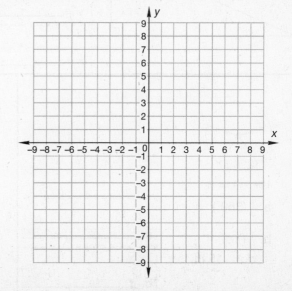

1.

	Percent	Actual Count
Original	100	
Change (+)	c	
New		

2.

height

shadow $\quad\underline{\quad}\ \underline{\quad}$

3. Graph the points and draw the line.

height (x)	length (y)
3	5
6	

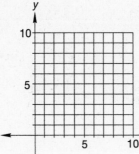

When $y = 2\frac{1}{2}$,

what is x? _____

A $2\frac{1}{2}$ ft. long shadow has a _____ ft. tall source.

Use work area.

4. Label the can and find the volume.

$h = 10$ cm $\qquad r = 3$ cm

$V = $ *area of base × height*

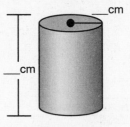
___ cm
___ cm

Leave π as π.

5. similar triangles
units are cm

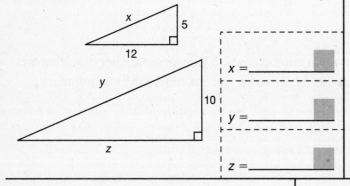
x
5
12
y
10
z

$x =$ _____

$y =$ _____

$z =$ _____

6. a. scale factor =

b. area smaller = _____

area larger = _____

c. $\dfrac{\text{area larger}}{\text{area smaller}} = (\text{scale factor})^2 =$ _____

Use work area.

7.

Use 3.14 for π.

a. $\frac{1}{5}(360°) =$

b. $\frac{1}{5}(\pi d) =$
$d = 15$ in.

a. _____

b. _____

8. $2x + 3y = 6$

x	y
0	
	0

x-intercept _____

y-intercept _____

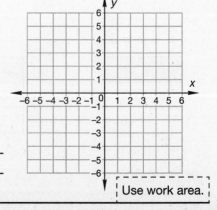

Use work area.

9. 70% of 110

10. *Factor perfect squares.*

$3\sqrt{27} =$

11. $\sqrt{2} \ \sqrt{22}$

12. $\dfrac{6xm}{12x^2} =$

13. $\left(\dfrac{2}{3}\right)^2 \left(\dfrac{1}{3}\right)^2 \left(\dfrac{4}{9}\right)^{-2} =$

14. $A = \dfrac{1}{2}(b_1 + b_2)h$

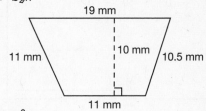

$A \ \bigcirc \ 2 \text{ cm}^2$

$2 \text{ cm}^2 \cdot \dfrac{\text{mm}}{\text{cm}} \cdot \dfrac{\text{mm}}{\text{cm}} = \underline{\hspace{1cm}} \text{ mm}^2$

$A = \underline{\hspace{3cm}}$

15. $2^2 + 2^2 =$

$(2\sqrt{2})^2 =$

These are the sides of a

_____ triangle because the

numbers fit the P_____ Theorem.

 Use work area.

16. $\dfrac{\text{mi}}{\text{hr}}$ to $\dfrac{\text{gal}}{\text{hr}}$

$\dfrac{60 \text{ mi}}{1 \text{ hr}} \cdot \dfrac{\text{gal}}{\text{mi}} =$

17. a. decimal

$6\overline{)1.000}$

b. percent

$\dfrac{1}{6} =$

c. rounded to thousandths

a. _____

b. _____

c. ___ . ___ ___ ___

18. Solve for *s*.

$A = \pi rs$

$s = \underline{\hspace{2.5cm}}$

19. *A, B,* and *C*

a. { ABC , ACB , _____ , _____ , _____ , CBA }

b. *P(ABC)* =

_____

20. Shaded area to nearest whole unit.

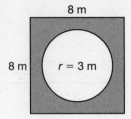

8 m

8 m   *r* = 3 m

Use 3.14 for π.

_____

21. Factor out −3.

$-3x^2 - 9x - 42 =$

−3 (_____)

22. $\frac{1}{2}w - \frac{2}{3} = \frac{2}{3}$

w = _____

23. $0.3m = 0.4m - 0.5$

m = _____

24. $5 + x^2 + 2x \longrightarrow x^2 + 2x + 5$

$x + x^2 - 1 \longrightarrow$ _____

25. The relationship _____

proportional.

_____

Probability of Dependent Events (page 557)

Sometimes the probability of one event depends on the outcome of another event.

- **Independent** probability events are events that do not affect each other.

    Flipping a coin and spinning a spinner are independent events because the outcome of the coin flip does not affect the spinner.

- The probability of independent events is the product of each individual event:

    P(coin and spinner) $= P$(coin) $\cdot P$(spinner)

    Example: A bag contains two white marbles and three blue marbles. If two marbles are selected, what is the probability of selecting two blue marbles if the first marble is replaced in the bag before the second draw?

    The events are independent. P(blue) for the first draw is $\frac{3}{5}$ because 3 of the 5 marbles are blue. P(blue) for the second draw is $\frac{3}{5}$ because there are still 3 blue marbles in the bag.

    P(blue and blue) $= P$(blue) $\cdot P$(blue)

    $$= \frac{3}{5} \cdot \frac{3}{5} = \frac{9}{25} = 0.36$$

- **Dependent** probability events are events that do affect one another.

- The probability of dependent events is still the product of each individual event, but the probability of the second event must be calculated *after the first event has happened.*

    Example: A bag contains two white marbles and three blue marbles. If two marbles are selected, what is the probability of selecting two blue marbles if the first marble is not replaced in the bag before the second draw?

    The events are dependent. For the first draw, P(blue) is $\frac{3}{5}$ because 3 of the 5 marbles are blue. Now there are 2 white and 2 blue marbles left in the bag. For the second draw, P(blue) $= \frac{1}{2}$ because 2 of the 4 marbles are blue.

    P(blue and blue) $= P$(blue) $\cdot P$(blue)

    $$= \frac{3}{5} \cdot \frac{1}{2} = \frac{3}{10} = 0.3$$

a. A spinner is spun twice. Are the events independent or dependent?

The events are _____ because the outcome of the first spin does not affect the second spin.

b. Four different cards lettered A, B, C, and D are face down on a table with the order scrambled. As a card is turned over it is left letter side up. Find each probability.

P(turning over A first) =

P(turning over A, then B) = P(turning over A first) · P(turning over B next)

$$= \frac{\quad}{4} \cdot \frac{\quad}{3} =$$

P(A, then B, then C) = P(A first) · P(B next) · P(C next)

$$= \frac{\quad}{4} \cdot \frac{\quad}{3} \cdot \frac{\quad}{2} =$$

P(A, then B, then C, then D) = P(A first) · P(B next) · P(C next) · P(D last)

$$= \frac{\quad}{4} \cdot \frac{\quad}{3} \cdot \frac{\quad}{2} \cdot \frac{\quad}{1} =$$

c. The four letter cards A, B, C, and D are face down on the table. Michelle turns over one card and finds that it is A. If she turns over the remaining cards one at a time, what is the probability that she turns them over in alphabetical order?
A is already out.

P(B, then C, then D) = P(B first) · P(C next) · P(D last)

$$= \frac{\quad}{3} \cdot \frac{\quad}{\quad} \cdot \frac{\quad}{\quad} =$$

d. In a bag are 6 marbles: 3 red, 2 white, and 1 blue. Three marbles are drawn one at a time without replacement. What is the probability of drawing red, then white, then blue?
P(R, then W, then B) = P(R first) · P(W next) · P(B last)

$$= \frac{\quad}{6} \cdot \frac{\quad}{5} \cdot \frac{\quad}{4} =$$

Recall that the probabilities of an event and its complement (**not** the event) add to 1. What is the probability of **not** drawing red, then white, then blue?
P(not "R, then W, then B") + P(R, then W, then B) = 1

P(not "R, then W, then B") = 1 − P(R, then W, then B)

$$= 1 - \frac{\quad}{\quad} =$$

e. Gerry's drawer has 2 black socks and 4 blue socks. If he selects two socks without looking, what is the probability they are **both black**?
P(black, then black) = P(black first) · P(black next)

$$= \frac{\quad}{\quad} \cdot \frac{\quad}{\quad} =$$

1. in.
    calories   —   —

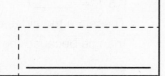

3.

	Percent	Actual Count
Original	100	
Change	c	
New		

2.

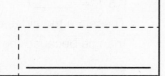
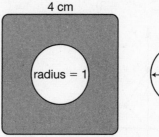

total distance: _____ mi

time up: $30 \text{ mi} \cdot \dfrac{1 \text{ hr}}{10 \text{ mi}} =$ _____ hr

time down: $30 \text{ mi} \cdot \dfrac{1 \text{ hr}}{30 \text{ mi}} =$ _____ hr

total time: _____ hr

average speed: $\dfrac{\text{mi}}{\text{hr}} =$

Use work area.

4.

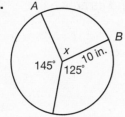

a. $m\angle x + 145° + 125° = 360°$

b. Use 3.14 for π

$AB = \dfrac{}{360°}$ (circumference)

a. _____   b. _____

5. shaded area to nearest cm^2.

4 cm

radius = 1   ←2 cm→

Use 3.14 for π

_____

6. a. $3 \text{ in.} \times \dfrac{\text{ft.}}{\text{in.}} =$ _____

    $V = lwh$

b. ft^3 to yd^3

_____ ft$^3 \cdot$ _____ $\cdot$ _____ $\cdot$ _____ $=$

a. _____

b. _____

7. similar triangles

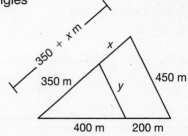

350 + x m

350 m   x   450 m

y

400 m   200 m

⊢____ m ⊣

$\dfrac{350}{400} = \dfrac{350 + x}{}$

$\dfrac{400}{y} = \dfrac{}{450}$

$x =$ _____

$y =$ _____

8. $5x - 7x \le -4 - (-4)$

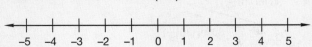

$x \ge$ _____

9. $1^2 + 2^2 =$ _____

$(\sqrt{5})^2 =$ _____

These are the sides of a _____

triangle because the numbers fit the

P_____ Theorem.

Use work area.

10. *proportion*

_____

11. yd^2 to ft^2

$4840 \ yd^2 \cdot$ _____ $\cdot$ _____ $=$

_____

12. $A(0,0)$, $B(0,5)$, $C(2,3)$
Translate $\triangle ABC \ (-2, -3)$.

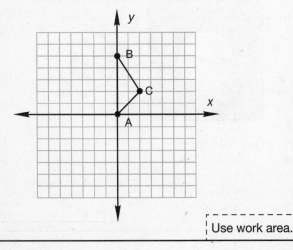

Use work area.

13. Name the shape and find its area.

$A = \dfrac{1}{2}(b_1 + b_2)h$

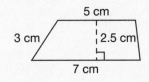

5 cm

3 cm   2.5 cm

7 cm

_____

14. *Factor perfect squares.*

$6\sqrt{12} =$

_____

15. $5\sqrt{5}\sqrt{5} =$

_____

16. $\dfrac{9x^2y^4 2m^{-1}}{2x^2y^3 9m^{-1}}$

17. $\dfrac{(-15)(10)}{-15 - 10} =$

18. *V = area of base × height*

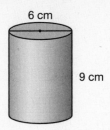

6 cm

9 cm

Use 3.14 for π.

19. $\overline{} \approx$
$$\frac{}{1000 \text{ cm}^3}$$

A $\frac{1}{2}$ **B** $\frac{1}{4}$ **C** $\frac{1}{5}$ **D** $\frac{2}{5}$

20. Graph both equations.

$y = -x - 1$

$y = mx + b$

$x + y = -1$

x	y
0	
	0

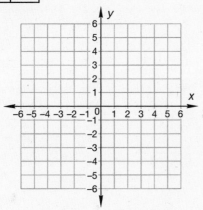

The graphs are _____.

Use work area.

21.

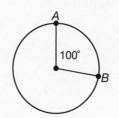

A

100°

B

A full circle is 360°

22. $\dfrac{0.2}{0.5} = \dfrac{8}{x}$

x = _____

23. $\frac{2}{3}x = \left(\frac{3}{2}\right)^{-1}$

$x =$ ______

24.
$$\begin{array}{r} 2x + 3y - 4 \\ x - 3y + 7 \\ \hline \end{array}$$

______

25. a. Estimate 1990 population.

$$\begin{array}{rr} & 1990 \\ - \underline{\qquad\qquad} & 1980 \end{array}$$

b. *In what decade do the graphs cross?*

a. ______

b. ______

• Selecting an Appropriate Rational Number (page 563)

Fractions, decimal, and percents are all forms of rational numbers that describe parts of a whole.

Teacher Note:
• Review "Fraction-Decimal-Percent Equivalents" on page 13 in the *Student Reference Guide*.

• Use **fractions** when the decimal or percent is a *repeating number.*

• Use **decimals** when other numbers in the problems have *decimal places.*

• Use **percents** when *comparing* parts of a whole or stating an *increase or decrease.*

• Use **fractions** when a number can be *divided evenly by the denominator* of the fraction.

Example: How much is 40% of $\frac{1}{2}$ of $12.60?

$12.60 has decimal places, so convert to decimals.

40 % of $\frac{1}{2}$ of $12.60	Given
$0.4 \times 0.5 \times$ $12.60	Converted to decimals
$0.2 \times$ $12.60	Multiplied 0.4 and 0.5
$2.52	Multiplied

Example: How much is $66\frac{2}{3}$% of $\frac{5}{6}$ of $12.60?

$66\frac{2}{3}$% and $\frac{5}{6}$ both convert to repeating decimals, so use fractions.

$66\frac{2}{3}$% of $\frac{5}{6}$ of $12.60	Given
$\frac{\overset{1}{2}}{3} \times \frac{5}{\underset{3}{6}} \times$ $12.60	Converted to fractions
$\frac{5}{\underset{1}{6}} \times$ $\overset{1.40}{12.60}$	Multiplied $\frac{2}{3}$ and $\frac{5}{6}$
$7.00	Multiplied

Practice Set (page 565)

a. Find 20% of $\frac{1}{4}$ of $12.00. _____

Use fractions because $12.00 can be divided evenly by 4.

_____ $\times \frac{1}{\underset{1}{4}} \times$ $\overset{3.00}{12.00}$ =

b. Find $33\frac{1}{3}$% of $\frac{3}{8}$ of $12.00. _____

Use fractions because $33\frac{1}{3}$% converts to a repeating decimal.

_____ $\times \frac{3}{8} \times$ $12.00 =

c. To find 80% of $21.50, would you convert 80% to a fraction or to a decimal?

$21.50 has decimal places, so use a _____.

d. To find 25% of $24, would you convert 25% to a fraction or to a decimal?

$24 can be divided evenly by 4, so use a _____.

e. Circle the most appropriate rational number to announce a discount of $14 from a regular price of $40?

A save $\frac{7}{20}$ **B** save 0.35   **C** save 35%

Written Practice (page 564)

1.

	Ratio	Actual Count
CDs		c
Cassettes		
Total		

_____

2.

	Percent	Actual Count
Made		
Missed		
Total	100	t

_____

3.

	Percent	Actual Count
Original	100	p
Change		
New		

_____

4.

a. *A full circle is 360°.*

b. Use 3.14 for π

$Arc = \dfrac{}{360°}$ (circumference)

a. _____

b. _____

5. new = 100% − _____ % = _____ %

Change to a decimal.

Area is related to scale factor squared.

(Scale factor)^2 = _____

Change to a percent.

reduction = 100% − _____ % =

6.

a. The triangles are similar because

corresponding _____ are

_____.

b. $x =$ _____ $y =$ _____

c. scale factor = _____

_____

Use work area.

7. *closed dot*

_____

8. monomial, binomial, or trinomial?

_____

degree: _____

$5 + x^2 - 2x \longrightarrow$ _____

⌐ ¬
¦ Use work area. ¦
L ⌐

9. Surface area

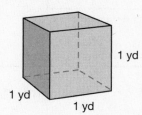

1 yd

1 yd

1 yd

_____ yd² · _____ · _____ =

_____ yd² | _____ ft²

10. $\sqrt{6}\sqrt{8} =$

_____

11. $3x + 2x^2 + x^2 - x =$

_____

12. $\dfrac{4x^2y^{-1}2x^3}{6x^4y^2} =$

_____

13. 50% of $\dfrac{2}{3}$ of $1.20

_____

14. $A(0, 0)$, $B(3, 3)$, $C(-4, 4)$

a. $AB^2 = 3^2 + 3^2 =$ _____

$AC^2 = 4^2 + 4^2 =$ _____

$BC^2 = 7^2 + 1^2 =$ _____

b. $A = \dfrac{1}{2}(AB)(AC)$

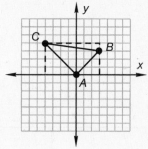

a. r _____

b. _____

15. a. longest size

b. perimeter

a. $BC =$ _____

b. _____

16. a. decimal

$$3\overline{)4.00}$$

b. percent

$$1\frac{1}{3} =$$

a. _____

b. _____

17. Use cents.

a. $\dfrac{\text{quarter}}{\text{dime}} =$

b. A dime is what percent of a quarter?

a. _____

b. _____

18. $A = \dfrac{1}{2}(b_1 + b_2)h$

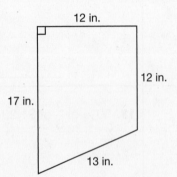

12 in.

12 in.

17 in.

13 in.

_____

19. Graph $y = x$

Solve $x + y = 0$ for y and graph.

$y =$

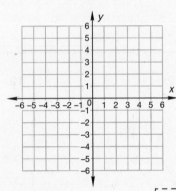

Use work area.

20. $a_n = 2n^2 - 1$

$a_{10} =$

$a_{10} =$ _____

21. $\dfrac{x}{5} = \dfrac{0.42}{0.3}$

$x =$ _____

22. $3x + 2 = x + 14$

$x =$ _____

23. $\dfrac{3}{4}x = \left(\dfrac{4}{3}\right)^{-2}$

$x =$ _____

24. $-\dfrac{x}{5} = 10$

$x =$ _____

25. Graph the data.

	Parts Red Paint (x)	Parts Yellow Paint (y)	$\frac{y}{x}$
1 gal	3	5	
2 gal	6	10	
3 gal	9	15	
4 gal	12	20	

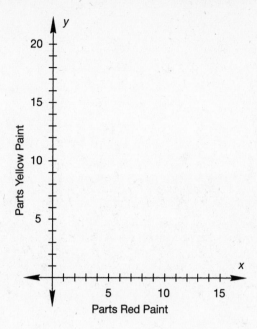

Is it proportional? _____

Constant = _____

equation: y =

Use work area.

L84-495

• Surface Area of Cylinders and Prisms (page 568)

Name _____

Teacher Note:
• Review "Geometric Solids" on page 30 in the *Student Reference Guide*.

Cylinders and prisms have congruent parallel bases connected by flat or curved faces.

• The **total surface area** of a solid is the sum of the area of each face or surface.

• The **lateral surface area** of a cylinder or prism is the surface area without the area of the bases.

  Total Surface Area = 2(area of base) + (lateral surface area)

• A shortcut to find the lateral surface area is to multiply the *perimeter* of a base by the height.

  Lateral Surface Area = perimeter of base × height

• We can substitute this formula into the formula for total surface area.

  Total Surface Area = 2(area of base) + (perimeter of base × height)

Example: Compute the surface area of this cylinder in terms of π.

The bases are circles with a diameter of 4 units.
Area of base = πr^2 = $\pi(2)^2$ = 4π units²

The perimeter of a base is the circumference of the circle.
Perimeter of base = πd = 4π units
Lateral Surface Area = perimeter of base × height
              = $4\pi × 5 = 20\pi$ units²
Total Surface Area = 2(area of base) + (lateral surface area)
              = $2(4\pi) + 20\pi = 28\pi$ units²

Example: A tent in the shape of a triangular prism is shown. What is the surface area of the tent in square feet?

The bases are triangles with b = 6 and h = 4.
Area of base = $\frac{1}{2}(bh)$ = $\frac{1}{2}(6 × 4)$ = 12 ft²

Perimeter of the base = 6 + 5 + 5 = 16 ft
Lateral Surface Area = perimeter of base × height
              = 16 × 7 = 112 ft²
Total Surface Area = 2(area of base) + (lateral surface area)
              = 2(12) + 112 = 136 ft²

Find the total surface area of these figures.

a. _____

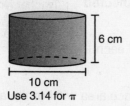

6 cm

10 cm

Use 3.14 for π

Surface Area = 2(area of base) + (perimeter of base 3 height)

b. _____

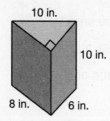

10 in.

10 in.

8 in.   6 in.

Surface Area = 2(area of base) + (perimeter of base × height)

c. What is the lateral surface area of the cylinder in problem **a**? _____

Lateral Surface Area = (perimeter of base × height)

d. What is the lateral surface area of the triangular prism in problem **b**? _____

Lateral Surface Area = (perimeter of base × height)

e. Find the **lateral surface area** of a 30-ft-high water tower with a 40 ft diameter.

Use 3.14 for π. _____

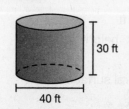

30 ft

40 ft

1. How many more pedestrians?

	Ratio	Actual Count
Cyclists		
Pedestrians		
Total		

Pedestrians

$-$ _____ Cyclists
_____

_____

2.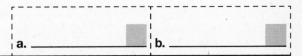

3 mi

a. $\dfrac{\text{min}}{\text{mi}}$

b. $\dfrac{\text{mi}}{\text{min}} \cdot \dfrac{\text{min}}{\text{hr}} =$

a. _____

b. _____

---

3. $16\dfrac{2}{3}\%$ of $3,000,000 =$ _____

I used _____ because
3,000,000 can be divided by 6.

Use work area.

4. circle divided into tenths

a. $\dfrac{1}{10}$ ( ) =

b. $Arc = \dfrac{circumference}{10}$

$d = 50$ in.

a. _____

b. _____

---

5. scientific notation

$0.001 =$

_____ $\times$ _____

6. similar triangles

a. $x =$ _____ $y =$ _____

b. corresponds to $\angle C$: $\angle$_____

c. scale factor = _____

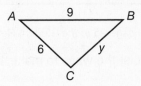

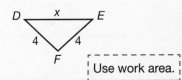

Use work area.

---

7. Use a calculator to find the length of the diagonal.

The diagonal is

about _____ in., so the

13 in. long frame _____ fit.

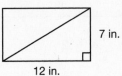

7 in.

12 in.

Use work area.

8. $2(x + 4) + 2(x + 3) =$

_____

---

9. $-2x + 1 > 1$

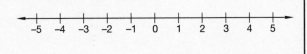

$x \le$ _____

10. *lateral surface area = perimeter of base $\times$ height*

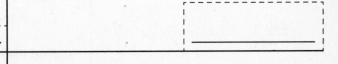

7 cm

11 cm

_____

---

11. Expand and write in descending order.

$-7x(5 - x)$

12.

$$\begin{array}{l} \text{2 red} \\ + \text{3 green} \\ \hline \text{total} \end{array}$$

$P(\text{green,green}) = \dfrac{}{} \cdot \dfrac{}{4} =$

13. $\sqrt{500} =$

14. $2\sqrt{5}\sqrt{20} =$

15. *See page 25 in the* Student Reference Guide.

a. List the ways to make 10 or more.

———, ———, ———,

———, ———, ———

b. $P(10 \text{ or more}) = \dfrac{}{36} =$

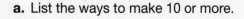

Use work area.

16.

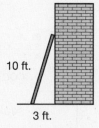

10 ft.

3 ft.

17. $\dfrac{\text{ft}}{\text{min}}$ to $\dfrac{\text{mi}}{\text{hr}}$

$\dfrac{440 \text{ ft}}{2 \text{ min}} \cdot \dfrac{}{} \cdot \dfrac{}{} =$

18. Graph $y = \dfrac{1}{2}x + 2$

Solve $x + y = 5$ for y.
Graph the line.

Find the intersection point.

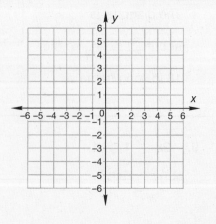

(———, ———)

19. I _____ the area

of the _____ from
the area of the trapezoid.

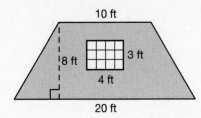

20. Measure in centimeters the longest side of
the trapezoid in problem 19.

_____ cm = 20 ft

$25 \text{ ft} \cdot \dfrac{\text{cm}}{\text{ft}} =$

21. $\dfrac{x}{3} = \dfrac{1.5}{0.5}$

$x =$ _____

22. $\dfrac{2}{3}x + 2 = \left(\dfrac{1}{3}\right)^{-1}$

$x =$ _____

23. $0.2x - 0.02x = 0.018$

$x =$ _____

24. $2x^2 - 2 = 48$

$x =$ _____, _____

25. R _____ the triangle across the
y-axis.

Use work area.

• **Volume of Pyramids and Cones** (page 574)

Name _____

Teacher Notes:
- Introduce Hint #55, "Comparing Volume of Related Solids."
- Review "Geometric Solids" on page 30 in the *Student Reference Guide*.

We can use what we already know about cylinders and prisms to find the volume of cones and pyramids

- Volume of a **cylinder** = area of base × height

- A **cone** is a geometric solid with one base and a curved side that goes up to a point.

- The volume of a cone is related to the volume of a cylinder with the same height and radius.

  Volume of a **cone** = $\frac{1}{3}$ (area of base × height)

  volume of cone = $\frac{1}{3} B \cdot h$

  $V = \frac{1}{3}\pi r^2 h$

- Volume of a **prism** = area of base × height

- A **pyramid** is a geometric solid with one base and triangular sides that meet at a point.

- The volume of a pyramid is related to the volume of a prism with the same height and base.

  Volume of a **pyramid** = $\frac{1}{3}$ (area of base × height)

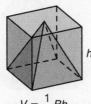

  $V = \frac{1}{3} Bh$

Example: Find the volume of this square pyramid.

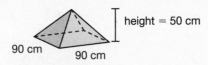

height = 50 cm

90 cm   90 cm

Volume $\frac{1}{3}$ (area of base × height)

$= \frac{1}{3}$ (90 cm)²(50 cm)

$= \frac{1}{3}$ (8100 cm²)(50 cm)

$= 135{,}000$ cm³

Find the volume.

a. Find the volume of a square pyramid with dimensions $\frac{1}{10}$ of the pyramid in the example.
edges of the base = 9 cm
height = 5 cm

Volume = $\frac{1}{3}$ (area of base × height)

= $\frac{1}{3}$ (9 cm)²(5 cm)

= $\frac{1}{3}$ (81 cm²)(5 cm)

= _____

The volume of the smaller pyramid is **what fraction** of the pyramid in the example?

$\frac{\text{smaller}}{\text{larger}}$ = $\frac{\underline{}}{135,000}$ =

The volume of the smaller pyramid is **what percent** of the volume of the pyramid in the

example? _____
Convert your fraction answer to a percent.

b. The area of the hexagonal base of a pyramid is $18\sqrt{3}$. The height is 12. What is the volume?

Volume = $\frac{1}{3}$ (area of base × height)

= $\frac{1}{3}$ ($18\sqrt{3}$ units²)(12 units)

= _____

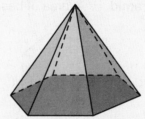

c. The diameter of the base of the cone is 20 inches. The height is 21 inches. What is the volume of the cone? Express the answer in terms of π and using 3.14 for π rounded to the nearest cubic inch.

Volume = $\frac{1}{3}$ (area of base × height)

= $\frac{1}{3}$ (π)(10 in.)²(21 in.)

= $\frac{1}{3}$ (π)(_____ in.²)(21 in.)

= _____ π in.³

Rounded volume = _____ in.³

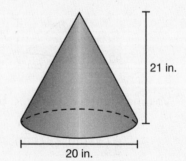

21 in.

20 in.

d. Using a 12-inch cube of clay, Lucian makes a 12-inch high pyramid with a 12-inch square base. What is the volume of the pyramid? _____

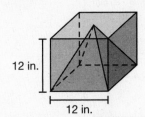

12 in.

12 in.

Does Lucian have enough clay from the original cube to make another pyramid the same size as the first?

Volume of prism = area of base × height

_____, because the volume of the cube is _____ times the volume of pyramid with the same base and height.

e. A party hat arrived in a cylindrical container in which it fit perfectly. If the volume of the container is 99 in.³, what is the volume of the cone-shaped hat? _____

Written Practice (page 578)

1.   8 lb 5 oz
      − 5 lb 15 oz

2.

	Percent	Actual Count
Original	100	
Change	c	
New		

3. circle divided into twelfths

  a. $\frac{1}{12}($ $) =$

  b. $\frac{1}{12}$(circumference)

    $d = 12$ in.

  a. _____

  b. _____

4. $V = \frac{1}{3}$ (area of base × height)

  $h = 4$ in.

6 in.

5. *lateral surface area = perimeter of base × height*
Use 3.14 for π.
Round to the the nearest cm².

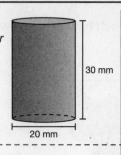

30 mm

20 mm

6. Write a proportion.

7. Add down.

$$3x - 2y - 4$$
$$\underline{x + 2y - 7}$$

8. a.

	Percent	Actual Count
Original	100	
Change		
New		n

b.

	Percent	Actual Count
Original	100	
Change		
New		

9. What percent boys?

11 girls
$\underline{+ \qquad \text{boys}}$
25 total

a. ____

b. ____

10. $\begin{matrix} \text{mi} \\ \text{\%} \end{matrix} \quad \dfrac{192}{75} = \dfrac{}{100}$

11. $a_n = 5n - 2$

____, ____, ____, ____

Use work area.

12. $\sqrt{5}\sqrt{15} =$

13. $3(-1) - 2\left(-\dfrac{1}{2}\right) =$

14. $33\frac{1}{3}\%$ of $\frac{4}{5}$ of $4.50

15. Solve for y.

$$y - 7 = 2x - 3$$

$y =$ _____

16. Is this a right triangle? _____

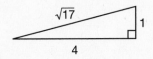

$(\sqrt{17})^2 =$ _____

$(4)^2 + (1)^2 =$ _____

Use work area.

17. 3 winners out of 21 cards

  a. $P(\text{win}) =$

  b. $P(\text{second win}) = \dfrac{}{20} =$

a. _____ **b.** _____

18. $\dfrac{\text{mi}}{\text{hr}}$ to $\dfrac{\text{ft}}{\text{min}}$

$$\dfrac{60 \text{ mi}}{1 \text{ hr}} \cdot \underline{\quad} \cdot \underline{\quad} =$$

19. a. $y = -x$

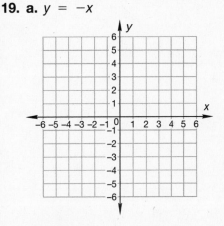

  b. Solve $x + y = 4$ for y.
  Then graph.

  c. Are the lines parallel, perpendicular, or

  oblique? _____

Use work area.

20. $\dfrac{2.7}{5.4} = \dfrac{3}{x}$

$x =$ _____

21. $1.2 - 3.4x = -5.6$

$x =$ _____

22. $\dfrac{4}{7} - \dfrac{3}{7}x = 1$

$x =$ _____

23. $17 - 2x = x - 7$

24. Label each view as front, top, or right side.

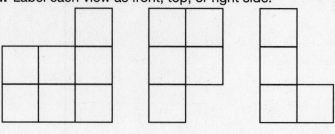

$x =$ _____

! Use work area. !

25. Each box has $V =$ _____ ft^3.

How many boxes are there in all?

There are two boxes you can't see.

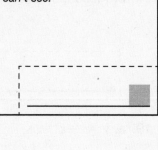

_____

• Scale Drawing Word Problems (page 580)

Name _____

Teacher Notes:
• Review Hint #47, "Scale Factor."
• Review "Scale Factor" on page 31 in the *Student Reference Guide*.

A map or a scale drawing is a small representation of a larger real-world object.

• The **scale** of a map or drawing is a *proportional relationship* from the drawing to the real object.

• Use the scale like a unit multiplier to answer questions.

> **Example:** Mary sketched a scale drawing of her dream garden using 1 inch to represent 2 feet. If the drawing of the garden is 8 inches long, how long will Mary's garden be?
>
> The question asks for the real length of the garden, so the answer will be in **feet**. Use the scale like a unit multiplier so that inches cancel and the answer is in feet.
>
> $$8 \text{ in.} \cdot \frac{2 \text{ ft}}{1 \text{ in.}} = 16 \text{ ft}$$
>
> If Mary's garden is 12 feet wide, how wide should the drawing be?
>
> $$\overset{6}{\cancel{12}} \text{ ft} \cdot \frac{1 \text{ in.}}{\underset{1}{\cancel{2}} \text{ ft}} = 6 \text{ in.}$$
>
> The question asks for the width on the drawing, so the answer will be in **inches**.

• In some cases you will have to use a ruler to measure part of a drawing. Then multiply by the scale to find the real dimensions.

> **Example:** Edmund wants to convert an attic to living space. He made a scale drawing with the scale 1 inch = 16 feet. What are the dimensions of Bedroom 2 excluding the closet?
>
> Use a ruler to measure the length and width of Bedroom 2 in inches.
>
> length: 1 inch   width: $\frac{3}{4}$ inches
>
> Use the scale to find the real length and width of the room
>
> $1 \text{ in.} \cdot \dfrac{16 \text{ ft}}{1 \text{ in.}} = 16 \text{ ft}$ $\dfrac{3}{4} \text{ in.} \cdot \dfrac{16 \text{ ft}}{1 \text{ in.}} = 12 \text{ ft}$
>
> length = 16 ft   width = 12 ft

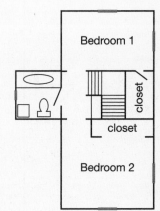

a. A map is drawn with a scale of 1 inch = 8 miles. Two towns $2\frac{3}{4}$ inches apart on the map are how

many miles apart? _____

$2\frac{3}{4}$ in. $\cdot$ $\dfrac{\text{mi}}{\text{in.}}$ =

b. Mariah is making a scale drawing of her apartment. Her apartment measures 36 feet long and 30 feet wide. She wants the drawing to fit on an 8.5 in.-by-11 in. piece of paper. Which of the following would

be a good scale for Mariah to use? _____

Find the scale that gives the largest drawing but still fits on the paper.

A 1 in. = 2 ft   **B** 1 in. = 3 ft   **C** 1 in. = 4 ft   **D** 1 in. = 6 ft.

36 ft $\cdot$ $\dfrac{\text{in.}}{\text{ft}}$ =   30 ft $\cdot$ $\dfrac{\text{in.}}{\text{ft}}$ =

c. Refer to the example of Edmund's attic. Find the actual length and width of Bedroom 1, without the closet. The scale is 1 in. = 16 ft.

Measure the length and width of Bedroom 1 in inches.

actual length: $\dfrac{\text{in.}}{}$ $\cdot$ $\dfrac{\text{ft}}{\text{in.}}$ = _____   actual width: $\dfrac{\text{in.}}{}$ $\cdot$ $\dfrac{\text{ft}}{\text{in.}}$ = _____

d. Mr. Kistler drew this scale drawing of his classroom to a scale of 1 cm = 3 ft. Measure the length and width of the drawing in centimeters, use the scale factor, and label the actual length and width of the classroom in ft.

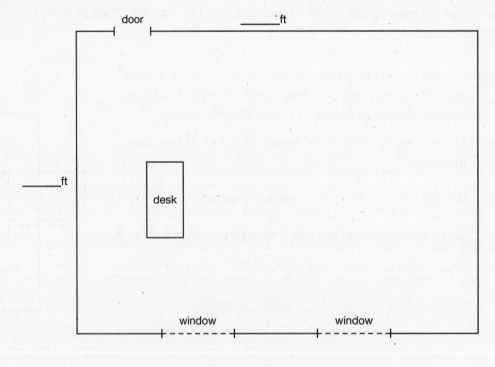

1. 1 in. = 2 ft

   a. 5 in. · —— =

   b. 12 ft · —— =

   a. _____

   b. _____

2. 1 in. = 5 ft

   a. 25 ft · —— =

   b. 2 in. · —— =

   a. _____

   b. _____

3. $19.53 → $20
$12.99 → $13
$26.90 → $27

Her estimate is _____ than

the actual total because she rounds each

number _____.

⌐ ‎ ‎ ‎ ‎ ‎ ‎ ‎ ‎ ‎ ‎ ‎ ‎ ‎ ‎ ‎ ¬
Use work area.

4. *Total the areas of each rectangle.*

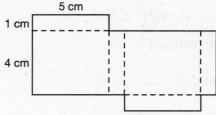

A 20 cm²   **B** 25 cm²

C 50 cm²   **D** 58 cm²

5. volume of cylinder and cone in terms of π

volume of cone $= \frac{1}{3}$ *(area of base × height)*

6 in.

4 in.

6. *surface area = 2(area of base) = (lateral surface area)*

Leave π as π.

7. Label the side lengths on the drawing.

$\frac{1}{2}$ in. = 1 ft

¦ Use work area. ¦

8. (1, 1), (0, −1), and (−2, 0)

a. fourth vertex: (,   )

b. side length: _____ units

c. area: _____ units²

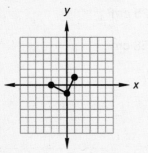

9. two A's out of 6

$P(A, \text{then } A) = \dfrac{}{6} \cdot \dfrac{}{5} =$

10. $2(x + 3) + 2(x + 4) =$

¦ Use work area. ¦

11. $x(x + 3) - 4(x + 3) =$

12. $3x^{-1}y^2x^3y^{-1} =$

13. $\sqrt{8}\ \sqrt{10}$

_____

14. $\dfrac{(-3) - (2)(-4)}{(-2) - (-1)} =$

_____

15. 50% of $33\frac{1}{3}$% of 1.2

_____

16. $AB + BC =$

$AC =$

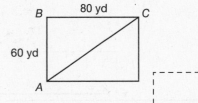

_____

17. circle divided into ninths

  a. $\frac{1}{9}($ $) =$

  b. $\frac{1}{9}$ *(circumference)*

  a. _____

  b. _____

18. a. m³ to yd³

  $1m^3 \cdot \dfrac{yd}{m} \cdot \dfrac{yd}{m} \cdot \dfrac{yd}{m} =$

  b. m³ to ft³

  Use the answer from **a** and round to the nearest ft³.

  _____ yd³ $\cdot \dfrac{ft^3}{yd^3} =$

  a. _____

  b. _____

19. Graph $y = x$

Graph $x + 2y = 6$.

Where do the lines intersect?

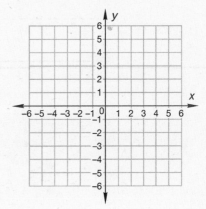

(_____ , _____)

20. $\dfrac{2.1}{1.4} = \dfrac{x}{6}$

$x = $ _____

21. $0.3x - 0.9 = 0.3$

$x = $ _____

22. $\dfrac{4}{5} - \dfrac{3}{5}x = \dfrac{3}{5}$

$x = $ _____

23. $\left(\dfrac{7}{2}\right)^{-1} = -\dfrac{1}{7}x$

$x = $ _____

24. $4(x - 3) + 5 = x + 2$

$x = $ _____

25. She swims 30 min per day for 4 days.

$\dfrac{5 \text{ laps}}{2\frac{1}{2} \text{ min}} \cdot \dfrac{\text{min}}{1 \text{ day}} \cdot \underline{\hspace{1cm}} \text{ days } = $

_____

● Review of Proportional and   Name _____
Non-Proportional Relationships (page 585)

We can tell if a relationship is proportional by looking at its graph, its equation, or a table of values.

• A proportional relationship has three properties:

   1. A proportion relates **two variables**, an input number (x) and an output number (y).
   If one variable increases, the other variable increases by a constant, k.
   If one variable decreases, the other variable decreases by the constant, k.

   2. In a table of the x and y values, every ratio of y to x (except when x is 0) reduces to the same number, k.

   $$\frac{y}{x} = k$$

   The constant, k, is called the **constant of proportionality.**
   k is a number, not a variable.

   3. A graph of the x and y values is a **line that intersects the origin (0, 0).**
   When one variable equals zero, the other variable also equals zero.

• Equation of a proportional relationship:

   $y = kx$

• Comparing this equation to the slope-intercept form of a line ($y = mx + b$), we see that k is the slope and the y-intercept is zero.

• An equation with a y-intercept other than zero, or an equation with any exponents is **not** a proportional relationship.

Practice Set (page 589)

a. In a proportional relationship, there are how many variables? _____

The graph of the relationship is what shape? _____

When one variable is zero, what number is the other variable? _____

b. An equation in the form $y = kx$ indicates a direct proportion. As x changes by 1, y changes by a constant factor, k. Circle the equation that indicates a direct proportion.
   A $y = 5 + x$ **B** $P = 4s$ **C** $A = bh$

c. The equation $y = kx$ transforms to $\frac{y}{x} = k$, which means that the ratio of y to x is constant. If $\frac{y}{x} = 3$, then which pair of (x, y) coordinates does **not** fit the relationship. Circle your answer.
   A (4, 12)   **B** (6, 18)   **C** (9, 3)

d. Which relationship below is **not** an example of a proportional relationship?

   A Distance and time when driving at a constant speed

   B Quantity and price when the unit price remains the same

   C Hours awake and hours asleep when the number of hours in a day remains the same

e. Circle the letter of the graph that shows a proportional relationship.

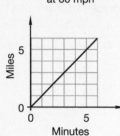 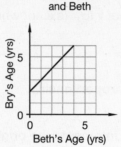 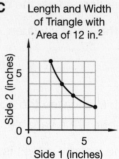

| **A** Distance Traveled at 60 mph | **B** Ages of Bry and Beth | **C** Length and Width of Triangle with Area of 12 in.² |

f. Circle the equation that is an example of a proportional relationship.

   A $d = 30t$ **B** $A = s^2$ **C** $P = 2l + 2w$

Written Practice   (page 590)

1. 0.5 in. = 1 ft

   a. 2.5 in. · ——— =

   b. 60 ft · ——— =

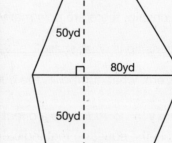

   a. _____

   b. _____

2. Add the areas of the two trapezoids.

40yd

50yd

80yd

50yd

60yd

3.

	Percent	Actual Count
Original	100	
Change		
New		n

_____

_____

4. perimeter

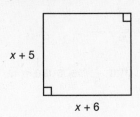

5. $-2x(3 + x - 3x^2) =$

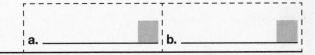

6. *lateral surface area = perimeter of base × height*
The base is an equilateral triangle.

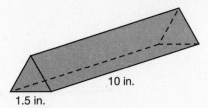

10 in.

1.5 in.

7.

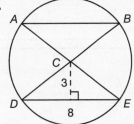

3 ft

3 ft

a. volume of cube

b. volume of pyramid $= \frac{1}{3}$ *(volume of cube)*

a. _____

b. _____

8.

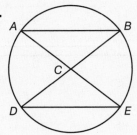

a. obtuse
central angles

b. acute
central angles

a. ∠ _____ and ∠ _____

b. ∠ _____ and ∠ _____

9.

A   B

C

3

D   8   E

a. area of △CDE

b. *C is the center, so CA and CB are radii.*

a. _____

b. _____

10.

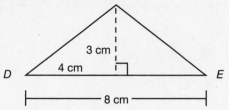

a. CD

b. diameter

a. _____

b. _____

11. Leave π as π.

$$\frac{\text{area of both triangles}}{\text{area of circle}} = \underline{\quad}$$

This fraction is _____ than $\frac{1}{3}$, because π is greater than 3.

Use work area.

12. similar triangles

b. $\dfrac{\text{perimeter of } ABC}{\text{perimeter of } DEF}$

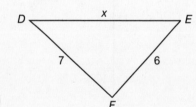

a. x = _____

y = _____

b. _____

13. $\sqrt{98} =$

_____

14. $4\sqrt{10} \ \sqrt{20} =$

_____

15. $\left(\dfrac{2}{3}\right)^{-2} + \left(\dfrac{3}{4}\right)^{-1} =$

_____

16. 150% of $\dfrac{3}{10}$ of 0.2

_____

17.

Tasks	Time	Ratio
3	18	
4	24	
5	30	
6	36	

This is a _____ relationship with a constant of _____.

Each task takes _____ seconds.

Use work area.

18. km to mi

Round down to tenths.

10 km · —— =

19. $\frac{5}{9}$

    a. percent

    b. decimal

    $\overline{)}$

    c. rounded to hundredths

a. _____

b. _____

c. _____ . _____ _____

20. Graph $y = x$ and $y = x + 2$.

Are the lines parallel, perpendicular,

or oblique? _____

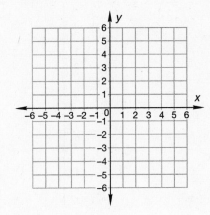

Use work area.

21. $\frac{2}{3}x + \frac{3}{8} = \frac{3}{4}$

x = _____

22. $\frac{2.7}{1.8} = \frac{x}{2}$

x = _____

23. $0.4 - 0.02x = 1.2$

x = _____

24. $\frac{2}{5}n = -18$

n = _____

25. Graph the data.

Amount of Detergent	$\frac{3}{4}$ c	$1\frac{1}{2}$ c	$2\frac{1}{4}$ c	3 c	$3\frac{3}{4}$ c
Number of Laundry Loads	1	2	3	4	5

The data is _____.

equation: y = _____

constant: k = _____

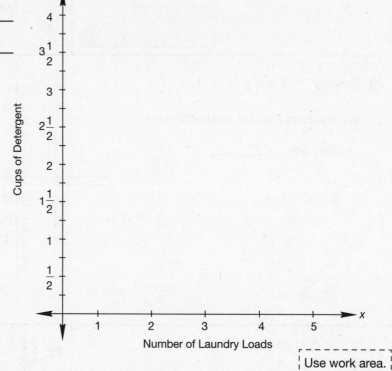

Use work area.

• **Solving Problems with Two
Unknowns by Graphing** (page 593)

Name _____

A system of equations is a set of two or more equations that use the same variables.

• In a **system of equations**, the x and y variables have the same value in both equations.

• A graph of an equation shows all the possible (x, y) pairs of numbers that work in the equation.

   If two equations are graphed on the same coordinate plane, the equations will usually **intersect,** or cross, at a single (x, y) point.

   This point of intersection shows the values of x and y that work for both equations at the same time. The x and y values **solve** the system of equations.

• To solve a system of equations,

   1. Write each equation in slope-intercept form. (Solve each equation for y.)

   2. Graph both equations on the same coordinate plane.

   3. Find the point where the lines intersect and write its coordinates (x, y).

   4. The x-coordinate is the solution for x. The y-coordinate is the solution for y.

Example: Theo is thinking of two numbers. He says that the sum of the numbers is 6. He also says that one number is 10 more than the other number. What are the two numbers?

$$\begin{cases} x + y = 6 \\ y = x + 10 \end{cases}$$

$y = x + 10$ is already in slope-intercept form.

$x + y = 6$ is not in slope-intercept form.

Solve $x + y = 6$ for y.

$x + y = 6$	Given equation
$y = -x + 6$	Subtracted x from both sides

Graph both the equations:

$y = -x + 6$	$y = x + 10$
Slope $= -1$	Slope $= 1$
y-intercept $= 6$	y-intercept $= 10$

The lines intersect at $(-2, 8)$. The only numbers that work in both equations are $x = -2$ and $y = 8$. Theo was thinking of the numbers -2 and 8.

We can check that this is correct by substituting in the original equations:

$-2 + 8 = 6$ and $8 = -2 + 10$.

Practice Set (page 595)

Solve each problem by graphing the system of equations.

a. Together Xena and Yolanda have $12. Yolanda has $6 more than Xena. How much money does each person have?

Xena: _____   Yolanda: _____

$$\begin{cases} x + y = 12 \\ y = x + 6 \end{cases}$$

Solve $x + y = 12$ for y.

$y = $

Now graph both equations.

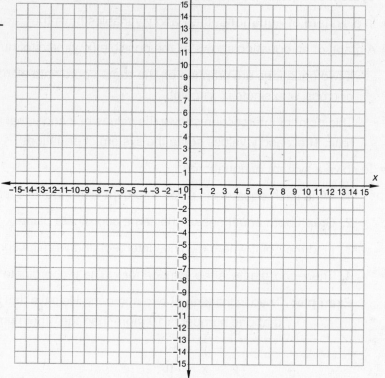

b. Nikki is thinking of two numbers. Their sum is 12. The greater number is double the lesser number. What are the two numbers?

$x = $ _____ $y = $ _____

$$\begin{cases} x + y = 12 \\ y = 2x \end{cases}$$

Solve $x + y = 12$ for y.

$y = $

Now graph both equations.

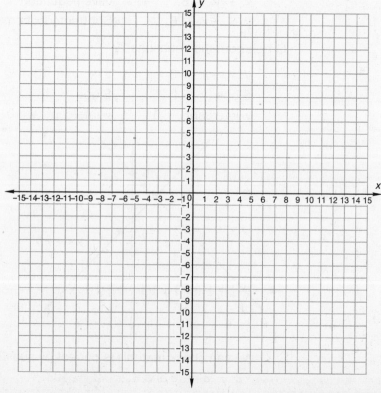

c. Look at the two equations and guess the solutions to this system of equations. Then graph the equations to check your guess.

$x =$ _____ $y =$ _____

$y = x$ so the numbers are equal.

$$\begin{cases} x + y = 6 \\ y = x \end{cases}$$

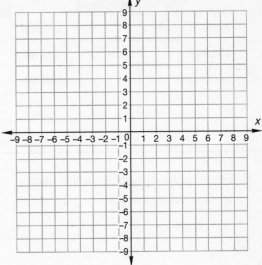

d. Look at the two equations and describe the numbers that will fit both equations.

The y number is _____ less than the x number,

and the numbers total _____.

Graph the equations to solve.

$x =$ _____ $y =$ _____

$$\begin{cases} y = x - 6 \\ x + y = 0 \end{cases}$$

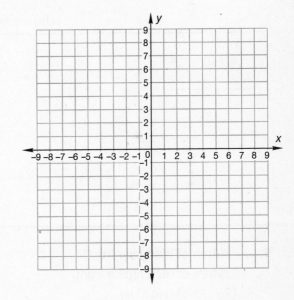

Written Practice   (page 596)

1. 1 in. = 4 ft

   a. 3.25 in. · —— =

   b. 6 ft · —— =

   a. _____

   b. _____

2.

	Ratio	Actual Count
Exuberant		e
Deflated		
Total		

_____

3.

	%	Actual Count
Original	100	
Change		
1st Year		f

	%	Actual Count
Original	100	
Change		
2nd Year		s

4. *Add the exponents.*

Use the proper form.

$$\frac{3.6 \times 10^3 \text{ sec}}{1 \text{ hr}} \cdot \frac{8.76 \times 10^3 \text{ hr}}{1 \text{ year}} =$$

$$\begin{array}{r} 8.76 \\ \times 3.6 \\ \hline \end{array}$$

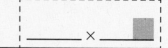 ——— × ———

5. Find 6 pairs of whole-number factors whose product is 90.

$$\frac{1}{\_\_}, \frac{90}{\_\_} \quad \frac{2}{\_\_}, \frac{}{\_\_} \quad \frac{}{\_\_}, \frac{}{\_\_}$$

$$\frac{}{\_\_}, \frac{18}{\_\_} \quad \frac{6}{\_\_}, \frac{}{\_\_} \quad \frac{}{\_\_}, \frac{}{\_\_}$$

Use work area.

6. m³ to cm³

$$1 \text{ m}^3 \cdot \underline{\quad} \cdot \underline{\quad} \cdot \underline{\quad} =$$

7.
$$\begin{array}{r} x + 2y - 4 \\ -x - y + 2 \\ \hline \end{array}$$

8. Add the volumes of a rectangular prism and a triangular prism.

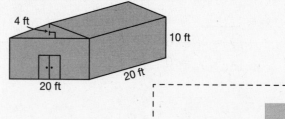

4 ft · 10 ft · 20 ft · 20 ft · 20 ft

9.
$$\begin{array}{r} 2(\text{Area of triangular front}) \\ 2(\text{Area of rectangular front}) \\ + \quad 2(\text{Area of one side}) \\ \hline \end{array}$$
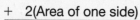

10. Find C to the nearest foot.

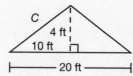

C · 4 ft · 10 ft · 20 ft

Width: C + 1 is the width of the roof.

Add 1 to C (for the overhang) _____ ft

Length: Add 2 to 20 (for the overhang) _____ ft

Area = 2(*lw*)

11.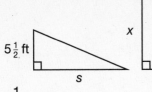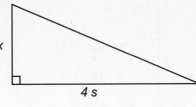

x

$5\frac{1}{2}$ ft

s

$4\,s$

$$\dfrac{5\frac{1}{2}}{s} = \dfrac{x}{4s}$$

Cross multiply and cancel the "s."

_____

12. *Factor perfect squares.*

$$2\sqrt{6}\ \sqrt{15} =$$

_____

13. $\sqrt{720} =$

_____

14. $(-12) + (-3)(-4) - (-5) =$

_____

15. $\dfrac{2}{3} \times 0.15 =$

_____

16. $1^2 + 7^2 =$

$(5\sqrt{2})^2 =$

These _____ the sides of a right triangle because the numbers fit the

_____ theorem.

17.

Minutes	Charge	$\dfrac{\$}{min}$
1	$1.10	
2	$1.20	
3	$1.30	
4	$1.40	

This _____ a proportional relationship.

Use work area.

Use work area.

18. Graph the equations.

$y = -x \qquad y = x$

Are the lines parallel, perpendicular, or

oblique? _____

Find the intersection point.

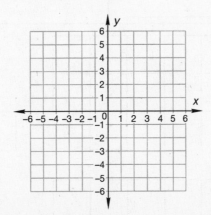

(_____ , _____)

19. Solve by graphing.

$$\begin{cases} x + y = 1 \\ x - y = 5 \end{cases}$$

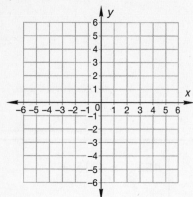

x = _____   y = _____

20. $\frac{8}{9}$

   a. percent

   b. decimal

   $\overline{)0}$

   c. rounded to two decimal places

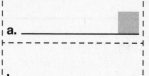

   a. _____

   b. _____

   c. ____ . ____

21. $\frac{0.5}{2.5} = \frac{x}{10}$

x = _____

22. $0.007x - 0.07 = 0.7$

x = _____

23. $x - 4 = 3x + 2$

x = _____

24. $\frac{5}{9}x - \frac{1}{3} = \frac{2}{3}$

x = _____

25. Label each view as top, front, or right-side.

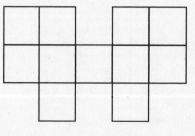

Use work area.

• Sets (page 599)

Name _____

Teacher Notes:
• Review "Number Families" on page 10 in the *Student Reference Guide*.
• Introduce reference chart, "Set Notation."

A set is a collection of elements written using braces, { }.

• The set of *integers* is expressed this way:

$$\{..., -3, -2, -1, 0, 1, 2, 3, ...\}$$

• The ellipsis (...) shows that the set goes on and on in the same pattern.

• Consider two sets, A and B.

$$A = \{1, 2, 3, 4\} \qquad B = \{3, 4, 5\}$$

• To show that an element is in a set, use the symbol $\in$. To show that an element is not in a set use the same symbol marked out, $\notin$.

$$3 \in A \qquad\qquad 3 \in B$$

3 is an element of both A and B.

$$2 \in A \qquad\qquad 2 \notin B$$

2 is an element of A. 2 is not an element of B.

$$6 \notin A \qquad\qquad 6 \notin B$$

6 is not an element of A or B.

• The **intersection** of sets is every element the sets have in common.

$$A \cap B = \{3, 4\}$$

The intersection of A and B is 3 and 4.

• The **union** of sets is every element in all the sets.

$$A \cup B = \{1, 2, 3, 4, 5\}$$

The union of A and B is 1, 2, 3, 4, 5.

• We did not repeat elements in the union. Write each element only once.

• Consider another set: set C.

$$C = \{1, 2\}$$

• All the elements of set C are in set A. Set C is a **subset** of A.

$$C \subset A$$

C is a subset of A.

• A **Venn diagram** shows relationships between sets using circles.

The Venn diagram shows sets A, B, and C.
Set C is completely inside A: **subset**
3 and 4 are in both A and B: **intersection**
1, 2, 3, 4, and 5 are all the numbers in A, B, and C: **union**

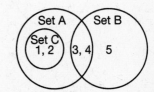

• The *intersection* of B and C contains **no elements**. A set with no elements is the **empty set**, $\varnothing$.

$$B \cap C = \varnothing$$

- The "Number Families" chart on page 10 in the *Student Reference Guide* shows some sets of numbers. These sets have special names:

Set	Symbol
counting numbers	$\mathbb{N}$
integers	$\mathbb{Z}$
rational numbers	$\mathbb{Q}$
real numbers	$\mathbb{R}$

Practice Set (page 602)

Use $\in$ and $\notin$ to tell whether each number is an element of the set of **integers**.

a. -1 _____ {integers}

b. 2 _____ {integers}

c. $\sqrt{3}$ _____ {integers}

Use the **subset** symbol $\subset$ to tell the relationship between A and B.

d. A = {all triangles}   B = {all polygons}

_____ $\subset$ _____

e. A = $\mathbb{R}$ B = $\mathbb{Q}$

_____ $\subset$ _____

f. A = {vowels}   B = {letters in the alphabet}

_____ $\subset$ _____

Write the elements of the sets in the correct places in the Venn diagrams. Then write the **intersection** of A and B.

g. A = {3, 6, 9, 12}   B = {5, 12, 15, 20}

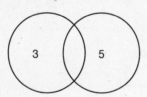

A ∩ B = {_____}

h. A = {all parallelograms}   B = {all trapezoids}

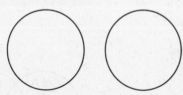

A ∩ B = ∅

Practice Set (continued) (page 603)

Write the elements of the sets in the correct places in the Venn diagrams. Then write the **union** of A and B.

i. A = {10, 20, 30}   B = {20, 30, 40}

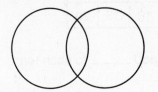

A ∪ B = { _____, _____, _____, _____ }

j. A = {2, 4, 6, 8, ...}   B = {4, 8, 12, ...}

A ∪ B = { _____, _____, _____, ... }

Written Practice   (page 603)

1. 1 in. = 10 ft

    a. 2.1 in. · ——— =

    b. 18 ft. · ——— =

    a. _____ **b.** _____

2. Answer in standard form.

    $(3.33 \times 10^{-22}g)(6.02 \times 10^{23})$

        3.33
    × 6.02

3.

	Percent	Actual Count
Original	100	
Change		
Total		t

4. Central angles

Every hour is $\frac{1}{12}$ (360°) = _____°.

At every half-hour, the hour hand has moved halfway

between numbers = _____°.

a.

b.

c.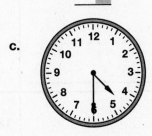

d.

Use work area.

5. Multiply the probabilities.

$$P(\text{H 5 times}) = \frac{1}{2} \cdot \underline{\quad} \cdot \underline{\quad} \cdot \underline{\quad} \cdot \underline{\quad} =$$

_____

6.

n	1	2	3	4
a_n	5	10	15	20

The rule is add _____ to each term

$a_n = $ _____

$a_{20} = $ _____

Use work area.

7. Draw the rectangle.

(3, 1), (2, −2), (−1, −1), (0, 2)

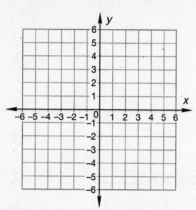

length = _____   width = _____

Use work area.

8. area of rectangle

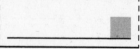
_____

9. $\dfrac{\text{rotations}}{\text{min}}$ to $\dfrac{\text{rotations}}{\text{sec}}$

$$\frac{60{,}000 \text{ rotations}}{1 \text{ min}} \cdot \underline{\quad\quad} = \frac{\text{rotations}}{1 \text{ sec}}$$

$$\frac{\text{sec}}{1 \text{ rotation}} =$$

_____

10. $(-3)^1 - 3^2 - (-3)^3 =$

_____

11. 75% of $\frac{2}{3}$ of $1.44

_____

12. $\sqrt{20{,}000} =$

_____

13. $2x^{-2}y^{-3}xy =$

_____

14. *Put the numbers in order.*

$\dfrac{1}{\rule{1.5cm}{0.4pt}}, \dfrac{}{\rule{1.5cm}{0.4pt}}, \dfrac{}{\rule{1.5cm}{0.4pt}}, \dfrac{}{\rule{1.5cm}{0.4pt}}, \dfrac{}{\rule{1.5cm}{0.4pt}}, \dfrac{}{\rule{1.5cm}{0.4pt}},$

$\dfrac{}{\rule{1.5cm}{0.4pt}}, \dfrac{}{\rule{1.5cm}{0.4pt}}, \dfrac{}{\rule{1.5cm}{0.4pt}}, \dfrac{6}{\rule{1.5cm}{0.4pt}}$

a. mean: _____   mode: _____

median: _____   range: _____

b. _____

Use work area.

15. a. Graph the points.

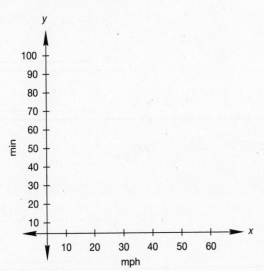

b. Use the graph to find min when

mph = 55 · _____ min

Use work area.

16. Solve by graphing.

$\begin{cases} y = x - 5 \\ x + y = 3 \end{cases}$

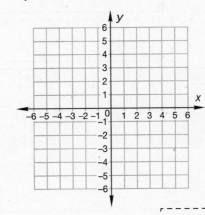

$y = $ _____

$x = $ _____

17. A = {2, 4, 6, 8, 10, 12}

B = {3, 6, 9, 12}

a. A∩B = {_____, _____}
   intersection

b. A∪B = {_____, _____, _____, _____,

   union

   _____, _____, _____, _____}

18. $\dfrac{mi}{hr}$ to $\dfrac{ft}{sec}$

$\dfrac{60\ mi}{1\ hr} \cdot \dfrac{hr}{min} \cdot \dfrac{min}{sec} \cdot \dfrac{ft}{mi}$

Use work area.

19. $\frac{2}{11}$

   a. percent

   b. decimal $)\overline{}$

   c. rounded decimal

   a. _____

   b. _____

   c. ____ . ____ ____ ____

20. a. Factor: $5m^2 - 40m + 5 =$

   b. Distribute: $7x(x - 3) =$

   a. _____

   b. _____

21. $\frac{1.5}{2.5} = \frac{3}{x}$

   $x =$ _____

22. $0.05 + 0.02x = 1.95$

   $x =$ _____

23. $\frac{4}{5} - \frac{2}{3}x = \frac{14}{15}$

   $x =$ _____

24. $-\frac{m}{3} = 3$

   $m =$ _____

25. a. h _____

   b. Which state? _____

   c. Each bar is one _____ year.

   d. A 15% increase is 115%.
      Multiply 1993 – 94 by 1.15. What year is close to that? _____

   e. The daily attendance _____ each school year.

Use work area.

• **Effect of Scaling on
Perimeter, Area, and Volume** (page 610)

Name _____

Teacher Notes:
• Review Hint #47, "Scale Factor."
• Review "Scale Factor" on page 31 in the *Student Reference* Guide.

The scale factor is the ratio of the dimensions of similar figures.

• A scale factor greater than 1 is an increase in size.

• A scale factor less than 1 is a decrease in size.

• The scale factor is also used to find the ratio of measures of the figures:

  Perimeter is related by the **scale factor.**

  Area is related by the scale **factor squared.**

  Volume is related by the **scale factor cubed.**

Practice Set (page 613)

a. If you know the scale factor between two polygons, describe how you can find the ratios of their perimeters and area.

The ratio of perimeters is the $\underset{s}{\_\_\_\_}\underset{f}{\_\_\_\_}$. The ratio of the areas is the scale factor $\underset{s}{\_\_\_\_}$.

b. The dimensions of a wallet-size photo are about **half** the dimensions of a 5 inch-by-7-inch photo. The **area** of a wallet-size photo is about what fraction of the area of a 5 inch-by-7-inch photo?

(scale factor)^2 = _____
Area is related by (scale factor)^2.

c. A triangle with vertices at (0, 0), (1, 0), and (0, 2) is dilated by a scale factor of 4. The **area** of the

dilated image is how many times the area of the original triangle?_____

d. Find the scale factor of the smaller rectangle to the larger rectangle. _____

4 in.

6 in.

2 in.

Find the ratios of the perimeters and areas of the larger rectangle to the smaller rectangle.
larger to smaller

perimeters: _____ to _____   areas: _____ to _____

e. Find the surface area and volume of a 1-inch cube and a 10-inch cube.

A cube has six equal square faces.

1-inch cube   **10-inch cube**

surface area: _____ ▪   surface area: _____ ▪

volume: _____ ▪   volume: _____ ▪

What is the ratio of the surface areas? $\dfrac{\text{smaller}}{\text{larger}} = $ _____

What is the ratio of the volumes? $\dfrac{\text{smaller}}{\text{larger}} = $ _____

f. One square has sides 10 cm long. A second square has sides **50% longer.** How long are the sides of

the larger square? _____ ▪

longer = 100% + 50% = 150%

What is the scale factor from the smaller to larger square written as a decimal? _____
Write 150% as a decimal.

What is the ratio of the areas of the smaller to larger square written as a decimal? _____

g. To celebrate her pizza shop's 10th anniversary, Blanca is offering "Double Your Dollar Days." During
this time, customers can get twice as much pizza for the price of a 10-inch pizza. What is the
approximate diameter of a pizza **twice the area** of a 10-inch pizza? (circle one)
Area is related by (scale factor)².
(scale factor)² = 2

scale factor = _____
diameter of larger pizza = scale factor × diameter of smaller pizza

A 12 in.   **B** 14 in.   **C** 16 in.   **D** 20 in.

h. If a **6-inch diameter** balloon holds a pint of water, how much water does a **6-inch radius** balloon

hold? _____ ▪

diameter of larger balloon = _____

scale factor = _____
Volume is related by (scale factor)³.

1. 16c = 1 gal

cups __2__ __16__
lb

2.

	Percent	Actual Count
Original	100	
Change		
New		

3. Estimate the sale price.

$23.95 →

discount = $33\frac{1}{3}$% of $ _____

4. 1 in. = 250 ft

a. 1000 ft · —— =

b. 0.5 in · —— =

a. _____

b. _____

5. V = area of base × height

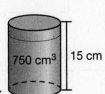

750 cm³   15 cm

a. The __V_____ and

__h_____ are given.

__D_____ the volume

by the height to find area of the base.

b. Solve for B.
V = Bh

a. _____   b. B = _____

6. How many cones can be filled with water from problem **5**?

Volume of cone = $\frac{1}{3}$Bh

_____

7. descending order

3(x − 4) + x(x − 4) =

_____

8. Find the area of the shaded square.

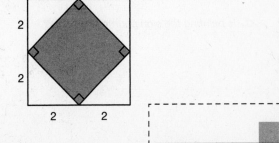

2

2

2   2

_____

9. radius of $A = x$
radius of $B = 2x$

   a. *Circumference is related by scale factor.*

   b. *Area is related by (scale factor)².*

   a. _____

   b. _____

10. $P(A, E, I, O, U) = \dfrac{\quad}{5} \cdot \dfrac{\quad}{4} \cdot \dfrac{\quad}{\quad} \cdot \dfrac{\quad}{\quad} \cdot \dfrac{\quad}{\quad}$

_____

11. **a.** triangle area

   b. circle area
      Leave π as π.

   c. $\dfrac{\text{triangle area}}{\text{circle area}}$

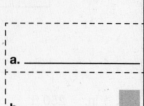
2 cm
2 cm

   a. _____

   b. _____

   c. _____

12. $3xyx - 2xy^2 + yx^2 =$

_____

13. $2\sqrt{8}\,\sqrt{18} =$

_____

14. 📖 *See page 615.*

   a. most = _____

      least = _____

   b.   Friday
      $+$ _____ Saturday

Use work area.

15. **a.** Find x.

   b. *Perimeter is related by scale factor.*

   c. *Area is related by (scale factor)².*

   d. *Is painting the sign perimeter or area?*

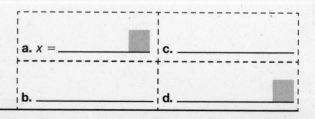
a. $x =$ _____   **c.** _____

b. _____   **d.** _____

16. Draw the triangle.

(0, 0), (2, 1), (−2, 4)

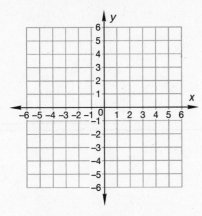

a. classify by angles

b. area

a. _____

b. _____

17. a. length of hypotenuse

b. perimeter

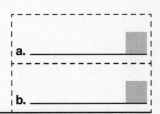

a. _____

b. _____

18. S = {M, W, F}

M = {T, W}

a. S∩M = {_____}

intersection

b. S∪M = {_____, _____, _____, _____}

union

Use work area.

19. cm³ to in³.

1 in. = 2.54 cm

Use a calculator and round to the nearest in.³

1000 cm³ · _____ · _____ · _____ =

_____

20. a. Factor: $4x^2 + 4x =$

b. Distribute: $-(x - 3)$

a. _____

b. _____

21. $\frac{5}{11}$

a. percent

b. decimal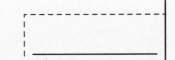

c. rounded decimal

a. _____

b. _____

c. _____ · _____ _____

22. $\frac{1.2}{1.6} = \frac{9}{x}$

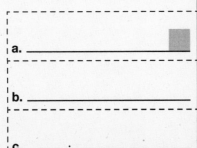

x = _____

23. $\frac{5}{6}x = \frac{1}{2}x + \frac{1}{3}$

24. $0.1 + 0.001x = 1.01$

$x = $ _____

$x = $ _____

25. Label the area of the large square and the length of the hypotenuse. Use the Pythagorean Theorem.

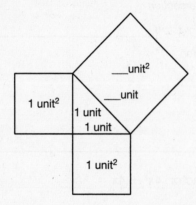

_____unit^2

_____unit

1 unit^2

1 unit

1 unit

1 unit^2

Use work area.

- **Area of Rectangles with Variable Dimensions**
- **Products of Binomials** (page 617)

The Distributive Property of Multiplication can be used to find area and the products of binomials.

- The **Distributive Property** spreads multiplication over addition or subtraction.

  $$(12)(x + 2) = (12 \cdot x) + (12 \cdot 2) = 12x + 24$$

- The Distributive Property can also be used to spread multiplication by more than one term.

- We replace (12) with $(10 + 2)$ and see if we get the same answer.

$(12)(x + 2)$	Given
$(10 + 2)(x + 2)$	$10 + 2 = 12$
$10(x + 2) + 2(x + 2)$	Distributive Property
$(10x + 20) + (2x + 4)$	Multiplied
$12x + 24$	Collected like terms

- A **binomial** is an expression made up of two algebraic terms.

- To multiply binomials, we have to use the Distributive Property like we did above.

  Example: Expand: $(x + 3)(x + 2)$

$(x + 3)(x + 2)$	Given
$x(x + 2) + 3(x + 2)$	Distributive Property
$x^2 + 2x + 3x + 6$	Multiplied
$x^2 + 5x + 6$	Collected like terms

  We multiply $(x + 2)$ by x and 3 separately, and then combine terms.

- Be careful with negative signs! Carry them with the numbers.

  Like signs $(+/+$ or $-/-)$ make a positive product.
  Unlike signs $(+/-$ or $-/+)$ make a negative product.

  Example: Expand: $(x - 3)(x - 4)$

$(x - 3)(x - 4)$	Given
$x(x - 4) - 3(x - 4)$	Distributive Property ($-$ stayed with -3)
$x^2 - 4x - 3x + 12$	$x \cdot -4 = -4x; -3 \cdot x = -3x; -3 \cdot -4 = +12$
$x^2 - 7x + 12$	Collected like terms

• A shortcut for multiplying binomials is to remember **FOIL**.

$$(x - 3)(x - 4)$$

F (Multiply **first** terms)	$x \cdot x = x^2$
O (Multiply **outside** terms)	$x \cdot -4 = -4x$
I (Multiply **inside** terms)	$-3 \cdot x = -3x$
L (Multiply **last** terms)	$-3 \cdot -4 = +12$
Add them all together.	$x^2 - 7x + 12$

Practice Set (page 620)

a. What is the area of this rectangle? Multiply the binomials. _____ + _____ + _____

$(x + 4)(x + 2)$

$x(x + 2) + 4(x + 2)$

$x^2 + 2x + 4x + 8$

(rectangle with top side labeled $x + 4$ and left side labeled $x + 2$)

b. What is the **area of a square** with a side length of $x + 4$? _____ + _____ + _____

$(x + 4)^2 = (x + 4)(x + 4)$

$x(x + 4) + 4(x + 4)$

c. Find the product: $(x + 2)(x + 5) =$ _____ + _____ + _____

$(x + 2)(x + 5)$

_____ $(x + 5) +$ _____ $(x + 5)$

Expand.

d. $(x + 1)(x + 3) =$ _____

$x(x + 3) + 1(x + 3)$

$x^2 + 3x + x + 3$

e. $(x + 4)(x + 7) =$ _____

_____ $(x + 7) +$ _____ $(x + 7)$

f. $(x + 3)^2 =$ _____

$(x + 3)(x + 3)$

g. $(x + 10)^2 =$ _____

h. $(x + 8)(x - 3) =$ _____

$x(x - 3) + 8(x - 3)$

$x^2 - 3x + 8x - 24$

i. $(x - 5)(x + 2) =$ _____

_____ $(x + 2) -$ _____ $(x + 2)$

j. $(x + 2)(x - 2) =$ _____

k. $(20 + 2)(20 - 2) =$ _____

Written Practice (page 621)

1.

	Percent	Actual Count
Original	100	
Change		
New		

2. 1 in. = 2 ft

12 ft · _____ =

7 ft · _____ =

length = _____

width = _____

3. *Total cost is 100% + 6% = 1.06*

4. $2 < x \le 5$

Graph $x > 2$ and $x \le 5$.

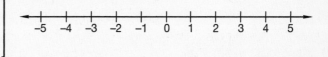

Use work area.

5.

Each hour is $\frac{1}{12}$ of the circle.

What is the angle?

What percent is $\frac{4}{12}$?

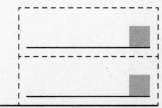

6. $A = \{1, 2, 3, 4, 5\}$

$B = \{2, 4, 6, 8, 10\}$

a. $A \cap B = \{$ ___ , ___ $\}$
intersection

b. $A \cup B = \{$ ___ , ___ , ___ , ___ ,

___ , ___ , ___ , ___ $\}$

union

Use work area.

7. area

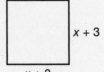
$x + 3$

$x + 3$

$(x + 3)(x + 3)$

$x(x + 3) + 3(x + 3)$

___ + ___ + ___

8. area

$(x - 1)(4x + 2)$

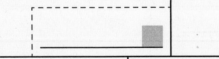 $x - 1$

$4x + 2$

___ $(4x + 2) -$ ___ $(4x + 2)$

___ − ___ − ___

9. Draw the rectangle. $(1, -3)$, $(4, 0)$,

$(0, 4)$, $(-3, 1)$

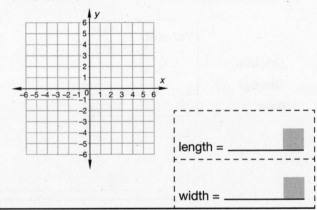

length = ___

width = ___

10. area

11. length of diagonal

A diagonal divides the rectangle into two right triangles.

12. perimeter of square

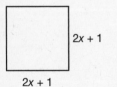
$2x + 1$

$2x + 1$

___

13. $d = 20$ in.

a. Estimate the percent. ___ %

b. area of triangle: ___

area of circle: ___

c. % = $\dfrac{\text{triangle}}{\text{circle}}$ = ___

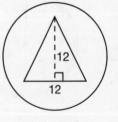
12

12

Use work area.

14. *The third side must be less than the sum of the first two sides.*

_____

15. $(\sqrt{5})^2 + (\sqrt{5})^2 =$ _____

$(\sqrt{10})^2 =$ _____

This _____ a right triangle

because the numbers fit the

P_____ Theorem.

Use work area.

16. ft³ to yd³

240 ft³ · _____ · _____ · _____ =

17. perimeter and area

$A = \frac{1}{2}(b_1 + b_2)h$

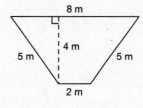

8 m

4 m

5 m   5 m

2 m

_____

_____

18. $\frac{1}{25}$

a. percent

b. decimal

a. _____

b. _____

19. $\frac{2.4}{1.8} = \frac{x}{6}$

$x =$ _____

20. $0.05 + 0.01x = 0.4$

$x =$ _____

21. $\frac{5}{3} + \frac{3}{4}x = \frac{5}{4}$

$x =$ _____

22. $3(x + 2) = 2x + 15$

$x =$ _____

23. volume of smaller and larger prisms
$V = Bh$

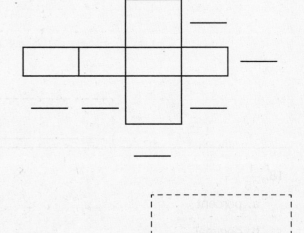

24. a. scale factor

   b. *Area is related by*
   (scale factor)².

   c. *Volume is related by*
   (scale factor)³.

a. _____

b. _____

c. _____

25. This is a net of the smaller prism. Label the side lengths.

_____

• Equations with Exponents
(page 624)

Name _____

Equations with exponents can be solved by finding the roots of both sides of the equation.

• Squaring a number changes a negative number to a positive.

$$5^2 = 5 \cdot 5 = 25 \qquad (-5)^2 = (-5) \cdot (-5) = 25$$

• An equation with a squared variable has two possible solutions.

$$x^2 = 25$$

$$x = 5 \text{ or } -5$$

• The solution can also be written

$$x = \pm 5$$

x is equal to plus or minus 5.

• A **quadratic equation** is an equation with a squared variable (exponent of 2).

• Solve quadratic equations in the same way as other equations:

1. Isolate the variable on one side of the equation.

2. Find both square roots.

3. Simplify the radical, if necessary. *(Factor perfect squares.)*

Example: Solve: $2x^2 + 7 = 23$

$2x^2 + 7 = 23$	Given
$2x^2 = 16$	Subtracted 7 from both sides
$x^2 = 8$	Divided both sides by 2
$x = \pm \sqrt{8}$	Took square root of both sides
$x = \pm 2\sqrt{2}$	$\sqrt{8} = \sqrt{4}\sqrt{2} = 2\sqrt{2}$

- For problems about the real world, sometimes only the positive or only the negative answer will make sense.

Example: The rectangles are similar.

Find x by solving this proportion.

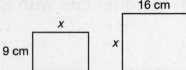

$$\frac{x}{16 \text{ cm}} = \frac{9 \text{ cm}}{x} \qquad \text{Given}$$

$x \cdot x = 9 \cdot 16$	Cross multiplied
$x^2 = 144$	Multiplied
$x = \pm 12$	Took square root of both sides
$x = 12 \text{ cm}$	The side length of a square must be a positive number.

Practice Set (page 626)

Solve each quadratic equation. Simplify radicals when possible.

a. $2x^2 - 3 = 29$

  $2x^2 = 32$

  $x^2 = 16$

  $x = \pm$ _____

b. $5x^2 + 6 = 16$

  $x = \pm$ _____

c. $-7x^2 + 8 = -13$

  $x = \pm$ _____

d. $8 = 4w^2 - 24$

  $w = \pm$ _____

e. $\dfrac{4}{x} = \dfrac{x}{9}$

  $36 = x^2$

  $x = \pm$ _____

f. $\dfrac{x}{3} = \dfrac{4}{x}$

  $x = \pm$ _____

g. Yoli arranges 121 square tiles into one larger square. How many tiles are along each edge of the larger square? _____

Area of square = 121 squares

1.

	Ratio	Actual Count
Recommended		
Did not		d
Total		

2. *total = 100% + 8.25% = 108.25%*

1.0825
× $10

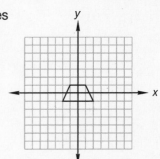

3. scale = 1:24

$10 \text{ in.} \cdot \dfrac{24}{1} =$

_____ in. $\cdot \dfrac{\text{ft}}{\text{in.}} =$

_____ in.

_____ ft

4. The quadrilateral has vertices (–2, –1), (2, –1), (1,1), and (–1, 1). Draw a dilation with scale factor = 2.

Area is related by (scale factor)².

$\dfrac{\text{bigger}}{\text{smaller}} =$

Use work area.

5. $-1 \le x < 5$

Graph $x \ge -1$ and $x < 5$.

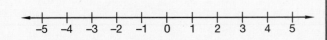

Use work area.

6. 25 letters

a. *decimal*

$P(\text{A, E, I, O, U}) = -$

b. *fraction*

A has been removed

$P(\text{E, I, O, U}) = -$

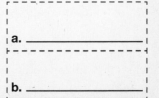

a. _____

b. _____

7. *See page 18 in the* Student Reference Guide.

_____

8. A = {2, 4, 6, 8, ...}
B = {1, 3, 5, 7, ...}

a. A∩B =
intersection

b. A∪B = {_____, _____, _____, _____, ...}
union

Use work area.

9. $x^2 + 1 = 50$

$x = \pm$ _____

10. $(x - 7)^2 = (x - 7)(x - 7) =$

_____ − _____ + _____

11. $(2x + 4)(x + 1) =$

_____ + _____ + _____

12. area

_____

13. area and perimeter

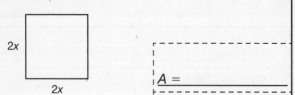

$A =$ _____

$P =$ _____

14. $\dfrac{\text{area of circle}}{\text{area of square}}$

Leave π as π.

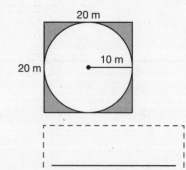

_____

15. $2\sqrt{12} + 4\sqrt{75} =$

_____

16. $-2x - 4 \geq x + 5$

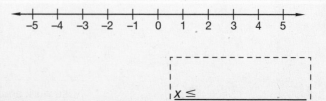

$x \leq$ _____

17. Solve by graphing.

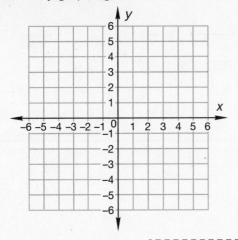

$$\begin{cases} x + 2y = 4 \\ x - y = 1 \end{cases}$$

x = _____

y = _____

18. 10.0 $\frac{gal}{min}$ Old

−2.5 $\frac{gal}{min}$ New

$\frac{gal}{min}$ Saved

$\frac{gal}{min} \cdot \frac{min}{1 day} \cdot \frac{days}{week} =$

_____

19. 0.875

a. percent

b. reduced fraction

a. _____

b. _____

20. Solve for s.

$A = 6s^2$

s = _____

21. surface area = 600 cm²

a. area of each face

b. edge length

c. volume

a. _____

b. _____

c. _____

22. $1.2x - 0.5 = x$

x = _____

23. $\frac{2}{3}x + \frac{3}{4} = \frac{3}{2}$

24. Solve by cross multiplying.

$$\frac{x}{3} = \frac{x+1}{2}$$

$$2x = 3(x + 1)$$

$x =$ _____

$x =$ _____

25. Use 1.41 for $\sqrt{2}$.

A 90 ft

B 127 ft

C 157 ft

D 180 ft

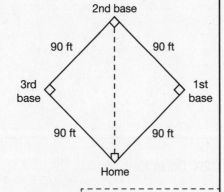

2nd base

90 ft   90 ft

3rd base   1st base

90 ft   90 ft

Home

_____

• **Graphing Pairs of Inequalities
on a Number Line** (page 629)

Name _____

Pairs of inequalities can be graphed on a number line to find their solution.

- A **pair** of inequalities shows a range of numbers.

  $3 < x \le 10$

- This pair of inequalities can be stated as two individual inequalities.

  $x > 3$ **and** $x \le 10$

  x is greater than 3 and x is less than or equal to 10.

- On a number line, the inequalities look like this

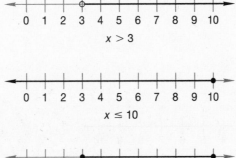

$x > 3$

$x \le 10$

$3 < x \le 10$

- In the last graph, the parts of the individual inequalities that go on and on are not there because x must make sense in both inequalities.

- Remember to use an open circle for < and > and a dot for $\le$ and $\ge$.

  Example: Graph the solution set of the inequality $-1 \le x < 5$.

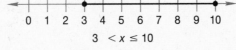

  The solution set is all the numbers *greater than or equal to -1 and less than 5*.

- A pair of inequalities linked by **or** has a different graph.

  Example: Graph this pair of inequalities: $x \le -1$ or $x \ge 3$

  The solution is all the numbers *less than -1 or greater than 3*.

Practice Set (page 631)

Graph each inequality on a number line.

a. $-3 < x < 3$

    *x is greater than –3 **and** x is less than 3.*

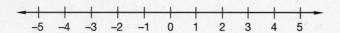

b. $x \leq -3$ or $x \geq 3$

    *x is less than or equal to –3 **or** x is greater than or equal to 3.*

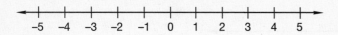

c. $5 < x \leq 10$

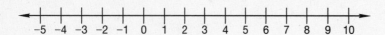

d. $x < 0$ or $x \geq 5$

e. A college will cancel a lab class if **less than 12 students** enroll. **No more than 30 students** can enroll in one lab class. Write an inequality that shows the numbers of students, *s*, that could be in the lab class. Graph the inequality.

    _____ *s* _____

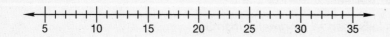

1.

	Percent	Actual Count
Made it		
Did not		d
Total	100	

2. Round $199 and $139.

	Percent	Actual Count
Original	100	
Change (−)	c	
New		

3. 1 in. = 1.5 ft

8 in. · ——— =

4. two number cubes

$P(\text{both odd}) = P(\text{odd}) \cdot P(\text{odd}) =$

5. a. Draw square *ABCD*.

A(0,2), B(2,0), C(0,−2), D(−2,0)

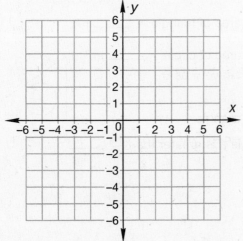

b. Turn your page until the square looks the same. How many degrees was that? _____

6 a. side of *ABCD*

b. area of *ABCD*

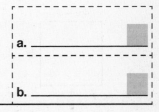

a. _____

b. _____

7. $x < -1$ or $x \geq 0$

x is _____ than _____ or x is

_____ than or equal to _____.

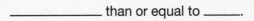

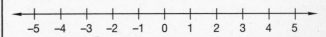

Use work area.

Use work area.

8. $A = \{5, 10, 15, 20, 25, 30, 35, 40, 45\}$

$B = \{15, 30, 45\}$

a. A∪B = { ——, ——, ——, ——, ——, ——, ——, ——, —— }
union

b. A∩B = { ——, ——, —— }
intersection

> Use work area.

9. $(x + 10)^2 = (x + 10)(x + 10) =$

—— + —— + ——

10. $(x - 10)^2 = (x - 10)(x - 10) =$

—— − —— + ——

11. $(x + 10)(x - 10) =$

—— − ——

12. area

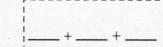

——————

13. Area and perimeter

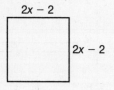

$A =$ ——————

$P =$ ——————

14. a. area of triangle = —— in.²

b. area of circle = —— in.²
Leave π as π.

c. $\dfrac{\text{circle}}{\text{triangle}} =$

Is this greater than $\dfrac{1}{4}$? ——

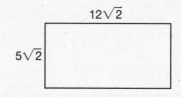

> Use work area.

15. $2\sqrt{27} + \sqrt{12} =$

_____

16. $x^2 + 1 = 50$

$x = \pm$ _____

17. $2^2 + 3^2 =$ _____

$4^2 =$ _____

If the triangle were a ^r_____ triangle, the longest side would be $\sqrt{13}$. The longest

side is _____ than $\sqrt{13}$, so the

triangle is obtuse.

Use work area.

18. $\dfrac{qt}{hr}$ to $\dfrac{cups}{min}$

$\dfrac{8\ qt}{1\ hr} \cdot \dfrac{hr}{min} \cdot \dfrac{cups}{qt} = \dfrac{cups}{min}$

Take the reciprocal to find $\dfrac{min}{cups}$. Round to

a whole number of minutes.

_____ min.

Use work area.

19. a. Factor: $5x^2 - 25x + 60$

b. Distribute: $-3x(3x - 1) =$

a. _____

b. _____

20. The net of the square pyramid has 4 congruent triangles and a square base.

a. area = _____ units²

b. Circle the solid this net creates.

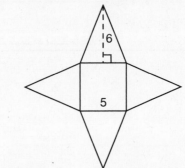

 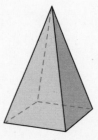 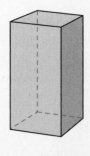

Use work area.

21. Similar trapezoids

    a. scale factor = _____

    b. The perimeter of the larger trapezoid is the

    perimeter of the smaller trapezoid times the

    _____

    _____ .

    Use work area.

22. Write as a decimal.
  Area is related by (scale factor)².

---

23. Percent greater
  (scale factor)² = _____

  Write as a percent.

  greater = _____% − 100% =

24. $2\frac{2}{3}$

  a. percent

  b. decimal

  c. rounded to
    hundredths

  a. _____

  b. _____

  c. _____

---

25. $2.3 - 0.02x = 0.5$

  $x =$ _____

• Slant Heights of Pyramids and Cones (page 634)

Name _____

For pyramids and cones, we use the Pythagorem Theorem to find slant height. We use slant height to find surface area.

• The height of a pyramid or cone is the perpendicular distance from the base of the solid to the apex (the point).

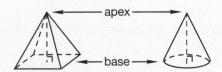

The height is used to calculate volume.

• The slant height of a pyramid or cone is the distance from the base to the apex along the outside surface.

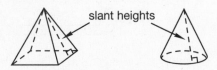

The slant height is used to calculate surface area.

• The height and slant height are related by the Pythagorean Theorem.

• The slant height is the hypotenuse of a right triangle that has the height as one leg and half the base as the other leg.

Example: Find the slant height of the cone.

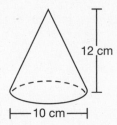

The diameter of this cone is 10 cm. Half of the base is the radius, 5 cm.
The radius, the height, and the slant height form a right triangle.

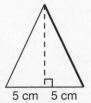

We use the Pythagorean Theorem to find the slant height of the cone.

$$a^2 + b^2 = c^2$$
$$5^2 + 12^2 = c^2$$
$$25 + 144 = c^2$$
$$169 = c^2$$
$$13 = c$$

The slant height is 13 cm.

Practice Set (page 636)

a. Describe the difference between the height and the slant height of a cone.

The _____ of a cone is the perpendicular distance from the center of the cone to the apex.

The _____ of a cone is the distance from the base to the apex along the outside.

b. Compared to the height of a pyramid, the slant height is
  A longer   **B** shorter   **C** the same
  The slant height is the hypotenuse of a right triangle.

For problems **c** and **d**, find the slant height. Label the right triangle to show the dimensions used in the calculations.

c. _____

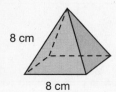

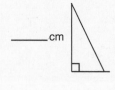

d. _____

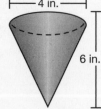

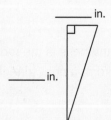

1. 20% of $45

2. 1 in = 2 mi

3. Find miles per gallon. Round the numbers.

23,742
−23,450

4. Find $\dfrac{L}{100 \text{ km}}$.

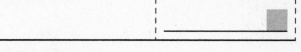

$$\dfrac{150L}{2500 \text{ km}} = \dfrac{}{100 \text{ km}}$$

5. two number cubes

$P(1, 1) = P(1) \cdot P(1) =$

6. $-4 < x \le -1$

x is greater than _____ and x is less than or

equal to _____ .

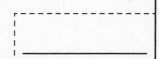

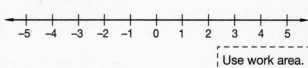

Use work area.

7. $E = \{..., -4, -2, 0, 2, 4, 6, 8, ...\}$
$F = \{..., -3, -1, 1, 3, 5, 7, ...\}$

a. How many elements are in E∩F? _____

intersection

b. E∪F is what set of numbers? 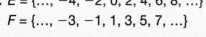 i_____

union

Use work area.

8. Rita forgot that a_____ is,
related by the scale factor

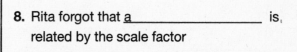
_____ .

Use work area.

9. Find the area of each circle in terms of π. How are the areas related? _____ and _____ total _____.

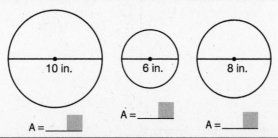

10 in.   6 in.   8 in.

A = _____   A = _____   A = _____

Use work area.

10.

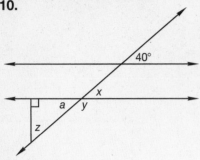

Find *x*.

Corresponding angles are congruent.

$x =$ _____

Find *y*.

Adjacent angles are supplementary.

$y =$ _____

Find *a*.

Vertical angles are congruent.

$a =$ _____

Find *z*.

The sum of the angle measures in a triangle is 180°

$z =$ _____

---

11. $2 + $1.60/mi

a.

(*x*) mi	(*y*) $
0	
1	
2	

b. equation

$y =$ _____ $x +$ _____

Use work area.

12. $(2x + 5)^2 = (2x + 5)(2x + 5) =$

_____ + _____ + _____

---

13. $(2x - 5)^2 =$

_____ + _____ − _____

14. $(2x + 5)(2x - 5) =$

_____ − _____

---

15. Area

_____

16. area and perimeter

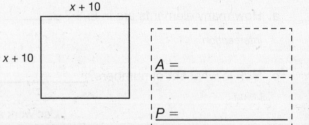

$A =$ _____

$P =$ _____

---

17. $2\sqrt{20} \sqrt{15} =$

_____

18. fraction and decimal

$\frac{1}{2}\% = 0.5\%$

_____

_____

---

19. Leave π as π.

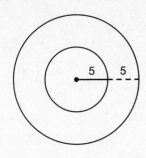

$$\frac{\text{small circle}}{\text{large circle}} =$$

20. Use 3.14 For π.

large circle − small circle =

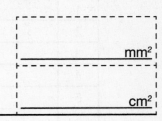

_____ mm² · $\dfrac{\text{cm}}{\text{mm}}$ · $\dfrac{\text{cm}}{\text{mm}}$ =

_____ mm²

_____ cm²

21. 📖 See *bottom of page 638.*
Use the Pythagorean Theorem and a calculator to find the height to the nearest tenth of a centimeter.

22. yd² to ft²

40 yd² · _____ · _____ =

23. This is a net of a cone.

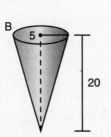

90°

20

a. The net will create which cone below?

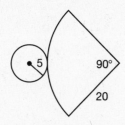

A 20

5

B 5

20

b. Surface area = _____

Area of circle with radius 5

$+ \left(\dfrac{90}{360}\right)$ Area of circle with radius of 20

Leave π as π.

Use work area.

24. $2x^2 = 50$

$\underline{x} = \pm$ _____

25. $f = \$2.50 + \$1.25\, n$

a.

n	f
0	
1	
2	
3	
4	
5	
6	

b.

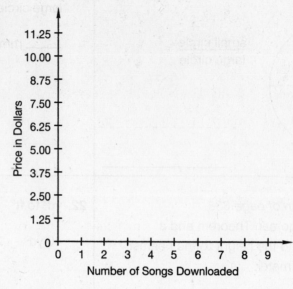

c. The graph _____ proportional

because it does not intersect the _____ .

**• Geometric Measures
with Radicals** (page 640)

Name _____

Finding the perimeter or area of some geometric figures involves multiplying, adding, or subtracting radicals.

• Radical expressions have a whole number and a radicand (number under the square root symbol).

• Radical expressions with the **same radicands** are like terms and *can be added*.

$$3\sqrt{2} + \sqrt{2} = 4\sqrt{2}$$

Both terms contain $\sqrt{2}$.

• Radical expressions with **different radicands** *cannot be added*.

$$5\sqrt{3} + 5\sqrt{2}$$

$5\sqrt{3}$ and $5\sqrt{2}$ cannot be added.

• **Factor perfect squares** to simplify radicals.

Practice Set (page 642)

Find the perimeter and area of each figure in units.

a. $P =$ _____ $A =$ _____

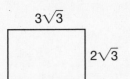

$3\sqrt{3}$

$2\sqrt{3}$

b. $P =$ _____ $A =$ _____

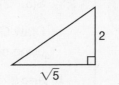

2

$\sqrt{5}$

c. What is the perimeter and area of a square with vertices at (2, 0), (0, 2), (–2, 0), and (0, –2)?

$P =$ _____ $A =$ _____

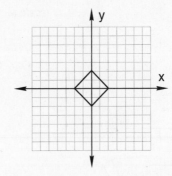

d. What is the perimeter and area of this square?

$P =$ _____ $A =$ _____

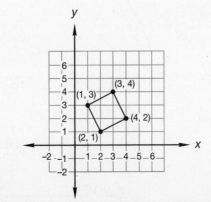

(1, 3)   (3, 4)

(4, 2)

(2, 1)

1.

	Percent	Actual Count
Correct		
Incorrect		i
Total	100	

_____

2.

	Percent	Actual Count
Original	100	
Change		
New		n

_____

3. 2 in. = 3 ft

12 ft · —— =

_____

4. lateral surface area

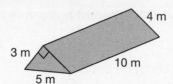

_____

5. total surface area

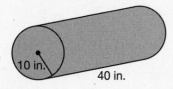

_____

6. a. Draw $QRST$:
Q(−1,1), R(3,1),
S(3,−2), T(−1,−2).

Draw $Q'R'S'T'$
using scale factor 3.

b. _Area is related by_

(scale factor)². _____

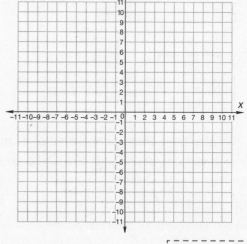

Use work area.

7. similar triangles

Solve for x.

$$\frac{6}{x} = \frac{15}{12 + x}$$

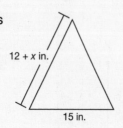

12 + x in.

15 in.

x in.

6 in.

$x =$ _____

$x + 12 =$ _____

8. 3 blue, 7 green
The marble is replaced after the first draw.
Write as fraction and decimal.

P(green, green) = —— · ——

_____

_____

9. Put the data in order.

$\underline{5}$, ___, ___, ___, ___, ___, ___, ___, $\underline{12}$

a. mean: _____ median: _____

mode: ___, ___, ___ range: _____

b. difference: _____

‹Use work area.›

10. $(4.88 \times 10^{-22}\text{g})(6.02 \times 10^{23}) =$

11. $x < -1$ or $x \geq 3.5$

x is less than _____ or x is greater

than or _____ to _____.

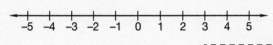

‹Use work area.›

12. $0.5 - 0.02x = 3.5$

$x =$ _____

13. $\frac{2}{7}x - \frac{1}{14} = \frac{1}{2}$

$x =$ _____

14. $3x + 2(-x + 3) = 17$

$x =$ _____

15. $4x^2 = 100$

$x = \pm$ _____

16. $F = \{2, 3, 5, 7, 8\}$ $S = \{3, 4, 5, 6\}$

a. $F \cap S = \{$ _____, _____ $\}$ *intersection*

This set is people who rated

_____ highly.

b. $F \cup S = \{$ _____, _____, _____, _____,

_____, _____, _____ $\}$ *union*

This set is _____ the

people surveyed.

‹Use work area.›

17. $(3x + 1)^2 =$

_____ + _____ + _____

18. $(x - 5)(x + 5) =$

_____ − _____

19. a. length = _____ 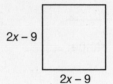 width = _____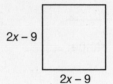

b. $P =$ _____ $A =$ _____

c. Count the squares and half squares to check the area.

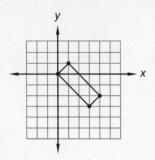

Use work area.

20. area and perimeter

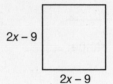

$A =$ _____

$P =$ _____

21. $\sqrt{196} - \sqrt{169} =$

_____

22. fraction

0.1%

_____

23. Label the front, side and top views.

a. **b.** **c.**

_____ _____ _____

d. Count cubes to find the volume. _____

Use work area.

24. Find the area of the figure.

Multiply the area by 4.

$$\frac{200 \text{ lbs}}{\text{area}} =$$

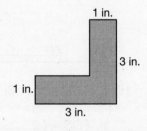

$$\frac{\text{lbs}}{\text{in}^2}$$

_____

25. area = 100 ft²

Double means the scale factor is 2.

Area is related by (scale factor)².

perimeter = 52 bricks

Perimeter is related by scale factor.

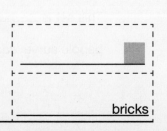

_____ bricks

• Recursive Rules
for Sequences (page 646)

Name _____

Teacher Note:
• Review Hint #53, "Finding Patterns in Sequences."

A sequence is an ordered list of numbers that follow a rule.

   $\{3, 6, 9, 12, ...\}$

• A table for this sequence showing the position, n, and the value, a, looks like this:

Term Position (n)	1	2	3	4	...
Term Value (a)	3	6	9	12	...

• A rule for this sequence is "Multiply the position of the term (n) by 3 to find the value (a)."
   The formula is
   $a_n = 3n$

• We can also write a rule that shows how each term relates to the previous term in the sequence. This is called a **recursive rule.**

• The recursive rule for this sequence is, "To make each term, add 3 to the preceding term."
   The recursive formula is
   $a_n = a_{n-1} + 3$

   The value of a_n is equal to the value of the preceding term (a_{n-1}) plus 3.

• Because each term depends on the preceding term, the first term must be given:
   $a_1 = 3$

• The recursive rule is written with both parts:
   $$\begin{cases} a_n = a_{n-1} + 3 \\ a_1 = 3 \end{cases}$$

• This formula makes the same table as the one above:
   $a_1 = 3$
   $a_2 = a_1 + 3 = 3 + 3 = 6$
   $a_3 = a_2 + 3 = 6 + 3 = 9$
   $a_4 = a_3 + 3 = 9 + 3 = 12$

• To write a recursive formula for a given sequence, find how each term is related to the next term. Find the pattern.

   Example: Write a recursive formula for the following sequence:
   $\{2, 4, 8, 16, 32, ...\}$

   Each term equals the preceding term **times two.**
   Write the first term, a_1.
   $a_1 = 2$

   Write the formula that will turn each preceding term (a_{n-1}) into the next term (a_n).
   $a_n = 2a_{n-1}$

- To find the value of a term in a recursive formula:

   1. Start with the first term, a_1.
   This value is given.

   2. Use the value of a_1 in the formula to find the value of a_2.

   3. Continue finding each term by using the preceding term.

   Example: Use this recursive formula to find the second and third terms in the sequence.

   $$\begin{cases} a_1 = 5 \\ a_n = 3a_{n-1} \end{cases}$$

   The first term is 5. Substitute 5 for a_1 to find a_2.
   $a_2 = 3a_{2-1} = 3a_1 = 3(5) = 15$
   $a_2 = 15$

   Substitute 15 for a_2 to find a_3.
   $a_3 = 3a_{3-1} = 3a_2 = 3(15) = 45$
   $a_3 = 45$

Practice Set (page 648)

a. Write a recursive formula for the following sequence:
$\{1, 4, 16, 64, ...\}$
Find the pattern.
Each term (a_n) equals the preceding term (a_{n-1}) times _____.

$$\begin{cases} a_1 = 1 \\ a_n = \underline{\quad} \, a_{n-1} \end{cases}$$

b. The terms of the following sequence are generated with the formula $a_n = 5n - 2$.
$\{3, 8, 13, 18, ...\}$
Write a recursive formula for the sequence.
Find the pattern.
Each term equals the preceding term plus _____.

$$\begin{cases} a_1 = \underline{\quad} \\ a_n = a_{n-1} + \underline{\quad} \end{cases}$$

c. One of the terms in the following sequence is 729. Write a recursive formula for the sequence and find the term that follows 729.
$\{1, 3, 9, 27, ...\}$
Find the pattern.
Each term equals the preceding term times _____.

$$\begin{cases} a_1 = \underline{\quad} \\ a_n = \underline{\quad} \, a_{n-1} \end{cases}$$

To find the term that follows 729, substitute 729 for a_{n-1}. _____

d. Which formula below generates the terms of the following sequence? (Circle one.)

{2, 3, 5, 9, 17, 33}

Find the pattern.

Each term is the preceding term times _____ and minus _____.

A $\begin{cases} a_1 = 2 \\ a_n = 2a_{n-1} - 1 \end{cases}$ **B** $a_n = 2n - 1$ **C** $\begin{cases} a_1 = 2 \\ a_n = a_{n-1} + 1 \end{cases}$

Written Practice (page 649)

1.

	Percent	Actual Count
Correct		
Incorrect		*i*
Total	100	

2.

	Percent	Actual Count
Last Year	100	
Change		
Now		*n*

3. *Multiply the probabilities.*

4. Put the data in order:

2 , _____ , _____ , _____ , _____ , _____ , 9

a. mean: _____ median: _____

mode: _____ range: _____

b. _____ **c.** _____

Use work area.

5. oats
granola _____ _____

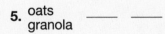

6. Label the measures on this net of the cylinder.

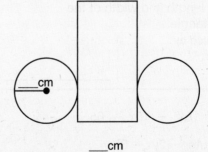

___cm

_cm

7. $\sqrt{2} + \sqrt{2}$ $\sqrt{4}$

↓ ↓

_____ ◯ _____

Find the lateral surface area and the total surface area. Use 3.14 for π.

LSA = _____

SA = _____

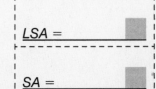

8. $-4 \leq x < -3$

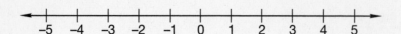

Use work area.

9.

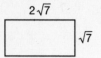

$2\sqrt{7}$

$\sqrt{7}$

a. area

b. perimeter

a. _____

b. _____

10.

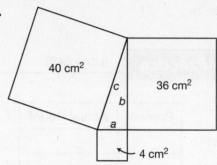

40 cm²

36 cm²

c

b

a

4 cm²

acute, obtuse, or right? _____

$a =$ _____

$b =$ _____

$c =$ _____

area = _____

11.

y

x

_____

Label the length and width of the larger rectangle.

Area is related by (scale factor)².

_____

12. a. Factor: $15x^2 - 10x - 65 =$

b. Distribute: $-(2y - 3) =$

a. _____

b. _____

Use work area.

13. $A = \{0, 1, 5\}$
$B = \{0, 2, 4\}$

a. $A \cap B = \{$_____$\}$
intersection

b. How many in $A \cup B$? _____

c. Is $A \cap B$ or $A \cup B$ both cities? _____

Use work area.

14. $\frac{1.2}{2.2} = \frac{6}{x}$

$x =$ _____

15. $0.4 + 0.01x = 0.13$

$x =$ _____

16. $x^2 + 1 = 10$

$x = \pm$ _____

17. $\frac{1}{3}x = \frac{2}{3}x + \frac{1}{6}$

$x =$ _____

18. $(2x - 3)^2 =$

_____ − _____ + _____

19. $(2x + 3)(2x - 3) =$

_____ − _____

20. area and perimeter of rectangle

$x + 1$

$x + 7$

$A =$ _____

$P =$ _____

21. $\frac{4.5 \times 10^{12}}{3.0 \times 10^{8}} =$

_____

22. $16\frac{2}{3}\%$ of $4.50

_____

23. *Substitute each term for* a_{n-1} *to find the next term.*

$$\begin{cases} a_1 = 4 \\ a_n = a_{n-1} + 3 \end{cases}$$

$\underline{\quad 4 \quad}, \underline{\quad\quad}, \underline{\quad\quad}, \underline{\quad\quad}$

Use work area.

24. $3(x - 5) > 2(5 - x)$

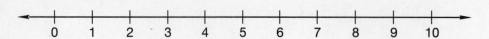

$x >$ _____

25. a. Is this a positive or negative correlation? _____

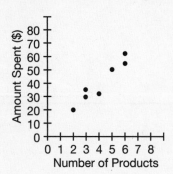

b. Use a ruler to estimate a line through the data. From your line, find the y-value for $x = 8$.

$y =$ _____

Use work area.

• **Relations and Functions** (page 651)

Name _____

A function is a rule that relates an input number (*x*) to an output number (*y*).

• For any input number, there can be only one output number.

  $y = 2x$
  When $x = 5$, $y = 10$.

• If *x* equals 5, *y* will always be 10 and *y* cannot be any other number.

• If an *x* makes more than one *y*-value, then the input-output rule is a **relation**, but not a function.

  Functions are special types of relations.

• Compare the tables:

x	y
0	−1
3	3
4	−1
6	4

x	y
0	−1
3	3
3	6
6	4

• The table on the left is a *function* because every *x*-value makes one *y*-value. The table on the right is a *relation that is not a function* because the *x*-value 3 makes two *y*-values, 3 and 6.

• This property of functions leads to the **vertical line test**:

  If a **vertical line** can be drawn through more than one point on a graph, the graph is a *relation*, but not a function.

• A vertical line is one *x*-value. If the line touches more than one part of the graph, that *x*-value makes more than one *y*-value.

Practice Set (page 654)

For **a–d**, write "function" or "not a function" for each graph or table.

a. _____

vertical line test

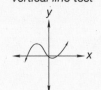

b. _____

c. _____

Every x-value can have only one y-value.

x	y
3	5
2	6
1	7
2	8
3	9

d. _____

x	y
2	5
3	4
4	5

1.

	Ratio	Actual Count
Martha		
Sister		
Total		t

2.

	Percent	Actual Count
Received		
Requested		q
Total	100	

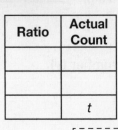

3. 8 blue, 2 green

   a. *P*(blue, blue) with replacement

   b. *P*(blue, blue) without replacement

4. Circle the correct terms.

relation or function?

vertical line test

linear or nonlinear?

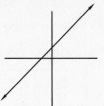

Use work area.

5. Circle the correct term.

relation or function?

vertical line test

linear or nonlinear?

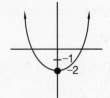

Use work area.

6. $\sqrt[3]{1000}$ = _____

Label the side lengths of this cube.

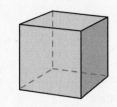

V = 1000 cm³

Use work area.

7. Write an equation for the table.

d	s
30	1
60	2
90	3
120	4

   $s =$ _____

8. *V* = *area of base* × *height*

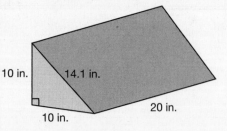

10 in.   14.1 in.

20 in.

10 in.

9. lateral surface area

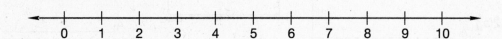

10. $x < 4$ or $x \geq 6$

x is _____ than 4 or _____ than or _____ to 6.

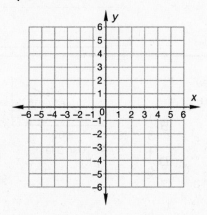

0 1 2 3 4 5 6 7 8 9 10

‾‾‾‾‾‾‾‾‾‾‾‾‾‾‾‾‾‾‾‾‾‾‾‾
¦ Use work area. ¦
¯¯¯¯¯¯¯¯¯¯¯¯¯¯¯¯¯¯¯¯¯¯¯¯

11. Graph the equations to solve.

$$\begin{cases} 4x + 2y = 8 \\ y = x + 1 \end{cases}$$

‾‾‾‾‾‾‾‾‾‾‾‾‾‾‾‾‾‾‾‾ ‾‾‾‾‾‾‾‾‾‾‾‾‾‾‾‾‾‾‾‾
¦ x = _____ ¦ ¦ y = _____ ¦
¯¯¯¯¯¯¯¯¯¯¯¯¯¯¯¯¯¯¯¯ ¯¯¯¯¯¯¯¯¯¯¯¯¯¯¯¯¯¯¯¯

12. Put the data in order:

   4
‾‾‾, ‾‾‾, ‾‾‾, ‾‾‾, ‾‾‾, 14 ‾‾‾

a. mean: _____   median: _____

   mode: _____   range: _____

b. _____

‾‾‾‾‾‾‾‾‾‾‾‾‾‾‾‾‾‾‾‾‾‾‾‾
¦ Use work area. ¦
¯¯¯¯¯¯¯¯¯¯¯¯¯¯¯¯¯¯¯¯¯¯¯¯

13. scale factor =

Area is related by (scale factor)².

‾‾‾‾‾‾‾‾‾‾‾‾‾‾‾‾‾‾‾‾‾‾‾‾‾‾
¦ _____ ¦
¯¯¯¯¯¯¯¯¯¯¯¯¯¯¯¯¯¯¯¯¯¯¯¯¯¯

14. $\dfrac{3.4}{4.4} = \dfrac{x}{22}$

‾‾‾‾‾‾‾‾‾‾‾‾‾‾‾‾‾‾‾‾
¦ x = _____ ¦
¯¯¯¯¯¯¯¯¯¯¯¯¯¯¯¯¯¯¯¯

15. $0.5x = 1.5 + 0.8x$

‾‾‾‾‾‾‾‾‾‾‾‾‾‾‾‾‾‾‾‾
¦ x = _____ ¦
¯¯¯¯¯¯¯¯¯¯¯¯¯¯¯¯¯¯¯¯

16. $\dfrac{2}{3}x - \dfrac{1}{2} = -\dfrac{1}{6}$

‾‾‾‾‾‾‾‾‾‾‾‾‾‾‾‾‾‾‾‾
¦ x = _____ ¦
¯¯¯¯¯¯¯¯¯¯¯¯¯¯¯¯¯¯¯¯

17. $3x^2 + 2 = 50$

‾‾‾‾‾‾‾‾‾‾‾‾‾‾‾‾‾‾‾‾
¦ x = ± _____ ¦
¯¯¯¯¯¯¯¯¯¯¯¯¯¯¯¯¯¯¯¯

18. $\begin{cases} a_1 = 5 \\ a_n = 2(a_{n-1}) \end{cases}$

$a_4 = 40$

$a_5 = 2(a_{5-1}) = 2(a_4) =$

$a_5 = \underline{\hspace{2cm}}$

19. area and perimeter

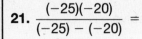

$x - 1$

$A = \underline{\hspace{3cm}}$

$P = \underline{\hspace{3cm}}$

20. $2\sqrt{3}\,\sqrt{3} =$

21. $\dfrac{(-25)(-20)}{(-25) - (-20)} =$

22. $\dfrac{wx^3y^4}{x^2y^2z^{-2}} =$

23. $\dfrac{\text{circle area}}{\text{triangle area}}$

A $\dfrac{1}{2}$ **B** $\dfrac{1}{3}$

C $\dfrac{1}{4}$ **D** $\dfrac{1}{9}$

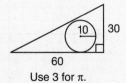

Use 3 for π.

24. $3 + 6 = \underline{\hspace{1cm}}$

The total of the two shorter sides of a triangle

must be \underline{\hspace{3cm}} than the third side, so this is not a triangle.

Use work area.

25. $(0, 4), (2, 0), (-2, 0)$

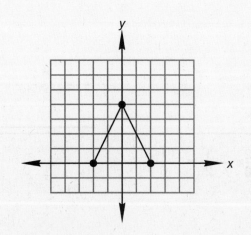

Use work area.

• Inverse Variation (page 658)

Name _____

The variation between two variables may be direct or inverse.

- In **direct variation,** the relationship between two variables is directly proportional.

- The ratio, or *quotient*, of y to x equals a constant, k. The graph of direct variation is a line.

  $y = kx$ or $\dfrac{y}{x} = k$

- For the example below, the constant, k, is 2.

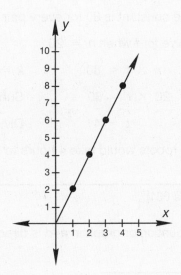

x	y	$\dfrac{y}{x} = k$
1	2	$\dfrac{2}{1} = 2$
2	4	$\dfrac{4}{2} = 2$
3	6	$\dfrac{6}{3} = 2$
4	8	$\dfrac{8}{4} = 2$

As one variable *increases*, the other variable *increases*.

- In **inverse variation,** the relationship between two variables is inversely proportional.

- The **product** of x and y equals a constant, k. The graph of inverse variation is a curve (non-linear).

- For the example below, the constant, k, is 12.

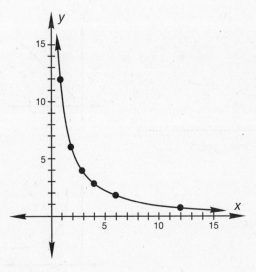

x	y	xy = k
1	12	$1 \cdot 12 = 12$
2	6	$2 \cdot 6 = 12$
3	4	$3 \cdot 4 = 12$
4	3	$4 \cdot 3 = 12$
6	2	$6 \cdot 2 = 12$
12	1	$12 \cdot 1 = 12$

As one variable *increases*, the other variable *decreases*.

- Many rate problems have inverse variation.

- Because the **product is constant**, we can solve for different variables.

Example: The number of robots *(n)* working and the amount of time *(t)* it takes to finish a job are inversely proportional. If it takes 10 robots 8 hours to finish a job, how long would it take 20 robots to finish the same job?

The relationship has a constant product: $n \times t = k$

One pair of numbers is $n = 10$ and $t = 8$.

$n \times t = k$	Inverse variation
$10 \times 8 = k$	Substituted given numbers
$80 = k$	Multiplied

The constant is 80 for every pair of *n* and *t*: $n \times t = 80$.

Solve for *t* when $n = 20$.

$n \times t = 80$	$k = 80$
$20 \times t = 80$	Substituted 20 for *n*
$t = 4$	Divided both sides by 20

20 robots would take 4 hours to finish the job.

Practice Set (page 661)

Tell whether each equation or graph in **a–d** is direct variation or inverse variation.

a. $\dfrac{y}{x} = k$ _____

　　constant ratio

b. $x \cdot y = k$ _____

　　constant product

c. _____

　　linear graph

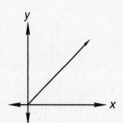

d. _____

　　non-linear graph

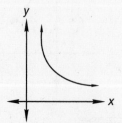

Practice Set (continued) (page 661)

e. Determine if the variables in tables 1 and 2 are inversely proportional.

1.

x	y	xy
1	6	$1 \cdot 6 = 6$
2	3	
3	2	

The variables have a constant

_____ so they are

_____ proportional.

2.

x	y	xy
1	3	$1 \cdot 3 = 3$
2	2	
3	1	

The variables do not have a constant

_____ so they are

_____ proportional.

f. If it takes 3 people (p), working at an equal rate, 5 hours (h) to complete a job, how long would it take

5 people to complete the same job? _____

$p \times h = k$

First, find k.

$3 \times 5 = k$

$k =$ _____

Substitute for k in the inverse variation equation.

$p \times h = k$

$5 \times h =$ _____

$h =$ _____

g. The volume of air (v) in a balloon and the air pressure (p) in the balloon are inversely proportional. If the

balloon is squeezed to $\frac{1}{2}$ its original volume, by what factor does the air pressure increase? _____

$v \times p = k$

$\left(\frac{1}{2}\right)v \times (\quad)p = k$

1. direct variation

cups $1\frac{1}{4}$ _____

% $\frac{}{10}$

2. inverse variation

$xy = k$

Find k.

$(12)(3) = k$

$k =$ _____

$xy =$ _____

$x(4) =$ _____

$x =$ _____

3. two number cubes

$P(3 \text{ or even}) = \frac{\quad}{\quad} \cdot \frac{\quad}{\quad} =$

4. Find the slant height of this cone.

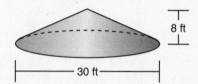

30 ft

8 ft

8 ft l

15 ft

$l =$

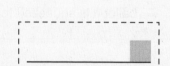

5. First find volume in ft³.

_____ ft³ · $\frac{100 \text{ lb}}{1 \text{ ft}^3}$ =

$V =$

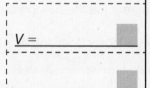

6. inverse variation

$xy = k$

First, find k.

7. Put the data in order.

_____, _____, _____, _____, _____

a. mean: _____   median: _____

mode: _____   range: _____

b. _____

Use work area.

8. **a.** Factor: $48x^2 - 24x - 36 =$

b. Distribute: $24\left(\frac{3}{8}x + \frac{5}{6}\right) =$

a. _____

b. _____

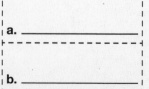

9. $7 \leq x < 10$

 x is greater than or equal to ____

 and x is less than ____ .

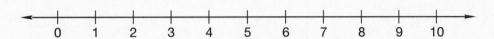

Use work area.

10. lateral surface area to the nearest cm²

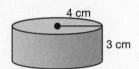

4 cm

3 cm

11. $4^2 + 5^2 =$ $6^2 =$

 Since $4^2 + 5^2$ is _____ than 6^2, the angle is less than a right angle and the

 triangle is _____ .

Use work area.

12. 📖 *See bottom of page 662.*

13.

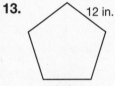

12 in.

window

 a. perimeter of window

 b. *Area is related by (scale factor)².*

 a. _____

 b. _____

14. $\dfrac{2.8}{4.8} = \dfrac{7}{x}$

 $x =$ _____

15. $0.0004x - 0.05 = -0.04$

 $x =$ _____

16. $\dfrac{5}{8} - \dfrac{1}{2}x = \dfrac{1}{2}$

 $x =$ _____

17. $\dfrac{x^2}{4} = 16$

 $x = \pm$ _____

18. $(2x + 1)(x - 1) =$

___ – ___ – ___

19. $(x - 7)^2 =$

___ – ___ + ___

20. area and perimeter

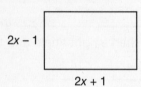

2x – 1

2x + 1

$A =$ _____

$P =$ _____

21. $\sqrt{8}\ \sqrt{6} =$

_____

22. $2x + y + x - y =$

_____

23. $\dfrac{m^{-3}xz^5}{m^3xm} =$

_____

24. $\begin{cases} a_1 = 1 \\ a_n = 2a_{n-1} + 1 \end{cases}$

$a_6 = 63$

$a_7 =$

$a_7 =$ _____

25. inverse variation

$xy = k$

a. $(6.0 \times 10^3)(9.0 \times 10^8) =$

b. Use your answer
from part **a.**

$\dfrac{}{3.0 \times 10^7} =$

a. _____ × _____

b. _____ × $\dfrac{mi}{hr}$

• Surface Areas of Right Pyramids and Cones (page 664)

Name _____

Teacher Note:
• Review "Geometric Solids" on page 30 in the *Student Reference Guide*.

The surface areas of pyramids and cones are related to the slant height and the measures of the base.

• The **slant height** is the distance from the edge of the base to the apex along the outside of the solid.

• The **lateral surface area** of a solid is the surface area *without the area of the base*.

Example: Find the lateral surface area of this pyramid with a slant height of 10 cm and a regular hexagonal base with sides 5 cm long.

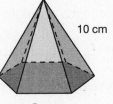

10 cm

5 cm

Lateral Surface Area of a Right Pyramid

$$A_s = \frac{ps}{2} \text{ or } \frac{1}{2}ps$$

A_s is lateral surface area
p is perimeter of base
s is slant height

First find the perimeter of the base. The base is a regular hexagon with 5-cm sides, so the perimeter is $6 \times 5 \text{ cm} = 30 \text{ cm}$.

Now use the lateral surface area formula:

$$A_s = \frac{ps}{2}$$

$$A_s = \frac{(30\text{cm})(10\text{cm})}{2}$$

$$A_s = 150 \text{ cm}^2$$

• The lateral surface area of a cone is also related to the perimeter of the base and the slant height.

• A cone has a circular base, so the perimeter is the circumference.

Example: Find the lateral surface area and the total surface area of this cone.

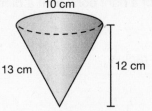

10 cm

13 cm   12 cm

Lateral Surface Area of a Right Cone

$$A_s = \pi rs$$

A_s is lateral surface area
r is the radius of the base
s is slant height

The diameter of the base is 10 cm, so the radius is 5 cm.

Now use the lateral surface area formula:

$$A_s = \pi rs$$

$$A_s = \pi(5 \text{ cm})(13 \text{ cm})$$

$$A_s = 165\pi \text{ cm}^2$$

The total surface area of the cone is the lateral surface area plus the area of the circular base.

$$A_{base} = \pi r^2$$
$$A_{base} = \pi (5 \text{ cm})^2$$
$$A_{base} = 25\pi \text{ cm}^2$$

total surface area $= A_s + A_{base} = 165\pi \text{ cm}^2 + 25\pi \text{ cm}^2 = 190\pi \text{ cm}^2$

Practice Set (page 667)

a. Describe how to find the lateral surface area of a right pyramid.

The lateral surface area is one half of the p_____ times the s_____ h_____.

b. Describe how to find the lateral surface area of a right circular cone.

The lateral surface area is pi times the r_____ times the s_____ h_____.

c. Find the **total surface area** of a square pyramid with base sides 5 inches long and a slant height of 4 inches.

The base is a square. Find its perimeter and area.

$P =$ _____

$A_{base} =$ _____   4 in.

                                    5 in.

Now use the lateral surface area formula:

$$A_s = \frac{ps}{2}$$

$$A_s =$$

$$A_s = \text{_____}$$

total surface area $= A_s + A_{base} =$ _____

d. Find the **lateral surface area** of a right cone with a diameter of 8 cm and a slant height of 12 cm. Leave π as π.

The diameter is 8 cm. Find the radius.

$r =$ _____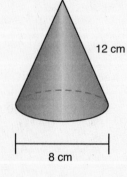

                                    12 cm

Now use the lateral surface area formula:

$$A_s = \pi r s$$

                                    8 cm

$$A_s = \pi (\quad \text{cm})(\quad \text{cm})$$

$$A_s = \text{_____}$$

1. Volume

$A_s = \pi rs$

$A = A_{base} + A_s$

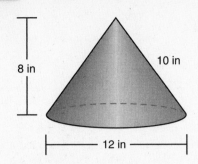

8 in

10 in

12 in

$V = $ ▢

$A = $ ▢

2.

	Percent	Actual Count
Bumpy		
Not Bumpy		
Total	100	t

▢

3.

	Percent	Actual Count
Last Year	100	l
Change		
This Year		

4. 2 red, 3 white, 5 blue

a. P(red, red) with replacement

b. P(red, red) without replacement

a. _____

b. _____

5. scale factor $= \dfrac{1}{18}$

Area is related by (scale factor)².

_____

6. scale factor = _____

Perimeter is related by scale factor.

Area is related by (scale factor)².

_____

_____

7. *Factor perfect squares.*

$\sqrt{12} + \sqrt{27} = $

_____

8. *vertical line test*

This _____ a function because a

v_____ line passes through more than one point on the graph.

Use work area.

9. Round to the nearest square inch.

A_s = perimeter of base $\times$ height

total area = $2A_{base} + A_s$

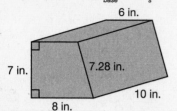

6 in.

7 in.   7.28 in.

10 in.

8 in.

---

10. $x < -12$ or $x \geq -6$

x is _____ than _____ or x is _____ than or equal to _____.

-15 -14 -13 -12 -11 -10 -9 -8 -7 -6 -5

Use work area.

---

11. a. slant height = _____

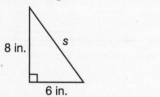

8 in. s

6 in.

b. area of one triangle = _____

s

12 in.

c. total surface area = _____

$A = A_{base} + A_s$

Use work area.

---

12. $P(\text{win}) = \dfrac{1}{3}$

$P(\text{win, win}) =$

---

13. a. $S = \{\text{perfect squares} < 100\}$

= {_____, _____, _____, _____, _____, _____, _____, _____, _____}

b. $C = \{\text{positive cubes} < 100\}$

= {_____, _____, _____, _____}

c. $S \cap C = \{$_____, _____$\}$

d. $S \cup C = \{$_____, _____, _____, _____, _____, _____, _____, _____, _____, _____, $\}$

Use work area.

14. $\dfrac{7.2}{4.8} = \dfrac{3}{x}$

_x_ = _____

15. $0.07 - 0.007x = 0.7$

_x_ = _____

16. $(3x - 4)(3x + 4) =$

_____ + _____

17. $(x - 11)^2 =$

____ – ____ + ____

18. area and perimeter

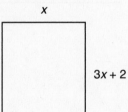

_x_

$3x + 2$

_A_ = _____

_P_ = _____

19. Put the data in order.

0.01, _____, _____, _____, _____, 1

mean: _____   median: _____

mode: _____, _____, _____

⌐ Use work area. ⌐

20. $\dfrac{72m^4x^3b^{-1}}{36m^3x^3b^2} =$

_____

21. $\dfrac{(-21) + (-24)}{(-21) - (-24)} =$

_____

22. $2x + 3y + 1 + x - 3y + 4 =$

_____

23. 50% of $\dfrac{2}{3}$ of 1.5

_____

24. inversely proportional

If the volume increases, does the pressure increase or decrease?

25. $k =$ _____

$y =$ _____

Bytes (x)	Bits (y)	$\frac{y}{x} = k$
1	8	
2	16	
3	24	
4	32	

Conversion of Bytes to Bits

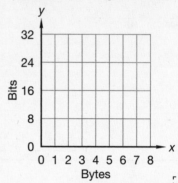

Use work area.

• Geometric Probability (page 675)

Name _____

Geometric probability is based on the area of two figures.

Teacher Note:
• Review "Geometric Formulas" on page 29 in the *Student Reference Guide*.

• The **probability** of an event is the *ratio* of the favorable outcomes to the total outcomes.

$$P = \frac{\text{favorable outcome}}{\text{total possible outcomes}}$$

• **Geometric probability** is the ratio of the *area* of a smaller figure to the *area* of a larger figure.

$$P = \frac{\text{Area of smaller figure}}{\text{Area of larger figure}}$$

• Imagine geometric probability as throwing a penny at a shape drawn inside an area of play. The probability of the penny landing in the shape is the geometric probability.

Example: What is the probability that an object that lands in the circle also lands in the square?

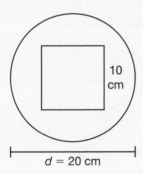

10 cm

$d = 20$ cm

Find the area of each figure.

$A_{\text{square}} = s^2$ $A_{\text{circle}} = \pi r^2$

$A_{\text{square}} = (10 \text{ cm})^2$ $A_{\text{circle}} = \pi(10 \text{ cm})^2$

$A_{\text{square}} = 100 \text{ cm}^2$ $A_{\text{circle}} = 100\pi \text{ cm}^2$

$$\text{Probability} = \frac{A_{\text{square}}}{A_{\text{circle}}}$$

$$= \frac{100 \text{ cm}^2}{100\pi \text{ cm}^2} = \frac{1}{\pi}$$

To approximate the value, use 3.14 for π.

$$\frac{1}{\pi} \approx 0.32$$

Practice Set (page 677)

Find the probability that an object that lands in the larger region will also land in the inner shape.

a. $P = \dfrac{A_{small}}{A_{large}} =$

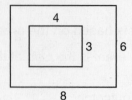

$A_{small} =$ _____ $A_{large} =$ _____

b. $P = \dfrac{A_{triangle}}{A_{square}} =$

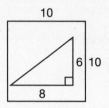

$A_{triangle} =$ _____ $A_{square} =$ _____

c. $P =$ _____

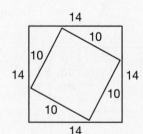

$A_{small} =$ _____ $A_{large} =$ _____

d. $P =$ _____

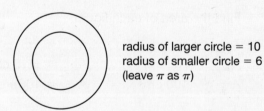

radius of larger circle = 10
radius of smaller circle = 6
(leave π as π)

$A_{small} =$ _____ $A_{large} =$ _____

e. Look back at the example. Which is greater, the probability that an object lands in the square or the probability that the object lands in the circle outside the square?

The probability of _____ in the square is greater.

The probability of landing in the square is about 0.32.

*The probability of **not** landing in the square is 1 – P(land in square).*

1. Label the dimensions of this prism.

$V = $ area of base × height

---

2. $P = \dfrac{A_{small}}{A_{large}}$

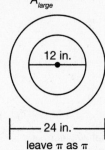

12 in.

|— 24 in. —|
leave π as π

3.

	Percent	Actual Count
Original	100	
Change		
New		n

---

4. 4 green, 3 blue
no replacement

a. P(green, blue) =

b. P(blue, green) =

c. P(green, blue) +
P(blue, green) =

a. _____

b. _____

c. _____

---

5. Similar figures

scale factor = _____

a. ratio of diameters

b. ratio of surface **areas**

a. _____

b. _____

6.

x	y	xy
2	30	2 · 30 =
3	20	
4	15	
5	12	

a. This is _____ variation because there is a

constant ^{p}_____.

b. If $x = 6$, then $y = $ _____.

Use work area.

---

7. 40, 45, 50, 55, 60

mean: _____   median: _____
mode: none

The mean is equal to the _____
because the numbers are equally
spaced.

Use work area.

---

8. 📖 *See the top of page 679.*

9.

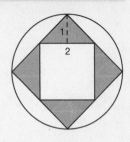

a. *The diameter is 1 cm plus halfway across the square.*

b. *The radius is 1 cm plus halfway across the small square.*

c. area

Leave π as π.

a. *d =* _____

b. *r =* _____

c. *A =* _____

10. a. area of one triangle

b. There are 4 triangles.

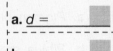
$$\frac{A_{triangles}}{A_{circle}} =$$

c. _____ is less than $\frac{1}{3}$ because π is

_____ than 3.

a. *A =* _____

b. _____

c. _____

11.

$$\frac{14.01 \text{ g}}{6.022 \times 10^{23}} =$$

_____ × _____ g

12. area and perimeter

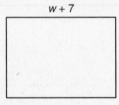

A = _____

P = _____

13. two number cubes

$P(>0 \text{ and } <7) =$

_____

14. Find *a.*

Alternate interior angles are congruent.

Then find *x.*

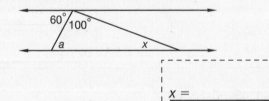

x = _____

15. $\frac{4.1}{5.1} = \frac{82}{x}$

x = _____

16. $0.04 - 0.003x = 0.4$

x = _____

17. $-\frac{1}{8} + \frac{1}{2}x = 0$

$x =$ _____

18. $(5x - 5)(5x + 5) =$

_____ – _____

19. $(x + 9)^2 =$

_____ + _____ + _____

20. $(-2)^2(4)^{-1} =$

_____

21. $\dfrac{3x^3}{2x^{-1}y} =$

_____

22. $\dfrac{(-2)(-3)(-4)}{-2 + (-3) - (-4)} =$

_____

23. $P = \dfrac{A_{triangle}}{A_{circle}}$

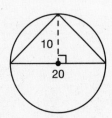

_____

24.

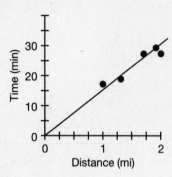

a. When $x = 1$, $y =$ _____

b. equation: $y =$ _____ x

c. Each mile takes about _____ minutes.

Use work area.

25. a. Which kind of variation? (circle one)
direct or inverse

b. Which is the constant? (circle one)

A walking rate   **B** walking time

C walking distance   **D** walking fit

Use work area.

• **Growth and Decay** (page 681)   Name _____

Exponential growth or decay can be found by repeatedly multiplying by the growth or decay rate.

• Consecutive terms in a geometric sequence have a constant *ratio.*

    1, 2, 4, 8, 16, . . .

    $\dfrac{2}{1} = 2$ $\dfrac{4}{2} = 2$ $\dfrac{8}{4} = 2$ $\dfrac{16}{8} = 2$

    In this example, the constant ratio is 2. Each term is 2 times the previous term.

    The terms get larger as the sequence goes on.
    This sequence is an example of **exponential growth.**

• In the geometric sequence below, the terms get smaller as the sequence goes on.

    128, 64, 32, 16, . . .

    $\dfrac{64}{128} = \dfrac{1}{2}$ $\dfrac{32}{64} = \dfrac{1}{2}$ $\dfrac{16}{32} = \dfrac{1}{2}$

    The constant ratio is 2. Each term is $\frac{1}{2}$ the previous term.

    This sequence is an example of **exponential decay.**

• Some real-world problems show exponential growth or decay.

    To solve growth and decay problems, make a table and multiply each number by the constant ratio to find the next number.

Practice Set (page 682)

a. Find the next term in this growth sequence. What is the constant ratio?

   16, 24, 36, 54, . . .

   $\dfrac{24}{16} =$ $\dfrac{36}{24} =$ $\dfrac{54}{36} =$

   constant ratio = _____

   Multiply 54 by the constant ratio to find the next term: _____

b. Find the next term in this decay sequence. What is the constant ratio?

   256, 192, 144, 108, . . .

   $\dfrac{192}{256} =$ $\dfrac{144}{192} =$ $\dfrac{108}{144} =$

   constant ratio = _____

   next term = _____

Practice Set (continued) (page 683)

c. The schools in an older community experienced a **decline** in the student population of 3% per year. If the decline continues at the same rate, and there are 5000 students in the community this year, about how many students will be in the community in three years? Round to the nearest hundred. _____

decline = 100% − 3% = 97%   *Change to a decimal.*

Multiply the number of students at the end of each year.

Years	Numbers of Students
0	5000
1	5000 × 0.97 = 4850
2	4850 × 0.97 =
3	

d. The number of bacteria in a culture increased from about 2000 to 4000 in one hour. Assuming the number of bacteria **grows exponentially,** how much longer will it take the number to increase to 16,000? _____

Find the constant ratio.

$$\frac{4000}{2000} =$$

Hours	Numbers of Bacteria
0	4000
1	4000 × _____ =
2	
3	

Written Practice   (page 683)

1. people ___ ___
   minutes

2.

	Percent	Actual Count
Not seen		n
Seen		
Total	100	

3.

	Percent	Actual Count
Original	100	
Change		
New		n

4. **a.** $a_n = 3n - 1$

$a_1 =$ _____ $a_2 =$ _____ $a_3 =$ _____

b. $\begin{cases} a_1 = 2 \\ a_n = a_{n-1} + 3 \end{cases}$

$a_2 =$

$a_3 =$

a. _____ , _____ , _____

b. __2__ , _____ , _____

5. 5 red, 4 yellow
no replacement

a. $P(R, Y) =$

b. $P(Y, R) =$

c. $P(R, Y) + P(Y, R) =$

d. P(not R and Y) $=$

  $1 - P(R, Y) - P(Y, R) =$

a. _____

b. _____

c. _____

d. _____

6. 1 ounce covers the small cube
Ratio of surface areas

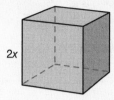

_____

7. perimeter and area of square

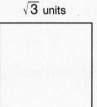

$\sqrt{3}$ units

$\sqrt{3}$ units

$P =$ _____

$A =$ _____

8. Is this a function? _____

vertical line test

linear or non-linear?

_____

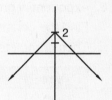

Use work area.

9. 4 green, 2 yellow, 6 gray
with replacement

P(green, gray) $=$

_____

10. a. slant height

b. $A_s = \pi r s$

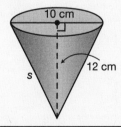

a. _____

b. _____

11. area and perimeter of rectangle

$l = 2w + 9$

$w = w$

$A =$ _____

$P =$ _____

12. *Use scientific notation.*

$$\frac{1 \cent}{\$1000} = \frac{1 \cent}{\cent}$$

_____ $\times$ _____

13. *Each edge is 1 unit.*

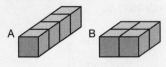

A   B

a. *Each cube is 1 unit³.*

$V_A =$ _____ $V_B =$ _____

b. *Each face has area of 1 unit².*

$A_A =$ _____ $A_B =$ _____

Use work area.

14. Reduce. Use the larger number.

$$\frac{40 \text{ ft}}{30 \text{ units}} = \qquad \frac{60 \text{ ft}}{40 \text{ units}} =$$

_____ ft = _____ units

15. exponential growth
Find the constant, *k*.
Then complete the table.

Time	Students
8 a.m.	4
9 a.m.	$4 \times k = 8$
10 a.m.	$8 \times k =$ ___
11 a.m.	
noon	

Use work area.

16. $a_n = 2n$

$a_1 =$ _____ $a_2 =$ _____
$a_3 =$ _____ $a_4 =$ _____

How do you make each next term? Add _____.

$$\begin{cases} a_1 = \underline{\quad} \\ a_n = a_{n-1} + \underline{\quad} \end{cases}$$

Use work area.

17. $-\dfrac{4}{3} + \dfrac{1}{12}x = -\dfrac{3}{4}$

$x =$ _____

18. $4x^2 = 64$

$x = \pm$ _____

19. a. factor: $32x^2 - 16x + 8 =$

   b. distribute: $\frac{1}{2}(3x - 6) =$

a. _____

b. _____

20. $(2x + 1)^2 = (2x + 1)(2x + 1) =$

_____

21. $(2x + 1)(2x - 1) =$

_____

22. $\dfrac{6x^4y^9}{3x^{-2}y^3} =$

_____

23. $33\frac{1}{3}\%$ of $\frac{3}{4}$ of 0.12

_____

24. *inverse variation*

   $yx = k$

   $y =$ people $x =$ hours

   First find k.

   _____ × _____ $= k$

   $k =$ _____

   Now find x when $y = 4$.

_____

25.  *See page 685.*

_____

- **Line Plots**
- **Box-and-Whisker Plots** (page 686)

Name _____

Teacher Note:
- Review "Statistics" on page 23 in the *Student Reference Guide.*

Line plots are graphs that use the number line to organize data.

- A **line plot** shows data on a number line.

  Every data point gets an X on the number line.

- It is easy to find the mode (most common number) on a line plot.

  Example: During physical fitness testing, students count the number of curl-ups they can do in one minute. The following totals were collected for the class. Graph the data on a line plot. (The data are in order from least to greatest.)

  26, 29, 32, 35, 36, 38, 38, 38, 39,
  39, 40, 40, 40, 40, 42, 42, 43, 45,
  45, 45, 46, 48, 50, 51, 52, 53, 55

Each data point is graphed with an X on a number line.

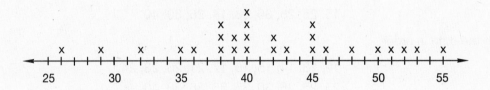

The mode is 40.

- A **box-and-whisker plot** also shows data on a number line.

- It is easy to find the median on a box-and-whisker plot.

- To make a box-and-whisker plot,

  1. Find the **median** (middle number).

  2. Find the middle number between the median and the lowest number.
  This is called the **lower quartile.**

  3. Find the middle number between the median and the highest number.
  This is called the **upper quartile.**

  4. Make a dot above the number line for the median, the lower quartile, and the upper quartile.
  Draw a "box" around these dots.

  5. Make a dot for the lowest number **(lower extreme)**. Make a dot for the highest number
  (upper extreme). Draw "whiskers" to connect the extremes to the box.

Example: Graph the physical fitness data on a box-and-whisker plot.

The data is still in order from least to greatest.

26, 29, 32, 35, 36, 38, 38, 38, 39,
39, 40, 40, 40, 40, 42, 42, 43, 45,
45, 45, 46, 48, 50, 51, 52, 53, 55

There are 27 data points, so the median is the 14th number. The median is 40. There are 13 data points above and below the median, so the quartiles are 7 numbers away from 40. The lower quartile is 38. The upper quartile is 46. The lower extreme is 26 and the upper extreme is 55.

We draw dots at all these points and make a box around the median and quartiles. Then we draw whiskers to the extremes.

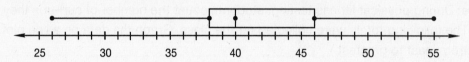

Practice Set (page 688)

In fitness testing, students did push-ups and recorded the number they were able to complete. The students' totals are recorded below.

12, 16, 21, 17, 23, 13, 23, 24, 35, 36,
15, 25, 25, 36, 38, 14, 26, 30, 40

First, we put the data in order:

12, 13, 14, 15, 16, 17, 21, 23, 23, 24,
25, 25, 26, 30, 35, 36, 36, 38, 40

a. Make a line plot of the data.

Put an X on the number line for each data point.

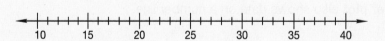

b. Make a box-and-whisker plot of the data.
Find the median. There are 19 data points, so the median is the 10th number.

median: _____

Find the quartiles. There are 9 data points above and 9 data points below the median. Start at the median and count **down** 5 numbers to find the lower quartile. Start at the median and count **up** 5 numbers to find the upper quartile.

lower quartile: _____   upper quartile: _____

The least number is the lower extreme. The greatest number is the upper extreme.

lower extreme: _____   upper extreme: _____

Now you can make a box-and-whisker plot.
Make a dot above the number line for each of the numbers you have found so far.
Draw a box around the median, lower quartile, and upper quartile.
Draw whiskers to the extremes.

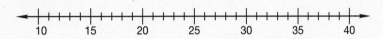

c. Which of these graphs quickly shows the median? _____ plot

Which of these graphs quickly shows the mode? _____ plot

Written Practice   (page 688)

1. Find the scale factor and ratio of the areas.

$2\frac{1}{2}$ in. $\longrightarrow$ 5 in.

$3\frac{1}{2}$ in. $\longrightarrow$ 7 in.

_____

_____

2.

	Percent	Actual Count
Passed		
Did not pass		
Total	100	t

_____

3. *total price = 100% + 8.25% = 108.25%*
108.25% of $100

4. $y = 2x + 35$

a.

x	y
1	
2	
3	
4	

b. Is this direct proportion?

_____

¦ Use work area. ¦

5. $y = 2x + 35$

a. Is this a function? _____

b. Is the equation linear or non-linear? _____

6. {1, 3, 5, 7, . . . }

a. This is the sequence of _____ numbers.

b. _____, _____, _____

c. $a_n = 2n - 1$
$a_{100} = $ _____

¦ Use work area. ¦

¦ Use work area. ¦

7. Volume

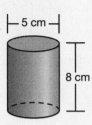

8. 1, 2, 3, 4, 5, 6, 7

no replacement

P(even, even) =

9. ratio of surface areas

30 cm → 60 cm

scale factor = _____

6 ounces cover the small pyramid.

10. a. Complete this drawing of a square pyramid.

b. Which figure is a net of the pyramid?

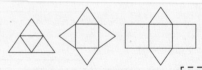

Use work area.

11. *The cone forms similar triangles.*

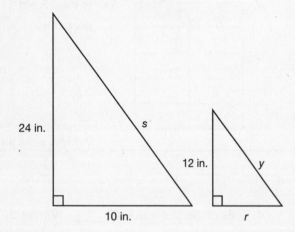

24 in.

12 in. y

10 in. r

s

a. Find s.

b. Find y · $\dfrac{s}{y}$ = —

c. Find r.

This is the radius, so the diameter is what?

a. _____

b. _____

c. _____

12. 1 oz = 30 cm³

total oz = 8 × 8 oz = _____ oz

$\dfrac{oz}{} \cdot \dfrac{cm^3}{oz}$ =

Round to the nearest cup.

$\dfrac{}{150}$ = —

13. *Composite numbers are 4 and 6.*

P(heads, composite) =

14. Put the data in order:

___0.5___, _____, _____, _____, ___7___

mean: _____   median: _____

mode: _____

Use work area.

15. $\dfrac{3.6}{2.6} = \dfrac{9}{x}$

$x =$ _____

16. $0.04x - 0.44 = 0.02x$

$x =$ _____

17. $-\dfrac{1}{3}x - \dfrac{3}{5} = \dfrac{1}{3}$

$x =$ _____

18. $x^2 - 16 = 9$

$x =$ _____ , _____

19. $(3x + 1)(x + 5) =$

_____

20. $(2x - 2)^2 =$

_____

21. $(6.0 \times 10^8)(5.0 \times 10^{-3}) =$

_____ $\times$ _____

22. $\dfrac{3x^{-2}\,y^5}{9x^3\,y^5} =$

_____

23. 75% of $\frac{5}{6}$ of 4.8

24. area and perimeter of rectangle

$l = 2x + 3$

$w = 2x - 3$

$A = $ _____

$P = $ _____

25.

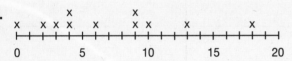

```
            x         x
  x   x x x     x     x x        x              x
  ├─┼─┼─┼─┼─┼─┼─┼─┼─┼─┼─┼─┼─┼─┼─┼─┼─┼─┼─┤
  0       5        10       15       20
```

Read the data from the line plot in order:

__0.5__, _____, _____, _____, _____, _____, _____, _____, _____, _____, __0.5__

median: _____   lower quartile: _____   upper quartile: _____

lower extreme: _____   upper extreme: _____

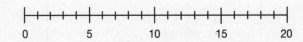

```
  ├─┼─┼─┼─┼─┼─┼─┼─┼─┼─┼─┼─┼─┼─┼─┼─┼─┼─┼─┤
  0       5        10       15       20
```

Use work area.

• Volume, Capacity, and Mass in the Metric System (page 691)

Name _____

Teacher Notes:

• Introduce Hint #56, "Gram/Kilogram Manipulatives."

• Review "Equivalence Table for Units" on page 1 in the *Student Reference Guide*.

The metric system has special qualities that relate water's volume, capacity, and mass under standard conditions.

• Measures are related by powers of 10.

   1 cm = 10 mm   1 kg = 1000 g

• Measures of volume (amount of space), capacity (amount of water), and mass (similar to weight) are all related.

Volume		Capacity		Mass of water
1 cm³	=	1 mL	=	1 g

   One cubic centimeter is one milliliter is one gram of water.

   This 1-cm cube takes up 1 cm³ and can hold 1 mL of water, which has a mass of 1 gram.

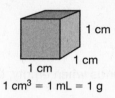

   1 cm
   1 cm
   1 cm
   1 cm³ = 1 mL = 1 g

• Because metric measures are related by powers of 10, we can make other equivalences by multiplying every measure by the same number.

• Multiply by 1000:

Volume		Capacity		Mass of water
1000 cm³	=	1 L	=	1 kg

   One thousand cubic centimeters is one liter is one kilogram of water.

Example: Malia wants to find the volume of a vase. She fills a 1-liter beaker with water and then uses all but 280 milliliters filling the vase. What is the volume of the vase? If the mass of the vase is 640 grams, what is the mass of the vase filled with water?

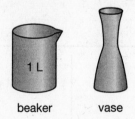

beaker   vase

1 liter is 1000 mL. Malia used all but 280 mL filling the vase.

1000 mL − 280 mL = 720 mL

She used 720 mL of water to fill the vase.

1 mL = 1 cm³, so the volume of the vase is 720 cm³.

Because 1 mL of water = 1 g, the water in the vase has a mass of 720 g.

The mass of the vase without water is 640 g, so the total mass is

640 g + 720 g = 1360 g.

Practice Set (page 694)

a. What is the **mass** of 3 liters of water? _____

      1 L = 1 kg

b. What is the **volume** of 2 liters of water? _____

      1 L = 1000 cm³

c. When the bottle was filled with water, the mass increased by 1 kilogram. How many **milliliters** of

water were added? _____

      1 kg = 1 L

d. An aquarium that is 25 cm long, 10 cm wide, and 12 cm deep can hold how many **liters**

of water? _____

      Find the volume in cm³.

      1000 cm³ = 1 L

e. If the aquarium in **d** weighs about 6 pounds when empty, then about how much would it weigh when

it is $\frac{3}{4}$ full of water? (Use 1 kg ≈ 2.2 lb.) _____

      Use your answer to **d**. Convert to kg and multiply by $\frac{3}{4}$, then add the weight of the aquarium.

      _____ kg . $\dfrac{\text{lb}}{\text{kg}}$ =

Written Practice (page 694)

1. Solve for *d*.

    c = π d

    Find *d* when c = 77 cm.

    Use $\frac{22}{7}$ for π.

    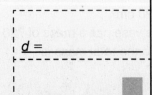
    d =

2. What percent is **not** shaded?

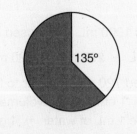

135°

3.

	Percent	Actual Count
Original	100	
Change		
New		n

4. Volume

Leave π as π.

2 in.

3 in.

5. Graph $y = 2x + 1$.

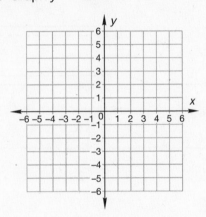

$(5, \underline{\hspace{1cm}})$

6. $a_n = 50 - 2n$

$a_{10} =$

$a_{20} =$

$a_{10} = \underline{\hspace{2cm}}$

$a_{20} = \underline{\hspace{2cm}}$

7. ratio of surface areas

scale factor $= \dfrac{1}{100}$

8. 4 green, 3 red, 5 white

no replacement

a. $P(\text{red, green}) =$

b. $P(\text{green, red}) =$

c. $P(\text{red, green}) + P(\text{green, red}) =$

d. $P(\text{not red and green}) = 1 - c =$

a. _____

b. _____

c. _____

d. _____

9. Draw a square with vertices at (2, 1), (–1, 2), (–2, –1), and (1, –2). Shade the four triangles.

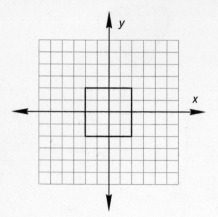

Use work area.

10. **a.** A_{large}

b. A_{small}

c. $P = \dfrac{A_{small}}{A_{large}}$

d. percent shaded

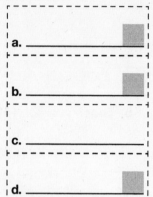

a. _____

b. _____

c. _____

d. _____

11. $\begin{cases} a_1 = 1000 \\ a_n = 1.05a_{n-1} \end{cases}$

$a_2 =$

$a_3 =$

$a_2 =$ _____

$a_3 =$ _____

12. scale factor = 4

_____

13. $\dfrac{4.2}{3.5} = \dfrac{x}{10}$

$x =$ _____

14. $0.03x - 0.5 = 0.01$

$x =$ _____

15. $\dfrac{2}{5}x + \dfrac{1}{2} = \dfrac{7}{10}$

$x =$ _____

16. $\dfrac{1}{2}x^2 = 50$

$x =$ _____

17. $(2x + 1)(x + 2) =$

18. $(x - 10)^2 =$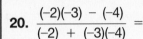

19. $\dfrac{2x^3m^{-1}}{6m^4x^2} =$

20. $\dfrac{(-2)(-3) - (-4)}{(-2) + (-3)(-4)} =$

21. 150% of $\dfrac{3}{4}$ of 2.4

22. $2\sqrt{6} \ \sqrt{12}$

23. area and perimeter of rectangle

$l = 2x - 1 \qquad w = x + 5$

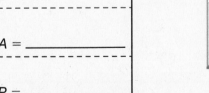

$A =$ _____

$P =$ _____

24. volume, capacity, and mass

$1000 \ cm^3 = 1 \ L = 1kg$

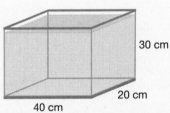

30 cm

20 cm

40 cm

25. 📖 *See the bottom of page 696.*

a. _____

b. _____

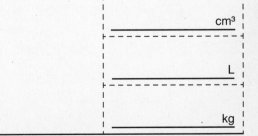

_____ cm³

_____ L

_____ kg

• Compound Average and Rate Problems (page 697)

Name _____

The average (mean) of a set of items is the quotient of the sum of the items divided by the number of items.

$$average = \frac{sum}{number} \qquad number \overline{)sum}^{\,average}$$

Teacher Notes:
• Introduce Hint #57, "Complex Average."
• Refer students to "Complex Average" on page 25 in the *Student Reference Guide*.

• To find the sum given the average and the number of items, multiply.

  Average × number = sum

• Keep these formulas in mind to find the average in multi-step average problems.

• In some problems, two sets of items with different average values have to make one final average.

• To find the average for all the items,

  1. Multiply to find the sum for each set.

  2. Add the sums.

  3. Divide by the number of items in both sets.

     Set *A*: average × number = sum *A*
     Set *B*: average × number = sum *B*
     total sum = sum *A* + sum *B*
     $$total\ average = \frac{total\ sum}{total\ number}$$

Example: Blanca bought 200 shares of XYZ stock at an average price of $54 per share. Later she bought 100 more shares at $60 per share. What was the average price per share Blanca paid for all 300 shares of XYZ?

There are two different sets of items. We find the sum of each set.

1st set	2nd set
200 shares at $54	100 shares at $60
200 × $54 = $10,800	100 × $60 = $6000

Add the sums and divide by all the items to find the average for all the shares.

$10,800 + $6000 = $16,800
200 + 100 = 300 shares
$16,800 ÷ 300 = $56

Each of the 300 shares cost an average of $56.

- In some problems, we have to find missing numbers that will make a target average.

   1. Multiply to find the sum of the target average.

   2. Multiply to find the sum of the numbers so far.

   3. Find the difference between **1** and **2**. This is the sum of the missing numbers.

   4. Find the average of the missing numbers, if necessary. (Read the problem carefully to know what to do.)

$$\text{target sum} = \text{target average} \times \text{numbers}$$
$$\text{so far sum} = \text{average so far} \times \text{numbers}$$
$$\text{missing sum} = \text{target sum} - \text{so far sum}$$
$$\text{missing average} = \frac{\text{missing sum}}{\text{missing numbers}}$$

Example: After three games of bowling, Gabe's average score was 88. What score does Gabe need to average in his next two games to raise his average to 90?

Gabe's target average is 90 over 5 games. Multiply to find the target sum:

$$90 \times 5 = 450$$

Gabe's average so far is 88 over 3 games. Multiply to find the sum so far:

$$88 \times 3 = 264$$

Find the difference:

$$450 - 264 = 186$$

The problem asks for the average over two games. Divide the difference by 2:

$$186 \div 2 = 93$$

Gabe must score an average of 93 in the next two games to get his target average of 90 over 5 games.

Practice Set (page 699)

a. Jarrod earns $12 per hour helping a painter and $15 per hour helping a carpenter. What is Jarrod's average hourly rate for the week if he helps the painter for 10 hours and the carpenter for 20 hours?

▨_____per hour

There are two sets: 10 hours at $12 and 20 hours at $15. Multiply to find the sum of each set. Then add the sums and find the average for all 30 hours.

$10 \times \$12 =$ ▨_____ $20 \times \$15 =$ ▨_____

b. Kaitlyn has a four-game average of 87. What does she need to average in her next two games to have

a six-game average of 90? _____

The target average is 90 for 6 games. The average so far is 87 for 4 games.
Multiply to find each sum. Then subtract the sums and find the average of 2 games.

$90 \times 6 =$ _____ $87 \times 4 =$ _____

c. Sonia covered 30 km for the fund raiser. She jogged the first 15 km in 2 hours and walked the rest of the distance in three hours. Find her average jogging speed, average walking speed, and average speed for the full 30 km.

jogging speed (km/hr): 15 km in 2 hr = _____

walking distance = 30 km − 15 km = _____

walking speed (km/hr): _____ km in 3 hr = _____

average speed = 30 km in 5 hr = _____

Written Practice   (page 699)

1. 4 blocks · $\dfrac{\text{sec}}{\text{block}}$ =

3 min = _____ sec

2.

	Ratio	Actual Count
Walked	1	w
Drove	44	
Total		

3.

	Ratio	Actual Count
Original	100	
Change		
New		

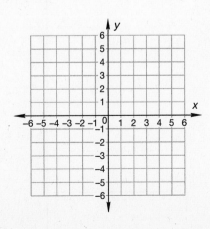

4. Solve by graphing.

$x + y = 4$ $2x - 4 = 2$

x	y
0	
	0

x	y
0	
	0

$x =$ _____

$y =$ _____

5. volume

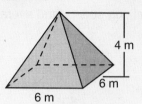

4 m

6 m

6 m

6. ratio of surface areas

scale factor = _____

7. $y = 1x + 10$

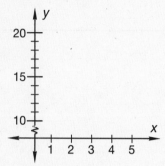

What point shows a four-topping pizza?

(4,   )

8. Put the data in order:

_____, _____, _____, _____, _____, _____

a. mean: _____   median: _____

mode: _____   range: _____

b. _____

Use work area.

9. 1, 2, 3, 4, 5, 6, 7, 8

a. $P(<3, <3) =$
without replacement

b. $P(<3, <3) =$
with replacement

c. $P(<3, <3 \text{ without}) \bigcirc P(<3, <3 \text{ with})$

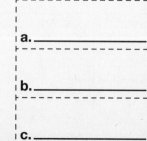

a. _____

b. _____

c. _____

10. circle divided into fifths

a. $m\widehat{AB} = \frac{1}{5}$ (   )

b. $AB = \frac{1}{5}$ (circumference)

$d = 10$ in.
Use 3 for π.

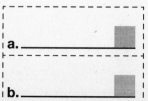

a. _____

b. _____

11.

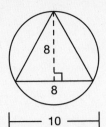

Use 3.14 for π.

$P(inside) \dfrac{A_{triangle}}{A_{circle}}$

$P(outside) = 1 - P(inside)$

I would select _____ because its

probability is g _____ .

Use work area.

12. *Complex average*

to lake: $24 \text{ mi} \cdot \dfrac{1 \text{ hr}}{8 \text{ mi}} = $ _____

from lake: $24 \text{ mi} \cdot \dfrac{\text{hr}}{\text{mi}} = $ _____

average $= \dfrac{\text{total distance}}{\text{total hours}}$

13. $\dfrac{5.1}{1.7} = \dfrac{3}{x}$

$x = $ _____

14. $0.02x + 0.1 = 1$

$x = $ _____

15. $5x^2 - 2 = 3$

$x = $ _____

16. $\dfrac{3}{7} + \dfrac{1}{3}x = \dfrac{10}{21}$

$x = $ _____

17. 10% of $\dfrac{1}{8}$ of 4.24

18. $\dfrac{16z^4 m^3}{56 m^{10} z^{-1}} = $

19. $\sqrt{1,000,000} =$

$\sqrt{1,000,000} = \sqrt{10^6}$

_____

20. $\sqrt{8} + \sqrt{8} =$

_____

21. *Complex average*

target average: 99 over 7 games

sum $= 99 \times 7 =$ _____
average so far: 103 over 3 games

sum $= 103 \times 3 =$ _____

missing sum $=$ _____ $-$ _____ $=$ _____

missing average $= \dfrac{\text{missing sum}}{4 \text{ games}} =$

⌐ Use work area. ⌐

22. *Find the pattern.*

5, 12, 19, 26, . . .

a. Start with _____ and add _____ to each term.

b. _____ , _____ , _____

c. Circle the equation that fits the sequence.

A $a_n = n + 7$ **B** $a_n = 7n + 2$

C $a_n = 7n - 2$ **D** $a_n = 5 + 7n$

⌐ Use work area. ⌐

23. $(3x + 1)^2 =$

_____

25.

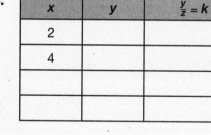

x	y	$\frac{y}{z} = k$
2		
4		

24. area and perimeter of rectangle

$l = 2x + 3$ $w = 2x - 3$

$A =$ _____

$P =$ _____

$k =$ _____

• Reviewing the Effects of Scaling on Volume (page 702)

Name _____

Teacher Notes:
- Review Hint #47, "Scale Factor."
- Review "Scale Factor" on page 31 in the *Student Reference Guide*.

The ratios between perimeters, areas, and volumes of similar figures can be determined by using scale factor.

- The ratio of the sides or edge lengths of similar figures or solids is the **scale factor.**

  The scale factor is almost always a number greater than 1 (going **from** a *smaller* figure **to** a *larger* figure).

  If the problem asks for the scale factor **from** a *larger* figure **to** a *smaller* figure, the scale factor will be less than 1.

- The scale factor relates perimeters, areas, and volumes of the similar figures.

  Perimeter is related by the scale factor.
  Area is related by the (scale factor)².
  Volume is related by the (scale factor)³.

- The amount of paint or tile needed to **cover** an object is an area problem: use (scale factor)².

- Weight, mass, and capacity depend on volume: use (scale factor)³.

Practice Set (page 703)

a. This 3-by-3 cube is constructed of 27 blocks. How many blocks are needed to construct a cube with

twice the dimensions of the original cube? _____

scale factor = _____
volume

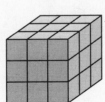

b. An architect builds a $\frac{1}{50}$ scale model of a proposed building for a client. The **volume** of the model is

what fraction of the volume of the proposed building? _____

c. The larger cylindrical container has dimensions 25% greater than the smaller container. The larger container will hold about **what percent more** flour than the smaller container? (Circle one.)

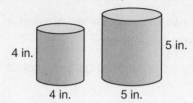

25% greater is 100% + 25% = 125%

scale factor = _____

volume

percent more = _____% − 100% = _____

A 25%   **B** 50%   **C** 100%   **D** 200%

d. A crate with the given dimensions will hold 24 cubes with 12-inch sides. How many 6-inch cubes will the crate hold? _____

scale factor (from 6-in. to 12-in.) = _____

volume

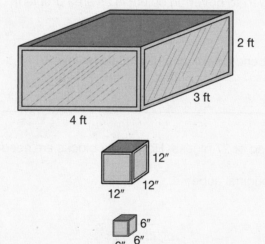

Written Practice   (page 704)

1. width of label = height of can
   length of label = circumference of
      can + 0.38 cm

   Use 3.14 for π.

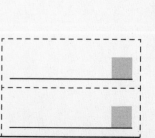

2. Solve by graphing.

$2c + 3r = 18$

c	r
0	
	0

$c + r = 18$

c	r
0	
	0

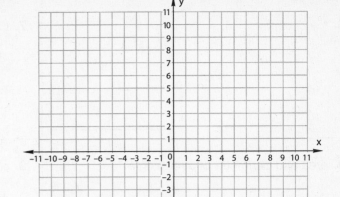

c = _____   r = _____

3.

	Percent	Actual Count
Forgot		
Did not forget		
Total	100	t

_____

4.

	Percent	Actual Count
Last Year	100	l
Change		
This Year		

_____

5. Solve by graphing.

$x + y = 3$

x	y
0	
	0

$2x + y = 8$

x	y
0	
	0

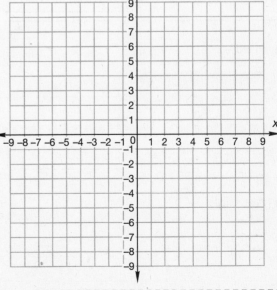

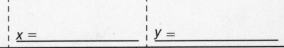

x = _____   y = _____

6. $(5y - 4)(5y + 4) =$

_____

7. $(5y + 4)^2 =$

_____

8. area and perimeter of a rectangle

$l = 5x$ $\qquad$ $w = 2x + 7$

$A =$ _____

$P =$ _____

9. *complex average*

$40 \times \$1.20 = \$$ _____

$60 \times \$1.10 = \$$ _____

total sum $= \$$ _____

$\text{average} = \dfrac{\text{total sum}}{\text{total plants}}$

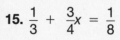

10. 1 kidney, 2 green, 2 pinto, 3 lima
no replacement
$P(\text{lima, pinto}) =$

A $\dfrac{3}{28}$ $\quad$ **B** $\dfrac{5}{8}$ $\quad$ **C** $\dfrac{3}{32}$ $\quad$ **D** $\dfrac{5}{32}$

_____

11. slant height

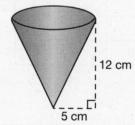

12 cm

5 cm

_____

12. $A_s = \pi r s$

_____

13. $3x^2 + 7 = 34$

$x =$ _____

14. $0.05x + 0.2 = 2$

$x =$ _____

15. $\dfrac{1}{3} + \dfrac{3}{4}x = \dfrac{1}{8}$

$x =$ _____

16. $\dfrac{3.2}{2.4} = \dfrac{6}{x}$

$x =$ _____

17. $\sqrt{50} + \sqrt{50}$

_____

18. $33\dfrac{1}{3}\%$ of $\dfrac{5}{8}$ of 2.4

_____

19. $1\dfrac{2}{3} \cdot \dfrac{3}{8} + 2\dfrac{1}{2} =$

_____

20. $\dfrac{42a^2bc}{49a^{-2}b^{20}} =$

_____

21. two number cubes
$P(\text{odd} > 4,\ \text{odd} > 4) =$

_____

22. scale factor = _____

Volume is related by (scale factor)³.

_____

23. a. scale factor

b. Area is related by (scale factor)².

c. Volume is related by (scale factor)³.

a. _____ b. _____ c. _____

24. Leave π as π.

   a. volume of larger cone

   b. volume of smaller cone

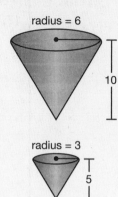

radius = 6

10

radius = 3

5

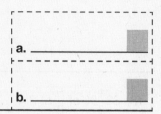

a. _____

b. _____

---

25. This shape is the larger cone minus the smaller cone.

   a. volume

     Leave π as π.

   b. volume to nearest ten in.³

     Use 3.14 for π.

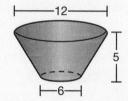

├──12──┤

5

├─6─┤

a. _____

b. _____

• Volume and Surface Area of Compound Solids (page 707)

Name _____

To calculate the volume and surface area of a complex shape, break the complex shape into a combination of simpler shapes.

Teacher Notes:
• Review "Geometric Formulas" on page 29 and "Geometric Solids" on page 30 in the *Student Reference Guide.*

• The activity on 📖 page 709 is optional.

• To estimate the volume or surface area of a real-world object, draw the object as several geometric solids, such as cylinders, prisms, pyramids, and cones.

• Then total the volume or surface area of the solids.

• Use the formulas from the *Student Reference Guide, p. 30.*

Practice Set (page 709)

a. This figure is composed of 1-inch cubes.

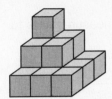

Find the volume. _____

Each 1-in. cube has a volume of 1 in.³.

Count the cubes (including the cubes you cannot see).

Build the figure out of blocks if you need help.

Find the surface area (but not the bottom). _____

Each face of a 1 in. cube is 1 in.².

Count the faces (including the faces you cannot see.)

b. This building can be drawn as several geometric solids.

Top view

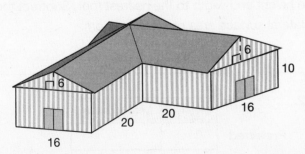 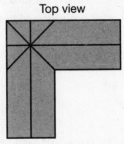

Think of the building as two rectangular prisms and two triangular prisms. The dashed lines show where a side of the prism is "inside" the building.

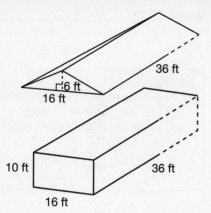 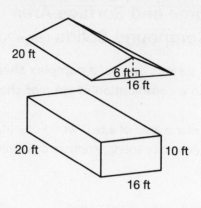

Find the volume of the rectangular part of the building: _____

Find the volume of each rectangular prism and add.

Find the surface area of the rectangular walls. _____

Find the surface area of the sides of each rectangular prism and add.

Do not use the part of the drawing that is "inside" the building.

c. Measure the length, width, and height of your classroom with a yard stick. Round measurements to the nearest foot.

length: _____   width: _____   height: _____

Find the volume of your classroom in ft³. _____

Find the total area of the walls in your classroom. _____

Measure the height and width of the doorway in your classroom. Round to the nearest foot.

height: _____   width: _____

Subtract the area of the doorway from the area of the walls to find an estimate of the lateral surface

area of the classroom: _____

If there are windows in your classroom, measure the height and width to the nearest foot. Subtract the area of the windows to get a better estimate of the lateral surface area of the classroom.

Written Practice (page 709)

1. $\dfrac{30 \text{ cups}}{45 \text{ min}} = \dfrac{\text{cups}}{15 \text{ min}} = \dfrac{\text{cups}}{1 \text{ hr}}$

A 15 cups in $\frac{1}{2}$ hr   **B** 35 cups in 1 hr

C 60 cups in $1\frac{1}{2}$ hr   **D** 50 cups in 1 hr

2.

	Ratio	Actual Count
Preferred		
Did not		n
Total	11	

_____   _____

3.

	Percent	Actual Count
Trade-in	100	t
Change		
Price		

4. $6x - 5y = 30$

x	y
0	
	0

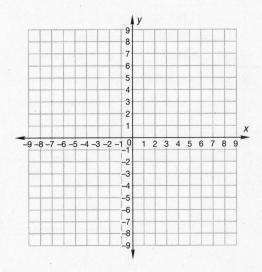

Use work area.

5. Solve by graphing.

$$\begin{cases} x + y = 4 \\ x - y = 6 \end{cases}$$

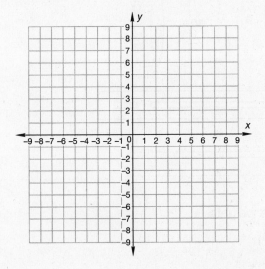

$x = $ _____

$y = $ _____

6. *inverse variation*

$xy = k$

$x = $ min $y = \dfrac{mi}{hr}$

First, find k.

7. Solve for x. Then graph.

$2(x + 3) < x + 7$

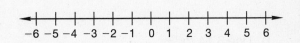

$x < $ _____

8. Solve by graphing.

$$\begin{cases} 2x + 7y = 6 \\ -x + y = -3 \end{cases}$$

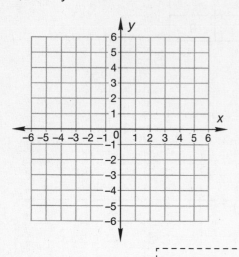

_x_ = _____

_y_ = _____

9. volume

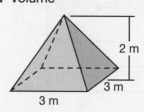

2 m

3 m

3 m

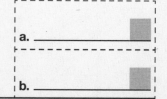

10. a. total volume of three cylinders

Leave π as π.

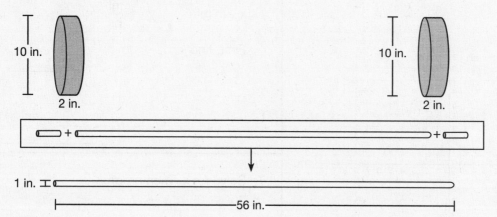

10 in.

2 in.

10 in.

2 in.

+   +

1 in.

|← 56 in. →|

The bar is only 56 in. long because 4 in. is "inside" the weights.

b. Use 3.14 for π.

$$\underline{\quad\quad} \text{ in}^3 \cdot \frac{0.3 \text{ lb.}}{1 \text{ in}^3} =$$

a. _____

b. _____

11. slant height

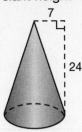

12. $A_s = \pi rs$

Use $\frac{22}{7}$ for π.

13. a. volume

Use $\frac{22}{7}$ for π.

b. volume of smaller similar cone

scale factor $= \frac{1}{2}$

a. _____

b. _____

14. a. Label the dimensions.

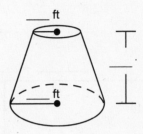

b. Use your answers to problem **13** to find the volume.

b. _____

15. $5m^2 + 3 = 83$

$m = $ _____

16. $0.1r + 2.5 = 3.1$

$r = $ _____

17. $\frac{1}{3} + \frac{1}{4}x = \frac{5}{6}$

$x = $ _____

18. $\frac{2.4}{1.8} = \frac{6}{x}$

$x = $ _____

19. $\dfrac{35w^5m^{-4}}{14wm^{-4}} =$

20. $66\dfrac{2}{3}\%$ of $\dfrac{3}{4}$ of \$0.72 =

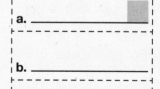

21. $(x + 3)(x - 3) =$

_____ − _____

22. $(x - 3)^2 = (x - 3)(x - 3) =$

_____ − _____ + _____

23. area and perimeter

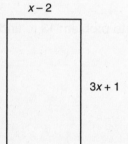

$x - 2$

$3x + 1$

$A =$ _____

$P =$ _____

24.

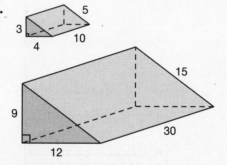

5
3
4   10

15
9
30
12

a. lateral surface area
   of smaller prism

b. scale factor

c. ratio of surface
   areas

a. _____

b. _____

c. _____

25. a. volume of larger prism

b. volume of smaller prism
   Use the scale factor.

c. ratio of volumes

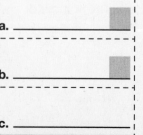

a. _____

b. _____

c. _____

Similar figures have corresponding dimensions that are proportional and are related by a scale factor.

Teacher Notes:
- Review Hint #47, "Scale Factor."
- Review "Scale Factor" on page 31 in the *Student Reference Guide*.

- The scale factor relates perimeters, areas, and volumes of similar solids.

  > *Perimeter is related by the scale factor.*
  > *Area is related by the (scale factor)^2.*
  > *Volume is related by the (scale factor)^3.*

- To calculate scale factor, the **dimensions must be written in the same units.**

- If the units are different, convert them with a unit multiplier.

  Example: An architect builds a scale model of a building she is designing. The scale of the model is 1 inch = 5 feet. What is the scale factor from the model to the building? The surface area of the building is how many times the surface area of the model? The volume of the building is how many times the volume of the model?

  > The scale 1 inch = 5 feet is given in different units: inches and feet.
  > Convert 5 feet to inches before finding the scale factor.
  >
  > 5 feet = 60 inches
  >
  > $$\text{scale factor} = \frac{60 \text{ in.}}{1 \text{ in.}} = 60$$
  >
  > *Area is related by the (scale factor)^2.*
  > The surface area of the building is 60^2 = 3600 times the surface area of the model.
  >
  > *Volume is related by (scale factor)^3.*
  > The volume of the building is 60^3 = 216,000 times the volume of the model.

Practice Set (page 714)

For problems **a–c,** use the scale factor to help you answer the question.

a. The two cylinders are similar. If the lateral surface area of the smaller cylinder is 20π in.^{2}, then what is the lateral surface area of the larger cylinder? _____ scale factor = _____

area

2   3

b. The volume of a model car built to a 1:20 scale is **what fraction** of the volume of the car? _____
The volume of the model is smaller than the volume of the car.

c. A toy doll modeled after an infant is a 1:3 scale model. The amount of material required to clothe the doll is about **what fraction** of the amount of material needed to cloth an infant? _____
Is clothing area or volume?

1.

	Percent	Actual Count
Blustery		
Not blustery		n
Total	100	

2. sales tax

$7\frac{1}{2}$% of $400

3. reflection across $y = 1$

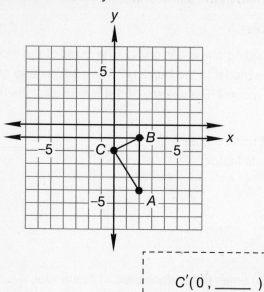

$C'(0, \underline{\hspace{1cm}})$

4. $3x + 5y = 15$

x	y
0	
	0

y-intercept: $(0, \quad)$

x-intercept: $(\quad, 0)$

5. $2x + 4y = -12$

	x	y
y-intercept	0	
x-intercept		0

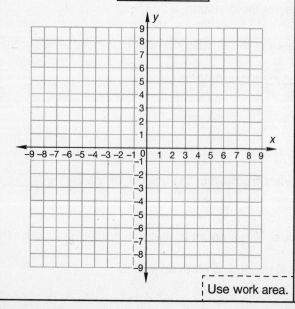

Use work area.

6.

```
  21 red
   5 blue
 +10 green
  36 total
```

a. $P(\text{red, blue}) = \dfrac{\quad}{36} \cdot \dfrac{\quad}{35}$

no replacement

b. $P(\text{blue, red}) =$
no replacement

c. $P(\text{red, blue}) +$
$P(\text{blue, red}) =$

d. $P(\text{not red and blue}) =$
$1 - c =$

a. _____

b. _____

c. _____

d. _____

7. Solve by graphing.

$$\begin{cases} x + y = 12 \\ y - x = 4 \end{cases}$$

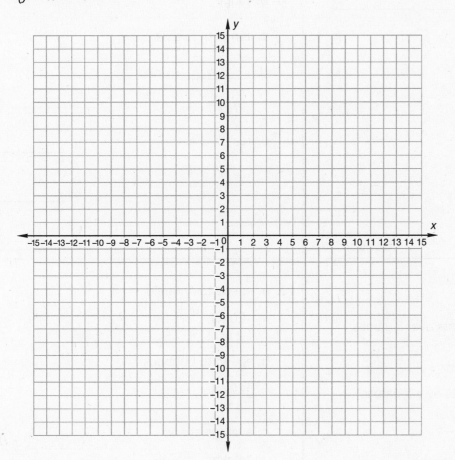

Marla is _____ years old.

$x = $ _____

$y = $ _____

8. a. scale factor from larger to smaller

 b. ratio of areas
 Use reciprocal of a.

 c. ratio of volumes
 Use reciprocal of a.

 a. _____

 b. _____

 c. _____

9. a. Volume of larger cone
 Leave π as π.

 b. Volume of smaller cone
 Use scale factor.

 a. _____

 b. _____

10. $a_n = 12 - 2n$

_____, _____, _____, _____, _____, _____

11. a. median

b. range

c. range of middle

d. _____ and _____

a. _____

b. _____

Use work area.

c. _____

12. *Complex average*

target average: 10 points over 5 games

sum = _____

average so far: 8 points over 3 games

sum = _____

missing sum = _____

missing average $= \dfrac{\text{missing sum}}{2}$

_____

13. a. speed to Amarillo

$\dfrac{120 \text{ mi}}{2 \text{ hr}} =$

b. speed to Lubbock

$\dfrac{120 \text{ mi}}{3 \text{ hr}} =$

c. average speed

$\dfrac{\text{total mi}}{\text{total hr}} =$

a. _____

b. _____

c. _____

14. 📖 *See the top of page 716.*

_____

15. $12x^2 + 2 = 50$

$x = \pm$ _____

16. $0.008m + 0.12 = 1$

$m =$ _____

17. $\frac{1}{8} + \frac{1}{3}x = \frac{11}{12}$

$x =$ _____

18. $\frac{5}{x} = \frac{2.7}{8.1}$

$x =$ _____

19. area and perimeter of rectangle
$l = 5x + 9 \quad w = 2$

$A =$ _____

$P =$ _____

20. $\frac{20x^4 m^{-2}}{4x^3 m^{-2}} =$

_____

21. 250% of $\frac{5}{6}$ of $0.48

_____

22. The carton is broken into a rectangular prism and a pyramid.

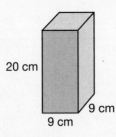

20 cm

9 cm
9 cm

height = 2 cm
slant height = 5 cm

9 cm
9 cm

Volume

_____

23. surface area

Do not count the top of the prism or the bottom of the pyramid.

24. 1000 cm³ = 1 L

L

25.

Day	Number of Visitors
M	
T	
W	
Th	
F	
S	

Use work area.

• Consumer Interest (page 717)

Name _____

Consumer interest is interest charged at a fixed or variable rate to a consumer who borrows money.

- In Investigation 10, we looked at **compound interest,** which is how money can grow at a percentage every year. The percentage is called the **interest**.

- Money that is borrowed is called a **loan.**

- Loans gain interest over time. The higher the interest rate (percentage), the more interest has to be repaid.

- Common reasons to borrow money are for mortgages (to buy a house) and for auto loans (to buy a car).

- Money borrowed on a credit card is another type of loan that gains interest.

- A loan is repaid over a period of time with monthly **payments.**

- A loan is completely repaid only when the payments total the amount borrowed *plus all the interest*

Practice Set (page 719)

a. Two families repaid their 30-year $300,000 mortgages. One family had a 6% loan that was repaid at about $1800 per month. The other family had a 7% loan that was repaid at about $2000 per month.

What was the difference in interest charges over the life of the loans? ⬛_____
Multiply the difference by the number of months.

$2000 − $1800 = ⬛_____

30 yr = _____ mo

b. Monthly mortgage payments vary with the length of the loan. The table below shows the approximate monthly payment on a $300,000 mortgage for 15 years and for 30 years at 7%.

Payback Period	Approximate Payment
15 yr	2700
30 yr	2000

What is the difference in interest charges over the life of the loan? ⬛_____
Multiply each monthly payment by the number of months. Then find the difference.

15 yr = _____ mo   30 yr = _____ mo

15-yr total = ⬛_____   30-yr total = ⬛_____

Practice Set (continued) (page 719)

c. Two friends each had an auto loan of $20,000. One was repaid at 8% in 3 years at about $625 per month, and the other at 8% in 5 years at about $405 per month. The total of the payments for the 5-year loan is how much more than the total for the 3-year loan? ______

3 yr = ______ mo   5 yr = ______ mo

3-yr total = ______   5-yr total = ______

d. The table shows the approximate monthly payments on a 5-year auto loan of $20,000 at two different interest rates.

Rate	Payment
8%	405
9%	415

Over the life of the loan, how much more is paid at 9% than at 8%? ______

5 yr = ______ mo

8% total = ______   9% total = ______

e. Find the monthly interest charge on a $12,000 credit card balance at 2% per month. ______

2% of $12,000

If the $12,000 balance is carried for a year, what is the total of the interest charges? ______

1 yr = 12 mo

Written Practice (page 719)

1. $\frac{220}{400}$ of 20,000

______

2. 2 × 12 min = ______

a. 3 × ______ min = ______

b. 4 × ______ min = ______

c. directly or inversely proportional?

a. ______

b. ______

c. ______

3. *Complex average*

two sets of averages

sum $A = 35 \times 4 =$ _____

sum $B = 42 \times 3 =$ _____

total average $= \dfrac{\text{total sum}}{\text{total days}}$

4. perimeter

$l = 12$ ft 9 in. $w = 11$ ft 4 in.

Simplify the mixed measure after adding.

5. a. Factor: $6x^2 - 9x =$

b. Distribute: $-2x \ (x - 3) =$

a. _____

b. _____

6. *See page 29 in the* Student Reference Guide.

$P = \dfrac{A_{\text{triangle}}}{A_{\text{parallelogram}}}$

7. Solve by graphing.

$\begin{cases} -2x + 3y = 18 \\ x + y = -4 \end{cases}$

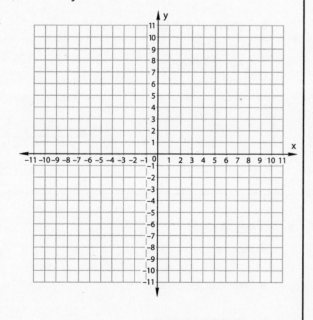

$x =$ _____

$y =$ _____

8. Solve by graphing.

$\begin{cases} x - y = 3 \\ 2x + 2y = 10 \end{cases}$

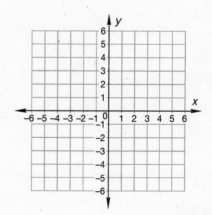

length: _____

width: _____

9. a. volume of larger pyramid

   b. Complete the net of the pyramid.

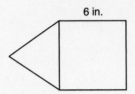
6 in.

a._____

10. a. slant height

4 in.   s

3 in.

b. $A_s = \dfrac{ps}{z}$

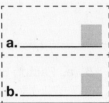
a._____

b._____

11. a. scale factor

   b. ratio of surface areas

   c. ratio of volumes

a._____

b._____

c._____

12. a. *Each hour is* $\dfrac{1}{12}$ *the circle.*

   b. length of arc to nearest inch
   $d = 12$ in
   Use 3.14 for π.

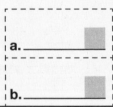
a._____

b._____

13. Interest is paid first.

   Find the interest: 2% of $4500 = $ ____

   $100 payment

   −____ interest

   ____ paid to balance

Use work area.

14. 3 red, 6 blue
   $P(\text{red, red}) =$

   a. with replacement

   b. no replacement

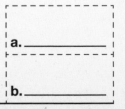
a._____

b._____

15. mean

$$
\begin{array}{r}
2.5 \\
3.6 \\
4.5 \\
+\ 5.5 \\
\hline
\end{array}
$$

_____ . _____

16. $(-1)^2 - (-1)^3 - (-1)^4 =$

_____

17. 20% of 108% of $20.00

 _____

18. $\dfrac{2.4 \times 10^6}{4.0 \times 10^{-2}} =$

_____ × _____

19. $\dfrac{36m^4b^2}{48m^{-1}b^5} =$

_____

20. $(3x + 1)(x - 3) =$

_____

21. $(x - x)^2 =$

_____

22. area and perimeter of rectangle

$l = 5x - 4$ $\qquad$ $w = 4x - 5$

$A =$ _____

$P =$ _____

23. $7x^2 - 50 = 650$

$x =$ _____

24. $0.04r - 0.2 = 1$

$r =$ _____

25. Which solid has these views?

Front

Top

Right Side

A

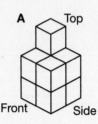

B

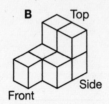

C

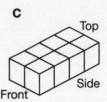

Some fractions convert to a decimal that repeats over and over without end.

• **Repeating decimals** are written with a bar over the **repetend,** the repeating part.

$$\frac{3}{11} \longrightarrow 11\overline{)3.000} \begin{array}{r} 0.2727 \\ \hline \end{array}$$

$$\frac{3}{11} = 0.\overline{27}$$

$$\begin{array}{r} 2.2 \\ \hline 80 \\ 77 \\ \hline 30 \\ 22 \\ \hline 80 \\ 77 \\ \hline 3 \end{array}$$

• To convert a repeating decimal with a bar to a fraction,

1. Write the variable *f* equal to the repeating decimal.

$f = 0.\overline{27}$

2. Count the number of digits under the bar. (In this case, 2 digits)

3. Multiply both sides of the equation by a power of 10 with that number of zeros. (**Shift** the decimal point.)

$100f = 27.\overline{27}$

4. Subtract the original equation from the shifted equation. The repeating part subtracts out.

$$\begin{array}{r} 100f = 27.\overline{27} \\ - \quad f = 0.\overline{27} \\ \hline 99f = 27 \end{array}$$

5. Divide to solve the equation for *f*. Reduce the fraction.

$$f = \frac{27}{99} = \frac{3}{11}$$

Practice Set (page 725)

Convert each repeating decimal to a reduced fraction.

a. $0.\overline{8} =$ _____

$f = 0.\overline{8}$

There is 1 digit under the bar, so multiply both sides by 10.
Subtract the original equation.

$$\begin{array}{r} 10f = 8.\overline{8} \\ - \quad f = 0.\overline{8} \\ \hline 9f = 8.\overline{0} \end{array}$$

$f =$ _____

b. $0.\overline{72}$ = _____

$f = 0.\overline{72}$

There are 2 digits under the bar, so multiply both sides by 100.

Subtract the original equation.

$$100f = 72.\overline{72}$$
$$- \quad f = \quad 0.\overline{72}$$
_____

c. $0.8\overline{3}$ = _____

There is 1 digit under the bar, so multiply both sides by 10.

$$100f = 8.3\overline{3}$$
$$- \quad f = 0.8\overline{3}$$
_____
$$99f = 7.50$$

$$f = \frac{7.5}{99}$$

Multiply by $\frac{10}{10}$ to clear the numerator of the fraction. Then reduce.

$$f = \frac{7.5}{99} \times \frac{10}{10} = \frac{75}{90} =$$

d. Write $33.\overline{3}\%$ as a repeating decimal, then as a reduced fraction.

$33.\overline{3}\% = 0.$_____ = _____

There is 1 digit under the bar, so multiply by 10.

e. Write $12.1\overline{2}\%$ as a repeating decimal, then as a reduced fraction.

$12.1\overline{2}\% = 0.$_____ = _____

f. The probability of rolling 8 with a pair of number cubes is $0.13\overline{8}$. About how many times would you expect to roll 8 in 180 rolls?

There is one digit under the bar, so multiply by 10.

$$10f = 1.3\overline{8}$$
$$- f = 0.13\overline{8}$$
_____
$$9f = 1.25$$

$$f = \frac{1.25}{9}$$

Multiply f by $\frac{100}{100}$ to clear the decimal in the numerator. Then reduce.

$$f = \frac{1.25}{9} \times \frac{100}{100} =$$

Finally, multiply by 180 to find the expected number of times an 8 is rolled.

16. 11 lb 7 oz
   − 7 lb 11 oz
   ⎯⎯⎯⎯⎯⎯⎯⎯

17. *Substitute for x and y.*

18. $(2x + 5)(2x − 5) =$

19. $(2x − 5)^2 =$

20. perimeter and area of rectangle

   $l = 6x + 1$ $w = 2x + 5$

$P =$ ⎯⎯⎯⎯⎯⎯⎯⎯⎯⎯

$A =$ ⎯⎯⎯⎯⎯⎯⎯⎯⎯⎯

21. $3x^2 − 8 = 100$

$x =$ ⎯⎯⎯⎯⎯⎯⎯⎯⎯⎯

22. $0.08 − 0.02x = 1$

$x =$ ⎯⎯⎯⎯⎯⎯⎯⎯⎯⎯

23. $3(x + 6) − 4x = 20$

$x =$ ⎯⎯⎯⎯⎯⎯⎯⎯⎯⎯

24. $\dfrac{1.6}{3.6} = \dfrac{x}{27}$

25. Label the front, top, and right side views.

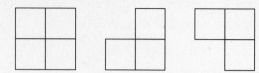

$x = \underline{\hspace{3cm}}$

Use work area.

• Volume and Surface Area of a Sphere (page 731)

Name _____

Teacher Note:
• Review "Geometric Solids" on page 30 in the *Student Reference Guide*.

There is a special relationship between the volumes of a cylinder, a cone, and a sphere.

• The volume of a cone is related to the volume of a cylinder with the same radius and height:

Volume of cone $= \frac{1}{3}$ (volume of cylinder) $= \frac{1}{3}$ (area of base $\times$ height)

$V = \frac{1}{3}\pi r^2 h$

• The volume of a sphere is also related to the volume of a cylinder with the same radius and height.

Volume of sphere $= \frac{2}{3}$ (volume of cylinder) $= \frac{2}{3}$ (area of base $\times$ height)

• The height of the sphere is equal to the diameter of the sphere: $h = 2r$. We substitute $2r$ for h to get the formula for volume of a sphere.

$V = \frac{4}{3}\pi r^3$

• Because the volume of a cone is $\frac{1}{3}$ the volume of a cylinder and the volume of a sphere is $\frac{2}{3}$ the volume of a cylinder, then together the cone and the sphere have the same total volume as a cylinder.

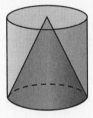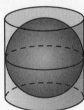

• The formula for the surface area of a sphere is related to the area of a circle.

• The surface area of a sphere is 4 times the area of a circle with the same radius:

Surface area $= 4\pi r^2$

Practice Set (page 734)

The cylinder below has a height equal to its diameter. In the cylinder is the largest sphere it can contain. Packing material is used to fill all the empty spaces in the cylinder. Use this information to answer problems **a** and **b**.

a. What fraction of the volume of the cylinder does the sphere fill up? _____

b. What fraction of the volume of the cylinder does the packing material fill up? _____

Practice Set (continued) (page 734)

Find the volume and surface area of each sphere.

$V = \frac{4}{3}\pi r^3$

$A = 4\pi r^2$

c. $V =$ ______

$A =$ ______

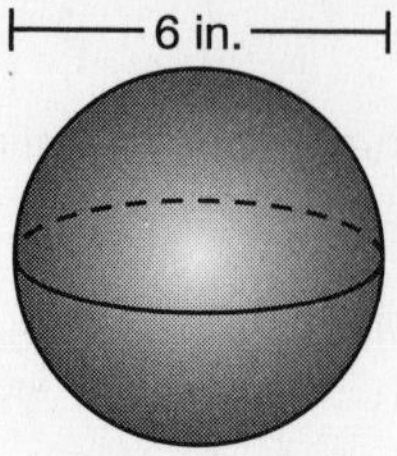

6 in.

Leave π as π.

d. $V =$ ______

$A =$ ______

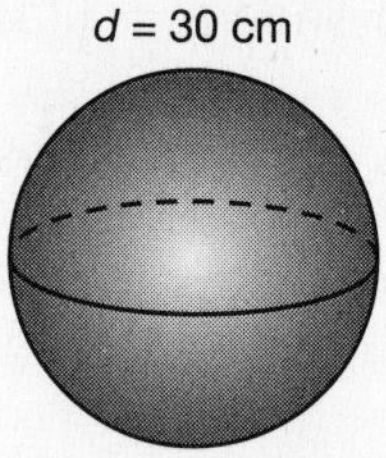

d = 30 cm

Use 3.14 for π.

Written Practice (page 735)

1.

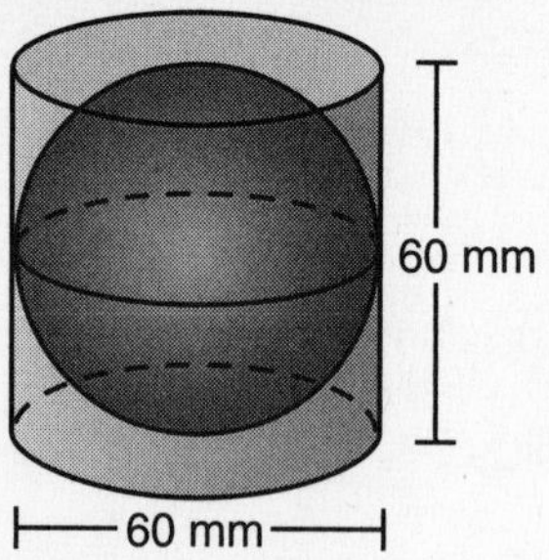

60 mm
60 mm

a. $V =$ (area of base) $\times$ height

b. $V = \frac{4}{3}\pi r^3$

c. What fraction of **a** is **b**?

a. ______

b. ______

c. ______

2. Leave π as π.

a. area of base of cylinder

b. $A = 4\pi r^2$

c. **b** is how many times **a**?

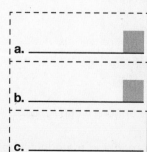

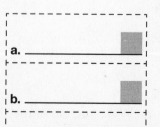

a. ______

b. ______

c. ______

3.

	Percent	Actual Count
Original	100	b
Change		
New		

4. Add down.

$$3a + 2b - 5$$
$$\underline{4a + 5b - 2}$$

5. $0.8\overline{3}$

One digit under the bar.

Multiply by ten.

$$10f = 8.3\overline{3}$$
$$\underline{-\quad f = 0.8\overline{3}}$$

6. Graph: $-4x + 3y = 24$

x	y	
0		y-intercept
	0	x-intercept

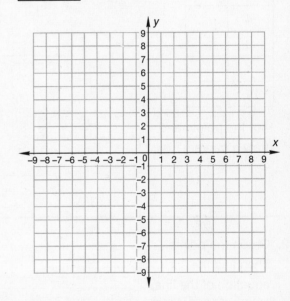

when $x = 12$, $y =$ _____.

Use work area.

7. $(x + 3)(x - 1) =$

8. Factor: $36x^2y - 24xy^2 =$

9. Find the probability of landing in the triangle

Leave π as π.

10. Is this a right triangle?

$$6^2 + 1^2 =$$

$$(2\sqrt{10})^2 =$$

11. Complete the table for the quadratic function.

$$y = -\frac{1}{16}x^2$$

x	y
−8	
−4	
0	
4	
8	

Plot the points and draw a curve.

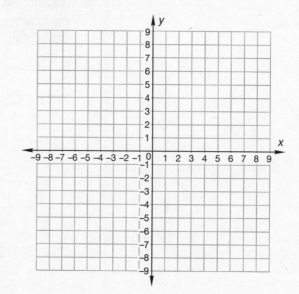

Use work area.

12. Graph the points. Then find the equation of the line. (2, 5) and (−3, −10)

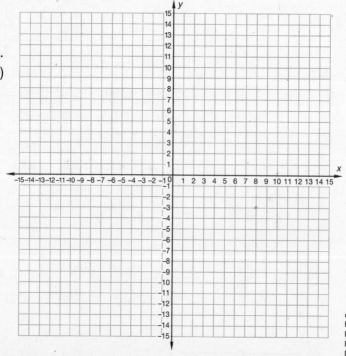

$y =$

© 2007 Harcourt Achieve Inc.

13. $5x^2 - 3 = 42$

$x = $ _____

14. $0.14 - 0.02x = 0.88$

$x = $ _____

15. $\dfrac{3}{4}x + \dfrac{1}{3} = \dfrac{5}{6}$

$x = $ _____

16. $\dfrac{2.42}{0.11} = \dfrac{44}{x}$

$x = $ _____

17. $2x - 5 < 3x - 7$

$x > $ _____

18. $4(2x - 3) = 4x - 4$

_____

19. $\dfrac{45x^5m}{9m^{-1}x} = $

_____

20. $\dfrac{(-2)(-3) - (-2)}{(-2) - (-3)} = $

_____

21. *Put in order.*

$\underline{\ 2.7\ }$, _____, _____, _____, $\underline{\ 4.6\ }$

mean (to one decimal place): _____

median: _____

mode: _____

Use work area.

22. Draw the rectangle:
$A(3, 0)$, $B(1, -2)$, $C(-2, 1)$, $D(0, 3)$

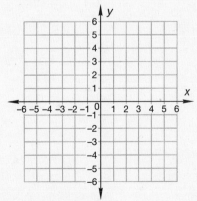

perimeter and area

$P = $ _____

$A = $ _____

23. Move every vertex 2 units right and 3 units up.

A'(,   )   B'(,   )

C'(,   )   D'(,   )

Use work area.

24. area and perimeter of a rectangle

$l = 3x + 1$ $w = 3x - 1$

A = _____

P = _____

25. a. Write an equation from the table.

$B =$ _____ A

b. Complete the table.

A	B	$\frac{B}{A} = k$
1	3	
2	6	
4	12	
5	15	

$k =$ _____

Use work area.

• Ratios of Side Lengths of Right Triangles (page 737)

Name _____

Teacher Notes:
• Review "Pythagorean Theorem" on page 29 in the *Student Reference Guide*.

• Introduce reference chart, "Trigonometric Ratios."

The ratios of the side lengths of right triangles have special propereties.

• A right triangle has one right angle and two acute angles.

• A right triangle has two legs and a hypotenuse.

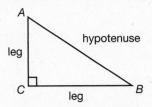

$\angle A$ and $\angle B$ are acute angles.

$\angle C$ is the **right** angle.

$\overline{AC}$ and $\overline{BC}$ are the legs (shorter sides).

$\overline{AC}$ is the hypotenuse (longest side).

• The legs of a right triangle are either **adjacent** to (touching) or **opposite** the acute angles.

$\overline{AC}$ is adjacent to $\angle A$.

$\overline{BC}$ is opposite $\angle A$.

$\overline{BC}$ is adjacent to $\angle B$.

$\overline{AC}$ is opposite $\angle B$.

• The ratios of sides of right triangles are important in **trigonometry,** a branch of mathematics that is used for many real-world situations.

> **Example:** Find the ratio of the length of the side **opposite** $\angle R$ to the length of the **adjacent** side. Then use a calculator to find the ratio to 3 decimal places.

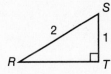

The side opposite to $\angle R$ is $\overline{ST}$. $ST = 1$.

The side adjacent to $\angle R$ is $\overline{RT}$. Use the Pythagorean Theorem to find RT.

$$a^2 + b^2 = c^2$$
$$(1)^2 + b^2 = (2)^2$$
$$1 + b^2 = 4$$
$$b^2 = 3$$
$$b = \sqrt{3}$$

$RT = \sqrt{3}$. The ratio of ST to RT is

$$\frac{\text{opposite}}{\text{adjacent}} = \frac{ST}{RT} = \frac{1}{\sqrt{3}}$$

Rounded to three decimal places, the ratio is 0.577.

Practice Set (page 739)

Find each ratio for the illustrated right triangle. Express each ratio as a fraction and as a decimal rounded to three decimal places.

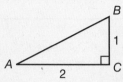

With respect to ∠A, find the ratio of the lengths:

a. Opposite side to adjacent side $\dfrac{BC}{AC}$

   fraction: _____   decimal: _____

b. Opposite side to hypotenuse $\dfrac{BC}{AB}$

   fraction: _____   decimal: _____

c. Adjacent side to hypotenuse $\dfrac{AC}{AB}$

   fraction: _____   decimal: _____

With respect to ∠B, find the ratio of the lengths:

d. Opposite side to adjacent side

   fraction: _____   decimal: _____

e. Opposite side to hypotenuse

   fraction: _____   decimal: _____

f. Adjacent side to hypotenuse

   fraction: _____   decimal: _____

Written Practice   (page 739)

1. $3880 = 20g + 1200$

2.

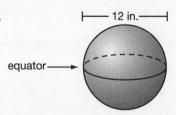

equator →

a. circumference

b. $A = 4\pi r^2$

g = _____

a. _____

b. _____

---

3. $V = \frac{4}{3}\pi r^3$

Use 3 for π.

Which is closest?

A 450 in^2 **B** 900 in^3

C 1200 in^3 **D** 7000 in^3

4. The surface area is the sum of 2 congruent trapezoids and 2 congruent triangles.

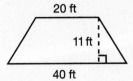

5. $0.\overline{81}$

Two digits under the bar.
Multiply by 100.

$100f = 81.\overline{81}$
$-\quad f = \quad 0.\overline{81}$

6. $3r + 5p - 4$
$\underline{2r - 4p + 4}$

7.

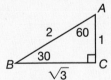

a. $\frac{AC}{AB}$

b. $\frac{BC}{AB}$

c. $\frac{BC}{AC}$

a. _____

b. _____

c. _____

8. a. $V = \frac{1}{3}$ *(area of base × height)*

b. ratio of surface areas

scale factor = _____

c. ratio of volumes

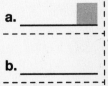

a. _____

b. _____

c. _____

Solve by graphing.

$$\begin{cases} x + y = 1 \\ -5x + 10y = -20 \end{cases}$$

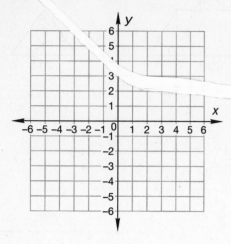

10. $y = 2x + 4$

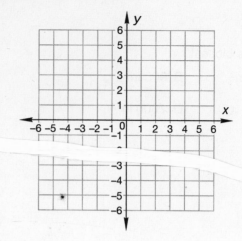

$x =$ _____

$y =$ _____

$(4, \underline{\hspace{1cm}})$

11. probability of landing in circle
Leave π as π.

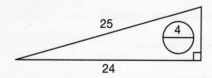

12. $\dfrac{24x^5y^{-9}}{32xy^{10}} =$

_____

_____

13. two number cubes

$P(<5, <5) =$

14. Graph the points. Then find the equation of the line.

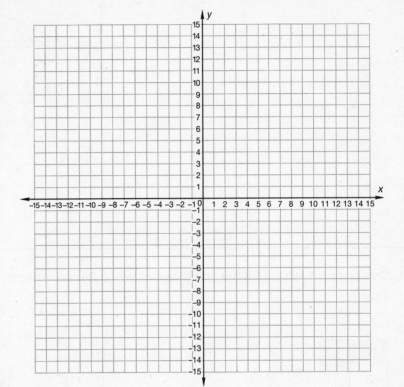

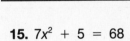

_____

$y =$ _____

15. $7x^2 + 5 = 68$

$x =$ _____

16. $0.4 - 0.03x = 1$

$x =$ _____

17. $\frac{5}{8}x - \frac{1}{3} = \frac{1}{2}$

$x =$ _____

18. $\frac{9.3}{6.3} = \frac{x}{21}$

$x =$ _____

19. Factor: $44x^2 - 22x + 33 =$

_____

20. $3(x - 7) \leq 5x + 1$

$x \geq$ _____

21. $5x - (-2) = 10x - 3(x + 1)$

$x = $ _____

22.

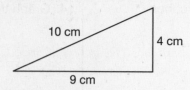

This _____ a right triangle because

$9^2 + 4^2 = $ _____ and $10^2 = $ _____.

Use work area.

23. Complete the table. Plot the points and draw a curve.

$y = -0.8x^2$

x	y
−3	
0	
3	

24. area and perimeter of a rectangle

$l = 5x + 4 \quad w = 4x - 5$

$A = $ _____

$P = $ _____

25. first 2 dog years = 10.5 years each
later dog years = 4 years each

a. 3 dog years

b. 10 dog years

a. _____

b. _____

Use work area.

• Using Scatterplots to Make Predictions (page 742)

Name _____

A scatterplot is a graph of points representing two variables which can be used to make predictions about future data.

Teacher Note:
• An activity takes the place of the Practice Set for this lesson.

• A scatterplot does not make an exact line because the points come from real-world data.

• Even though the scatterplot does not make a perfect line, the plot can still tell if the two variables are **correlated.**

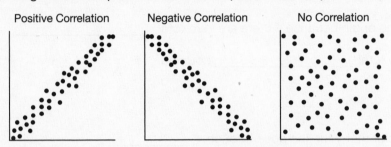

Positive Correlation   Negative Correlation   No Correlation

The scatterplot on the left shows a **positive correlation.** As one variable increases, the other variable also increases. An estimated line through the points has a *positive slope.*

The scatterplot in the middle shows a **negative correlation.** As one variable increases, the other variable decreases. An estimated line through the points has a *negative slope.*

The scatterplot on the right shows **no correlation.** The plot shows no relationship between the two variables.

• To estimate a line on a scatterplot, use a ruler to draw a line that goes through or near as many points as possible.

Activity: *Using a Scatterplot to Make Predictions*

The students in Mrs. Takeyama's class wanted to find a relationship between the number of letters in a random part of a book and the number of vowels in that same part of the book. Each student selected a book and a few sentences from the book at random. Then each student counted the number of total letters in the sentences and the number of vowels in the sentences. Finally, each student plotted a point using his or her data.

The scatterplot below shows the number of letters counted on the *x*-axis and the number of vowels counted on the *y*-axis.

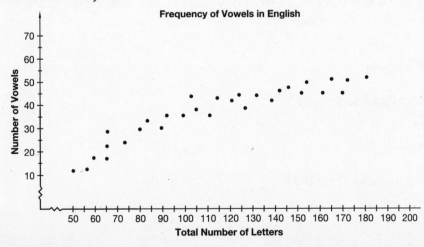

1. Describe the relationship on the scatterplot.

   As the total number of letters increases, the number of vowels _____.

2. Does the scatterplot show positive correlation, negative correlation, or no correlation?

   _____

3. Use a ruler to estimate a best-fit line on the scatterplot. Should the line pass through the origin? Why?

   The line should pass through the origin because if there are zero total _____

   counted, there will also be zero total _____ counted.

4. Find the slope of your best-fit line. slope = _____

   - Pick a point on the scatterplot that your line goes through. (_____, _____)

   - The line also goes through the origin, (0, 0), so the slope will be $\frac{y}{x}$.

   - Convert the slope to a percent.

   - Round to the nearest percent. slope = _____%

   - What does this number mean?

   - This number is the _____ of the total letters that are _____.

5. Open your textbook to any page. Pick two sentences from that page and count the total number of letters in the sentences. Do not count spaces or punctuation. Leave your book open; you will need to find the same sentences again.

   - total number of letters = _____

   - Use your percent from exercise **4** to predict the number of vowels in your sentences. Round to the nearest whole number.

   - predicted number of vowels: _____

   - Count the number of vowels in your sentences.

   - actual number of vowels: _____

   - Was your prediction close to the actual number? _____

Written Practice (page 745)

1.

	Percent	Actual count
Before	100	
Change		
After		*a*

2. *Complex average*

30 min = _____ hr

_____ hr × 8 $\frac{mi}{hr}$ = _____ mi

_____ hr × 6 $\frac{mi}{hr}$ = _____ mi

total mi = _____

average = $\frac{\text{total mi}}{\text{total hr}}$

3. 213 mL − 150 mL   1 mL = 1 cm^3

4. $3x + 4y - 5$
$4x + 3y + 2$

5. $4m - 5y - 6$
$2m - 4y - 6$

6. $\left(-\frac{2}{3}\right)^2 =$

7. $\left(-\frac{2}{5}\right)^0 =$

8. $(x - 1)(x - 10) =$

9. Leave π as π.

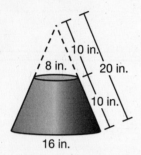

a. lateral surface area of big cone

b. lateral surface area of small cone

c. a − b =

a. _____

b. _____

c. _____

10. a. scale factor

b. ratio of surface areas

a. _____

b. _____

11. area of shaded region
Leave π as π.
Units are cm.

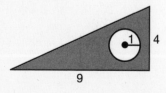

_____

12. a. $\frac{BC}{BA}$

b. $\frac{BC}{AC}$

a. _____

b. _____

13. Complete the table. Plot the points and draw the curve.

$y = -0.5x^2$

x	y
–4	
–2	
0	
2	
4	

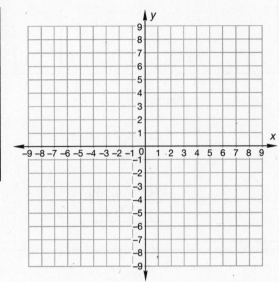

14. y–intercept = _____

slope = $\dfrac{\text{rise}}{\text{run}}$ = _____

Use work area.

y = _____

15. $-2x^2 + 11 = 3$

x = _____

16. $0.3 - 0.02x = 0.4$

x = _____

17. $\dfrac{3}{4}x + \dfrac{1}{3} = \dfrac{7}{12}$

x = _____

18. $\dfrac{2.8}{3.5} = \dfrac{x}{5}$

x = _____

19. Factor: $27x^2 + 18x - 81 =$

_____

20. $7(3 - x) < 3 - x$

$x >$ _____

21. $2x - (-3x) = 7x - 2$

x _____

22. $\dfrac{32m^4b^{-4}}{20b^4m} =$

$x =$ _____

23. $0.41\overline{6}$

One digit under the bar.
Multiply by 10.

$10f = 4.16\overline{6}$
$\underline{f = 0.416}$

_____

24. _Put in order._

$\underline{9.8}$, _____, _____, _____, $\underline{10.8}$

Round to one decimal place.

mean: _____

median: _____

25.

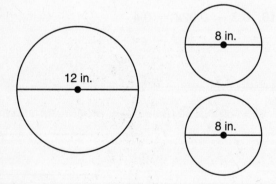

12 in.

8 in.

8 in.

Leave π as π.

12-in. area = _____

8-in. area = _____

Are two 8-in. pizzas more or less pizza than one 12-in. pizza? _____

Use work area.

• **Calculating Area as a Sweep** (page 748)

Name _____

Area can be modeled as the sweep of a broom.

• Imagine pushing a broom across a floor.

• The area swept by the broom is a rectangle with width equal to the width of the broom and length equal to the distance the broom is pushed.

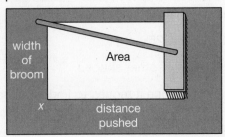

• Now imagine pushing a broom that has one end nailed to the floor. The broom sweeps out part of a circle.

• The area swept by the broom equals the width of the broom times the **average** distance the broom moves.

• One end of the broom does not move at all (zero distance) and the other end moves part of a circumference.

• For problems about "sweeping," a segment is the "broom."

> **Example:** As radius $\overline{CA}$ turns, it sweeps the area of a circle. The radius is a "broom" turning around the center of the circle.

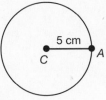

How wide is the broom (radius $\overline{CA}$)?
The radius is 5 cm.

How far does point *A* move in one full turn?
Point *A* is the outside edge of the radius. It moves around the circumference of the circle.

> Circumference $= \pi d = \pi(10 \text{ cm}) = 10\pi$ cm

How far does point C move in one full turn?

Point C is the center of rotation, so it does not move. It moves zero distance.

What is the average distance the points from A to C move during one full turn?
Find the average of the distance for point A and point C.

$$\text{average} = \frac{(10\pi \text{ cm} + 0 \text{ cm})}{2} = 5\pi \text{ cm}$$

The area is the product of the average distance (5π cm) and the radius (5 cm).

$$A = (5\pi \text{ cm})(5 \text{ cm}) = 25\pi \text{ cm}^2$$

This is the same distance the area formula would give us:

$$\text{Area of circle} = \pi r^2 = \pi(5 \text{ cm})^2 = 25\pi \text{ cm}^2$$

- The idea of sweeping can apply to the areas of other shapes.

- Multiply the width of the "broom" by the distance it moves to find the area.

Practice Set (page 751)

a. Imagine a broom steadily narrowing from 12 in. to 0 in. as it sweeps 10 in. to form a triangle. Describe how to find the area of the triangle.

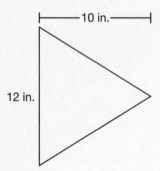

M_____ the length the broom sweeps, _____ in., by the average width of the broom,

6 in. The area is _____ in.^{2}.

b. Segment AB is 5 cm long and the diameter of the cylinder is 10 cm. Describe how to calculate the lateral surface area of the cylinder. Find the lateral surface area expressed in terms of π.

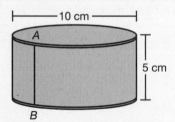

M_____ the width of the broom, _____ cm, by the distance the broom sweeps, which

is the C_____ of the cylinder.

$C = \pi d = \pi(10 \text{ cm}) =$ _____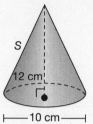

lateral surface area $= (5 \text{ cm})($ ___ $\text{cm}) =$ _____

c. How long is the **slant height** of this cone? _____

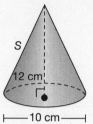

S

12 cm

├── 10 cm ──┤

If the slant height sweeps around the cone, what is the **average distance** it moves?

The top of the slant height would not move.

The bottom of the slant height moves around the circumference of the base.

$C = \pi d = \pi($ ___ $\text{cm}) =$ _____

average distance $= \dfrac{\_\_ + 0}{2} =$ _____

What is the lateral surface area of the cone? (Use 3.14 for π.) _____

Multiply the slant height by the average distance.

d. Write the formula for the lateral surface area of a cone.

$A =$ _____

Use the formula to find how many square inches of paper are used to make a paper party hat

of these dimensions. _____

7 in.

├── 6 in. ──┤

Written Practice   (page 752)

1.

	Percent	Actual Count
Occupied		
Not Occupied	*n*	
Total	100	

2. *complex average*

$14 \times 5 =$ _____

$28 \times 2 =$ _____

Total sum $=$ _____

average $= \dfrac{\text{total sum}}{\text{total days}} =$

3. Solve for c.

$$300 + 4c = 416$$

_____

4. $(3x^3)^4 =$

_____

5. $(2y^4)^5 =$

_____

6. $2m - 3x + y$
   $\underline{2m + 3x - y}$

_____

7. $3w - 4x - y$
   $\underline{3w + 4x - y}$

_____

8. $\left(-\dfrac{1}{3}\right)^3 =$

_____

9. $\left(-\dfrac{3}{2.1}\right)^0 =$

Any number to the zero power equals what?

_____

10. $\dfrac{48wx^2y^{-1}}{32x^2y^2} =$

_____

11. $a_n = 2n + 3$
   $5, 7, 9, \ldots$

  a. $a_{100} =$

  b. _What n gives $a_n = 99$?_

  a. $a_{100} =$ _____

  b. $n =$ _____

12. $4x + 2y = -12$

x	y
0	
	0

y-intercept: (0,   )

x-intercept: (, 0)

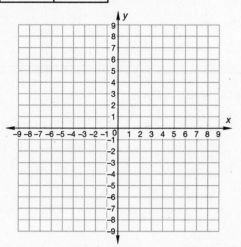

Use work area.

13. scale factor = $3\frac{2}{3}$

ratio of surface areas

_____

14. ratio of volumes

Which is closest?

A $3\frac{2}{3}$ **B** 25   **C** 50   **D** 100

_____

15. Graph the rectangle.

$A(-3,0)$, $B(-5,4)$, $C(-3,5)$, $D(-1,1)$

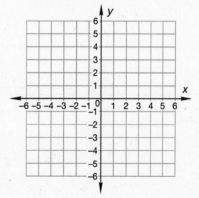

$P = $ _____ $A = $ _____

16. Use the coordinate plane in problem **15.**
Reflect the rectangle across the *y*-axis.

Each vertex will move to the other side of the y-axis.

The y-coordinates will not change.

$A'($, $)$ $B'($, $)$

$C'($, $)$ $D'($, $)$

Use work area.

17. Write an equation for the line.

slope = $-\frac{1}{2}$

y-intercept = 2

$y = $ _____

18. $3x^2 + 7 = 34$

$x =$ _____

19. $\frac{1}{5}x + \frac{1}{3} = \frac{4}{3}$

$x =$ _____

20. $\frac{x}{3} = \frac{12}{x}$

$x =$ _____

21. $1 + 0.05x = 0.2$

$x =$ _____

22. $3m + 5 = -1$

$x =$ _____

23. $-2 < x \le 3$

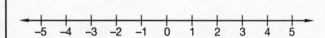

Use work area.

24. area and perimeter of a rectangle
$l = 4x + 2 \quad w = 4x - 2$

$A =$ _____

$P =$ _____

25. Give answers in terms of π and rounded to the nearest in².

width of the "broom" = 2 in.
The "broom" sweeps the circumference.
radius = 6 in.

_____

_____

• **Relative Sizes of Sides and Angles of a Triangle** (page 754)

Name _____

The lengths of the sides of a triangle are related to the measures of the angles in the triangle.

> The **longest side** of a triangle is *opposite* the **largest angle**.

> The **shortest side** of a triangle is the *opposite* the **smallest angle**.

Teacher Note:

• Review "Angles" on page 27 in the *Student Reference Guide.*

• Remember that the sum of the angle measures of a triangle is 360°.

Example: List the sides of this triangle in order from shortest to longest.

$m\angle R = 59°$ and $m\angle Q = 61°$. The sum of all three angle measures is 180°, so

$$m\angle P = 180° - (59° + 61°) = 60°$$

$\angle R$ is the *smallest* angle in the triangle, so the side opposite $\angle R$ is the *shortest* side: $\overline{PQ}$
$\angle Q$ is the *largest* angle in the triangle, so the side opposite $\angle Q$ is the *longest* side: $\overline{PR}$
The size of $\angle P$ is *between* $\angle R$ and $\angle Q$, so the length of $\overline{RQ}$ is *between* $\overline{PQ}$ and $\overline{PR}$.
In order of length, the sides are:

> side $\overline{PQ}$, side $\overline{QR}$, side $\overline{PR}$

• This also works the other way.

• The measures of the angles of a triangle are related to the lengths of the sides in the triangle.

> The **largest angle** of a triangle is *opposite* the **longest side**.

> The **smallest angle** of a triangle is *opposite* the **shortest side**.

Example: The lengths of sides of $\triangle ABC$ are given. List the angles in order of size from smallest to largest.

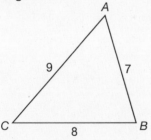

The *shortest* side is $\overline{AB}$, so the *smallest* angle is $\angle C$.
The *longest* side is $\overline{AC}$, so the *largest* angle is $\angle B$.

$\overline{BC}$ is in *between* $\overline{AB}$ and $\overline{AC}$, so $m\angle A$ is in *between* $m\angle C$ and $m\angle B$.
In order of size, the angles are:

> $\angle C, \angle A, \angle B$

Practice Set (page 756)

For **a** and **b** refer to figure *ABCD*.

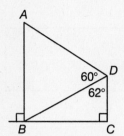

a. Find the measures of ∠*CBD*, ∠*DBA*, and ∠*DAB*.

The sum of the angle measures in a triangle is 180°.

m∠*CBD* = _____ ▨   m∠*DBA* = _____ ▨   m∠*DAB* = _____ ▨

m∠CBD + m∠DBA = 90°

b. Write these segments in order from shortest to longest.
$\overline{AB}, \overline{AD}, \overline{BD}, \overline{BC}, \overline{DC}$

AD does not equal BC, even though m∠BDC = m∠DBA.

_____, _____, _____, _____, _____

c. Which angle in △*WXY* is the smallest angle? ∠ _____

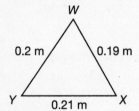

d. Find $\overline{WY}$ if $\overline{AC}$ is 6.4 cm.

$\overline{WY}$ = _____ ▨

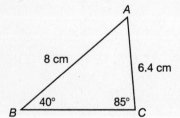

Find the measures of ∠A and ∠X.

The triangles are similar. Write a proportion.

1.

	Percent	Actual Count
Filled		
Not Filled		
Total	100	t

2. $m = 700 + 5a$

3. Guess and check to solve.

$\begin{cases} u + d = 21 \\ 5u + 10d = 160 \end{cases}$

$u =$ _____

$d =$ _____

4.

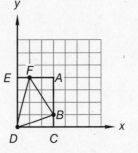

5. Use the Pythagorean Theorem to find the side lengths.

Sides: _____, _____, _____

Angles: _____, _____, _____

The smallest angle is opposite the shortest side.

Use work area.

6. $4m\,(3m^2 - 2) =$

7. $(2x - 4)^2 =$

8. $(4x^2)^3 =$

9. $\left(-\dfrac{2}{5}\right)^3 =$

10. $\left(\dfrac{-2}{1.1}\right)^0 =$

11. $\dfrac{25m^4b^2}{35b^{-1}m} =$

- - - - - - - - - - - - - - -
_____

12. $-2x + 5y = -20$

x	y
0		y-intercept (, 0)
	0	x-intercept (0 ,)

Use work area.

13. perimeter and area of rectangle
$A(0, 0), B(-2, -2), C(-3, -1), D(-1, 1)$

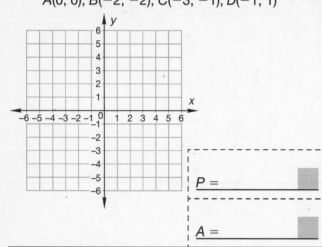

$P =$ _____

$A =$ _____

14. _Turn your page $\frac{1}{4}$ turn clockwise to see what the rotated rectangle should look like._

$A'(\quad , \quad)$ $\qquad B'(\quad , \quad)$

$C'(\quad , \quad)$ $\qquad D'(\quad , \quad)$

Use work area.

15. area and perimeter of rectangle
$l = 5w - 6 \qquad w = w$

$A =$ _____

$P =$ _____

16. $7^2 + 24^2 =$

$25^2 =$

Use work area.

17. slope $= -2$
y-intercept $= 4$

$y =$ _____

18. Complete the table. Plot the points and draw the curve.

$y = -\dfrac{1}{9}x^2$

x	y
-6	
-3	
0	
3	
6	

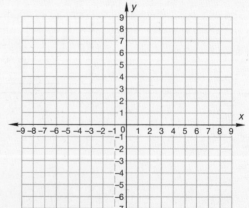

Use work area.

19. $1.1\overline{6}$

One digit under the bar

Multiply by 10.

$10f = 11.6\overline{6}$

$\quad f = 1.1\overline{6}$

_____

20. $-x^2 - 9 = -25$

$x = $ _____

21. $\frac{1}{3}x - \frac{1}{2} = \frac{1}{12}$

$x = $ _____

22. $\frac{1.2}{3.2} = \frac{3}{x}$

$x = $ _____

23. $3x + 5 > 4x$

$x < $ _____

24. 📖 *See the bottom of page 757.*

_____

25. Write as a reduced mixed number.

Cancel matching zeros.

$\dfrac{25,000}{600} =$

The whole number part is the number of hours.

The fraction part is the part of an hour (minutes).

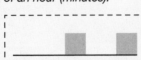

Division by zero is not allowed.

• We say that division by zero is **undefined**, which means it does not make sense.

$$\frac{6}{0} = ? \qquad 0\overline{)12}^{?} \qquad 10 \div 0 = ? \qquad \frac{0}{0} = ?$$

• We must make sure our equations and expressions never allow zero in the denominator.

• To do this, for variable expressions and equations, use a "not equal to" ($\neq$) sign for the value of the variable that would make the denominator equal to zero.

> **Example:** If we were asked to graph the following equation, what number could not be used in place of the variable?
>
> $$y = \frac{12}{x + 2}$$

If $x = -2$, then the denominator would equal zero.

$$y = \frac{12}{x + 2} \qquad \text{Given equation}$$

$$y = \frac{12}{(-2 + 2)} \qquad \text{Substituted } -2 \text{ for } x$$

$$y = \frac{12}{0} \qquad \text{Simplified}$$

x cannot be equal to -2.

$x \neq -2$

> **Example:** Find the numbers that may not be used in place of the variable.
>
> $$\frac{1}{x^2 - 9}$$

When $x = 3$ or -3, the denominator would equal zero.

$$x \neq 3, -3$$

Practice Set (page 761)

a. Use a calculator to divide several different numbers of your choosing by zero. Remember to clear the calculator between calculations. What answer is displayed? _____

b. If we attempt to form two division facts for the multiplication fact $5 \times 0 = 0$, one of the arrangements is not allowed. Circle the division that is not allowed.

A $\frac{0}{5} = 0$ **B** $\frac{5}{0} = 0$

c. Under what circumstances does the following expression not equal 1? Why?

$$\frac{x - 1}{x - 1}$$

If $x =$ _____, then the expression is a division by _____.

For the following expressions, find the number or numbers that may not be used in place of the variable. Use the "not equal to" sign ($\neq$).

d. $\dfrac{5}{x}$

$x \neq$ _____

e. $\dfrac{2}{x - 3}$

$x \neq$ _____

f. $\dfrac{b}{2w}$

$w \neq$ _____

g. $\dfrac{y + 3}{2y - 8}$

$y \neq$ _____

h. $\dfrac{16}{x^2 - 4}$

$x \neq$ _____ , _____

i. $\dfrac{3ab}{c}$

$c \neq$ _____

1.

	Percent	Actual Count
Original	100	
Change		
New		n

2. The figure shows the lateral surface area of an unrolled cone.

12 cm

120°

a. *The figure is part of a circle.* $A = \dfrac{}{360°}(\pi r^2)$

b. The formula for lateral surface area of a cone is: $A = \pi r^s$

Use your answer from **a.** for A and solve for r. Then find the circumference.

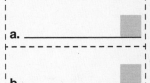

a. _____

b. _____

3. $\begin{cases} n + q = \underline{\hspace{1cm}} \\ 5n + 25q = \underline{\hspace{1cm}} \end{cases}$

Guess and check to solve.

$n = $ _____

$q = $ _____

4. a. $\left(\dfrac{3}{2}\right)^{-2} =$ **b.** $\left(\dfrac{3}{5}\right)^{-1} =$

c. $(5)^{-2} =$ **d.** $\left(\dfrac{1}{2}\right)^{-3} =$

a. _____ **b.** _____

c. _____ **d.** _____

5. $\dfrac{24x^5b^{-1}}{18xb^4} =$

6. $\left(-\dfrac{3}{5}\right)^0 =$

7. $(5r^3)^2 =$

8. $4x(2x^3 + 3) =$

9. 7 + 3m − 5x
3 − 3m + 2x

_____

10. *division by zero*

$$\frac{2y}{x(2-x)} =$$

x ≠ _____ , _____

11. (x + 2)(x − 6) =

_____

12. −5x + 7y = 30

x	y
0	
	0

y-intercept: (0,   )
x-intercept: (,0)

Use work area.

13. Write each answer as a decimal.

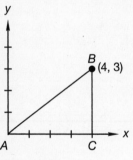

from ∠A

a. $\dfrac{\text{opposite}}{\text{hypotenuse}}$

b. $\dfrac{\text{adjacent}}{\text{hypotenuse}}$

c. $\dfrac{\text{opposite}}{\text{adjacent}}$

a. _____

b. _____

c. _____

14. *Turn your page a $\frac{1}{2}$ turn to see what the rotated triangle will look like.*

A′(,   )

B′(,   )

C′(,   )

Use work area.

15. area and perimeter of a rectangle

l = 2x + 7

w = 2x − 7

A = _____

P = _____

© 2007 Harcourt Achieve Inc.

16. Complete the table. Plot the points and draw the curve.

$y = x^2 - 4$

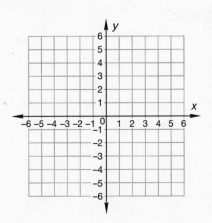

x	y
-2	
-1	
0	
1	
2	

17. *slope* $= \dfrac{rise}{run}$

y-intercept $= 8$

$y = $ _____

18. $-2x^2 + 5 = -3$

$x = $ _____

19. $\dfrac{1}{5} + \dfrac{1}{2}x = \dfrac{3}{20}$

$x = $ _____

Use work area.

20. Factor: $32x^2 - 8x + 24 = $

_____

21. $0.2 + 0.02x = 3$

$x = $ _____

22. $4x > 6x + 6$

$x < $ _____

23. $3x - 7 = 5x + 3(x - 4)$

$x = $ _____

24. area of shaded region in terms of π

The height of the triangle is also the radius of the circle.

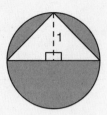

25. total spent

100% + 20% = 120%

120% of $38.50

We use significant digits to tell the accuracy of a measurement.

• Most measurements are not exact.

• The segment below is 8.9-cm long.

• If we looked at the segment and the ruler with a magnifying glass, we might see that the segment is not exactly 8.9-cm long.

• The ruler does not have marks for hundredths of a centimeter, so the best we can measure the segment is 8.9 cm.

• The number of digits used in a measurement is called the number of **significant digits**.

• Rules for counting significant digits are:

  1. Count all non-zero digits.

  2.54 has **three** significant digits.

  2. Count zeros that are between non-zero digits.

  10.7 has **three** significant digits.

  3. Count ending zeros in a *decimal* number.

  1.20 has **three** significant digits.

  120 has only two significant digits.

  4. Do not count zeros if there is not a non-zero digit to the left.

  0.023 has **two** significant digits.

  1.023 has four significant digits.

  5. If a number is written in scientific notation, ignore the power of 10 for counting significant digits.

  1.20×10^3 has **three** significant digits.

  6. **Exact** numbers have an unlimited number of significant digits. Exact numbers are conversion rates.

  12 in. = 1 ft is a exact conversion.

- When calculating with significant digits, it is important to write the answer with the correct number of digits.

- When multiplying or dividing, the product or quotient has only as many significant digits as the measurement with the **least number** of significant digits.

> **Example:** If the 8.9-cm segment is divided into 4 equal parts, what would be the length of each segment?
>
> $8.9 \div 4 = 2.225$
>
> 8.9 cm has two significant digits. 4 is an exact number, so it has an unlimited number of significant digits. The answer will have the same number of significant digits as the measurement with the least number of significant digits.

Write 2.225 cm with two significant digits:

2.2 cm

- When adding or subtracting, the sum or difference may have only as many *decimal places* as the measurement with the **least number** of *decimal places*.

> **Example:** A test tube contained 6.24 mL of liquid before it was heated and 4.6 mL after it was heated. How many mL of liquid evaporated?
>
> First subtract the measurements.
>
> $6.24 - 4.6 = 1.64$
>
> 4.6 mL has one decimal place. 6.24 has two decimal places. The answer will have the same number of decimal places as the measurement with the least number of decimal places.
>
> Write 1.64 mL with one decimal place:
>
> 1.6 mL

Practice Set (page 766)

Write the number of significant digits for each measurement.

a. 10.68 sec

_____ significant
digits

b. 0.063 L

_____ significant
digits

c. 4.20 kg

_____ significant
digits

d. 1.609×10^3 m

_____ significant
digits

Perform each calculation and express each answer with the correct number of significant digits.

e. 3.6 cm · 4.2 cm = _____

*A product has the same number of significant digits as the measurement with the **least** number of significant digits.*

f. $\dfrac{16.4 \text{ m}}{1.2 \text{ sec}}$ = _____

*A quotient has the same number of significant digits as the measurement with the **least** number of significant digits.*

$1.2 \overline{)16.4}$

g. 1.24 g + 6.4 g + 5.1 g = _____

*A sum has the same number of **decimal places** as the measurement with the least number of decimal places.*

    1.24
    6.4
  + 5.1
  _____

h. 0.249 L − 0.12 L = _____

*A difference has the same number of **decimal places** as the measurement with the least number of decimal places.*

    0.249
  − 0.12
  _____

Written Practice (page 766)

1.

	Percent	Actual Count
Last Year	100	
Change		
This Year		t

_____

2. Find *d* when $m = 27$.

$m = 15 + 4d$

_____

3. a. _____

b. _____

c. _____

Use work area.

4. *complex average*

$10 \times \$18 = \$$_____

$6 \times \$20 = \$$_____

total sum $= \$$_____

$\text{average} = \dfrac{\text{total sum}}{\text{total gallons}}$

5. Factor:

a. $9a^2 - 12a =$

b. $8x^3 + 12x^2 =$

a. _____

b. _____

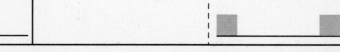

6. a. $(4)^{-2} =$

   b. $\left(\dfrac{1}{3}\right)^{-3} =$

   c. $\left(\dfrac{2}{5}\right)^{-2} =$

a. _____

b. _____

c. _____

7. $\left(-\dfrac{1}{9}\right)^{0} =$

_____

8. $(3x^5)^3 =$

_____

9. $7m^2(3m + 5) =$

_____

10. $(6x + 5m + 3) + (3m + 1 + 4x) =$

_____

11. $A = 4\pi r^2$

Round to the nearest ten in².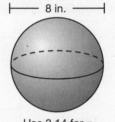

| 8 in. |

Use 3.14 for π.

_____

12. $V = \dfrac{4}{3}\pi r^3$

Round to the nearest ten in³.

_____

13. area and perimeter of a rectangle

   $l = 2x + 9 \qquad w = x + 7$

$A =$ _____ $P =$ _____

14. Write answers as decimals rounded to the thousandths place.

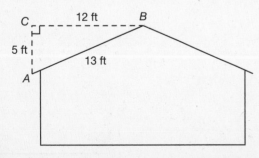

from $\angle A$

  a. $\dfrac{\text{opposite}}{\text{adjacent}}$

  b. $\dfrac{\text{opposite}}{\text{hypotenuse}}$

a. ___ . ___ ___ ___

b. ___ . ___ ___ ___

15. *division by zero*

$$\frac{x + 4}{2x - 6}$$

$\underline{x \neq}$ _____

16. Complete the table. Plot the points and draw the curve.

$y = -x^2$

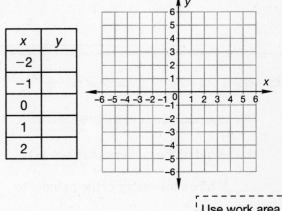

x	y
−2	
−1	
0	
1	
2	

Use work area.

17. slope $= \frac{2}{3}$

y-intercept $= \frac{19}{3}$

$\underline{y =}$ _____

18. *Put in order.*

$\underline{98.2}$, _____, _____, _____, $\underline{99.0}$

mean: _____   median: _____

mode: _____

Use work area.

19. $-3x^2 + 50 = -25$

$\underline{x =}$ _____

20. $\frac{4}{5} + \frac{1}{3}x = \frac{23}{30}$

$\underline{x =}$ _____

21. $\frac{2.4}{4.4} = \frac{x}{33}$

$\underline{x =}$ _____

22. $3x < 5x - 8$

$\underline{x >}$ _____

23. $(x + 3)(x - 1) =$

----

24. $(2x - 5)^2 =$

----

25. *volume of a cone* $= \frac{1}{3}$*(volume of cylinder)*

The _____ has more ice cream.

The height of the cone would have to be

_____ times the height of the cylinder to

have equal volume.

Use work area.

• **Sine, Cosine, Tangent** (page 768)   Name _____

Teacher Note:
• Students will need a calculator with trigonometric function keys.

The sine, cosine and tangent of an angle in a right triangle tell us about the side lengths of the triangle.

• A right triangle has one right angle and two acute angles.

• A right triangle has two legs and a hypotenuse.

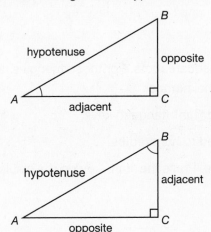

∠A and ∠B are acute angles. ∠C is the right angle.

$\overline{AC}$ and $\overline{BC}$ are the legs (shorter sides). $\overline{AC}$ is the hypotenuse (longest side).

• The legs of a right triangle are either **adjacent** to (touching) or **opposite** the acute angles.

$\overline{AC}$ is adjacent to ∠A. $\overline{BC}$ is opposite ∠A.

$\overline{BC}$ is adjacent to ∠B. $\overline{AC}$ is opposite ∠B.

• The ratios of the lengths of the sides of a right triangle have special names: the **sine**, the **cosine**, and the **tangent**.

Trigonometry Ratios

Name	Ratio
sine	$\dfrac{\text{opposite leg}}{\text{hypotenuse}}$
cosine	$\dfrac{\text{adjacent leg}}{\text{hypotenuse}}$
tangent	$\dfrac{\text{opposite leg}}{\text{adjacent leg}}$

Example: Find the sine, cosine, and tangent of ∠A.

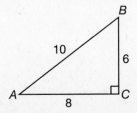

The leg adjacent to ∠A is $\overline{AC}$. The leg opposite ∠A is $\overline{BC}$. The hypotenuse is $\overline{AB}$.

$$\text{sine } \angle A = \frac{\text{opposite}}{\text{hypotenuse}} = \frac{6}{10} = 0.6$$

$$\text{cosine } \angle A = \frac{\text{adjacent}}{\text{hypotenuse}} = \frac{8}{10} = 0.8$$

$$\text{tangent } \angle A = \frac{\text{opposite}}{\text{adjacent}} = \frac{6}{8} = 0.75$$

- The ratios are written as decimals.

- The sides of some triangles will have lengths that are square roots. For those triangles, use a calculator to find the sine, cosine, or tangent rounded to a decimal number.

- Many calculators have "sin" (sine), "cos" (cosine), and "tan" (tangent) keys.

    Example: Find the tangent of a 22° angle rounded to hundredths.

    Enter "22" for the measure of the angle. Press the "tan" key on the calulator. You can read the answer from the display.

    tan 22° = 0.404026225...

    Round to hundredths.

    tan 22° = 0.404026225... = 0.40

- The ratios of sides found using a calculator can be used to solve problems about missing sides in right triangles.

    Example: Basil is 100 feet away from a tall tree. The angle to the top of the tree is 22°. Find the height of the tree.

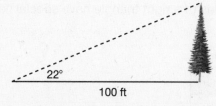

22°

100 ft

The diagram shows that the height of the tree is the *opposite* leg of a right triangle, and the distance to the tree is the *adjacent* leg of a right triangle. Substitute tan 22° = 0.40 from the calculator.

$$\text{tangent } 22° = \frac{\text{opposite}}{\text{adjacent}} = \frac{\text{height}}{100 \text{ ft}} = 0.40$$

Use the variable t for the height of the tree. Solve for t.

$$\frac{t}{100} = 0.40$$

$$t = (0.40)(100) = 40$$

The tree is about 40 ft tall.

Name the trig function for each ratio.

a. _____ $\dfrac{\text{opposite}}{\text{adjacent}}$

b. _____ $\dfrac{\text{opposite}}{\text{hypotenuse}}$

c. _____ $\dfrac{\text{adjacent}}{\text{hypotenuse}}$

For **d–f** refer to this triangle. Write each ratio in **fraction form**.

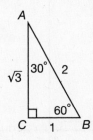

d. What is the sine of ∠ B? _____

$$\text{sine } \angle \;=\; \frac{\text{opposite}}{\text{adjacent}} \;=\; \frac{AC}{AB}$$

e. What is the cosine of ∠ B? _____

$$\text{cosine } \angle B \;=\; \frac{\text{adjacent}}{\text{hypotenuse}} \;=\; \frac{BC}{AB}$$

f. What is the tangent of ∠ B? _____

$$\text{tangent } \angle B \;=\; \frac{\text{opposite}}{\text{adjacent}} \;=\; \frac{AC}{BC}$$

Use a calculator with trig functions to find the following. Round to the nearest thousandth.

g. What is the sine of ∠ A? _____

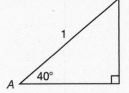

h. What is the tangent of ∠ B? _____

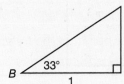

i. The height of the kite is the side *opposite* the 42° angle. The known side (100 ft) is the side adjacent.

Find the height of the kite. _____

$$\tan 42° \;=\; \frac{\text{opposite}}{\text{adjacent}} \;=\; \frac{\text{height}}{100 \text{ ft}}$$

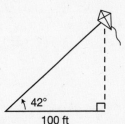

Use a calculator to find tan 42° to the nearest hundredth. Write a proportion and solve for the height of the kite.

1.

	Percent	Actual Count
Last Year	100	*l*
Change		
This Year		

2.  G→ 438 mi ←K

438 miles
− _____ Gerry's miles
_____ Kay's miles

average = $\dfrac{\text{Kay's miles}}{4 \text{ hr}}$

3. 9:42:30 a.m. to 9:43:00 a.m. = _____ sec

9:43:00 a.m. to 10:00:00 a.m. = _____ min

10:00:00 a.m. to 1:00:00 p.m. = _____ hr

1:00:00 p.m. to 1:17:00 p.m. = _____ min

1:17:00 p.m. to 1:17:15 p.m. = _____ sec

4. a. $1000 × 1.5%

b. $20 − **a**

c. $1000 − **b** =

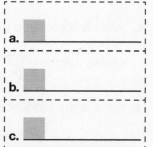

a. _____

b. _____

c. _____

5. $(3x^4y^5)(-2x^2y^4) =$

6. $(5x^3m)(-5x^3m) =$

7. $5x^2(3x + 2) =$

8. $(4x^5)^2 =$

9. $2x + 3y - 7$
$\underline{ x - 3y + 2}$

10. a. $(3)^{-3} =$

b. $\left(\frac{1}{5}\right)^{-2} =$

a. _____

b. _____

11. a. $\left(-\frac{2}{5}\right)^{0} =$

b. $\left(\frac{3}{7}\right)^{-2} =$

a. _____

b. _____

12. Draw the front (trapezoid) and right-side (rectangle) views.
Label the measures of the sides.

Use work area.

13. *volume = area of base × height*
The trapezoid is the base.

14. a. total surface area
2 trapezoids
2 rectangular sides
rectangular bottom
rectangular top

b. Each sheet of plywood is 32 ft². Round your answer up.

a. _____

b. _____

15. area and perimeter of a rectangle
$l = 2x - 1$ $w = x + 2$

$A =$ _____ $P =$ _____

16. slope = 1
y-intercept = -6

$y =$ _____

17. Factor: $8x^3 + 4x^2 + 12x =$

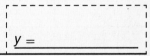

18. Use 1.732 for $\sqrt{3}$.
Round to thousandths.

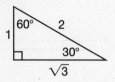

a. sine 60° =

$$\frac{opposite}{hypotenuse}$$

b. tangent 60° =

$$\frac{opposite}{adjacent}$$

c. cosine 60° =

$$\frac{adjacent}{hypotenuse}$$

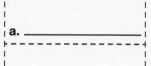

a. _____

b. _____

c. _____

---

19. $5x^2 + 3 = 48$

$\underline{x =}$ _____

20. $\dfrac{1}{2} + \dfrac{1}{6}x = \dfrac{1}{3}$

$\underline{x =}$ _____

---

21. $0.2 - 0.03x = 2$

$\underline{x =}$ _____

22. $2x + 3 = 5x + 6$

$\underline{x =}$ _____

---

23. $-5x + y = 10$

x	y
0	
	0

y-intercept: (0,   )
x-intercept: (,0)

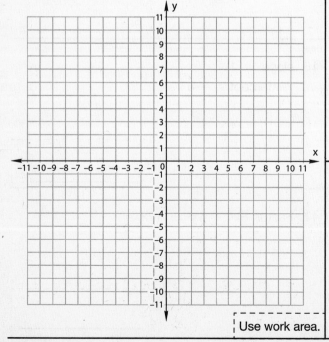

Use work area.

24. Complete the table. Plot the points and draw the curve.

$y = 3x^2$

x	y
−1	
0	
1	

Use work area.

25. 📖 See the bottom of page 772.

_____

• Complex Fractions (page 773)

Name _____

The numerator and denominator of a fraction can be other fractions, or expressions using fractions.

• The bar in a fraction shows division.

$$\frac{3}{4} \longrightarrow 3 \div 4$$

• To divide *by* a fraction, **flip** the fraction and multiply.

$$\frac{3}{4} \div \frac{1}{2}$$

$$\frac{3}{2\cancel{4}} \times \frac{\cancel{2}^{1}}{1} = \frac{3}{2}$$

• A **complex fraction** has a fraction as its numerator, denominator, or both.

   1. Rewrite a complex fraction as a division.

   2. Flip the denominator and multiply.

   Example: Simplify:
   $$\dfrac{\frac{1}{5}}{\frac{2}{3}}$$

$$\dfrac{\frac{1}{5}}{\frac{2}{3}} \longrightarrow \frac{1}{5} \div \frac{2}{3}$$

$$\frac{1}{5} \times \frac{3}{2} = \frac{3}{10}$$

• The percent symbol, %, shows a denominator of 100.

• Simplify percents by rewriting as a complex fraction.

   Example: Change $28\frac{4}{7}\%$ to a fraction and simplify.

$$28\frac{4}{7}\% = \dfrac{28\frac{4}{7}}{100} \longrightarrow 28\frac{4}{7} \div 100$$

$$\frac{\cancel{200}^{2}}{7} \times \frac{1}{\cancel{100}_{1}} = \frac{2}{7}$$

Simplify.

a. $\dfrac{\frac{2}{5}}{\frac{2}{3}}$ $\longrightarrow$ $\dfrac{2}{5} \div \dfrac{2}{3}$

$\downarrow$ $\downarrow$

$\dfrac{2}{5} \times \dfrac{3}{2} = \underline{\hspace{1cm}}$

b. $\dfrac{30}{\frac{5}{6}}$ $\longrightarrow$ $30 \div$

c. $\dfrac{\frac{1}{2} - \frac{1}{3}}{\frac{1}{2} + \frac{1}{4}}$

Simplify the numerator and denominator first.

$\dfrac{1}{2} = \dfrac{}{6}$ $\dfrac{1}{2} = \dfrac{}{4}$

$\underline{-\dfrac{1}{3} = \dfrac{}{6}}$ $\underline{+\dfrac{1}{4} = \dfrac{}{4}}$

Change each percent to a fraction and simplify.

d. $14\dfrac{2}{7}\% = \dfrac{14\frac{2}{7}}{100}$ $\longrightarrow$ $14\dfrac{2}{7} \div 100$

$\downarrow$ $\downarrow$

$\dfrac{100}{7} \times \dfrac{1}{100} =$

e. $8\dfrac{1}{3}\% = \dfrac{8\frac{1}{3}}{100}$

f. $4\dfrac{1}{6}\% =$

Written Practice (page 776)

1.

	Percent	Actual count
Original	100	
Change	c	
New		

2. a. $\dfrac{6\%}{12} = \underline{\hspace{1cm}}\%$

b. $300{,}000 \times $ **a** $=$

c. $1798.65 - $ **b** $=$

d. $300{,}000 - $ **c** $=$

Round to the nearest hundred dollars.

a. _____

b. _____

c. _____

d. _____

3. *Freddy can be faster or slower than Elizabeth.*

faster:

Elizabeth ├──────── 9 mi ────────┤

Freddy ├──────────── 9 + 3 mi ────────────┤

$$\text{speed} = \frac{\text{mi}}{1\frac{1}{2}\text{ hr}} = \frac{\text{mi}}{1\text{hr}}$$

slower:

Elizabeth ├──────── 9 mi ────────┤

Freddy ├──── 9 - 3 mi ────┤

$$\text{speed} = \frac{\text{mi}}{1\frac{1}{2}\text{ hr}} = \frac{\text{mi}}{1\text{hr}}$$

Use work area.

4.

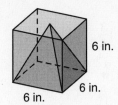

6 in.

6 in.

6 in.

a. volume of cube

b. volume of pyramid

c. What fraction of the cube is **not** the pyramid?

a. _____

b. _____

c. _____

5. slant height and lateral surface area

Use square roots in your answers.

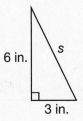

6 in.

s

3 in.

$s =$ _____

$A =$ _____

6. Factor: $6x^3 + 3x^2 + 9x =$

_____

7. $(4x^5y)(-2x) =$

_____

8. $(-2m^2b^5)(-m^3) =$

_____

9. $-2x^3(x + 1) =$

_____

10. $(4x^5)^3 =$

_____

11. a. $\dfrac{1\frac{1}{2}}{1\frac{3}{4}}$ → $1\frac{1}{2} \div 1\frac{3}{4}$

$$\underline{\hspace{1cm}} \times \underline{\hspace{1cm}} =$$

b. $\dfrac{16\frac{2}{3}}{100}$ → $16\frac{2}{3} \div 100$

$$\underline{\hspace{1cm}} \times \dfrac{1}{100} =$$

a. _____

b. _____

12. a. $\left(\dfrac{1}{9}\right)^0 =$

b. $\dfrac{6x^5m^2}{9x^5m} =$

a. _____

b. _____

13. $(1 - 2x + 3m) + (4m + 5x - 6) =$

_____

14. $(3m + 1)^2 =$

$\underline{\hspace{1cm}} + \underline{\hspace{1cm}} + \underline{\hspace{1cm}}$

15. Use 1.414 for $\sqrt{2}$

a. tangent 45°

$\dfrac{opposite}{adjacent}$

b. sine 45°

$\dfrac{opposite}{hypotenuse}$

c. cosine 45°

$\dfrac{adjacent}{hypotenuse}$

a. _____

b. _____

c. _____

16. area and perimeter of a rectangle
$l = 7w + 9 \quad w = w$

$A =$ _____

$P =$ _____

17. $-5x^2 + 9 = -36$

$x = \pm$ _____

18. $3(x - 1) = 4x - 9$

$x =$ _____

19. $\frac{3}{7}x - \frac{1}{14} = \frac{1}{2}$

$x =$ _____

20. $\frac{3.5}{1.4} = \frac{x}{4}$

$x =$ _____

21. $(7, -14)$ and $(0, 7)$

y-intercept $= 7$

slope $= \dfrac{\text{rise}}{\text{run}} = \dfrac{7 - (-14)}{0 - 7} =$

$y =$ _____

22. Solve by graphing.

$\begin{cases} 3x - 4y = 12 \\ x + y = 4 \end{cases}$

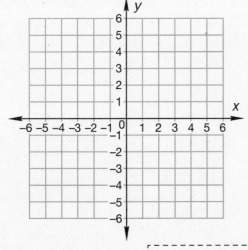

$x =$ _____

$y =$ _____

23. Square $ABCD$ has vertices $A(3, 0)$, $B(4, -3)$, $C(1, -4)$, and $D(0, -1)$.

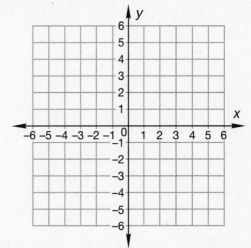

perimeter and area

$P =$ _____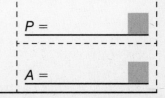

$A =$ _____

24. Translate *ABCD* so that *A'*(0, 3).

B'(,) *C'*(,) *D'*(,)

25.

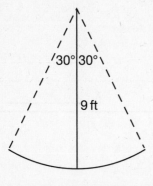

The distance the pendulum travels is part of a c_____.

The total degree measure of the arc is _____°.

The distance is $\frac{}{360°}(2\pi r)$, which is about _____ ft.

• **Rationalizing a Denominator**   Name _____

(page 778)

Fractions are usually written without square roots in the denominator.

• Square roots in the numerator are okay.

• **Rationalizing a denominator** takes a square root out of the denominator of a fraction.

• **Multiply the numerator and the denominator by the square root.**

Example: Rationalize the denominator of the fraction: $\dfrac{3}{\sqrt{5}}$

Multiply by $\dfrac{\sqrt{5}}{\sqrt{5}}$ to rationalize the denominator.

$$\frac{3}{\sqrt{5}} \cdot \frac{\sqrt{5}}{\sqrt{5}} = \frac{3\sqrt{5}}{5}$$

Practice Set (page 779)

Rationalize the denominator of each fraction in **a–h**.

a. $\dfrac{3}{\sqrt{2}} \cdot \dfrac{\sqrt{2}}{\sqrt{2}} = \dfrac{}{2}$

b. $\dfrac{4}{\sqrt{2}} \cdot \dfrac{\sqrt{2}}{\sqrt{2}} = \dfrac{}{2}$

c. $\dfrac{1}{\sqrt{3}} \cdot \dfrac{}{} = \dfrac{}{3}$

d. $\dfrac{2}{\sqrt{3}} \cdot \dfrac{}{} = \dfrac{}{3}$

e. $\dfrac{8}{\sqrt{8}} \cdot \dfrac{\sqrt{8}}{\sqrt{8}} = \dfrac{8\sqrt{8}}{8} =$

f. $\dfrac{5}{\sqrt{10}} \cdot \dfrac{}{} = \dfrac{}{} =$

g. $\dfrac{\sqrt{2}}{\sqrt{3}} \cdot \dfrac{\sqrt{3}}{\sqrt{3}} = \dfrac{}{3}$

h. $\dfrac{2\sqrt{3}}{\sqrt{2}} \cdot \dfrac{}{} = \dfrac{}{} =$

1.

	Percent	Actual count
Last Year	100	
Change		c
This Year		

_____

2. a. $\dfrac{6\%}{12} =$

a. _____

b. $\$20,000 \times \mathbf{a} =$

b. _____

c. $\$608.44 - \mathbf{b} =$

c. _____

d. $\$20,000 - \mathbf{c} =$

Round to the nearest hundred dollars.

d. _____

3. Mariya folded _____ items.

Irina folded _____ items.

Irina folded $\dfrac{\text{items}}{8 \text{ minutes}} =$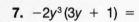

_____

4. $\dfrac{x^{-5}m^3}{m^2z^{-3}} =$

_____

5. $\dfrac{4x^2r^{-2}}{2x^{-1}r^3} =$

_____

6. $3x^2y\,(-2y^3) =$

_____

7. $-2y^3\,(3y + 1) =$

_____

8. a. $(4)^{-1} =$

b. $(5r^4)^3 =$

a. _____

b. _____

9. a. $\left(\dfrac{1}{5}\right)^0 =$

b. $\left(\dfrac{2}{5}\right)^{-2} =$

a. _____

b. _____

10. $5 - 4x - (2x - 1) =$

_____

11. a. $\dfrac{\frac{3}{4}}{6} \longrightarrow \dfrac{3}{4} \div 6$

$\dfrac{3}{4} \times \text{—} =$

b. $\dfrac{3\frac{1}{3}}{100} \longrightarrow 3\frac{1}{3} \div 100$

a. _____

b. _____

12. Rationalize the denominator.

a. $\dfrac{1}{\sqrt{2}} \cdot \dfrac{\sqrt{2}}{\sqrt{2}} =$

b. $\dfrac{1}{\sqrt{3}} \cdot \text{—} =$

a. _____

b. _____

13. Use 1.414 for $\sqrt{2}$.
Round to the nearest thousandth.

$\dfrac{1}{\sqrt{2}} =$

_____

14. Factor: $10x^3 - 8x^2 - 6x =$

_____

15. $(2x + 9)^2 =$

_____

16. $4x^2 - 9 = 91$

$x =$ _____

17. $0.2x + 0.8 =$

$x =$ _____

18. $\dfrac{1}{8}x + \dfrac{3}{4} = 2$

$x =$ _____

19. $-2(x + 3) = -x$

$x =$ _____

20. area and perimeter of a rectangle

$l = x \qquad w = 2x - 13$

$A =$ _____

$P =$ _____

21. slope = $-\dfrac{1}{2}$

y-intercept = 2

$x =$ _____

22. Write as a fraction and as a decimal to the nearest thousandth.

sine 30° = $\dfrac{\text{opposite}}{\text{hypotenuse}}$ =

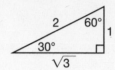

_____
_____

23. Find AC.
Units are inches.

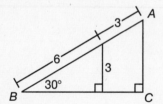

$\dfrac{6}{} = \dfrac{6+3}{AC}$

_____

24. area of shaded region
Leave π as π.

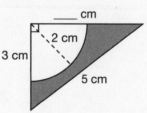

The unshaded part is $\dfrac{1}{4}$ circle.

_____

25. Cancel units.

$0.75 \text{ sec} \cdot \dfrac{60 \text{ mi}}{1 \text{ hr}} \cdot \dfrac{\text{hr}}{\text{min}} \cdot \dfrac{\text{min}}{\text{sec}} \cdot \dfrac{\text{ft}}{\text{mi}} =$

_____

Investigations
1-12

• The Coordinate Plane (page 68)

Name _____

- A **coordinate plane** is a grid formed by two perpendicular number lines.

- The *x*-axis is the *horizontal* number line.

- The *y*-axis is the *vertical* number line.

- The **origin** is the point at which the *x*-axis and the *y*-axis intersect.

> **Teacher Notes:**
> - Introduce Hint #30, "Rectangular Coordinates."
> - Refer students to "Rectangular Coordinates" on page 18 in the *Student Reference Guide*.
> - Students may use a straightedge to draw lines on coordinate planes.
> - These worksheets provide space to complete the activity. If additional coordinate planes are needed, see Lesson Activity 1.

- **Coordinates** are two numbers that tell the location of a point.

    They are always written as a pair of numbers in parentheses, such as (3, 2).

    The first number (*x*-coordinate) shows *horizontal* direction and distance from the origin.

    The second number (*y*-coordinate) shows *vertical* direction and distance from the origin.

    The sign of the number indicates the direction.

- Positive coordinates are up or right.

- Negative coordinates are down or left.

    The origin is at point (0, 0).

- **Quadrants** are the four regions of the plane divided by the two axes.

    Quadrants are numbered *counterclockwise* starting at upper right.

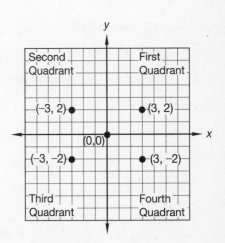

Example 1: Find the coordinates of the vertices of △ABC on this coordinate plane. Then count squares and half squares on the grid to find the area of the triangle in square units.

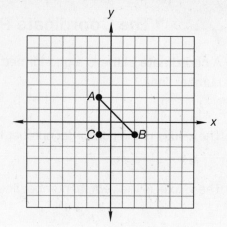

Point *A* (–1, 2)

Point *B* (,   )

Point *C* (,   )

x-coordinate of a point: Start at the origin (0, 0).

Count horizontally to the point. Right is positive; left is negative.

y-coordinate of a point: Start at the origin (0, 0).

Count vertically to the point. Up is positive; down is negative.

Area: _____ units²

Count each full square in the triangle as one square unit.
Count each half square in the triangle as a half square unit.
Find the total area.

• We can **graph** pairs of related points from a table by reading the *x*- and *y*-numbers as coordinates for points.

Example 2: Graph pairs of numbers from this table on the coordinate plane.

• Each row in the table names a point.

• Start at the origin (0, 0).

• Count 2 units left for –2.

• Count 1 unit down for –1.

• Draw a point at (–2, –1).

• Draw points for the other rows in the table.

x	y
1	2
2	3
3	4
4	5

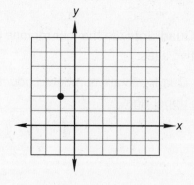

1. Graph and label the following points on a coordinate plane:

   a. (3,4)   **b.** (2, −3)   **c.** (−1, 2)   **d.** (0, 4)

   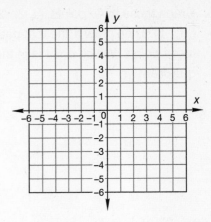

   - Start at the origin.
   - To graph (3, 4) move right along the horizontal *x*-axis three units.
   - From there, turn and move up four (4) units.
   - Draw the point.
   - Label the point with the coordinates (3, 4).
   - Now do the same for the other coordinate points.

2. Explain how you located the point (2, −3) in problem 1.

   I started at the _____. I counted _____ units to the

   right on the x-axis. From there I counted 3 units _____ and drew the point.

3. The vertices of square *ABCD* are located at *A*(2, 2), *B*(2, −1), *C*(−1, −1) and *D*(−1, 2). Draw the square and find its perimeter and area.

   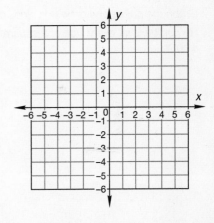

   - Graph
   - Draw the square
   - The side of each small square is one unit.
   - Add all the units along the edges of the square to find

     the perimeter. _____units

   - Multiplying length by width (or count the enclosed squares)

     to find the area. _____units²

4. Which vertex of square *ABCD* in problem 3 is located in the **third quadrant**?

   vertex _____

5. Graph these three points: (4, 2), (2, 0), and (−1, −3). Then draw a line that passes through these points. Which point is in the **fourth quadrant**? (,   )

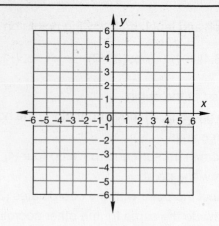

6. One vertex of a square is the origin. Two other vertices are located at (−3, 0) and (0,−3). What are the coordinates of the fourth vertex? (,   )

Graph the points and draw two sides of the square. Remember that every side of a square is the same length.

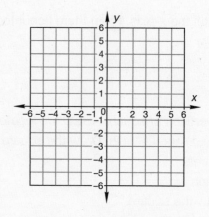

7. Find the **perimeter** and **area** of a rectangle whose vertices are located at (3, −2), (−2, −2), (−2. 4), and (3, 4).

Perimeter: _____ units   Area: _____ units²

Graph the points. Count to find the perimeter and area.

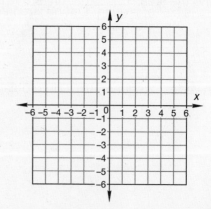

8. Points (4, 4), (4, 0), and (0, 0) are the vertices

   of a triangle. Graph the triangle.

   Find the **area** of the triangle by counting the

   whole squares and the half squares.

   _____ units²

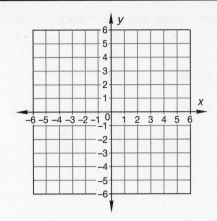

9. The point (–3, 2) lies in which quadrant?

   quadrant ___

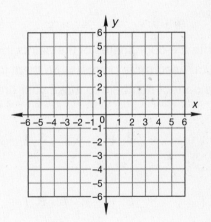

10. A pint is half of a quart. Letting *x* represent
    the number of pints and *y* the number of
    quarts, we can make a table of *x, y* pairs.
    Graph the pairs from this table on a
    coordinate plane.

x	y
0	0
2	1
4	2
6	3

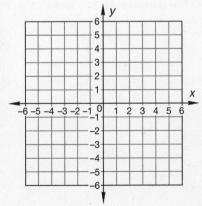

11. Graph these points and connect the dots in order.

1. (0, 4)   **2.** (–3, –4)   **3.** (5, 1)

4. (–5, 1)   **5.** (3, –4)   **6.** (0, 4)

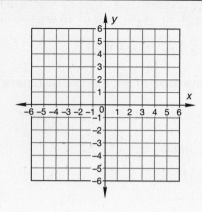

12. Make a connect-the-dots drawing using at least 6 different points on this coordinate plane.

Write the coordinates of the points in order. If you need more points, write them in with the correct numbers to make your drawing.

1. (,   )   **2.** (,   )   **3.** (,   )

4. (,   )   **5.** (,   )   **6.** (,   )

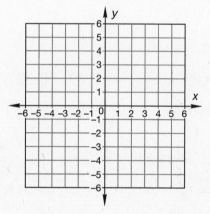

• **Pythagorean Theorem** (page 132)

Name _____

• Right triangles have special parts.

• The *longest side* of a right triangle is called the **hypotenuse**.
   The hypotenuse is opposite the right angle.

• The *two shorter sides* of a right triangle are called the **legs**.
   The legs are the sides that form the right angle.

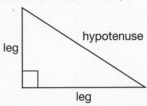

• The **Pythagorean Theorem** says that the sum of the squares of the legs of a right triangle equals the square of the hypotenuse.
   Every right triangle obeys the Pythagorean Theorem.

• The Pythagorean Theorem is usually written with *a* and *b* for the legs and *c* for the hypotenuse.
   $a^2 + b^2 = c^2$

Example 1: This right triangle has sides of 6 cm, 8 cm, and *c*. The squares drawn on the triangle show that the square of 6 is 36 and the square of 8 is 64. Find c^2.

• Pythagorean Theorem: $c^2 = a^2 + b^2$

$c^2 = 36 \text{ cm}^2 + 64 \text{ cm}^2 = $ _____

• Take the square root of c^2 to find *c*.

$c = $ _____

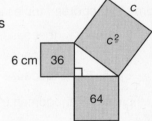

Example 2: This right triangle has sides of *a*, 12 in., and 13 in. The squares drawn on the triangle show that the square of 12 is 144 and the square of 13 is 169. Find a^2.

• Pythagorean Theorem: $a^2 + b^2 = c^2$
$a^2 + 144 \text{ in.}^2 = 169 \text{ in.}^2$

$a^2 = $ _____

• Take the square root of a^2 to find *a*.

$a = $ _____

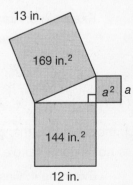

1. Write the name of the property of right triangles illustrated in examples 1 and 2.

   P_____   T_____

2. What is the name for the two sides of a right triangle that form the right angle? l_____

3. What is the name for the side of a right triangle that is opposite the right angle? h_____

4. Write the Pythagorean Theorem as an equation. Use the letters a and b for the shorter sides of a right triangle and c for the longest side of a right triangle.

   _____ + _____ = _____

5. Draw squares on each side of this triangle. Find the area of each square.

   $12^2 =$ _____ in.² $16^2 =$ _____ in.²

   $c^2 =$ _____ + _____ = _____ in.²

   Find c (square root). $c =$ _____

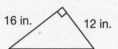

6. Use the Pythagorean Theorem to find a.

   $b^2 =$ _____ $c^2 =$ _____

   $a^2 +$ _____ = _____

   $a^2 =$ _____

   $a =$ _____

- **Pythagorean triples** are three whole numbers that fit the Pythagorean Theorem. Some Pythagorean triples are show below.

      3, 4, 5   (because 9 + 16 = 25)
      5, 12, 13   (because 25 + 144 = 169)
      8, 15, 17   (because 64 + 225 = 289)

- Multiples of Pythagorean triples are also Pythagorean triples.

      3, 4, 5
      6, 8, 10   (3, 4, 5 times 2)
      9, 12, 15   (3, 4, 5 times 3)

   Example 3: Are the numbers 2, 3, and 4 a Pythagorean triple? _____

   Does $2^2 + 3^2 = 4^2$?

   $2^2 + 3^2 =$ _____ + _____ = _____

   $4^2 =$ _____

- If the sides of a triangle do not fit the Pythagorean Theorem, the triangle is **not** a right triangle.

   Example 4: Cassidy sketched a triangle and carefully measured the sides. Is her triangle a right triangle? _____
   Do the sides fit the Pythagorean Theorem?

   $7^2 + 7^2 =$ _____ + _____ = _____

   $10^2 =$ _____

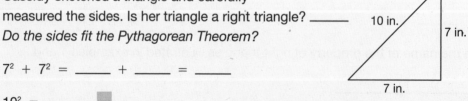

7. Write a multiple of 5, 12, 13 that is a Pythagorean triple.

5,   12,   13

↓   ↓   ↓

10, _____, _____

8. Are the numbers 8, 15, and 17 a Pythagorean triple? _____
Does $8^2 + 15^2 = 17^2$?

$8^2 + 15^2 =$ _____ + _____ = _____

$17^2 =$ _____

9. Does a right triangle with the dimensions 8 cm, 9 cm, and 12 cm exist? _____
Do the sides fit the Pythagorean Theorem?

$8^2 + 9^2 =$ _____ + _____ = _____

$12^2 =$ _____

• Builders can use the Pythagorean Theorem to tell whether they have
made a right angle. If the length of the hypotenuse is too long, the angle is
too big. If the length of the hypotenuse is too short, the angle is too small.

10. Britney is framing a wall. She wants the angle at *C* to be a right angle.
She marks point *A* 8 feet from *C* and point *B* 6 feet from *C*.
She measures from *A* to *B* and finds the distance is 10 ft $1\frac{1}{2}$ in.

   • Is the distance from *A* to *B* too long or too short to be

     a right angle? _____

     $6^2 + 8^2 =$ _____

     The distance from *A* to *B* should be _____ ft.

   • Should Britney push *B* toward *A* or pull *B* away from *A* to make a right angle?

     Because the distance from *A* to *B* is too _____, Britney should _____ *B* toward *A*.

• Many right triangles have side lengths that are not whole numbers. In these cases, leave the side length as an irrational number (in a square root sign).

Find the irrational number that represents the length of the unmeasured side of each triangle.

11. *One leg is 2 units and the other leg is 1 unit.*

$2^2 + 1^2 = \sqrt{}$

$a = \sqrt{}$ units

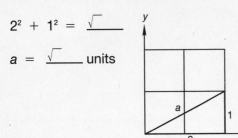

12. $a^2 + b^2 = c^2$

$b = \sqrt{}$

Activity: Pythagorean Puzzle

• Materials required:
  Copy of Investigation Activity 3
  Scissors

1. Cut out the squares from the legs (shorter sides) of the right triangle.

2. Cut along the lines of the squares to make eight triangles.

3. Use the triangles to cover up the square on the hypotenuse of the right triangle. The triangles should not overlap. Use all eight triangles.

• Classifying Quadrilaterals (page 197)   Name _____

- A **quadrilateral** is a four-sided polygon. There are many types of quadrilaterals.

- This chart from the *Student Reference Guide* shows the different types of quadrilaterals:

Teacher Notes:
- Introduce Hint #43, "Classifying Quadrilaterals."
- Refer students to "Classifying Quadrilaterals" on page 16 and "Quadrilaterals" on page 18 in the *Student Reference Guide.*
- Review "Angles" on page 27 in the *Student Reference Guide.*
- Students will need a calculator for question 15.

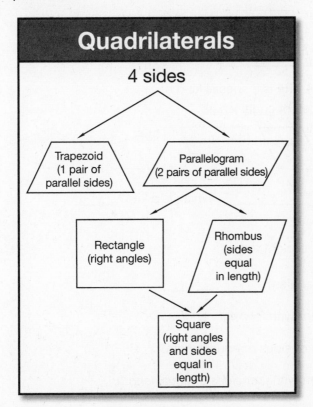

- Use the letters of the quadrilaterals below to answer the questions.

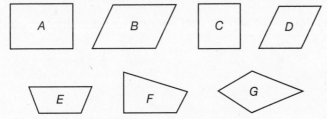

1. Which figures have *two pairs* of **parallel** sides?   _____, _____, _____, _____

3†. Which figures have *no pairs* of **parallel** sides?   _____, _____

- Quadrilaterals can be sorted by the number of pairs of parallel sides.

- A **parallelogram** is a quadrilateral with *two pairs* of *parallel* sides.

4. Which of the figures *A–G* are parallelograms?   _____, _____, _____, _____

†Question numbers correspond to question numbers in the Course 3 **Saxon Math** textbook.

- Parallel sides of a parallelogram have equal lengths.

- A **trapezoid** is a quadrilateral with *one pair* of *parallel* sides.

5. Which of the figures A–G is a trapezoid? _____

- The parallel sides of a trapezoid are **not** equal in length.

- If the non-parallel sides of a trapezoid are equal in length, it is an **isosceles trapezoid.**

- A **trapezium** has *no pairs* of *parallel* sides. A **kite** is a special kind of trapezium that has two pairs of adjacent sides of equal length.

     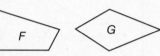

6. Which of the figures A–G are trapeziums? _____, _____ Which is a kite? _____

- Quadrilaterals can be sorted by the number of right angles.

7. Which of the figures A–G have four right angles? _____, _____

- A **rectangle** is a special kind of parallelogram with *four right angles.*

- Quadrilaterals can be sorted by the number of sides of equal length.

- A **rhombus** is a special kind of parallelogram with *four sides of equal length.*

8. Which of the figures A–G have four sides of equal length? _____, _____

9. Which figure in A–G is both a rectangle (four right angles) and a rhombus (four sides of equal length)? _____

- A **square** is both a rectangle and a rhombus.

- A Venn diagram may be used to show relationships between quadrilaterals. The letters in the Venn diagram refer to figures A–G.

- Each circle in the Venn diagram shows a special type of quadrilateral. Notice that some letters are inside more than one circle.

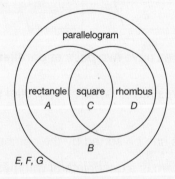

Refer to the Venn diagram and to figures A–G to answer questions 10–14.

10. Which figure is a parallelogram but not a rectangle or a rhombus? _____

11. Which figure is a parallelogram and a rhombus but not a rectangle? _____

12. Which figure is a parallelogram and a rectangle but not a rhombus? _____

14. Which figures on the Venn diagram are not parallelograms? _____, _____

• The rectangle below is called the "Golden Rectangle." It is often used in art and architecture.

$$1 + \tfrac{1}{2}(\sqrt{5} - 1)$$

1

• Notice that the width is 1, but the length is an irrational number.

15. Use a calculator to find the length of the golden rectangle to the nearest tenth. (Ask your teacher for help if you have trouble.) _____

16. Multiply the width and the length of the golden rectangle by 10 to find whole numbers that approximate the side lengths of a golden rectangle.

width: _____   length: _____

• A model of a rectangle can be made out of straws and pipe cleaners (Figure J). When the sides are shifted, the angles change (Figure K).

Figure J

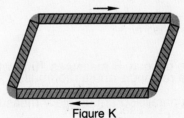

Figure K

Refer to figures J and K to answer problems **17–27.**

17. Is figure K a rectangle (four right angles)? _____

Is figure K a parallelogram (two pairs of parallel sides)? _____

18. Did the lengths of the sides change when the angles changed? _____

19. Does the perimeter of figure K equal the perimeter of figure J? _____

20. Does the area of figure K equal the area of figure J? _____
This figure might help you decide if the area changed.

Figure J   Figure K

21. As the sides of figure K are shifted and the obtuse angles become larger and the acute angles smaller, how does the area change?

The area gets _____.

22. The four angles of figure J total how many degrees? _____
Figure J has four right angles.

23. What is the sum of the angles in figure K? _____
It has the same sum as the angles in figure J.

25. Put the tip of your finger on a corner in figure J. Trace around two angles of the figure. You have traced a half turn. If you kept tracing the sides, your finger would go back in the opposite direction.

How many degrees is half a turn? _____

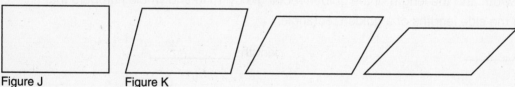

Figure J   Figure K

26. In figure K, the measure of an obtuse angle and an acute angle together total how many

degrees? _____
Two angles make a half turn.

27. If an obtuse angle of figure K measures 100°, what does an acute angle measure? _____

28. Figure *ABCD* is a parallelogram. Angle *A* measures 70°. What does ∠*B* measure? _____
Adjacent angles in a parallelogram total 180°.

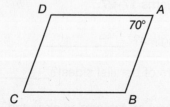

29. In parallelogram *ABCD*, ∠*A* measures 70°. What does ∠*D* measure? _____

30. Use the information from questions 28 and 29 to find the measure of ∠*C*. _____

- A figure has **reflective symmetry** if it can be divided in half by a line so that the halves are mirror images.

- This triangle has reflective symmetry.

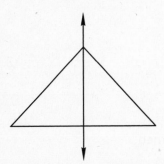

- The line that divides the triangle into mirror images is a **line of symmetry**.

- Some quadrilaterals have lines of symmetry.

Draw the lines of symmetry on each figure below. One figure has no lines of symmetry.

31.

How many lines of symmetry? _____

32.

How many lines of symmetry? _____

33.

C

How many lines of symmetry? _____

35. Do the lines of symmetry for figure *A* pass through sides, angles, or both? _____

36. Do the lines of symmetry for figure *D* pass through sides, angles, or both? _____

37. Do the lines of symmetry for figure *C* pass through sides, angles, or both? _____

A figure has rotational symmetry if its image reappears more than once as the figure is rotated a full turn.

• We show a square being turned below.

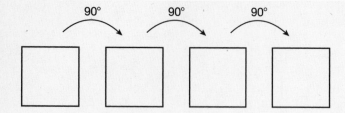

• Every time the square is turned 90°, it looks the same as it did before it was turned.

• A square has **rotational symmetry.**

• Because the square looks the same four times as it makes one full turn, we say the square has rotational symmetry of **order** four.

Circle "yes" or "no" to tell whether each figure has rotational symmetry. If a figure has rotational symmetry, tell its order.

38. Yes / No   order: _____

39. Yes / No   order: _____

41. Yes / No   order: _____

42. Yes / No   order: _____

• Drawing Geometric Solids (page 271)

Name _____

- **Plane figures** are geometric shapes that are two-dimensional (flat). Examples of plane figures are rectangles, hexagons, and circles.

- **Geometric solids** are three-dimensional figures.

- Two **faces** meet at an **edge**. Two edges meet at a **vertex**.

- A **polyhedron** is a type of geometric solid in which *every face is a polygon*. A polyhedron has no curved edges.

— face
— edge
— vertex

- This table shows names and examples of some geometric solids:

Teacher Notes:
- Introduce Hint #48, "Geometric Solids (Manipulatives)," and Hint #49, "Faces on a Cube."
- Refer students to "Geometric Solids" on page 30 in the *Student Reference Guide*.
- ETA Relational GeoSolids and unit cubes can be found in the Adaptations Manipulative Kit.
- The extensions are optional.

Geometric Solids

Polyhedron (pl. polyhedra)		A general term that identifies a solid with faces that are polygons. A polyhedron has no curved surfaces or edges.
Prism		A type of polyhedron with parallel congruent bases.
Pyramid		A type of polyhedron with lateral surfaces that narrow to a point (apex).
Cylinder		In this book we will use the term **cylinder** to refer to a right circular cylinder as illustrated.
Cone		In this book we will use the term **cone** to refer to a right circular cone as illustrated.
Sphere		A smooth curved solid every point of which is the same distance from its center.

© 2007 Harcourt Achieve Inc.

- Look at the prisms in the table. A prism has two **bases** (the tops and bottoms of the figures) that are *parallel* and *congruent (same size and shape)*.

- We name prisms by the shape of their bases:

1. A triangular prism has how many faces, edges, and vertices?

   The bases of this prism are the top and bottom.

   faces: _____

   edges: _____

   vertices: _____

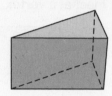

2. Name each figure.

   A r_____ prism

   B p_____

   C c_____

   D t_____ prism

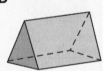

   Which figure is not a polyhedron?_____

- Because geometric solids are three-dimensional, we have to uses tricks to draw them on a flat two-dimensional surface like a piece of paper.

Triangular Prism

Rectangular Prism

Hexagonal Prism

- Notice that some of the edges of the geometric solids are drawn with dashed lines. These edges are "hidden" from view on the back of the solid.

- **Parallel projection** is one way to draw prisms and cylinders.

- Prisms and cylinders both have congruent parallel bases, so we start there and then draw lines for the visible and "hidden" edges.

Activity 1: *Sketching Prisms and Cylinders Using Parallel Projection*

Follow the instructions to complete each geometric figure. Use a ruler or straightedge to make straight lines.

Rectangular Prism

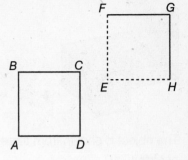

- Draw lines to connect *D* to *H*, *C* to *G*, and *B* to *F*.

- Draw dashed lines to connect *A* to *E*.

Is base *ABCD* or base *EFGH* "in front"? base _____

Triangular Prism

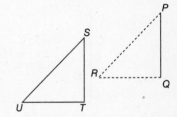

- Draw lines to connect *P* to *S*, *Q* to *T*, and *R* to *U*.

Which edge that you drew is "hidden"? _____

Cylinder

- Draw an **ellipse** (a "flattened" circle) for the second base of the cylinder.

  Is the top base or the bottom base hidden? _____

- Pyramids and cones have only one base. We start by drawing the base and then connecting the base to a point called the **apex.**

Activity 2: *Sketching Pyramids and Cones*

Follow the instructions to complete each geometric figure. Use a ruler or straightedge to make straight lines.

Rectangular Pyramid

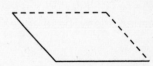

- Draw lines from each vertex of the base to the apex. *One of the lines will be a dashed line.*

Cone

- Draw lines from opposite sides of the ellipse to the apex.

- **Multiview projection** displays a three-dimensional object as if a person was looking directly at it from three viewpoints: the top, front, and side.

- An **isometric**, or angled, view is also included. Hidden edges are not shown in the isometric view.

Activity 3: *Create a Multiview Drawing*

This is the isometric view of an object:

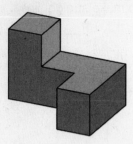

The object is shown from three viewpoints below. Label each figure with its viewpoint: **top, front,** or **side.**

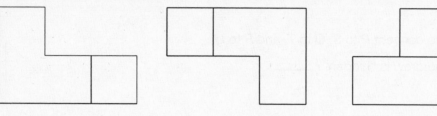

_____   _____   _____

extensions

1. Build the object from Activity 3 using unit cubes. In Activity 3, the object is shown from the top, front, and right sides. The object can be drawn from three other viewpoints. Sketch each viewpoint.

   Bottom

   Back

   Left Side

- When we look at objects in the real world, things that are farther away from us appear to be smaller. This is called **perspective**.

- We can draw geometric solids with perspective by using a **vanishing point**.

Activity 4: *One-Point Perspective Drawing*

Follow the instructions to complete this perspective drawing of a trapezoid.

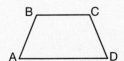

- Draw a line from every vertex of the trapezoid to the vanishing point (point *X*).

- Draw a point anywhere on line *AX*.

- Draw a line that is parallel to $\overline{AB}$ from your point to line *BX*.

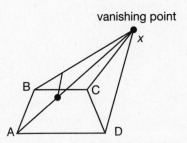

- Continue drawing lines to complete the trapezoidal prism.

- Erase the lines that go from the "back" of the trapezoidal prism to the vanishing point.

- Can you tell which lines in the trapezoidal prism are "hidden"? Erase those lines and replace them with dashed lines.

Graphing Transformations (page 342)   Name _____

- Transformations are ways to change the position and size of a geometric figure. We can graph transformations on a coordinate plane.

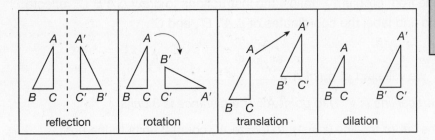

| reflection | rotation | translation | dilation |

- Reflection, rotation, and translation are **congruence transformations** because the **image** (new figure) is congruent to the original figure.

- Dilation is a **similarity transformation** because the image is similar to the original figure. The size has changed.

- A reflection is a flip of a figure across a line.

1. △ABC has vertices at A(−2, 6), B(−5, 2), and C(−2, 2). Follow the instructions to draw △ABC reflected (flipped) over the x-axis. Name the reflection △A′B′C′. First find the coordinates of A′, B′, and C′.

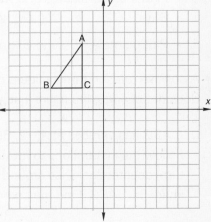

- To find the coordinates of A′ we will start at point A.

- Find the distance from A to the x-axis. The distance is 6 units.
  The distance from A to the x-axis is the y-coordinate.

- Since point A is 6 units above the x-axis, to locate A′, count 6 units below the x-axis.

  Because we are reflecting across the x-axis, A′ will be the same distance below the x-axis as A is above the x-axis.

- Now we have flipped point A vertically over the x-axis. Label this point A′.

- Write the coordinates of A′: A′(−2,−6)
  The x-coordinate does not change. Since this is a vertical flip the y-coordinate changed.

- Find the coordinates of B′ and C′.
  B′(−5,   )   C′(−2,   )

- Plot points A′, B′, and C′ and draw △A′B′C′.

2. Compare the coordinates of the two triangles.

   The _____-coordinates are the same number but have different signs.

   The _____-coordinates did not change.

3. Using the same coordinate plane from problem 1, follow the instructions to draw △$A'B'C'$ reflected (flipped) over the line $x = 1$. Find and label the coordinates of △A'', B'', and C''.

   • Draw a vertical line at $x = 1$.

   • To find the coordinates of A'' we will start at point A'.

   • *Find the distance from the vertical line ($x = 1$) to point A'. The distance is 3 units.*

   • Since point A' is 3 units to the left of the line ($x = 1$), to locate A'', count 3 units to the right of the line.
     Because we are reflecting across the x-axis, A'' will be the same distance right of $x = 1$ as A' is left of $x = 1$.

   • Now we have flipped point A' horizontally over the line ($x = 1$). Label this point A''.

   • Write the coordinates of A'': $A''(4, -6)$
     The y-coordinate does not change. Since this is a horizontal flip, the x-coordinate changes.

   • Find the coordinates of B'' and C''.
     $B'' (\quad, 2)$ $C'' (\quad, 2)$

   • Plot points A'', B'', and C'' and draw △$A''B''C''$.

• A *positive rotation* turns a figure *counterclockwise* around a **point of rotation**. The point of rotation does not change; the figure just spins counterclockwise around the point of rotation.

4. △ABC has vertices at $A(-2, 6)$, $B(-5, 2)$, and $C(-2, 2)$. Follow the instructions to rotate △ABC 90° (one quarter turn) counterclockwise around the origin. The rotated image is △ABC. Find the coordinates of A, B, and C.

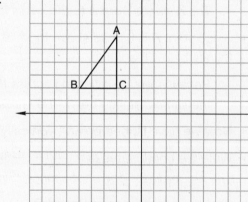

   • Get a piece of tracing paper and put it over the coordinate plane.

   • Trace the x- and y-axes but do not label them. Then trace △ABC.

   • Place the tip of your pencil on the origin. Turn the tracing paper 90° counterclockwise (a quarter turn) so that the y-axis aligns with the x-axis.

   • Label the horizontal axis on the tracing paper x and the vertical axis y.

   • Use the traced image to plot points A', B', and C' and draw △$A'B'C'$ on the coordinate plane.
     $A'(-6, -2)$ $B'(-2, \quad)$ $C'(\quad, -2)$

5. Follow the instructions to rotate △ABC 180° counterclockwise around the origin on the same coordinate plane. The rotated image is △A"B"C". Find the coordinates of A", B", and C".

- Put a piece of tracing paper back over the coordinate plane and trace a triangle on top of △ABC.

- Place the tip of your pencil on the origin. Turn the tracing paper 180° (a half turn).

- Label the x- and y-axes on the tracing paper.

- Use the traced image to plot points A", B", and C" and draw △A"B"C" on the coordinate plane.
   A"(2, −6)   B"(5,   )   C"(, −2)

• Translations (sliding a figure without flipping or turning) can be described with coordinates (a, b), where a is the change in the x-coordinate and b is the change in the y-coordinate.

6. △ABC has vertices at A(−2, 6), B(−5, 2), and C(−2, 2). Follow the instructions to draw △ABC translated 7 units to the right and 8 units down, or (7, −8). Find the coordinates of A', B', and C'.

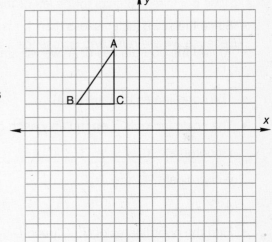

- Every point on △ABC will shift 7 units right and 8 units down.

- To find the coordinates of A' start at point A.

- The coordinates of A are (−2, 6).

- Add (+7) to the x-coordinate: −2 + 7 = 5
  Add (−8) to the y-coordinate: 6 + (−8) = −2

- Write the coordinates of A': A'(5, −2)

- Find the coordinates of B' and C'.
  B'(2,   )   C'(, −6)

- Plot points A', B', and C' and draw △A'B'C'.

7. Again, △ABC has vertices at A(−2, 6), B(−5, 2), and C(−2, 2). Follow the instructions to draw △A'B'C' so that A' is shifted to the origin. Find the coordinates of B' and C'. Describe the translation with coordinates.

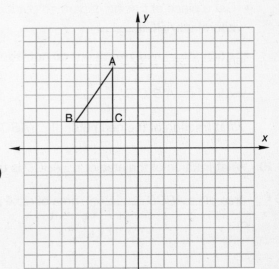

- First find the translation of A to A'.

- Write the coordinates of A: (−2, 6)

- Write the coordinates of A' which is the origin (0, 0).

- Find the translation from (−2, 6) to (0, 0).
  Use x-coordinate: −2 + x = 0   x = 2
  Use y-coordinate: 6 + y = 0   y = −6

- Describe the translation with coordinates: (,   )

- Apply the translation to B and C to find the coordinates of B' and C'.
  B'(−3,   )   C'(, −4)

- Plot points A', B', and C' and draw △A'B'C'.

- A dilation is a transformation in which the figure gets larger. Dilations have a scale factor greater than 1.

- A contraction is a transformation in which a figure gets smaller. Contractions have a scale factor less than 1.

- Dilations and contractions are centered on a point. If the point is the *origin,* we can **multiply the coordinates by the scale factor** to find the new coordinates for the figure.

8. $\square ABCD$ has vertices at $A(6, 4)$, $B(6, -2)$, $C(-2, -2)$, and $D(-2, 4)$. Follow the instructions to draw $\square ABCD$ using a scale factor of $\frac{1}{2}$, with the center of contraction at the origin. Find the coordinates of the vertices of $\square A'B'C'D'$.

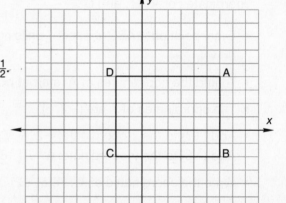

- Since the scale factor is less than 1, $\square A'B'C'D'$ will be smaller than $\square ABCD$.

- To find the coordinates of A' we will start at point A.

- The coordinates of A are $(6, 4)$.

- The scale factor is $\frac{1}{2}$, so multiply each coordinate by $\frac{1}{2}$.

  x-coordinate: $6 \times \frac{1}{2} = 3$

  y-coordinate: $4 \times \frac{1}{2} = 2$

  $A'(3, 2)$

- Find the coordinates of B', C', and D'.

  $B'(-3, \quad)$ $C'(\quad , -4)$ $D'(\quad , \quad)$

- Plot points A', B', C', and D'. Draw $\square A'B'C'D'$.

9. What fraction of the dimensions of $\square ABCD$ are the

dimensions of $\square A'B'C'D'$? _____

length of $\square ABCD$ _____

width of $\square ABCD$ _____

length of $\square A'B'C'D'$ _____

width of $\square A'B'C'D'$ _____

What fraction of the perimeter of $\square ABCD$ is the perimeter of $\square A'B'C'D'$? _____

10. What fraction of the area of $\square ABCD$ is the area of $\square A'B'C'D'$? _____

area of $\square ABCD$ _____   area of $\square A'B'C'D'$ _____

Follow the instructions to graph each transformation.

11. △*XYZ* has vertices at *X*(−2, 5), *Y*(−5, 2), and *Z*(−2, 2). Draw △*XYZ* reflected (flipped) across the x-axis. Find and label the coordinates of *X'*, *Y'*, and *Z'*.

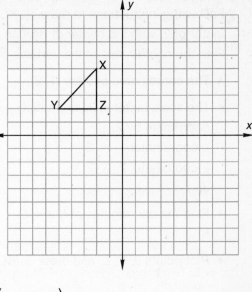

- Find the distance from the x-axis to point *X*. The distance is 5 units.

- Change the distance **above** the x-axis, 5, to a distance **below** the x-axis: −5. Label this point *X'*. *Because we are reflecting across the x-axis, X' will be the same distance below the x-axis as X is above the x-axis.*

- Now we have flipped point *X* vertically over the *X*-axis.

- Write the coordinates of *X'*: *X'*(−2,   )
  The x-coordinate does not change.

- Find the coordinates of *Y'* and *Z'*. *Y'*(,   )   *Z'*(,   )

- Plot points *X'*, *Y'*, and *Z'* and draw △*X'Y'Z'*.

12. △*PQR* has vertices at *P*(3, 0), *Q*(3, −5), and *R*(6, 0). Follow the instructions to rotate △*PQR* 90° counterclockwise around point *P*. The rotated image is △*PQR*. Find the coordinates of *P*, *Q*, and *R*.

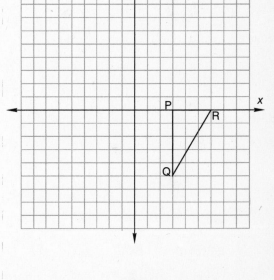

- Get a piece of tracing paper and put it over the coordinate plane.

- Trace △*PQR*. Do not trace the x- and y-axes.

- Place the tip of your pencil on point *P*. Turn the tracing paper 90° counterclockwise. Side *PQ* on the tracing paper should align with the x-axis.

- Use the traced image to plot points *P'*, *Q'*, and *R'* and draw △*P'Q'R'* on the coordinate plane.
  P'(3, 0)   *Q'*(8,   )   *R'*(, 3)

13. △*DEF* has vertices at *D*(−2, −2), *E*(2, −2), and *F*(0, 2). Follow the instructions to draw △*DEF* after a translation of (5, 3). Find the coordinates of *D*, *E*, and *F*.

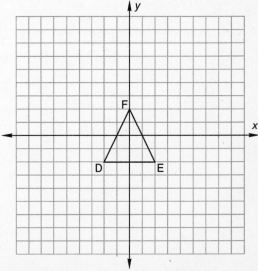

- Every point on △*DEF* will shift (5, 3), or 5 units right and 3 units up.

- The coordinates of *D* are (−2, −2).

- Add (+5) to the x-coordinate: −2 + (+5) = +3
  Add (+3) to the y-coordinate: −2 + (+3) = +1

- Write the coordinates of *D*: *D*(3, 1)

- Find the coordinates of *E* and *F*.
  D(,   )   *F*(,   )

- Plot points *D*, *E*, and *F* and draw △*DEF*.

14. △JKL has vertices at J(1, 2), K(−1, −2), L(1, −2).
Follow the instructions to draw △JKL using a scale
factor of 2, with the center of dilation at the origin.
Find the coordinates of the vertices of △JKL.

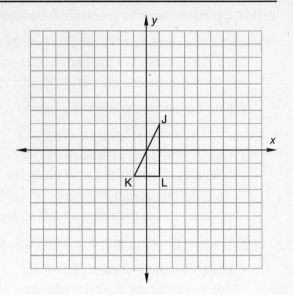

- The coordinates of J are (1, 2).

- The scale factor is 2, so multiply each
  coordinate by 2.
  x-coordinate: 1 × 2 =
  y-coordinate: 2 × 2 =
  J(,   )

- Find the coordinates of K and L.
  K(,   )   L(,   )

- Plot points J, K, L and draw △JKL.

•Collect, Display, and Interpret Data (page 412)

Name _____

- **Statistics** is the science of collecting and interpreting data.

- Statistics are used to draw conclusions about data and to make predictions based on the data.

- The **population** is the group of people that researchers want to study.

- If a population is a large number of people, it is not practical to study each person. So researchers survey a **sample**, or a part of the population.

- Researchers must be careful to choose a sample that is **representative** of the entire population. For example, surveying only girls for a study on all eighth-grade students is *not* a representative sample.

- Researchers must also be careful to ask questions in a way that avoid **bias** or slant toward a particular point of view. For example, the question, "Which do you like more: water or a cool, sweet glass of lemonade?" is biased towards the lemonade because of the words used.

- The managers of a theme park plan to build a new restaurant, and the managers want to know what kind of restaurant their customers want. The managers decide to ask every park visitor (the whole population) which restaurant they would like to have built.

    1. What are some problems with surveying the entire population?

       The s_____ would take a long time, and some customers might not want to take the survey.

    2. The theme park managers decide to survey just the people in one of the other restaurants already in the park. Why might this sample not be representative of the population?

       The customers at one r_____ could have different preferences than the p_____ as a whole.

    3. Josh took a survey of his class. He asked each classmate "Which restaurant would you like to eat at in a theme park: a sandwich shop, a fish and chips shop, or a pizza parlor?" He tallied the data in the frequency table below. Total each tally and write the total in the column labeled "Frequency."

Restaurant	Tally	Frequency
Sandwich Shop		
Fish and Chips		
Pizza Parlor		

Josh wants to display his data on a **bar graph**. Complete the bar graph below by drawing bars to the correct height.

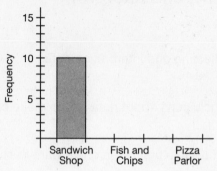

4. **a.** Which type of restaurant was the most popular in Josh's survey? _____

   b. If Josh surveyed customers at the theme park instead of his classmates, why might the results be different?

   Every person in Josh's class is a student.

   At the theme park Josh would survey s_____ and adults.

   An a_____ might make different restaurant choices than a _____.

- **Qualitative data** is data that falls into categories, such as type of restaurant. Bar graphs are often used for showing qualitative data.

- **Quantitative data** is data made up of numbers, such as the height of every student in a classroom.

- A **histogram** is used to display the data quantitative data that is divided into *intervals*.

   5. A movie theater collected data on the ages of customers attending a new movie. The ages are listed in order below.

   7   8   8   9   9   9   10   10   11   12
   12   12   13   14   15   16   16   17   18   20
   23   28   32   33   34   34   35   37   40   41
   48   51   53   57   58   62   68   70   72   75

Divide the data into 15-year intervals by tallying in the frequency table below. Total each tally in the column labeled "Frequency." Then complete the histogram to display the data.

Age	Tally	Frequency
1–15		
16–30		
31–45		
46–60		
61–75		

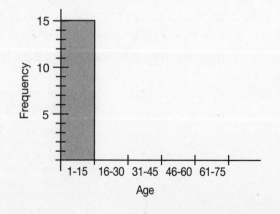

- An **opinion survey** is used to find out what *percent* of a population likes or dislikes an idea. An opinion survey asks people to answer a question with "yes," "no," or "I don't know."

- We often display the results of an opinion survey on a **circle graph** (pie chart).

- The entire circle represents the whole population, 100%. Each sector of the circle is a percent of the whole.

- Remember that a sector of a circle covers part of the circle. We can find the central angle of a sector by multiplying 360° by the percent of the sector.

6. Kira asks 30 students "Would you rather have math class in the morning or the afternoon?" Kira tallies her data in the frequency table below. Total each tally, find the percent of the students for each row, and calculate the central angle for each sector. Then, label the sectors of the circle graph with the percent and the answer each sector represents.

Response	Tally	Frequency	Percent	Angle of Sector
Morning	~~IIII~~ ~~IIII~~	10	$\frac{10}{30} = \frac{1}{3} = 33\frac{1}{3}\%$	$\frac{1}{3}(360°) = 120°$
Afternoon	~~IIII~~ ~~IIII~~ ~~IIII~~			
Don't know	~~IIII~~			

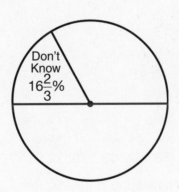

7. One hundred eighth graders were surveyed and asked what extra-curricular activities they planned to be involved with in high school. The students were given several choices and could select as many as they wanted. The results are shown below.

music	卌 卌 卌 卌 卌 II
sports	卌 卌 卌 卌 I
service clubs	卌 卌 卌 卌 卌 卌 III
student government	卌 卌 卌
other	卌 卌 III

a. Would a histogram be appropriate for this qualitative data?

_____, because a h_____ is used for quantitative data.

b. Would a circle graph be appropriate for this data?

_____, because a circle graph shows parts of a w_____ circle. Students were allowed to make more than one choice, so the parts will not add to a whole.

c. Total each tally and graph the data on the bar graph below.

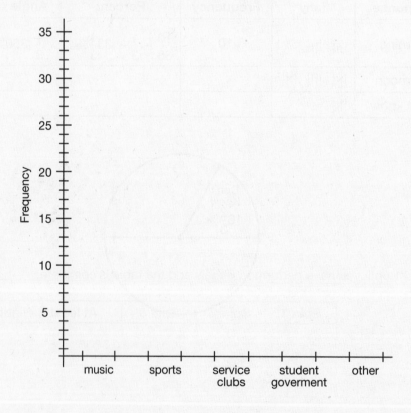

• Probability Simulation (page 476)

Name _____

- A cereal company makes this claim on its cereal boxes:

  "One in three boxes contains a free movie pass!"

- The **theoretical probability** of getting a free movie pass is $\frac{1}{3}$.

- This does *not* mean that if someone buys three boxes of cereal then he or she is certain to get a movie pass. The person could be unlucky and buy three boxes that do not contain a movie pass.

Teacher Notes:

- Review Hint #45, "Probability."

- Review "Probability, Chance, Odds" on page 25 in the *Student Reference Guide*.

- Students will need a spinner divided into thirds and a coin to complete this Investigation.

Activity 1: *Probability Simulation*

- This activity will **simulate** buying three of the cereal boxes.

- Get a spinner that is divided into thirds (three equal sectors).

  Mark "Winner" in one sector.

  Mark "Not a Winner" in the other two sectors.

- Your spinner should look like this:

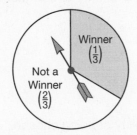

1. Simulate buying 3 cereal boxes by spinning the spinner 3 times.

   For each spin, record "W" (for winner) or "N" (for not a winner) in the table.

   In the "At least one winner?" column write "yes" or "no," depending on whether there were any winners in the three-spin trial.

2. Repeat step 1 until you have performed 6 trials and the table is complete.

	Spin 1	Spin 2	Spin 3	At least 1 winner?
trial 1				
trial 2				
trial 3				
trial 4				
trial 5				
trial 6				

3. Compute the experimental probability of having at least one winner after purchasing 3 cereal boxes. Total the "yes" entries in the last column and divide by the number of trials.

   P(at least one movie pass in three boxes) $= \dfrac{\text{number of "yes"}}{\text{number of trials}} =$

Answer these questions about the simulation in Activity 1.

1. What did one spin of the spinner represent?

   <u>B</u>_____ one cereal box

2. What did each three-spin trial represent?

   Buying _____ cereal boxes

3. What did the spinner stopping on "winner" represent?

   Getting a _____ in a cereal box

4. What did the spinner stopping on "not a winner" represent?

   _____ getting a movie pass in a cereal box

5. Tell if the following tools could have been used instead of a spinner to conduct the cereal box simulation. Explain why or why not.

   Can you use the tools to find a $\frac{1}{3}$ probability?

   a. Two red cards and one black card

   _____, because the black card has _____ probability of being chosen.

   b. A coin

   _____, because a heads or tails is _____ probability.

   c. Three red marbles

   _____, because the marbles are all the same.

   d. One red, one white, one blue marble

   _____, because one of the marbles could _____ the winner.

   e. A number cube

   _____, because selecting 2 out of 6 numbers has a _____ probability.

INVESTIGATION 8

• Scatterplots (page 538)

- When collecting data in a real-world situation, the data points will usually not graph to make a perfectly straight line.

- We can graph real-world data on a **scatterplot** and estimate a line to understand the general trend of the data.

Teacher Notes:
- Review Hint #45, "Probablity".
- The graphing calculator activity on 📖 page 542 is optional.

- Mr. Lopez's physical education class did laps around the track. Each student recorded the total time and the number of laps he or she completed. A plot of the data is shown to the right of the table. The number of laps is the x-axis. The time is the y-axis.

Number of Laps	Time (min)
3	9
4	8
2	3
6	12
5	15
4	7
2	4
6	15
3	7
5	11
6	7

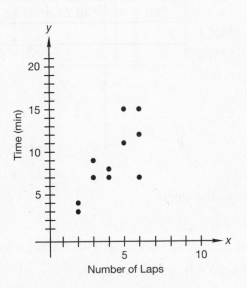

The graph is a scatterplot because the data do not line up perfectly.

- The data points do show a **correlation:** the more laps (x-coordinate), the longer the time (y-coordinate).

- We look at the data and use a ruler to draw a line that passes near all of the points.

  We call this a **best-fit line.**

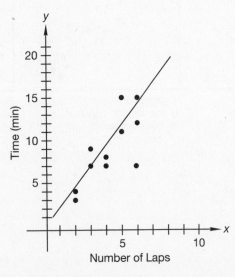

- The best fit line is just an estimate. Other lines could have been drawn that pass near or through the data points. There is no exact correct answer.

- Look at point (6, 7) on the graph. This point represents running 6 laps in 7 minutes.

- Point (6, 7) is an **outlier.** An outlier is a data point that is far away from all the other points.

- When estimating a line, do not consider data points that are far away from the others (outliers).

- We can find an equation of the line we drew on the graph.

    1. Start with the one point that the line passes through. This point is (3, 7).

    2. Then estimate another point on the line. The point (6, 14) seems to be on the line.

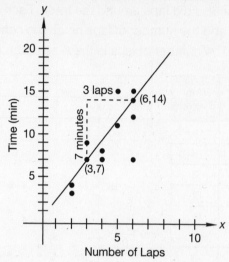

    3. Now estimate the slope:

    $$m = \frac{7}{3} = 2\frac{1}{3}$$

    4. The *y*-intercept appears to be zero, so the equation of the line is $y = 2\frac{1}{3}x$

    This means the ratio of time to laps is about $2\frac{1}{3}$ min/lap.

- Data on a scatterplot can show a **positive** correlation, **negative** correlation, or **no** correlation.

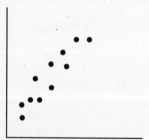

Positive correlation
as one variable increases,
so does the other

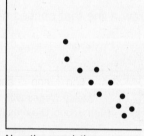

Negative correlation
as one variable increases,
the other decreases

Zero correlation
no linear relationship

Example: Determine whether the wages of college graduates and the wages of high-school graduates in the listed jobs are correlated. If so, find the equation of an estimated line.

Median Weekly Earnings, 2000

	High School Diploma ($)	Bachelor Degree or Higher ($)
Cashier	303	384
Cook	327	396
Computer Programmer	864	1039
Data-Entry Keyers	475	514
Designers	633	794
Electricians	714	976
Police	726	886
Legal Assistants	563	725
Real Estate Sales	614	918

A graph of this data with an estimated line is shown below. There is a positive correlation for the data, because the line has a positive slope.

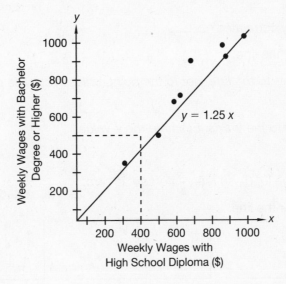

- We see that the line passes through about (400, 500). The line also goes through (0, 0). So the slope is about

$$m = \frac{500}{400} = 1.25$$

- The equation of the line is

$$y = 1.25x$$

- This means that college graduates earn about 1.25 times (25% more than) the money that high-school graduates make in the same job.

Activity: *Make a Scatterplot and Graph a Best-fit Line*

Dana records the number of multiplication problems she completes correctly in every 30 seconds. Is the time spent working and the number of multiplication problems positively correlated?

- The table below shows Dana's total time in minutes and the total number of multiplication problems completed during that time.

- Plot the data on the graph and estimate a straight line through the data. Use a ruler to draw a straight line. The line should intersect the origin.

Time (min)	Problems Completed
½	5
1	9
1½	10
2	14
2½	18
3	20

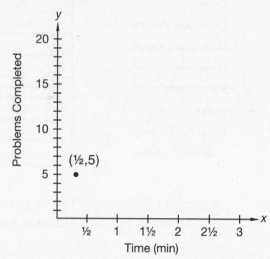

7.   Is the data positively correlated? _____

Find an equation for the line.

*Go up from 2 minutes to the **line**, not to the point, unless your line passes exactly through the point (2, 14).*

From the line go left to the y-axis. Estimate the y-value.

slope = $\dfrac{\rule{1cm}{0.4pt}}{2}$ =

The line goes through (0, 0), so the y-intercept is zero.

Write an equation for the line.

$y = $ _____

8. Freddy ran for eight minutes wearing a heart rate monitor. He checked his pulse every minute of his run. Freddy's heart rate at each minute is charted below. Make a scatterplot of the data.

Minutes Run	Heart Rate
1	95
2	110
3	133
4	142
5	150
6	158
7	170
8	175

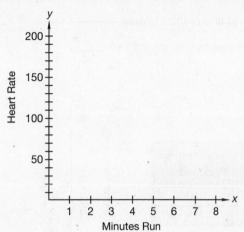

Estimate a best-fit line on the graph.

Is the correlation positive or negative? _____

What does the slope of the line represent?

As Freddy runs longer, his heart rate _____ .

What does the *y*-intercept of the line represent?

When Freddy is not running, his heart rate is about _____ .

If Freddy kept running for 30 minutes, would his heart rate continue to increase at the same rate?

_____, his heart rate would _____ less and less.

9. Shayna conducted a survey to find out how much money her customers are willing to pay for a new item. She charted the number of people willing to buy the item for each proposed price. Make a scatterplot for the data.

    Estimate a best-fit line on the graph.

    Is the correlation positive or negative? _____

Proposed Price ($)	Number of Purchasers
1.00	10
1.50	9
2.00	6
2.50	5

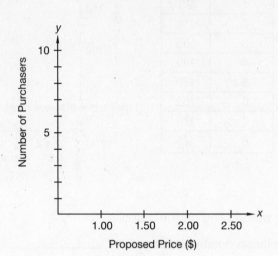

• Sampling Methods (page 606)

Name _____

• A **population** is the whole group of people that researchers want to study.

• Every ten years, the U.S. Census Bureau conducts a study by surveying every resident in the United States.

This study is called a **census study**. It includes every person in a population.

A census study gives accurate results because everyone in the population takes part in the survey.

Teacher Notes:
• Students will need a copy of Investigation Activity 8, available in *Saxon Math Course 3 Instructional Masters,* to complete this Investigation.
• The graphing calculator exercise in the Activity on 📖 page 607 is optional.

• For instance, the Census Bureau reported that for a one-way trip to work, the average nationwide commute time was 24.3 minutes in 2003.

Nationwide
24.3 min

• A census study takes a lot of time and money, so most researchers cannot use a census study.

• Instead researchers choose a **sample** of a population. A good sample is **representative**, or similar to, the larger population.

• The American Community Survey randomly selected households from across the nation to participate in a similar commute study. Individual state and city averages vary from the nationwide average:

New York	Nebraska	Chicago	Tulsa
30.4 min	16.5 min	33.2 min	17.1 min

• These commuting averages may have accidentally been a result of surveying people who do not represent the population. For example, in Chicago, it is possible that only people with long commute times were surveyed.

a. If researchers had surveyed only people who live in Nebraska for the national commute time

average, what would the national average have been? _____

b. How is the average different from the real national average? The average commute time for

Nebraska is _____ than the national average.

• Researchers often select a **random sample** from the population to make sure the sample is representative.

One way to select a random sample is to assign a number to each member of the population and then randomly select numbers.

Activity: *Random Number Generators*

A health food store wants to test its consumers' response to a new product. The researcher assigned a number to each person in the customer database and used a random number generator to select a sample of customers.

Customers

00	Strickler	10	Smith
01	Sanchez	11	Zamora
02	Tsing	12	McNelly
03	LaBrado	13	Jensen
04	Poth	14	Gomez
05	Barrell	15	Rathod
06	Jo	16	O'Grady
07	Joslen	17	Barreto
08	Cheung	18	Davis
09	Clark	19	Lee

1. Follow the instructions to select five names from the list using a random number table.

   • Get a copy of Investigation Activity 8.

   • Close your eyes and put a finger on any part of the table.

   • Write down the number your finger is on.

   • Go down to the next number in the table and write that number.

   • Keep moving down the table and writing the numbers until you reach the bottom of the table.

   • Your list of numbers may look like this:

   07365195578245

   • Divide your list of numbers into pairs of numbers from right to left. Write each pair in the blanks below. If you do not have enough numbers, you may have to use the table again.

   _____, _____, _____, _____, _____, _____, _____, _____, _____, _____, _____, _____

   • Cross out any pairs of numbers that are greater than 19. Record the remaining numbers in these blanks.

   _____, _____, _____, _____, _____

   • If you did not get five pairs of numbers that are less than 19, make more pairs of numbers from the table.

   • Match up the pairs of numbers with the names in the customer list. Write the five randomly sampled names below:

   _____   _____   _____

   _____   _____

2. Another way to select a sample is by **systematic sampling,** in which subjects are chosen from a list with equal spacing.

- Choose a number from 1 to 9. Look at the customer list and write down the name of the

  person with that number. _____

- Count down the list by your number to find another name. If you get to the last name on the

  list, keep counting and go back to the start of the list. _____

- Keep counting down the list by your number to get three more names. Skip names that you have already selected.

  _____

  _____

  _____

- Five customers out of 20 is not a very large sample.

- The best way to avoid **sampling error** is with a large, random group.

Example 1

Identify a problem with each sampling method below. Describe a better sampling method for each situation.

- **a.** *Matthew wants to know the percentage of students at his middle school who favor school uniforms. He decides to ask everyone in his English class whether or not they favor school uniforms.*

  - Matthew should survey his entire school, not just his English class.

  - This kind of sampling is called convenience sampling, because Matthew did what was easiest, not what was best.

  - A better method would be stratified sampling.

  - Matthew could divide the school into three parts, or strata: the 6th graders, 7th graders, and 8th graders. Then he could survey a random part of each strata.

- **b.** *In response to requests for a new softball diamond, the city council would like to know how important building a softball diamond is to the residents. They ask researchers to conduct a phone survey by randomly selecting 20 names from the phone book.*

  - Surveying 20 people in a city is a small sample. This may not give a reliable result. It is possible that all 20 people would like softball much more than the city as a whole.

  - Surveying 200 or 2,000 people would make a much better sample.

- After a sample is selected, the survey questions must be written.

- When a survey question might push people to answer one way or the other, the question is **biased.**

Example 2

Consider the following questions proposed for a survey about a new softball diamond. Select the least biased question and explain.

1. *Wouldn't you like a new softball diamond at Filly Park?*

2. *Which of these describes your desire for a softball diamond at Filly Park: I do not want one / I feel indifferent to the idea / I would like one / I want one built soon.*

3. *The city pays for many services under a tight budget, like street lighting, crossing guards in front of schools, and park maintenance. How important is it to you that the city build a softball diamond at Filly Park?*

- Only **question 2** is a non-biased survey question.

- The way **question 1** is written assumes that people will answer "yes."

- **Question 3** describes problems with the city's budget and may cause people to answer "no."

Write a survey question about school uniforms for Matthew to ask the students at his school.

Are you for or _____ wearing school uniforms?

Write a biased survey question about school uniforms.

Don't you think school uniforms are _____?

Gillian wants to survey the 8ᵗʰ graders in her school about a class trip over Spring Break. Answer these questions to help Gillian plan her survey.

- What population is being studied? _____ in Gillian's school

- If there are 600 8ᵗʰ grade students in Gillian's school, what would be a good sample size?

  _____

- How should the sample be selected? ͬ_____

- What question should Gillian ask?

  Are you _____ or against a class trip over Spring Break?

- Can you think of a different way of asking the question that might make more people answer "yes"?

  Wouldn't it be _____ to take a class trip over Spring Break?

- Can you think of a way of asking the question that might make more people answer "no"?

  Do you want to take an expensive _____?

© 2007 Harcourt Achieve Inc.

• Compound Interest (page 670)

Name _____

• Money deposited in a bank grows over time according to the interest rate.

Principal is the amount of money originally deposited.

Interest is the amount the money earns over time. Interest is written as a percent and calculated as a decimal.

Simple interest is a percentage of the principal only.

Compound interest is a percentage of the principal and any interest earned.

> **Teacher Notes:**
>
> • Refer students to "Simple Interest" on page 23 in the *Student Reference Guide*.
>
> • Check students' calculators before teaching the method described in this lesson. See instructions for your calculator if the keystroke sequence described in this lesson does not work for you.

• This example shows 5% simple interest and compound interest on $100 principal over three years.

Simple Interest	
$100	Principal
$5	1st year (5% of $100)
$5	2nd year (5% of $100)
+ $5	3rd year (5% of $100)
$115	total after three years

Compound Interest	
$100.00	Principal
+ $5.00	1st year (5% of $100)
$105.00	total after 1 year
+ $5.25	2nd year (5% of $105)
$110.25	total after 2 years
+ $5.51	3rd year (5% of $110.25)
$115.76	total after 3 years

With simple interest, $100 grows to $115 after three years.

With compound interest, $100 grows to $115.76 after three years. Money grows more quickly with compound interest.

• The difference between simple interest and compound interest is small at first, but the difference grows larger over time.

This table shows the simple and compound interest on the same amount over 50 years.

Total Value of $100 at 5% Interest

Number of Years	Simple Interest	Compound Interest
3	$115.00	$115.76
10	$150.00	$162.89
20	$200.00	$265.33
30	$250.00	$432.19
40	$300.00	$704.00
50	$350.00	$1146.74

- To calculate the **total** after a percent increase:

  1. Add the percent increase (the interest) to 100% (the principal).

  total increase = increase % + 100%

  2. Change that number to a decimal and multiply the starting amount.

  Example: Over the last century, the stock market's average annual (yearly) rate of return has been about 10%. Make a table that shows the value of a $1000 investment growing 10% each year after 1, 2, 3, 4, and 5 years.

  The yearly increase is 10%, so the total yearly increase is

  $$10\% + 100\% = 110\% = 1.1$$

  To find the total after each year, multiply the starting amount from each year by 1.1. The principal is $1000.

  $$1^{st} \text{ year total} = \$1000 \times 1.1 = \$1100$$
  $$2^{nd} \text{ year total} = \$1100 \times 1.1 = \$1210$$
  $$3^{rd} \text{ year total} = \$1210 \times 1.1 = \$1331$$
  $$4^{th} \text{ year total} = \$1331 \times 1.1 = \$1464.10$$
  $$5^{th} \text{ year total} = \$1464.10 \times 1.1 = \$1610.51$$

  Make a table with these values.

**Total Value of $1000 at
10% Interest**

Number of Years	Compound Interest
1	$1100.00
2	$1210.00
3	$1331.00
4	$1464.10
5	$1610.51

- Compound interest takes a lot of multiplication, so **use a calculator**.

Activity: *Calculating Interest and Growth*

1. Perform the calculations in example 1 with a calculator by using the multiplication sequence shown below:

$$1000 \times 1.1 \times 1.1 \times 1.1 \times 1.1 \times 1.1$$

Do the numbers shown after each multiplication match the numbers in the table? _____

- Notice that 1.1 is a **repeated factor**. Repeated factors are grouped with exponents. For instance, $2 \times 2 \times 2 = 2^3$. The interest calculation above can be written with an exponent:

  $$1000 \times (1.1)^5$$

2. Some calculators have an exponent key. The key is labeled "x^y" or "y^x". Ask your teacher to help you find the exponent key.

Use this formula to calculate compound interest with the exponent key: $V = P(1 + I)^n$
- V is the total value.
- P is the principal.
- I is the interest rate written as a decimal.
- n is the number of years.

Find the value (V) of $1000 ($P$) growing 10% ($I$) each year after 5 years (n) using the exponent key.

The money increases by 10% each year, so the increase is

$$100\% + 10\% = 110\% = 1.1$$

Follow the steps:
- Enter "1000" for the principal.
- Press "×" for multiplication.
- Enter "1.1" for the interest.
- Press "x^y" for the exponent.
- Enter "5" for the number of years.
- Press "=" to get the total value.

What number did you get? _____

3. Use a calculator and the exponent key for the following problem.
If a 25-year-old invested $1000 in a mutual fund that averaged 10% return per year, what would be the value of the investment when the person was 65? Round the answer to the nearest thousand dollars.

From the problem, what is P, the principal? _____

What is I, the interest rate? _____ Write I as a decimal. _____

Add 1 (for 100%) to I. _____

What is n, the number of years? _____

Follow the steps to use the formula: $V = P(1 + I)^n$
- Enter "1000" for the principal.
- Press "×" for multiplication.
- Enter "1.1" for the interest.
- Press "x^y" for the exponent.
- Enter "40" for the number of years.
- Press "=" to get the total value.

What total value did you get? ■ _____

Round the value to the nearest thousand dollars. ■ _____

Use a calculator with an exponent key for exercises **4** and **5**.

4. Find the value of a $4500 investment earning 5% compound interest after 100 years. Round the answer to the nearest thousand dollars.

   What is P? _____

   What is I? _____   Write I as a decimal. _____   Add 1 to I. _____

   What is n? _____

   Follow the steps to use the formula: $V = P(1 + I)^n$
   - Enter "4500" for the principal.
   - Press "×" for multiplication.
   - Enter "1.05" for the interest.
   - Press "x^y" for the exponent.
   - Enter "100" for the number of years.
   - Press "=" to get the total value.

   What total value did you get? _____

   Round the value to the nearest thousand dollars. _____

5. Find the difference in value, after 30 years, of a $5000 investment earning 6% compound interest and a $5000 investment earning 5%.

   What is P? _____   What is n? _____

   I is 6% (0.06) for one value and 5% (0.05) for the other.

   Find the 6% interest value first.
   - Enter "5000" for the principal.
   - Press "×" for multiplication.
   - Enter "1.06" for the interest.
   - Press "x^y" for the exponent.
   - Enter "30" for the number of years.
   - Press "=" to get the total value.

   Write the value at 6% interest. _____

   Find the 5% interest value next.
   - Enter "5000" for the principal.
   - Press "×" for multiplication.
   - Enter "1.05" for the interest.
   - Press "x^y" for the exponent.
   - Enter "30" for the number of years.
   - Press "=" to get the total value.

Write the value at 5% interest. ▪▪▪▪▪▪▪▪

Now find the difference between the 6% and 5% values. ▪▪▪▪▪▪▪▪

- The **Rule of 72** is a Rule that gives an *estimate* of the time it takes for an amount of money to *double*.

- To use the Rule, **divide 72 by the interest percent**.

  Example 2: Apply the Rule of 72 to estimate how quickly an investment will double at 6% interest.

  The rule of 72 says to divide 72 by the interest rate. 72 divided by 6 is 12. So the investment should double about **every 12 years**. We can use this estimate to make a table.

  Approximate Value of $1000 Investment at 6% Compounded Annually

Growing at 6% for (Years)	0	12	24	36
Value of Account	1000	2000	4000	8000

6. Refer to the table in example 2. Predict the value of $1000 growing at

   12% interest for 36 years. ▪▪▪▪▪▪▪▪
   The money is growing twice as fast as in the example 2.

7. Use the Rule of 72 to estimate the value of $1000 growing at 12% over 36 years.
   Divide 72 by the interest to find the doubling time. Then complete the table.

Growing at 12% for (years)	Value ($)
0	$1000
6	$2000
12	
18	
24	
30	
36	

8. Compare the growth rates at 6% in the table in example 2 and at 12% in the table in exercise **7**.

The 12% rate grows much _____.

- Compound interest is an example of **exponential growth.** The graph of exponential growth is a curve.

- Direct variation is an example of **linear growth**. (Linear means "line.")

- This graph compares exponential and linear growth.

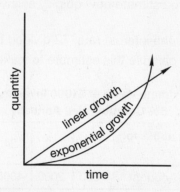

9. *A property owner was going away on business for three weeks and wanted to hire a person to care for the property. Two people applied for the job. The first person wanted to be paid $100 per day. The second person wanted a penny the first day, two cents the second day, four cents the third day, and so on, **doubling** every day for three weeks. Which person should the property owner hire?*

3 weeks = 21 days
The first person wants $100 per day. The total over 21 days is $_____.

The second person wants to double his fee every day: 2^{n-1}, where *n* is the number of days. Use a calculator to find 2^{n-1} for a total of 21 days.

2^{20} = _____ ¢

Divide by 100 to change to dollars: $_____

Should the property owner hire the first person or the second person? _____

10. At a steady growth rate of 1.2%, about how long would it take for the world's population to double?

_____ years
Use the Rule of 72.

11. If a country's energy needs increase at 3% per year, then its energy needs will double in about how

many years? _____ ▨
Use the Rule of 72.

• Non-Linear Functions (page 727)

Name _____

- The picture below shows a ball pushed off a 48-ft-tall building.

- Every half second the height of the ball is recorded.

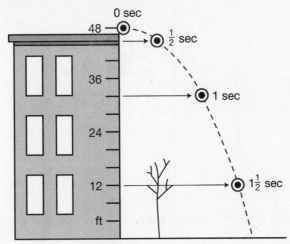

- The ball does not make a straight line to the ground. It makes a curve.

- This kind of curve is called a **parabola**. The graph of functions with the variables y and x^2 make a parabola.

Activity 1: *Modeling Freefall*

1. Use the picture of the ball falling off a building to fill in this table. The height of the ball is h and the time in seconds is t. Every mark on the building is 4 feet.

t	h

2. Complete this table by substituting the x-values into this function.

   $y = -16x^2 + 48$

x	y
0	
$\frac{1}{2}$	
1	
$1\frac{1}{2}$	

Graph the points.

feet

50
40
30
20
10
0

0    $\frac{1}{2}$ 1 $1\frac{1}{2}$ 2

seconds

- The two tables are the same. The function models the falling ball.

- The function is called a **quadratic function** because it has an x^2 term.

- This graph shows the function including *x*- and *y*-values less than zero.

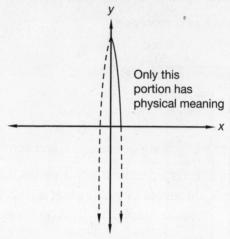

Only this portion has physical meaning

For the falling ball, why wouldn't we include the parts of the graph that are dashed lines?

Time and height cannot be n_____ numbers in this situation.

- The quadratic function is a **non-linear** function because the graph of the function is not a line. (Linear means *line*.)

- The height of the ball does **not** change at a constant rate. Instead, it falls faster and faster as it speeds up over time.

Activity 2: *Using the Graph of a Quadratic Function*

Leslie held a softball 5 ft above the ground and threw it straight up at 32 ft/sec. She predicts that the height *(h)* in feet of the ball at *(t)* seconds could be described by this function:

$$h = -16t^2 + 32t + 5$$

3. Substitute the values for *t* from the table into the equation. Record the height of the ball at 0, 1, and 2 seconds.

t	h
0	
1	
2	

4. Plot the points *(t, h)* on this graph.

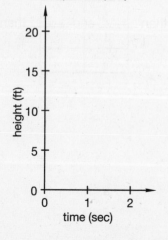

What is the greatest height of the ball from the table? _____

When is the ball at this height? _____

About when does the ball hit the ground (*h* = 0)?

The ball hits the ground a little after _____ seconds.

Look at the graphs in Activities 1 and 2. How are the paths of the balls different?

In Activity 1, the ball starts at the _____ and falls down.

In Activity 2, the ball starts at the bottom, goes _____, and comes back _____.

• The graph of every quadratic function is a parabola with a **vertex** that is the maximum or minimum value of the function. In Activity 2, the vertex of the function is (1, 21).

Activity 3: *Maximization*

Uriel has 20 yards of fencing, and he would like to use it to enclose a rectangular plot of land for a garden. He wonders what the rectangle's dimensions would have to be to contain the **maximum area** with his length of fence.

Uriel drew a rectangle and named one side length *x*. Since half the perimeter of the rectangle is 10 yards, he reasoned that the other side length must be 10 − *x*.

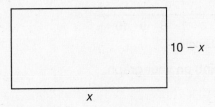

$10 - x$

x

Using *x* and *x* − 10 as the length and width, the area is

$$A = lw$$
$$A = x(10 - x)$$
$$A = 10x - x^2$$

The equation is a quadratic function.
What values for *x* make sense in this equation?

Side lengths have to be positive numbers, so *x* must be greater than _____ and _____ than 10.

Write a pair of inequalities to show the range of *x* values. _____ < *x* < _____

5. Use the area function to complete the table.

What dimensions give maximum area?

x	A
2	16
3	21
4	
5	
6	
7	
8	

l = _____ ▨   *w* = _____ ▨

What shape is this? _____

6. Plot the points (*x*, *A*) on this graph.

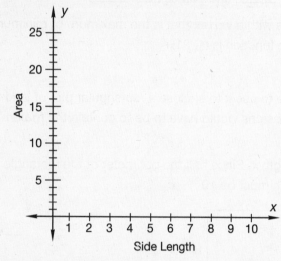

Label the vertex (highest point) on your graph.

• Proof of the Pythagorean Theorem (page 782)

Name _____

• A **proof** is a series of mathematical steps that show how a particular idea must be true.

• Proofs can be algebraic or geometric.

• In this Investigation, we will make an algebraic proof of the Pythagorean Theorem.

• The Pythagorean Theorem states that the lengths of the legs in a right triangle are related to the length of the hypotenuse:

$$a^2 + b^2 = c^2$$

• This equation is where our proof should end.

• We start with the diagram of the right triangle below.

• The right angle is $\angle C$. The acute angles are $\angle A$ and $\angle B$.

• The length of the hypotenuse is c. The length of the leg opposite $\angle A$ is a. The length of the leg opposite $\angle B$ is b.

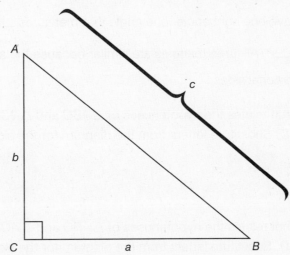

1. Trace this triangle on another sheet of paper.

2. Write the angle and side labels on your triangle to match the triangle on this page.

3. We need to draw a perpendicular segment from the hypotenuse, $\overline{AB}$, across the triangle to C. The corners on a ruler are right angles. Put a ruler on your drawing so that the end of the ruler is along $\overline{AB}$ and the other side goes through the right angle, C. Use the ruler to draw a straight line from $\overline{AB}$ to C. Label point D where the segment intersects $\overline{AB}$.

4. There are now two small right triangles inside the large triangle. Draw the right angle symbol at D. Label the distance from B to D as x. The entire length of $\overline{AB}$ is c, so the rest of the distance is $c - x$. Label the distance from A to D as $c - x$.

• We need to show that the two smaller right triangles and the large right triangle are all similar to each other.

• Similar triangles have *congruent angles*.

5. What is the sum of the two acute angles in a right triangle?

    The sum of the three angle measures of any triangle is _____°. A right angle measures _____°.

    So the sum of the two acute angles in a right triangle is _____°.

6. Label the degree measure of ∠B as $m°$.

    If ∠B in △ABC measures m degrees, then how many degrees is the measure of ∠A?

    $m∠A = $ _____° $- m$.

    Label the degree measure of ∠A.

7. If the measure of ∠B is m and the measure of ∠A is $90 - m$, then what is

    a. m∠BCD? _____°

    b. m∠ACD? _____°

8. Are all three triangles similar? Explain.

    All three triangles have one right angle, one angle that measures _____°, and one angle that

    measures 90 − _____°. All three triangles are similar because the angles are <u>c</u>_____.

• Similar triangles have proportional sides.

9. Write a proportion that relates the hypotenuses of △ABC and △BCD to the corresponding legs of △ABC and △BCD. Substitute letters from the diagram for the side lengths.

    $$\begin{array}{cc} & \text{hyp} \quad \text{leg} \\ \triangle ABC & \dfrac{c}{a} = \dfrac{BC}{BD} = \underline{} \\ \triangle BCD & \end{array}$$

10. Write a proportion that relates the hypotenuses of △ABC and △ACD to the corresponding legs of △ABC and △ACD. Substitute letters from the diagram for the side lengths.

    $$\begin{array}{cc} & \text{hyp} \quad \text{leg} \\ \triangle ABC & \dfrac{c}{b} = \dfrac{AC}{AD} = \underline{} \\ \triangle ACD & \end{array}$$

11. Cross multiply each of the proportions from **9** and **10**.

$$\frac{c}{a} = \frac{a}{x} \qquad\qquad \frac{c}{b} = \frac{b}{(c-x)}$$

$$cx = \underline{\hspace{1.5cm}} \qquad\qquad c^2 - cx = \underline{\hspace{1.5cm}}$$

12. After cross multiplying, the term cx appears in both equations. In the first cross product, $cx = a^2$. Substitute a^2 for cx in the second equation.

$$c^2 - \underline{\hspace{1.5cm}} = \underline{\hspace{1.5cm}}$$

13. Solve the equation from **12** for c^2.

$$c^2 =$$

What is this equation called? _____

• This completes an algebraic proof for the Pythagorean Theorem.